The Psychology of Thinking

The Psychology of Thinking

LYLE E. BOURNE, JR.
University of Colorado

BRUCE R. EKSTRAND
University of Colorado

ROGER L. DOMINOWSKI
University of Illinois at Chicago Circle

PRENTICE-HALL, INC., Englewood Cliffs, New Jersey

PRENTICE-HALL SERIES IN EXPERIMENTAL PSYCHOLOGY
James J. Jenkins, Editor

© 1971 by Prentice-Hall, Inc., Englewood Cliffs, New Jersey

All rights reserved. No part of this book may be reproduced in any form or by any means without permission in writing from the publisher.

13-736702-3

Library of Congress Catalog Card Number: 79-135409

Printed in the United States of America

Current printing (last digit)
10 9 8 7 6 5 4

PRENTICE-HALL INTERNATIONAL, INC., *London*
PRENTICE-HALL OF AUSTRALIA, PTY. LTD., *Sydney*
PRENTICE-HALL OF CANADA, LTD., *Toronto*
PRENTICE-HALL OF INDIA PRIVATE LIMITED, *New Delhi*
PRENTICE-HALL OF JAPAN, INC., *Tokyo*

Contents

Foreword, ix

Preface, xi

I Introduction and Orientation

ONE
Psychology and the Concept of Thought, 3

The Nature of Thinking, 4
Development of Thinking, 12
Aims and Plan of the Book, 17

TWO
History and General Theoretical Systems, 20

Antecedents of Scientific Psychology, 21
The Beginnings of an Independent Psychology, 24
Later Developments, 26
The Psychology of Thinking in America, 30
Summary, 38

II Problem Solving

THREE
Understanding Problem Solving: Preliminary Considerations, 41

Types of Problems and Solution Processes, 41
Methods for Studying Problem Solving, 49   Summary, 63

FOUR
Theories of Problem Solving, 64

Three Theoretical Views, 65   Summary, 78

FIVE
Empirical Studies of Problem Solving: The Task, 80

Characteristics of the Problem Situation, 80
Characteristics of the Solution, 90

SIX
Empirical Studies of Problem Solving: The Problem Solver, 98

Individual Differences Among Problem Solvers, 99
Transfer Effects in Problem Solving, 104   Summary, 117

III Verbal Learning

SEVEN
Tasks, Variables, and Processes, 121

Tasks and Methods, 122
A Modest Theoretical Orientation, 126
The Associative Process, 130
Major Verbal-Learning Variables, 133   Summary, 143

EIGHT
Verbal Learning: The Relationship to Thinking, 144

Transfer of Training, 144   Mediation, 151
The Adequacy of S-R Analyses: Selected Problems, 153
Summary, 173

IV Concept Formation

NINE
The Nature of Concepts, 177

Formal Characteristics of Concepts, 177
Conceptual Behavior, 182
Methodological Considerations, 185   Summary, 192

TEN
Contemporary Theories of Concept Formation, 194

Section I: The Theories, 194
Theory of Associations, 194   Theory of Hypotheses, 196
Theory of Mediation, 199
Theory of Information Processing, 202

Section II: Preliminary Evaluation of Theories, 205
Conceptual Issues, 206   Empirical Issues, 207
Summary, 222

ELEVEN
Empirical Studies of Conceptual Behavior: The Problem Solver, 223

Performance, 223
General Characteristics and Processes of the Learner, 234
Development of Conceptual Behavior, 244
Summary, 252

TWELVE
Empirical Studies of Conceptual Behavior: The Task, 254

Complexity of the Response System, 254
Properties of the Concept, 257
Properties of the Stimulus, 261
Informative Feedback, 271
Timing of Critical Events, 274   Summary, 280

V Language

THIRTEEN
Language and Thought, 285

Some Basic Research Findings, 285
The Linguistic Relativity Hypothesis, 292
Language and Thought—Additional Considerations, 301
Summary, 307

FOURTEEN
Language: A System for Thinking, 308

Competence and Performance, 308
Levels of Linguistic Analysis, 310   Semantics, 328
The Development of Language, 332   Summary, 342

VI Conclusion

FIFTEEN
Concepts, Thoughts, and Behavior, 345

Thinking and Behavior, 345   Learning to Think, 348
Learning and Using Concepts, 348   Final Remark, 353

Bibliography, 355

Author Index, 375

Subject Index, 379

Foreword

It will come as no surprise to the reader to hear that American psychology in the 1970's is in a period of rapid and dramatic change. To some of the psychologists who are involved, it is merely a period of accelerated change in the normal evolution of science; to other psychologists, it is a period characterized by a major shift in emphasis toward cognitive psychology; to still others, it is a period of active revolution in psychological content, experimentation and theory. The labels are arbitrary, of course, and the task of assigning the correct one can best be left to history. The facts that stimulate all of these comments justify each of the labels to some extent. Under a variety of pressures, originating both inside and outside of the discipline, American psychology has begun a reexamination of its prevalent assumptions about the nature of psychological theory, the nature of experimentation and the very nature of the subject matter itself. New possibilities are being entertained and old formulations are being studied in new lights. Certain subject matters, particularly perception and cognition, which were regarded only yesterday with great suspicion, are now being given serious attention. New forms of experimentation are emerging and there is a flowering of demonstrations that point to complex "mentalistic" phenomena that cry for examination and explanation.

One of the problems facing the discipline is that of integrating the new with the old, trying to keep that which is good while going forward to that which is better. Thomas Kuhn, the philosopher of science, refers to this as the "rewriting" of the history of the science. I might add that this kind of rewriting is important, constructive, and just downright hard to do. Among the "revolutionaries" there is little sentiment to retain ties with the past and an unbecoming willingness to sweep the boards clean. This posture leads to spirited confrontations such as those recorded in Dixon and Horton's *Verbal Behavior and General Behavior Theory* where the new psycholinguists collided head on with the traditional views of the learning theorists and the verbal learners. The view does not lend itself to integration however. Among the "evolutionaries," on the other hand, there is a similar willingness to deny anything new is happening at all and a firm assertion that nothing of any importance needs to be changed. This view also resists integration.

To the "moderates," then, falls the task of trying to reinterpret old facts and integrate old materials in the newer frameworks. In this fashion they try to advance and develop the field. It is precisely this task that Bourne, Dominowski and Ekstrand have undertaken. All of these young men were trained in traditional paradigms and they understand them thoroughly. All of them have moved on in their research and thinking beyond their training in significant ways. *Purposes, intentions, knowledge, structures, relations* and *skills* have made an appearance in both their theory and research, but their attitude toward the past has been to recode and reinterpret it rather than abandon it.

It was fascinating to me to watch the changes that occurred in the authors even during the writing of the book. At one point the entire outline was discarded and a new structure was hammered out. On another occasion, we met together for three days to see if we all understood the changes that had gone on in each other as a result of the production of the first draft of the text itself. New insights appeared and were incorporated into the text; the view of old materials changed and altered until some chapters, already written, were abandoned or completely rewritten in the light of new understandings. The experience for the authors and editor was truly educational and even a little inspirational.

The book is a bridge between the old theories, old data and old positions and the newer theories and views still struggling to emerge. There is, of course, no pretense that a final, definitive position has been achieved. The book is rather a *work in progress*, frozen for the moment for the service and guidance of the reader. It joins other books in this experimental psychology series (Jakobovits and Miron, 1967, Dixon and Horton, 1968, and Dember and Jenkins, 1970) in the attempt to move toward a constructive cognitive psychology that is firmly based in data and criticism. It is my hope that the next edition will be almost as different from this one as this book is from the traditional accounts of thinking of the American behaviorists in the "great age of learning theory" in the 1940's.

I think the authors have made a vital contribution to the work of our time that tries to reexamine the cognitive processes. I cannot imagine a better book for the student of today who wants to get started toward bettering his own understandings and preparing to make his own contributions.

JAMES J. JENKINS
University of Minnesota
Minneapolis

Preface

There has been a noticeable increase in the number of psychological studies of thinking during the past two decades. Not only has the amount of research increased, but theories of thought and types of investigation have changed. In this book an attempt is made to relate these many research findings to the various conceptions of the nature of thinking.

In selecting topics for presentation, we have been guided by the idea that thinking is most closely related to problem solving. In addition to considering behavior in rather obvious problem situations, we have stressed the problem-solving aspects of verbal learning, concept formation, and linguistic behavior. Throughout the book, we have emphasized the role of a person's knowledge, skills, and intentions in his thoughtful behavior. For this reason, considerable attention is devoted to conceptual systems and to language, because these are major components of human knowledge.

Our analysis of thought has been especially influenced by a colleague at Colorado, Peter Ossorio. Peter has made available to us several unpublished manuscripts on problems and issues related to this text, among which the most helpful were *Persons* (1966), *Notes on behavior description* (1969), and *Meaning and symbolism* (1969), all published in mimeograph. Peter's face-to-face discussions with us and comments on our early drafts were invaluable. We have borrowed freely of his ideas and suggestions, though we take full responsibility for all distortions, misinterpretations, and misrepresentations of his work.

We are indebted to James J. Jenkins for his critical comments, suggestions, and general encouragement during the writing of the book. For their assistance in typing the manuscript, we are grateful to Karen Gordon, Betty MacDonald, and particularly to Judy Bowman, who did a major share of the work. Finally, we thank our colleagues who have helped shape our ideas about thinking and our wives for tolerating us during the agonizing hours of preparation and writing.

LYLE E. BOURNE, JR. / BRUCE R. EKSTRAND / ROGER L. DOMINOWSKI

The Psychology of Thinking

I Introduction and Orientation

One Psychology and the Concept of Thought

"Thinking" is one of the those mysterious concepts that everyone understands and no one can explain. The more we study it, the cloudier it seems. We know the word, *thinking*, from everyday discourse. As we grow up, we all learn to use this word properly in reference to the behavior of others and ourselves. Viewed in this manner, there is nothing peculiarly difficult or uncertain about the meaning of thinking. But thinking is also a scientific concept, an object of investigation and theorizing by psychologists. Strangely enough, it is in the scientific idiom that most of the confusion about thinking seems to develop.

The status of thought as an object of psychological inquiry is an enigma. On the one hand, it presents a challenging set of questions with intrinsic fascination to almost everyone who comes into contact with the psychology. On the other hand, progress toward any kind of systematic, general understanding of the phenomena in question has been tortuously slow. Significant insights have been rare and, until recently, sustained programs of research have been practically nonexistent. As an unfortunate result, the literature is still fragmentary and disorganized.

It has been argued that psychology, in its present stage of progress, simply isn't ready to undertake a rigorous investigation of so complex a phenomenon as thinking. Most psychologists readily admit to incomplete knowledge about the so-called simple processes, such as learning and perception. If it is further assumed that complicated behaviors are essentially compounds of elementary processes, then it might be unrewarding to embark now on the study of thinking. The counter argument is that there is no sound basis for judging the readiness of psychology to undertake a study of thinking. Furthermore, there is no guarantee that a thorough investigation of elementary behavior will even set the stage for a better understanding of complex processes; such processes may be fundamentally different. Most important, however, is the fact that a survey of the field reveals evidence of an increasing, serious interest by research-oriented psychologists in the problems of thinking; the beginnings of a substantial experimental and theoretical literature have appeared. The primary purpose of this book is to organize available information and to set it forth in an integrated fashion. Whatever systematization we can accomplish should provide a clearer view of the nature of thinking and prove useful to those research workers with sufficient temerity to attack the imposing problems still to be solved.

Thus, we will attempt to give an adequate rendering of current psychological knowledge about thinking, including the special interpretations that various investigators and theorists have advanced for their data. It should be clear from the outset, however, that our review is necessarily selective and suffers the inevitable biases of a point of view. Although it is unlikely that any attempted justification will have widespread acceptance, it seems reasonable to outline some of the principles that have guided our approach.

THE NATURE OF THINKING

Definitions of Thinking

While the difficulties of precise definition are generally acknowledged (e.g., Voss, 1969), there seems to be no shortage of definitions of thinking in the psychological literature. Before presenting our own, we shall look at some of the characteristics that repeatedly appear in these definitions.

Whatever else is said, thinking is typically described as a *complex, multifaceted,* human *activity*. For example, Gagné (1959) asserts that every instance of thinking probably involves some serialized components of stimulus categorization, hypothesis formulation, and decision making, interpolated between the presentation of a problem and its attempted solution. This stands in contrast to other human activities, e.g., rote memorization, in which the number and variety of component activities are relatively small.

More often than not, definitions make note of the apparent fact that much of what goes on in thinking is *invisible*. Haber (1969) speaks of the internal or implicit actions of processes that run their course in advance of any performance by the thinker. How these processes are to be described is not completely clear, their detailed specification being the primary goal of psychological research and theory. For the most part, however, the processes are described in behavioral terms, e.g., "sorting stimuli," "storing" (memorizing), "scanning a list in memory," "deciding," "executing," and the like, and are sometimes referred to as "miniature performances" (Mandler, 1962; McGuigan, 1966).

Some writers conceptualize the internal attributes of thinking as *physiological* or quasi-physiological, as in Osgood's theory (1957) of encoding physical energies of the external environment into the internally organized receptor, neurological, and motor events.

A third characteristic often mentioned is the status of thinking as a *causal* agent, as a determiner of behavior. Behavior, identified exclusively with performance (responses or bodily movements), is said by Newell (1969), among others, to be the simple product of causative, underlying processes, to which any of its instances can be easily and immediately reduced. This conception is, of course, implicit in Osgood's definition as well.

Finally, there is the often tacit assumption that thoughtful behavior is at least partly related to stimuli *without any immediate physical presence*. Part of what governs the activity does not exist in the external "here and now." The thinker might use his *memory;* he might *anticipate* events yet to happen; he might *imagine* possibilities which never have occurred. Theorists typically manufacture an internal "here and now" to take account of these possibilities. For example, Bruner (1964) speaks of internal activities involving the manipulation of *enactive* (or motor), *iconic* (or perceptual), or *symbolic* (or linguistic) images.

These are a sample of properties that are most commonly attributed to thinking, as a psychological concept. With some simplification, they can be put together to form a composite definition: *Thinking is a complex, multifaceted process. It is essentially internal (and possibly nonbehavioral), involving symbolic representations of events and objects not immediately present, but is initiated by some external event (stimulus). Its function is to generate and to control overt behavior.* This expression seems straightforward enough, a reasonable working hypothesis. But is it?

Problems of Definition. Despite superficial appearances, neither the foregoing definition nor its derivatives is a useful starting point for research. Indeed, such a definition creates more problems than it solves.

Consider that the foregoing definition makes it easy to forget the obvious fact that the term *thinking* is commonly used to describe behavior. It implies that statements such as "He is thinking" or "He is a thoughtful person," as descriptions of a behaving individual, are at best vague, imprecise, and nonscientific. It asserts that the real referent of thinking, whether we realize it or not, is a set of invisible activities going on inside the organism. Therefore, if we subscribe to that definition, we implicitly designate thinking to be some kind of nonbehavioral phenomenon. We permit a distinction between behavioral events and thinking, giving thinking the status of a cause of behavior. At the same time we have safely (for the definition) or dangerously (for the science) removed thinking from any possibility of direct empirical observation (or, in some cases, tossed it like the hot potato it is to the members of some other discipline, such as physiology, which we hope is better equipped to get at the internal workings of the "thinking" organism).

This line of reasoning seems dubious. We need to try another approach. How do we decide in any case whether we have an example of thinking? Somehow we have the capability of making that discrimination. We do it always on the basis of a person's behavior and our knowledge of his situation and his history. No amount of looking inside the organism, or speculating about internal processes, is as relevant to the use of the term *thinking* as are the history, current circumstances, and behavior of the person in question. *Thinking is purely and simply a behavioral concept,* and any other use of the term is either a corruption or the substitution of a different concept. And treating it as a behavioral concept in no way strips it of scientific meaning.

The Scope of Thinking and Behavior. How can thinking be a matter of behavior when the outward signs of thought are often so minimal and when the thinker's eventual performance (if any) is so simple in character? To answer that, let us consider an example. Imagine a mathematician proving a theorem, who spends much of his time leaning back in his chair, head cupped in his hands, and eyes closed, and whose only overt activity is an occasional scribble of pencil on paper. Would you say he was thinking? Probably! Then is it conceivable that all the obviously complex, intricate, high-level things that go on are reflected in his behavior, for example, the simple act of writing on paper? The answer to that is yes and no. No one would say that thinking reduces to the bodily movements that accompany the writing of equations on paper; surely, there is more to thinking than that. But so too is there more to the term *behavior* than that. The mathematician's behavior entails more than an overt performance (and its accompanying achievement, a written-out solution). We believe that the intricacies of what the mathematician did, that is, his thinking or thought processes and corresponding performance, are reasonably and naturally classified as behavioral phenomena.

Let us investigate this further. Perhaps we need a better understanding of the term *behavior* itself. When we talk of behavior, it is common to give a performance description, e.g., "He scribbled on paper." In some psychological theorizing, behavior is equated, either implicitly or explicitly, with performance, i.e., with overt responding. Performance and behavior become one and the same, indistinguishable. If that is our impoverished concept of behavior, it is easy to see the need for other processes, which then must be presumed to be nonbehavioral, to explain what is happening. Obviously, the mathematician's pencil scratches do not give a complete account of his problem-solving activities. Other events and processes—thinking—must enter in. The mathematician "perceived the problem"; had some motivation to work on it; developed, visualized, or imagined alternative possible solutions; decided among them; and tried them out implicitly. Only after he had something that seemed to work, after he had solved the problem in his head, so to speak, did he engage in any overt action. If behavior is performance, then, necessarily, these other processes and events which precede performance and make performance possible—thinking—must be a cause of behavior, and not behavior *per se*. A careful elucidation of these antecedent, thinking processes might help not only to provide a means of controlling behavior but also to explain why behavior is what it is.

This analysis leads us unfortunately to seek explanations for something we have not yet adequately described. Logic demands description before explanation, and good description sometimes accomplishes explanation simultaneously. What is needed first is a reasonable system for describing behavior. There is no logic or evidence that requires the classical equation of behavior with performance. Indeed some performances are not real behaviors. Imagine, for example, that the mathematician is really dead or, better, that he is a life-like dummy and that his performance (even his handwriting) is controlled by a puppeteer through an intricate network of strings. Would it now make sense to talk of the mathematician's behavior? We can talk of the activity of his arms and fingers but not sensibly of *his* (as a person) *behavior*. In other cases, the same performance might be an aspect of any one of several alternative behaviors. Did the mathematician write a solution to a problem, a note to his wife, a reminder to himself about a different matter? Clearly one has to use more than just performance concepts to give an adequate description of a behavior.

Behavior Description. What does it take to give a behavior description? We propose that, to approximate completeness, any description must take account, implicitly or explicitly, of at least four parameters: *knowledge, skill, intention,* and *performance* (Ossorio, 1966). For any process to qualify as a behavior at all, something must either be said or be understood about what the behaving persons knows, what he knows how to do, what he wants to do, and what in fact he does (and the attendant achievement). Any description that fails to mention one or more of these parameters, such as the traditional theoretical description which is given only in action terms, is at best incomplete and at worst irrelevant, i.e., not a description of behavior at all.

Reconsider the thoughtful mathematician. What makes his behavior sensible is not just the visible activity, although that is certainly a part of it. What makes it an example of a meaningful behavior is that it is a real person with particular skills, knowledge, and intentions who engages in that activity. What qualifies the whole episode as a case of "mathematical problem solving" is that the various parameters fit that description. Here is a person who has the requisite knowledge, skills, and intentions to address mathematical problems and who performs, in this instance, in a way that recognizably qualifies as using those characteristics. (If we want more evidence, of course, it is reasonable to ask additional questions, such as "What are the man's qualifications? Education? What did he scribble on paper, equations or doodles?" We presume for sake of this example that, on all counts, the answers are compatible with the description, mathematical problem solving.)

Knowledge, skills, and intentions are not nonbehavioral mechanisms that produce performance (behavior). Neither are they causal, antecedent events or processes which effect (or affect) performance (behavior). They are, rather, part and parcel of behavior itself. Any discussion of real behavior will implicate each of them.

What has been said so far amounts neither to a proposition nor to a theory in the usual sense. It is rather a conceptual-terminological system for sensible systematic discourse about the topic of this book and about the domain of behavior, in general. We present it not as something subject to empirical test, nor as a competitor to traditional theory (as outlined in general terms above and exemplified in detail in subsequent chapters), but as a logically complete and consistent way to proceed. Throughout this text, when we speak of a behavior we have in mind not just an overt movement, a response, or a performance, but rather an instance of a complex concept having cognitive, skillful, intentional, and performative properties. As the discussion develops, we shall see that this system leads to a rule-following model of the behaving organism with the characteristics of recursiveness and reflexivity which are necessary to generate and therefore to account for the infinity of real or possible behaviors of a single human being.

Thinking as a Behavior Description. If we adopt this conceptual system, then clearly there is reason to be suspicious about the previously given definition of thinking, emphasizing complex, implicit, enabling processes. That definition supplies an answer, even before a proper question has been asked. The first thing we need is a description of what is to be explained.

To find out what a term means, it is reasonable to ask how it is used. When is it an appropriate description and when not? What kind of discrimination does it codify? The reply, in this case, is that we use *thinking* typically to characterize a kind of achievement by a person, involving a change in his behavior potential. The term is particularly relevant in the context of a problem, as when a person "tries to think" of plausible solutions. It is the "thought that occurs" to him as he tries to solve the problem, the achieved change in his potential to behave, which is the phenomenon of primary interest.

In a derived sense, thinking is a term used to characterize certain behavioral episodes. It is a conspicuously noncommittal description. It does not tell much beyond the fact that the person is real and awake and is behaving intentionally and intelligibly under the circumstances. To say, "He is thinking," is analogous to statements like "He is telling" or "He is getting." It is not very specific but, when the term is used appropriately, there is little else to be said. After all, if we were in a position to say more—as, for example, "He's really adding up a column of numbers in his head" —we would not need to use the more general term, thinking, in the first place.

Try this on the illustrative mathematician. While he sits, rocked back in his chair, *thinking* is surely the apt description and there is little else to be said. His circumstances give rise to a problem and his history qualifies him as a problem solver. He is thinking about a problem and how it might be solved. His visible activity level is minimal, though he *is* performing (sitting is a kind of performance). Of course, the real payoff for describing his behavior as thoughtful vis-à-vis some mathematical problem comes over the longer term when he produces a solution or an attempt or says he was trying to solve the problem. That will usually close off any further questions about the correctness of the description.

Thus, we would say that, rather than being a complex, covert computing process which can never be seen (unless we specify its physiology), thinking is a simple noncommittal way to describe a behavior which, like all behavior, is completely observable. The goal of research is not to explain or define the phenomenon away by saying that thinking is really some other kind of process. The goal is to elucidate those properties of the thinker and his circumstances—knowledge, skill, intention, and performance—in such a way as to permit a more detailed description, e.g., "He calculated the sum," or "He integrated by parts."

Other Uses of Thinking. Relying, as we do, on a descriptive, natural language approach to the topic, we need to contend with the fact that *thinking* has an apparent multitude of uses. It is applied not only to the problem solver, but to other behaviors in the following ways as well:

1. I think (believe) it is time to go.
2. To think of (anticipate) changing schools is frightening.
3. He did it without thinking (unintentionally).
4. Can you think of (remember) his address?
5. The idea is unthinkable (unacceptable).
6. Can you think of (imagine) what it would be like to be rich?

It might be argued from these examples that thinking, as a concept, is too vague or inexplicit to be meaningful or scientifically useful. How indeed can one investigate such a variable form of behavior?

There is no need to make a detailed argument in reply. First, although there are several senses in which the term is used, for all practical purposes, it is usually clear which sense is intended. Thinking in the sense of problem solving, which is the major focus of our discussion, is rarely confused with the other possibilities. Second, there is a common feature among these uses which ought not to be neglected. They all entail behavior which is impossible to characterize in a physical, "here-now" idiom. They involve knowing, cognition, and ideation in contrast to automatic performance. The study of thinking as a problem-oriented behavior ought to be of some relevance to thinking in each of its various senses.

A Definition. Now that we have rejected the more or less "established" point of view, where are we left as regards a definition of thinking? There are several things that can be said: (1) Thinking is a way of characterizing a behaving individual. (2) It codifies an operative potential for a certain range of behavior on the part of that individual. (3) It is typically applicable when the circumstances are problematical and it makes sense to say that the person is working on the problem. (4) The characterization, "He is thinking" (or anything more specific) is minimally governed by performance standards. Logically, he might be thinking whether his activity level is high *or* low. However, engaging in other activities —pacing up and down, for example—while thinking will often lead the observer to describe the subject as doing that (pacing) rather than thinking. The question of minimal performance standards comes up here because it is under this condition, when there is nothing else that a person could reasonably be said to be doing, that we feel most free to say that what he is doing is thinking. (5) Thinking, like all behavior, is elucidated in a rule-following model, having knowledge, skill, intention, and performance parameters.

We can give no definition of thinking in the classical form, "Thinking is . . . ." Judging by the voluminous deliberations of a recent conference of psychologists on the topic of thinking (Voss, 1969), it is doubtful that any such definition can command more than a modicum of support and agreement among the experts. What thinking "really is" can be settled neither by definition nor by empirical research anyway. Arbitrary definitions tend to impose constraints, leading to the exclusion from research or theory of valid examples. To say on the other hand that we must establish the limits only via empirical research is to adopt a preliminary "know-nothing orientation" toward the topic which proceeds in ignorance of the logical status of thinking as a concept in human behavior.

Our plan is merely to list some of the salient attributes of the concept of thinking and to proceed henceforth with examples. We will let the examples speak for themselves and invite the reader to judge their relevancy and centrality. We take the goal of research on this topic to be the elaboration and systematization of rule-form descriptions of human behavior in problematic circumstances, and not the identification of underlying causes of behavior.

Examples of Thinking

The number of possible examples of human thinking is indefinitely large. Indeed, there is hardly a case of human action to which the concept of thought is inappropriately applied. Even in a test of simple reaction time, a person's response might on occasion be "thoughtful" (Sternberg, 1966). Obviously, there is no way to deal with all examples, and that in itself might make questionable the wisdom of any approach based on instances. Fortunately, it is neither necessary nor even desirable to consider all examples. Concepts are not explicated by the totality of possible examples. On the contrary, the totality is generated from the concept, which itself is derived (abstracted) from a few examples. No one learned the concept *dog* from contact with all dog objects. A few exemplars were sufficient to provide the general knowledge necessary to discriminate on all subsequent occasions. And so it is with thinking: we need to consider relatively few examples, and we have tried to select those that are the most useful.

Many examples of thinking, such as daydreaming or hallucinating, have not been studied in any significant experimental sense. Little beyond the obvious can be said in those cases. Our approach will be to work intensively with a few examples, chosen primarily because they represent indisputable cases of thinking and because a substantial body of knowledge about them does exist. The examples are taken from the research areas typically referred to in psychology as *problem solving, concept formation, verbal learning,* and *psycholinguistics*. Because the labels fall considerably short of reflecting the scope of the area and issues involved, it is helpful at this point to elaborate briefly on each of these topics.

Problem Solving. We say that a "problem" exists whenever it is clear that (1) a person is trying to attain some goal, or to change his present circumstances into some specifiably different situation, (2) his initial attempts fail to accomplish this end, and (3) two or more alternative courses of action are possible. It might be added that problems exist partly because of the limited ability of human beings to use available information and to consider simultaneously all possible courses of action. This fact leads directly to the concept of *strategies,* which are more or less efficient, systematic methods for dealing sequentially with response possibilities in a problematic situation.

The term *problem solving* is often used synonymously with the entire set of events which has been labeled here *goal-directed thinking*. In this discussion, however, because of methodological considerations and the status of contemporary research, problem solving is defined in a somewhat more limited sense, as an aspect of thinking involving both the formulation of and selection among possible responses in a problematic situation. Many of these ways of performing, including the correct one(s), might have been learned previously by the subject, so that the problem is in effect solved upon his discovery of the appropriate performance.

When problem solving is so defined, its principal distinguishing characteristic is the emphasis on *discovery* of correct solutions. This distinction is reflected in procedures used in experimental work. In studies of language and concept formation, the subject is typically given preliminary instructions about, and sometimes experience with, the kind of performance required by the task, so that his principal achievement is to learn to make these responses appropriately, i.e., at the correct stimulus. In studies of problem solving, similar information is likely not to be given, or, indeed, the subject might be misinformed concerning some crucial aspect of the situation, so that he must discover the correct performance for himself.

Conceptual Behavior. All behavior is in a sense conceptual. We respond not to the uniqueness in our circumstances but to the regularities—the categories, the sequences, and the functions—of objects and events in the world. It is easy to show that the full capacity of any normal human being for making discriminations is generally not exercised. Consider that, when the circumstances are conducive, a person can make seven million color discriminations alone. That our behavior is not always contingent on these distinctions is obvious. Rather it seems more appropriate to describe human behavior as a matter of responding to each situation as an example of a more general case, principle, rule, or concept. This is the way we deal with the tremendous diversity of stimulation encountered in everyday life.

In psychology, the phrase *conceptual behavior* implies the learning or utilization of categories or principles. The term *concept*, although widely used in a variety of ways, represents for present purposes a general description applicable to a variety of distinguishable states of affairs. These states, commonly called *instances of the concept*, are grouped together, ordered, or otherwise arranged on some basis, such as the existence of common attributes or characteristics or some other relationship among the instances. In a sense, a *concept* codes many objects or events according to some principle or set of principles, which might, for example, define a small number of categories, and thereby simplify the existing circumstances of a person.

Verbal Learning and Psycholinguistics. The relation between thinking and language has been a matter of speculation and dispute throughout history (Carroll, 1964) and is hardly the kind of question we can hope to settle in this text. It is clear, however, that there is no way to divorce a discussion of thinking from considerations about language. Furthermore, there is an impressive body of information collected in studies of language and verbal learning which describes unique features of thoughtful behavior. Contemporary research in verbal learning represents the most refined extension of the principles of associationism to be implicated in analyses of thought. The work in verbal learning, at the same time, provides an illustration of the strengths and weaknesses of purely associative interpretations of behavior. It is obviously pertinent to review this literature in detail.

We take a relatively general, yet simple, point of view with respect to the relation between language and thinking. Both concepts are treated as being essentially applicable to behaving individuals. Saying something is a form of behavior and saying something is accomplished by speaking (or writing, etc.), which is the performative aspect of that behavior. For an individual to speak is for him to participate in a public, social, rule-governed form of behavior. The most outstanding characteristic of this form of behavior is that it codifies distinctions of all kinds. Thus, the individual who says "cat" (e.g., in "the cat pressed the bar") is ipso facto distinguishing cats from noncats and doing so in an explicit and public way. Among the important distinctions codified in particular languages are the distinction between language and nonlanguage; between behavior and nonbehavior; between the behaving individual and the behavior of that individual; between actual behavior and proclivities, capabilities, and potentials for behavior; between one particular behavior and another particular behavior; between thought and nonthought; and between one particular thought and another particular thought. Note that within-category distinctions are crucial. If we could not distinguish one behavior from another behavior or one sort of behavior from another sort of behavior we would have lost the category of "behavior" entirely.

Likewise, if we could not distinguish one thought from another we would have lost the category of "thought" entirely. In this respect, then, language is essential for thought. However, thought is also essential for language, since knowledge is essential for behavior, including verbal behavior. "Speaks" refers to an aspect (performance) of behavior, not a behavior per se. There could be no such behavior as that which has the performative aspect "speaks" if that behavior did not also have other aspects, including the cognitive aspect of making distinctions of some sort. Those distinctions must be operative and not merely potential. A person who *knows* that Peking is the capital of China is eligible to engage in behaviors which depend on that knowledge. On a given occasion, however, he may be unable to engage in such behaviors because the knowledge is not available. However, if at a given time he *thinks* (realizes, is aware) of Peking as being the capital of China, then at that time he is not merely eligible, but fully prepared to engage in these behaviors. The difference between knowing a fact and thinking of it is like the difference between merely owning a hammer and having it in one's hand. Thus, reference to the concepts an individual has, to the knowledge he has, and to the thoughts that he has are all ways of characterizing his behavior potential, and they differ from one another in that they form a series going from more noncommittal (concept) to least noncommittal (thought). It is because all behavior requires some *operative* distinction that all behavior, including verbal behavior, can be looked upon as "thoughtful" or as "an expression of what he had in mind."

Thus, language and thought are mutually implicative. The relation is a systematic, logical one which can be delineated only by introducing other related concepts such as behavior, the parameters of behavior, and the role of observation and description of behavior as special cases of behavior. This view of the relation of thought to language contrasts with two more common views: (1) that there is a simple and direct logical connection, comparable to the connection between buying and selling or between a batter and a bat in baseball; (2) that there is a causal or geographical relation, so that one occurs at the place where the other one occurs, for example, that the process of (implicit) speech is part of a larger process of producing thoughts or that thinking is a process which is part of a larger process that produces speech performances. Thus, the present view of the mutual implication is one which permits us to say that infants and other species of individuals think even though they do not speak. We merely say that it could not (logically) be the case that *anyone* (infants or otherwise) thought without speaking if *no one* could speak.

In the simplest analysis, the linguistic system consists of conceptual elements (a lexicon) and their relations (a grammar). It gives the way human beings have for characterizing the objects, events, processes, and states of affairs that comprise their circumstances. The major point of interest in this text will be the nature of linguistic codes and the variables influencing the manner in which they are learned and subsequently used in solving problems.

Comment. The parametric analysis of behavior and of "thought," as a locution for referring to distinctions (concepts) which the individual is fully prepared to act on at a given time, clarifies the variety of ordinary language expressions in which the term "think" or "thought" appears. In particular, it helps us to see why there is such a strong connection between thinking and problem solving: if behavior is a function of the values of five parameters—knowledge, skill, intention, performance, and achievement—then the variance among behaviors will in general be distributed across the five parameters. It follows that, by eliminating variance due to any one parameter, the contribution of the remaining parameters will be increased. Now, except in special circumstances, the achievement variance which we take note of is restricted to those achievements which are the expression of motivation and competence rather than luck, chance, coincidence, etc. Likewise, we generally ignore performance variance. Moreover, we can severely restrict skill variance by "trivializing" the level of skill required for performance which is successful. Thus the major remaining sources of variance are motivation and cognition. "Problem solving" reduces the motivational variance by definition. To the extent that a group of subjects is engaged in the same problem-solving task, their operative motivation is substantially the same. With this parameter pinned down, then, indeed, behavior variance is primarily a function of the cognitive parameter, and reference to the subjects' thoughts and thinking is simply the standard way of referring to operative values of the cognitive parameter. Thus, a "problem-solving" format in experimentation is methodologically appropriate for studying "thinking," though there remain, to be sure, a variety of technical considerations having to do with sampling of tasks, instructions, individual differences, etc.

Other Examples. As noted earlier, many (and possibly all) areas of psychological research are rich with examples of thinking, and so the limitations on this review are at least partly arbitrary. One notable omission is the topic of decision making and judgment, which has become a matter of increased interest to psychologists in recent years (Beach and Peterson, 1967). Another is the currently popular analysis of memory into perceptual and cognitive components of varying degrees of permanency (Atkinson and Schiffrin, 1968). Desirable as the inclusion of these topics might be on other grounds, we find them to be pedagogically less useful than the examples we have chosen to emphasize. We believe, however, they require no unique psychological principles, and it is possible to outline the essential work on decision making, memory, and other relevant topics within the context of the primary examples: language, concept formation, and problem solving.

DEVELOPMENT OF THINKING

Thoughtful Behavior

Consider the massive difference between a newborn human infant, who is capable of only a few primitive activities, and a normal adult, who routinely exhibits intricate skill, sometimes shows immediate comprehension of new facts, and occasionally demonstrates original problem-solving performance. The neonate starts essentially at zero and his learning to behave in any way is slow and tortuous. The adult, in contrast, has a large repertoire of behaviors, and new learning is easy and often insightful. The difference, in part, can be attributed to the adult's greater ability to think. How does this ability come about? This is a question which will be addressed in the context of specific forms of behavior later, but it might be helpful at this point to make a few general remarks.

Part of the development of thinking, of course, has to do with biological maturity. All the various systems of the body—sensory, neural, and motor—are intimately involved in behaving and therefore in thinking. One must be "mechanically equipped" to think. Behavior, however, is not a mechanism. It is more akin to the functional properties of a mechanism. Furthermore, in view of the abstract, recursive, conceptual nature of adult behavior, there is clearly more to it than mere passive, seemingly predetermined biological growth.

The basis of psychological change is personal history, experience, and learning. A person gains knowledge and skills by observation and by practice. Each new fact and skill adds to his behavioral repertoire and contributes to a basis for further development.

To make note of the fact that, at any given time, a person, even a child, does not engage all of his knowledge and skills and yet "still has them," it is commonly said in psychological theory that the knowledge and skills are represented symbolically, in memory. They are there as a reserve, to be called upon as circumstances demand. In any particular circumstance, a person might be said "to search through his memory, to select an appropriate symbolic representative, and to output a particular performance based on that representation." These and similar activities, said to take place internally and invisibly, are generally referred to as symbolic processes, i.e., as operations on the organism's repertoire of symbolic representations.

While it is clear that a person does accumulate and remember ways of behaving and normally does behave in a way that is consistent with his present circumstances, there is no clear evidence in logic or in data that these behaviors are really internal physical units that get stored, processed, searched for, selected, and invoked by some set of internal storage or processing devices. That argument only leads to regressive questions about the mechanisms underlying the mechanisms. It is not an accident that the description of symbolic processes (the functions of some alleged symbolic device) is given in behavioral terms, such as storing, sorting, and selecting. That in itself is a strong clue that, rather than being functions of a device at all, they are functions of a person, i.e., part and parcel of or, better, parameters of his behavior.

A Symbolic Representation of Skill. Mandler (1962) has given the following account of the compounding and integration of primitive activities into complex, skillful behavior. In any task to be learned or problem to be solved, a person might begin by making discrete, crude and, almost always, somewhat disorganized responses. If the task is not completely beyond his capabilities, we can expect that some of his activity will be correct (or approximately so) and thus followed by reinforcement or confirming informative feedback. Eventually, incorrect responses are eliminated, and proper performance (which may consist of a series of responses) becomes relatively stable. At this point, Mandler describes the various components of the total activity required by successful performance in the task as well integrated. Integration in this sense implies that responses which were previously unrelated to each other have become organized into a single functional unit. The entire response sequence is elicited as a unit by some stimulus or situation, much as the individual components were earlier.

There are many examples of this phenomenon: the hungry rat that threads its way swiftly through the alleys of a complex maze which may involve a dozen or more choice points and cul de sacs; the college sophomore serving in a rote learning experiment who recites a long string of nonsense syllables in some arbitrary order prescribed by the experimenter; or the mathematics teacher who presents without notes the steps of a logical proof for a complicated theorem. In any of these examples, it is unlikely that the performer was miraculously transformed instantaneously from a naive organism to one capable of running off the proper response sequence without error. The skill was acquired through practice. Even though the person might in some cases be capable at the outset of making each of the appropriate responses, the sequence must be learned, organized, or integrated. As these examples suggest, integration can take place on many different levels of complexity. Thus, the emission of some rudimentary vocalization, such as "da-da," can be integrated in much the same way as reciting an entire list of nonsense syllables or speaking a complete sentence.

The feature of Mandler's proposition which is critical for present purposes is that, as a response unit becomes integrated, there develops a correlative "symbolic" representation (within the learner) which can function independently of its overt movement counterpart. The symbolic representation allows the person to "think" about responding without necessarily moving a muscle. The existence of many symbolic representations of skill (plus the knowledge of their respective effects or outcomes) opens the way for some of the complex phenomena we have subsumed under the heading, thinking. The person has in his repertoire certain ways of behaving from which alternative courses of action can be formulated. If one of these alternatives is appropriate in some new problem and if the person chooses to follow it, he might appear, to an observer, to solve the problem insightfully.

Two points are worth noting about Mandler's proposal, which has been somewhat freely translated for present purposes. First, it deals with the acquisition of specific skills, acquired in the context of a single task with relatively unchanging physical features. The skill developed is correspondingly rather narrow and might not apply to a wide range of tasks. We shall consider another idea next which deals with a broader kind of skill, based not on physical attributes but on relations between attributes.

Secondly, while the proposal does allow for a symbolic representation of skill (the symbolic analogue of a well-integrated performance), there is no corresponding representation of the person's knowledge of that skill, i.e., when it is appropriately employed, what its effects are (were, or are likely to be), etc. That parameter appears to be assimilated to the stimulus. If there is enough physical similarity between the present stimulus and the original learning situation (how much is left unspecified), the analogue and its accompanying performance are automatically invoked. This feature in Mandler's proposal is a near-universal characteristic of psychological theories of learning and thinking.

Acquisition of a More General Competence. Harlow (1959) has characterized the ability to think in terms of more general skills which clearly transcend the particular (physical) attributes of a problem and are based on principles or concepts which encompass the correct performances for a class of tasks. The analysis is based on an extensive series of experiments, mostly with monkeys but occasionally with young children, aimed at demonstrating that organisms can be trained to think (follow rules). The paradigm of these experiments can be illustrated with the following simple example. The subject is presented initially with a discrimination learning task in which he is required to learn to choose one of two different stimulus objects. Hidden under one of the objects is some valued incentive, such as a grape for the monkey or a piece of candy for the child. On each trial (or presentation of a pair of objects), the subject is allowed one choice or response. If the chooses correctly, he gets the incentive; if he chooses incorrectly, he gets nothing. This procedure continues until the subject masters the problem (or for some predetermined number of trials). Next, the subject is presented with a second two-choice discrimination problem, in which the stimulus objects are different. Learning is carried to the same criterion. The procedure is repeated for still another problem with novel stimulus objects. Always the same principle for solution holds, i.e., one object is consistently associated with reward throughout the trial series.

The number of problems presented will depend on several factors, including the species and sophistication of the organism used as subject. Beginning with naive monkeys, several hundred such problems may be constructed and used. Changes in a subject's performance across a series of problems are the data of interest and, as one might expect, a general positive transfer effect is observed. Efficiency of performance improves measurably on each successive problem. Whereas during the initial problems in the series, the subject might take many trials to achieve a solution (to choose consistently the rewarded object), the subject's performance on later problems shows an insight-like leap from chance probability of being correct on Trial 1 to perfect responding from Trial 2 on. If the performance measure is the percentage of correct responses within a group of subjects, Trial 1 yields a value near 50 per cent, because with any new pair of stimuli only half the subjects are likely to guess which of the two is correct. Trials 2 through n, however, yield a value at or near 100 per cent. Figure 1-1 presents some

FIGURE 1–1. *A family of learning set curves, showing the performance (percentage of correct responses over six successive trials) of rhesus monkeys on several hundred two-choice discrimination problems.*

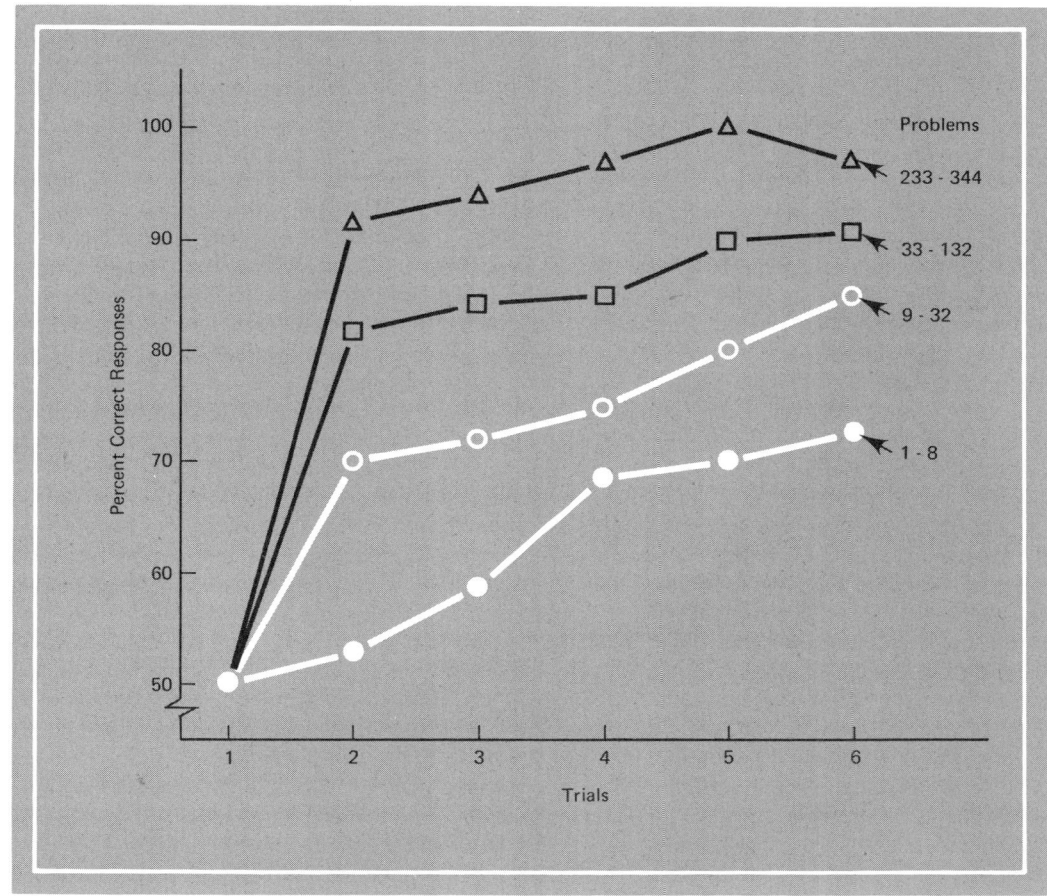

Source: Data are redrawn from H. F. Harlow, Learning set and error factor theory. In S. Koch, ed., *Psychology: A Study of a Science.* New York: McGraw-Hill Book Co., 1959.

data reported by Harlow from such an investigation. Over the course of several problems it seems fair to say that the subject learns or catches on to a principle or general rule for responding in this simple situation. The principle is based on the fact that reward is regularly associated with one of the two stimulus objects. The rule describing performance may be stated in the following way: Choose either stimulus on the first trial; if correct, continue to choose the same object; if incorrect, switch and consistently choose the other.

Harlow described the process which takes a learner from trial-and-error to insightful performance as the formation of a learning set. A learning set is conceived, by Harlow, as

Psychology and the Concept of Thought 15

a set of habits, organized internally (like symbolic analogues), which allows efficient performance on each new problem of a given type. Although the learner begins with a disorganized, unsystematic approach to a particular kind of problem, if he is given the opportunity to practice on several of them successively, he will build up a plan or integrated system for responding that will be generally useful in other problems of the same type. A repertoire of learning sets, according to Harlow, provides the bases for thinking, especially by human beings.

Learning sets, and their corresponding principles, are not limited to simple problems like two-choice discrimination learning. Harlow has shown their development in a variety of tasks, such as the *oddity problem,* which requires a response to the unique member of an array of three or more objects, and the *reversal problem,* wherein the reward is switched periodically from one stimulus object to the other. On a more complex level, experiments have indicated a general improvement in the ability of human beings to form or utilize concepts based on some principle such as the existence of common stimulus elements within all instances of the concept. Examples are common in everyday behavior. Learning how and when to apply a certain mathematical equation is a familiar educational experience. As students, we all remember solving "rate problems," e.g., if Mr. X drives his auto at an average speed of 50 miles per hour (R), how far will he travel (D) in five hours (T), using the formula, $D = R \times T$? All of these and many others illustrate the utilization of a principle which is learned or acquired through practice and experience. Each principle holds for a class of problems and is, in essence, independent of the particular concrete elements—stimulus objects, numbers, etc.—which are involved. Operating in every case is the formation and subsequent utilization of a skill which Harlow calls a learning set. Just as with Mandler's symbolic analogue, it might be noted, the invocation of a learning set is not said to be a matter of the subject's knowledge, but is left rather to the control of physical stimulus events.

Comment. Cognitive process is only one of several terms that has been used to refer to the nonperformance aspects of thinking. The literature of psychology contains many others. Any reader who takes time to explore firsthand the research and theory in the area can expect to come across such terms as organization mechanisms, mnemonic devices, plans, hypotheses, schemata, heuristics, strategies, transformations, symbolic structures and processes, analogic structures, expectancies, and mediating mechanisms, just to name a few that enjoy some currency. This, of course, well illustrates the difficulty of trying to organize the field and to understand the interrelationships among empirical findings and theoretical positions. For the sake of consistency, in the bulk of the following discussions we use the term *cognitive processes,* except where explicit reference is made to the work of an experimenter who has a convincing reason for using a different label.

The Emphasis on Learning. Almost all descriptions of the development of cognitive behavioral processes (as exemplified by Mandler and Harlow) emphasize the importance of learning as a precursor. An organism's capacity for complex behavior is prescribed by the repertoire of knowledge and skills, of cognitions and competences, he has acquired. When a person encounters a novel problem or task, he performs in ways which have been successful in the past and, if necessary, builds upon these behaviors to form (to learn) different and possibly higher order competences. Out of experience come more and more highly organized behavior patterns, befitting current and probably future problems. This line of reasoning argues for a hierarchical model of behavior in which simple activities are integrated into sequences or classes which, in turn, are organized into more complex, higher order conceptual units.

In essence, we would accept Harlow's conclusion that people learn the knowledge and skills that constitute thoughtful behavior. Thinking is largely a matter of acquiring problem-solving competence. This conclusion has tempted some (e.g., Staats, 1968) to speculate that all cognitive processes, and all thinking, originate in and can be accounted for by simpler learning processes, such as conditioning. This, in turn, implies that the laws of learning apply directly to thinking and that one can understand thinking in terms of these more elementary principles. While there is an apparent continuity in behavior from simple learning to complex mental activity, the evidence that all thinking is a compounding of elementary processes is not compelling. The principles by which we learn should be consistent with those which pertain to thinking, but need not necessarily exhaust them. We can probably expect that studies of learning will aid in an understanding of thought, but also that the reverse is just as true, i.e., that studies of thinking will shed light on "simpler" learning processes. In the following chapters, discussion will be oriented around a description of the essential properties of thinking and how they appear to be related to learning; it will leave reason to question, however, the sufficiency of simple learning as an explanation for thought.

"Uncontrolled" Thought Processes. As a final note, mention should be made once again of the fact that much of what we call thinking in ordinary language might have little obvious movement, outcome, or directionality to it. Day-dreaming, being "lost in thought," free associating, all have a more or less nonpurposive flavor and might not be accompanied by any apparent intentional action. The relevant descriptive distinction is between cases of "thinking about x," with which this book is primarily concerned, and merely "thinking."

The scientific study of thinking began with an emphasis on a kind of "free" or "uncontrolled" thinking. But free thinking is an activity which is particularly unaffected by the person's immediate surroundings. This makes the problems of experimental analysis worse than they are otherwise, which are formidable enough. Although there is little experimental evidence to report, what is available is consistent with the orientation outlined here or with empirical evidence from studies of directed thinking. The few normative studies of free thinking that have been made, e.g., studies of verbal associations, provide no reason to attribute any unique properties to behavior in such situations which do not also pertain to directed thinking.

AIMS AND PLAN OF THE BOOK

This book aims at providing a resume of what psychologists know or speculate about thinking. The approach is not exhaustive, but rather emphasizes a selected set of examples. We hope to sample and to integrate sufficient information to provide the reader with an understanding of the way scientific psychology conceptualizes one of its most important problems and the degree to which it is capable of contributing to an understanding of it.

Preliminary discussions should have made clear the virtual impossibility of formulating a definition of thinking suitable for scientific purposes, that is, entirely consistent with the opinions of all workers in the area. The crux of the problem is that thinking is a noncommittal term which covers a variety of behaviors. Moreover, much of what a person is doing while thinking is silent, giving the investigator little movement-type data to work with and leaving the distinct (and correct) impression that a lot more is going on than we could ever hope to capture in an analysis of movement. The purpose of this review is to elucidate our use of the term and to do that scientifically by relying on experimental data and theory. We believe that the eventual elucidation will be a rule-following model, specified by knowledge, skill, intention, and performance parameters. But this is clearly not the modal position in psychology today and we shall want to develop alternative positions which have also been applied to the empirical examples we have selected.

Chapter 2 deals with matters of general history. The discussion will be limited in several ways. First, although there is considerable evidence in the writings of philosophers and natural scientists, dating from the days of pre-scientific psychology, of interest in all facets of human and animal behavior, this chapter will set forth only the important historical landmarks of the last 100 years or so. Prior to this point in time there was really little factual information relevant to thinking, and most discussions, although profound, were entirely speculative in nature. Substantial reviews of psychological issues and the antecedents of scientific psychology are already available, and we could not hope, in the brief space of a single chapter, to match the quality of presentation that has already been achieved (Boring, 1950).

Chapter 2 will touch only the highlights of early research and theory on thinking, consisting primarily of a general discussion of matters which are not specific to the various aspects of thinking or subareas which are treated in detail in later chapters. In this, we will include outlines of some conceptualizations of thought processes which contrast with the one adopted for purposes of organization in the present volume. The aim of the chapter is primarily to provide an appreciation and understanding of the developments within psychology, in general, which have set the stage for the rigorous science of thinking which now appears to be a reality.

The next twelve chapters, the body of the book, divide into four sections, each devoted to a distinct area of research. Each section attempts to inform the reader on three main issues: (1) the current status of empirical work in the area, including some discussion of research methods where necessary, (2) the best developed theoretical ideas for organizing research findings, and (3) the manner in which the area connects with and exemplifies the concept of thinking. The format of the sections will vary, because the way in which these points are best addressed differs among the topics, but the purpose is basically the same in each.

The areas to be covered have already been outlined. The first topic, covered in Chapters 3, 4, 5, and 6, is problem solving. This might seem like an unnatural place to begin, for, as we have noted, problem solving is often used as a synonym for the entire process of goal-directed thinking and, in its most creative form, is extremely complicated and intricate. To date, however, psychological research on problem solving has been surprisingly simple in its conception and structure and the issues under investigation have been correspondingly limited. As a consequence the field is not well developed and is best treated as a preliminary to the more complex questions that have been considered in other areas.

The treatment of language is divided into two sections, Verbal Learning (Chapters 7 and 8) and Language (Chapters 13 and 14). The first section reviews those aspects of the classic approach to verbal learning and verbal behavior which seem to embody and exemplify thought processes, and it shows clearly that even in the highly refined, highly mechanized routines designed to study simple, fundamental associations—the linkage of two verbal items by rote memorization—the existence and influence of thought by the learner cannot be avoided. There are several good examples, such as the so-called mediational phenomena and subjective organization of verbal materials, that demonstrate the point. Many of these follow directly from research on problem solving which often utilizes simple linguistic tasks, e.g., the anagram.

The findings reviewed in this section are, in a sense, a spin-off from studies with a basically different purpose. They do not represent a direct experimental attack on thinking. There is some scientific research with the primary aim of explicating the relation between linguistic activities and thinking. Because this is a more recent and more complicated endeavor and not always easy to rationalize with the classical approach to verbal behavior, it is considered in a separate section, Chapters 13 and 14. This work is based as much or more in linguistics as it is in orthodox psychology and is fundamentally concerned with the functions of language, i.e., coding and describing, and their manifestations in all behavior, including thinking.

Between the two sections, a field which appears to have a relation to both kinds of verbal behavior, namely concept formation, will be surveyed, Chapters 9, 10, 11, and 12. The relation should be clear in advance. Whether we have a case of subjective organization of apparently unrelated nonsense items, or the effects of syntactical structure on the recognition of substantive messages, concepts—systematic ways of treating a variety of distinguishable objects or events—are clearly involved. What we know about the learning and utilization of concepts helps to understand and to integrate work on many aspects of verbal behavior. In fact, it will appear from this that at least in some cases the major differences between the classical, associational approach to verbal activities and the newer, linguistics-based approach which seems more directly pointed at the language-thought relation are largely terminological and a matter of emphasis.

Chapter 15 is an overview. Rather than summarize the material in preceding chapters, however, it offers a modest proposal, arising from the general orientation laid out in this chapter, for reducing, organizing, and in general for talking systematically about thinking. The proposal is a system for describing conceptually the cognitive and competence aspects of thoughtful behavior, thereby suggesting some interpretations of empirical findings. While we cannot offer a complete theory, we can try to make clear both the complexity and the elusiveness of the issues, and what we think research to date has contributed to their clarification. We can also suggest in this context some possible directions for future research.

Two History and General Theoretical Systems

There is an intensive search by modern psychologists for the rules, the laws, or the principles by which people think. Even as recently as the nineteenth century, however, philosophers accepted the idea that formal logic represented the laws of thinking. Logic was supposed to reveal in some sense the essence of human thought and reasoning, the processes and products of the mind. Of course, it was obvious to logicians and psychological philosophers that, in their behavior, human beings exhibit all sorts of violations of logic. To find examples of irrational behavior was and is no problem at all. And this, it would seem, should constitute adequate falsification of any theory that identifies thinking with logic. But the philosophers and psychologists of the day operated on rather different assumptions than most of their modern counterparts. These early workers conceived of man dualistically; they assumed an independence of mind and body. There was, therefore, no reason to expect that bodily action would correspond strictly to mental processes. Thus, although reason and logic might be violated by a person's acts, the operations of his mind could still be rational.

Once the enterprise of scientific psychology began to function in earnest, it became clear that the dualistic philosophy was a hindrance to productive work and an obstacle to scientific progress. It was rejected, rather uniformly, by psychologists and philosophers alike. The rejection was so violent in some quarters that the concept of mind itself was ruled out as illegitimate and nonscientific. That is part of another story, however, to be told in a separate section. We need only say here that scientific psychology very early accepted a unity, cohesion, and continuity of behavior involving both symbolic activity (the modern counterpart of mind) and bodily movement.

Although logicians, as well as psychologists, recognized in the nineteenth century that mental activity was more than logic could represent, no one would claim, even today, that logic is entirely irrelevant to human thought. In a sense, logic is a description of rational, self-consistent thinking—how man ought to think, if not how he actually *does*.

Logical principles are not natural laws; they don't describe behavior except in special cases. They are, however, baselines against which the validity or adequacy of human reasoning can be checked. Logicians can hardly explain the various fallacies that characterize the behavior of human beings. This residue of illogic is left to the psychologist to explore.

The intent of this chapter is to describe the recent history of the psychology of thinking. We must begin several hundred years ago to discover the important antecedents of a formal and independent experimental psychology, for these imposed a strong commitment and serious constraints on the study of thinking.

ANTECEDENTS OF SCIENTIFIC PSYCHOLOGY

Associationism

By far the most important precursor of the scientific psychology of thinking is a tradition within philosophy which extends backward in time at least as far as Aristotle. This is the movement commonly known as *Associationism,* particularly as that doctrine was developed and argued by the empiricist moral philosophers of Great Britain. It is this movement which provided a research orientation for most early experimental psychologists; this is the movement which gave the psychology of learning and thinking most of its important problems and defined its essential content.

Locke. We pick up the tradition first in the writings of a seventeenth-century Englishman, John Locke. For Locke, psychology was the study of the mind or mental life, which he conceived as a complex, though analyzable, structure. The mind, wrote Locke, is a manifold of ideas, some simple and others complex. The idea is the irreducible unit of the mind; by definition, it is a concept or a meaning or an item of knowledge. Anything in the mind or within the realm of consciousness is held to be analyzable into its component elements. The empiricism in Locke's position comes from his insistence that ideas are not innate, but rather arise through experience, i.e., empirically. The mind, at the outset, is a blank slate—from Aristotle, a *Tabula Rasa*—and on this slate, experience enscribes its message. Locke's associationism is embodied in the notion that simple ideas bind together to form more complex ones; it is these, of course, which are the subject of analysis.

Locke described simple ideas as elemental and unanalyzable. They were able to enter into association with other ideas, according to certain laws or principles, to form compounds; thus the term "mental mechanics" has sometimes been applied to the associationism of Locke and his followers.

According to Locke there are two sources of simple ideas. First, ideas arise from sensations or the products of an organism's sensory apparatus. This is a fairly obvious source and occasioned little criticism or objection from the thinkers of the day. The second source was the mind itself, through reflection upon its own activity. In a sense, Locke was saying here that the mind is capable of being conscious of its own activity, an assumption which stands at the very basis of the unique experimental method of the yet-to-be-founded "new" psychology, introspection. Since the mind was thought by some to be independent of overt action, the only way its content and function could be known is through the individual's ability to describe it, and this presumes an awareness of mental life. Later, when the introspective technique failed to turn up any conscious content in the mind during the performance of certain tasks which required thinking, the downfall of dualism and attendant assumptions about conscious content of the mind were a foregone conclusion. Associationism, in somewhat revised form, and the empirical approach have been with us through modern time, however, and continue to do psychology some good service.

Berkeley, Hume, and Hartley. Though the

principles of association were implicit in the writings of Locke, it was George Berkeley and David Hume who really developed them into an integral part of British empiricism; and even later in the eighteenth century it was Hartley who publicized the principles widely and turned them into accepted philosophical doctrine. Among the many laws which were thought to govern the association of ideas, images, and other types of mental elements, several have stood the test of time and continue to provide serviceable interpretations of learning, memory, and thinking today. These include (1) *contiguity*—two ideas that occur together in time or space tend to be associated or linked; (2) *similarity*—the more two ideas are similar, the greater their chance of being associated; and (3) *repetition*—the more often two ideas occur together the greater the strength of their association. In the writings of these philosophers, it is clear that the association of ideas is thought to make up the whole of mental life. That is, the mind follows a course established in the experience of an organism, proceeding from idea to idea according to how these ideas have been associated in the past. David Hartley most clearly laid the groundwork for this process, the train of thought, when he discussed the possibility not only of simultaneous associations—the substructure of a complex idea—but also of successive associations.

The Mills. The development of associationism did not cease with the writings of Hartley; indeed, it did not reach its apex as a philosophical school until the time of James Mill. James Mill, his son John Stuart Mill, and later Wilhelm Wundt turned this early philosophy into a sophisticated, formal theory, capable of systematic research. This is the story of the first half of the nineteenth century.

Mill, the elder, brought associationism to its fulfillment and nearly to the brink of an experimental psychology. Mill accepted the tenets of his predecessors, assuming that sensations and ideas were the fundamental classes of elements in the mind. Further, he proposed that sensations were the primary elements of consciousness, from which ideas were derived. Sensations produce ideas. The processes of association pertained to ideas, with contiguity being the basic principle. Perhaps most relevant to the soon-to-be-established science of psychology was Mill's discussion of the strength of associations between ideas and his suggestion of probable measures or indices. Although not a researcher himself, Mill provided some real leads for the scientist interested in mental processes. Mill's criteria of strength are not unfamiliar to the modern researcher: (1) *permanence*—the more persistent an association, the greater its initial strength; (2) *certainty*—the more confident the individual of the association, the greater its strength; and (3) *facility*—the greater the speed and effortlessness with which an association arises, the greater its strength.

Mill's writings are of importance to the science of psychology in at least two other respects, both concerning theoretical matters. One needs only to elaborate slightly Mill's definition of an idea to produce the modern concept of a mediator. For Mill and many modern thinkers, sensation begets some internal symbolic or mediating process—an idea. For the modern theorist, the mediator intervenes between input to an organism and eventual movement. There is nothing in Mill's proposition which directly links the idea with resultant response, although the step is rather obvious. Second, Mill's conception of the complex idea, as an additive compounding of simpler ones through association, is the essence of many modern conceptions of meaning.

In Mill, the younger, we find an even more direct appeal to the researcher to begin his attack on the problems of psychology. J. S. Mill's associationism is slightly but importantly different from his father's. Significant points of departure are: (1) his resurrection of similarity, intensity, and frequency as principles by which associations are formed in the mind; (2) his allowance for the existence of ideas without preceding sensations, or meanings without attendant images; and (3) his insistence that complex ideas can be in actuality more than an additive mixture of simpler elements. On this latter point, J. S. Mill seems to suggest that simpler ideas lose their identity when entering into a compound and can produce a molar thought which, as the Gestalt psychologists were later to argue, is different from the sum of its parts. The argument is not unlike Mandler's (1962) concept of the symbolic analogue, a mental unit representative of a well-integrated set or series of individual responses. For Mill, this necessitated something more than analysis if one is to understand the mind. The researcher, he warned, ought to study complex ideas in and of themselves as well as their constituent elements.

We have barely touched the highlights in this brief description of associationism and yet have given it perhaps more space than is appropriate. Left aside are many men, not only British but also French and German, who contributed significantly to empiricism and associationism; they include men like Kant and Herbart, who discussed nativistic contributions to the mind, levels of consciousness of ideas, and the apperceptive mass—a composite of simultaneously conscious ideas. But we have, in this survey, the essence of scientific psychology's philosophical preparation for the study of thinking, clearly one designed to emphasize empiricism, experience, and learning and to minimize the importance of nativism and the biological contributions to mental life. Before reviewing the work of the very earliest experimental psychologist, we return briefly to the seventeenth century to pick up a philosophical position on mental activity which was nonassociational in nature.

Faculty Psychology and the Scottish School

One major source of contemporary competition for associationism, within philosophy, was provided by a group of intellectuals who became known collectively as the Scottish School. Dissenting from the associational analyses, philosophers of this orientation conceptualized the mind as a set of faculties or powers which operate on incoming sensations. Their major objection to associationism was its emphasis on atomism in mental activity, which appeared to violate the orthodox religious notions of unity in mind and soul. Thomas Reid was the earliest important representative of this tradition, his most relevant writings appearing in the last half of the seventeenth century. In his works are descriptions of some 30 powers, such as self-preservation, pity, imagination, judgment, and memory, which are said to form the basis of mental activity. From this list, the later phrenologists attempted the discovery and identification of brain areas which were associated with mental powers.

The real antagonism between faculty psychology and associationism was seriously compromised by Thomas Brown early in the eighteenth century. Although trained in the Scottish tradition and holding to the notion of mental faculties, Brown found it necessary to invoke some principle such as association to account for the succession of thoughts which seemed to be typical in mental life. Beyond this, he is commonly given credit for being the first writer to treat explicitly and rigorously the secondary or nongeneral laws of association. That is, Brown concerned himself with the specifics of associations and with such problems as why one idea occurs when several seem to be possible. He proposed a series of laws which guided associational processes and accounted for the finer differentiation of ideas. Among these were relative frequency, recency, and vividness; within a set of alternative ideas, that one which stands highest on these scales will occur. We might note that all these concepts are familiar to the modern associationist interested in fundamental problems of learning and thinking. Brown's philosophy is interestingly close to that of James Mill, who was more in the mainstream of British associationism and empiricism.

THE BEGINNINGS OF AN INDEPENDENT PSYCHOLOGY

Thinking and the Formal Psychology of Wundt

In any historical account of psychology, no matter what the focal area, it is difficult to avoid the name of Wilhelm Wundt. Although there were others in the nineteenth century who contributed measurably to the establishment of a scientific psychology, Wundt is generally credited with founding the discipline, not only because his was the first bona fide psychological laboratory, but also and more importantly because he was the first to develop and maintain a systematic and concerted program of research on a range of psychological problems. Wundt was a systematist—tireless, prolific, and deeply committed. While the work of his laboratory at Leipzig was not inaugurated until 1879, Wundt himself began writing about psychology in the early 1860s. The philosophy which guided the research of Wundt and most of his students from 1880 on had fairly well been formulated prior to that time.

Psychological Dualism. Wundt was a dualist, who argued the separatism and independence of mind and body. The mental world is the world of experience, i.e., that which we know or of which we are consciously aware. Although the events of the mind and body might parallel one another, they do not interact nor exert any mutual causal influence. Wundt thought the job of a scientific psychology to be one of understanding the structure and processes of the mind and argued strongly that the proper and perhaps only approach was through introspection. Because of its emphasis on mind structure, the name *Structuralism* is often used in reference to Wundt's psychology and that of his students. The pattern of research emanating from Wundt's laboratory appears to have three phases: (1) an attempt to analyze conscious experience into elements; (2) an exploration of the elements in an effort to determine their function, mainly in associational processes; and (3) a study of the associations in hopes of uncovering fundamental principles which describe their formation and action. Only one kind of psychological explanation was acceptable: complex events and processes are to be understood in terms of the simpler ones of which they are composed and from which they are derived. Obviously, Wundt was strongly influenced by the empiricist-associationist movement in England.

Structuralism and Associationism. Despite the apparent similarity, there were basic differences between Wundt's conception of psychology and that of the associationist. Wundt brought to psychology the techniques of science; he was convinced of the adequacy of experimentation, realized in the procedure of introspection, as a means of understanding the mind. He sought the true irreducible elements of the mind through this technique, beginning with the exploration of sensory processes. From the research and writings of Wundt's group came evidence for a variety of mental elements: (1) *sensations*, the primary conscious data; (2) their purely mental counterparts, *images*; and (3) a kind of affective constituent called *feelings*. Despite the appellation—structuralism—Wundtians thought of the mind as a rather active mechanism. Their evidence generally led them to an acceptance of the laws of association, as descriptive of this activity. Beyond this, however, their system made allowance not only for the association of inputs to the mind, through sensation and perception, but also for associational processes, carried out by the mind itself, on the apperceptive mass of conscious data already in the mind.

The Nature of Thinking. As mentioned, the bulk of research in Wundt's laboratory dealt with sensory and perceptual processes. There was, in addition, some work on problems such as span of attention and reaction time. Very little emphasis was placed on memory and none at all on the so-called higher mental processes such as thinking—the focal issue in this book. Wundt himself ruled higher mental processes out of his laboratory because he felt them inaccessible to experimental investigation. To employ successfully the primary method of experimental psychology, namely, introspection, the observer experiencing the critical event or process must know what to watch for. Thought processes, according to Wundt, are complex and capricious. They lack the stability necessary for precise observation and therefore cannot be introspected. Being vague or ephemeral, thoughts were considered to achieve a sufficient constancy to be recognized and observed only when externalized and agreed to consensually as in a society. Thinking was, for Wundt, a kind of social psychological problem best studied naturalistically. He went to considerable pains to ensure that such thought processes did not enter his laboratory as a subject of experimental inquiry.

Wundt seemed to be saying that one must approach thought through the investigation of social and cultural processes, probably through natural and historical investigation, but that it is a mistake to believe that introspective laboratory studies will yield anything meaningful. These arguments on thinking are, at least to a modern viewer, unjustified. Yet the Wundtian system, taken as a whole, remained the most important force in psychology through the first decade of the twentieth century, perhaps until the rise of Behaviorism in America. Fortunately, some of Wundt's students and contemporaries did not rigidly adhere to his pronouncements on the nature of higher processes, and the scientific study of thinking began elsewhere only shortly after the establishment of Wundt's lab.

The Beginnings of a Scientific Study of "Higher Mental Processes" and Thinking

Attempts to study thinking in the laboratory with the prized structuralist techinque, introspection, contributed as much as any other factor to the dissolution of Wundtian psychology. Even the Herculean efforts of the more sophisticated and erudite students from the Leipzig laboratory, who carried on that program of research in many Western universities, were unable to withstand the onslaught of evidence delimiting the value of the structuralist orientation toward psychology.

Act Psychology. It should be made clear that there were other movements afoot within psychology before the turn of the century. Perhaps the most influential of these, in historical perspective, has been called *Act psychology*. Act psychologists questioned the structuralist emphasis on elements and on the content and static structure of the mind. They argued that psychologists might more profitably study mental functions or mental processes—the directed, ongoing activities of organisms. In contrast to Wundt, Act psychologists de-emphasized associationistic principles of mental activity, supplementing them with more complex organizational processes. They attempted to change the focus of research from "thought" to "thinking."

Although this school contributed little experimentation, it did offer a new perspective on psychology and on the study of thinking. It provided a reasonable alternative to the predominant structuralist viewpoint. It supplied the impetus for later developments such as the investigation of unconscious and of motivational aspects of thinking at Würzburg, the elaboration of a prototypical information processing theory of thinking by Otto Selz, and the use of a phenomenological approach by Gestalt psychologists. Each of these developments, as we shall see, has had an important impact on contemporary research and theorizing.

Ebbinghaus. On the empirical side prior to 1900, there is need to be concerned with the efforts of only one man, Hermann Ebbinghaus. It might be that Ebbinghaus was unaware of Wundt's dictum declaring the inaccessibility of higher mental processes to experimentation. Surely it didn't stop him from undertaking a prodigious program of research on verbal memory. Indeed, the impetus to this research, which is reflected in the methods used, came directly from Gustav Fechner, the first and most important student of psychophysics.

Ebbinghaus was—in fact had to be—an innovator. No one provided a precedent for his kind of experiment. He set for himself the task of studying how associations are formed. He developed measurement techniques, experimental procedures, and learning materials which were not only original but continue in heavy use even today. For a variety of reasons, the associations he chose to work with were verbal. Bothered by the strong possibility that any meaningful verbal materials would already be highly associated in the mind of the subject through past experience, he invented a verbal unit known as the nonsense syllable. Such an item consists (for English-speaking people) of three letters—a consonant, a vowel, and a consonant, in that order—which constitute neither prefix, suffix, nor word. Learning associations to these, Ebbinghaus reasoned, would be unaffected or uncontaminated by past experience (at least less so) than would meaningful words. Lists of these nonsense syllables comprised much of the material learned in his experiments, although it should be noted that on occasion, unfamiliar poetry was also used.

Ebbinghaus developed several methods of presenting materials and testing for the strength of associations learned and their retention through time. With these techniques, he was able to demonstrate several important principles of memory still recognized today. For example, he showed the effectiveness of repetition or frequency as a determiner both of association strength and retention. He studied variables, such as number of items to be learned, for their influence on time to learn and demonstrated the apparent existence not only of direct associations between successive items in a list but also of remote associations between nonadjacent items and backward associations. Perhaps his most famous finding was the classical "forgetting function" showing the decline of association strength over a time interval devoid of practice. Ebbinghaus' program of research on verbal memory was presented in a monograph, *On Memory,* which first appeared in 1885, only six years after the founding of the Leipzig laboratory. What is perhaps even more remarkable is that Ebbinghaus' efforts were accomplished without the benefit of a laboratory and with the services of only a single subject, Ebbinghaus himself.

Although he is no doubt best known in psychology for his study of memory, and for the path opened thereby to the rigorous study of higher mental processes, Ebbinghaus had other extensive interests. Among his related contributions was the development of a test of verbal intelligence which slightly antedated Binet.

LATER DEVELOPMENTS

Würzburg School

Oswald Külpe, despite the fact that he was a Wundt-trained, "tough-minded" experimental psychologist interested primarily in the content of the mind, was another who was unwilling to exile thought from the laboratory. And the more he and his students studied the attributes of thought, the further they moved from hard-line structuralism toward the softer, process-oriented Act psychology.

In the first decade of this century, Külpe and his collaborators at Würzburg reported a series of introspective studies on higher mental processes. The tasks posed for introspecting subjects in these experiments were rather simple thought problems involving judgment and controlled association—hardly the kind of problems used in modern studies of thinking. But they were sufficiently complex to give the subject some pause; responses, answers, or solutions were not automatic. The initial experiments raised questions about whether all the important components of thinking (1) were conscious and (2) fit into the commonly accepted categories of elements, sensations, images, and feelings. Introspective and retrospective descriptions by subjects of the content of consciousness during thinking often indicated a richness of sensations and images, as a structuralist would expect. But rather than being rationally composed and clearly directed toward problem solution, this mental activity was often without much organization and apparently unrelated to the eventual response. Yet out of it came a solution, and almost always the correct one.

Logic, Reasoning, and Imageless Thought. Evidence from the Würzburg school put the lie to the notion that human thinking and reasoning can be described in terms of rationally or logically related constituent elements. It questioned seriously the notion that all the fundamentals of thinking are conscious and to be found in the associatively complex structure of compounded elements. Though critics doubted whether all of mental content was reported by subjects in these experiments, the repeatability of Würzburg findings strongly implied that thinking is at least in part unconscious, motivated, process-like, and imageless.

Whether thought is sometimes imageless remained a controversial issue until it became obvious that the entire structuralist orientation toward psychology was a deadend. Wundt never accepted the evidence from Würzburg, claiming that introspection is useless for studying unpredictable mental processes, such as thinking, which prevent the subject from focusing his attention in advance on the significant phenomena. E. B. Titchener, a Wundt-trained psychologist who dominated orthodox psychology in the United States, accepted some of these findings but argued that the imageless and unconscious aspects of thought reported by subjects were in reality the associated context or meanings of sensory and imaginal events. In this development, Titchener espoused a context theory of meaning which held that the meaning of any idea derives from a background or context of associated ideas, conscious or unconscious, these associations arising either naturally or through prior experience. The Würzburg experiments obviously did not settle the issue, but they did show the inadequacy of introspection and structuralism to account for such an important psychological phenomenon as thinking.

Determining Tendencies. In addition, these studies made a more positive contribution by pointing up the important role of motivational factors in thinking and in behavior generally. H. J. Watt, working in the Würzburg laboratory, noted that the time needed to complete even the simplest thought problems might be long enough to introduce a contaminating memory factor into introspection. That is, perhaps the subject cannot report all conscious experience because some passes from memory before he can describe it. To minimize memory effects, Watt divided the problem into four periods: (1) *preparation*, during which the subject was given instruction as to the type of response required, e.g., "Give an association which is a subordinate of the stimulus word"; (2) *presentation* of the stimulus word, e.g., "Animal"; (3) the subject's *search for a proper response;* and (4) the *response* itself, e.g., "Horse." The subject was asked to introspect separately on each period, but in successive problems. With this technique, Watt discovered that Period 3 was often devoid of conscious content, the response occurring in an almost automatic fashion. There was far more content to report during Period 1. Conscious thinking, so it would seem, takes place in advance of the actual problem, i.e., the presentation of the stimulus. The purpose (or task), *Aufgabe,* as it was called, is established during Period 1, allowing the remainder of the thought process to proceed uninterrupted.

Narziss Ach, continuing this line of research, argued that the *Aufgabe* gives rise to unconscious determining tendencies, or preparatory sets which govern the course of consciousness and behavior. Ach set the stage for what is accepted almost universally in modern psychology—the unity of thinking and acting. According to Ach, the determining tendency, supplied during the preparation period, potentiates a certain set of associations and corresponding acts, so that when the stimulus arrives the subject's response is constrained to a certain subset of associations which are allowable under the *Aufgabe*.

Timing Mental Events. Külpe is perhaps less well known for another contribution to the study of higher mental processes. The mid-nineteenth century had seen the development of precise techniques for measuring the speed of human reaction to environmental events. From the notion of a *personal equation* employed by astronomers to correct for individual human differences in the temporal recordings of celestial events came a *mental chronometry* (Boring, 1950) or system for measuring the time characteristics of the mind. F. C. Donders, a Dutch psychologist, constructed the system on the assumption that the duration of mental events can be computed from the difference between simple reaction time and speed of reaction in situations which require some intervening process or processes. For example, to measure discrimination time, an experimenter would determine both the speed of reaction to a single stimulus, such as light onset (simple reaction time) and the speed of reaction in a similar task, wherein the subject must respond to only one of two or more stimuli (discrimination plus reaction time). In the second task, it is assumed that the subject must discriminate between or among the stimuli before responding. Only after such discrimination can he respond properly. If one assumes that the second task involves the compounding in additive fashion of two events, discrimination plus reaction, then it follows that time for discrimination is the difference between the speeds of reaction in the two tasks. By similar reasoning, procedures were adopted for measuring mental events other than discrimination, such as choice, association, judgment, and the like. Wundt, himself, accepted the possible validity of this technique, despite his aforementioned proclamation on the difficulties of dealing with higher mental processes in the laboratory. The notion of compounding mental events, embodied in this system, is of course not inimical to the general tenor of Wundt's associationistic philosophy.

It is difficult to deny the plausibility of conceptual arguments in favor of mental chronometry. On the more practical side, however, experimenters had to contend with horrendous variability in their reaction time data —variability not only between subjects but also within the same subject from time to time. Moreover, it became clear that reaction times of any sort were notoriously affected by practice, fatigue, attention, and other extraneous factors.

Külpe's insight pointed up an additional problem in the assumptions of the subtractive procedure. He argued—and the later evidence of both Ach and Watt supported the notion—that adding components to the simple reaction time situation did more than introduce another step in a chain of mental events intervening between stimulus and reaction. The effect of these additional components was to change the task substantively. More specifically, the nature of the task, given to the subject through preliminary instruction, established a preparatory set. Each task produced a different set or predisposition to respond. The important differences between simple and other reactions were not, at least according to introspective reports, to be found in the number of mental components between stimulus and response but in terms of the events preceding the stimulus. Further, no counterparts of discrimination, choice, etc., were found in the consciousness of subjects serving in these tasks. Külpe's critique, of course, bears not on the reaction time procedure nor on the measurements so determined. As a matter of fact, the results of early experiments seem to hold up exceptionally well. Even today, the reaction time experiment is an important tool in the repertoire of the experimental and applied psychologist. It is the interpretation of these data as measures of the duration of mental events to which Külpe took exception, and our modern evidence and theories are more in tune with him than with mental chronometry.

Some Developments in British Psychology

A good deal of space has been given to the start provided for psychology by German philosophers and scientists. The significance of this work notwithstanding, it was the development of an informal psychology in Great Britain that shaped the nature of the early American discipline as much as any other influence. This state of affairs is even more enigmatic when it is recognized that virtually all prominent American psychologists prior to 1900 received their formal introduction to and training in psychology from Wundt. There is insufficient space to describe most of what was going on in Britain during the last half of the nineteenth century. To understand American psychology, however, it is mandatory that certain events be given brief mention.

Darwin and Evolution. There are three events to be noted, which obviously are not unrelated. The first two were the result of a growing emphasis, generated by the theory of evolution and Darwin, on the consideration of living organisms (man included) and their environments as an interacting system. One key notion for psychology which derives directly from such an orientation is the denial of a separate creation for all the various species of animals and the substitutive idea of phylogenetic origination and continuity. Man ought not to be considered entirely apart from lower organisms; his anatomy, his physiology, his behavior are in many ways a product of an evolutionary process which produces increasing complexity and differentiation in animal forms. In a sense, man's lineal ancestors are the lower animals and, depending upon the closeness of the relationship, one can expect to find structural and functional similarities between man and other species. To put it another way, man evolved gradually over the millennia from lower forms. This notion was instrumental in focusing the attention of researchers on animal behavior and in generating a comparative psychology, for (assuming the theory) such a study could tell us much about human beings. The study of thinking in lower animals helped significantly to define the general nature of symbolic processes.

The second important notion from evolutionary theory is that of environmental adaptivity and organismic flexibility. The organism best equipped to change with his environment, to fit in under wide variations in external conditions, is the organism best able to survive and perpetuate its form and species. This notion brought to focus not only the biological structure of beasts but also, more compellingly than ever before, the function of these structures. The important question became: Of what use are the biological (and psychological) capacities which are the equipment of an organism?

Individual Differences. The last event to be mentioned was largely the product of another great British natural scientist, Francis Galton. Galton, in part as a consequence of his acceptance of the theory of evolution, became interested in the capacities of human beings to function in and adapt to their environments. Although he had ancient predecessors, it is probably fair to say that he demonstrated most clearly the real possibility of testing for behavioral capacities of men. In this he made perhaps three significant contributions to American thought: (1) an emphasis on performance, which after all is what a test measures—thus the focus swung away from intangible mental events to a more complete conception of behavior; (2) an underlining of the importance of individual variations and differences among organisms rather than an exclusive concern with the "generalized mind"; and (3) the development of some original quantitative techniques for description and analysis of behavior. Galton, of course, is primarily recognized in this area for his formulation of the underlying assumptions and techniques of correlation, i.e., the degree to which two (or more) characteristics of an organism vary together, or are co-related.

It is a travesty to leave British psychology at this point, for its influence on the development of modern psychology is not nearly so limited. But, more recent, and even more important events are yet to be described, and that task will be long and involved.

THE PSYCHOLOGY OF THINKING IN AMERICA

Despite their hard-line training in the German tradition, pioneer American psychologists were quick to pick up the leads of Darwin, Galton, and a handful of other British thinkers. Except for Titchener's group, early American psychology was more functional than structural, and, although continually revised in the light of new scientific evidence, remains in the functionalist tradition today. What this means, in brief, is a greater concern with the *Whys* and *Hows* of consciousness and behavior than with the *Whats*. Emphasis is on the functional significance of the "mind," on its role in the adaptation of an organism to its environment, and on its properties as a concept which describes behavior.

To say that this trend is attributable primarily to British influence should not be taken to mean that early American psychologists were merely followers. There were people in the United States prior to 1900 who had full-blown interests in scientific psychology. The brevity with which their influence is described here is no reflection of their significance in the field.

William James

No history of psychology would be complete or accurate without some description of the work of William James. He contributed broadly to the discipline, and, despite the fact that his significant publications appeared before the turn of the century, his works are popular and his ideas remarkably relevant even today. James would hardly qualify as an empirical researcher; he did no experiments of consequence. He was more an innovator, theorist, and systematist. His position, set forth in his *Principles of Psychology* (1890), was neither Structuralist, evolutionary, nor process-oriented, and yet it contained a little of all of these and more. He conceived of mind as an array of functions before any popularity had come to Act psychology, of consciousness as a dynamic stream of interacting events (with no rigid structure) before the performance of the Würzburg experiments, and of psychology as the study of adaptive processes before the advent of Functionalism as an American school. As a pragmatist, James attempted to explain both behavior and consciousness through a conception of the mind as a biological organ whose function(s) can be used for contending with an environment. Other than its greater intricacy and complexity, the mind is no different from other bodily structures, such as, say, the heart or the lungs, which play vital roles in the functioning of the whole organism. The mind, according to James, has evolved in man to the point where its functions are more versatile and pervasive than any other single organ. Whereas James contributed most directly to the establishment of a functionalist tradition in American psychology, it is not difficult to detect his influence in later Behaviorism and Gestalt psychology which were also functionally oriented.

Functionalism

If there ever was a formal school of Functionalism, it arose with the influence of John Dewey at the University of Chicago just before the turn of the century. The "school" was never a cohesive system, as was Structuralism under Wundt, but rather represented a protest, sponsored by James and Dewey, against Structuralism and its insistence on the exclusive study of consciousness and elementism. Its identity with Chicago was short-lived, as Functionalism quickly spread to Columbia and other American universities with formal psychology programs of training and research. Its substance was taken from the principles of James and embellished by the insights and findings of Dewey and his students and colleagues.

The Significance of Consciousness. Perhaps the greatest effect of these psychologists was their ability, through denial of the all-important role of consciousness, to lift the lid which had suppressed some of psychology's most significant problems. Obvious as it might be to the modern student that learning and its various forms—motivation, problem solving, and the like—are basic and important processes in the discipline, these were simply not recognized by the psychologist of 1900 as part of the content of the field. Using a greater amount of common sense than was typical of psychologists of that day, functionalists showed the way to less artificial, more real-life-like psychological problems. Their de-emphasis of consciousness and interest in behavior opened up comparative psychology, child psychology, and the study of individual differences, to mention the broader substantive areas, as well as educational and other applied psychologies.

The importance of consciousness was not disputed by the early functionalists, but its position as the *primary* problem for psychology was. Although the implications were much broader, consciousness was treated by the functionalist much as the mediators are treated in modern psychological theory. That is, consciousness was said to play a role as a set of intervening events or processes between environment and the organism's reaction to it. Consciousness assists the organism in its adaptation to the environment. This principle, coupled with the general idea that function and purpose of mind and behavior were the matters to be explained, meant that the last vestiges of dualism—the separation of mind and body—had been exorcised.

John B. Watson assisted in the later process. Watson was as thoroughly convinced that mind had no place in psychology as Wundt was that mind was the only important subject matter. To Watson, the growing evidence on the nervous system, its structure, and function meant that the mind as such could be completely replaced by a biological substructure of behavior. Mind and consciousness became "taboo" words, and movement became the only datum of psychology. Introspection was replaced entirely by objective observation. Watson took his degree under the functionalists at Chicago and within 10 years had followed the pendulum to its opposite extreme from Structuralism, establishing a school of Behaviorism which ruled mind and consciousness out of the psychological laboratory. But this is part of another story which will be picked up shortly.

Dewey and Problem Solving. Before turning to the later functionalists, it is worth mentioning that Dewey took a position with respect to directed or goal-oriented thinking much like the one outlined in the first chapter of this book. According to Dewey (1910), one can conceive of this process as a multistage affair describable as follows: (1) the recognition of a problem, or a "felt difficulty"; (2) the location and definition of the problem or the isolation of relevant features; (3) the formulation of possible, alternative solutions; (4) mulling over or reasoning through the various possibilities to determine the most likely one; and (5) testing the selected solution. One clearly recognizes in this analysis the major elements—conceptual behavior, coding and language, problem solving, and decision making—which are the primary topics of discussion in this text.

Stages of thinking have been prime targets for speculation by many people over the years. Graham Wallas, for example, after surveying anecdotal evidence on the symbolic processes of many creative scientists came to the conclusion that common to all creative acts are the four stages: (1) *preparation;* (2) *incubation*—a mulling over period; (3) *illumination* or *insight*—the conception of a solution; and (4) *verification*. We shall have more to say about the contribution of such speculation where appropriate in later chapters.

Later Functionalism

As mentioned, Functionalism was not long limited to Chicago. Another early locus for functionalists and their research was Columbia University, where, around 1900, Cattell, Woodworth, and Thorndike came together.

Thorndike. E. L. Thorndike pioneered the experimental study of animal behavior and intelligence (1898). For this purpose he devised a number of puzzle or problem boxes from which confined animals had to discover a means of escape. A variety of species, from cats to monkeys, were used as subjects. In part, his intent was to develop means for studying animal behavior in the laboratory, rather than relying exclusively, as his predecessors had, on anecdotal and naturalistic observation.

From his observations of how subjects escaped from puzzle box confinement—by pressing levers, pulling strings, scratching ears, or the like—Thorndike came to the conclusion that problem solving, at least in lower animals, proceeded on the basis of trial and error. There appeared to be no reasoning underlying the process of discovery exhibited by his animals. There were marked individual differences in the speed with which subjects reached a solution to the problem, but no indication that any saw through the problem, solving it in a purposeful, insightful fashion. Further, on subsequent presentations of the same problem to the same subject, there was little indication of immediate utilization of the solution performed on the preceding occasion.

Thorndike continued this line of research through the first decade of this century and from it developed a mechanistic theory of learning, some principles of which are central to modern behavior theory. For example, he concluded that learning and problem solving are, in general, gradual processes based on the increasing strength of a connection between the stimulus situation and a certain response or set of responses. This connection between stimulus and response is strengthened through two basic laws (Thorndike later elaborated and modified his theoretical system markedly), namely, the law of repetition or exercise—on which he concurred with Ebbinghaus—and the law of effect. The latter principle bears strong resemblance to the modern-day principle of reinforcement. It states, in brief, that an act or response which is followed by a pleasurable state of affairs (reward) tends to become associated with the stimulus situation effective at the time of its occurrence; conversely, the connection between a response which is followed by an annoying state of affairs (punishment) and the stimulus to which it occurs tends to be weakened. The emphasis, of course, is on behavior and the association of stimulus and response, rather than on the association of ideas or other mental events. In the work of Thorndike, which he called *Connectionism,* we have a clear separation from earlier forms of associationistic psychology.

Thorndike's experiments and interpretation were controversial for perhaps two reasons. First, his emphasis is clearly on the response or motor factors involved in learning. Trial and error, according to Thorndike, is to be found in the overt muscular activity of an organism. Perceptual, symbolic, and central processes played little or no role in his interpretation of problem solving. Behaviorists were quick to espouse the same point of view, but other functionalists, such as Woodworth, and particularly the Gestalt psychologists argued cogently for the importance of other factors. Second, many later researchers claimed that the nature of the experimental situation and problems used by Thorndike prevented his animals from behaving in any way other than trial and error. That is, Thorndike had, by and large, required responses which were unfamiliar to subjects at the outset, such as pulling a string, thus requiring the animal not only to discover the response but actually to learn to make it within the problem situation. If Thorndike had used familiar responses, to be employed in some novel way, the chance of an insightful, rational solution rather than blind fumbling and trial and error might have been enhanced. As we shall see, a number of researchers spent considerable effort attempting to demonstrate insightful solutions to problems by both animals and man. Further, Thorndike's tasks, according to some critics, disguised the relevant relations which the subject must perceive and "understand" before the problem can be solved insightfully. For example, in those cases where the animal had to pull a string to release a latch on the door to the confining box, the string-latch attachment could not be seen. Allowing the subject to perceive the relevant features of a problem might conduce, some argued, to insightful problem solving.

Thorndike himself often wrote as if he were convinced that animal behavior was not mediated by ideas or "symbolic processes." Responses are linked and made directly to the stimulus situation as it is sensed by the subject. Because data from human beings often appeared similar in form to those of animals, he was led to believe that essentially the same learning principles were fundamental among all species. Critics have allowed the possible necessity of Thorndike's simple laws in an account of complex human behavior, but have strongly questioned their sufficiency.

Behaviorism

As mentioned, John B. Watson was educated in the tradition of psychological Functionalism. *Behaviorism*, which he is usually credited with founding, was in essence a functional psychology. Whereas the typical functionalist admitted the data of consciousness into his intrepretative system, however, Watson did not, or at least tried not to. For the functionalist, behavior (generally equated with the organism's movement) was important as an indicator of the underlying state and process of the organism's mind; for the early behaviorist, action, movement, or behavior itself was the focus of attention, the primary datum. Depending on the extremity of his stand, a behaviorist might consider consciousness to be either inaccessible, unimportant, irrelevant to psychology, or nonexistent. In any case, he would claim that there is no point in trying to understand consciousness when the real data of psychology are open, observable, and available to direct measurement and investigation. Vague inferences to conscious states were excess baggage, according to Watson. Knowledge of the regularities of organismic movement is all that one really needs to be concerned with.

Watson on Thinking. It is difficult at first to resolve the extreme Watsonian position with the crassly apparent fact that much of animal and human behavior is symbolic, i.e., without gross motor accompaniments. Watson and other behaviorists, however, did not deny either the existence or the importance of these symbolic events. They merely refused to conceive or to speak of them as mentalistic entities such as images, feelings, or associations. Watson, for example, balked at Thorndike's early law of effect which attributed feelings of satisfaction or annoyance to an organism as a consequence of environmental happenings; these states were subjective and essentially unmeasurable. Rather, the behaviorist translated states of consciousness into implicit behaviors. Feelings, images, thoughts, etc., were said to be units of physical, though covert, behavior, which, if we knew when, where, and how to look, would be found to be just as recordable and reliable as the grosser forms of movement.

According to Watson, we should eventually find out that much of what is considered in a mentalistic sense to be thinking is in reality "implicit" or miniaturized motor activity, largely in the voice mechanism. Words are responses we have learned to apply to objects and events in the environment. They can be called symbols, in the sense that they "stand for" or represent things which they themselves are not. We can, then, "think" of these objects or events in terms of their verbal counterparts. When we "think to ourselves" about them, we are merely suppressing the overt verbal responses to the point where they become difficult or impossible for others to detect. But, with appropriately sensitive recording and measuring apparatus, we should find evidence of them in tiny laryngeal movements. Thus, according to Watson, much of what we call thinking is primarily subaudible speech. If there is thought, there must be a physical representation of it somewhere within the organism, a conception which fits with the essential creed of Behaviorism.

There are other points to be made in this brief description of Watson's system. First, it is totally mechanistic. Behavior is conceived as a complicated physical system. We can speak of its building blocks as elementary reflexes (response units which occur automatically in the presence of a specifiable stimulus), although it would be possible to dig deeper into the physico-chemical bases of these actions. Leaning on the work of Pavlov, which was becoming well known in the United States at the time, Watson argued that complex acts of behavior are actually compounds of reflexes, some unconditioned but mostly learned (or conditioned) in a certain stimulus context. Complex behavior is a concatenation of many reflex building blocks. Second, Watson stressed peripheral, i.e., muscular or kinesthetic and glandular, integrators of behavior. Responses themselves provide stimuli which cue the organism as to what to do next. Thus, a single external signal, such as the opening of a door to a confining chamber, might trigger off in a trained rat a rather complex behavioral sequence which takes the animal through a complicated maze pathway to some other chamber located several feet away. The responses made by the animal might seem automatic and independent, but in reality, according to behavioristic analysis, they are well organized in the sense that each provides the guiding stimulation for the next response in the chain. It is because of this that Behaviorism is said to espouse a peripheral or *motor theory* of thinking, with the important activities being muscular or glandular, rather than a central or ideational theory, which often carries the implication of central brain processes as the behavioral integrators.

Experiments on the Motor Components of Thinking

Many experiments have provided evidence on the intimate interplay between symbolic activity and movement. We shall cite a few briefly, even though this discussion begins to impinge on more current than historical areas of interest. Jacobsen, who interestingly enough was trained by the structuralist Titchener at Cornell, reported a series of experiments in the late 1920s and early 1930s which concern the thinking-acting relationship. Jacobsen developed a technique for physically relaxing human subjects. Introspective reports from his subjects indicated that mental activity, e.g., thoughts and feelings, generally diminished in quantity with relaxation. They reported that inner speech and imagery were typically reduced or impossible in a state of deep relaxation. When these subjects were instructed to imagine or think of certain events or actions, however, their thoughts were almost invariably accompanied by patterns of electrical activity recorded from particular muscular loci associated with the imagined process. For example, when a subject was instructed to think of flexing his right forearm, electrical signs of muscular activity were picked up from that arm, but not from other locations such as the left arm. When asked to imagine the Eiffel Tower in Paris, electrodes on the subject's brow gave evidence of incipient scanning movements of the eyes. Jacobsen's results seem clearly to indicate that specific patterns of muscular activity accompany and correlate with the content of thought processes. From this he drew the conclusion that thought was movement and that thought and muscular relaxation were incompatible.

Freeman (1931) reported some complementary experiments which appeared to indicate that elementary mental activity, such as adding numbers in one's head or completing jig-saw puzzles, could be facilitated by inducing in the subject an increase in generalized muscular tonus. Freeman's concept of a facilitating tonus for thought and action is the forerunner of the modern notion that arousal or activation serves as a necessary support for performance (Malmo, 1959). Freeman noticed that muscle tension was typically increased in subjects with increased incentives to perform well.

Somewhat later, Max (1937) conducted a study of muscular activity in the limbs of a group of deaf-mutes who had learned to converse through a sign language using their hands. Records of electrical activity were taken during both sleep and waking hours. Such activity generally decreased during sleep but there were occasional bursts which were apparently associated with dreaming. Max tried waking subjects during bursts and during periods of relative quiet, asking them whether they were dreaming. In some 85 to 90 percent of cases, subjects replied affirmatively upon being wakened during bursts and negatively during quiet. While working on simple problems of arithmetic, roughly 85 percent of deaf-mute subjects showed muscular activity in the hands while only 30 percent of normals did.

Finally, there is the evidence of Schilling (Boring, 1950) that speech-like movement, e.g., activity in the lips or throat, occurring during silent reading facilitates the understanding of the material being read.

An Evaluation. It seems likely that there are muscular (especially vocal) correlates of thinking. It might be that mental activity is in some sense dependent on specific muscular tonus. But the evidence has not been sufficient to convince all psychologists that thought and action are identical or that thought can be completely represented by patterns of peripheral activity. A strong version of such a position would imply (nonsensically) that the same peripheral activity, such as reciting the first law of thermodynamics, by two different individuals or even by the same individual at different times is an index of the same thought. Though it is possible to teach this principle by rote to a child, it is unlikely that it carries the same degree of understanding as that identified with the recitation of a theoretical physicist. The muscular activity recorded in the above-mentioned and other similar experiments might in fact be merely an overflow phenomenon; that is, as thinking occurs, its neurological correlates develop and send weak signals to respond to the muscles and glands. These peripheral organs are thereby activated during thinking, but comprise no essential part of it. This description represents the antithesis of Behaviorism and the issue still remains to be resolved. Some intermediate position might be closer to the truth, such as one which allows for facilitative support of thinking provided by some (optimal) level of muscular tonus, but would also admit the important role of central, neurological events in the whole ongoing process.

Latter-day behaviorists, of which there are many among modern psychologists, have more or less come around to such a position. Rather than ignoring consciousness, the modern behaviorist claims to objectify it. The mentalistic terminology of Structuralism and early Functionalism is rejected. In its place the neobehaviorist introduces "intervening variables," i.e., constructs, guesses, hypotheses about what's going on inside the organism, which serve as a theoretical explanation of overt performance. There is a fine line, of course, between such theorizing and the mentalistic speculation of earlier psychologists. About all that can be said at this point is that the present-day behavior theorist is somewhat more concerned with tying down his mentalism to observable input (stimulus) and output (response). His inferences to internal activity give the appearance of being more firmly based in objective and measurable data.

Gestalt Psychology

Another form of protest against Structuralism was *Gestalt psychology,* which emerged as a contemporary of Behaviorism but argued a quite different point of view. The fundamentals of this system are almost entirely the product of three men, Max Wertheimer, Kurt Koffka, and Wolfgang Köhler, who were colleagues briefly in the early 1910s at Frankfurt, Germany. The notions of Gestalt theory originated in Germany but were brought to the United States later in this century, when all three founders immigrated. Like the other schools we have outlined, Gestalt psychology attempted to deal with the full range of psychology. Only a summary of its contributions to the study of thinking can be given here, however.

The name, Gestalt, is a German word with no precise English equivalent, but is usually translated as "organized whole" or as "configuration." The name captures the essence of the Gestalt protest against Structuralism. Gestalt psychologists argue that psychological experience is not made up or compounded of static, discrete, and denumerable elements, which come and go in time, but rather consists of an organized but dynamic and ever-changing field of events which interact or mutually affect each other. When an organism experiences his environment, so the argument goes, he does not perceive or react to individual elements, but rather to the whole configuration of environmental forces. Properties of the whole psychological field are different from the simple sum of its parts; these properties emerge from the combination and interaction of parts. Gestalt psychology can be characterized as anti-elementarist; sensations, perceptions, images, associations, reflexes, and the like were not accepted as meaningful psychological units. To understand psychological processes, one must consider a system of stimulation in which the alteration of any part can affect all other parts. It is also nativistic, in the sense that the principles governing behavior are said to be part of the natural make-up of the organism rather than learned or otherwise gained through experience.

To illustrate the argument, Gestalt psychologists often point to perceptual phenomena such as apparent movement—the subject of Wertheimer's paper in 1912 which is often cited as the first treatise in Gestalt theory (Boring, 1950). It is well known that if two lights are properly spaced and blink on and off with appropriate timing, one continuous light moving from side to side is seen, rather than two discrete, alternating stimuli. The experience of apparent movement, which is the principle underlying moving pictures, is surely different from what one would expect from the simple perception of the two contributing parts alone.

In historical perspective, Gestalt psychology seems to deal primarily with perception, the principles of which are often presumed to be basic to all other psychological processes. Actually, Gestalt theory was self-consciously general, attempting to treat a wide range of psychological phenomena, including learning, thinking, motivation, and the like. Its emphasis on perception was more than anything else a product of its attack on and rejection of Wundt and Structuralism. The Gestalt psychologist's chief research technique is based on phenomenological reports by subjects of experiences under controlled stimulus conditions. Most results are in the form of free description of immediate experience, without interpretation. This differs from introspection in that (1) no attempt at analysis into formal elements is made and (2) reports from naive (rather than trained) observers are considered valid.

Gestalt Description of Thinking. The processes involved in thinking, from a Gestalt point of view, can be described as follows. A problem is said to exist when there are unresolved *tensions* or *stresses,* resulting from some interaction of perceptual and memory factors, in the individual's environment. The word, stress, is used in Gestalt theory as a hypothetical construct, but is said to involve a competition of forces as in actual physical stress. Thinking occurs as the stresses work themselves out, thus forcing certain organismic activity. Past experience with related problems is no guarantee of solution. The solution seemingly arises from the stresses in the problem as perceived, just as apparent movement arises under appropriate viewing conditions. Thinking, then, is a process of resolving field stresses. But solution, of course, does not always occur, at least not immediately. The problem solver might have to restructure the environment, i.e., look at it from several angles, before the interaction of events forces a clear picture of the solution. Further, he might require external direction which acts to readjust a system under tension. When the proper way of looking at the problem is achieved, however, solution appears almost automatically—in an instant of insight. Clearly, there is a strong relation between thinking and perception. They are governed, according to Gestalt theory, by essentially the same principles, the major difference being that thinking goes on at a more symbolic (or internal) level and is less under the control of external events.

Experimental Work. The most influential Gestalt work on thinking was that of Köhler who, during the years just prior to and during World War I, studied the performance of captive apes in a set of problematic situations graduated in difficulty. As an example, there were several problems in which the animal was required to use one or more sticks as tools to rake in food which was out of reach beyond the bars of his cage. Köhler observed considerable activity in subjects which could be called overt trial and error, in Thorndike's sense. Yet, fundamentally, Köhler's work is the antithesis of Thorndike's Connectionism; rather than acquiring some useful habit over a series of experiences with a given problem, Köhler's subjects almost invariably undertook the proper behavior or response sequence leading to solution after insight into the problem. Köhler reported that his subjects might hit upon the solution to a problem accidentally, but, once having seen the problem in its proper perspective, could repeat the solution without hesitation on subsequent occasions.

Wertheimer's research into thinking consisted of little more than a few simple demonstrations of the importance for learning of "seeing through" or understanding a task. Wertheimer's contention, which has been fairly well borne out by later, more substantial experimentation, was that rote learning, though possible, is vastly inferior to learning based on an understanding of the organization, meaning, and applicability of the material studied, especially insofar as later use in transfer and retention situation is concerned. Duncker (1945), a latter-day Gestalt psychologist, also contributed significantly to the study of thinking. Part of his work concerned the role of restructuring or reorganization in the production of insight into problem solution. His more influential work, however, dealt with a form of behavior known as *functional fixedness*—a mental set which reduces the tendency to use a given object in a necessary way as a result of some prior function which it has served. We shall have more to say about this phenomenon in later discussions, for it remains an interesting empirical problem today.

An Evaluation. Undeniably, Gestalt psychologists have contributed significantly to knowledge of the symbolic processes. Their insistence on the fundamental and basic importance of insight as a principle of learning, however, has unfortunately resulted in strong reactions from those who conceptualize new learning as a gradual process. The ensuing controversy over whether learning and problem solving are based on trial and error or insight is, of course, a far too simple way of looking at behavior. In any given situation, one might observe either type of behavior depending on a number of factors, such as whether or not the relationship between solution and the response required to produce it are clear and comprehensible. Whereas Thorndike might find gradual learning in a situation which requires an animal to scratch its right ear in order to gain release from a confining cage, Köhler is equally likely to find insightful learning in a task requiring the use of sticks to rake in food.

Reasons for such controversies are not always clear in retrospect. But it helps to understand that at the time Gestalt psychology arrived in this country, experimentalism was firmly in the grip of Behaviorism, which viewed the organism much as a machine, subject to the various sources of external stimulation and reacting to them in an essentially automatic fashion. The doctrine of Behaviorism had fairly well stripped animal and man alike of any "higher processes," and surely to the behaviorist insight must have smacked of a return to mentalism. Yet, insightful learning is a common experience, which is verifiable in the laboratory without much difficulty. Gestalt theory, although its principles were sometimes inexplicit, helped psychology to achieve a more balanced and realistic point of view with respect to complex human behavior than would have been possible through a strict Behaviorism.

SUMMARY

We have described briefly some of the more influential points of view in the history and development of the modern psychology of thinking. Each has supplied significant information to the body of knowledge about thinking, either through its emphasis on some particular but otherwise neglected facet of the problem or by its method of collecting and analyzing relevant data.

We have witnessed marked changes in the predominant research orientation, from the investigation of images and other classifiable mental elements to the analysis of behavior and the processes which seem to underlie it. The major schools have disappeared, as such, from psychology. The modern psychologist might lean in the direction of one or another general orientation, but it has become increasingly more apparent that no single orientation, centering on a small set of simple principles, can account for the vast and variegated knowledge presently available. Rather some complex theory, which might borrow principles from a variety of different points of view, is necessary for a successful summary and organization of knowledge. But, theoretical differences among psychologists do exist, and there remain many unsolved problems. These, as well as the better understood relationships, will be discussed in detail in the following chapters.

II Problem Solving

Three Understanding Problem Solving: Preliminary Considerations

In Chapter 1, a problem situation was described as one in which (1) a person is trying to attain some goal, (2) his initial attempts fail to accomplish this end, and (3) at least two, and commonly a large number of alternative courses of action are possible. This characterization can be applied to a great many situations, and, indeed, the multiplicity of problems makes the development of a unified account of problem solving quite difficult. That is, in attempting to state how a person solves a problem, one must consider the generality of the statement. As a description becomes more detailed, it also becomes less general; the details of solving a problem such as finding a mislaid book are quite different from those of discovering a proof to a problem in symbolic logic. The trick is to develop a system of classifying problems, problem solvers, and routes to solutions which is simultaneously abstract enough to possess some generality and detailed enough to provide useful information. Since no commonly agreed upon classification currently exists, one feature of the study of problem solving is a disturbing variety of tasks and resultant descriptions.

One of the purposes of this chapter is to present some ways of classifying problem-solving situations, both to aid in assimilating the research findings to be presented later and to indicate the scope of the present treatment. In addition, attention will be given to some general ideas about problems held by researchers in this field and to the methods they use to conduct their investigations. Chapter 4 contains summaries of several theoretical positions, while research findings will be reviewed in Chapter 5. Let us begin by considering ways in which investigators have characterized problem solving.

TYPES OF PROBLEMS AND SOLUTION PROCESSES

Three Views of Problem Solving

The views to be presented are essentially introductions to theoretical formulations.

They are given at this point because they provide an overview of the domain of problems and because the kind of task an investigator uses seems to depend upon the view he adopts. In considering these descriptions, keep in mind that they are not mutually exclusive, about which more will be said later.

Problem Solving as Perceptual Reorganization. In Chapter 2, Gestalt psychology was characterized as having a strong perceptual emphasis. The Gestalt approach to thinking advanced the idea that problems exist because people perceive the requirements of some situation incorrectly. A solution, therefore, requires a change in perception. As it is applied to problem solving, the term "perception" has at least two meanings. In some instances perception refers to the organization of stimulus elements (or attributes) into some pattern, as when one perceives a square. Scheerer (1963) has used the term in this manner; one of the problems he discussed is presented in Figure 3-1.

Given this display, the problem is to connect the nine dots by drawing four continuous straight lines without lifting the pencil from the paper. The problem is difficult presumably because most people perceive the dots as a square and confine their lines within its boundaries; solution requires extending lines beyond the boundaries of the "square." (The solution is left to the reader.) As another example, consider the problem of using six matches to form four equilateral triangles, each side of which is equal to the length of a match. This problem is impossible to solve as long as one perceives the triangles in only two dimensions. The solution requires the use of three dimensions (see Figure 3-2). It seems clear that solution in these cases requires a restructuring of the stimulus pattern.

The second meaning of perception is a more general one and refers to an awareness of some attribute of an object or situation, rather than to organization of the stimulus pattern as an object. Relationships among objects are stressed, and perceiving seems similar to "realizing" or "understanding." An-

FIGURE 3–1. The "Square" problem requires the subject to connect the nine dots with four continuous lines drawn without lifting the pencil from the paper.

FIGURE 3–2. The "pyramid" required in order to construct four equilateral triangles from six matches.

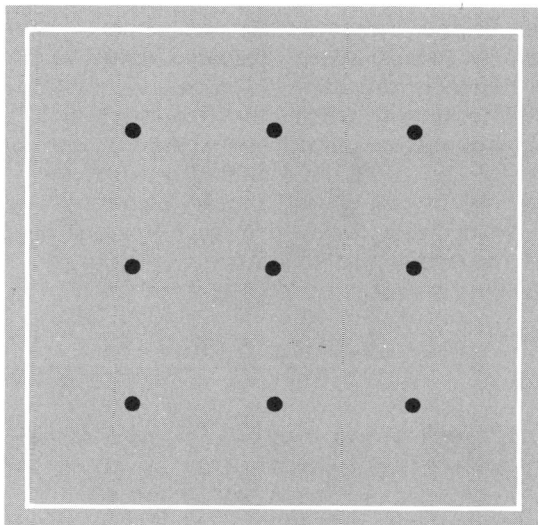
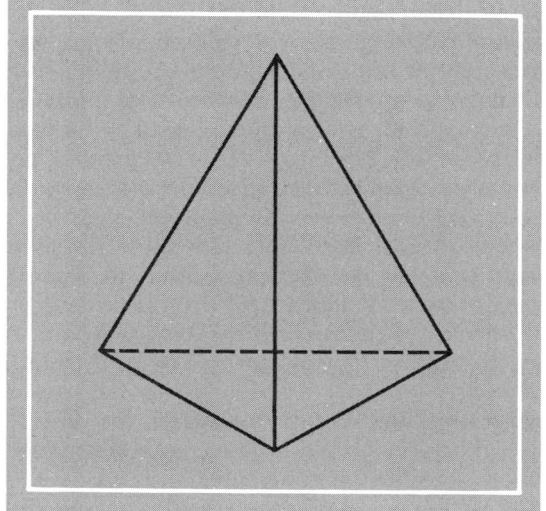

FIGURE 3–3. The "Ring-and-Peg" problem can be solved by using a piece of string to tie the two sticks together.

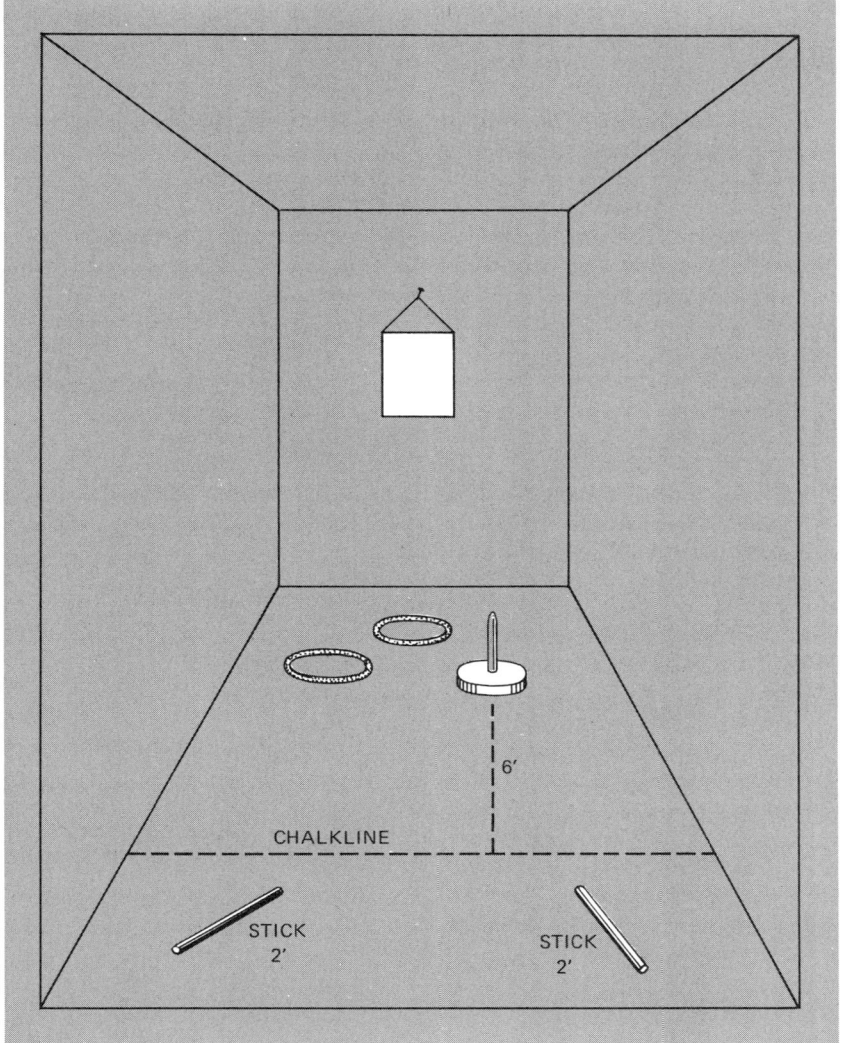

Source: Adapted from M. Scheerer, Problem-solving. *Scientific American*, 1963, **208**, 120. Copyright © 1963 by *Scientific American*. All rights reserved.

other of Scheerer's problems illustrates this meaning of perception (Figure 3-3).

The problem requires the subject to put two rings on a peg from a position six feet away. To accomplish this, the subject needs a tool to extend his reach; a satisfactory tool can be constructed by tying two short sticks together with a string, all of which are available. The critical object is the string—when it hangs alone on a nail in the wall, the problem is easy. But, when the string supports a mirror or sign, over half the college students given the problem failed to solve it within 20 minutes. Perceiving the string as "something to hang things with" interferes with perceiving it as "something to tie things with."

The examples provide a persuasive argument for dscribing problems in terms of the subject's perception of the situation and for studying how his perception can be changed in order that the problem is solved.

The next viewpoint to be considered has a rather different emphasis.

Problem Solving as Associative Arousal. Whereas a perceptual approach to problems stresses the influence of the situation on the problem solver's behavior, associative approaches emphasize the role of past experience. The basic idea is that a new task will be a problem for a person if his previous experience has resulted in the establishment of inappropriate behavioral tendencies which are "stronger" than those required to achieve the desired outcome. In other words, problems exist because subjects' prior learning produces negative transfer (interference) in new situations (Schulz, 1960).

In contrast to the intuitive and introspective connotations of a perceptual emphasis, associative definitions of problems seem rather formal and abstract. This results from the use of the "stimulus-response" terminology of behaviorism, which was initiated in a reaction against the "mentalism" of introspection. As was pointed out in Chapter 2, early behaviorist accounts were in terms of peripheral processes, but more recent associative views give great emphasis to "mediating processes."

The essential feature of an associative view is the response hierarchy. At the simplest level, this concept refers to the notion that a stimulus is associated with a number of responses and that the strength of association varies. Thus, these responses can be ordered in terms of strength, forming a hierarchy. A problem is said to exist when the strongest response is incorrect, and solution involves the arousal of successive responses in the hierarchy until the correct response is elicited. With this view, research emphasizes the identification and establishment of response hierarchies and the relation of these hierarchies to the solution of problems.

It seems appropriate at this point to consider the meanings of the terms "stimulus," "response," and "association." These terms were initially employed in the description of classical conditioning, in which case they have rather clear interpretations. A stimulus is something like a bell or light, a response is salivating or blinking an eyelid, and strength of association is indexed by response probability, response latency, or response amplitude. For example, the strength of association between a bell and salivation could be determined by measuring (1) *probability*—the likelihood that salivation will occur when the bell is rung; (2) *latency*—the amount of time occurring between the ringing of the bell and the beginning of salivation; or (3) *amplitude*—the amount of salivation that occurs. The construct "strength of association" implies that response probability, latency, and amplitude may be used interchangeably. That is, for a given stimulus, responses may be ordered in terms of probabilities, latencies, or amplitudes, and the theory assumes that these orderings will exhibit a high degree of correspondence with one another.

In applications of associative theory to problem solving, the assumption that response probability and latency are highly correlated is critical (response amplitude is seldom, if ever, encountered). The assessment of response hierarchies is almost always based on probabilities (responses are ordered in terms of relative frequencies of occurrence). The critical assumption is that when a problem is presented, the most probable response will have the shortest latency, the second most probable response the second shortest latency, and so forth. You should keep in mind that there is no logical necessity that probabilities and latencies be related in this fashion.

The terms "stimulus" and "response" have quite different meanings when used to describe problem solving than when used to describe conditioning. The "stimulus" in a problem situation is virtually equivalent to "the problem as presented" or a collection of poorly defined stimulus elements. A "response" is a way of "trying to solve the problem" which has no close connection to the operation of any particular muscles or glands. Consequently, although the terminology of conditioning is used in describing problem solving, the meanings of the terms have changed.

With these qualifications in mind, let us consider an associative description of problem solving which includes mediating processes. What Maltzman (1955) hypothesizes is roughly as follows: A stimulus might be directly associated with a particular response, but the more likely chain of events consists of a stimulus, a mediating response, and a more specific response elicited by the mediator. A general diagram of this type of organization is presented in Figure 3-4.

The meaning of the term "mediating response" must be explicated. In most treatments, a mediating response is a more abstract analog of a response. That is, a mediating response is an internalized, less detailed version of an overt response, at least at one level of discourse. In the most general terms, the distinction between mediating responses (r_g's) and (R's) is that an r_g is more abstract or broader than its associated R (the internal-overt distinction does not hold over all possible levels of discourse). For example, there are many ways to join two pieces of rope such as by tying a knot, employing a clamp, or gluing; in an associative description, these particular methods (tying, clamping, gluing) would be designated as R's, whereas the mediating response, r, would be associated with their commonality, joining. The diagram in Figure 3-4 implies that, before thinking of tying two pieces of rope together, a person would first think of joining them, and that the response of thinking of joining them would lead to the responses of tying, clamping, etc., with varying probabilities. A response which precedes and leads to another response is a mediating response.

With these definitions in mind, let us consider how Figure 3-4 describes problems. The problem situation, consisting of instructions, objects in the environment, and the current state of the subject, is symbolized by S_A, S_B, and S_C. Each of these elicits one or more mediating responses (r_g's). Each mediating response has stimulus properties (symbolized s_g); that is, each r_g is capable of eliciting a number of more particular responses (R's) which are equivalent with respect to achieving some specified goal. Thus, each mediating response is the anticipation of some goal and leads to the occurrence of specific ways of achieving that goal.

The description is completed by stating that the mediating responses can be ordered in terms of strength of association to the stimulus complex and that the particular responses in any hierarchy can be ordered in terms of strength of association to the stimulus properties of the mediating response. The implication of this compounding of hierarchies is this: For a particular response (e.g., R_3) to occur, the appropriate mediating response (r_{gb}) must be aroused and other responses (R_1 and R_2) more strongly associated with r_{gb} must already have occurred. The mechanism proposed to govern the rearrangement of response hierarchies in problem situations will be considered in the next chapter.

We must note that the associative description given above is oversimplified on two important counts. First, what was called a particular response (R) could sometimes be another mediating response (e.g., there are numerous ways of tying a knot) and, in principle, the length of a chain of mediating responses has no upper limit. The present relevance of pointing out the likelihood of more complicated sequences of behavior is simply to indicate that Figure 3-4 depicts a very uncomplicated situation. A second limi-

FIGURE 3-4. *A compound response hierarchy.*

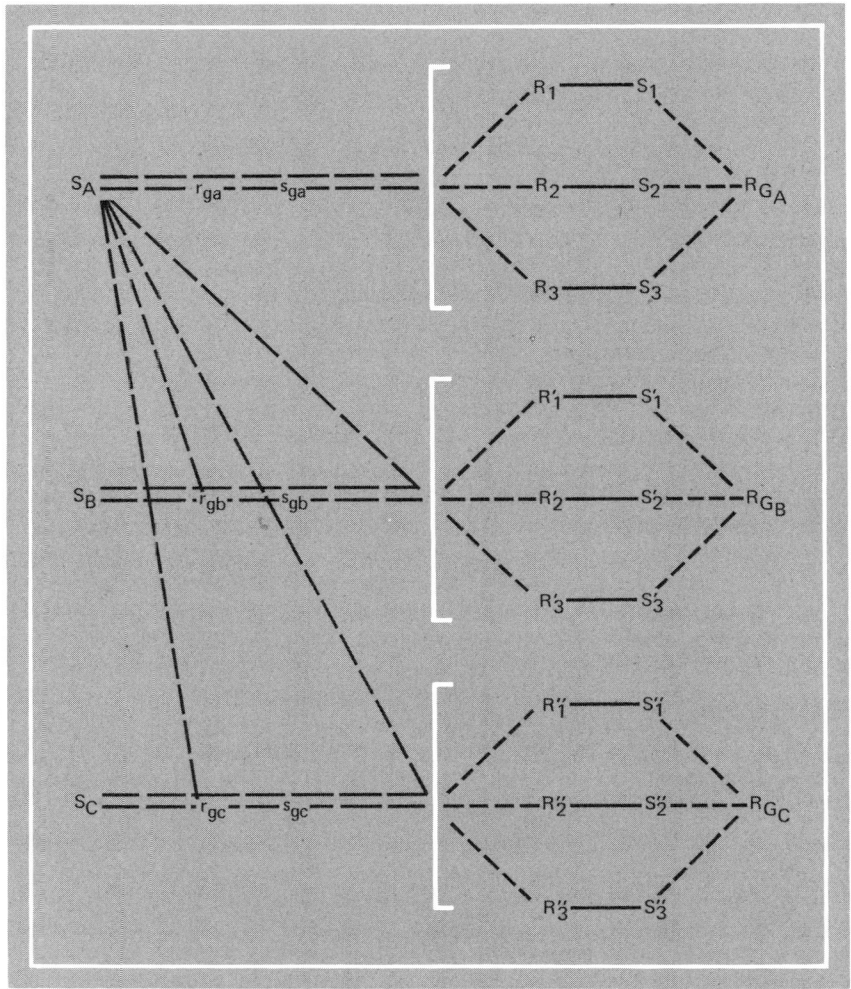

Source: Adapted from I. Maltzman, Thinking: From a behavioristic point of view. *Psychological Review,* 1955, **62**, 275-86. Copyright 1955 by the American Psychological Association and reprinted by permission.

tation of this presentation is that "responses" of any level of generality can be and are organized into a very large (theoretically infinite) number of sets or hierarchies with overlapping memberships. You will find in Chapter 4 that attempting to utilize stimulus-response terminology to describe such more complicated situations seems to lead to a cumbersome account.

Problem Solving as a Search Process. Advocates of an information-processing view of problem solving make use of a "maze model" of problems (Feigenbaum and Feldman, 1963). A problem is said to exist when a person is faced with the task of choosing one from a number of possible alternatives. Some emphasis is given to the influence of the number of alternatives on problem solving, but greatest interest lies in the process of searching among the alternatives and evaluating them with respect to the solution requirements. For problems such as choosing a move in a game of chess or checkers or selecting the next step in a mathematical proof, the process of selecting the best or correct alternative can be complicated indeed. Attention has been focused on the strategies that can be used to limit search in efficient ways, and a primary research technique is to program computers to solve problems, utilizing strategies discovered from observing human problem solvers working on the same tasks.

To summarize the discussion to this point, researchers have tended to adopt one of three points of view toward problem solving. A perceptual orientation leads to theoretical accounts emphasizing the problem solver's reorganization of the problem situation, the use of introspective accounts, and interest in the effect of variations in problem presentation on solution difficulty. In marked contrast, associative descriptions of problems are couched in "impersonal" stimulus-response terms and lead to a concern about variations in associative strength, utilizing learning concepts such as reinforcement, extinction, and generalization. The characterization of problem solving as a search process results in the attempt to discover the various strategies that problem solvers might use in selecting and evaluating alternative approaches to solutions.

As noted earlier, the viewpoints are not necessarily contradictory, and a researcher need not choose one to the total exclusion of the others. However, each investigator must decide how he will think and talk about problem solving, and the different emphases of these viewpoints probably reflect different conceptions of what is important in solving problems. It is also possible that a particular view is most advantageous for studying a certain type of problem. Ways of classifying problem types constitute the next topic for consideration.

Characteristics of Problems

In the discussion to follow, a number of problem attributes will be described. Although each characteristic will be presented in either-or terms, this is done for expository purposes only. Actual problems do not come in clear-cut categories, of course. Rather, the attributes provide a rough, imperfect means of getting some idea of the kinds of problems that theories have been designed to account for and that investigators have used in their research.

Well-Defined and Ill-Defined Problems. In distinguishing between well-defined and ill-defined problems, concern is directed toward the degree of constraint imposed on the problem solver. As an example of a well-defined problem, consider a task which sometimes appears on exams in elementary statistics: Prove: $\Sigma x^2 = \Sigma X^2 - (\Sigma X)^2/N$. The problem solver is given a very clear starting point (the left side of the equation), a very clear finishing point (the right side), and is required to abide by the rules of mathematics in bridging the gap. The solution to the problem is known (to the instructor), and any solution attempt can be unambiguously judged as right or wrong. In contrast, consider the problem, "Find a way to improve the quality of life." In this case, the problem solver would probably have a number of questions to ask of the source of this problem: "What do you mean by the quality of life?" "Whose life?" "Starting with what conditions?" "Can I invent things that don't exist?" "How long can the change take?" Under these circumstances, either the problem source must further define the problem, or the problem solver must define the problem for himself, hoping that his definition and his solution (given that definition) are acceptable. It is quite possible that a person might offer a solution that is judged satisfactory by some, but considered a failure by others.

These examples indicate the enormous variation possible in the degree of specification of a problem. As suggested above, for ill-defined problems, a very important part of the person's task is to define the problem in a potentially fruitful manner. Problems of this sort are often described as requiring *creative problem solving* for their solution. Reitman (1965), who provides an extensive discussion of this issue, has pointed out that most research on problem solving has dealt with fairly well-defined problems. Consequently, most of what is known about problem solving concerns finding solutions in highly specified situations, and solution attempts can be reliably scored as right or wrong.

Distinguishing between well-defined and ill-defined problems has an important implication for assessing the adequacy of descriptions of problem solving. For an ill-defined problem, the solution process must be more complex than for a well-defined problem. Consequently, a description of problem solving based on the study of simple, well-defined problems might represent only a small part (perhaps even a trivial part) of an adequate description of the process of solving an ill-defined problem.

Selection or Production of Solutions. A distinction somewhat related to the previous topic is whether or not a problem will be solved. As an example of a problem which is virtually certain to be solved, imagine a string of lights connected in series, in which all bulbs will fail to light if one is burned out. If the string is plugged in and fails to light, the problem is to find the burned-out bulb (or bulbs), assuming that this is the only possible reason for failure. By systematically checking each bulb, the problem will eventually be solved. For a problem which might be failed, consider the following: "What was the name of the German scientist who measured the speed of a nervous impulse in the middle of the 19th century?" The answer is Helmholtz, and there are at least two reasons why a person might fail this problem regardless of the amount of time he is given to work on it. He simply may not ever have been exposed to this fact, or he may "know" the answer but be unable to recall it. Generally, if the solution to a problem is contained in some fashion in a set of alternatives provided for the problem solver, the problem will be solved. The possibility for failure is increased in relation to the extent that the problem solver must recall or create the solution.

When a researcher can be confident that subjects will eventually solve a problem, his interest is usually directed toward how long people take to reach the solution, how many steps or selections they require, and the methods they use to search through the alternatives. When a problem requires subjects to produce their own alternatives, an investigator is often limited to determining how many people solve the problem (within some time limit, determined ultimately by the experimenter's patience). A considerable number of the tasks researchers use are of this latter type—"you either get it or you don't." An important feature of such tasks is that the investigator typically does not know much about what the subject is doing other than that he is thinking, and data collection involves simply whether a solution occurred, and, if it did, how much time was used.

One or Many Solutions. Most experimental tasks have a single solution, and the subject's task is to discover it. In some situations, however, subjects are asked to produce as many answers as they can, and interest is directed toward the number and quality of the solutions produced. Actually, some of these latter tasks do not have the characteristics of a typical problem. The subject may be given a task as simple as "name uses for a hammer" and each answer he gives is, in a sense, correct. The researcher often will want to find out simply how unusual the answers are, although sometimes criteria of adequacy or practicality will also be applied. Although the generation of many alternatives is often involved in finding the single correct answer to a problem, the considerations relevant to performance on a task with a single correct answer are different enough from those pertaining to situations in which any answer is "correct" that research on these two types of tasks will be treated separately in Chapter 5. A task having many solutions which are then judged against various criteria has the features of an ill-defined problem, in distinction to the well-defined nature of most experimental problems.

New or Old Solutions. Some problems require for their solution only that the subject recall something he has previously learned, a type of behavior that has been termed *reproductive problem solving* (Maier, 1940). An example of this type of problem would be requiring a subject to say some particular animal name beginning with *b;* the problem solver has previously learned a number of animal names and knows what it means for a name to begin with *b*. His attempts at solution may be described as searching among the animal names he is able to recall for those starting with *b,* saying each one until he says the "correct" one as defined by the experimenter (e.g., *beaver*). In contrast, *productive problem solving* is said to involve the integration of previously unrelated experiences. Maier proposed that solution is not guaranteed by the simple availability of these experiences, arguing that some *direction* is required for the proper integration to take place. The description of productive problem solving also suggests that more complex solutions are characteristic of this type of behavior in contrast to simple solutions in reproductive problem solving. There is perhaps an inevitable confounding of familiarity and simplicity since, as Mandler (1962) suggests (see Chapter 1), a complex sequence of activities seems to become integrated as a unit when well practiced. In problem situations, it is often difficult to

specify the degree of complexity of a solution, which suggests that dealing with the productive-reproductive distinction in terms of new versus old solutions will be adequate for present purposes.

METHODS FOR STUDYING PROBLEM SOLVING

A Survey of Experimental Tasks

Most experimental problems are fairly well-defined and have a single solution, with the result that researchers study the discovery of known solutions rather than the formulation and solution of problems with uncertain solutions. Solving the problem may require either selection from a specified set of alternatives or production of potential solutions. When production is required, the solution may vary from a rather familiar, "old" solution to a productive, "new" combination of ideas. The relationship between these problem attributes and the kinds of tasks which have been employed is indicated in Table 3-1. In addition to the tasks given in Table 3-1, researchers have sometimes employed problems which are already familiar, such as arithmetic problems, while other tasks have been used so infrequently that they will be described only when the research based on them is presented. What will now be considered are those tasks which have been created primarily for research purposes and which have been used with some regularity.

Search Tasks. The major feature of this class of problems is that the alternatives are clearly specified and usually provided for the subject, who must select the one or more which meet the requirements set by the experimenter. Included in this category are troubleshooting tasks requiring the subject to locate a defective component in some apparatus (as in the string of lights described earlier), jigsaw puzzles, and light-and-switches tasks. The latter problem involves an apparatus in which

TABLE 3-1. A Rough Classification of Problems

	Well-Defined Problems				Ill-Defined Problems
SELECTION	PRODUCTION				(All require production of a new solution, or have an uncertain solution)
Simple search tasks	One Solution		Many Solutions		
	New	Old	New	Old	
	Insight problems	Anagrams Complex search tasks	Originality tasks	Multiple-solution anagrams	

each of a number of switches is connected to more than one of a number of lights, with the subject required to turn switches until a specified pattern of lights is produced. Some search tasks are presented in verbal form, as when the subject is given a set of criteria and is then asked to find in a list of items the one satisfying those criteria. Since, for problems of this type the set of alternatives is known, solution is virtually guaranteed, with quality of performance judged on the basis of speed of solution or number of choices to solution. The experimenter can also analyze sequences of selections in an attempt to identify strategies used by subjects in working on the problem.

The above statement about the certainty of solution needs some qualification—solution is guaranteed only if the number of alternatives is small enough to allow a systematic check of all possibilities, and if the subject uses this method and can remember (or has a record of) previous choices in order to avoid repetitions. A search process through which all possibilities are considered in some systematic fashion is called an *algorithm*. Such methods guarantee success if a solution exists and if sufficient time is allowed. If the number of alternatives is large, an algorithmic search might require more time than the subject is willing to spend or than the experimental session affords. It is characteristic of human problem solvers that they tend not to use algorithmic methods in solving problems. Rather, they tend to use rules of thumb or other devices to limit search in some way; such techniques are called *heuristics*. Searching for a solution by a heuristic method can lead to a very efficient solution, but it can also lead to no solution at all.

Consider the example of working on a jigsaw puzzle. Assume that the problem solver has decided to start with a piece of the border with one red edge and seeks to locate the piece fitting the red edge. An algorithmic method of solving this small problem would be to take each remaining piece in turn, attempting to fit it in all possible ways, until a fit is found. It is highly unlikely that this method would be used. It is more likely that a person working on this problem would limit his search in some way, such as by looking only for pieces with a straight edge characteristic of border pieces and with a red edge and by attempting to fit only the red edge of any piece selected to the red edge of the starting piece. Most of the time, such a technique will work very well, but it will fail if the fitting edges are not of the same color.

Insight Problems. Perhaps the best example of a type of problem for which there is no guarantee of solution is the class known as *insight problems*. Although some of these problems involve the rearrangement of a perceptual display, those most frequently used require the subject to use an object in an unusual way. One such problem is the "two-string" problem. Imagine a room with two strings hanging from the ceiling—the task is to tie the two strings together. However, the strings are too far apart for a person to simply grasp one and walk to the other. There are a number of ways to solve the problem; one could pull one string from its mooring and take it over to the other, but this solution is usually not allowed by the experimenter (also, subjects typically assume that the strings must remain attached). If the subject could extend his reach, such as with a rake, the problem could be solved in this way, but there is typically no such tool available. The situation is usually set up such that the only possible solution is to tie an object to one string, set it swinging, then walk to the other string and wait for the swinging string (the pendulum solution). The likelihood of the solution occurring depends on what objects are available; as indicated earlier, those objects in the room are not commonly used as pendulum weights (switches, relays, pliers). The important feature of this problem is that the experimenter gives very little indication of what responses are permissible, thus solving depends on the subject's thinking of the correct type of solution attempt. Within the 15-minute time limit commonly used, about 85 percent of college students will solve this problem (Duncan, 1961).

A second example of an insight problem is the "candle" problem (see Figure 3-5). The subject is given a candle, a small box, some tacks, and some matches, with the instruction to affix the candle to the wall in such a way that it burns freely without dripping wax on the table or floor. In solving this problem, the critical object is the box, which must be attached to the wall with tacks and used as a platform for the candle (a rather unusual use for a box). As with the two-string problem, the subject gets little indication of how he ought to proceed, and solution depends on his thinking of the correct use. Although success in this task depends on the way in which the problem is presented, the candle problem seems to be of the same general level of difficulty as the two-string problem, with a noticeable number of failures under the 15-minute time limit. This fact, that insight problems are not always solved in the time allowed, should be remembered when evaluating research employing these problems. Furthermore, there is minimal performance involved in the subject's behavior (he might just stare at the materials for a considerable period), and describing his behavior more precisely than simply as "thinking" is a difficult task for the investigator.

Word Problems. A great many problems can be given in verbal form to human adults, and the characteristics of these problems vary considerably. However, a type of task which has been used with some frequency requires the subject to discover a word meeting certain stated criteria (as, for example, "I've chosen an animal starting with *b*. What is it?"). Since word problems can be presented as either production or selection tasks (by providing a list of possible answers), the possibility of comparing the two types of presentation exists, although direct comparisons have rarely been reported.

The most popular word problem has been the *anagram,* in which the subject is given a set of letters (e.g., *l-c-b-k-a*) and asked to make an English word *(black)*. Since the anagram provides a finite number of letters, a possible solution algorithm would be to generate all possible permutations of the letters, considering each as a potential solution. The efficiency of such a method will vary considerably with the number of letters presented; with only three letters, there are only 6 possible orders, but the number of orders increases to 120 with five letters, and to 720 with six letters. Anagrams of five letters have been used most often, and there is good evidence indicating that subjects, rather than generating permutations of the letters, try to generate words and subword letter sequences based on their knowledge of the vocabulary of the language. These

FIGURE 3–5. The candle problem. The upper panel shows the equipment available for mounting a candle on a wall. The lower panel shows the solution.

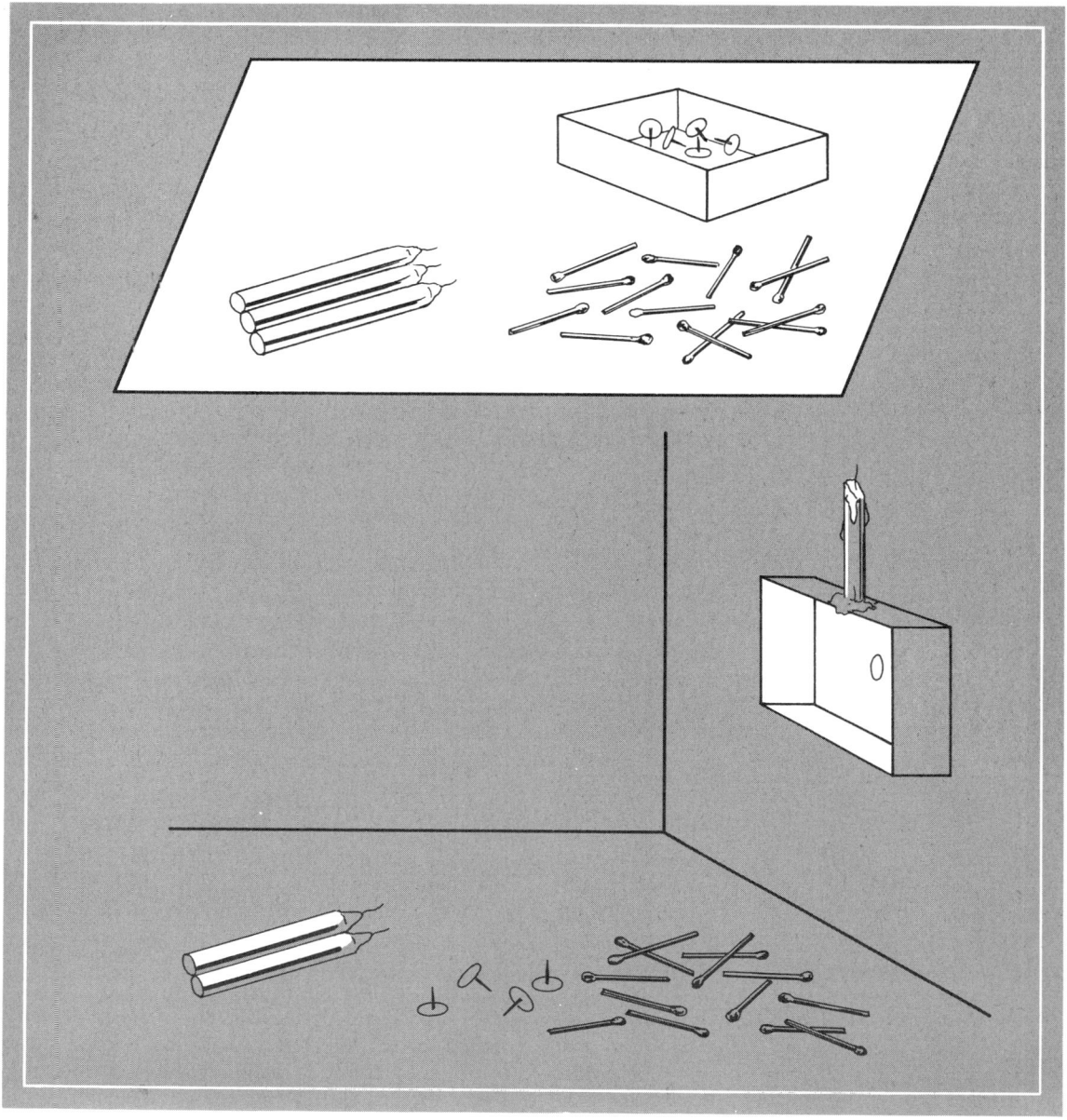

problems are fairly easy, with many solution times of less than a minute, but there will also be a considerable number of failures after four minutes' working time.

Analysis of Problem Types. An important question is whether the different problem types represent merely various situations in which essentially the same behavior will occur or whether different behaviors are involved. Of course, at the most detailed descriptive level, differences are inevitable, but, unfortunately, little effort at the more general theoretical level has been directed toward the similarities of the solution processes for different tasks. If anything, the use of different problems has been associated with different descriptive accounts (Table 3-2).

Search tasks have been generally employed within the context of an information processing approach, and interest has been directed toward the identification of search patterns and the effects of varying the number of alternatives. Insight problems were developed by Gestalt psychologists and have been described as requiring productive thinking. Research with these problems has emphasized the effects of direction-giving hints and variation in problem presentation. Although information processing terms were used in describing anagrams, the use of these problems has usually been combined with an associative orientation, and solving word problems has been viewed as reproductive problem solving. The reasons for this emphasis are fairly clear: Word problems allow experimenters to relate problem difficulty to the characteristics of well-established associative hierarchies based on experience with the language, and solving these problems seems to involve a process of recalling rather than recombining previously learned responses into new combinations. As mentioned earlier, an investigator's conception of the behavior he studies has a sizeable influence on the manner in which he conducts research (selecting tasks, variables), an influence which is perhaps no better exemplified than in the study of problem solving.

Research Methods

In this section, some of the more formal features of research on problem solving will be discussed, separate from the fact that different studies often involve different problems. Studies of problem solving tend to be primarily concerned with either a detailed description of the process by which a problem is solved or the identification of variables which affect the difficulty of a problem. The most frequently used measure of problem difficulty is solution time, and the temporal characteristics of problem solving will be discussed, as well as some suggestions for the interpretation of solution time.

Hypotheses Testing and Process Tracing. In studying problem solving, two questions

TABLE 3–2. Relationship Between Approach to Problem Solving and Kind of Problem Employed

	APPROACH TO PROBLEM SOLVING		
Tasks	Gestalt	Associative	Information Processing
Simple search tasks	No	Yes	Yes
Insight problems	Yes	Yes	No
Anagrams	Yes	Yes	Yes
Complex search tasks	No	No	Yes
Originality tasks	No	Yes	No
Ill-defined problems	?	No	Yes

may be asked: "How do people solve this problem?" and "What affects the difficulty of this problem?" In the long run, these questions are like two sides of a coin, since, if one identifies a variable which changes problem difficulty, he has also discovered something about how people solve the problem, albeit by indirect means. The reasons that these questions are distinguished is that they reflect differences in the kinds of performance indicators that investigators choose to obtain.

In a process-tracing experiment, the researcher makes an effort to obtain as much direct information as he can about the process of solving the problem. Any task in which the subject must make a sequence of choices or in which he can request new items of information provides the experimenter with data from which he can infer the process of solution. Strategies can be identified in certain patterns of choices, provided the investigator has some idea of what to look for. This technique has been employed to some extent with simple search tasks, but the greatest use of this method has been made in the study of conceptual behavior. Notice that whenever a task requires the subject to provide a record of choices, the investigator gets information relevant to both questions stated above, since the number of choices is a measure of difficulty while the sequence of choices gives an idea of the process of solution.

With problems in which the subject is essentially required only to produce a final answer, process tracing requires extra effort, and the usual procedure has been to ask the subject what he is doing, perhaps also why. Such questions can also be used with problems in which the subject makes a series of choices. One can ask why a particular choice is being made or what has been learned from a given move. A study by Gagné and Smith (1962) of the "pyramid puzzle" illustrates this use of the technique. The problem situation consists of a number of discs stacked according to size, the largest on the bottom, on one of three circles (Figure 3-6).

The subject's task is to get the discs stacked in exactly the same order on Circle B, moving only one disc at a time, moving discs only from one circle to another (Circle C may be used), and never placing a larger disc on top of a smaller disc. To illustrate this rule, if the subject moves the smallest disc to Circle B, then his only allowable move with the next smallest disc is to Circle C. The problem is difficult, and performance can be measured in terms of the number of unnecessary moves as well as in terms of solution time. Of present interest is the effect of requiring subjects to state a reason for each move. It was found that subjects in this verbalization condition made fewer unnecessary moves but took more time in solving training problems, compared to those who had no such requirement. The additional time taken by verbalizing subjects was simply a result of the fact that it takes time to state a reason. On a transfer problem on which no subject was required to verbalize, those who had previously stated reasons performed much better, both in terms of fewer unnecessary moves and faster solution times. At the end of the experiment, all subjects were asked to state a rule about how such problems should be solved, and their answers were judged for adequacy (there is a way to solve these problems with no unnecessary moves). Subjects who had been required to verbalize during training generally gave better answers than those who had not.

Gagné and Smith suggested that subjects who had been required to give reasons for moves were more likely to analyze the problem and try to find "good" reasons and, consequently, were more likely to discover the general principles which could be used for maximally efficient performance. Of particular importance for the present discussion is what the subjects said when they gave reasons for their own moves. The experimenters report that most of these verbalizations were not very illuminating (e.g., "only possible move," "just to try it," "to get at the larger disc"). The point is that these verbalizations are what an investigator would examine to get an idea of how the subjects were working on the prob-

FIGURE 3–6. *The "Disc transfer" or "Pyramid" problem requires the subject to move the discs from Circle A to Circle B, moving only one disc at a time and never placing a larger disc on top of a smaller one.*

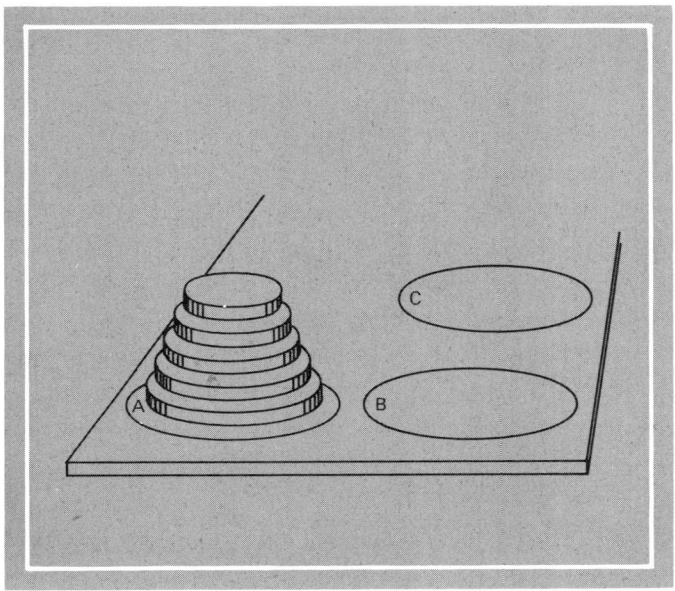

lem and, as has just been indicated, he might not find out very much.

You should not conclude that it is useless to ask problem solvers to "think out loud," since in many situations useful information can be obtained. Rather, considerable caution must be used in interpreting such verbalizations. A second example will solidify this argument. Mayzner, Tresselt, and Helbock (1964) attempted to get "thinking aloud" protocols for anagram problems. Since the commonly used five-letter problems are too easy for this purpose (the solution occurs so rapidly that the subject has great difficulty telling how he achieved it), these investigators used six-letter anagrams which are considerably more difficult. This change in the problem is what is important. There is strong (indirect) evidence that subjects try to solve five-letter anagrams to a large extent by thinking of words having one or more of the anagram letters as possible solutions. Yet, Mayzner et al. reported that only about one-third of their subjects' vocalizations were words. Other research indicates that construction of subword letter sequences takes on greater importance as the number of anagram letters increases (Kaplan and Carvellas, 1968; Rhine, 1959). Thus, the content of verbalizations is likely to change with the number of letters in the anagram, yielding information of limited usefulness.

There are a number of experimental tasks which seem to be "too easy" to obtain much information about the process of solution from what subjects say (they have little to say). As the last example indicates, making the problem more difficult to "slow subjects down" in order that they can tell the experimenter how they are proceeding risks the danger that the solution processes for the harder and easier problems are importantly different. There is always the possibility that requiring subjects to say what they are doing changes the manner in which they work on the problem. Despite these problems, and despite the fact that the psychologists' task is to describe subjects' behavior whether or not the subjects can describe their own behavior, it is undoubtedly true that the technique of asking people how they solve problems has been too little used. This is the result of the behavioristic influence on experimental psychology. In Chapter 2, it was pointed out that early behaviorism rejected introspection totally, and this mistrust of "what people tell you about what they are doing" persists today, although in less extreme fashion. Consequently, in most studies of problem solving, researchers have limited their data collection to measuring how many people solve a problem or how long solution takes, which leads to a different kind of research.

Research in which some variable is manipulated and differences in problem difficulty observed is directly related to the question, "What makes a problem difficult?" Indirectly, such research contributes to a description of problem-solving behavior, by filling in the blanks in a chain of reasoning indicated by "If the difficulty of the problem was affected by _____, then people must solve problems by _____." Investigations primarily directed toward the determination of the influence of some variable on problem difficulty are here termed "hypothesis-testing" studies. Some characteristic of the problem situation, broadly conceived, is varied, and interest is directed toward any differences in solution time or solution probability that result. The characteristic may refer to the instructions given, some attribute of the required solution, or the type of subject given the problem.

Hypothesis-testing studies exhibit considerable variability. In some cases, some quantified variable, such as the number of alternatives provided, is varied and the experimenter is able not only to state whether this variable affects problem difficulty but also to give some indication of the functional (mathematical) relationship between the manipulated variable and the index of problem difficulty. However, the majority of studies are simpler in design; two or three conditions differing "qualitatively" are compared (e.g., three different kinds of instructions), and the kind of statement that the researcher can make is noticeably less precise than a mathematical function. Since measures of the probability of solution or solution time are characteristic of hypothesis-testing studies of problem solving, we need to discuss these measures. Before doing so, however, we will present a discussion placing these measures in the total context of the study of problem solving.

Stages in Problem Solving. Several proposals concerning the stages of problem solving were presented in Chapter 2; as noted at that point, speculation about this issue has occurred for quite some time. The topic of present concern is a proposal made by Johnson (1955), because his ideas provide an interesting framework in which to interpret measures of problem difficulty such as solution time. Johnson divides problem solving into three stages: preparation, production, and judgment. During the preparation period, the subject must get some idea of what the problem is—what is given, what the criteria of a solution are, etc. Earlier in this chapter it was pointed out that most researchers have studied "well-defined" problems in which the subject is "fully prepared" for the problem by the experimenter who poses it. Consequently, little is known about the preparation stage.

The production stage refers to the consideration of alternative approaches to a solution and the generation of potential solutions. When a problem solver has produced a potential solution, he must judge its adequacy, leading him into Johnson's third stage. With these stages in mind, consider the typical procedure followed in the measurement of time to solution. The experimenter first fully informs the subject about the problem, then gives a "start" signal and begins timing. Some time later (regardless of what happens during the working period), the subject presumably tells the experimenter the correct solution, the timing period is terminated, and a "solution time" is recorded. It is clear that, according to Johnson's system, this solution time includes both production time and judgment time, since the subject presumably had not only to come up with the correct answer but also to judge it as worthy of offering to the experimenter. However, most interpretations of solution time have dealt only with the production of solutions; apparently, researchers have not considered judgment of great importance or have assumed that judgment adds some relatively small, constant amount to all solution times. This assumption may be incorrect, as the following research suggests.

In a series of ingenious studies, Johnson and his coworkers have attempted to demonstrate the independence of the proposed three stages of problem solving. Johnson and Jennings (1963) required each of a number of college students to read a story (preparation), write five titles for the plot (production), and select the best title as his final solution (judgment). Each stage was separately timed, and the investigators were interested in determining whether individual differences in the three time measures were related to each other. The results indicated that the three parts of the solution process were independent of each other in this sense—preparation times could not be predicted very well from judgment times, etc. Thus, subjects who took a relatively long time to produce their potential solutions were not characterized by relatively long judgment times; rather, their judgment times varied over a wide range in an unpredictable fashion.

What are the implications of Johnson's three-stage proposal? It seems that the identification of three problem-solving stages should stimulate investigators to consider carefully which parts of the solution process interest them. As noted earlier, most researchers have ignored preparation time; they have either assumed that preparation is constant over conditions and subjects, or they have manipulated preparation, primarily through different instructions. Johnson's analysis leads to an interesting speculation regarding the effects of instructions. Suppose that one set of instructions leads to shorter measured solution times than another, indicating that production-judgment is faster with the first mentioned instructions. However, Johnson's three-stage proposal suggests that, to compare total problem-solving performance in the two conditions, one should include the time taken for instructions (preparation). It seems likely that "better" instruction would ordinarily take more time to administer, probably because it would include more information about the problem or some guidance as to solution methods. Unfortunately, experimenters manipulating instructions typically do not report the time required for various instructions, making such an overall comparison impossible. The examination of instructional effects serves as an excellent example of the value of considering Johnson's three-stage analysis.

In addition to ignoring preparation time, most investigators seem also to have ignored judgment time. Differences in measured solution times have systematically been interpreted in terms of production speed, with judgment assumed to add at most a small constant to the measurement. The research by Johnson and Jennings indicates, however, that judgment times vary among subjects and are not consistently related to production times. Furthermore, a human subject might well make an error in judging the adequacy of a solution; the most critical difficulty arises when a subject fails to offer a solution because he has incorrectly judged it to be wrong. Attributing this subject's long solution time (or failure) to deficiencies in production is clearly incorrect; as an example, subjects who have failed an anagram problem, when told the solution, sometimes say, "I thought of that, but didn't think it was a word, so I didn't say it." To summarize this discussion, the time a subject takes to give a solution to the experimenter is ordinarily interpreted in terms of the production of that solution, and the adequacy of this interpretation depends on the validity of two assumptions: (1) that preparation was complete at the beginning of the measured time period, and (2) that judgment of a potential solution increases solution time by a relatively small and constant amount. Because of the lack of relevant data, the validity of these assumptions must be judged separately for each problem encountered.

Solution Probability as a Function of Working Time. In the hypothesis-testing studies which compose a large part of the research on problem solving, a comparison is made of the difficulty of problems under two or more conditions. Problem difficulty may be measured in terms of solution time or, if a fixed amount of working time is allowed, by the number of solutions (solution probability).

FIGURE 3-7. Production curves of cumulative number of responses as a function of working time.

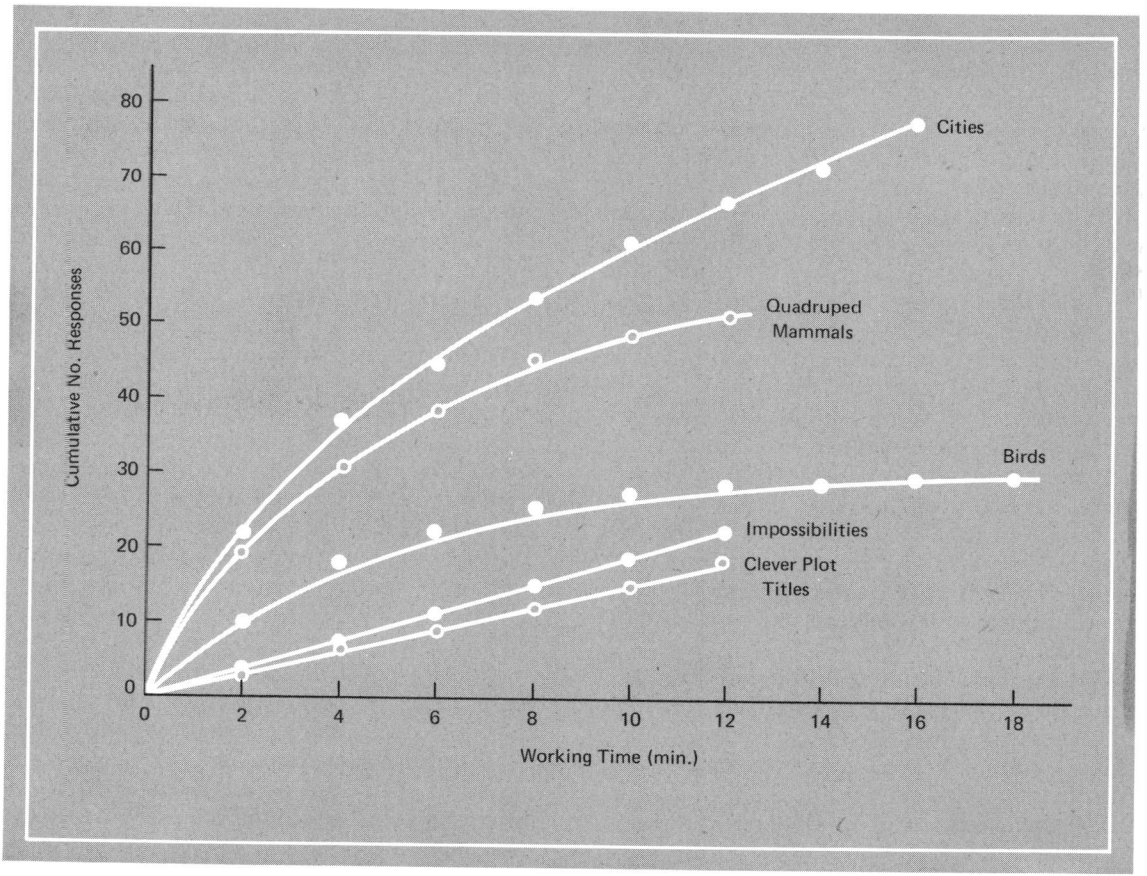

Source: From P. R. Christensen, J. P. Guilford, and R. C. Wilson, Relations of creative responses to working time and instructions. *Journal of Experimental Psychology,* 1957, **53**, 82-88. Copyright 1957 by the American Psychological Association and reprinted by permission.

It will be instructive to examine the relationship between these two measures.

What is the relationship between the number of responses produced and the amount of time that the subject has spent producing them? Christensen, Guilford, and Wilson (1957) studied this relationship for a variety of free-responding tasks (note that these were not problems in the usual sense). For tasks requiring the recall of previously learned information (reproductive thinking) such as the names of birds, makes of cars, and names of quadruped mammals, answers were produced at a steadily decreasing rate (Figure 3-7). In contrast, the rate of production for tasks involving unusual, clever, or "creative" responses is approximately constant over time. In addition to demonstrating that one can

FIGURE 3–8. The relation between cumulative solution probability and working time for anagram problems of two levels of difficulty.

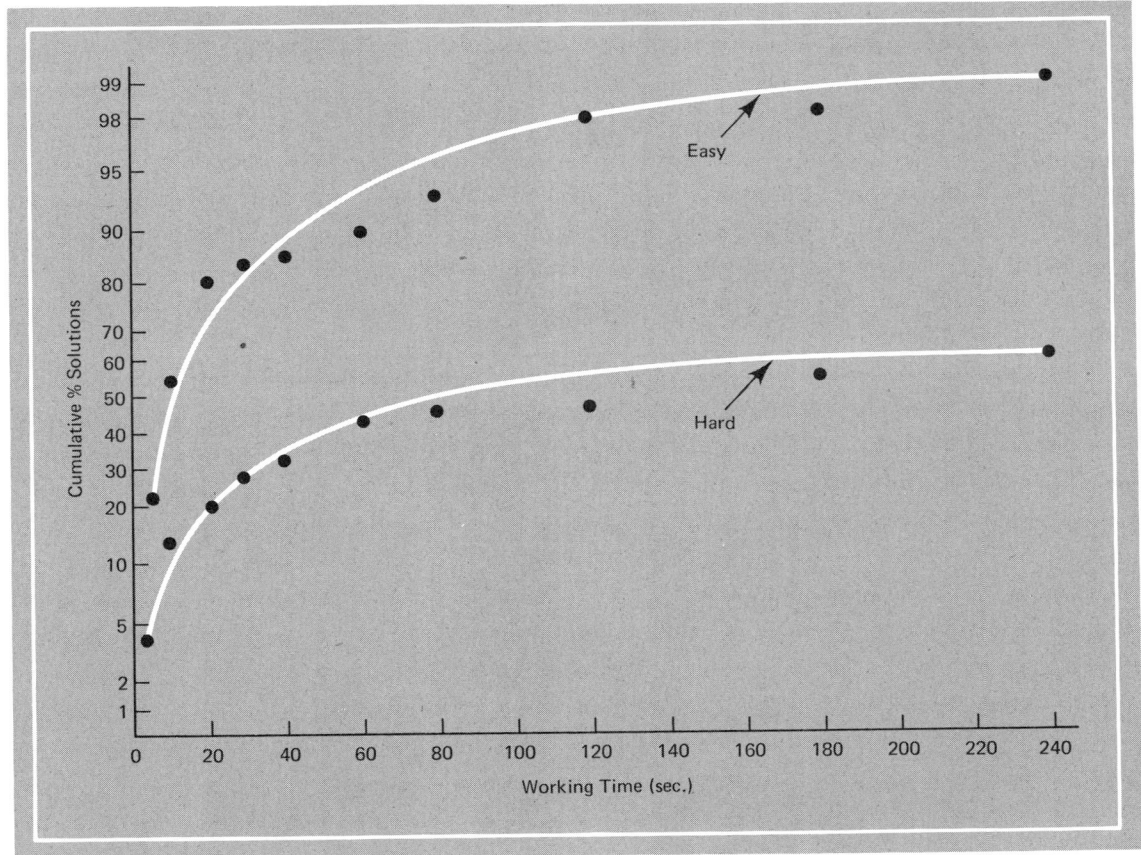

Source: Adapted from M. S. Mayzner and M. E. Tresselt, Anagram solution times: A function of letter order and word frequency. *Journal of Experimental Psychology,* 1958, **56,** 376-79. Copyright 1958 by the American Psychological Association and reprinted by permission.

distinguish kinds of behavior on the basis of the way in which output changes over time, these findings imply that solution probability will be related to working time in similar fashion. This implication is based on the assumption that, even when working "quietly" on a problem, a subject is producing potential solutions in much the same way as he says them aloud when asked to do so. If so, then changes in solution probability over time for a problem requiring reproductive thinking should have the same curvilinear form as the functions for the recall tasks in Figure 3-7.

Direct evidence has been reported for two types of problems. Figure 3-8 presents changes in solution probability over time for anagram problems of different difficulty levels. There are two pieces of information in this display. First, the data suggest that solving anagrams resembles recalling previously learned responses, since the relationships with working time are similar for these two behaviors. The second point is that the difference between the problems is clearly evident at the outset and is virtually unchanged by including longer solution times, within the total time allowed. Thus, the problems differ in difficulty, and the difference lies in the likelihood of reaching an early solution rather than in changes in solution probability over longer working times.

Similar findings have been reported for an insight problem (the two-string problem) and are depicted in Figure 3-9. This figure indicates that men do better than women and that solution probability is curvilinearly related to working time for both groups. Again, the difference between the groups is evident at the outset and does not change as longer times are considered. Earlier it was pointed out that solving insight problems has been considered productive thinking—the production of some new combination of ideas, which seems consistent with the requirement of discovering an unusual use for an object. However, the data in Figure 3-9 do not support such a description, since the relationship between solution probability and working time for the two-string problem resembles those found with anagram solving and reproductive output tasks rather than those for giving unusual responses.

Let us return to the relationship of solution probability and working time. The data for both anagrams and the insight problem suggest that differences between conditions (types of problems or types of subjects) will be evident in solution probabilities after a short working time and will be virtually unaffected as more time is allowed, within limits. Obviously, if enough time is allowed, virtually all subjects in all conditions will eventually solve the problem. The implication is that, if all an investigator wants to find out is whether solution is easier to obtain in one condition compared with another, the most efficient procedure would be to compare solution probabilities after a relatively short, optimum working interval. The optimum time limit will vary with the type of problem, e.g., 30 seconds for five-letter anagrams, perhaps 3 minutes for the two-string problem.

Keep in mind that the immediate goal of hypothesis-testing research is to determine whether problem-solving efficiency differs under various conditions. The researcher's responsibility is to conduct his investigation in such a manner that a fair test for a difference can be made. What this means is that, if the test is to be based on solution probabilities, enough subjects must be given the problem under the various conditions to enable the calculation of reliable solution probabilities. For example, one can hardly have much confidence in the finding that two out of five subjects solved in one condition (solution probability is .40) and four out of five subjects solved in another condition (solution probability is .80). However, if the probabilities were based on a greater number of subjects, perhaps 50 in each condition, one's confidence that a difference exists would be much greater.

The reason that relatively many subjects are needed to calculate reliable solution probabilities is that the researcher obtains a minimum amount of information from each indi-

FIGURE 3–9. *The relation between cumulative solution probability and working time for the "two-string" problem.*

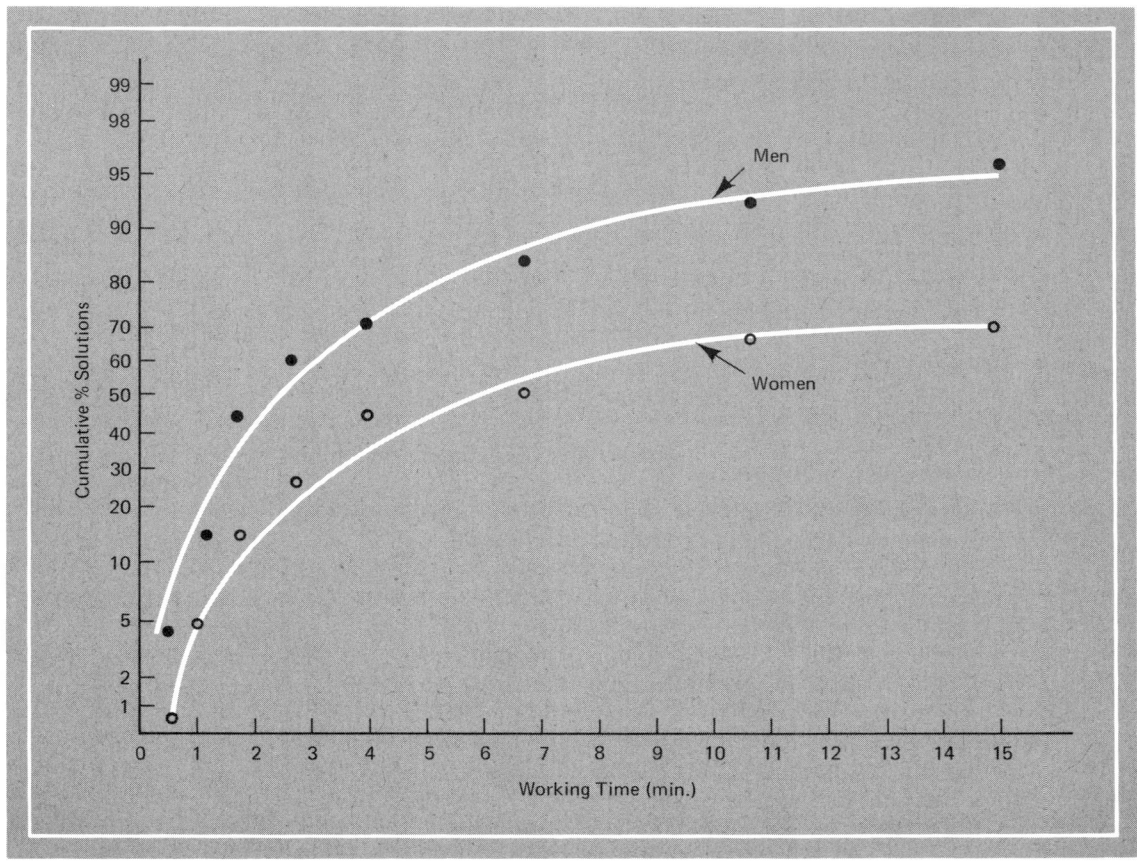

Source: Adapted from C. P. Duncan, Probability vs. latency of solution of an insight problem. Reprinted by permission of the author and publisher from *Psychological Reports,* 1962, **10**, 119-21.

vidual—whether or not he solved. An investigator can garner more information from each subject if he measures solution time, but the attempt to do so is hindered by the fact that some subjects may fail to solve. The functions of Figures 3-8 and 3-9 may be described by stating that the longer a person has worked on a problem without solving it, the longer he will have to continue working to reach the solution. You may recall from introductory psychology that the best average of a group of scores under most circumstances is the arithmetic mean and that, to calculate the mean, one needs to know the value of each individual score. Thus, if an experimenter wanted to compare solution times in two conditions, the best test he could make would be to compare the mean solution times for those conditions.

However, if some subjects fail to solve (have unknown solution times), calculating the mean is, strictly speaking, impossible. Consequently, comparing conditions in terms of solution times has often been based on medians (the median being the "middle" score), which is not a very sensitive test.

The discussion of solution time and solution probability has been somewhat prolonged for a very simple reason. If a researcher fails to find a difference between conditions, there is always the possibility that he failed to make a sufficiently sensitive test. There have been a considerable number of "no-difference" findings reported in the research literature on problem solving and, for some of these, the judgment that an inadequate test was conducted appears plausible.

An Interpretation of Solution Time. Most investigators interpret solution time as indicative of the difficulty of producing the solution to a problem. The question arises as to why solution times are longer in one condition than in another. Restle and Davis (1962) have provided some fruitful insights into this question. Their method of analysis consists of developing mathematical models appropriate to various problem-solving situations. The details of their analysis will not be presented; a brief sketch of their formulation will be given, then attention will be directed toward an interesting outcome of their work.

To begin, assume that a problem solver is attempting to produce a "one-step" solution (there is only one thing to be discovered). For purposes of analysis, working time may be divided into short, equal intervals of some arbitrary duration. In any interval, there is a certain probability (ϕ) that the subject will solve the problem and probability $(1 - \phi)$ that he will fail. Assuming that ϕ remains constant over time intervals, the probability that the problem will be solved in the nth time interval is given by the equation:

$$P(n) = \phi (1 - \phi)^{n-1}.$$

In examining this equation, note that for solution to occur in the nth interval, the subject must fail to solve in the first $n - 1$ intervals, with probability $(1 - \phi)^{n-1}$ and then solve in the nth interval, with probability ϕ. This equation indicates one way in which solution times can be affected: Decreasing ϕ increases the number of time intervals needed to reach a given level of cumulative solution probability. That is, the probability that the problem is solved by the end of the fourth time interval is equal to the sum of the probabilities for intervals 1, 2, 3, and 4. The probability of solving in the first interval is ϕ, for the second interval $\phi (1 - \phi)$, for the third $\phi (1 - \phi)^2$, etc. As an example, if $\phi = .5$, the probability that the problem will be solved in the first four intervals is .97, while it is only .76 if $\phi = .3$. Thus, solution times will be shorter as the probability of solving the problem in any time interval increases.

Restle and Davis extended this analysis to problems requiring multiple-step solutions, with the following simplifying assumptions: (1) Each stage is equally difficult. (2) Performance on one step is independent of performance on another. (3) The steps must be completed in succession. The result of this extension is that, for any given value of ϕ, solution times will be longer as the number of steps in the solution increases. The analysis thus far demonstrates a point of considerable importance for understanding the effects of variables on problem-solving efficiency. Solution times are a function of both the number of steps in the solution process and the probability of completing a step within a given time interval. Thus, when an experimenter finds solution times different under various conditions, it would be illuminating if he could determine whether this difference represents a change in the number of steps to solution, or the speed with which a step can be completed, or both. (The same general argument, but not the formulas presented, applies if the experimenter measures solution probability for a fixed amount of time.)

In the further extension of their analysis to

the continuous measurement of time (rather than dividing time into arbitrary intervals), Restle and Davis provide a potentially useful analytic tool. If the conditions of their model are met, the number of steps in a solution process can be estimated by the equation:

$$k = (\bar{t})^2 / s_t^2$$

This equation can be read: The estimate of the number of steps (k) to achieve the solution of a problem is equal to the square of the mean solution time ($\bar{t}$) divided by the variance of the solution times (s_t^2). The variance of a set of scores is the square of the standard deviation, which you may remember from introductory psychology.

Let us consider an example of the use of this formula. Restle and Davis describe the "rope" problem: "A prisoner attempted to escape from a tower, finding in his cell a rope which was half long enough to permit him to reach the ground safely. He divided the rope in half, tied the two halves together, and escaped. How could this have been?" The answer is that the rope was divided lengthwise. This problem was assumed to be a "one-step" problem, since solution depended on this single idea. This problem was given to a large number of college students, with the result that the mean solution time was 131 seconds, the standard deviation 116 seconds. Using the formula given above, the estimated number of steps is $(131)^2 / (116)^2 = 1.3$ steps, which is not far from the one step assumed.

Although the estimate of the number of steps must be viewed cautiously, since the assumptions of the model may not be adequately met, a comparison of estimates from various conditions seems less susceptible to error. Restle and Davis applied the formula to several problems of varying complexity and obtained good correspondence between estimates based on the formula and the judged number of steps, particularly in terms of the order of different conditions. The general point of this discussion is that an investigator often has some idea about the variable he manipulates, i.e., whether it affects the number of steps to solution or the speed of completing a step. A simple comparison of average solution times is ambiguous with respect to this interpretation. Application of the Restle-Davis formula, if possible, can provide the researcher with additional information on which to base his conclusions.

SUMMARY

Before going on to the consideration of the theories and findings relevant to problem solving, it will be helpful to summarize briefly what has been presented thus far. Attention has been given to the wide variety of problems used in experimentation and to some characteristics that may be used to classify problems into types. Most experimental tasks are well-defined problems; the problem situation is clearly specified for the subject and a definite solution is possible. Discovering the solution may involve selecting from a set of alternatives provided, or the subject may be required to generate potential solutions from the information provided. Although some work has been done on tracing the process of solution, most researchers have limited their observations to comparing the difficulty of problems under various conditions. Problem difficulty is indexed by solution probability or solution time, and there is the suggestion that, when problem difficulty differs between conditions, the difference is apparent in the probabilities of rapid solution. Solution difficulty has typically been interpreted as reflecting the difficulty of producing the answer, with the subject's preparation assumed to be complete because of instruction and little attention paid to the evaluation of potential solutions. Finally, an investigator's choice of variables and experimental tasks seems to depend on his conception of problem solving—whether his description emphasizes perception, associative arousal, or information processing (search).

Four Theories of Problem Solving

In the previous chapter, several theoretical differences were hinted at when the various definitions of problems were discussed. The theories to which these definitions lead are the topic of the present chapter. Before describing them, we shall make a few general statements setting the background for a theoretical analysis.

Obviously, the long term goal of research is to create an accurate description of the behavior under study. In this effort, any theory that is proposed has a dual responsibility: to account for previous findings and to predict new outcomes (guide future research). With respect to these criteria, evaluating theories of problem solving is particularly troublesome. Recall that most investigators have compared the difficulty of problems under various conditions and have obtained little additional information about what the subject is doing. A theory is expected to specify in some sense how any differences in problem difficulty were produced by the manipulation of the independent variables. But many differences in problem difficulty are compatible with two or more theories, thus not discriminating among them. Furthermore, different theories have been largely based on the manipulation of different independent variables in different problem situations. Each approach has stayed within its self-determined boundaries, with little effort directed toward crossing these boundaries. Therefore, the question of whether or not Theory A could account for the data used to support Theory B can rarely be answered.

Each of the theories to be discussed consists of a description of a process or orderly sequence of events, some of which are covert, assumed, or imagined, leading to the solution of a problem or to some attempt at solving a problem. Since parts of this process are typically not directly observable, choosing among postulated processes is often difficult. Clearly, if a theory states that a particular sequence of behavior should occur and a record of the appropriate behavior is available, comparing the prediction with the record is straightforward. What is lacking for many problems is the record.

In the absence of direct confrontations, comparing theories must be accomplished by examining their internal characteristics and their breadth. A theoretical approach applied to one situation at a time must also be held accountable for specifying how the individual descriptions combine into a general account. The theory which explains a larger number of findings is preferred to one which explains a lesser number. Finally, any description must be evaluated in terms of its predictions, its implications for future research. Once the data are in, one can always construct an explanation, but that explanation is more useful if it suggests an additional test based on new data.

Three theoretical views will be described: Gestalt, associative, and information processing. In the long run, no current theory can be expected to persist in its present form. Our purpose, both in examining existing theories and in surveying research findings, should be to think of ways in which the postulates of different approaches might be combined into an improved description or to devise new, more powerful approaches. This will prove to be both challenging and interesting.

THREE THEORETICAL VIEWS

Gestalt Theory

Gestalt descriptions of problem solving were discussed in Chapter 2, and it must be admitted that this approach has perhaps more historical than current significance. That is, there is little research currently being conducted under the direct influence of Gestalt theory. However, some of the ideas of Gestalt theory have been incorporated into information processing theory, a relatively recent development, and Gestalt theory gave rise to some research questions that are still of interest.

In Chapter 3, mention was made of the emphasis placed by Gestalt theory on the perceptual aspects of problem solving, with perception used in two ways. With respect to perception as the organization of a (usually visual) stimulus pattern, little more has been done than to demonstrate that perceptual influences can affect problem difficulty (as in the case of the "square" problem, Figure 3-1). It is in the broader, somewhat metaphorical sense of "functional perception" that Gestalt ideas have received most attention. Interest has been directed toward how a subject "views" or formulates a problem and changes his formulation in the attempt to find a solution.

Insight Versus Trial and Error. Early Gestalt theorists emphasized that problem solving is a directed activity in which the subject makes solution attempts based on some formulation of the problem. This description was contrasted with the "overt, trial-and-error" model initially proposed by Thorndike. As pointed out in Chapter 2, whether one will observe insightful problem solving or gradual improvement in performance seems to depend in part on the characteristics of the problem situation and of the subject. However, the influence of Gestalt theory on other positions should not be missed—more recent associative theories have dealt almost exclusively with symbolic processes rather than peripheral motor activity. The old issue of insight versus trial and error at the level of motor activity has been resolved with the realization that both are possible. In fact, information processing theorists have proposed that the "either-or" characterization of the issue is not particularly fruitful. They suggest that "degrees of insight" be considered and relate this to the use of heuristics in problem solving. If a problem is characterized in terms of a number of alternative solution possibilities, the degree of insight is indicated by the reduction in the number of alternatives that are actually tried. In other words, if a problem solver reaches a solution by mechanically testing each alternative in turn, his behavior would be described as not very insightful. In contrast, if a subject limits his search on the basis of some fruitful hypothesis, he would be characterized as exhibiting greater insight into the problem.

At a very general level, trial and error plays a part in any description of problem solving. The most general meaning of trial and error is simply that solution attempts are made without prior knowledge that they will be successful, and this is the essence of a problem. The postulation of trial and error in thinking is in no way incompatible with a description of the subject's behavior as the active generation and checking of hypotheses (Campbell, 1960). However, there can be disagreement among theorists as to the nature of solution attempts in a trial-and-error process, that is, whether solution attempts are best described as responses or hypotheses or strategies, etc.

Describing a solution as insightful has typically been taken to mean, in addition to a lack of overt trial and error, that the subject will have perfect retention of the solution. Recall that Kohler's apes were able to repeat a solution without hesitation when the problem situation was reintroduced. Modern investigators of human problem solving seem to assume that this facet of insight applies to their subjects. For virtually all of the tasks described in Chapter 3, researchers have *not* studied the behavior of the subjects who are given a problem a second time, apparently assuming that subjects would find the problem trivial. It seems reasonable to describe this behavior on the part of researchers as indicating at least some tacit acceptance of the Gestalt idea that insightful problem solving characterizes adult human subjects.

Direction in Problem Solving. For a Gestalt notion that has engendered some controversy among investigators, let us turn to the concept of "direction" in problem solving. Gestalt theorists emphasized productive thinking (the combining of past experiences in new ways) and held that simply having had the necessary experiences does not guarantee that one will combine them in the appropriate manner, or in any manner whatever. In addition to relevant experience, productive thinking is assumed also to require *direction,* which is not itself considered a result of learning. Direction is a function of the characteristics of the problem situation and refers to the ways in which the subject perceives (interprets) the problem. Just as there are "perceptual forces" in the presentation of the nine dots of Figure 3-1 leading to the perception of a square, there are, by analogy, "forces" present in any problem situation which lead to particular formulations of the problem. If the subject changes his interpretation of the problem situation, or if the problem situation is changed for the subject, new direction is provided for problem-solving attempts. Emphasizing direction has led to a concern for the effects of varying the presentation of a problem, to the attempt to characterize subjects' solution proposals in terms of direction, and to research on the effects of *direction-giving hints.* Findings relevant to the effects of varying problem presentation will be presented in Chapter 5, and the effects of hints will be discussed shortly. For the moment, let us consider how subjects' solution attempts are characterized.

Functional Value. In discussing subjects' attempts at solving a problem, Duncker (1945) classifies proposals in terms of their "functional value," which is the general means by which the problem solver tries to reach a solution. This classification scheme can be illustrated with examples from Duncker's "radiation problem": A tumor exists in a person's stomach. By stipulation an operation is impossible, and rays of sufficient intensity to destroy tissue must be used to eliminate the tumor. However, no damage must be done to healthy tissues. How can this be accomplished? Proposals such as "send the rays through the esophagus," "expose the tumor by operating," "move the tumor to the exterior" are said to embody the *functional value* "avoid contact between the rays and healthy tissue." Other approaches include desensitizing healthy tissue and reducing the intensity of the rays on the way to the tumor. The functional value of a subject's proposal indicates the way in which he is directing his problem-solving efforts at the moment. In Duncker's experiments, the subject and the experimenter engage in conversation, the subject proposing, the experimenter responding. For example, should the subject propose exposing the tumor by operating, the experimenter would remind him that an operation is impossible.

Duncker describes the process of solution as the productive reformulation of the problem. When the subject redefines the original problem (destroy the tumor, etc.) more specifically (avoid contact), the possibility of a workable solution to the problem might be increased. Duncker suggests that the general properties of a solution (functional values) typically precede the specific method. For example, in the "radiation problem," the solution lies in reducing the intensity of the rays on the way to the tumor. A subject who proposes turning down the rays until they reach the tumor, then increasing their intensity (which he is told cannot be done) has found an essential property of the solution (reducing intensity) but has not yet discovered the right way to accomplish this redefined goal (which is by sending a broad band of weak rays which intersect at the point of the tumor). One can distinguish among errors, a "good" error being one exhibiting the correct functional value but the wrong specific method, as in the previous example.

Trial-and-error descriptions of problem solving imply that the subject does *not* necessarily move closer to the solution as he continues working on a problem, and such descriptions might seem in opposition to the Gestalt idea of productive reformulations of the problem. However, reformulations are productive only to the extent that they are more specific, and Duncker does not state that a subject moves continuously closer to the solution. Rather, his subjects exhibited considerable shifting among functional values, including shifting from a wrong method having the right functional value (for example, the sequence "turn the rays up when they reach the tumor" followed by "expose the tumor by operating"). Thus, Duncker's description merely indicates that, to solve a problem, it must be reformulated in a more productive way, and that the general form (functional value) of the solution will typically precede the occurrence of the correct specific method having that functional value.

One of the weaknesses of Gestalt theory is that it includes little specification of what will lead a subject to reformulate a problem in a particular manner (if at all). As mentioned earlier, information processing theory has much of the flavor of Gestalt theory but is more specific. Gestalt theory seems to be limited to the statement that reformulations will occur in reaching a solution, but this is not a proposal that readily suggests research questions. One aspect of Gestalt theory that has been researched concerns the implication that "forcing" the subject to change his formulation of the problem should affect his performance. This implication has been tested in research involving hints and instructions.

Effects of Hints. According to Gestalt theory, when a subject is given a problem, he will formulate the problem for himself based on his past experience and the characteristics of the situation. There is no guarantee that appropriate direction will occur nor, if it does, any indication of when it will happen. If the subject has formulated the problem in a manner having the wrong functional value, he should be aided by shifting his direction. Assuming that a problem is difficult (subjects will need to reformulate), it is then possible that the experimenter can increase the likelihood of solution by encouraging subjects to shift their approach to the problem. Furthermore, if the experimenter provides a hint which leads toward the correct functional value, performance should be facilitated.

In considering the effects of hints on problem solving, two questions must be kept in mind: Does the hint provide direction? If so, will that direction aid solution of the problem? Clearly, if subjects do better when given a hint, the answer to both questions must be "yes." However, if a hint fails to facilitate performance, this could mean either that the hint failed to provide direction or that the direction provided did not aid solution of the problem. Such ambiguity seems to characterize research on this issue.

It appears that rather general hints such as "don't be blind to unusual possibilities" or "think of new ways of using objects" do not facilitate solution of the two-string problem (Duncan, 1961). These hints might be viewed as too general to provide any direction, and it can be argued that their failure reflects more a poor choice of hints than a weakness in Gestalt theory. However, research employing more specific hints has yielded only slightly more satisfactory results.

Two insight problems, the "two-pendulum" problem and the "hatrack" problem, require that two boards be wedged between the ceiling and floor of a room and joined together with a C-clamp (in the "hatrack" problem, the clamp also serves as the hook). Several investigators have studied the effect of giving a "ceiling hint," telling the subject that the ceiling must be used to solve the problem. Sometimes the "ceiling hint" was found to facilitate performance (Burke, Maier, and Hoffman, 1966; Maier, 1930), but on other occasions the hint made no difference (Saugstad, 1957; Weaver and Madden, 1949).

The study of Burke, et al. (1966) yielded results most compatible with Gestalt theory, but also indicated the complexities involved in evaluating the effects of hints. These investigators found that both the "ceiling hint" and the "clamp hint" (that the clamp must serve as the hook on the hatrack) changed subjects' attempts at solution (provided direction) and increased the probability that the problem would be solved. Furthermore, the hints had greater effect when given at the outset of the problem, before the subject had a direction, than when given after some time had been spent on the problem, when the subject presumably already had a direction which the hint must overcome. However, the results also indicated that hints can lead in false directions or be ignored. These complexities and the fact that researchers using essentially the same procedures have failed to obtain the same results make drawing any conclusion quite difficult. It must be pointed out that when hints have been found to be ineffective, comparisons were based on differences in solution probability after relatively long working times, which does not allow a very sensitive test for a difference. Unfortunately, this consideration does not explain the contradictory findings, since the same technique has been used in studies finding hints to facilitate performance. What appears to have happened is that researchers, faced with these perplexing, inconsistent results, have lost interest in the issue of direction-giving hints and also in the theory which led to the issue.

Summary of Gestalt Theory. Gestalt theory is characterized by the use of subjects' reports of their solution processes and by the description of problem solving as an active, reformulating search process. In these respects, it is the forerunner of information processing theory, to be presented later. The most distinctive features of the theory are (1) the identification of *insightful problem solving,* (2) an emphasis on *direction* in productive thinking, and (3) the analysis of solution attempts in terms of their *functional values.* Insight is currently viewed as existing in degrees, dependent on the amount of reduction in overt trial and error. Attempts to evaluate the idea that direction can be provided by hints and instructions have yielded ambiguous findings, with a resultant loss of interest in the concept itself. In the next chapter, research on a phenomenon stemming from Gestalt theory will be described, namely, *functional fixedness,* which is the tendency to persist in "perceiving" an object as serving one function when solution of a problem requires a different function. In general, the influence of Gestalt theory on modern researchers seems largely indirect in that most investigators accept (perhaps unwittingly) a number of the points that Gestalt theorists fought hard to establish, but few use the theory in a formal sense.

Theory of Associations

The associative approach to problem solving may be generally depicted as the attempt to extend the principles of classical and instrumental conditioning to the solving of problems. The basic component of associative theory is the response hierarchy, which was described earlier (see Figure 3-4). In this scheme, responses are organized into classes by means of a common mediating response (r_g) and problem solving is viewed as the rearrangement of the hierarchy of response sets or the rearrangement of responses within a set or class. There have been several different applications of associative theory to thinking. In this section, formulations concerning problem-solving set, increasing the originality of behavior, and creative behavior will be discussed. Before considering these applications, a more general statement of associative theory made by Maltzman (1955) will be described.

Reinforcement, Extinction, Recovery, and Generalization. In the associative model, the functional description of the subject at the beginning of a problem is in terms of a hierarchy of response classes, each with its own mediating response and with a hierarchy of individual responses within each class. The principles governing the operation of this system are those of conditioning: (1) *probability of occurrence*—a response that is reinforced increases in strength; (2) *extinction*—a response of some strength that is not reinforced will decrease in strength; (3) *spontaneous recovery*—with the passage of time following extinction, a response will regain some strength (spontaneous recovery); and (4) *changes in associative strength*—any change in the associative strength between a stimulus and a response will result in like changes in associations between that stimulus and "similar" responses and between that response and "similar" stimuli.

The last-named principle refers to generalization of changes in associative strength. "Similarity" is usually described in terms of "physical identity" of stimuli and responses. There are difficulties in this formulation—a "stimulus" is actually a concept, likewise a "response," and the meaning of "physical similarity" of concepts is by no means clear. Also, we must keep in mind the rather loose usage of the terms "stimulus" and "response" in describing problem solving, as mentioned in Chapter 3. The point of the present discussion is that, in associative descriptions of problem solving, emphasis is given to "mediated generalization"—generalization through the mechanism of the mediating response. Of particular relevance is the proposal that responses are similar if they are associated with the same mediating response. The importance of this feature will become apparent as associative theory is described.

By definition, the first response to occur in a problem situation will be the dominant response in the dominant response hierarchy. According to the definition of a problem, this response will be unsuccessful (will be extinguished), suffering a reduction in its effective strength. This extinction effect will generalize to the mediating response, and through it to other members of the same response hierarchy. Over time, spontaneous recovery of associative strength is assumed to occur for these responses. The second response to occur might be the second strongest response in the dominant response hierarchy; if it is also unsuccessful, extinction again would occur and would generalize. Eventually, the cumulative effects of extinction would reduce the effective strength of this class below that of the *original* second-most-dominant hierarchy, and so on. Thus, for example, if a problem required for its solution a low-ranking response in the dominant hierarchy, the problem might prove fairly difficult because the effective strength of this response would be reduced considerably by the mediated generalization (through the r_g) of the inhibitory effects of extinction of the stronger responses in that same hierarchy. Solution would not occur until (1) spontaneous recovery of effective strength had occurred for the originally dominant response hierarchy, (2) the effective strength of the particular response required had recovered to a point higher than that for previously stronger responses in that hierarchy, and (3) responses in other hierarchies had been weakened sufficiently by failure and mediated generalization of extinction effects. Because of these requirements, it is possible that solution might not occur at all.

Additional ways in which compound response hierarchies can be rearranged employ the same basic principles. When a particular response is reinforced through success, two effects are expected: (1) that response will move up in the response hierarchy to which it belongs, and (2) through mediated generalization, the strengths of all the responses in that class will be increased, i.e., that hierarchy will move up in the hierarchy of hierarchies. Direct elicitation of the mediating response produces an immediate increase in effective strength for the associated class of responses. In Maltzman's view, an important function of instructions is the elicitation of mediating responses.

COMMENT. These principles seem to afford a means of predicting the difficulty of problems and, presumably, the order in which solution attempts will occur. However, the utility of this approach depends on first identifying the compound habit-family hierarchy for a given situation, then on a precise specification of the effects of reinforcement, extinction, generalization, and recovery. This has proved difficult, with the consequence that tests of associative theory have largely dealt with responses in a single class or with differences between classes, but not with both simultaneously. Thus, while associative theory contains a set of principles governing responding (in contrast to Gestalt theory, which does not specify how successive reformulations occur), the theory has not been applied in more than a general way to relatively complex problem-solving situations. It is not clear how the response-hierarchy concept can be applied to problems having really new solutions (presumably the "response" does not yet exist). Furthermore, as Maltzman indicated, the compound hierarchy we have been considering is oversimplified, since any number of the responses we have described as particular responses might well be anticipatory responses for another class of responses, and so on. Nonetheless, the theory has been applied to various kinds of behavior, and it is these extensions that we will now consider.

Problem-Solving Set. "Set" is generally defined as a tendency to respond to a situation in a particular way. With this general definition, almost any response bias qualifies as a *set,* yet it seems more profitable to distinguish between tendencies to make a specific response and tendencies to make a specific type of response. To make set a concept separate from the general class of responses, set should be related to Duncker's functional value, or the mediating response of associative theory. This is especially true in view of the associative approach to the phenomenon of problem-solving set. Associative theorists have attempted to determine whether the principles of learning apply to sets. To make this a meaningful question, set must refer to something other than just any type of response tendency; if it does not, the question has already been answered—learning does occur.

The reason for pointing out this distinction is that some studies of problem-solving set have in fact established very specific response tendencies, in which case it seems unnecessary to use the special term "set." Therefore, the term "set" is most appropriately related to a class of responses, a relationship that obviously involves the mediating response in associative theory. This theory predicts how sets might develop, since the reinforcement of a specific response will, through mediated generalization, increase the strength of the entire class (in fact, classes) of responses to which that specific response belongs. Applying associative learning principles to the establishment of sets is straightforward, since the effects of number of training trials, extinction, recovery, etc., can be determined. This research has been based largely on anagram solving, with relationships among the denotative meanings of solutions serving as the basis of sets (e.g., animal names, flower names). Thus, the basic notion is that, should the solution to an anagram be the word *horse*, the strengths of other animal names will be increased when a subsequent problem is presented. Sets have often been studied in the context of negative transfer situations; a set is established, then followed by a problem requiring a solution from a different response class.

Originality Training. Behavior which is uncommon under the conditions in which it occurs and which is at least minimally relevant to those conditions is called "original" (Maltzman, 1960). The associative explanation of originality is very similar to the account of problem-solving set. In this case, responses are viewed as organized on the basis of "strength" rather than denotative meaning. In particular, low-strength responses are assumed to be associated with each other, such that the occurrence of one or a number of low-strength responses increases the probability that other low-strength responses will occur subsequently. For example, *sturgeon* has low probability of occurring in response to the statement, "Name a fish," and *zither* has low probability of occurring when "Name a musical instrument" is the "stimulus." The assumption is that the occurrence of *sturgeon* in response to the first instruction increases the probability that *zither* (or some other low-strength alternative) will be given when the name of a musical instrument is requested. Since originality is typically studied in a free-responding situation, any response is correct; consequently, techniques must be devised for getting low-strength responses to occur. Once a number of original responses have been made to occur, the question is whether original responses will occur when free-responding is allowed in a new, transfer situation. Obviously, an equally important question involves identifying techniques which will elicit original responses in the first instance.

The extension of associative theory to originality can be used as a point of departure for discussing some of the difficulties of the theory. When applied to problem solving, the theory views responses as organized primarily on the basis of denotative meaning (for verbal responses), and reinforcement consists essentially in making a response meeting the requirements set by the experimenter. When applied to the free-responding situation, responses are viewed as organized on the basis of strength, and, as noted earlier, all responses are technically correct. How is it then that uncommon responses can be reinforced more than common, high-strength responses? To account for this, the theory introduces the concept of self-reinforcement, that is, the mere occurrence of a response is reinforcing. Additionally, it is postulated that an uncommon response is more self-reinforcing than is a common response. It is obvious that the meaning of reinforcement has been changed; it no longer involves something the experimenter does but is tied soley to the subject's behavior. Indeed, under the definition of reinforcement used for problem solving (meeting the experimenter's requirements), we would have to say that, in the free-responding situation, uncommon responses become dominant over common responses even though both are *equally* reinforced. To tie together the two meanings of reinforcement conceptually, it becomes necessary to demonstrate that uncommon responses are more reinforcing than common responses in a manner independent of the finding that uncommon responses occur more frequently with training. Otherwise, the use of the term "reinforcement" in discussing originality training becomes redundant with the observation that a change has occurred.

As Maltzman (1960) has noted, the intraverbal associations possessed by an adult human are enormously complex, and it is possible that every verbal response is associated in some way with every other verbal response. The theory should indicate why mediated generalization is determined by similarity of denotative meaning in one situation, but by similarity of "strength" in another. One way of controlling the kinds of changes which take place is through instructions (e.g., "look for animal names" or "give uncommon responses"), which is compatible with the theory, since instructions are assumed to elicit responses directly (although the characterization of instructions as a "stimulus" seems to be an oversimplification). The theoretical problem lies in accounting for such changes in the absence of appropriate instructions to use a particular kind of mediation. Until this is accomplished, the total description offered by associative theory seems to include a generalization process without bounds. Realize that the problem of specifying how mediated generalization is restricted is not necessarily insoluble within associative theory; rather, it is a problem which must be faced by the theory.

Creativity. In the applications of associative theory presented thus far, emphasis has been directed toward the identification of response hierarchies for various situations and the demonstration that these hierarchies can be altered in ways consistent with associative learning principles. The present topic is Mednick's (1962) analysis of "creative behavior," with an emphasis on measuring stable individual differences. The concepts of original behavior and creative behavior are closely related, and some terminological confusion exists. Mednick defines *creative behavior* as behavior that is uncommon and relevant, which is virtually identical to Maltzman's definition of original behavior. For Mednick, original behavior is simply uncommon, while Maltzman views creative behavior as uncommon, relevant, and *valued by society*. A major point to be remembered is that characterizing behavior as creative involves someone's judgment (Maltzman prefers society, whereas Mednick uses the experimenter). In practice, the discrepancy is not large since investigators of original behavior have typically used tasks for which criteria of relevance are minimal and, as mentioned earlier, virtually any response can be viewed as "relevant" (to illustrate, what is an "irrelevant" free association?). When researchers concern themselves with creative behavior, criteria of relevance are usually more stringent and rather obvious. Nonetheless, the reliance on judgment in identifying creative behavior, with the attendant problem of deciding whose judgment to employ, continues to be a source of difficulty in such investigations.

Mednick defines *creative thinking* as the formation of associative elements into new combinations which either meet specified requirements or are otherwise useful. The degree of creativity is directly related to the degree of remoteness of the elements which are combined (for example, applying a concept from chemistry to history would be more creative than applying it to biology). A creative solution can occur through serendipity (accidental contiguity of elements), similarity of elements, and mediation (elements are combined because they elicit common associations). The likelihood of a creative solution depends on the number of associative elements a person possesses and their uncommonness, among other factors given less stress. Since a creative solution requires combining remotely associated elements, a person's chances of success increase as his associative hierarchies include more and more uncommon elements.

Actually, these two features of creativity can be separated. As Mednick points out, a highly creative individual might have a concentration of associative strength in a relatively small number of responses (steep hierarchy), but his responses might be very different from normative associations. Such a person might produce one creative solution, but his successive solutions will resemble the first. (Mednick suggests that some novelists exhibit such behavior in that later novels seem like slightly changed versions of the first.) The type of person likely to be creative repeatedly is one who has a flat associative hierarchy, i.e., weaker dominant responses and a distribution of associative strength over a larger number of uncommon responses. It is this latter type of creativity that has been most emphasized and toward which Mednick's measure of creativity has been directed.

Mednick proposed that a test of creative behavior must present items from remote associative clusters and require the person to find a mediating link which combines the items in a way meeting specified requirements. In the attempt to avoid materials biased in favor of one or another kind of specific experience, Mednick chose to use verbal items, based on the assumption that these items will reflect trans-situational experience for persons from the same (USA) culture. Furthermore, consistent with his analysis in associative terms, the basis for combining the items is purely associative rather than being based on relations such as superordination of common functional properties. Each item on his *Remote Associates Test* consists of three words, each of which is associated to some degree with a fourth word which a person must discover. As an example, consider the words *rat, blue,* and *cottage;* what word serves as an associative link among these words? The answer in this case is *cheese,* which occurs with relatively low frequency as a free-associative response to each of the three words provided (notice that the kind of relationship between the answer and the three words of the item is not the same in all cases).

Summary of Associative Theory. The essence of associative theory is that problem solving can be adequately described as *S-R* associations, including mediating connections (r_g-s_g), the establishment and operation of which is governed by the principles of conditioning. Kendler and Kendler (1962) have pointed out that problem solving includes horizontal processes (chaining of associations over time) and vertical processes (the simultaneous operation of multiple associations). The analysis of set concerns horizontal processes, since it is directed toward the temporal order of responses in a problem situation. Performance on an item of the Remote Associates Test exemplifies a vertical process, since the person presumably associates simultaneously to three stimuli. The approach has generated considerable research, with varying degrees of success. The primary shortcoming of the theory is incompleteness, indicated by a lack of consideration, except in general terms, of relationships among different response hierarchies. To an extent, neither Gestalt nor associative theory has attempted a specific account of the ordinal characteristics of problem solving when complicated sequences are involved. Gestalt theory simply states that reformulations will occur and, while associative theory suggests that switching from one response hierarchy to another will be determined by mediated generalization, no specific predictions have been made. Therefore, while associative theory makes testable predictions concerning differences in overall difficulty, it has dealt largely with simple problems, and its application to more complex problems remains to be attempted.

Theory of Information Processing

In the past decade, considerable effort has been directed toward programming computers to solve problems, leading to an information processing approach to the study of problem solving. Although information processing has been closely identified with computer simulation, other theorists have contributed to the development of this position (deGroot, 1966; Miller, Galanter, and Pribram, 1960). The theory has been applied to a variety of problems, including chess, checkers, arithmetic, and logic, as well as to concept attainment, which will be discussed in a later section. As indicated by this list, the theory has been directed toward complex problems requiring rather lengthy solution sequences. The method of evaluating the theory has been primarily to program a computer to solve a problem and then to compare its performance with that of human Ss.

The idea is to write a theory program that will guide a computer through a sequence of steps similar to (or simulating) the behavior of a real person working on some task. Writing such a program is not easy. Until we know more of what human beings actually do, there will remain a large number of possibilities. But it is the opinion of many psychologists that once a program is achieved that adequately mimics the relevant aspects of an organism's behavior, it will not only be a useful theoretical device (for controlling the organism and making predictions about his future behavior) but will also constitute a genuine explanation of his immediate behavior. From this, the inference is often drawn that many of the functional properties of the computer are identical to those of the living organism.

As is suggested above, a computer can be programmed to simulate a large number of behavioral processes. It can form associations, test hypotheses, compare items of information, remember, and so on. One could write a program resembling theories of association, of mediation, of strategy selection and test, and of other possibilities. In this sense, the approach is fundamentally indifferent to the basic assumptions made by the theorist. It turns out, however, that most computer models have depicted problem solving as an active process of formulation and evaluation. The subject is assumed to have a variety of information processing skills and is expected to generate a complex, highly integrated series of operations in the course of achieving problem solution. Some general features of these models will now be described.

Algorithms and Heuristics. With respect to information processing, a problem exists when a subject is required to choose the (or a) correct alternative from several that are placed before him (Feigenbaum and Feldman, 1963). There is no problem if only one alternative exists, for it must be chosen. Although the number of alternatives is important, information processing theorists have been more interested in how a problem solver would evaluate the properties of the alternatives in order to make a choice and in the difficulty imposed by this evaluation.

Consider a chess or checker player having the problem of choosing a move at any point in the game; in principle, any move can be related to the eventual outcome of the game, win, lose, or draw. However, the evaluation of an alternative is exceedingly complex. For each of the player's possible alternatives, his opponent has a number of replies, to each of which he has a number of rejoinders, to each of which his opponent has a number of replies, etc. Therefore, the selection of an alternative leads to a geometrically expanding "tree of possibilities," each branch eventually leading to a win, lose, or draw. The difficulty lies in examining all of these "paths through the maze" and in combining their outcomes in a manner suitable for selecting among the immediate alternatives.

As we said in the last chapter, a method which systematically considers all possibilities with respect to their eventual outcomes is called an *algorithm*. In principle, algorithms can be specified for chess, checkers, and other problems, but it is doubtful that they could be realized for any but the simplest problems. The reason of course is that the number of alternatives is too large. For example, it has been estimated that there are 10^{120} different paths through a chess maze, but less than 10^{16} microseconds available in a century to explore them (Newell, Shaw, and Simon, 1963). As a further example, the complete exploration of every possible path through a checker game involves about 10^{40} alternatives; at three choices per millimicrosecond, evaluation would require 10^{21} centuries (Samuels, 1963). These astronomical figures clearly make the point—there is simply not enough time for algorithmic solutions to problems of this type.

The alternative is to limit the search in some way, to explore potentially fruitful paths and ignore those likely to be blind alleys. Techniques which limit the search for solutions in problem spaces are called *heuristics* (heuristic methods). As Feigenbaum and Feldman (1963) have pointed out, a heuristic does not guarantee the optimal solution or, indeed, any solution at all; rather, heuristics offer solutions that are good enough most of the time. Two implications of this emphasis on heuristics are that the intelligent programming of a problem-solving machine must involve heuristics, and that human problem solvers use heuristics.

Describing problem solving in terms of heuristics leads to the task of specifying what heuristics are employed in the solution of problems. These vary in generality; for example, the chess-playing heuristic "consider only moves which do not place a piece in jeopardy of capture" has no counterpart in the heuristics for the solution of logic problems. However, there are information processing mechanisms that are common to the various situations, and the consideration of these mechanisms will characterize the approach.

Search-Scan Schemes. The solution of a problem typically involves the generation of subproblems to be explored. An executive process is specified which controls the order in which subgoals are attempted. An important feature of this process is the "search-scan scheme" (Simon and Newell, 1964). *Searching* involves the exploration of a subgoal, e.g., determining the consequences of a particular move in chess, or trying a particular method of proof in solving a logic problem. *Scanning* concerns the generation, comparison, and selection of alternative directions of search. The process of problem solving consists of alternating between searching and scanning, and the characteristics of this alternation determine the effectiveness of the process. If search persists too long, solution attempts become stereotyped (or, perhaps, functionally fixed). Search can be terminated by local or internal processes, e.g., in applying the heuristic "cease exploring moves to which the opponent has more than two replies," the exploration of a particular subgoal may yield no moves passing this criterion. A function of the executive process is to terminate search by employing more general stop rules, e.g., "explore no subgoal beyond seven steps." Clearly, if search is too often interrupted to scan alternative directions, particular subgoals will be inadequately explored, and the problem solver will exhibit indecisiveness. Thus, a certain balance must be incorporated between searching and scanning. An important point is that this balance must be specified in order for a problem-solving program to operate. Such specificity is characteristic of only information processing approaches.

Means-End Analysis. If a problem is defined in terms of a specified situation and a nonidentical desired situation, the solution process consists of reducing the differences between these two states. There must be a discrimination process which detects one or more differences between them, and associated with each difference is a set of operators which are possibly relevant to reducing the difference. A "means-end analysis" program tries to remove a difference by applying potentially relevant operators. Such behavior is clearly relevant to problems requiring proofs and can be seen as well in game playing problems. Once a desired board position in a game of chess or checkers is generated, the problem consists of determining the differences between the present board position and the next desired position, then of finding means of proceeding from one to the other. Miller, Galanter, and Pribram (1960) have suggested that this process serves as the basic functioning unit, naming it the TOTE (Test-Operate-Test-Exit). An initial test for a difference is made; if a difference exists, an operation is performed, followed by another test. If the test reveals that a difference still exists, another operator is called into play, but if the test shows "no difference" the process terminates (the problem is solved). TOTEs are hierarchically arranged, since the attempt to reduce an overall difference can lead to the specification of intermediate states varying in similarity to the given and desired states. Proceeding from one intermediate state to the next requires means-end analysis, with more specific TOTEs guided by (related to) the more general means-end analysis.

Planning Processes. The term "planning process" refers to the technique of eliminating some of the detail of a problem, effectively creating a simplified problem whose solution might be used to guide the solution of the original, more complex problem. For example one might attempt to determine a winning sequence from a midgame board position in a game of chess while ignoring pawns in the center of the board. Having found a successful sequence, one can then determine whether this plan or a modification of it will work for the total problem. In solving an anagram, selecting only some of the letters from the anagram and trying to think of words with these letters exemplifies a planning process.

Working Backwards. In the attempt to restrict the search for solutions to those more probably fruitful, a useful technique is working backwards from the desired state to the problem state. Consider a problem in which statement A is given, statement B to be proved. The solver might notice that proving B is trivial from statement C, then attempt to determine whether he can proceed from A to C. Further, the proof of C might be straightforward from statement D, etc. In a game of chess, a player might notice that winning is certain from a particular board position, then proceed by determining how one might produce that position from another, etc., in a sense checking to see if the current position is generated by this process. Although there is no requirement that one proceed *only* in backward fashion (which seems unlikely), it is clear that including this heuristic in a solution attempt will keep the solution process directed toward subproblems whose solution will lead to success on the total problem.

Although the working-backwards technique seems most applicable to situations in which the problem is to discover a method for proceeding from known initial and desired states, analogous processes may operate for other problems as well. For example, there is considerable evidence to suggest that, in solving anagrams, Ss think of words, comparing them to the anagram for a possible match. A working-forward method for this problem is to generate letter sequences until a word is produced; it seems likely that solution ordinarily consists of some alternation between these processes (see Johnson, 1966; Miller, Galanter, and Pribram, 1960).

Learning and Changes in Organization. Information processing descriptions postulate an organization of processes without saying much about how such an organization might have arisen. However, given some initial organization, statements are made concerning how the program is changed by experience. Solution attempts and their outcomes are stored, such that a subproblem encountered a second time in the course of a solution attempt will be remembered as "tried and failed," and thus will not be tried again. Both specific and general information is stored, the former exemplified by remembering particular board positions and their evaluations or specific proofs. Learning through generalizations occurs through changes in evaluation formulas or through remembering which theorems have proved successful in the past in conjunction with particular methods. A heuristic included is the process of trying methods in order of their probabilities of success in previous problems (the response hierarchy notion of associative theory). The programming of learning in a checkers-playing program has been described by Samuels (1963), together with some evidence of improved play over a series of games. Similarly, Newell, Shaw, and Simon (1958) have shown that the storage of previously proved theorems produces profound changes in the problem-solving capabilities in the Logic Theorist, their program for proving theorems in symbolic logic. Thus, while information processing theory has dealt primarily with describing how an existing organization of problem-solving processes operates, some attempts have been made to specify how this organization might be changed.

Summary of Information Processing Theory. The problem-solving computer programs constructed by information processing theorists are far more specific than the descriptions offered by either Gestalt or associative theory. To the extent that the programs accurately simulate human behavior, the descriptions they provide must be preferred. Two challenges yet to be faced by information processing theory are a specification of how the organization underlying behavior develops and a delineation of processes for simple problems such as anagrams and insight problems in a manner consistent with what is known about how human subjects solve such problems.

The advantage accruing to information processing theory, because of the complexity and specificity of the programs these theorists have created, has already been noted. Remember that there is no necessary connection between information processing theory and computer programming, thus, the advantage could be due more to the technique than to the theory itself. However, it seems that information processing theory does contain a larger set of concepts of greater flexibility and specificity than the other theories we have considered. Interestingly, the complexity of information processing theories has often been held against them. Influenced by the law of parsimony, many researchers tend to be suspicious of complexity in theoretical systems. But, while we have no clear evidence at the moment, it does seem a safe bet that the eventual account of human behavior will be at least as complicated as the most complicated psychological theory yet envisioned.

The use of a computer program as a theoretical device must be viewed with some caution. Creating a computer program to solve problems is an achievement which, in itself, is of uncertain relevance to understanding human behavior on the same problem, since the two types of problem solvers might operate in quite different ways. As stated earlier, most programmers have made use of what they can find out about how human beings solve problems in creating their programs, thus tending to minimize the discrepancies between the program and behavioral processes. Even with this constraint, some difficulties remain.

Reitman (1965) has suggested that, as simulations of human thinking, most computer programs have at least two deficiencies. First, the typical program is rigidly sequenced, continuing a particular routine until it is completed, while the typical human problem solver is quite distractable, both by external stimuli and by ideas "unrelated" to the problem he is working on. In other words, the computer program works on one thing at a time while the human works simultaneously on several things, either productively or unproductively, within a given time period. Second, computer programs typically have perfect access to previous information, while humans lose information over time. These difficulties do not seem to be serious problems for the theorist. Identifying deficiencies regarding distractability and forgetting presupposes that broader aspects of the description of problem-solving processes are adequately specified; thus, it is a good theory that is being questioned. Furthermore, distractability, nonsequential processing, and forgetting can be programmed, as Reitman has demonstrated. His book contains a description of a program with these characteristics as well as a lengthy discussion of the techniques of computer simulation and its implications for theories of thinking.

One additional possible pitfall concerning

the analogy between computer and human being must be mentioned. It is tempting—especially when some success in simulating the performance of human beings is achieved—to conclude that the properties of the computer and the subject are alike, that human beings must have structural components like computers and that, once we understand the structural features (neurophysiology?) of an organism, we will know all there is to know about his behavior (Newell, 1969).

This form of argument is dubious. The operations carried out by the computer are clearly analogous to human behavior, not human physiology. Insofar as the computer accurately mimics behavior it might be said to be doing things that real people do. But the essential features of a description of that process are functional and behavioral, not physiological or physical. The computer mechanism itself, while indispensable as a tool, is quite dispensable to the theory of human behavior.

The computer operates as a rule-following system. Theorists try to program the computer to operate in a way which is consistent with the rules of human behavior. To the extent that they are successful, the computer will arrive at answers and solutions (outputs) like those of human beings. It is the functional properties of the *program*—including those which are normally implicit—which are relevant to psychology and which constitute the analog of human behavior.

SUMMARY

The three theories outlined in this chapter represent different approaches to the study of problem solving and thinking in general. Of the three, two will be encountered repeatedly throughout the text—associative theory and the theory of information processing. Gestalt theory was never fully developed and, with the exception of emphasizing "learning through understanding" and organizational changes in perceptual memory, has not been applied to verbal learning, conceptual behavior, and language. Information processing theorists owe allegiance to Gestalt ideas and have built upon and extended those ideas. Therefore, the major theoretical contrast throughout the text is based in the comparison of the concepts and principles of information processing theory (including some Gestalt ideas) with those of associative theory.

It is possible to point out similarities among the theories, which leads one to wonder how different they *really* are. For example, Duncker's concept of *functional value* resembles the mediating response of associative theory. The heuristic "try methods on the basis of how successful they have been in the past" resembles the response hierarchy of associative theory. The Gestalt notion of reformulating the problem in more specific ways is like the planning process of information processing theory. Although such similarities exist, the differences must not be ignored. It is unlikely that Gestalt theorists would agree that shifts in approaches to a problem are governed by the principles of extinction, generalization, and recovery as associative theory postulates. In information processing theory, changes in direction are described in terms of strategies, and it seems doubtful that terms such as strategy, heuristic, and executive process can be translated into associative theory.

When one kind of behavior is described in terms originally used to describe another kind of behavior, one must carefully consider the extent to which the terms retain their original meanings. As has already been noted, the Gestalt use of the term "perception" when applied to problem solving seems somewhat metaphorical, and the meanings of "stimulus" and "response" in associative descriptions are not very clear. In the literature review to follow, research is described which is directed toward the question of how well the analogies fit. Little of this research has stemmed directly from information processing theory, since this approach is a recent development and most of the investigators' effort has gone to working out the details of computer programs rather than extensive research with human subjects. It would be a good exercise to attempt to describe the information processing systems required to account for the results to be presented.

Five. Empirical Studies of Problem Solving: The Task

In this chapter, the findings of psychological investigations of problem solving will be presented. As the research is described, keep in mind that many of the results, although obtained under the impetus of a particular theory, are consistent with several points of view. In addition, pay close attention to the task on which a given finding is based, since, as indicated earlier, a number of results are based on a single problem or a single type of problem. Obviously, the generality of such findings is open to question.

Most experimental studies of problem solving may be characterized as follows: The experimenter defines a problem for the subject who is required to find a solution based on that initial information. This can be contrasted with studies of conceptual behavior in which interest lies in how the subject utilizes information about the solution that is obtained gradually (in a series of informative steps). Consequently, investigations of problem solving typically involve a comparison of the relative difficulty of a task (measured in terms of solution time or solution probability) under various conditions rather than an attempt to obtain performance measures indicative of the strategies subjects use.

The review to follow is based in a straightforward manner on the description of a problem as a situation which the subject must respond to or modify in order to discover a solution meeting specified requirements. The first topic concerns how the difficulty of a problem is affected by its presentation (the characteristics of the problem situation). This will be followed by a description of research identifying the attributes of solutions which affect problem difficulty. The general orientation of this chapter is depicted in Figure 5-1.

CHARACTERISTICS OF THE PROBLEM SITUATION

Upon presentation of a problem, the subject has the task of finding a solution based on the information he has been given. In examining the characteristics of the problem situation, we are concerned with what the task is like at the outset—what the subject is given to work with. One problem character-

FIGURE 5–1. Variables involved in the description of problem-solving tasks.

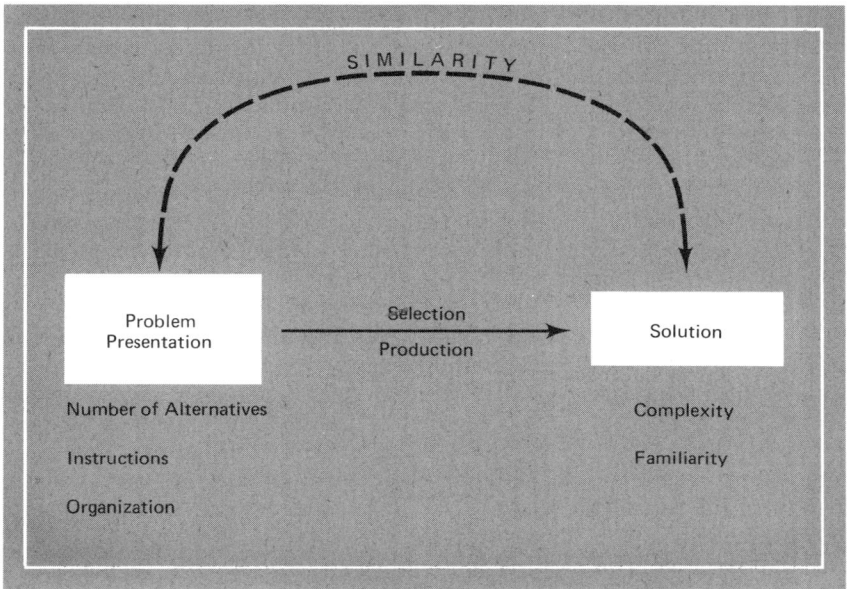

istic of importance is the size of a problem, which is suggested by the "maze" model of problems used in information processing theories: If the problem presents the subject with a set of alternatives from which he must select the correct one, then the difficulty of his search should be affected by the number of alternatives that must be considered. A second problem characteristic is suggested primarily by Gestalt theory: As the degree of organization of the problem situation increases, does it become more resistant to the changes necessary for solution? The final problem characteristic to be discussed is the similarity of the problem situation to the desired solution. Concern for this feature is expressed in both Gestalt and information processing theories, since both view problem solving as the process of moving from an initial (problem) state to a final (solution) state. These three attributes of problems—the size of a problem, the degree of its organization, and the similarity of the problem to the solution—will be considered in turn.

The Size of a Problem

It is not particularly surprising that the difficulty of a problem increases with its size. Research on this topic has been concerned with determining the precise relationship between size and difficulty. In order to make this determination, it must be possible to specify the size of a problem. Because of this requirement, studies of problem size have been based on search tasks for which alternatives are provided. Manipulations have involved the number of switches on a lights-and-switches apparatus (Davis, 1967), the number of visual patterns from which one must be selected to match a test pattern (Neimark and Wagner, 1964), and the number of pieces in a jigsaw puzzle (Solley and Snyder, 1958). The results indicate that solution difficulty increases as a roughly linear function of the amount of *information* in the problem. The amount of information is not equal to the number of alternatives (n), but rather to $log_2 n$ (the number of times 2 must be multiplied by itself to yield the number of alternatives). To grasp the meaning of this relationship, consider problems having 2, 4, 8, 16, and 32 alternatives, respectively (these numbers are equivalent to 2^1, 2^2, 2^3, 2^4, and 2^5). The increase in difficulty from one problem to the next largest one would be constant (increasing from 2 to 4 increases difficulty as much as changing from 16 to 32).

As indicated earlier, it is sometimes difficult to determine the size of a problem, usually because the alternatives being considered by the problem solver are not known to the investigator and thus cannot be enumerated. This research problem is illustrated by studies of problem size utilizing anagrams. What are the alternatives to be varied in number for anagram problems? Investigators have designated the number of permutations (rearrangements) of the anagram letters as the number of alternatives, but this characterization is likely to be in error. Counting anagram permutations is based on the assumption that subjects solve anagrams by permuting the anagram letters until a rearrangement is found that meets solution criteria (an English word). However, research on anagram solving indicates that people think of words in attempting to solve anagrams, often on the basis of one or a few of the anagram letters. Consequently, the accurate description of the size of an anagram problem involves some weighted function of the number of subword letter sequences that a subject might choose from and the number of words that he can think of for any sequence.

The problems involved in determining the number of alternatives for anagrams are exemplified in a study by Kaplan and Carvellas (1968) in which solution times were obtained for anagrams having from three to ten letters. To give some idea of the range of variation involved, for three, six, and ten letters respectively, the number of permutations varies from six to seven hundred to several million, and the amount of information varies from about two to seven to over twenty units (bits). Although solution difficulty increased with the number of anagram letters, the functional relationship did not at all resemble a linear relationship between difficulty and amount of information. Difficulty increased rapidly from three to six letters, more slowly thereafter. Kaplan and Carvellas identified a number of factors which complicate any interpretation of their findings. For example, the number of words available in English increases up to word lengths of six or seven letters, decreasing thereafter (what weight should be given to these "alternatives"?). For longer problems, subjects tended to deal with groups of letters such as prefixes and suffixes rather than with individual letters or other combinations. Finally, the method of solution changed with the number of letters; for shorter problems, subjects tried to think of words after very little rearrangement of any of the anagram letters, while for longer problems the reverse was true.

Although this research fails to provide a way of calculating the size of anagram problems with any accuracy, it does point to a number of pervasive features of human thinking. In trying to solve anagrams, subjects make use of what they know about English, and one must consider how this knowledge is organized. When people try to remember new information, they often organize it into "chunks" of various sizes. (Research on organization in learning will be presented in Chapter 7.) What is observed in anagram solving is the use of these chunks—the important point is that their content varies considerably. Sometimes the subject deals with a single letter as a unit, but he also utilizes frequent letter combinations (such as *ch*, *er*), suffixes, and short words as units. A second point is that subjects' strategies must be considered; these data indicate that strategies varied from trying to solve the whole problem in one step (for short anagrams) to working on the problem a part at a time (for longer anagrams). Realize that there is extensive use of "planning processes" evident in these data; a subject might take only a few of the letters provided and try to think of a word with those letters, subsequently checking to see if the solution to this simpler problem is also the solution to the entire problem. Further evidence on how the organization of subjects' knowledge and their strategies affect anagram solving comes from additional studies on the size of anagram problems.

Ronning (1965) reasoned that some permutations of anagram letters would not be tried because subjects know they begin with letter sequences not found in words (for example, one would not consider any sequence starting with *hk*). As more permutations could be ruled out, there would be fewer "real" alternatives, and solution should be easier. Ronning found that high rule-out problems were solved in less time than low rule-out problems. In a similar study, Tresselt and Mayzner (1968) found that solution times were longer for anagrams with five different letters (e.g., *ndyac—candy*) than for anagrams with one repeated letter (e.g., *paple—apple*). It was pointed out that the number of distinct anagram permutations is reduced from 120 with five different letters to 60 when one letter is repeated. Of course, there are other differences as well, such as fewer ways to start a word and perhaps fewer words with repeated letters. It is also possible that subjects' strategies may change when a letter is repeated, focusing on the positions for that letter, whereas choices among five different letters are based on different considerations. That the number of anagram permutations is itself of minimal importance is indicated by the results of another investigation.

In a study employing a different method, Dominowski (1968) compared performance on anagrams when various kinds of additional letter-sequence information were provided. Some subjects were given only the anagram (e.g., *keroj*); others received the anagram and were told the position of one letter in the word (e.g., *keroj* and _ _ k _ _), while in another condition subjects were told one bigram of the word but not its position (e.g., *keroj* and *ok*). Given a five-letter anagram, there are 119 anagram permutations remaining, one of which is the solution word (e.g., *joker*); knowing either the position of one letter or one bigram (but not its position) leaves only 24 possible permutations. Thus, it might be expected that both kinds of additional information would facilitate solving to the same extent. As predicted, bigram information facilitated performance very much, but information about the position of one letter was of no overall advantage. This suggests that bigram information is compatible with the strategies subjects use for these problems, whereas single-letter-position information is not. There was also an indication that subjects changed their strategies in order to make use of information about the position of a letter since, toward the end of the series of 36 problems that all subjects received, those receiving information about letter position began solving faster than subjects given just the anagram.

One other finding of this study is related to the way in which people organize and utilize their knowledge about word structure. Telling a subject either the first or last bigram in the solution word (e.g., *jo* or *er*) resulted in much better performance than telling him either of the middle bigrams (e.g., *ok* or *ke*), when the position was indicated and when it was not. This finding supports the idea that it is easier to recall a word from knowledge of either end than from information about the middle. Studies directly concerned with word recall have demonstrated that the order of decreasing importance of the fragments of a word is beginning, end, middle (Brown and McNeill, 1966; Horowitz, White, and Atwood, 1968).

These studies demonstrate the importance of problem size as a determinant of problem difficulty and illustrate the complexities involved in identifying the alternatives that subjects consider in working on various problems. To characterize adequately the set of solution possibilities for any but the simplest search tasks, one must take into account the subject's knowledge relevant to the task, how that knowledge is organized, and how the utilization of that knowledge will vary with different solution strategies. As a consequence, these studies raise many more questions than they answer, although the questions posed seem to be directed toward fruitful research. The findings on problem size also provide a convenient means of discussing the effects of instructions, which will now be considered.

Effects of Instructions. One of the more potent variables in problem solving concerns the manner in which the subject is prepared for his task. Solution times would certainly be longer and more variable if subjects were placed in the problem situation without any instruction—telling them to "make a word from the letters presented" or to "turn switches until lights 3 and 7 are on" saves a considerable amount of time. It is clear that instructions serve to limit the possible interpretations of the experimental situation and thus limit the courses of action that the subject considers. A number of investigations have been concerned with the effects of instructing the subject beyond telling him that a problem exists for him to solve, what the problem situation is, and what requirements a solution must meet.

Since problem difficulty is directly related to problem size, it would be expected that the difficulty of a problem would decrease as the subject is given more information about the problem, because additional information should serve to eliminate from consideration a number of solution alternatives. This appears to be true, as evidenced by studies employing the lights-and-switches problem (Davis, 1967; Davis, Train, and Manske, 1968; Duncan, 1963). Recall that with this apparatus, each light is controlled by more than one switch and each switch is connected to more than one light. Subjects who are informed of the connections solve more rapidly than those who must find out what the connections are as well as what the right combination of switches is. In studies of anagram solving, very powerful sets have been established by telling subjects to look for a particular kind of word, such as animal names. Such instructions result in much faster solutions (Safren, 1962) when the only possible solution is that suggested by the instructions or in an increased tendency for subjects to find the set solution when another solution is also possible (Maltzman, Eisman, and Brooks, 1956). For example, the anagram *ehros* has two solutions, *horse* and *shore*; subjects told to look for animal names are much more likely to give *horse* as their solution than subjects simply given the anagram.

Do not assume, however, that providing additional information will always lead to better performance. Recall that researchers employing direction-giving hints have assumed that such hints would limit the subject's behavior in productive ways but have often found that hints have no effect on problem-solving efficiency. In a study with high school students as subjects, Corman (1957) found that giving more information about a rule for solving problems (which involved changing matchsticks from one pattern to another in a specified number of moves) facilitated performance for subjects of high intelligence but tended to impair performance for those of lesser intelligence. These results indicate that problem solvers are not always able to make use of additional information.

Another point to keep in mind is that an experimenter's instructions form part of the context in which the influence of other variables will be evaluated. Davis, Train, and Manske (1968) found that the effects of some variables changed with the amount of information the subject had about the lights-and-switches task. For example, increasing the number of available switches resulted in more switch presses being made and more time being taken to solve the problem for subjects who did not know the light-switch connections. But, for subjects who knew the connections, this manipulation affected only the time they required, having no effect on the number of switch presses they made. The essential points is that to the extent that different investigators use different instructions, even though each researcher gives all of his subjects the same information, comparing the results of their investigations becomes more difficult.

A rather subtle way in which instructions can influence behavior is through the experimenter's giving the subject some indication of the difficulty of the task. Experimenters often tell the subject the maximum amount of time allowed for the problem or make some general statement such as "these problems are difficult." Several findings indicate that subjects' performance tends to be determined partly by their expectations for success (Aronson and Landy, 1967; Tombaugh and Tombaugh, 1963). Although solution times have not always been affected, one experiment indicates what can happen (Aronson and Landy, 1967). Subjects were given a task that could be completed within 5 minutes; those who were told they had 15 minutes took longer to complete the task than those "given" 5 minutes. Furthermore, this difference also occurred on a second task for which no differential instructions were administered. Suggesting to the subject that a task is difficult may have a number of effects, such as changing his strategy (he looks for more complicated solutions), affecting his attitude toward the task (he decides to work more slowly), or raising his anxiety level; choosing among these possibilities requires more information than is presently available. The general point should not be missed: If investigators pay little attention to their instructions, this feature of an experiment may vary in important ways from one study to the next, and the effect of some variable that the researchers *do* attend to may vary with instructions. Consequently, results may appear to be contradictory when they are not.

Organization of the Problem Situation

Based on the idea that problem solving consists of changing an initial situation (the problem) into a desired situation (the solution), investigators have attempted to identify the characteristics of a problem which will affect the difficulty of reorganization. Although several different variables have been studied, they have in common an emphasis on the degree or quality of organization of the problem situation, with the expectation that as a problem becomes better organized, it will be harder to rearrange. All of the research to be presented has concerned anagram solving, with the characteristics of the anagram being of interest.

Words as Anagrams. An issue raised several decades ago by Gestalt psychologists concerned the relative difficulty of word and nonsense anagrams. Although anagrams are usually nonsense letter sequences, it is possible to present one word as the anagram (e.g., *thing*) and require the subject to make another word from the letters (*night*). If words are better organized, more meaningful structures than nonsense letter sequences, then word anagrams should be harder to solve. Early studies produced inconsistent results, but Beilin and Horn (1962) employed greater control over other variables affecting anagram difficulty and found that word anagrams were more difficult. This finding has now been replicated with a variety of procedures (Beilin, 1967; Ekstrand and Dominowski, 1968).

Although it is safe to conclude that word anagrams are harder than nonsense anagrams, the interpretation of this difference poses some knotty problems. Words and nonwords differ on a multitude of attributes, which makes identification of the critical variable(s) quite difficult. The most obvious difference is that words have denotative meanings and nonwords do not. However, partly because psychologists have attempted to avoid the problem of explaining the meaning of *meaning* (a problem to arise again in Chapter 14), and partly to avoid special interpretations of the word-nonword difference if a more general explanation applies, investigators have proposed a number of other interpretations which apply to the difference between word and nonsense anagrams as well as to differences among nonsense anagrams. Most of these proposals will be considered shortly; for the moment, an attempt to extend a Gestalt principle of perception to the word-nonsense anagram difference will be described.

One possible explanation for the word-nonsense anagram difference is to characterize word anagrams as better organized *visual* stimulus patterns which are thus more difficult to rearrange. Ekstrand and Dominowski (1965) reasoned that, if this were true, then increasing the separation of anagram letters in a visual presentation should facilitate the solution of word anagrams more than solution of nonsense anagrams. According to the Gestalt principle of proximity, increasing the separation of the elements of a visual pattern should decrease the cohesiveness or organization of the pattern. If words are well organized visual stimuli, then increasing the spacing of the anagram letters should reduce the degree of organization and make the anagram easier to rearrange. In contrast, nonsense anagrams, which are presumably poorly organized even with close proximity of the letters, should be relatively unaffected by changing the spacing. Word and nonsense anagrams were presented with zero, five, or ten typewriter spaces between letters (e.g., *worth*, *w o r t h*, etc.). Contrary to the expectation, degree of spacing had only small, inconsistent effects in general and did not differentially affect the difficulty of word and nonsense anagrams. Let us now turn to other proposals.

Additional Factors in Anagram Organization. Mayzner and Tresselt (1959) proposed that the degree of organization of an anagram could be indicated by considering how often successive letters in the anagram occurred in that order in the English language. The idea is that, if successive letters occur often in that order in the language, the subject will tend to leave them in that order, but, if they occur infrequently, the subject will look for more likely combinations. For example, in the anagram *kjeor* (solution: *joker*), this analysis leads to the prediction that the subject will tend to leave *or* as is, since *or* is a frequent bigram in English, but he will break up *kj* and look for other combinations with these letters.

The extension of this argument to the word-nonsense anagram difference is that word anagrams are more likely to contain high frequency bigrams than are nonsense anagrams (which is generally true), and that word anagrams are more difficult for this reason rather than because they have meaning. Unfortunately, this explanation does not seem to work, for two reasons. First, word anagrams have been found to be more difficult than nonsense anagrams even when problems are selected such that the frequencies of the constituent bigrams are equal for the two types of anagrams. Second, manipulating the bigram frequency characteristics of nonsense anagrams has produced inconsistent results. Although Mayzner and Tresselt (1959, 1966) found anagrams containing high frequency bigrams to be harder, other investigators have obtained either no effect of this variable or a very small effect (Dominowski, 1967; Stachnik, 1963). Since bigram frequency effects cannot be used to account for the word-nonsense anagram difference, other interpretations must be considered.

One promising approach is based on considering the pronounceability of anagrams and was suggested by Hebert and Rogers (1966): The easier an anagram is to pronounce, the harder it will be to rearrange and thus to solve. With nonsense anagrams, this idea has empirical support, as indicated by a study by Dominowski (1969).

Dominowski's procedure was first to identify anagrams varying in pronounceability and having the same solution word (Table 5-1). Then, an attempt was made to change the pronounceability of the anagrams, testing to determine if their solution difficulty was also changed. The results were clear cut. Anagrams rated as easy to pronounce were both pronounced more rapidly and solved more slowly than those rated hard to pronounce. Practicing at pronouncing the anagrams re-

TABLE 5–1. Anagrams Differing in Pronounceability but Having the Same Solution

Easy-to-Pronounce	Hard-to-Pronounce
WIHEG	EHIWG
FEHRS	RSFHE
CEVRO	OEVRC
UDTOB	DTUOB
FLENO	LFNEO
ROYNA	RNYAO
HPROC	RPCOH

sulted in faster pronunciation speeds and slower solution times for anagrams at both levels of rated pronounceability. Thus, making anagrams easier to pronounce made them harder to solve. What remains to be determined is whether word and nonsense anagrams will differ in difficulty when pronounceability is controlled. Realize that should pronounceability prove to be a viable explanation for the word-nonsense anagram difference, the validity of the initial Gestalt analysis would be upheld, although perhaps not as initially expected. The reason is that to describe a letter sequence as easy to pronounce is to characterize it as easy to organize into a cohesive pattern, to deal with it as a unit.

Similarity to the Solution

It would be expected that the difficulty of a problem would decrease as the problem situation becomes more similar to the solution state. The idea is that, as similarity increases, less change is required to go from the problem to the solution. In investigating this proposal, researchers face the problem of characterizing the degree of similarity between the problem and solution states. For some tasks, judgments of similarity are possible, but there would be a clear advantage to identifying the bases for such judgments. Research on this topic has been limited to the study of the similarity of an anagram to its solution word and to the study of functional fixedness.

Anagram-Word Relations. Mayzner and Tresselt (1958) created some "hard" and "easy" letter orders for anagrams, with "hard" orders judged by them to be less similar to word letter order than "easy" orders. They suggested that easy orders probably required fewer letter rearrangements to get from the anagram to the word. In an attempt to develop a generally applicable index of anagram-word similarity, Dominowski (1966) proposed that anagram letter orders be characterized by the number of letter moves required to produce the word order, disregarding the spacing between letters and the distance letters are moved. According to this system, for the word *brown,* the anagram *rownb* requires one move (*b* to the front), while the anagram *rbwno* requires two moves (*b* to the front and *o* between *r* and *w*). In one of Dominowski's experiments, college students were given three minutes to work on a sheet containing thirty five-letter anagrams, with the number of required letter moves varying over conditions. The mean number of solutions was 15.4 for one-move orders, 3.1 for two-move orders, and 5.4 for three-move orders (unfortunately, an interesting letter order requiring four moves was not included—*nworb*). Although one-move orders were much easier than orders requiring more letter moves, problem difficulty was not simply related to the number of required moves.

There are several possible explanations for the lack of a simple relationship between letter moves and problem difficulty. One alternative is that the number of letter moves adequately indicates the similarity of the anagram to the solution, and that problem difficulty is not simply related to the degree of similarity between the problem and solution states. However, it seems more likely that number of letter moves does not adequately represent the similarity of the anagram to the solution word. Number of letter moves is obviously a gross index—perhaps the distance a letter must be moved is important (Hunter, 1961).

In retrospect, it seems that the use of number of letter moves might be based on very tenuous assumptions. The subject does not know how many letters or which letters must be moved to go from the anagram to the solution word, yet the prediction that one-move orders will be easiest implies that the subject will move the "right" letters. If anagram orders requiring different numbers of moves are examined, one finds that one-move orders tend to have more letters in their correct positions and tend to preserve the letter sequences of the word. Thus, it is possible that the effect of number of letter moves has little to do with a process of moving letters as such. Rather, the subject might try to think of words based on what the anagram looks like and, as more of the word is contained intact in the anagram, his solution attempts are more likely to be successful (for example, in viewing *rownb, rown* might make the subject think of *brown,* which he then notices can be spelled with the letters provided, rather than his engaging in the process of moving *b* to the front).

Finally, there is anecdotal evidence that judged similarity is not simply related to the number of letter moves. Two researchers (Cohen, 1968; Ronning, 1965), in describing how they constructed anagrams for their studies, indicated that they tried to make the anagrams as dissimilar as possible from the word. They created mostly two-move orders, which suggests that the reverse of a sequence (which three-move orders tend to be) might be more similar to the original sequence than a less structured rearrangement. Is 12345 more similar to 54312 or 24351? Although the research on letter moves indicates that problems which are quite similar to the solution are easier than those less similar, the precise relationship between problem difficulty and problem-solution similarity is not yet known.

Perceptual Functional Fixedness. The solution of insight problems requires using an object in a relatively unusual fashion, and it might be expected that solution will be more difficult if the problem presentation emphasizes the ordinary function of the object. Stressing the ordinary function of the critical object can be viewed as an attempt to make the problem situation *less* similar to what is required for solution.

A number of studies have compared different presentations of the "candle problem," focusing on the use of the box as a support for the candle (see Figure 3-5). Solution of this problem is much easier when the box is presented empty compared to performance when the box is presented filled with tacks (Adamson, 1952; Glucksberg, 1962). An explanation usually offered for this difference is that presenting the filled box tends to fixate the subject's perception of the box on its function as a container, thus delaying his perceiving the box as a platform for the candle. Glucksberg and Weisberg (1966) suggested a different interpretation, based on the finding that subjects who fail to solve this problem often do not report the presence of the box when asked to describe the materials, or describe it in an undifferentiated fashion ("a box of tacks"). Their suggestion was that the increased difficulty found with the filled box was not due to a lack of perceiving the appropriate function for the box, but rather to a lack of noticing the presence of the box as a separate object. Consistent with their interpretation, Glucksberg and Weisberg found that solution of the candle problem was facilitated by separately labeling each object when the problem was presented (e.g., the box was labeled "BOX").

Glucksberg and his associates have pursued their investigations of the effects of labeling and similarity with a different problem for which the traditional functional fixedness notion seems more applicable. The subject is given the task of constructing an electrical circuit—connecting a battery, switch, and light bulb—but insufficient wire is provided to complete the connections. Solution of the problem requires that a metal tool such as pliers, a wrench, or a screwdriver be used in place of the missing wire. For this problem, it is doubtful that subjects fail to notice the presence of the tool; rather, they fail to distinguish between properties of the object relevant to its usual function and those relevant to its novel function (conducting electricity).

Several different manipulations have been tried with this problem. Attempts to differentiate the handle and the blade of the screwdriver or to vary the similarity of the blade and the wires on the basis of visual cues such as color have met with only partial success. The more interesting research is concerned with the role of verbal processes in perception. Simply labeling the screwdriver and the wires with their ordinary English names does not affect problem difficulty, but separately labeling the blade and handle of the screwdriver facilitates solution (Glucksberg and Danks, 1967). This effect is the same as that obtained when the compound percept "box of tacks" is differentiated by giving the box a separate label. In another experiment, the critical object was either a wrench or pliers, and subjects were required to refer to the object with one of two names, *wrench* or *pliers*; in all cases, the wires were called by their ordinary name. The idea was that using the tool as a substitute for the wires would occur more readily when their names were similar (*pliers* and *wires*) than when their names were different (*wrench* and *wires*). Notice that the experimenters assumed that *wrench* and *wires* are acoustically dissimilar even though both begin with *w*. The results supported their expectation—calling the tool *pliers* facilitated solution of the problem, even when the object was a wrench.

These studies demonstrate that solution of insight problems is noticeably affected by the kinds of labels applied to the objects presented, and they indicate that perception is strongly influenced by verbal processes. There appear to be two ways in which labels can affect problem solving. Problem difficulty is lessened when an object, or part of an object, typically not noticed is made salient by having a separate label (*box* in the candle problem, *blade* in the circuit problem). A different effect of labels is to increase the likelihood that the subject will think of the correct function for an object, as exemplified by the facilitation which occurred when the critical object and the object to be substituted for were given similar names (*pliers* and *wires*). This research will be mentioned again in Chapter 13, in a general discussion of the way in which language serves as an encoding system for a person's environment.

Comment

The characteristics of the problem situation presented to the problem solver influence his behavior in several ways. When given a problem, the subject is faced with finding the solution in a set of real or imagined solution possibilities, and the difficulty of a problem increases as a direct function of the amount of information or uncertainty that he must deal with. An important determinant of the nature of the set of alternatives that the subject will consider is the instructions provided by the experimenter. Generally speaking, as the subject is given more information about the problem, he will consider a smaller set of solution alternatives and will find the problem easier to solve. However, the presentation of a problem can emphasize ideas which will misdirect the subject—stressing the ordinary function of an object when an unusual function is required impairs solution. A problem situation having a high degree of similarity to the solution state will more readily lead to the solution, as indicated by the ease with which one-move anagrams are solved. It appears that the better organized a problem situation is, the more resistant to change it is, resulting in greater problem difficulty. Finally, research in this area illustrates the complexities involved in adequately characterizing a problem. The researcher cannot simply attend to physical features of the situation but must consider how the subject will interpret the problem based on his knowledge and the strategies he employs in seeking a solution.

CHARACTERISTICS OF THE SOLUTION

In discussing the interpretation of solution time in Chapter 3, it was pointed out that solving a problem will take longer if the solution requires more steps, or if a step is more difficult to complete, or both. An obvious research tactic is to vary the number of steps required in a solution process and determine how solution time is affected. The other research goal is to identify variables which affect the speed of completing a step. It seems that little research has been explicitly directed toward this goal.

Considerable research has been done on a class of problems which may include both of the foregoing, namely, the relationship between the difficulty of discovering a solution and the familiarity of that solution to the subject. Most studies have involved fairly simple problems, such as anagrams, with the familiarity (language frequency) of the solution word being the variable of interest. One way to interpret the effect of familiarity on problem difficulty is to assume that solving involves a single step (e.g., finding the word), in which case familiarity would be viewed as affecting the speed of completing that step. Alternatively, solving can be construed as a search process, with familiarity affecting the order of searching and thus the number of steps to solution. Clearly, the meaning of a "step" is a matter of definition, and it is probably always possible to imagine a "step" of any size as composed of some number of smaller "steps." Whether the number of steps or the speed of completing a step is emphasized in interpretations of familiarity, effects seem to depend on whether the subject is required to produce or select the solution. When the task requires only that the solution be selected from a list of alternatives, familiarity is viewed as affecting the order of search. When the subject is required to produce the solution, familiarity might influence both the order in which potential solutions will be generated and the difficulty of generating an alternative for consideration. The possible differences in the effects of familiarity on selection and production tasks will be stressed when research on familiarity is presented. First, studies obviously concerned with the number of steps in a solution process will be described.

Solution Complexity

Increasing the number of steps required to solve a problem is expected to increase the difficulty of the problem, and research findings support this expectation. The more interesting aspect of this research concerns the nature of the increase in difficulty produced by requiring more steps. With some tasks, it appears that each additional required step simply adds a constant amount to problem difficulty. For lights-and-switches problems, the number of switches which must be used to produce the desired light pattern can be varied. Measures of problem difficulty (number of switch-turns or time to solution) are linearly related to the number of required switches (Davis, 1967; Davis, Train, and Manske, 1968). With reasoning problems (such as the "rope problem") used by Restle and Davis (1962) in their analysis of problem solving, solution time was linearly related to the estimated number of steps. However, other investigators have found problem difficulty to increase more rapidly than the required number of steps.

Hayes (1965) devised the "spy problem" to study the effects of varying the number of steps in a solution. The subject was told to imagine that he was running a spy ring and that, for security reasons, not all spies could talk with each other. After learning which other spies each spy could talk with, the subject was required to get a message from one spy to another, solving the problem "in his head." Solution times became more than proportionally longer as additional steps were required in the communication chain. A similar finding was reported by Gagné and

Smith (1962) for the disc transfer problem described in Chapter 3 (Figure 3-6). With this task, the number of required moves is equal to $2^n - 1$, where n is the number of discs. Thus, as the number of discs increases from 2 to 3 to 4, the number of required moves increases from 3 to 7 to 15. Gagné and Smith found that the number of moves subjects made in solving a problem increased more rapidly than the number of moves required.

Why does increasing the number of required steps for solution sometimes produce a linear increase in difficulty, sometimes a positively accelerated increase? In Chapter 3, it was pointed out that Restle and Davis' model was based on the assumption that the various steps in a solution process were equally difficult and independent of each other; if this is true, then each additional step will simply add a constant amount to problem difficulty. It appears that this description applies to the problems used by Restle and Davis as well as the lights-and-switches task. However, it does not accurately characterize either the "spy problem" or the disc transfer problem.

Hayes (1965) found that subjects worked faster on steps near the end of a solution chain—all steps were not of equal difficulty. Since both long and short solution chains included "near" steps, but only long chains had "far" steps which are completed more slowly, long chains averaged more time per step overall. Hayes also suggested that steps near the end were easier because they could be planned during earlier steps, thus indicating that the steps were not independent of each other. In the disc transfer problem, successive moves are clearly connected—what the subject can do at any point depends on what he has done before. Furthermore, the degree of error possible increases with the number of discs; a wrong move early in the solution process is likely to require more moves to correct the error as the number of discs to be moved increases. Therefore, increasing the number of required steps in a solution process always leads to greater problem difficulty, but whether this increase in difficulty is linear or positively accelerated depends on the relative difficulty of the steps and their interrelatedness.

Solution Familiarity

Incorporated into both associative and information processing theories is the idea that subjects, in attempting to solve a problem, will try various alternatives in an order determined by familiarity. Information processing theory includes "trying first an old, familiar method" as one of a number of heuristic principles, and associative theory is built around the concept of a response hierarchy. Recall that a response hierarchy exists when a number of responses have differential strengths of association to a stimulus (differential probabilities of occurrence) based on different frequencies of occurrence (or reinforcement) in the past. A basic assumption of associative theory is that the order of responses in terms of probabilities is also the order in which those responses will occur in a problem situation. Testing this idea requires that the researcher be able to specify the frequencies for the various alternative solution possibilities. Because of this requirement, most research on the effects of prior solution frequency (solution familiarity) has been based on tasks requiring the discovery of a word or letter combination, since it is relatively easy to obtain frequency information for these items.

The most common method of indicating the frequencies for different items has been to make use of population norms (Table 5-2). Some normative data stem from analyses of samples of printed matter such as books, magazines, and newspapers, while other norms have been gathered by having large groups of subjects respond under various instructions. With all these techniques, the result is a list of items and their frequencies of occurrence in the sample.

An assumption underlying the use of such norms is that ordering the items in terms of

TABLE 5–2. Sources of Frequency Information for Verbal Items

Source	Type of Information
Battig and Montague (1968)	Naming items in categories (college students)
Cohen, Bousfield, and Whitmarsh (1957)	Naming items in categories (college students)
Kucera and Francis (1967)	Analysis of English
Mayzner and Tresselt (1965)	Language frequencies for letters and letter combinations
Palermo and Jenkins (1964)	Word associations (fourth grade to college)
Russell and Jenkins (1954)	Word associations (college students)
Thorndike and Lorge (1944)	Language frequencies for English words

relative frequency for the group is equivalent to ordering them in terms of relative frequency for a "typical" subject. To illustrate, assume that each individual in a large group of college students has given one free association to the word *blue*. Tabulating frequencies indicates that *sky* was given 200 times, *cheese* 55 times, *moon* 12 times, and so on. What do these figures indicate about the relative probabilities of occurrence for the "typical" individual? Presumably, the "average person," if asked to give a large number of free associations to *blue*, would duplicate the relative probabilities of the group. However, this does not appear to be true, primarily because an individual's later responses are influenced by his earlier answers (Duncan and Wood, 1966); group norms are based on subjects' giving one or very few answers and thus do not reflect this influence.

There are two points to this discussion. First, the use of population frequencies to characterize response hierarchies for the purpose of making predictions about the order of responding in a problem situation involves some "technical" error. That is, the frequencies are not exactly correct because the norms do not reflect the influence of earlier responses on later answers, an influence which will be present in the problem-solving situation. The second point is more important—the fact that a subject's earlier answers affect his later ones indicates that, at best, only a general correspondence is possible between any indicated response hierarchy and the order of responses in a problem situation. The response hierarchy depicts the probabilities of occurrence for various alternatives in the context of the initial situation, not in the context of the initial situation and previously tried alternatives. Of course, associative theory characterizes problem solving as the rearrangement of hierarchies but, as indicated in Chapter 4, does not include any precise statement of the sequence of changes that will occur. In brief, using normative frequencies to determine the effects of solution familiarity is limited to the comparison of widely separated frequency levels, and any results provide only partial information about the solution process.

Effects of Word Frequency. Attempts to relate problem difficulty to differences in solution frequency have been most successful with problems requiring the subject to produce a word as the solution. If words are emitted in order of frequency, then problems with high-frequency solutions will be solved faster (or, with a fixed amount of time allowed, more often) than problems with solutions of lower frequency. Evidence supporting this prediction has been obtained in many studies of anagram solving, which consistently show that problem difficulty is inversely related to the language frequency of the solution word. For example, in a study by Mayzner and Tresselt (1959), four different frequency levels were compared: 100 or more occurrences per million words in printed English (e.g., *chair*), 50 to 99 per million (*model*), 1 per million (*jaunt*), and less than 1 per million but more than 1 per 4 million (*triad*). The mean solution times, in order, were 96, 76, 138, and 148 seconds. Thus, while there was a considerable difference in difficulty between very frequent and very infrequent solution words, there was a reversal of the general trend for the two highest frequency levels. This reversal probably indicates nothing more than the lack of fine-grain precision associated with the use of normative frequencies.

Further evidence on word-frequency effects with anagrams has been obtained with problems having more than one solution (e.g., *necoa* can be solved with either *canoe* or *ocean*). If subjects are required to find only one solution, high-frequency alternatives are given more often than low-frequency alternatives (Mayzner and Tresselt, 1966). When multiple solutions are given, the more frequent words tend to be given earlier (Johnson and Van Mondfrans, 1965). Duncan (1966*a*) also studied the relationship between frequency and order of responding with a task in which subjects were given a stimulus word from the Russell and Jenkins (1954) norms and were allowed up to three guesses to produce some particular response. Unknown to them it was either the most frequent associate (Group 1) or the second most frequent associate (Group 2). Duncan reasoned that if subjects guess in order of frequency, there should be a greater chance of success on the first guess if the desired answer is of high frequency. If the first guess is wrong, subjects are assumed then to try lower-frequency alternatives; consequently, success on later guesses should be more likely if the answer is of lower frequency. Results generally supported his analysis: On the first guess, Group 1 achieved more correct answers than Group 2, but on guesses two and three, the groups were about equally successful, with Group 2 doing slightly better.

While these results support the notion that subjects will try alternatives roughly in order of frequency when working on a problem, additional factors which complicate this relationship have been identified. Duncan (1966*b*) has pointed out that the idea that alternatives will be tried in order of frequency applies to those the subject *actually* considers, not to the set of alternatives that *might* be considered. The distinction is between what a subject knows and has potentially available and what he actually recalls in the problem situation (Table 5-3). The number of items recalled is likely to be less than the number that could be recalled. There is no guarantee that a particular word will be included among those

TABLE 5–3. *Hypothesized Dual Effect of Item Frequency on Problem Solving, Using the Example of "Thinking of an Animal Name" (Fictitious Data)*

Subject's Knowledge of Animals	Names Recalled in Problem Situation
(Arranged in order of frequency)	(Arranged in order of occurrence)
VERY FREQUENT: Horse, Dog, Cow, Monkey, Cat, Tiger, Elephant, Mouse	Horse, Cow, Monkey, Tiger, Mouse, Muskrat, Llama, Buffalo
************************************	
INFREQUENT: Gerbil, Lynx, Muskrat, Whale, Llama, Orangutan, Mole, Buffalo, Otter, Gazelle	

recalled, and Duncan's work suggests that high-frequency alternatives are more likely to be recalled. Subjects were given word problems having two answers and were asked to find both of them (for example, "find a tree name starting with *w* and having six letters" has the answers *willow* and *walnut*). For each of 17 such problems, the two words differed in language frequency; subjects were able to produce high-frequency alternatives 58 percent of the time, but could produce low-frequency alternatives only 37 percent of the time. What this suggests is that a problem having a low-frequency solution which the subject must produce will be difficult for two reasons: (1) The subject is less likely to recall the solution during the problem session. (2) If he recalls the solution, it is likely to occur later in the solution process. One implication of this analysis is that different effects of varying frequency should be observed when the subject need only select the correct alternative from a list provided, compared to requiring the subject to recall the solution. The available evidence supports this expectation.

Frequency Effects with Selection Tasks. If the subject is required only to select the correct alternative from a list provided, variations in the frequency of the correct answer should affect only the order in which items will be chosen. Discovering a low-frequency solution should require more selections than finding a higher-frequency answer, but the difficulty associated with low-frequency solutions should not be as great as when the subject has to recall any alternatives he will consider. The results of a study by Dominowski (1965) indicate that the effects of varying frequency are quite different in selection tasks. Subjects were given a set of five bigrams varying in language frequency (*er, ea, et, em, ew*) and were instructed to select the "correct" bigram in as few guesses as possible. Ten such problems were presented; five different conditions were created by varying the rank, based on frequency, of the correct bigram (e.g., in Condition 3, the correct bigram for each problem was the one with the third highest language frequency). On the first problem, the number of errors to solution was inversely related to the frequency of the correct alternative, as expected if subjects tend to guess in order of frequency (Figure 5-2). But, on later problems the relationship between errors and the relative frequency of the correct item changed. As indicated in Figure 5-2, selecting the item with the lowest frequency in the set was no longer the most difficult problem; rather, choosing the item with medium language frequency proved most difficult. This suggests that after the first problem, subjects had some idea of the relative frequency of the correct item and tried to guess the alternative representing that rank. The difficulty of choosing the item with medium frequency indicates either that it was difficult to get an idea of the relative frequency of the answer in that condition or that subjects had some notion of the frequency of the answer but couldn't figure out which item in a set had the third highest frequency.

The latter interpretation is supported by the findings of Jurca and Duncan (1969). In their study, a problem consisted of presenting five words varying in language frequency; in different conditions, subjects were told to guess either the first, second, third, fourth, or fifth most frequent word. The task was easy if the subject had to guess either the most frequent or the least frequent word, being more difficult if the item to be guessed had medium frequency. These results indicate that the relationship between difficulty and the frequency of the correct alternative will be curvilinear if the subject knows the frequency of the answer and is required only to select it from a set of items provided. A curvilinear relationship will be apparent immediately if the subject is told which relative frequency is correct; in the absence of such instructions, the subject will identify the correct relative frequency over a series of problems and use this information to improve his performance. Effectively, the subject will learn

FIGURE 5–2. Number of errors made in finding solutions of different relative frequencies.

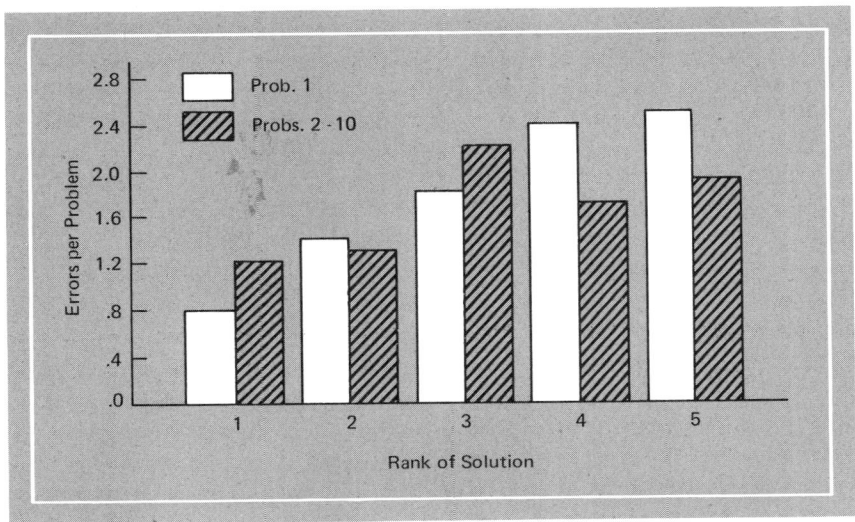

Source: Adapted from R. L. Dominowski, Problem difficulty as a function of relative frequency of correct responses. *Psychonomic Science*, 1965, 3, 417-18.

a relative-frequency concept ("the least frequent item is correct").

If selecting a low-frequency solution becomes easier once the subject learns that the answer is of low frequency, the possibility is suggested that a similar phenomenon might occur when the solution must be recalled from memory. There are no studies directly concerned with this idea, but Duncan (personal communication) has provided some relevant data from his study on thinking of words (1966b). As mentioned earlier, each of his problems had two answers differing in language frequency (e.g., *willow* and *walnut* as answers to "give a tree name starting with *w* and having six letters"). Duncan compared performance in a condition in which subjects were told the high-frequency solution and asked only for the low-frequency alternative (Group L) with performance when the low-frequency solution was given and the high-frequency was asked for (Group H). Duncan reports that, first, there was no improvement in performance over 17 problems for either group and, second, that Group H was more successful throughout than Group L. Keeping in mind that this was only a rough, post hoc analysis, these data suggest that subjects might improve in discovering a low-frequency solution when they are selecting from specified alternatives but not when they must recall the solution from memory.

One reason why it should be hard to get better at producing low-frequency solutions also accounts for the difficulty of selecting a medium-frequency answer from a set of alternatives. The difficulty of selecting a correct answer is directly related to the number of similar alternatives contained in the set (Duncan, 1967). Thus, when given five alternatives and told to choose the one with the third highest frequency, a subject finds the task difficult because that item is "surrounded" by items of similar frequency. In like fashion, if a subject knows that he must produce a low-frequency solution, part of his difficulty is due to the fact that there are a great many low-frequency alternatives in most sets. If a subject is asked to think of the name of a common tree, the possibilities are probably limited to *maple, oak, elm,* and *pine,* but if he is asked to produce an uncommon tree name, there are many more possibilities (e.g., *catalpa, aspen, eucalyptus, magnolia, juniper, linden,* etc.). In addition to the difficulty imposed by the larger problem space associated with low-frequency solutions, there is also the problem that low-frequency items are harder to recall.

In summary, when a problem solver is required to recall a solution from memory, difficulty is roughly an inverse function of the frequency (familiarity) of the solution. With selection tasks, this relationship is complicated by differences in the discriminability of alternatives at various frequency levels. Frequency effects are usually attributed to the production stage of problem solving. Johnson, Lynch, and Ramsay (1967) have shown that frequency can also affect judgment. One of their tasks required subjects to compare two letter sequences (e.g., *buxom* and *bxuom*) and decide whether the letter orders were the same or different. One sequence was always a word, while the other was sometimes a repetition of the word, sometimes a scrambled version of the word. Subjects performed this task more rapidly when the words were of high frequency and made more errors when the words were of low frequency. Applying this finding to anagram solving, part of the reason why solution times are faster for high-frequency words is that the subject, once he thinks of the solution, is more likely to make a rapid and accurate comparison of the word with the anagram.

Frequency Effects with Part-Solutions. Solving anagrams is considerably easier when the solution is a high-frequency word, compared to discovering a low-frequency solution. Mayzner and Tresselt (1962) extended this idea to part-solutions, reasoning that solution words containing high-frequency letter sequences (e.g., *water, house*) should be easier to discover than words with low-frequency sequences (e.g., *judge, fruit*). Since research on this proposal has yielded inconsistent results, it will be only briefly described. Some studies have yielded small to moderate differences favoring words containing high-frequency bigrams as easier, but in other studies no difference has been observed. There are several problems involved in studying this effect. Should all letter sequences be given equal weight? Apparently not; Mayzner and Tresselt (1966) suggest that the initial bigram should be given the greatest weight and, as mentioned earlier in this chapter, other evidence indicates that both ends of a word are more importantly involved in solving than sequences in the middle. Is frequency a reasonable measure? The argument against its use (Dominowski, 1967) is most easily illustrated by an extreme example: *qu* doesn't occur very often in printed English, but, if a subject is given an anagram containing *q* and *u*, he is almost certain to form *qu*. Finally, the importance of constructing bigrams in solving anagrams has not been adequately determined, and there is some evidence indicating that bigram construction is a step that can sometimes be skipped. If so, then manipulating bigram characteristics is likely to yield inconsistent results, which is what has happened.

Availability of Functions. The last topic related to solution familiarity concerns the solution of insight problems. Saugstad (1955) spoke of the "availability of functions" for solving an insight problem, with the implication that these functions are either available or not, in contrast to the concept of relative familiarity applied to solutions of word problems. The "either-or" formulation has led to ambiguous results and seems to be an inadequate way of approaching the relationship between availability and problem-solving efficiency. The standard research technique has been to ask subjects to list uses or functions for a number of objects, including the one to be used in the insight problem. This assessment takes place prior to presenting the problem, and performance on the problem is related to performance on the availability test. There are two methodological weaknesses in this research. First, the fact that a subject doesn't give a particular use for an object on an availability test does not mean that this function is unavailable to him in all situations. The problem situation might well suggest uses for an object that are not prompted in the context of an availability test, as the Gestalt concept of *direction* implies. Second, these studies have largely involved a comparison of the number of solvers after fairly long working time, an insensitive method. These inadequacies limit the value of this research.

In studies by Saugstad (1955) and by Saugstad and Raaheim (1957), subjects who gave appropriate uses on the availability test were more likely to solve the related insight problem than those who scored zero on the test. It is worth noting that a considerable proportion of zero scorers did solve the problem, indicating the lack of precision of the availability test. This lack is emphasized in the findings of Duncan (1961) and Staats (1957); in both studies, almost no subjects gave appropriate uses on an availability test, and almost all subjects solved the problem. In other words, failing to give an appropriate use on an availability test seems not to be of crucial importance, except that such failure might be indicative of a somewhat lower likelihood that a problem requiring that use will be solved. The more interesting finding is that some subjects who do give appropriate uses subsequently fail to solve the problem, or that differences in problem-solving success can be observed between groups of subjects who give evidence of having the relevant functions available (Duncan, 1961; Maier and Burke, 1966). This finding supports the Gestalt contention that simply having had the relevant experience (having the appropriate functions available) does not guarantee that solution will occur. Availability is necessary but not sufficient; what may be needed in addition is the proper *direction* from the problem context. Maier and Burke suggested that the major difference between solvers and nonsolvers of an insight problem lies in the selection of experiences relevant to the solution.

Comment

Research on solution characteristics has dealt with two broadly defined variables: solution complexity and solution familiarity. Increasing the number of required steps in a solution process appears to produce a linear increase in solution difficulty if the steps are equally difficult and can be completed independently, but produces a positively accelerated increase if success on one step affects the chances for success on another. The findings regarding solution familiarity are based almost exclusively on finding solutions to simple, verbal problems and thus possess unknown generality. However, the results are reasonably consistent. If solving a problem involves recalling solution alternatives from memory, difficulty is roughly inversely related to the familiarity of the solution. If solution requires only selection of the correct alternative from a set provided, familiar solutions will still be easier to find than unfamiliar solutions, but discovering low-frequency solutions can also become less difficult if the subject knows that an uncommon alternative is correct.

Six Empirical Studies of Problem Solving: The Problem Solver

Having surveyed the various ways in which the difficulty of a problem is affected by the features of the initial problem situation and the attributes of the solution which must be produced, we will now consider those characteristics of problem solvers that are related to problem-solving efficiency. Individual differences in problem-solving efficiency are likely to be related to differences in relevant knowledge, skills involved in formulating a problem, search strategies, etc. Because of the lack of information about how subjects attempt to solve simple problems, little has been done to interrelate various kinds of behavior in the problem situation. This state of affairs is in direct contrast to that regarding conceptual behavior, where considerable effort has been expended to find out how subjects try to identify concepts (their strategies) and to determine whether various strategies are associated with different levels of efficiency. Performance on simple problems has been related primarily to rather obvious measures such as intelligence, sex, age, and general motivational level. Much of the information does not help to understand how the problems are solved; for example, if one finds that males are more likely to solve a problem than females, this finding by itself is not very useful because the investigator must determine why males and females differ, and there are many possible reasons, e.g., differences in relevant knowledge, skills, or in general the subject's personal history.

A final point concerns the proposed goal of this research, namely to identify the correlates of problem solving. As should now be obvious, there is an enormous variety of problems, and it would be naive to expect that some people are consistently better or worse for all possible problems. Each type of problem doubtless requires different kinds of behavior, thus individual differences in performance will not be stable from one problem type to the next, and the correlates of problem-solving efficiency will change with the problem. In this regard, individual differences in anagram-solving efficiency appear to be reliable (Johnson, 1966), but performance on one insight problem seems unrelated to performance on another (Adamson, 1952; Duncan, 1961). The findings to be presented should be viewed with these limitations in mind. The relationships between problem solving and general ability, age, sex, and motivational level will be described. Finally, because so much of the research on simple problem solving has been based on either anagrams or insight problems, the correlates of performance in these situations will be listed.

INDIVIDUAL DIFFERENCES AMONG PROBLEM SOLVERS

Differences in General Ability

Performance on tests of general mental ability (intelligence) has typically been found to be positively related to problem-solving efficiency. Subjects who score higher on intelligence tests also perform better on anagrams (Mendelsohn, Griswold, and Anderson, 1966) and on lights-and-switches problems (French, 1958). Results with insight problems have been inconsistent and indicate that conclusions should be drawn with considerable caution. In one study, subjects with higher test scores solved problems more efficiently (Maltzman, Eisman, and Brooks, 1956), but in another no relationship between intelligence test scores and problem solving was observed (Burke and Maier, 1965). Different intelligence tests and different problems were used in these investigations, thus the reasons for the discrepant results are difficult to identify. Since it has also been found that performance on one insight problem is unrelated to performance on another, perhaps these results suggest that the class of insight problems is too broadly defined; unfortunately, how the class should be subdivided more meaningfully is not apparent. In general, it is not surprising that performance on intelligence tests is related to problem solving, since such tests tap a wide variety of behaviors, and it seems reasonable that some part of the test would sample behavior similar to that involved in solving the problem (for example, vocabulary in the case of anagram solving).

Age Differences

Although no attempt has been made to construct a "developmental psychology of problem solving," in contrast to the situation with respect to conceptual behavior (see Chapter 12), the results of several studies can be combined to suggest a relationship between age and problem solving, which should be interpreted with appropriate caution. Problem-solving efficiency appears to improve with age through early adulthood subsequently to deteriorate (Birren, Jerome, and Chown, 1961; Weir, 1967). Age changes in problem solving probably resemble those found on intelligence tests, an analogy which provides a useful caution, since Wechsler (1958) has shown that age changes on intelligence tests vary considerably from one part of the test to another.

The utility of including subjects of different ages is illustrated by a study by Beilin (1967), who compared anagram solving by subjects ranging in age from 8 to 14 years. He found both that overall performance improved with age and that the difference in solving word and nonsense anagrams increased with age. While the overall improvement can be attributed to increases in vocabulary and perhaps to practice in solving verbal problems, the differential change for word and nonsense anagrams raises an interesting question. What happens during that time span which results in less improvement for word anagrams than for nonsense anagrams? While no ready answer is available, Beilin's finding places another restriction on any explanation for the word-nonsense anagram difference. For example, if pronounceability is the reason that word anagrams are harder, then it must also be true that the difference in pronounceability between words and nonsense strings increases between 8 and 14 years of age.

Sex Differences

There are numerous reports that males are superior to females in solving insight problems (e.g., Duncan, 1961; Staats, 1957). The reasons for this difference are not clear; one might expect that males are simply more likely to think of object functions more relevant to solving, but Duncan obtained evidence not supporting this idea. He found that males and females were equally likely to give relevant uses for the critical object on an availability test, thus the fact that males typically solve the problem in roughly half the time taken by females cannot easily be explained in terms of differences in availability of functions. With other kinds of problems, sex differences in performance are less evident. Although performance on arithmetic subtests of intelligence tests favors males (Wechsler, 1958), other studies have revealed few sex differences on such tasks (see Duncan, 1959). Males and females perform equivalently on lights-and-switches problems (Davis, 1967) and on anagrams (Mendelsohn, Griswold, and Anderson, 1966). It is clear that no simple, general statement can be made about sex differences in problem-solving efficiency; furthermore, when differences are observed, they seem difficult to explain in terms of differences in abilities related to reaching a solution.

One interesting proposal which has some support is based on the idea that solving problems is associated with the masculine role in our culture. If so, then females might expect that, being females, they probably won't do very well on a problem, and consequently they perform relatively poorly (remember that performance is affected by expectations regarding success). Milton (1957) investigated this proposal by giving a test designed to measure a person's degree of identification with the cultural male sex role; of course, males as a group score higher, but there are individual differences both among males and among females. Milton found that, for both males and females, problem-solving efficiency was directly related to the degree of masculine role identification. The results indicated that, if one could compare males and females with equal degrees of identification with the masculine role, the two sexes would perform equally well. This attitudinal interpretation of sex differences is also supported by findings that females profit from discussions which may be viewed as changing their attitudes toward problem solving (Carey, 1958; Hoffman and Maier, 1961).

Motivational Differences

In many psychological descriptions of behavior, motivation plays an important part by interacting with prior experience to determine the characteristics of performance. One formulation that has considerable empirical support is the *Yerkes-Dodson law*, which states that there is some optimal level of arousal for any task. In other words, the function relating quality of performance to level of arousal will have an inverted-U shape; performance will first improve, then deteriorate as arousal varies from its lowest to highest levels. An important point is that the optimal level of arousal depends on the task; consequently, a generally optimal level of motivation cannot be specified.

One factor determining the optimal level of arousal for a task is the difficulty of the task. The idea is that the motivational level must be high enough that the correct habits are aroused but not so high that additional, competing habits are also brought into play. Consequently, as the difficulty of a task increases, a lower level of arousal is likely to be optimal. Another way to view motivational effects is to describe motivational changes as affecting the differences among habits in terms of "strength." To illustrate this idea, imagine a task in which only two habits are likely to be aroused, one stronger (more likely) than the other. Increasing the motivational level is predicted to magnify the difference in strength between these two habits, the strong one becoming relatively stronger, the weak habit relatively weaker. If the initially strong habit is correct, increasing the motivational level should facilitate performance, but if the weak habit is correct, the increase in motivation will impair performance (Spence, 1956). To summarize this discussion, if a task is difficult, increasing arousal is likely to impair performance, but, if a task is somewhat easier, moderate increases in arousal might facilitate performance; extreme increases will also impair performance due to the arousal of additional competing habits.

Investigations of motivational effects on problem solving have taken two forms. One method has been to identify subjects having different levels of general arousal, usually on the basis of a test of general anxiety, then to correlate individual differences in arousal with individual differences in problem-solving efficiency. An alternative procedure involves creating conditions designed to produce different levels of arousal, such as by giving stress-inducing instructions or offering money for superior performance. One difficulty with many investigations stems from the fact that the level of performance depends on the general arousal level of the subject, the motivational characteristics of the problem-solving situation, and task difficulty. Consequently, if an investigator attends only to one of these factors, no clear expectation regarding the effects of variation in that factor can be stated. These complications will become apparent as the research is described.

Anxiety and Stress. A number of studies have been concerned with the relationship between general anxiety and problem solving, with the general conclusion that performance on problem-solving tasks (including anagrams and insight problems) is not simply related to individual differences in general anxiety (Maltzman, Eisman, and Brooks, 1956; Mendelsohn, Griswold, and Anderson, 1966; Staats, 1957). However, if subjects are differentiated on the basis of test anxiety (the tendency to become anxious in test situations) rather than on general anxiety, high-test-anxious subjects usually perform more poorly (e.g., Harleston, 1962; Russell and Sarason, 1965). Thus, it appears that in order to predict a subject's performance on a problem simply on the basis of his tendency to become anxious, one must determine the subject's propensity for anxiety in stressful (test) situations rather than relying on measures of general anxiety. This suggests that the cues (whatever they may be) present in a problem situation are an important determinant of a subject's motivational level.

Some indication of how the motivational properties of the problem situation function can be provided by considering the expected effects of giving a stress-inducing instruction to problem solvers. The expectation is that giving such an instruction is more likely to impair the performance of high-test-anxious subjects because these subjects are already highly motivated, and the additional arousal produced by instructions is likely to push their motivational level past the optimum. It is difficult to predict what should happen for low-anxious subjects, since the prediction depends on the relationship between their "base" arousal level and the optimum arousal level (for example, it is possible that the increased arousal produced by instructions could move them to the optimal level, thus facilitating performance).

The gross expectation is that stress-inducing instructions should impair the performance of high-anxious subjects to a greater extent. Sarason (1961) obtained results consistent with this expectation; telling subjects that anagrams measured intelligence increased the performance difference favoring low-anxious subjects. However, Russell and Sarason (1965) found no effect of any sort as a function of giving "neutral" versus stressful instructions. Since there were differences in the task and the general experimental situation between these two studies, it is quite possible that the findings are not contradictory—both the optimal level of arousal for the task and the levels produced by the experimental manipulations may differ in these investigations.

Investigators have repeatedly found that failure adversely affects problem solving (Feather, 1966; Solley and Stagner, 1956). This effect has several possible interpretations. The frustration produced by failure may increase the subject's level of arousal and, if later problems are difficult, magnify this difficulty by increasing the potency of competing responses relative to the solution. Alternatively, failure may produce an increase in the number of competing habits. As a further possibility, failure may result in a reduction in the subject's expectancy of success, leading to less effort being expended or to less appropriate attempts at solution (looking for solutions that are too complex for the later problems).

Functional Fixedness and Arousal. Glucksberg (1962) made use of the fact that the box-filled and box-empty versions of the candle problem differ in difficulty to investigate the interaction of motivational effects with task difficulty. His study was related to the proposition that increases in arousal make strong habits stronger, weak habits weaker. If so, increasing the subject's motivational level with the box-filled version of the problem should impair performance, since the subject should have a greater tendency to fixate on the box as a container, making it more difficult to think of it as a platform for the candle. No specific prediction can be made for the box-empty version, since the exact strength of the correct response is not known; increasing arousal might have no effect or facilitate performance. Motivation was manipulated through instructions; in the "low-arousal" condition, subjects were given rather typical, "neutral" instructions, whereas subjects in the "high-arousal" condition were told that they could earn a monetary reward (up to $20) if they solved rapidly. Results confirmed expectations: high arousal impaired solution of the difficult box-filled version, but increasing arousal had no effect on performance with the easy, box-empty version. Alternatively, the difference in difficulty between the two versions (the functional fixedness effect) was greater with the high-arousal level. The full complexity of the relationship between motivation and task difficulty is indicated by the results of a study by Tecce (1965), who gave the two versions of the candle problem to subjects at three levels of general anxiety. The functional fixedness effect was greatest for subjects of high or low anxiety, smallest for medium-anxious subjects.

Even greater breadth and complexity for motivational effects are illustrated in a study by Suedfeld, Glucksberg, and Vernon (1967). These investigators used a tactual form of the candle problem in which the subject is blindfolded, making perception of the objects dependent on physical contact. With this version of the problem, Glucksberg (1964) has shown that solution usually follows an adventitious contact with the box, a finding with important implications for the effects of varying motivation. In most problem-solving situations, physical activity is of no concern and, in discussing motivational effects, one is concerned with whether the motivational level is sufficient to arouse the correct habit, whether the level is so high that additional competing habits will be aroused, and so on. However, with the tactual form of the candle problem, for which physical activity is an important consideration, an additional factor comes into play. Increasing arousal leads to greater physical activity, which in this case should increase the subject's chances of making contact with the box, which, in turn, will facilitate solving the problem. The overall effect of increasing motivation is thus the combined result of increased activity (helpful) and increased competition (harmful).

Motivation was manipulated in two ways: (1) Subjects were given either the neutral or the monetary-reward instructions used by Glucksberg (1962), and (2) subjects either did or did not experience 24 hours of sensory deprivation before receiving the problem. The combinations of these variables yielded three motivational levels: low (neither deprivation nor monetary incentive), medium (deprivation only, or incentive only), and high (both deprivation and incentive). The results are depicted in Figure 6-1. As indicated, the functional fixedness effect was greater with either high or low motivation, a finding similar to Tecce's (1965) and giving further support to the idea that performance is related to motivation according to an inverted U-shaped function.

Correlates of Anagram Solving

A great deal of research on problem solving has been based on anagrams, and it will be helpful to indicate the correlates of anagram solving in order to shed some light on what is involved in solving these problems. As mentioned earlier, individual differences in anagram solving appear to be reliable and are related to differences in intelligence, particularly knowledge of vocabulary. Mendelsohn, Griswold, and Anderson (1966) showed that subjects with small vocabularies (relative to other college students) do poorly on anagrams, while those with larger vocabularies can do well but might also do poorly. The point is that familiarity with words is only one attribute of a good anagram solver.

Mendelsohn, et al. proposed that shifting attention is also important, both in terms of

FIGURE 6–1. *The effect of level of arousal on solution times for hard (box-filled) and easy (box-empty) versions of the candle problem.*

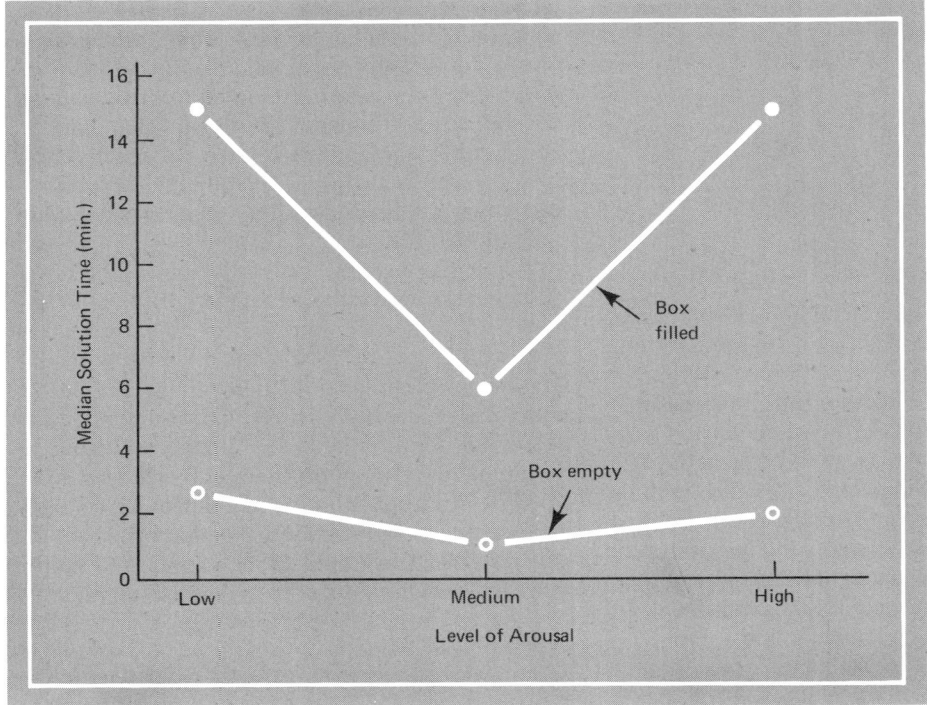

Source: From P. Suedfeld, S. Glucksberg, and J. Vernon. Sensory deprivation as a drive operation: Effect upon problem solving. *Journal of Experimental Psychology*, 1967, **75**, 166-69. Copyright 1967 by the American Psychological Association and reprinted by permission.

repeatedly examining the anagram for new cues to solution and in terms of generating a variety of possibilities based on any cue. Their analysis is supported by the finding that anagram performance is positively related ($r = +.40$) to scores on a test requiring the implicit transformation of visual displays (see also Gavurin, 1967) and to scores on the Remote Associates Test ($r = +.43$). These investigators view the Remote Associates Test as requiring rather common associates and tapping individual differences in the ability to form and evaluate hypotheses about solutions efficiently. This interpretation, it should be noted, is quite different from that of Mednick (1962) who created the test. In summary, these results suggest a description of anagram solving in terms of the subject's *knowledge* of the language and his *skills* related to selecting cues and generating alternative solution possibilities in an efficient manner.

Correlates of Insight-Problem Solving. Insight problems seem, at first glance, to resemble "real-life" problems more than anagrams, and it would be expected that useful information of considerable generality could be obtained by using these tasks. Unfortunately, the concept of an "insight problem" may be too broad, since it seems that different tasks within this class involve unrelated behaviors. For example, as noted above, performance on one insight problem appears unrelated to performance on another. Whether or not efficiency in solving insight problems is related to intelligence seems to depend on which insight problem is used. A positive relationship might be expected between insight-problem solving and performance on the Remote Associates Test, since both presumably involve thinking of unusual responses, but the two behaviors appear to be unrelated to each other (Danks and Glucksberg, 1966).

There are only two reliable findings concerning insight problems: males solve such problems more efficiently than females, and the functional fixedness effect varies with motivational level. However, despite considerable research with these problems, psychologists do not have a good idea of what is involved in solving insight problems. Burke and Maier (1965), after an unsuccessful attempt to relate a number of measures of intellectual ability and flexibility in thinking to performance on an insight problem, suggested that the behavior observed with insight problems may be different from that seen in other problem-solving situations. If this is so, a researcher might still study insight-problem solving for its own sake, but the general usefulness of his findings is quite limited.

Comment

The purpose of trying to identify the correlates of problem solving is to get information about the solution process and also to find suggestions for ways to improve subjects' problem-solving efficiency. Unfortunately, little progress has been made. The information available is imprecise, and many of the relationships do not help much to understand the solution process. For example, finding that problem solving is related to intelligence, sex, or age is only a preliminary step, since one must determine more precisely why these relationships exist.

Some promising findings have been reported. For example, anagram solving is related to subjects' knowledge of vocabulary and ability to shift attention while working on the problem. Would people become better anagram solvers if their vocabulary levels were deliberately increased? How would one go about making a problem solver better able to shift attention and avoid fixation? Attempts to change problem-solving behavior through various kinds of experiences or training methods are the next topic for consideration.

TRANSFER EFFECTS IN PROBLEM SOLVING

A great deal of interest has been focused on the influence of past experience on problem solving. Some of the findings previously described have involved transfer of previous experience outside the laboratory to the problem situation (e.g., word frequency effects, words as anagrams). In the present section, emphasis will be on short-term transfer effects produced by giving problem solvers different kinds of experiences in the laboratory prior to attempting a test problem. Prior experience can produce either facilitation (positive transfer) or impairment (negative transfer), and research has been concerned with identifying those conditions under which various kinds of transfer will occur.

Studies of transfer in problem solving can be roughly sorted into two classes to distinguish between prior experience which involves problem solving and prior experience of a different sort (e.g., watching a demonstration, being taught a solution method). In the first instance, attention is directed toward practice effects; the subject is given the opportunity to work on a number of problems, and the researcher looks for changes in the subject's behavior as practice continues. In the latter case, the researcher makes some deliberate attempt to change the subject's problem-solving behavior, often using a training method which does not itself require the subject to solve problems. With both kinds of transfer, an important determinant of the effects of prior experience is the specificity of the relationship between the prior experience and the problem subsequently presented. For example, in studying practice effects, a researcher might simply give subjects a series of anagrams and, if asked to state the relationship between problems, would answer, "They are all just anagrams." This relationship can be contrasted with a set of anagrams in which the solutions are semantically related (e.g., all animal names) or in which the relationship of the anagram letter order to the word letter order is constant (e.g., the first anagram letter is always the third letter of the word).

Emphasizing the specificity of relationships brings up a methodological issue. If an experimenter wants to determine the effect of a rather specific relationship, he must be sure to isolate that effect. For example, suppose the anagram *pleap* (solution: *apple*) is given to one group of subjects as their first problem, but another group receives this problem after working on a series of anagrams whose solutions are all names of fruits. If these two groups perform differently on the test problem, it would not be possible to determine whether the difference is due to the second group's simply having worked on a series of anagrams or to their having worked on a series of anagrams with similar solutions. To isolate the effect of working on problems with "similar" solutions (e.g., all animal names), the researchers should compare subjects who have worked on a series of anagrams having animal names as solutions with subjects who have worked on a series of anagrams having a variety of solutions, to equate these groups in terms of experience with anagrams as such. In a number of studies of practice effects and, particularly, training effects, the treatments given to various groups differ in complex ways, which makes it difficult to identify the critical differences.

Practice Effects

When the only relationship among a series of problems is that they are all the same type of problem, any change observed is called "learning to solve." If a more specific relationship obtains, changes are attributed to the acquisition of problem-solving "sets." The difference between *learning to solve* and the effects of *set* is obviously the generality of the relationship among the problems. If a subject learns to solve, it must mean that he has learned some general rule or strategy which can be successfully applied to the entire class of problems, whereas a set usually involves a fairly specific solution rule which will aid in solving some problems but hinder solving others.

Learning to Solve. Although simple practice effects are commonly observed with conceptual and verbal-learning tasks, the likelihood of observing such effects in problem solving seems to depend on the type of problem. It has usually been found that subjects do not improve over a series of anagrams (e.g., Dominowski, 1968; Mayzner and Tresselt, 1962) or over a series of word-guessing problems (Battig, 1957; Duncan, 1966b). Little relevant research has been done with insight problems, but Duncan (1961) found that subjects who solved an unrelated insight problem before attempting the two-string problem did no better than those given only the two-string problem. These negative findings must be interpreted cautiously, since they are primarily incidental results from studies not designed for investigating learning to solve and in which fairly small amounts of practice were given. Also, the subjects were college students, and it is possible that most of their improvement in problem solving might have taken place before they entered the laboratory.

With problems in which sequences of choices occur, learning to solve has been observed with some regularity. Subjects improve over a series of lights-and-switches problems (Davis, 1967), other search tasks (Neimark, 1961), and the game of twenty questions (Taylor and Faust, 1952), with some exceptions in the last case (Bendig, 1957). Strategies varying in effectiveness have been identified for these tasks, and improvement generally reflects increased used of better approaches to the problem.

While it is tempting to suggest that perhaps there is no general strategy or skill that applies to all anagrams or to all insight problems, caution must again be emphasized. With more standard learning tasks, general practice effects have been found to depend on both the number of tasks encountered and the amount of practice gained on each task (Duncan, 1958; Morrisett and Hovland, 1959). The importance of these factors is illustrated by the studies of the game of "twenty questions." Bendig (1957) used a modified version of the game, allowing only five questions per game, and found no improvement over three games. In contrast, Taylor and Faust (1952) allowed up to thirty questions per game and observed improvement over sixteen games. It appears to be critical that the subject actually solves each problem, rather than just work on it, and that he is given a variety of problems. In the studies of anagrams, word-guessing tasks, and insight problems, relatively few problems were given, and subjects did not solve all problems. Consequently, the question of whether *learning to solve* can occur with such problems remains open.

Problem-Solving Set. The development of a *set* is related to more specific interproblem relationships than is learning to solve. Research has been done on three kinds of set: a category set with anagrams (e.g., all solutions are animal names), a letter-order set with anagrams (the same rearrangement applies to all problems), and a method set with water-jar problems. A water-jars problem is a modified arithmetic problem in which the subject is told the capacities of three jars and is required to measure a specified amount. For example, given jars holding 18, 43, and 10 pints, how would one measure 5 pints of water? The solution is to fill the 43-pint jar, then pour water from it into the 18-pint jar once, into the 10-pint jar twice (43 − 18 − 10 − 10 = 5). A method set is established by giving a number of problems having the same solution method (e.g., largest minus the medium minus the smallest twice).

The study of set has usually been guided by associative theory, in which set is related to mediating responses. A category set fits this conception nicely, with the category name (e.g., *animals*) mediating the production of particular items from the category (e.g., *horse, tiger,* etc.). It is somewhat more difficult to imagine the class of responses associated with a letter-order or method set; rather, it seems easier to characterize these sets in terms of the adoption of a solution rule of a high degree of specificity. Kaplan and Schoenfeld (1966) demonstrated just how specific a letter-order set can become in photographing subjects' eye movements while they were solving anagrams. The development of set was indicated by the adoption of distinctive eye-movement patterns, namely looking at the anagram letters in the order in which they appeared in the solution word. It seems likely that a similar specificity characterizes method set for water-jar problems.

Problem-solving set has often been described in negative terms, the notion being that subjects who develop sets are rigid (Luchins and Luchins, 1959). This description seems inadequate for two reasons. First, the attempts to use set as a measure of rigidity have not always been successful (Levitt, 1956). Second, whether a set will facilitate or impair problem solving depends on the applicability of the set to the problem; perhaps the negative connotations of set have arisen because many studies of set have been designed to show negative transfer.

The standard procedure for studying set has been to give a series of training problems all having the set solution, followed by a test problem or problems. The test may either be a problem with two solutions, the set solution and another, often simpler, solution, or it may be an "extinction" problem requiring a new solution. Interest has been centered on extending associative learning principles to sets. The strength of a set should increase with the number of training problems, facilitating solution of a problem requiring the set solution, impairing performance on an "extinction" problem requiring a different solution. It has further been argued that completing the "extinction" problem should reduce the strength of a set to the same low level, regardless of the original amount of training (Gardner and Runquist, 1958). Evidence related to these predictions is presented in Figure 6-2. The results were generally in accord with expectations; although performance on a "post-extinction" problem requiring the set solution tended to be better with higher degrees of original training (contrary to expectations), the differences were not statistically reliable. Further support for the acquisition-extinction analysis of set was obtained by Runquist and Sexton (1961), who found that a rest after an "extinction" problem produced spontaneous recovery of set.

Although these findings support an associative analysis of set, other results are difficult to reconcile with this analysis. For example, conditioning usually occurs more rapidly with moderate temporal separation of training trials (distributed practice) than with closely spaced trials (massed practice), but set is stronger after massed presentation of training problems than after distributed practice (Kendler, Greenberg, and Richman, 1952). It would be expected that additional set-inducing trials after an extinction problem should strengthen a set, but such additional practice does not affect the strength of set (Bugelski and Huff, 1962). Adamson (1959) tested another conditioning principle, that partial reinforcement leads to greater resistance to extinction than does continuous reinforcement. In his study, some subjects used the same solution method on all twelve training problems, while others used this method on six problems randomly mixed with six other problems each requiring a different method. On extinction problems requiring new solutions, the partially reinforced subjects performed more poorly, as expected. However, Mayzner (1955) and Mayzner and Tresselt (1956) found exactly the opposite—more set for subjects given continuous training. The reasons for these discrepant results are not apparent, but, in any case, characterizing a mixed training series as equivalent to partial reinforcement seems questionable. Not only is the set solution not reinforced on some problems, but different solution methods are reinforced; Mayzner and Tresselt clearly considered mixed training as developing alternatives to compete with the set solution.

How can these findings be accounted for? No complete explanation is possible (partly because of contradictory findings), but a description which is consistent with many of the results can be outlined. Adopting a set

FIGURE 6–2. *The effect of number of training problems on performance on the last training problem, an extinction problem requiring a new solution, and a post-test problem requiring the set solution.*

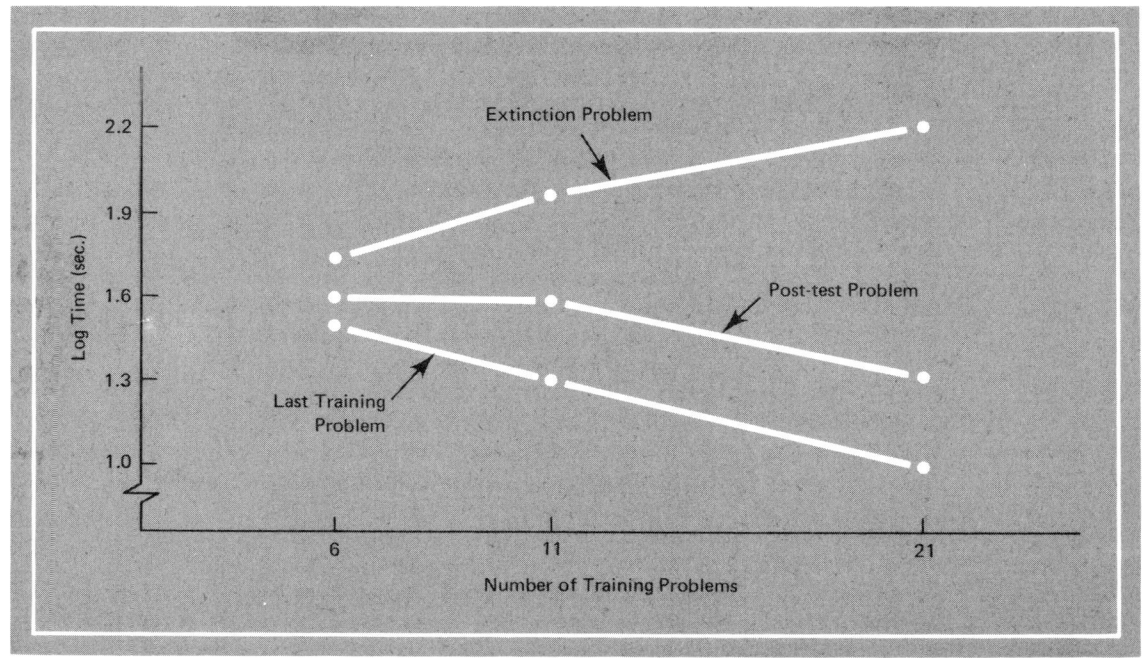

Source: From R. A. Gardner, and W. N. Runquist, Acquisition and extinction of problem-solving set. *Journal of Experimental Psychology,* 1958, **55**, 274-77. Copyright 1958 by the American Psychological Association and reprinted by permission.

is like discovering a concept; the commonality or regularity existing among the training problems is the basis of the set. Identifying the regularity will be easier if the training problems are presented in close succession rather than separated in time, as in distributed practice, or by problems having different solution characteristics, as in mixed training (Underwood, 1952). Increasing the complexity of the set solution should make identification of the regularity more difficult, resulting in a slower adoption of the set, as Bugelski and Huff (1962) demonstrated. As more training problems (exemplars of the concept) are given, it becomes more likely that a subject will notice the regularity and adopt the set. Once the set is adopted, additional training should have little effect.

If a problem solver has been exposed to a series of problems that can be efficiently solved by a simple solution rule (and has discovered that principle), he should be more likely to look for such regularities when a different series of problems is presented. Jacobus and Johnson (1964) obtained such a result; subjects who were first given set training with anagrams were more likely to adopt a set with water-jars problems than subjects given only set training with water jars. The description of the development of set as a process of noticing regularities and adopting a solution method based on them does not require that subjects be able to provide this description of their own behavior for the experimenter. However, Davis and Hess (1962) did find that none of their subjects developed efficient sets below the level of awareness, as indexed by subjects' reports.

Training and Transfer

Attempts to change problem-solving behavior through prior training have involved a wide variety of techniques, ranging from trying to prompt the specific solution to a problem, through teaching solution principles, to having subjects free associate in the hope that they will be more "original" when a problem is subsequently presented. Most investigations have been concerned with attempts to facilitate problem solving, with the notable exception of functional fixedness, which will be considered first.

Functional Fixedness. As a perceptual effect, functional fixedness has already been described—an insight problem is more difficult if the presentation emphasizes an ordinary function for the critical object. As a transfer effect, functional fixedness refers to inhibition in using an object in one function due to recent use of that object in another function (Duncker, 1945). Most researchers have examined subjects' choices of objects in solving an insight problem, usually the two-string problem.

The standard procedure is as follows: The two-string problem is given with both a small electric switch and a small relay available for use as weights to make a pendulum of one string. Prior to the problem, some subjects use the switch to complete an electrical circuit, some use the relay, and others do nothing. The essential finding is that subjects given experience in using one object to complete the circuit tend to use the alternate object to solve the problem, while those just given the problem use each object with equal frequency (Birch and Rabinowitz, 1951).

It is important to note that functional fixedness occurs only when transfer is from an ordinary use of an object to an unusual use. Van de Geer (1957) found that prior use of an object to solve a problem (unusual use) had no effect on its subsequent ordinary use, while Duvall (1965) found facilitation with this sequence of experiences. In a similar vein, Ray (1965) found that functional fixedness could not be produced if the object were highly rated for use in solving the problem. Also, if the subject receives training in unusual uses for the object in addition to using it in an ordinary fashion, functional fixedness is reduced (DiVesta and Walls, 1967a; Flavell, Cooper, and Loiselle, 1958).

Although functional fixedness is sometimes considered a special case of problem-solving set, there are reasons to keep the concepts separate. Functional fixedness refers to an inhibitory effect on problem solving involving perception of the same object in different situations, while set concerns the adoption of the same solution method in different problems, which can aid or impair solution depending on the relationship between the problems. More importantly, functional fixedness and set are differently affected by certain variables. Anderson and Johnson (1966) gave subjects repeated experience with the ordinary function of an object, analogous to set-inducing trials. They found that varying the temporal separation of these experiences produced no change in the amount of functional fixedness observed, in contrast to the greater amount of set found after massed practice, compared to distributed practice. Also, set and functional fixedness exhibit different forgetting functions. If a two-day interval occurs between experience in the ordinary use of an object and presentation of the test problem, functional fixedness is greatly reduced. But, the amount of set does *not* decrease when a comparable delay is introduced between set-inducing training and a test problem. These results thus indicate that set and functional fixedness represent different kinds of behavioral tendencies.

Priming of Solutions. On the basis of the strong effects of solution familiarity on problem difficulty, it would be expected that increasing the familiarity of a solution during a training session should facilitate problem solving. With anagrams, having subjects learn word lists including the solutions results in positive transfer to subsequent problem solving (Dominowski and Ekstrand, 1967). This is true even if subjects are merely exposed to the solutions without instructions to learn and without any indication of the connection between the word list and the anagrams (Mendelsohn and Griswold, 1964). It is also possible to produce effects such as those resulting from sets. Subjects who are shown words associated with the solutions during a training period solve anagrams much faster than control subjects without training, and almost as fast as those shown a list of the solutions (Dominowski and Ekstrand, 1967). As an analogy to the negative effects of set, showing words unrelated to the solutions, but telling subjects that associations exist, leads to subsequent impairment in anagram solving.

Priming effects have also been observed with insight problems, but with less regularity. Judson, Cofer, and Gelfand (1956) found that having subjects learn a word list containing a critical sequence (*rope, swing, pendulum*) facilitated their performance on the two-string problem, but Maltzman, Bellon, and Fishbein (1964) were unable to replicate this result. A quite direct attempt to prime the solution of the two-string problem by giving practice in using the critical object as a pendulum weight does produce positive transfer (DiVesta and Walls, 1967a). Maltzman, Brooks, Bogartz, and Summers (1958) were able to facilitate solution of the two-string problem by providing subjects with unusual uses for the critical object in a prior training session. In an interesting twist on the effects of exposure, requiring subjects to repeat a critical word (*swing*) a number of times in rapid succession—a procedure which leads to loss of meaning for the word (semantic satiation)—results in impairment of performance on the two-string problem (Wakin and Braun, 1966).

A number of other attempts have been made to facilitate solution of insight problems, including demonstrating critical functions, having subjects work on simpler versions of the problem, and having them list uses for the critical object. The findings with respect to these manipulations are so inconsistent that one can have no confidence that any of them work. Such ambiguity suggests that researchers have inadequately characterized the behavior involved in solving insight problems, perhaps also the likely effects of their training methods.

Transfer of Principles. An issue which stems primarily from the Gestalt attack on associative approaches to problem solving concerns the relative effectiveness of training by memorization versus learning principles. That is, a subject may learn the solution to a problem by simply memorizing it, or he may be taught a principle or technique which will enable him to generate the solution to the training problem (and presumably also solutions to other problems). A wide variety of tasks has been used in studies related to this issue, including translation of codes, tasks requiring matchsticks to be rearranged from one pattern to another, and card tricks (e.g., the subject is asked to arrange a deck of four red and four black cards such that, if he alternates between placing the top card on the table and placing the top card at the bottom of the deck, the cards on the table will have the pattern RBRBRBRB; the correct deck order is RRBRRBBB).

The solution principles that a subject learns can have varying degrees of appropriateness to subsequent problems. The comparison of principle training with memorization has yielded some inconsistencies, but one generalization does have some support. Although the different methods of training may be equivalent in terms of recall of the training solution and performance on very similar test problems, there is a tendency for subjects taught solution principles to perform better on transfer problems that are similar to but slightly more difficult than the training problem (Forgus and Schwartz, 1957; Hilgard, Irvine, and Whipple, 1953). However, if the transfer problems are much more complex or fairly dissimilar, learning solution principles will not produce positive transfer unless additional instruction is given (DiVesta and Walls, 1967b; Goldbeck, Bernstein, Hillix, and Marx, 1957; Scandura, 1966).

There are several limitations to keep in mind when interpreting the effects of principle training. For example, principle training is likely to take more time than memorization, which counteracts any advantage on transfer performance due to principle training. Greater control over the degree of learning of principles seems necessary, since some researchers have attributed lack of transfer to inadequate learning of principles (Burack and Moos, 1956). Other investigators have suggested that principle training may result in subjects' being able to state the principle while being unable to use the principle to advantage in solving problems (Corman, 1957; Gagné and Smith, 1962). It has been proposed that subjects will be better able to use a solution principle if they are required to discover it during training rather than if they are told the principle. This proposal has only moderate support; in some cases, better retention and transfer are observed when principles are discovered (e.g., Haselrud and Meyers, 1958), but in others, discovering principles and being taught principles yield equivalent transfer effects (e.g., Forgus and Schwartz, 1957). It seems that if any difference will be observed, principle training will produce better transfer than memorization, and discovery of principles will yield better transfer than teaching of principles. However, in each comparison, the condition associated with superior transfer is also the condition likely to require more training time. Finally, the lack of consistency in these findings indicates that useful distinctions could be made among various solution principles or techniques in terms of adequacy and among training methods in terms of efficiency.

Facilitating Original and Creative Behavior

Original and creative behavior is valued in our society and has been a topic of great interest among psychologists in the past decade. Although originality has been studied primarily in laboratory settings, studies of creativity vary considerably. No attempt will be made here to provide a complete description of the ideas and research in this area; relevant discussions are available elsewhere (Guilford, 1968; Wallach and Kogan, 1965; Taylor, 1962). Rather, emphasis here will be directed toward those aspects of originality and creativity most closely related to problem solving and, in particular, to the attempts which have been made to change this behavior.

An *original response* is one which is statistically infrequent; the originality of a response is inversely related to the frequency with which it is given by a representative group of subjects. Recall that original responses are also described as minimally relevant to the situation, but that, in practice, criteria of relevance play a small part in measuring originality. For behavior to be termed creative, it must be original (statistically infrequent), and, in addition, a problem must be solved or some other criteria of relevance or practicality must be met. Since originality is one of the characteristics of creative behavior, some correspondence between original behavior and creative behavior might be expected. Furthermore, both kinds of behavior might have something in common with problem solving, especially if a problem requires an uncommon solution.

Mednick's (1962) analysis of creativity can be used to indicate the relationships that might be expected among original behavior, creative behavior, and problem solving. According to Mednick's proposal, a highly creative individual is one who has a "flat" associative hierarchy characterized by relatively weak dominant responses, a large number of responses, and a rather even distribution of response "strength" within the hierarchy. Less creative people are described as having "steep" hierarchies with very strong and stereotyped dominant responses and relatively few weaker responses of low strength. Examples of "flat" and "steep" hierarchies are depicted in Figure 6-3.

As you may recall from Chapter 3, Mednick's analysis led him to construct the Remote Associates Test, in which a person must discover a fourth word associatively related to each of three other words he is given. Mednick reasoned that a person capable of producing more associations and more original associations would be more likely to produce the word linking the three words of an item on the test. In like fashion, if a problem requires an unusual solution, the problem solver capable of generating more alternatives and more original alternatives should be more likely to reach the solution (an analysis which seems readily to apply to insight problems). This much is theory; the evidence, some of which

FIGURE 6–3. Hypothetical associative hierarchies for the stimulus word table.

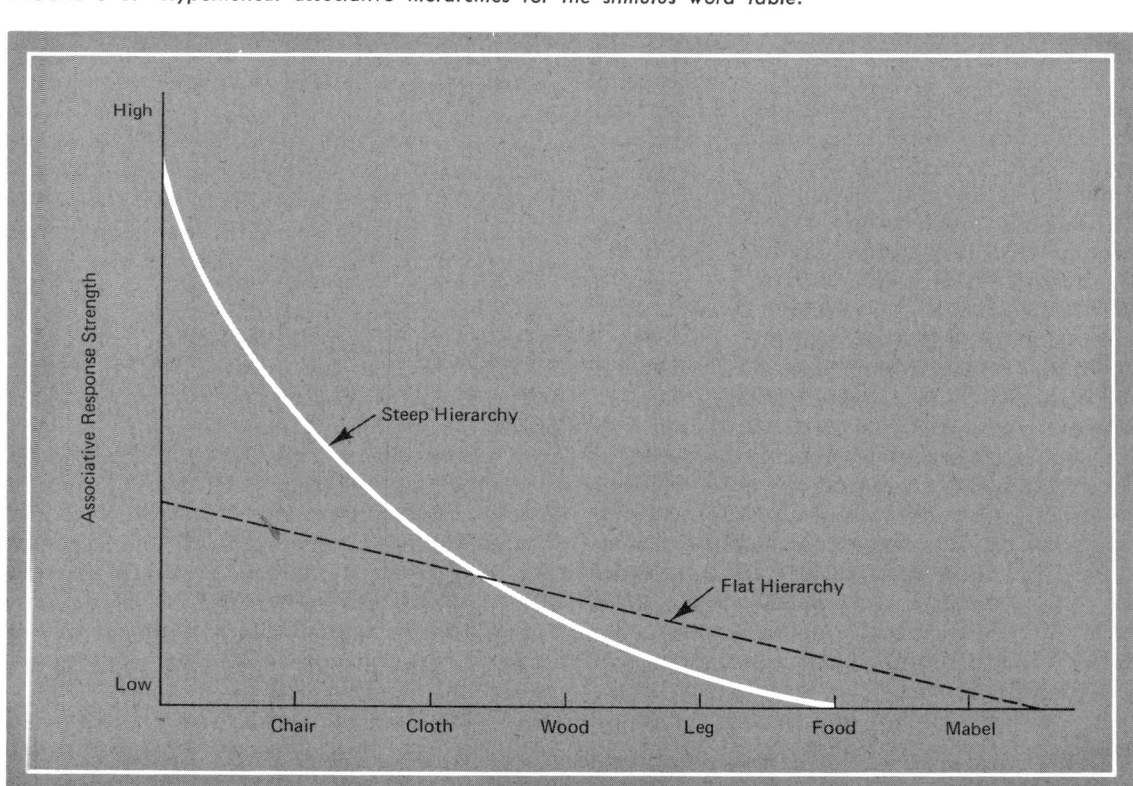

Source: From S. A. Mednick, The associative basis of the creative process. *Psychological Review*, 1962, **69**, 220-32. Copyright 1962 by the American Psychological Association and reprinted by permission.

has already been presented, indicates that this theoretical analysis is incomplete.

Original behavior is typically studied in situations in which subjects are asked to free associate, give uses for objects, generate plot titles, and so forth. In such situations, the originality of performance increases as subjects continue working. That is, early responses are common or stereotyped, whereas later responses are more original (Wallach and Kogan, 1965; Wilson, Guilford, and Christensen, 1953). Keep in mind that an original response is one that is statistically infrequent; however, original responses tend to be rated as "unusual" by judges. People who give more answers also give more original responses; in other words, one can tell how original a person's answers are by determining how many answers he gives (relative to other individuals).

Let us now turn to the more critical questions. Do people who give more original responses also perform better on the Remote Associates Test? Mednick's analysis predicts that they would, but the evidence tends to indicate otherwise. Although Mednick reported some preliminary findings of a positive relationship between test performance and the production of original associates, Maltzman, Belloni, and Fishbein (1964) found that high and low scorers on the Remote Associates Test had virtually identical associative hierarchies, in terms of originality, in giving six successive associations to stimulus words. More generally, individual differences in output on free-responding tasks seem to be essentially unrelated to individual differences in performance on tasks having a specific solution, including the Remote Associates Test (e.g., Taft and Rossiter, 1966; Wilson, Guilford, and Christensen, 1953). Is performance on Mednick's test related to solving insight problems, as was suggested? The answer was given earlier: Danks and Glucksberg (1966) found no relationship.

In summary, although producing responses that are original is a necessary component of producing creative responses, it appears that individual differences in originality account for a very small part of differences in creativity. As Gestalt theorists suggested in their analysis of productive thinking, simply being able to produce many ideas and original ideas does not guarantee that relevant ideas will be generated or appropriately combined when criteria of practicality or problem solution are applied. Generating a creative idea, because the idea must satisfy some criterion of relevance, resembles solving a problem, although a problem might require a rather ordinary solution. Some relationship between these behaviors is indicated by the finding that subjects who give a solution judged "creative" to a problem having other solutions also perform better on several problems, each of which has a single, objective solution (Maier and Janzen, 1969). Two comments about the Remote Associates Test seem in order. First, performance on the test is related to performance in several fields. For example, high scorers on the test tend to be more productive researchers as indicated by criteria such as publications and patents (Mednick and Mednick, 1967). Second, Mednick's analysis of performance on the test is generally not supported by the evidence. Rather than emphasizing the similarities of original behavior and test performance, stressing their differences seems more appropriate. Studies of transfer effects support the distinction.

Prompting Original Behavior. It is fairly easy to make people more original (as it has been defined here). The most direct approach is to *ask* them to be original in giving uses for objects, titles for plots, etc. Compared to subjects instructed simply to give uses for an object, those instructed to be original give a smaller number of uses but a larger number of original uses (Manske and Davis, 1968). Similar results have been reported with respect to the effects of instructions to be "clever" in producing plot titles (Christensen, Guilford, and Wilson, 1957).

A different approach to increasing originality is based on the fact that subjects produce more original responses as they continue working on the task. The standard procedure has been to present stimulus words repeatedly, with subjects required to give a different association to each presentation (Maltzman, (1960). Of course, successive associations tend to be more original; primary interest lies in the transfer effects of such training. This training procedure has been found to increase originality on subsequent free-association tests (e.g., Maltzman, Bogartz, and Breger, 1958) and on giving uses for objects (e.g., Maltzman, Simon, Raskin, and Licht, 1960). The importance of repeated responding to the same stimulus word was demonstrated by Maltzman et al. (1960). A training procedure involving associating once to each of 125 words was compared with the standard procedure of associating 5 times to each of 25 words, giving a different association each time. Both procedures resulted in greater originality on a subsequent free-association test, but only the repeated-responding procedure yielded more original behavior in giving uses.

Maltzman's associative interpretation of these findings was outlined in Chapter 3. The occurrence of an original response is viewed as self-reinforcing, and associative connections are postulated among original responses. Consequently, the occurrence of some original responses should increase the likelihood that other original responses will occur via mediated generalization. Other researchers have suggested that originality transfer effects are related to subjects' expectancies regarding the task they are to perform.

Levy (1968) proposed that the effectiveness of originality training is a function of the degree to which the role of an original person is described for the subject. He found that originality on a training task and on a transfer test was an increasing function of the amount of original-role information provided. A role interpretation is consistent with the effects of instructions to be original, but the more interesting feature of this view concerns the effect of reinforcement. Levy found that simply giving verbal reinforcement ("good, fine") for unusual responses during training (without instructions about playing an original role) resulted both in increased originality and in subjects' perceiving their role in the experiment as that of an original person. The greatest originality and transfer occurred when subjects were both instructed to play an original role and reinforced for unusual responses during training; Levy's interpretation is that reinforcement provided information about how well subjects were playing the role. It is important to note that Levy obtained increased originality on a transfer test without requiring subjects to give different responses to repeated presentations of stimuli during training. His results emphasize once again the importance of instructions in determining behavior and indicate the utility of considering subjects' expectancies in descriptive accounts.

Although these findings are encouraging, there are limitations on the effectiveness of these training procedures. Maltzman's standard training procedure has not always increased originality on other tasks (Maltzman et al., 1958), and practice at giving uses does not appear to produce transfer effects to either uses tests or free association (Maltzman et al., 1960). An important question is whether or not such techniques can be used to facilitate behavior other than that of simply giving original responses. Earlier in this chapter, it was pointed out that neither free associating nor giving uses, even with instructions to be original, seems to have any facilitating effect on solution of insight problems.

Transfer to the Remote Associates Test. Based on the (apparently incorrect) idea that success on the Remote Associates Test is largely a function of producing unusual associations, originality training would be expected to facilitate test performance. However, associative practice with stimulus words unrelated to test solutions has no effect on test performance (Caron, Unger, and Parloff, 1963; Maltzman, Belloni, and Fishbein, 1964).

If subjects associate to a word related to the solution of a test item just prior to attempting the item, then facilitation is observed and is directly related to the number of associations they are asked to give (Maltzman, Belloni, and Fishbein, 1964). But, simply increasing subjects' tendencies to give unusual associations does not aid test performance.

Additional studies have produced further complexities. Freedman (1965) argued that Maltzman's training technique was ineffective because success on the test requires thinking of many associations, including common ones, in a short time, rather than producing unusual associations. Freedman proposed that giving subjects practice in producing short bursts of associations would facilitate test performance, and he obtained evidence supporting his expectation. By any method of analysis, one must concede that the Remote Associates Test is most like itself, yet Maltzman, Belloni, and Fishbein (1964) found that practice on a number of test items had no effect on subsequent performance on other test items. While these findings seem to defy explanation, the essential point of this discussion should not be missed. Techniques which quite readily increase the production of original responses do not facilitate performance on the Remote Associates Test. Some reasons for the differential effects will now be presented.

Increasing Creativity. Why should it be so easy to increase originality yet so difficult to increase creativity? The answer seems to be that there are a great many original or unusual ideas, but only a very few, perhaps only one, will also meet the criteria of relevance or practicality imposed on a creative response. Suppose that there are 10,000 original ideas potentially available, 2 of which meet the criteria of revelance needed for a creative solution, and suppose further that a subject, in a typical working period, will produce 20 of these ideas. His chances of producing a creative idea are about 1 in 250. If he doubles his output of original ideas, which would not be easy but could be accomplished, his chances of generating a creative idea improve to about 1 in 125. The point is that, despite a huge increase in originality, the subject would still be very likely to fail to produce a creative idea.

Varying the instructions given to subjects in a free-responding task yields results consistent with this analysis. Subjects instructed to be original in listing uses for an object give more original uses, as mentioned earlier, but they produce no greater number of "creative" (original *and* practical) uses than subjects given ordinary instructions (Manske and Davis, 1968). In other words, most original ideas are impractical. A similar finding was obtained by Johnson, Parrott, and Stratton (1967), who compared the quality of solutions given by subjects instructed to give only one solution to that for subjects asked to give many solutions. The multiple-solution group produced a greater number of superior solutions, even though the average quality of their solutions was lower. Thus, instructions to produce many solutions yielded more solutions at all quality levels. An interesting finding concerned a third group instructed to produce many solutions and then select the best; their selections were better than others they produced but not as good as those produced by the single-solution group. It was suggested that training in judging the quality of one's solutions might be needed to produce solutions of high quality.

This emphasis on instructions and judgment is relevant to the idea of "brainstorming" proposed by Osborn (1957), which has led to the development of courses in creative thinking. *Brainstorming* is characterized by instructions to produce a large quantity of ideas, to think of "wild" ideas, to withhold judgment of the quality of ideas (criticism), and to think of ways of improving ideas proposed by others or of combining two or more ideas. Subjects taking courses based on these ideas usually score higher on various tests of creativity than those not enrolled (Parnes,

1962), but these differences are difficult to interpret because of the complexity of the treatment. Preliminary analyses have indicated that such courses have little effect on academic achievement (Parnes, 1962), but it is not clear what effect should be expected, if any. Other studies have been concerned with some of the features of brainstorming.

In brainstorming, participants are encouraged to think of "wild" ideas, based on the assumption that more creative ideas will be produced. However, subjects instructed to "use their wildest imagination" in listing uses for objects, although producing the largest total number of uses, give no more "creative" uses than any other group (Manske and Davis, 1968). Another feature of brainstorming is the avoidance of criticism; the notion is that judging the quality of ideas will inhibit production and thus creativity. It appears that imposing judgmental restrictions does reduce the number of ideas produced. Instructing subjects to be both original and practical in listing uses results in fewer uses being given (Manske and Davis, 1968), and practice in judging plot titles produces a slight decrease in the number of titles subsequently written for a test story (Johnson and Zerbolio, 1964). However, there is no reduction in the number of good (original and useful or relevant) ideas produced in either case.

Brainstorming also involves working in groups, with emphasis on the advantage of having one person's production stimulated by the ideas of other members of the group. Quite in contrast to this proposal, Taylor, Berry, and Block (1958) found that, while groups of four were superior to individuals working alone; the pooled efforts of four individuals working alone were much better than those of real groups in terms of number of ideas, number of unique ideas, and quality of ideas. These investigators suggested two reasons that brainstorming might be inhibited in groups. One is that, despite instructions to avoid criticism, participants might feel less free from criticism in groups than when they work alone. The second is that members of a group tend to adopt the same set or approach to a task, which is likely to reduce the number of different ideas produced. As often seems to be true of complex treatments, these results demonstrate that, while brainstorming courses might improve the production of creative ideas, the various features of the course can facilitate, impair, or have no effect on this behavior.

An important feature of brainstorming and other training techniques is extended practice. More original and more creative ideas will be produced as the amount of time spent working on the task increases. The rate of producing clever or "creative" ideas appears to be fairly constant over the working period, with no indication that subjects are running out of ideas (see Figure 3-7). Thus, keeping people working on a task for an extended period, even past the point at which they feel their supply of ideas has been exhausted, is likely to result in the production of more creative ideas.

Providing a changed context for subjects to work in can also have positive effects. Davis and Manske (1966) instructed subjects to imagine themselves in a particular situation (for example, at a picnic) and to list uses for an object (e.g., a screwdriver) in that situation. Compared to subjects simply asked to list uses, those given a situational set produced more uses, more original uses, and more creative (original and useful) uses. It was suggested that the improved performance was due to the subjects' being forced to consider previously unrelated ideas contiguously.

Mednick (1962) noted that one way to achieve a creative solution is through accidental contiguity of remote ideas. He gave the example of a scientist who keeps a fishbowl filled with slips of paper, each containing some concept or fact. At regular intervals, the scientist draws some slips from the bowl and tries to find a relationship among the concepts or facts selected. The results of the study by Davis and Manske (1966) suggest that such techniques might well lead to productive outcomes.

Comment

A number of general statements can be made about transfer effects in problem solving. It is clear that transfer depends on specificity of the relationship between prior experience and the transfer task. For example, if a subject works on a series of problems that can be solved by using a specific solution rule or technique, he will adopt this method, with the result that performance on problems for which the method is appropriate will be facilitated, but performance on problems requiring different approaches will be impaired. In contrast, if the only relationship among a series of problems is that they are of the same type, changes in problem-solving behavior are less likely to occur, although subjects do sometimes learn strategies which can be applied to a broad class of problems.

The probable effects of deliberate attempts to train subjects to solve problems vary in similar fashion. Training will produce positive transfer if, during training, the subject is familiarized with the solution to a problem or learns a principle which can be applied rather straightforwardly to a test problem. If the principle requires modification to be applied to a test problem, then positive transfer is less likely. Finally, training which, at best, could be expected to produce only a very general kind of transfer (such as by increasing the subject's tendency to produce original ideas) tends to have little effect on subsequent problem solving. The research on original and creative behavior suggests why this should be the case. In any situation, many original ideas are possible, but only a very small number of these will also satisfy criteria of relevance or practicality. Thus, while it is fairly easy to increase the production of original ideas, the chances of generating a creative idea or the specific idea required to solve a problem are rather remote.

SUMMARY

In this section, an attempt will be made to summarize briefly the findings of research on problem solving, to suggest some directions for future research, and to indicate how problem solving is related to verbal learning, conceptual behavior, and language. A problem exists when an initial state must be altered, and the subject must find the correct way to produce the desired change by perhaps first generating and then selecting from a number of alternative courses of action. Solving the problem will be more difficult as the number of alternative solution possibilities increases. If the subject is given additional information about the problem or has learned or been taught an appropriate solution method, the number of alternatives that he will consider will be reduced, and he will solve the problem more efficiently. Familiar or simple solutions will be found more easily than unusual or complex solutions. The way in which the problem is presented may suggest certain courses of action which can either mislead or aid the subject in finding the solution; some problem situations are so well organized that they seem to inhibit the subject's thinking of ways to alter them and find a solution. A problem solver's chances for success are clearly dependent on the amount of relevant knowledge he possesses and, perhaps more importantly, on his skills in selecting the right ideas; in addition to such ability factors, the subject's motivational level must be appropriate for the task. In describing the subject, not only must one pay attention to the influence of long term experience, but one must also consider any changes in knowledge, skills, or motivation that have been produced by very recent experiences.

The precision and generality of the information relevant to the several parts of this description vary considerably. The task for future research is to refine the information about each part of the description and to fit the pieces together into an adequate theory of problem solving. With respect to this endeavor, three comments seem in order. First, investigators must concern themselves with developing a useful taxonomy of problems. Achieving this goal will be dependent on creating an accurate picture of each task and on research deliberately directed toward identifying the similarities and differences among problems. Second, there appear to be no good reasons for continuing to investigate one factor at a time. Rather, interactions among variables should be studied, particularly those between "task" factors and "subject" factors. Third, researchers ought to obtain more information about the solution process, rather than limit data collection to indices of difficulty. Interrogating subjects or using tasks which "automatically" provide such information are two ways of satisfying this criterion. Researchers have simply been negligent in not using these techniques. Finding out how subjects approach a problem can enable an investigator to identify a potentially useful "subject" factor to be included in subsequent studies. Of course, describing the solution process is the basic goal of research, and any method which might provide relevant data should be tried.

These suggestions for research specify methods already in frequent use in the study of conceptual behavior. In this field, researchers employ only a small number of well-characterized tasks, tend to perform complex experiments, and make a noticeable effort to determine how their subjects work on the tasks. The advantages of this approach will be obvious when conceptual behavior is discussed in later chapters.

In discussing problem solving, frequent references were made to the relationship among ideas or the organization of a subject's knowledge. Traditionally, the study of verbal learning has been viewed as providing information about how this organization should be characterized and how it develops with experience. These topics will be discussed in the chapters to follow. Furthermore, research based on the more recent view of verbal-learning tasks as problems will be described. According to this view, the subject comes to a learning task with a wealth of knowledge and skills and makes use of these in trying to discover an efficient way of learning the material.

Concern for the organization and use of knowledge leads quite naturally to the topic of language; Chomsky (1968) has proposed that an understanding of human mental organization depends on an understanding of human language. Some examples of the influence of language on problem solving have already been cited (e.g., words as anagrams, labels, and functional fixedness). In later chapters, interest will be centered on what it means to know a language and how a person acquires this knowledge. Some aspects of language acquisition have been viewed as concept attainment (e.g., learning the meanings of words), while other aspects can be fruitfully described as the acquisition of a rule for performing a creative act—generating grammatical sentences. As these behaviors are described, look for characteristics of problem solving and attempt to determine whether the important features of a problem situation can be identified in verbal-learning, conceptual, and linguistic tasks.

III Verbal Learning

Seven Tasks, Variables, and Processes

Is solving a problem really a matter of eliciting the correct associations? Is the stream of conscious thought really a concatenation of associations? As we have indicated in Chapter 2, associationism represents the most important philosophical precursor of the scientific psychology of thinking. As developed by the British empiricists, the formation of associations was the fundamental process in acquiring knowledge, and the exercise of associations was thought itself. As we have seen in the preceding chapters on problem solving, modern analyses of thinking have been strongly influenced by this tradition. Under this view the analysis of the basic process of association then becomes a major goal of a scientific analysis of thinking. The empirical analysis began, as we have seen, with the work of Hermann Ebbinghaus on the nature of verbal learning and memory. It is to that tradition that we now turn our attention.

In this chapter, we will examine the tasks that are customarily employed in verbal-learning research, the variables known to influence the rate of learning, and the processes that are invoked to explain verbal-learning phenomena. The major goal of verbal-learning research has been to understand the conditions for the formation and utilization of associations; the goal has not been to understand verbal behavior in general. Verbal-learning research *per se* should not be expected to contribute directly to an understanding of linguistic behaviors such as speaking and understanding grammatical sentences. In a very real sense, the ultimate applicability of the concepts and phenomena of verbal learning will be principally toward an understanding of human thought, and not toward the understanding of linguistic behavior, except indirectly through the interaction of language and thought. From the basic philosophy of associationism, the study of thinking must begin with a thorough analysis of associations, and modern research on verbal learning represents the most sophisticated and rigorous analysis of associations that is being done today.

TASKS AND METHODS

Types of Tasks

Paired-Associate Learning. The most often employed task in verbal-learning research is paired-associate learning. The very name of the task seems to embody the basic goal of verbal-learning psychology. A pair of verbal items is presented to the subject and his task is to develop an association between them. Thus, we might present the subject with two nonsense syllables, *BOT* and *DAP*, allow him to study the pair for some specified amount of time, and then test him to see if an association was formed. The test would most likely consist of presenting one of the items and asking the subject to say the other one; we present *BOT* and see if the subject says *DAP*. The original thinking is that if an association has been developed, presentation of one item will elicit the other item, or it will tend to be followed by the subject's saying the other item (to state a more conservative view). It can be seen, then, that paired-associate learning seems to be studying the most basic process of thinking, stripped of all its glamour.

In actual fact, a paired-associate experiment almost always employs a list of several associations. A typical paired-associate task is illustrated in Table 7-1. Briefly, there is a list of pairs of words, the left-hand member of each pair is typically called the stimulus and the right-hand member is the response. The stimulus, of course, is the item that is

TABLE 7-1. Two Presentations Methods for a Typical Paired-Associate Learning Task

List of Pairs	Anticipation Method	Recall Method
		----------------
grass-chalk	grass	study trial
house-loyal	grass-chalk	----------------
mountain-horse	house	grass-chalk
table-window	house-loyal	house-loyal
rug-fog	mountain	mountain-horse
top-baseball	mountain-horse	table-window
	table	rug-fog
	table-window	top baseball
	rug	----------------
	rug-fog	end study; begin test
	top	----------------
	top-baseball	house
		rug
		table
		grass
		top
		mountain

The center column illustrates the sequence of events under the anticipation method, and the right-hand column illustrates the recall method. The events are presented one at a time, usually at a controlled rate with a machine called a memory drum.

presented to the subject during a test for association, and the response is the item that the subject is supposed to say; for example, on test trials, when the experimenter presents the stimulus *grass,* the subject must say *chalk* in order to be correct. Typically, the stimuli are presented in a random order and in a different order on each trial of the task. As in most verbal-learning tasks, learning is indexed by the number of correct responses on each trial or by the number of trials it takes for a subject to reach some arbitrary performance criterion, usually one perfect recitation of the list.

Two presentation and test methods customarily employed in paired-associate learning are illustrated in Table 7-1. In the *anticipation method,* the stimulus is presented and the subject attempts to anticipate the correct response. This is followed by presentation of the correct response paired with the stimulus. The subject sees *grass,* attempts to respond, and then sees *grass-chalk.* The first interval, in which only the stimulus is presented, is known as the anticipation interval and it constitutes the test for learning. The second interval, when *grass-chalk* is presented, is the study interval during which time the subject receives feedback about his response and attempts to memorize the pair.

The second method is known as the *study-test method* or the *recall method.* This method completely separates the study and test portions of the task. The subject is first shown all of the pairs in the list for a study trial. This is followed by a test trial where the stimuli are presented one at a time and the subject attempts to give the correct response for each stimulus. The subject, however, does not get information about the correct response until the next study trial. Interestingly, despite this lack of immediate feedback, the recall method typically leads to slightly faster learning than the anticipation method (Battig, 1965; Cofer, Diamond, Olsen, Stein, and Walker, 1967).

The major advantage of the paired-associate task is that it seems to identify the stimulus clearly and it makes a clear distinction between stimuli and responses. The experimenter, therefore, has a reasonably good idea as to what the stimulus is for each response, and since the stimuli are different from the responses, he can manipulate stimulus variables independently of response variables. These distinctions and manipulations are important if one has a theory that involves these entities and their properties.

Serial Learning. Serial learning presents the subject with the task of learning a list of items in the exact order in which they were presented. The experimenter selects a list of items, randomly orders them, and then presents the list to the subject in this order on every trial. For example, the list might consist of *grass, chalk, house, mountain, loyal,* and *horse.* In the anticipation method, the subject sees the units, one at a time, in order; as each unit appears he attempts to anticipate the next unit in order. In the recall method, the experimenter shows the list for a study trial after which the subject tries to say (or write down) the units in order without any feedback from the experimenter until the next study trial. Ostensibly, each item is the stimulus for the next item, which in turn is the stimulus for the succeeding item. Thus each item is both a stimulus and a response, making independent manipulation of stimulus and response variables impossible in a serial-learning task. Although this is similar to the technique originally used by Ebbinghaus, this task has fallen into disfavor as a means for analyzing associative learning.

Free-Recall Learning. Free-recall learning is similar to serial learning in that the subject is confronted with a list of items and is required to learn them. However, free recall does not require that the subject recall the units in the order in which they were presented. He is free to recall them in any order he wishes, and typically the experimenter presents the items in a different order on each trial. In this task, it is not at all clear what is associated with what as we will see in the next chapter.

Associative Matching. The associative matching task is very much like the paired-associate task, differing only in the manner of testing. In matching, as the name implies, one tests the subject by presenting him with the stimuli and the responses (typically in two separate columns on a sheet of paper), and his task is to match each response with its stimulus. Matching is most often done with the alternate study and test procedure; however, some work has been done using an anticipation technique where one stimulus is presented along with perhaps three alternative responses and the subject must select the correct one from among the three. It then becomes identical to the multiple-choice or multiple-guess tests that are so infamous among college students.

Verbal-Discrimination Learning. Verbal-discrimination experiments typically confront the subject with a list of pairs of verbal units. The subject, however, is not required to learn an association between the two members of a pair. Instead, the experimenter has arbitrarily selected one unit in each pair as the correct unit and the subject must learn which unit is correct for each pair. This, of course, can also be done with triplets or quadruples, etc. A pair might be *grass-loyal* and for that pair, *loyal* might be the correct unit. In the anticipation method, the subject sees *grass-loyal* and attempts to select the correct unit, after which the experimenter indicates which of the two words was the correct one. In the recall method, the subject is shown each pair on a study trial with the correct item indicated by underlining. This is followed by a test trial where each pair is presented (without underlining) and the subject attempts to say the correct item in each pair. The subject is thus learning to discriminate between two verbal items such that he can say one of them (the correct item) and inhibit saying the incorrect item—hence, the name verbal discrimination.

The Two-Stage Analysis of Paired-Associate Learning

The paired-associate task has become the model for verbal-learning research. That is, a major goal in verbal-learning research is to determine what processes are involved in learning a paired-associate list, what variables influence paired-associate learning, and how the variables exert their influence on such learning.

In 1959, Underwood, Runquist, and Schulz proposed a two-stage model of paired-associate learning that has subsequently had great theoretical usefulness in the analysis of verbal learning. The first stage is known as the *response-learning* stage. During this stage, the subject learns what the responses are in the list. Referring to Table 7-1, the subject is learning that the responses are *chalk, loyal, horse, window, fog,* and *baseball,* a rather easy task for most college students. But suppose the responses were six trigrams of maximum difficulty, *JZH, ZHQ, HJZ, ZJQ, QHJ,* and *JQZ.* Now just learning what the six responses are becomes a very burdensome task.

The second stage is known as the *associative stage,* the stage during which an association is learned between each stimulus and its response. At the end of the response-learning stage, the subject knows that *chalk, loyal, horse,* etc., are the responses but does not know which response goes with which stimulus word. It is during the associative stage that he "connects" each response that has been learned with its stimulus.

The two-stage model merely says that both kinds of learning are necessary before the subject can perform correctly in a paired-associate task; it does not say that the two stages are completely separated in time. That is, response learning is not necessarily completed before the onset of associative learning. For example, the subject may be associating a learned response word with its stimulus before he has learned all of the other response words in the list. In addition, it is possible that part of a response is learned and associated with its stimulus before the entire response is acquired. Suppose the pair was *grass-JZH;* the subject might know that *grass* goes with a trigram that begins with *J* before he has learned the other two letters in the trigram.

The major value of the two-stage analysis comes from the fact that variables can have different effects on the two stages, perhaps facilitating one and inhibiting the other. Thus, the overall effect of a variable on paired-associate learning may be obscured and perhaps not even noticed due to the counteracting effects. One might then erroneously conclude that the variable was of no interest in verbal learning. It is necessary, therefore, to attempt to determine the effect of the variable separately for the two stages or components of paired-associate learning. Free-recall learning presumably is closely related to the response-learning stage of paired-associate learning such that if a variable is known to inhibit or retard free recall, it will probably inhibit the response-learning stage of paired-associate learning (see Ekstrand, 1966). Similarly, associative matching is presumably measuring the associative-stage component of paired-associate learning without the response-learning component since the subject is provided with a list of responses in the matching task. Thus, if a variable inhibits or retards matching performance, it will probably inhibit the associative stage of paired-associate learning. By determining the independent effects of a variable on response learning (using free recall) and on associative learning (using matching), one can then make a prediction about the effect of this variable on overall paired-associate learning.

An example of the direct application of this strategy to the analysis of the effect of a variable on paired-associate learning comes from the work of Underwood, Ekstrand, and Keppel (1965). The variable in question was *conceptual similarity*. This refers to the fact that some or all of the words in a paired-associate list are similar to each other in that they are instances of the same concept. For example, high conceptual similarity might be defined by the fact that all of the words in the list were names of animals. Underwood, Ekstrand, and Keppel demonstrated that high conceptual similarity facilitated free-recall learning (i.e., it is easier to learn a list of animal names than a list of unrelated words) and that it retarded the acquisition of a matching task. From these results one can now predict the effect of increasing conceptual similarity on overall paired-associate learning. If the conceptual similarity is manipulated in the paired-associate task on the response side only (all responses are the names of animals, but the stimuli are not conceptually related) we can expect that (1) increasing the similarity will facilitate the response-learning stage, but (2) this will be accompanied by a corresponding interfering effect on the associative stage. The net effect of these two opposing trends will determine the effect on overall learning. In the Underwood, Ekstrand, and Keppel experiment, the net effect was essentially zero, indicating counteractive cancelling of the positive effect on response learning by the negative effect on associative learning.

The two-stage analysis has an additional implication which may be seen if one attempts to predict the overall effect of conceptual similarity when it is manipulated on the stimulus side of a paired-associate list (e.g., all the stimuli are animal names and the responses are unrelated). Presumably, the subject learning a paired-associate list does not have to learn what the stimuli are in the list, i.e., there is no stimulus-learning stage. As a result there will not be a positive effect of conceptual similarity to cancel out the negative effect on associative learning expected on the basis of the matching experiment. Therefore, we can predict that increasing the conceptual similarity of the stimuli will result in an overall reduction in the speed of paired-associate learning. This is exactly what Underwood, Ekstrand, and Keppel found. The two-stage analysis of paired-associate learning implies that whenever a variable is known to affect both response learning *and* associative learning, the effect of manipulating this variable will depend on whether it is varied among the stimuli or among the responses. If the variable influences only associative learning, then the implication is that the variable will have about the same effect on the stimulus side as on the response side. If the variable affects only response learning, it will have an effect on paired-associate learning only if it is manipulated on the response side.

There has been some concern expressed about the fact that the two-stage analysis of paired-associate learning ignores stimulus-learning processes. For example, it is known that subjects often learn a great deal about the stimuli—after learning a paired-associate list they can recall rather well what the stimuli were (Newman and Gray, 1964). While the nature of the paired-associate task may seem to make stimulus learning unnecessary, subjects apparently do learn something about the stimuli as units. Furthermore, recent evidence indicates that at the very least, the subject must learn enough about a stimulus so that he can recognize it on a later trial as being a stimulus he saw earlier. If he fails to recognize an old stimulus, he will not be able to respond at any level above chance correctness (Bernbach, 1967; Martin, 1967). Furthermore, stimulus-oriented processes seem to assume more importance as the similarity of the stimuli is manipulated, as, for example, when all the stimuli are animal names.

Some theorists have suggested that the subjects must complete a stimulus differentiation or discrimination stage in order to overcome the generalization that might result among similar stimuli. Suppose the stimuli were those trigrams mentioned earlier: *JZH, ZHQ, HJZ, ZJQ, QHJ,* and *JQZ*. These units are so similar that subjects might have difficulty telling one from the other. Perhaps the subject must learn to discriminate among the various stimuli before he can proceed to associate a particular response with a particular stimulus and perform correctly. Without the discrimination, the amount of generalization among the stimuli would be massive and would prevent the subject from responding reliably.

One could argue, however, that this discrimination process is really just a part of the associative stage or a description of what might go on during the associative stage and is not a separate stage in itself. The question would probably be settled if we could demonstrate that there are variables which have one effect on a stimulus-discrimination stage and a different effect on an associative stage. Such a demonstration would clearly make it useful to identify a stimulus-discrimination stage (or a stimulus-recognition stage or a stimulus-differentiation stage) separate from the associative stage. Verbal-discrimination learning may be of some use in the study of stimulus-oriented processes, for it may be measuring a stimulus discrimination process free from any response learning or associative learning. This is because the verbal-discrimination task does not require the subject to learn any responses or associations.

Generally, it will probably be worthwhile to entertain the notion of some kind of stimulus-learning process, realizing that such a process may not be independent of the associative stage. For a recent review of the work on stages of paired-associate learning and paired-associate learning research in general, the reader should consult the excellent summary provided by Battig (1968). Battig has suggested *ten* possible processes in paired-associate learning!

A MODEST THEORETICAL ORIENTATION

At this point it will be convenient to present a small bit of theory around which the reader may wish to organize his thinking about verbal learning. Verbal-learning theorists have placed heavy emphasis on mediational mechanisms of one variety or another. Basically, a mediating response can be defined as a response that possesses stimulus properties, i.e., a response that may serve as a stimulus for another response. What will be presented here is a particular variety of mediational theory developed specifically for verbal-learning phenomena. It has proved useful in developing an understanding of these phenomena and therefore deserves our consideration. It will also provide the reader with a good example of the general type of theory that is used in verbal learning, based on strictly associative principles.

When a stimulus unit (e.g., the word *loyal*) is presented to a subject, he must make some response in the act of perceiving the unit. He must encode that stimulus in some manner that results in the stimulus' being represented "inside his head." It is easiest to think about this response as the perceptual response to a verbal unit. This has been called the *representational response* (Bousfield, Whitmarsh, and Danick, 1958), the response required to represent the external stimulus in the internal environment. Typically, these perceptual or representational responses are veridical (truthful) perceptions with respect to what the experimenter intends the stimulus to be. Thus, presenting the word *loyal* will result in the representational response of *loyal* (it is as if the subject says to himself, "loyal"). However, we can imagine situations where this response is not a veridical representation of the external stimulus but represents some misperception or transformation of the stimulus. If the stimuli are those highly similar trigrams, *JZH, ZHQ, HJZ*, etc., it could easily happen that the representational response to *JZH* could turn out to be something like *JZQ*. Or as suggested by Deese (1965), subjects can respond to very rare words as if they were not so rare words (e.g., *abbess* gets represented as *abyss*). Transformations of the stimulus also result when a subject represents a letter sequence as a word, as, for example, when the subject represents the trigram *JOK* as the implicit representational response of *joke* and not as a spelled trigram, *J-O-K*. With certain materials, great differences can be expected depending on whether the subject represents the stimulus by spelling or by pronouncing.

A second kind of implicit response occurs to the stimulus properties of the representational response. Since the representational response possesses stimulus properties, it meets the definition of a mediational response, a response that can serve as a stimulus for another response. Underwood (1965) has put the label, *implicit associative response,* on the response to the stimulus properties of the representational response. The associative response to a representational response is likely to be a response with strong pre-existing associative strength to the representational response. For example, if the representational response is *loyal,* the implicit associative response might be *faithful.* As Underwood indicates, if the representational response is a word, the implicit associative response is most likely to be a frequent response to that word in a free-association test. Presentation of the word *table* will thus result in the representational response of *table* which will probably be followed by the implicit associative response of *chair.* It is also possible that several associative responses are made to a representational response under some circumstances, i.e., each implicit associative response is a mediational response that can lead to still another associative response. The sequence of these associative responses must be inferred from other performances, of course, most likely from continuous free-association norms where the subject is presented one word and is required to "reel off" a series of associations. The information available about the structural nature of associations (Deese, 1962 and 1965) also contributes toward an identification of these implicit-associative-response sequences.

Underwood (1965) has presented evidence supporting the utility of this concept in the interpretation of verbal memory. Briefly, subjects were read a list of 200 words, and as each word was read they were required to indicate whether or not the word had occurred earlier in the list. Underwood reasoned that presentation of the word *hot* would result in the representational response *hot* followed most likely by the implicit associative response *cold.* If later in the list the word *cold* was actually presented, it would result in the representa-

TABLE 7–2. An Illustration of the Procedure Designed to Produce False Recognitions

Words Presented	Representational Response	Possible Implicit Associative Response	Relation
hot · · · · · ·	hot	cold	antonym
Test: cold	cold	hot	
dark heavy lamp match · · · · · ·	dark heavy lamp match	light light light light	converging associates
Test: light	light	dark	
maple oak elm birch · · · · ·	maple oak elm birch	tree tree tree tree	superordinate
Test: tree	tree	oak	
atom cabin germ gnat village · · · · ·	atom cabin germ gnat village	small small small small small	sense impression
Test: small	small	large	

The solid arrows indicate the basis for confusion that would lead to a false recognition as suggested by Underwood (1965). The dashed arrows indicate an alternative explanation of the confusion.

tional response *cold* and the subject would then attempt to determine if *cold* had occurred earlier. If *cold* had occurred earlier as an implicit associative response, the subject could be expected to confuse it with the highly similar representational response of *cold,* leading him to indicate that indeed *cold* had occurred earlier in the list. In other words, Underwood was asking if the presentation of *hot* would lead the subjects to believe (at some later time) that *cold* had actually been presented. The results of the study strongly supported this hypothesis; subjects very often would indicate that a word had occurred earlier when in fact it did not (a false recognition). Only a strong associate of the word had occurred earlier. Table 7-2 presents the general sequence of events Underwood used to produce these false recognitions.

Underwood demonstrated that false recognition behavior occurred for three classes of word relationships (see Table 7-2): (1) antonyms, where the subjects would falsely recognize *cold* if it were preceded by *hot;* (2) converging associates, where subjects would falsely recognize *light* if it were preceded by *dark, heavy, lamp,* and *match,* all of which elicit *light* in free association; and (3) superordinates, where subjects would falsely recognize the word *tree* if it were preceded by *maple, oak, elm,* and *birch.* This false recognition of superordinates suggests that instances of a concept will implicitly suggest the concept name. Finally, Underwood attempted to demonstrate false recognition behavior for a fourth class of words, sense impressions. However, subjects did not falsely recognize *small,* for example, when it was preceded by *atom, cabin, germ, gnat,* and *village,* all of which elicit the sense impression of *small*. Recently, however, Kimble (1968) has been able to demonstrate false recognition of sense impression responses.

One could argue, alternatively, that what really happened in the Underwood and Kimble studies was a result of the test for the earlier occurrence of the implicit associative response. In Table 7-2, the solid arrows indicate the basis for the false recognition suggested by Underwood. The dashed arrows, however, indicate an alternative basis for the confusion. Thus, when the test word *cold* was presented, two things could have explained why the subjects said it had occurred earlier when in fact only *hot* had occurred: (1) there was a confusion of the representational responses of *cold* with the earlier implicit associative response of *cold* given to *hot,* the basis suggested by Underwood; or (2) the test word *cold* could have elicited *hot* as an implicit associative response which was then confused with the earlier occurrence of *hot* as a representational response, indicated by the dashed arrow in Table 7-2. Note that this explanation would not apply to the sense impressions and remember that Underwood did not find false recognitions for this class of words.

Recently, Anisfeld and Knapp (1968) have tested this alternate interpretation of Underwood's experiment by using unidirectional associates (e.g., *how* elicits *now,* but *now* does not typically elicit *how*). By examining Table 7-3, it can be seen how unidirectional associates allow for the separation of the two explanations of false recognitions. In the upper portion of the table, Situation A, *how* comes before *now* in the list and the solid arrow indicates that the basis for confusion suggested by Underwood is present in this situation. The lower portion of the table, Situation B, illustrates the events when *now* precedes *how.* Here the dashed arrow indicates that false recognition should occur if the alternate interpretation is correct. The results showed that only Situation A resulted in false recognitions of the test words providing strong support for the mediational model suggested by Underwood.

As we will see, the concept of an implicit associative response is an extremely useful explanatory device for many verbal-learning phenomena. It is also important to realize that implicit associative behavior (mediation) is an important aspect of what many theorists

TABLE 7–3. *Two Situations for the Production of False Recognitions with Unidirectional Associates*

Words Presented	Representational Response	Presumed Implicit Associative Response
(A) how	how	now
⋮		
now	now	never
(B) now	now	never
⋮		
how	how	now

Anisfeld and Knapp (1968) found false recognitions only in Situation A.

---

mean by thinking. To illustrate, one could say that Underwood demonstrated that presentation of *hot* can make the subject *think* of *cold*, i.e., he demonstrated that subjects are thinking while performing a word-recognition task. Jenkins (1963), in his review of mediation effects, has suggested that "associative arousal" or mediation processes are important aspects of problem-solving and hypothesis-formation tasks. And, as we will see in later chapters, mediational constructs have played important explanatory roles in conceptual behavior. Such mediation views of thought suggest that we must thoroughly understand implicit associative behavior if we are to understand thinking. In principle, there is much to be found out about human thought from the study of verbal-learning phenomena, because so much of verbal-learning behavior requires the postulation of something like implicit associative behavior, and other activities governed by stimuli which have no current physical presence.

THE ASSOCIATIVE PROCESS

The Role of Contiguity

The British associationist philosophers suggested several laws governing the formation of associations. Foremost among these was the *law of contiguity*. This law implied that if two ideas occurred together in space and time —if they were spatially and temporally contiguous—the ideas would become associated. No other consequences were necessary for the formation of an association. With the advent of modern learning theory and the principles of reinforcement, a controversy arose concerning the sufficiency of pure contiguity. Many theorists took the position that some kind of reinforcement must be operative for the development of an association. In verbal-learning tasks, however, it has been difficult to conceptualize what a reinforcement might consist of. The two units of a paired-associate item are certainly spatially and temporally contiguous, but where is the reinforcement that would explain the association? Some theorists have merely identified information feedback as a reinforcement in such situation; perhaps the subject "reinforces himself" when he finds out that he made a correct response. Such interpretations of reinforcement make it extremely difficult to determine whether contiguity alone is sufficient for the establishment of an association.

Contiguity does, however, appear to be sufficient. In 1964, Spear, Ekstrand, and Underwood presented evidence that strongly suggests that reinforcement is not a necessary condition for the formation of associations. These researchers had subjects learn a verbal-discrimination task consisting of 12 pairs of low-frequency words to a criterion of two successive perfect trials. The verbal-discrimination task allows for repeated contiguous presentations of two words without requiring that the subject learn an association between them. The question was, Would the repeated contiguity establish an association? If it did, the nature of the verbal-discrimination task would make it extremely unlikely that any reinforcement of such an association had taken place. To test for the association, the subjects were transferred to a paired-associate task after completion of the discrimination task. For some of the subjects, the paired-associate pairs were identical to the pairs in the discrimination list (appropriate pairs). For other subjects, the items from the discrimination pairs were rearranged into different pairs for the paired-associate task (inappropriate). Still a third group served as a control; these subjects learned a discrimination list that was completely different from the paired-associate list.

The learning curves for the three groups on the paired-associate transfer task are presented in Figure 7-1. If the contiguity in the discrimination task had resulted in an association, we would expect the appropriate group to do quite well in the transfer task, and we would expect the inappropriate group to do poorly, since the first-task associations would likely interfere with the formation of new and different associations with the same units. As Figure 7-1 clearly illustrates, this is exactly what happened. Spear and his associates interpreted these data to mean that contiguity alone is sufficient for the establishment of an association. Thus, in paired-associate learning we can assume that the repeated contiguity of the two units in a pair is sufficient to establish an association.

The Role of Mediation

However basic the law of contiguity may appear, subjects do seem to learn paired associates by other means, the most important of which appears to be mediation. Consider the pair *heavy-dark*. The stimulus word, *heavy*, could easily suggest the mediator, *light*, which is already associated with the response word, *dark*. In other words, the implicit associative response (IAR) to the stimulus serves as a mediator between the stimulus and response. The subject sees *heavy*, thinks *light*, which then suggests *dark*.

Mediation is undoubtedly an important process in verbal learning. If the subject comes to the experiment with associations that will facilitate his performance, we can be fairly sure that these associations will be operative in the experiment. In different terms, we can be sure that the subject will use his associative knowledge to make the task as easy as possible.

The heavy use of mediation in paired-associate learning has been documented by many investigators (e.g., Bugelski, 1962; Underwood and Schulz, 1960) who have asked their subjects how they went about learning each pair. Adams and Montague (1967), for example, found that only about one-third of the pairs in their experiment were learned without any mediational "aids" as judged by subject reports. Such pairs are said to have been learned by "rote memorization," meaning most likely that contiguity was the basis of the learning. The contiguity would come from seeing the pair on the memory drum and from the sub-

FIGURE 7–1. The transfer results of an experiment demonstrating association by contiguity.

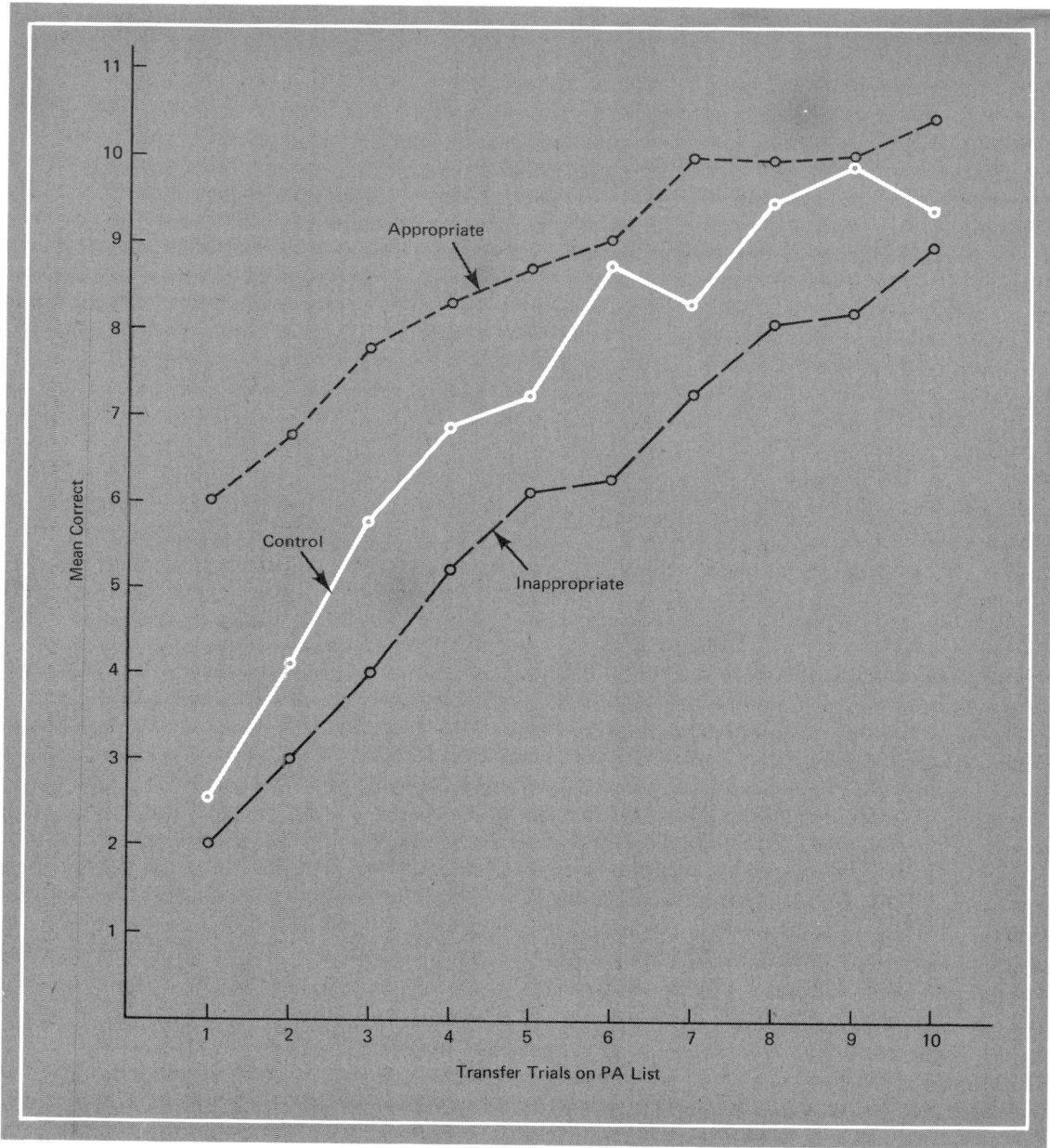

Source: From N. E. Spear, B. R. Ekstrand, and B. J. Underwood, Association by contiguity. *Journal of Experimental Psychology*, 1964, **67**, 151-61. Copyright 1964 by the American Psychological Association and reprinted by permission.

jects' rehearsing the pair, i.e., saying the pair to themselves over and over. Adams and Montague classified the reported mediators into four categories. Table 7-4 presents an example of each category, and the proportion of paired-associate items learned by the various means. The subjects report sentence-like mediators more often than any other type, suggesting that linguistic knowledge is relevant to this task. Adams and Montague refer to the mediational aids as *natural language mediators,* further emphasizing the role that prior linguistic knowledge and ability may play in the associative process. Such subjective reports on the mediational aids employed by subjects when they are learning verbal tasks again indicate that these tasks cause the subjects to think.

We have stressed the importance of describing the knowledge that a subject possesses if we are to understand his behavior. In verbal-learning theory, the subject's knowledge is presumed to be basically an enormous set of associations that he has learned (originally by contiguity) throughout his life. In the above example of mediated learning, the knowledge with which the subject enters the experiment is considered to be an association between *heavy* and *light* and another association between *light* and *dark*. With this associative knowledge, the subject can learn the pair *heavy-dark* quite rapidly, because all the associations that are necessary have already been formed before the experiment begins. The real question, however, is: To what extent can we explain behavior by postulating that knowledge consists only of associations regardless of the complexity of these associations?

MAJOR VERBAL-LEARNING VARIABLES

In this section we will examine the effects of three major variables in verbal-learning research. Each of the variables is a task variable, i.e., a variable with respect to the nature of the verbal material to be learned. The first two variables, meaningfulness of the units and similarity of the units to each other, are the two most powerful variables determining the speed of learning. The third, the level of abstractness of the units, is of special interest because it seems to imply most clearly that the behavior of subjects in verbal-learning experi-

TABLE 7–4. Types of Frequency of Mediational Aids (Natural Language Mediators)

Type of Mediation	Sample Pair	Sample Report	Proportion of Pairs
Sentence Association	Inshore-Victor	I thought of troops landing on a shore	.358
Word Association	Retail-Wealthy	Money	.162
Sound Association	Retail-Fatal	The two words sound alike	.075
Letter Association	Portly-Unearned	P-U	.059
Learned by Rote			.332
Forgot How Pair Was Learned			.010

From J. A. Adams and W. E. Montague, Retroactive inhibition and natural language mediation, *Journal of Verbal Learning and Verbal Behavior,* 1967, 6, 528-35. Copyright © 1967 by Academic Press.

ments is to a large extent predicated on thought.

Meaningfulness

Defining Operations. It is difficult to specify the meaning of meaningfulness. For example, consider two three-letter units, *JZH* and *JOB*. *JZH* is rather low in meaningfulness and *JOB* rather high, as we could surmise from looking in a dictionary. But *IBM* is not in the dictionary and it certainly is more meaningful than *JZH*. How do we establish this? About the only way is to have subjects rate (scale) these units as to how meaningful they are. At this stage, the scaling operations define the variable of meaningfulness. A great deal of such scaling work has been done, and almost all memory materials, including random shapes, have been scaled for meaningfulness. In addition, there has been a great deal of research devoted to determining the variables that underlie the dimension of meaningfulness (see Underwood, 1966; and Underwood and Schulz, 1960). Several candidates are available: (1) *Pronounceability*—there is a high correlation between ratings of pronounceability and ratings of meaningfulness. Clearly, *JOB* is much easier to pronounce than *JZH*. (2) *Number of associations*—there is also a high correlation between the number of free associations subjects can give to an item and the rated meaningfulness of the item as one can see by trying to free associate to *JZH* and *JOB*. Perhaps, then, meaningfulness is determined by the extent to which an item evokes associates from a subject, i.e., makes him think of other things. (3) *Familiarity*—there is also a high correlation between ratings of how familiar an item is (how frequently it has been encountered) and how meaningful it is rated. Moreover, there is a substantial correlation between actual counts of the frequencies of units in the English language and meaningfulness ratings of these units. Certainly you have seen *JOB* or heard it much more often than you have seen or heard *JZH*.

These three variables, pronounceability, number of associates, and familiarity, are the major correlates of rated differences in meaningfulness. These variables are all so highly correlated with each other that it is not an easy task to separate them for individual study. For example, it is not easy to manipulate pronounceability while holding the number of associates the units elicit constant. If a unit is easily pronounced it is usually rather familiar and probably elicits a fair number of associates. Even if one could find such a set of items that differed on pronounceability but not on number of associates, one could argue that it would be such an unusual set of items that no generalization to other items is reasonable. The available data just do not indicate clearly what the relevant variables underlying meaningfulness are. As a result we will have to consider the variable of meaningfulness as multidimensional. Perhaps all three major candidates are involved in determining the overall meaningfulness rating of an item, and perhaps each variable is more important in some circumstances than in others.

One interesting possibility is that the meaningfulness of an item is determined by the relationship of that item to the linguistic structure and habits of the rater. For example, Greenberg and Jenkins (see Jenkins, 1966) have analyzed nonsense syllables for their relationship to English spelling and linguistic pronounceability defined in terms of the sounds units of the English language (phonemes). The results of their complex analysis indicated a very strong positive relationship between ratings of meaningfulness and the closeness of the unit to the linguistic structure of the English language. In simple terms, the more a syllable looks or sounds like an English word, the higher its rated meaningfulness. Since familiarity of an item and the number of associates it elicits can probably be related to the linguistic usage of that item, it seems quite possible that the most crucial attribute of meaningfulness could be linguistic structure and behavior.

FIGURE 7–2. *A schematized illustration of the effects of meaningfulness on paired-associate learning.*

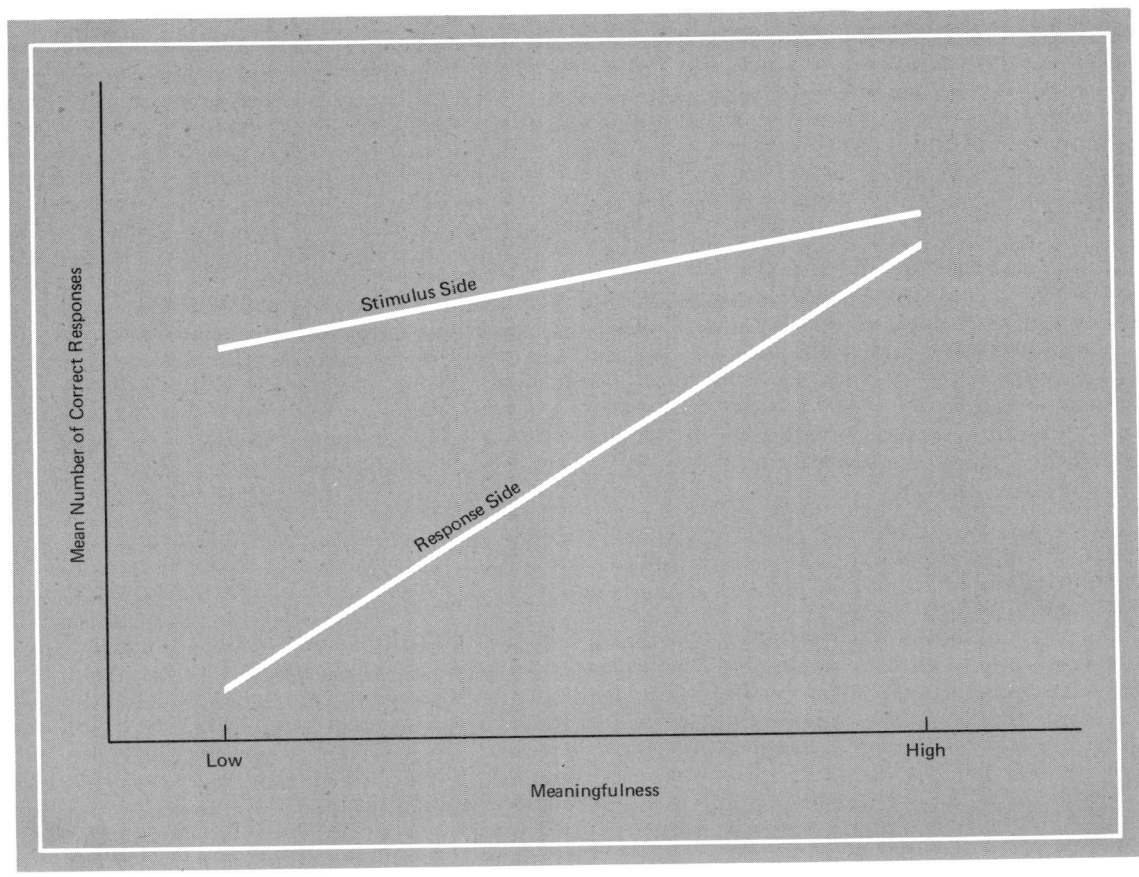

Source: From B. J. Underwood, *Experimental Psychology*, 2nd ed. New York: Appleton-Century-Crofts, 1966 (Figure 11-2, p. 471.)

Meaningfulness and Learning. As is easily surmised, meaningfulness is positively related to learning rate. Increasing the meaningfulness of the units to be learned from very low to very high will result in a large increase in the speed of learning. In paired-associate learning, the effect of meaningfulness depends on whether it is manipulated on the stimulus or response side of the list. A schematized version of the findings taken from Underwood (1966) is shown in Figure 7-2. The facilitating effect of increasing meaningfulness is greater on the response side than on the stimulus side. Since we also know that meaningfulness facilitates free-recall learning and associative matching, the explanation of this differential effect is readily apparent considering the two-stage analysis of paired-associate learning. Meaningfulness, when manipulated on the response side, facilitates both the response-learning stage and the associative stage. When manipulated on the stimulus side, it facilitates only the associative stage. Since it has two beneficial effects on the response side and only one on the stimulus side, we would naturally expect a bigger overall effect on the response side. Note, however, the implicit assumption of this interpretation that the associative stage effect is of roughly equal magnitude on the stimulus and response side.

The theoretical scheme involving representational and implicit associative responses can help us to understand the facts of meaningfulness as well as contribute to an analysis of the variables underlying meaningfulness. For example, units very low in meaningfulness may be difficult to learn because the representational response to them is not stable over time (e.g., to the stimulus *JUK* we might respond on one trial with something like "juck" and on the next trial with "juke"). Obviously, it will be difficult to learn items and associate them if we do not respond to them in a consistent manner (see Martin, 1968). The attribute of familiarity represents this feature most clearly. That is, by becoming familiar with a unit we probably come to represent that unit in a reliable fashion (after a few trials we would respond consistently with "juck" or "juke").

The attribute of pronounceability would be important with respect to how much information can be encoded in a single representational response. If the unit is easy to pronounce, one response will encode all of the letter information; if it is difficult to pronounce as a unit (e.g., *JZH*) we would have to make a more complex three-letter response in order to encode the stimulus. If immediate memory is of limited capacity, the benefits of pronounceability are obvious. Pronounceability will also affect the reliability of the representational response as would familiarity. Items very easy to pronounce will be pronounced in the same way each time; however, there is probably a middle range of pronounceability, exemplified by *JUK*, where the item can be pronounced but a problem arises because it can be pronounced in more than one way. Again, if the manner of pronunciation of such an item were not reliable, difficulty would certainly develop in learning and associating such items.

The attribute of meaningfulness dealing with the number of associates that are elicited by the item immediately suggests that the importance of the concept of implicit associative responses. Meaningful items will elicit many associative responses and will therefore be readily assimilated into the existing structured associative repertoire. Remember that subjects report a great deal of mediational activity when learning paired associates. Obviously, if an item elicits many implicit associative responses, the probability is high that at least one of them would serve as a strong mediator between that item and its response. With respect to the role of linguistic habits and meaningfulness, remember that the sentence mediator was the most frequent device used by subjects, so that items that are a part of our language repertoire or closely related to it would be expected to be easy to learn. Sentence mediators might be quite inefficient if the items being mediated are not part of the linguistic repertoire. Thus, *the retail merchant was wealthy* would mediate the pair *retail-wealthy* quite well, but *the JUK was BOT* would probably not mediate the pair *JUK-BOT* very well.

Viewed in this manner, all attributes of meaningfulness may be important, although for different reasons. Familiarity, pronounceability, and relationship to the English spelling and sound system would have marked effects on the nature of the representational response. Number of associates and relationship to the semantic and syntactic habits of the subject would affect the implicit associative or mediational behavior. In any case, we must conceive of meaningfulness as a multidimensional attribute of a verbal unit, and we probably should entertain the idea that different dimensions of meaningfulness will be important in different kinds of learning situations.

Similarity

An even more potent learning variable is the similarity of the units to be learned to each other and to things that have been learned before. Most of the verbal-learning research on similarity deals with similarity defined within the list being learned; however, research on transfer of training has dealt heavily with effects of similarity defined between two or more lists. Several classes of similarity can be identified and are worthy of separate analysis because the different classes have different effects on learning.

Formal Similarity. Formal similarity is defined by some kind of actual physical similarity among the units. Two kinds are typically distinguished: (1) *orthographic,* where the similarity is in terms of repeated identical letters in the various units (e.g., *JZH, ZJQ, QHZ, ZQH, HQJ, JQH*), and (2) *acoustic,* where the similarity is defined in terms of similar sounding letters or units (e.g., when pronounced as English letters of the alphabet, *BJY* and *GKI* are acoustically similar to each other while *BJY* and *ZNX* are not). Formal similarity retards both free-recall and paired-associate learning and the magnitude of the effects can be enormous. The above list of trigrams composed exclusively of the letters *Z, J, Q,* and *H* would be practically impossible for college students to memorize, whether these were the units of a free-recall list or the stimuli of a paired-associate list or the responses of a paired-associate list. Acoustic similarity also inhibits learning, and the exact nature of the errors the subject will make can be predicted from the acoustic relationship. For example, in learning *BJY* and *GKI,* the subject might make the error *BJI* but would be very unlikely to make the error *BJK* or *GBI* (see, for example, Conrad, 1964; Wickelgren, 1965).

The difficulty produced by high formal similarity must arise from either misperception of the items (nonveridical representational responses) due to their physical similarity and the imperfect sensory and perceptual abilities of the subject or from primary stimulus and response generalization. A very clear demonstration of this generalization has been presented by Abbott and Price (1964). They demonstrated that when a trigram is used as the conditioned stimulus in an eyelid conditioning experiment, generalization of the eyelid response occurs to other similar trigrams, and the amount of generalization is directly proportional to the number of letters that the trigrams have in common. There is no doubt that heavy generalization among all the units in a high formal similarity list takes place during learning and that the amount of this generalization will be the major factor in determining the difficulty of list learning.

Semantic Similarity. Semantic similarity exists when two units are judged similar to each other, not because of any physical, external similarity inherent in the units, but because the units have similar dictionary meanings (e.g., *huge, tremendous, gigantic, stupendous, massive, immense, colossal, prodigious, whopping*). Now, obviously, for the similarity to obtain, the subject must bring (transfer) to the learning situation a certain amount of relevant prior experience (e.g., he must speak the English language). In other words, the subject must respond to the words such that the meaning of the word is apparent in some way. Just what that way of responding is constitutes the major problem in the psychology of meaning and is one of the most difficult and evasive concepts in psychology. Semantics, the science of meaning, presently is grappling with these problems but an answer, in terms of a general theory of meaning, seems to be a long way off. In any case, we can agree tentatively with Vygotsky (1962) that one of the closest places of contact between language and thought is in the area of semantics. Using the meaning of a word is a thought process, for the meaning is in no sense contained in the nature of the physical configuration of the letter. It must somehow be a product of the knowledge of the subject with respect to that configuration.

In verbal learning, semantic similarity differs from formal similarity in that semantic similarity facilitates free-recall learning, whereas formal similarity retards free-recall learning. Semantic similarity, like formal similarity, retards associative learning (Underwood, Runquist, and Schulz, 1959). As a result of this differential effect of semantic similarity, the effect of this variable on paired-associate learning in general will depend on whether it is manipulated on the stimulus side or the response side. On the response side, the positive effect on response learning will be cancelled or reduced by the negative effect on associative learning. On the stimulus side, no such cancelling will occur and only the negative effect on associative learning will be apparent. Thus, semantic similarity will retard paired-associate learning more if it is manipulated on the stimulus side than on the response side.

Conceptual Similarity. We have already mentioned conceptual similarity and its effects on paired-associate, free-recall, and associative learning. Again, conceptual similarity is defined by the fact that the various items in a list can be viewed as instances of the same concept (e.g., all the words in the list are names of animals). Remember also that the basic learning effects of conceptual similarity are identical with the effects of semantic similarity, i.e., both are positively correlated with the ease of response learning and negatively correlated with the ease of associative learning. This suggests the possibility that one type of similarity might be reducible to an instance of the other type. Semantic similarity could be a special case of conceptual similarity. Thus, *large, huge, tremendous, gigantic*, etc., are instances of a concept we might label *large*. Or, conceptual similarity could be a special case of semantic similarity. Conceptual similarity among a set of words is certainly in some sense based on semantics, the meanings of the words. Thus, in some sense, *dog, cat, horse,* and *cow* are semantically similar.

Conceptual similarity is of special interest here because of the obvious relationship between the work in verbal learning and the work in concept attainment. By studying the effects of conceptual similarity on verbal learning we can expect to contribute to the study of conceptual behavior; likewise, the study of conceptual similarity in verbal learning will benefit from the knowledge gained from research in concept attainment. Moreover, it is obvious that subjects who are faced with a learning task involving high conceptual similarity behave in a manner reflecting the organized, structured nature of thinking. The study of conceptual similarity in verbal learning stands out as a clear example of the existence of thinking in the context of learning. In free-recall tasks, for example, subjects typically respond on test trials in a manner that reflects the categories represented in the list of words being learned. If the list consists of forty words which represent four instances of each of ten concepts (e.g., four animal names, four country names, etc.) the subject will cluster the instances in recall according to the concepts (Bousfield, 1953). He will write down all the country names together and all the animal names together and so on, even though the list was scrambled during the study trials.

Mediated Generalization and Similarity. By examining the role of the implicit associative response, we can better see the possibility for subsuming semantic similarity under conceptual similarity. When all the words in the list are names of animals, we can expect that the associate to the representational response of each word will be *animal*. In the case of semantic similarity, perhaps all the words with similar meanings tend to elicit as an associate the word most representative of the meaning suggested. *Huge, tremendous, immense, gigantic* might all implicitly elicit *large*. The first thing that we might expect to happen here (based on the false recognition experiments) is that the subject would think that *large* itself was actually in the list when in fact it was not. He would then recall the word *large*, making what is known as an intrusion error. Both Deese (1959) and Weingartner (1964) have presented strong evidence for such intrusions in the case of associated lists of words. Weingartner had subjects learn a free-recall list consisting of 15 strong associates to the word *sleep*, and 15 associates of the word *sour* but not including the words *sleep* or *sour*. Nevertheless, 37 percent of the intrusions in recall were intrusions of the word *sleep*, and 18 percent were intrusions of *sour*. Certainly we could expect similar results for semantically similar words. For conceptually similar word lists we probably would not expect subjects to intrude in recall with the category name; we might expect them to think of the category name at recall but not to write it down because they know that all the words in the list were instances. In semantic similarity the category name (*large*) would also be an instance of the concept; this is not true of conceptual similarity.

If all the words in a list elicit the same implicit associative response, we can expect difficulty in associative learning. The common associative response will be a nondifferentiating response and it will therefore be most difficult to learn a different response for each instance. In order to associate a different response with each concept instance, the subject would have to extinguish responding with the common response or he would have to respond with additional associative responses that differentiate each animal instance from all the others. In other terms, the difficulty in learning comes from *secondary* or *mediated generalization* among the words as opposed to the primary generalization that is operating in formal similarity. *Gigantic* and *tremendous* are not physically very similar to each other, but a response conditioned to one will generalize to the other. This generalization is based on previous learning (i.e., learning something about the meaning) and is therefore referred to as secondary generalization. The major theory of secondary generalization is the mediation hypothesis which suggests that the generalization is a result of the subject's making a mediational response to the physical stimulus (e.g., presentation of *gigantic* results in the mediational response *large*), and this explains the origin of the term "mediated generalization." Since the generalization appears to be due to the word meaning, the term *semantic generalization* is also common. If the subject doesn't make the mediating response (e.g., he doesn't speak English), generalization will not occur.

We must consider three major ways in which mediated generalization could take place among a list of words that are semantically similar (see Table 7-5). Two of the ways are dependent on direct associations between the stimulus items. Suppose *gigantic* and *tremendous* are strong associates of each other and suppose we condition an overt response such as finger withdrawal to the stimulus word *gigantic*. In Panel A of Table 7-5 we see that one way to explain the subsequent generalization to the stimulus word *tremendous* is to suggest that during the initial training stage, the response was actually being conditioned to *tremendous* at the same time as it was being conditioned to *gigantic*. This is due to the fact that the implicit response of the subject was *tremendous* which then became contiguous with the withdrawal response. The response will then be made in the test stage to the stimulus *tremendous*, because the association, *tremendous*—finger withdrawal, was reinforced and learned in the training stage (contiguity would also be important). This is sometimes referred to as *parasitic reinforcement* taking place in the training stage. The implicit response of *tremendous* is like a parasite on the word *gigantic* so that reinforcing one is like reinforcing the other.

In Panel B we see that it is not absolutely necessary to postulate the existence of parasitic reinforcement. Here the mediation takes place during the test stage. The test stimulus *tremendous* elicits *gigantic* (as an implicit as-

Tasks, Variables, and Processes 139

TABLE 7–5. *Three Alternative Descriptions of the Process of Mediated Generalization*

Stimulus	Implicit Associative Response	Overt Response
A		
Training: Gigantic	→ tremendous	→ lift finger
Test: Tremendous	→ none necessary	→ lift finger
B		
Training: Gigantic	→ none necessary	→ lift finger
Test: Tremendous	→ gigantic	→ lift finger
C		
Training: Gigantic	→ large	→ lift finger
Test: Tremendous	→ large	→ lift finger

sociative response) which is already conditioned to withdrawal so that withdrawal takes place in the test stage. Note that the arrangements of both Panels A and B require direct associations between the words, the difference being that in Panel A the implicit associative response is necessary only in the training stage, while in Panel B it is necessary only in the test stage.

In contrast, the description suggested in Panel C does not require any direct association between the stimulus words, but it requires implicit associative behavior in both the training and test stages. Perhaps *gigantic* and *tremendous* do not elicit each other, but they elicit the common response *large*. Then, parasitic reinforcement will result in *large* being associated with finger withdrawal in the training stage. In the test stage, *tremendous* will elicit *large* as an implicit response which will then mediate the withdrawal response.

The three descriptions presented in Table 7-5 all seem to be appropriate, but in different circumstances. For our purposes, however, we must remember that A and B will work only if there are direct associations among the stimulus words, while C requires no direct associations, only a common mediating response. In the case of semantic similarity, it is probably true that the words are strongly associated with each other directly (*gigantic, large, tremendous, huge*, etc., all elicit each other with some reasonable strength). Thus, both A and B are viable candidates for explaining the mediated generalization with semantic similarity that could produce the increased ease of free recall and the decreased ease of associating a different response to each stimulus. Description C would also be applicable to semantic similarity if all the words elicited some common response (perhaps all the words suggest *large* or *bigness*). However, in conceptual similarity, C is the most likely candidate for explaining the mediated generalization, because the words are not likely to be highly associated with each other. If the list contains all animal names such as *dog, cat, horse, cow, rabbit, armadillo, elephant*, then the fact that all the words elicit *animal* is going to be most important, which implies the sequence outlined in C. Complexity arises from the fact that even in conceptual similarity the words are likely to be somewhat directly associated with each other. For example, *dog* and *cat* are very strongly associated with each other as are *horse* and *cow;* so, A and B are again possible explanations of the mediated generalization. In order to test for the adequacy of C, one has to have a set of words that all elicit a common response but that are not directly associated with each other. The common mediating response is necessary for C, and the lack of direct associations is necessary if one wants to exclude the possibility of having the generalization take place through A or B. Such a list of words is rather difficult to find.

Wood and Underwood (1967), in a very clever experiment, did find such a list of words using the sense impression norms. For example, *chalk, snow, milk,* and *sheet* all elicit the sense impression of *white,* but they are not directly connected with each other. Thus, if subjects are asked to learn such lists and if evidence of mediated generalization is obtained, then it is reasonable to exclude A and B as possibilities and to suggest that C is responsible. The problem with sense impressions is that apparently the subjects do not readily give them as implicit responses (recall that Underwood did not find false recognition of sense impressions). Wood and Underwood overcame this problem by presenting appropriate colored patches alongside of each stimulus word. Subjects learned a list of words which included a group of "white words," a group of "red words," "yellow words," etc. When a red word (e.g., *blood*) was presented, alongside it was a patch of red paper designed to suggest the mediating response, *red,* to the subject. The results showed that when appropriate patches were paired with the words, mediated generalization took place, as inferred from free-recall performance, superior to that taking place in a group learning without the colored patches. These findings strongly suggest that description C is a possible means of producing mediated generalization.

Abstract versus Concrete Words

Finally, a third variable of obvious importance to the problem of language and thought is the degree to which the words being learned are abstract or concrete in meaning. In 1965, Paivio presented evidence clearly indicating that word abstractness is an important variable in paired-associate learning. The most recent work suggests that abstractness is a more potent variable than meaningfulness. Concrete words (low abstractness) are words that have objective referents that can be pointed to, for example, *tree, house, pencil, chair,* and *door.* In contrast, abstract words—*idea, truth, beauty, justice, freedom*—have no such referents. The distinction is also an important one for the study of semantics. How does one learn the meaning of an abstract word? You might be able to teach a child the meaning of *chair* by pointing repeatedly to physical referents (chairs) while saying the word *chair,* but no such process seems possible for truly abstract words.

Paivio had subjects learn a 16-pair paired-associate list composed of abstract and concrete words. There were four types of pairs in the list, resulting from the factorial combination of stimulus abstractness (high or low) and response abstractness (high or low). Thus, there were four pairs of the concrete-concrete variety, four concrete-abstract pairs, four abstract-concrete pairs, and four abstract-abstract pairs. The results in terms of mean total correct responses in four trials on each of the four types of pairs are shown in Table 7-6, where it can be seen that stimulus abstractness was a very important determinant of paired-associate learning, whereas response-term abstractness was not so effective. Both stimulus and response abstractness had significant effects on learning rate, with concrete words being learned faster than abstract words; but the effect was much more pronounced on the stimulus side. This differential effect of abstractness on the stimulus and response side is extremely interesting for it cannot be attributed to a difference in the level of meaningfulness of abstract and concrete words. Typically, concrete words are rated as more meaningful than abstract words (Paivio presented just such rating results). However, since we know that stimulus meaningfulness is less important than response meaningfulness in paired-associate learning, we cannot argue that Paivio's results are explainable by the fact that his abstract and concrete words differed on meaningfulness as well as abstractness; for, if the results were

TABLE 7–6. Mean Total Correct Response in Four Trials as a Function of Stimulus and Response Abstractness

Stimulus Abstractness	Response Abstractness		
	Abstract	Concrete	Total
Abstract	6.05	7.36	13.41
Concrete	10.01	11.41	21.42
Total	16.06	18.77	

From A. Paivio, Abstractness, imagery, and meaningfulness in paired-associate learning. *Journal of Verbal Learning and Verbal Behavior,* 1965, *4,* 32-38. Copyright © 1965 by Academic Press.

due to meaningfulness and not abstractness, Paivio would have found a bigger effect of response-term abstractness than of stimulus-term abstractness.

Paivio argues that the effect is due to imagery—the concrete words were rated much higher than the abstract words on an imagery scale. The argument runs like this: Imagery is important mainly on the stimulus side of paired-associate lists, the stimulus words suggesting an image to the subject which serves as a mediator between the stimulus and response. Responses that suggest images (concrete responses) are not so important, for the response image would not be aroused until the response occurs in some fashion, and if the response occurs, the subject is either correct (if it occurs as his verbal response) or he is too late (if it occurs when the shutter on the memory drum lifts and tells him what the correct response was). In other words, an image is most important in the associative stage, and mainly if it is an image readily triggered by the stimulus word, and an image which suggests the response word to the subject. Note that this argument suggests that stimulus properties are more important than response properties in the associative stage, in contrast to the traditional notion that the two are of equal importance in determining the ease of association.

Assuming that stimulus imagery is the relevant attribute, there are several ways one could explain the beneficial effects of such imagery. (1) Stimulus images might be just distinctive implicit responses, minimizing the effect of any stimulus similarity that is present. For example, *icy* and *frigid* are semantically similar, but the images they might arouse could be quite different, the former an image of lots of icicles hanging from a roof and the latter an image of an emotionally unresponsive woman. The distinctive images might then obviate the usually interfering effect of this semantic similarity. (2) Stimulus images might serve as excellent "pegs" upon which to "hang" the response word. The images might be easily modified to include the response word. For example, the pair *icy-rug* could be learned by thinking of a winter image of a rug left out on a clothesline with icicles hanging from it. (3) The image of a stimulus might be an initial implicit response that is more likely to produce additional verbal mediators, one of which might already be connected to the response word.

It also is possible to argue that the image itself does not really occur during paired-associate learning. Perhaps words that are rated high in imagery are also words that elicit many implicit responses. Thus, explanation (3) is applicable, the only difference being that the image itself is not the predecessor of the mediational responses. Obviously, it is difficult to determine whether implicit nonverbal images are actually responsible for the facilitation that takes place when the concreteness of the learning materials is increased. In any case, an impressive array of work continues to be consistent with just such an imagery hypothesis (e.g., Paivio and Madigan, 1968; Paivio, Smythe, and Yuille, 1968). Anyone attempting to explain this evidence on the basis of purely *verbal* mediation will be confronted with an enormously difficult chore.

SUMMARY

In this chapter, we have examined the basic principles derived from the verbal-learning laboratory. The basic tasks used in verbal-learning research have been described. We have also seen that contiguity and mediation are the two most important associative processes in verbal-learning theories. Finally, the major variables of *meaningfulness, similarity,* and *abstractness* have been examined.

The emphasis in this chapter has been on purely associative principles. As we have indicated, verbal-learning research has been heavily dominated and directed by associative theories of behavior. The knowledge possessed by a subject is construed as basically associative in nature. In the next chapter, however, we will see that difficulty arises when one attempts to explain all of verbal-learning behavior on the basis of purely associative constructs. It will become quite obvious that subjects think while learning and that this thinking cannot always be easily described in associative terms, even with the flexibility of mediational constructs. We can expect verbal-learning research to continue to contribute to our understanding of thought, not only because such research will contribute to our understanding of associations, but also because verbal tasks tap and often tax the cognitive abilities of the learner.

Eight Verbal Learning: The Relationship to Thinking

In this chapter, we will examine selected problems, concepts, and phenomena from the verbal-learning laboratory. We have selected topics that seem most closely related to problem solving, concept formation, and thinking in general, and topics which seem to illustrate most clearly the role of thinking in verbal learning.

The discussion begins by treating two important areas of investigation in the verbal-learning laboratory that are also important constructs in the psychology of thinking: transfer of training and mediation. These two topics are closely related because, as we will see, mediational processes are important to an understanding of transfer and transfer is always involved when mediation is presumed. Both concepts are directly relevant to thinking because each is often involved in explanatory models for thought.

TRANSFER OF TRAINING

It is quite obvious that thinking is influenced by previous learning. Solutions that have worked in the past are likely to be tried on similar problems in the future. Experience is important because it results in learning that can be transferred to future situations in order to make the future much more pleasant. The whole idea of education is predicated on transfer of training; it is hoped that one learns things in school that will be important in his later behavior. Obviously, if there were no transfer of learning from one situation to the next, life would be incredibly difficult, consisting of an endless series of frustrating problems, each one always having to be solved "from scratch." This obviously crucial role of transfer requires that we attempt to understand the laws of transfer, if we are to understand thinking.

Operational Definition of Transfer

The operational definition of transfer of training is illustrated in Table 8-1. An experimental group is given two tasks, A and B, while the control group is given only Task B.

TABLE 8-1. *The Operational Definition of Transfer of Training*

	Task A	Task B
Experimental	Yes	Yes
Control	No	Yes

The intent is to see if the experimental group is affected by the previous experiences of Task A, i.e., Do these subjects learn anything while completing Task A that is transferred to Task B? The groups are compared on the second task. If the experimental group is superior to the control group on Task B, *positive transfer* is defined. If the experimental group is inferior to the control, *negative transfer* is defined. In positive transfer, the inference is that something about Task A was beneficial to performance on Task B, and the experimental subjects transferred this beneficial learning to the second task where they then had an advantage over the control subjects. In negative transfer, experimental subjects have presumably learned something in Task A that interferes with the performance of Task B. The similarity of Task B to Task A results in the subjects' transferring this negative component to the second task which leaves them at a disadvantage compared to the control subjects.

Finally, we must also remember that certain components of Task A may facilitate performance on Task B while other components may interfere. The advantage of the experimental group over the control group will be the net result of the transfer of the positive and negative components. When the experimental and control groups do not differ on Task B performance, two explanations are always possible: (1) there is no transfer from Task A to Task B, or (2) there is substantial transfer between the two tasks but the transfer is a mixture of positive and negative effects which cancel each other out.

As an example of transfer in problem solving, consider the priming study of Dominowski and Ekstrand (1967). Task B was to solve anagram problems. For one group of experimental subjects, Task A consisted of listening to a list of the solution words to the Task B anagrams. Obviously, we would expect positive transfer for this group. Task A for another experimental group was to listen to a list of words which the subjects thought were associates of the solutions but in fact were unrelated to the solutions. Certainly, it is reasonable to predict that this might produce negative transfer. The results did indeed support these predictions. Many studies of thinking can profitably be viewed as studies of transfer of training. This seems particularly true for studies of problem solving.

In fact, Schulz (1960) has suggested that much of what goes on in problem solving can fruitfully be viewed as negative transfer. Problems are often problems because of negative transfer. We are confronted with a problem to solve (Task B) and perhaps the reason it is a problem is that we transfer components from past experience which interfere with the solution to the problem at hand. Consider the candle-mounting problem (Fig. 3-5) that is used in research on functional fixedness (see Chapters 3 and 5). As you will recall, the task, which is analogous to Task B in a transfer design, is to mount a candle on the wall using only the equipment shown in the upper panel of Figure 3-5. The solution is shown in the lower panel. The problem boils down to "discovering" that the box, which is ostensibly just a container for the tacks, is required for mounting the candle. Thus, we could conceive of a subject's previous experience with boxes as containers for things as constituting Task A—learning that boxes are containers. Transferring this experience with boxes to the candle problem results in interference with discovering that the box can be used as a platform. Presumably, someone who had had no previous experience with boxes as containers but lots of experience with boxes as platforms, would experience positive transfer, and for such a subject the candle problem would be no problem at all.

The Analysis of Transfer

The Basic Paradigms. Paired-associate learning tasks have proved convenient and useful in the study of transfer of training, and much of what we know about transfer has been learned from the verbal-learning laboratory. In a paired-associate task, the subjects encounter a series of pairs of items, each item being symbolized as A-B. The A and B units might be words, nonsense syllables, trigrams, etc. In following the A-B list with a second paired-associate list, we might make changes in either the stimulus terms (A terms) or the response terms (B terms). The basic variable in such transfer situations is similarity, and it is convenient to think of a gradient of similarity between the stimuli of the two lists and between the responses of the two lists. This gradient would range from identical items in the two lists, through various degrees of similarity, down to completely dissimilar items in the two lists. In the jargon, similarity is indicated by the number of prime markers alongside the letter; thus A and A' are highly similar, A and A" not quite as similar, and so on; the more prime marks the less the similarity until the items are completely dissimilar, at which point the letter is changed.

The final complication comes from the various dimensions of similarity that could be manipulated between the two lists. The similarity between A and A' could be formal (*XKQ* and *XQK*), semantic (*gigantic* and *large*), acoustic (*hate* and *eight*), or conceptual (*tulip* and *daisy*). Finally, verbal-learning investigators have been interested in the case where no obvious dimension of similarity exists between two items but the items are associated with each other to varying degrees (e.g., *food-eat*). One may think of a dimension of "associative similarity" in such cases, the similarity being determined by the extent to which such items elicit the same associates, i.e., *food* and *eat* are associatively similar to the extent that the free associations to *food* are also given as free associations to *eat* (see Deese, 1965).

Armed with all these dimensions of similarity which can be varied independently on the stimulus and response sides of paired-associate lists, the verbal-learning psychologist sets out to examine transfer from one list to another. For example, symbolizing the first list as A-B, and varying only stimulus similarity, the second lists would be A-B again, A'-B, A"-B . . . . . C-B. Varying only response similarity would yield second lists such as A-B, A-B', A-B", A-B''' . . . . . A-C. Such manipulation yields the basic transfer paradigms that have been most thoroughly studied: A-B, A-C; A-B, C-B; A-B, A-B'; A-B, A'-B; and A-B, C-D. These paradigms are illustrated with semantic similarity in Table 8-2 along with a unique paradigm of interest, the A-B, A-Br paradigm, where the *r* refers to "re-paired," meaning that the A and B terms are identical in both lists, but they are paired differently in the two lists.

Looking at Table 8-2 we can see that all the paradigms start with the same first list but transfer to different second lists. In actual practice, the lists are presented in the reverse order so that all the paradigms end up with the same second list, the variations among the paradigms being introduced in the first list. This is done so that the paradigms can be compared directly on second-list performance, where the lists being learned are identical, so that differences in performance must be due to the differences in the relationship between first and second lists and not to the fact that there are differences in the second lists per se.

Transfer is typically measured by employing the A-B, C-D paradigm (presumably zero similarity) as the control paradigm, rather than having a control group that learns no first list at all. This is because of a distinction that can be made between *specific* and *nonspecific* transfer effects. In learning any two paired-associate lists there is positive transfer from the first to the second due to factors known as *warm-up* and *learning to learn*. Warm-up implies a beneficial effect due merely to getting ready for a task; you warm-up for learning on A-B which helps you learn C-D

TABLE 8–2. *Basic Transfer Paradigms Illustrated with Semantic Similarity*

Paradigm Symbol	First List	Second List	Specific Factors in Transfer	Direction of Transfer Effect
A-B, A-C	large-house	large-street	forward	negative
A-B, C-B	large-house	street-house	backward response learning	negative positive
A-B, A-B′	large-house	large-home	forward backward response learning	positive positive positive
A-B, A′-B	large-house	big-house	forward backward response learning	positive positive positive
A-B, A-Br	large-house table-rock	large-rock table-house	forward backward response learning	negative negative positive
A-B, C-D	large-house	street-apple	———	control

compared to someone attempting C-D without being ready. But notice that the warm-up is not specific to the paradigm relation; you could have warmed-up on list Q-P or X-Y. Therefore, warm-up is called a nonspecific transfer component. Similarly, while learning A-B, you probably learn something about how to learn paired-associate lists in general (perhaps mediational aids, learning strategies, or rules) which will help you learn C-D compared to someone who attempts the C-D list without any paired-associate experience. This is known as learning to learn, and it too is a nonspecific transfer component because you could have accomplished the same thing by learning any paired-associate list. The A-B, C-D paradigm provides subjects with the warm-up and learning-to-learn experience common to all the other paradigms so that differences between the A-B, C-D paradigm and the others are not due to these factors. Any transfer differences that exist are then said to be specific to the lists and relationships involved, thus defining specific transfer effects.

The results of numerous studies of the various basic paradigms (see Kjeldergaard, 1968; Underwood, 1966) generally indicate that when compared to the A-B, C-D control paradigm, the following paradigms produce overall negative transfer: A-B, C-B; A-B, A-C; and A-B, A-Br, in order of increasing amount of negative transfer. The A-B, A-B′ and A-B, A′-B paradigms produce large amounts of positive transfer. A careful analysis of the paradigms also indicates, however, that there are typically both positive and negative effects involved, the overall transfer depending on the net result.

Transfer—the Two-Stage Analysis. It is helpful in understanding such transfer results to call on the two-stage analysis of paired-associate learning. The first stage is response learning (i.e., learning what the B terms are). If the B terms are carried over to the second list, we can expect the subject to transfer the response learning from List 1 to List 2, circumventing part of the List 2 task, and thereby benefiting substantially from the List 1 experience with the B terms. The second stage is associative learning, learning the A-B associations. This appears to be bidirectional learning since not only does A come to "elicit" B as a response (the so-called forward association, A-B) but B comes to elicit A (the backward association, B-A). Now if you have learned A-B and are asked to perform A-C, we can expect that the forward, A-B association will interfere with the performance of A-C, producing negative transfer. With respect to the backward association, consider the A-B, C-B paradigm. In the first list you learn the backward association B-A and in the second list you learn the backward association B-C. Clearly B-A should interfere when you are learning B-C in the second list, producing negative transfer.

Thus, at least three factors are of major importance in attempting to determine the amount of transfer that will occur (see Martin, 1965): (1) transfer of response learning, (2) transfer of forward associations, and (3) transfer of backward associations. The net transfer will be the sum of the positive and negative effects of these three components. The components for the basic paradigms together with their presumed effects (positive or negative) are listed in Table 8-2.

Take, for example, the A-B, C-B paradigm where we can expect a positive-transfer component due to the transfer of response learning and a negative effect due to interference from the List 1 backward associations during List 2 learning. Since the A terms which are responsible for eliciting the forward associations do not appear in List 2, the forward associations are not a factor in the observed transfer. The net transfer then will depend on the relative magnitude of the positive effect of transferred response learning and the negative effect of backward interference. If the B responses were extremely difficult to learn in List 1 then it will be extremely beneficial to have accomplished this when beginning List 2, since the control subject will have to accomplish this learning "from scratch." This large positive effect will more than counteract the negative interference from the B-A associations and net positive transfer will result. If, however, the B responses are very easy to learn, transfer of response learning will be of only slight value since the control subject can quickly accomplish this response learning. Then, the negative interference from B-A associations will overpower the small positive effect of transferred response learning and net negative transfer will result. In most verbal-learning situations, response learning is not that difficult so that some net negative transfer usually occurs with the A-B, C-B paradigm. But whenever the response learning is difficult, we can expect positive transfer in this paradigm.

The A-B, A-C paradigm, on the other hand, is almost always a negative transfer situation. Whenever new responses must be made to old stimuli that tend to elicit interfering responses, we can expect negative transfer from the forward association. Since the B terms do not occur in the second list, we cannot expect transfer of response learning nor transfer of B-A associations.

Finally, the A-B, A-Br paradigm produces maximal negative transfer in paired-associate experiments. Here there is negative transfer from both the forward and backward associations. Some of this interference will be counteracted by the transfer of response learning since the same responses occur in both lists, but this will generally not be of sufficient magnitude to counteract the interference. Again notice that if the response learning were extremely difficult, having accomplished it in List 1 would be of tremendous value in learning List 2, a situation that could conceivably result in positive transfer in the A-B, A-Br paradigm since the forward and backward interference would be more than counteracted.

Positive Transfer—Mediation and Generalization. The last two paradigms to be discussed are the A-B, A-B' and the A-B, A'-B cases. Both of these paradigms produce marked positive transfer when compared to the A-B, C-D control paradigm and this is not surprising from an intuitive point of view. Certainly learning *large-home* will be facilitated if you have already learned *large-house*. The stickler comes when we attempt to explain why. At this point the picture becomes even more complicated because it appears that different principles are involved depending on whether orthographic and acoustic similarity or semantic, conceptual, and associative similarity are involved. With orthographic and acoustic similarity, transfer appears to be best explained by the basic principles of stimulus and response generalization. Thus a response learned to the stimulus XKQ will generalize to similar stimuli such as XQK, the amount of such stimulus generalization being a function of the degree of similarity (Abbott and Price, 1964). This along with the positive transfer effect from response learning will explain the positive transfer in the A-B, A'-B paradigm. Similarly, if you have learned to say XKQ to some stimulus, this should generalize to responses similar to XKQ (response generalization) producing a positive effect in second list response learning and associative learning. This can explain the positive transfer in the A-B, A-B' paradigm.

However, the situation appears to be distinctly different when the other varieties of similarity are involved. This difference is best illustrated with associative similarity. Assume List 1 contains the pair *door-eat* and List 2 contains *door-food;* thus we have an A-B, A-B' case. Now this produces positive transfer, but certainly not because *eat* and *food* are physically similar stimuli (i.e., they are neither orthographically or acoustically similar). We cannot invoke primary stimulus or response generalization along some physical dimension of similarity.

Instead, the transfer is said to be produced by mediated generalization, and this brings us to the importance of mediation in transfer. In this example, a mediating response (a hypothetical covert response with stimulus properties) is presumably responsible for the positive transfer. Since *eat* and *food* are strongly associated, we can expect that presentation of *eat* might lead to the mediating response (what we have earlier called the implicit associative response) of *food*, and likewise presentation of *food* would lead to the implicit response *eat*. Now, the positive transfer could be produced by these implicit mediational responses in one or both of the following ways: First, while a subject learns *door-eat* in List 1, *eat* may be eliciting *food* as an implicit associative response which is then contiguously associated with *door*. When *door-food* occurs in List 2, our subject finds it an extremely easy task, because *door-food* was actually being learned during List 1 (parasitic reinforcement). Notice here that the crucial mediational responding occurs during List 1 learning. The alternative interpretation suggests that the mediational responding takes place during List 2 learning. Having learned *door-eat*, the subject now encounters *door-food*. On test trials the appearance of *door* elicits the implicit response *eat* due to first-list learning and *eat* then elicits the response *food* due to the prior association that exists between these items. The same kind of mediational processes are presumed to operate in the A-B, A'-B paradigm. Also the mediational explanation is easily applied to the cases of semantic and conceptual similarity. The reader should attempt a mediational analysis of these situations for himself armed with the three models of mediation presented earlier in Table 7-5.

We agree with Schulz (1960) that our understanding of thinking will be enhanced by applying a transfer-of-training analysis. A great deal of thinking can be viewed as attempts on the part of the subject to bring his past experience to bear on the present task. The success of such efforts should be more accurately predictable once we fully understand the transfer relationship between the relevant and irrelevant aspects of previous learning and the stimulus situation confronting the problem solver. The subject in Luchins' set experiments with the water jars (see Chapter 6) is confronted with a series of similar problems, each of which requires the same solution formula (largest — medium — smallest twice). Suddenly he is presented with still another similar problem which can be solved more easily by the formula, medium — smallest, although the longer method still works. If the situation is viewed as analogous to the A-B, A'-B paradigm, it is easy to see why the subject will respond with the familiar but longer solution instead of the shorter, new solution. Here A and A′ represent the similar problem situations and B represents the response, longest — medium — smallest twice. Since the problems are quite similar, we can expect the response to generalize. The problem situation has become associated with the long solution, not with medium — smallest. Suppose instead that on the crucial problem only the new formula will work. Now we have a similar problem to which a new response must be made, or an A-B, A′-C paradigm. Certainly we can expect negative transfer from the prior experience with the longer formula which will probably be tried and retried by the subject who just can't believe it won't work.

What Is the Response? In attempting to extend our transfer analysis to complex thinking we are faced with an old problem in psychology, namely the definition of the word *response*. Above, we spoke of longest — medium — smallest twice as if it were a single response, when obviously it is a complicated set of responses that occurs when a subject solves a water-jar problem with this formula. We have also spoken of words as responses in verbal-learning experiments; but, to respond by saying the word *hypochondriacal* is not to make a single response, for a complex chain of articulatory responses is necessary. When a subject responds with the trigram, *JZH*, just how many responses has he really made? Early in learning, *JZH* seems to be performed as if it were a three-response serial list. But, after several trials, the response is "integrated" and seems to be performed as if it no longer consists of three letters but instead is a single response. This integration is perhaps most apparent in motor skills, where, for example, swinging a golf club appears to be a single response for a professional golfer, but a series of smaller, jerky responses for the duffer. The learning that is involved when a series of responses comes to be performed as if it were

a single response is called *response integration*, and this construct has played a crucial but subtle role in S-R theory. By postulating response integration, S-R theory can begin to tackle such complex areas of problem solving as we have seen with the example of solving water-jar problems. Without response integration, such theories would have great difficulty in describing very simple learning phenomena. But usually, the process of integration is merely postulated and ignored until the definition of a response is challenged. We obviously have a very poor understanding of what happens when response integration takes place and how it happens, and until we understand this process, S-R theories will have ignored an extremely important part of any performance situation.

Response integration appears intuitively to be a valid learning process. It certainly seems to be a necessary component for an association theory of complex behavior, for it allows the theorist a great deal of flexibility in his definition of a response. Small chains of responses at one level of analysis become single responses at the next higher level of analysis due to response integration. In speaking, for example, a set of articulatory movements is integrated into a single phoneme, a set of phonemes is integrated into a single syllable, and a set of syllables is integrated into a single word. Indeed, low-frequency, multisyllable words such as *hypochondriacal* and *antidisestablishmentarianism* may not have been integrated to the point of a single response, but instead are more likely to be performed as a set of syllable responses. The problem of response integration is a sticky one, but if one is going to invoke this construct in his explanations, he should not ignore his responsibility for explaining response integration itself. In any case, with the great flexibility provided by such a construct, one can attempt to apply S-R principles to more complex phenomena, and the relevance of transfer-of-training research to problem solving is a fine example of this.

MEDIATION

The concept of mediation has played a crucial role in all S-R analyses of thinking. Basically, such theories imply that thinking is implicit, covert responding that is instigated by external stimulation. In turn, this implicit responding results in implicit stimuli which may elicit overt responses. Suppose you classically condition a subject to blink his eye each time the external stimulus (symbolized by capital S) *hot* is presented. Subsequently, you present a different S, the word *cold,* and you find that your subject blinks (he makes the appropriate external response, R). Now it is difficult to explain such generalization of responding from *hot* to *cold* on the basis of primary stimulus generalization since the two words are neither orthographically nor acoustically similar. In such cases, the behavior has been interpreted as due to *mediated generalization,* a concept we have examined earlier. Presentation of *cold* (S) leads to the implicit response *hot* (r, implicit events being represented in small letters) due to the strong pre-existing association between *hot* and *cold* and due to the "priming" effect of having recently seen *hot.* This implicit response serves a stimulus function or it has stimulus properties (s) which elicit the external response (R) of blinking because the subject has been conditioned to blink to the stimulus *hot.* According to mediation theory, then, the sequence of events is as shown in Figure 8-1. The behavior is said to be mediated by the implicit events. The subject blinks to the stimulus *cold* because both blinking and the word *cold* have been associated with the word *hot* which serves as the mediating (intervening) link between the stimulus *cold* and the eyeblink. The mediator *hot* is represented twice in the figure because it serves first as a response and then as a stimulus thus giving us a mediating response: a response that can serve as a stimulus. Many more than one mediating sequence (r-s) can and often is assumed to intervene between S and R.

Mediation Paradigms

The experimental investigation of mediation phenomena has been one of the major points of interest to verbal-learning psychologists. Sophisticated treatments of this work have been presented by Jenkins (1963) and Kjeldergaard (1968). There are three basic types of mediation paradigms: (1) chaining, (2) stimulus equivalence, and (3) response equivalence. In verbal learning these are usually studied by appropriate manipulation of the relationships among a series of consecutively learned paired-associate lists. The three paradigms are represented in Table 8-3 each as a succession of three paired-associate lists beginning with a list of A-B associations. Mediation is inferred on the basis of performance on List 3. If mediation is operative, performance on List 3 should surpass that of a control condition which did not learn the relevant associations in List 1 or List 2. It is also common to infer one of the steps from association norms; thus, A-B might be *hot-cold,* and the subject would then learn just the second and third lists in the laboratory.

The chaining paradigm is the most straightforward mediation situation. Here the learning of the first two associations will permit the operation of a simple chain on the test list: *hot* (S) elicits *cold* covertly (r), the stimulus properties of *cold* (s) then elicit the correct overt response (R), *dax.*

In the stimulus-equivalence paradigm, *hot*

FIGURE 8-1. Sequence of events in simple mediation.

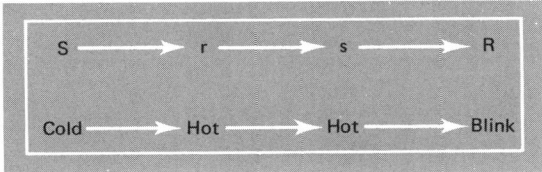

TABLE 8–3. Basic Mediational Paradigms

	List 1	List 2	List 3 (test)
Chaining Inferred[1]	A-B Hot-Cold	B-C Cold-Dax	A-C Hot-Dax
Stimulus Equivalence Inferred	A-B Hot-Cold	C-B Dax-Cold	A-C Hot-Dax
Response Equivalence Inferred	A-B Hot-Cold	A-C Hot-Dax	B-C Cold-Dax

[1] When the A-B link is inferred from association norms, subjects learn only Lists 2 and 3 in the laboratory.

and *dax* are said to become equivalent because they both have been stimuli for the response *cold*. The fact that facilitation occurs on List 3 implies a general principle that is often used by mediation theorists to explain behavior in other situations: two stimuli that have been associated with the same response become associated with each other. There are at least two possible explanations of stimulus equivalence: (1) during List 3 learning, *hot* elicits *cold* implicitly which via the backward association from List 2 suggests the correct response, *dax*; and (2) during List 2 learning, *cold* elicits *hot* so that both *cold* and *hot* are contiguously paired with the List 2 stimulus, *dax*. This contiguity produces an association (parasitic reinforcement) between *dax* and *hot* during List 2 learning which is then transferred to List 3, producing the facilitation on List 3.

In the response-equivalence paradigm, *cold* and *dax* are said to become equivalent because they have both been associated with the same stimulus, *hot*. Response equivalence implies another general principle: two responses that have been associated with the same stimulus become associated with each other. Again two mechanisms of mediation are possible: (1) during List 3 learning, presentation of the stimulus *cold* elicits the mediational response *hot* which in turn elicits the correct response, *dax*, due to List 2 learning; and (2) during List 2 learning, presentation of the stimulus *hot* elicits the implicit associative response, *cold*, which is then paired contiguously with *dax*. This contiguity produces an association (again parasitic reinforcement) between *cold* and *dax* while the subject is learning *hot-dax*. The *cold-dax* association is then transferred to List 3 where facilitation in List 3 learning will occur.

It is important to note that mediated behavior implies the operation of transfer of training, and as a result it is necessary to understand the principles of transfer in order to understand the conditions under which mediation can be expected. For example, the first two stages in the response-equivalence paradigm constitute an A-B, A-C paradigm which is known to produce negative transfer. In this paradigm, learning of A-C is also known to produce extinction or unlearning of A-B (Barnes and Underwood, 1959), a fact which could easily prevent or retard the operation of mediation in the third stage of the response-equivalence paradigm. In other words, the situation is complex when three-stage paradigms are involved. Nevertheless, mediation (as judged by positive transfer in stage three learning) usually occurs in the three-stage paradigms. Horton and Kjeldergaard (1961) compared eight different three-stage paradigms and found evidence for positive transfer in stage three learning for six of the paradigms. The differences among the paradigms, however, were not significant. If one proceeds undaunted to four-stage mediation paradigms, the results do not show strong evidence for mediational effects (Jenkins, 1963). In the four-stage designs, the transfer relationships become extremely complex, making it difficult to determine the conditions for successful mediation or the reason for failure.

Mediational responding plays a crucial role in thinking in the views of S-R theorists. And, assuming that most mediational responses are linguistic in character, the problem of the relation between language and thought reduces to the role of mediation in thinking for many theorists. Later in this book we will encounter the mediational analysis of the Kendlers (e.g., Kendler and Kendler, 1962) in connection with conceptual behavior. Similarly, many (particularly Luria, 1961) have spoken of the directive function of "internal speech" and to the mediational theorists this simply means that the implicit speech responses are the stimuli for overt behavior. In problem-solving research, mediational responding also assumes a critical role. Here, problems exist because the stimulus situation does not elicit the appropriate or necessary mediational responses, as, for example, in the candle problem where the box may elicit the implicit response "container" or no response, rather than the appropriate mediator, "platform." As long as mediation continues to be a crucial explanatory construct in S-R theories of complex behavior, the verbal-learning research on mediation should contribute greatly to our understanding of such behavior.

THE ADEQUACY OF S-R ANALYSES: SELECTED PROBLEMS

What Is the Stimulus?

If S-R association theory is to explain any behavior adequately it is obvious that we must be able to delineate the exact nature of the stimulus. If we cannot pinpoint the stimulus, it seems rather fatuous to expect a stimulus-response theory to explain the behavior. Earlier in this chapter we have seen that the definition of a response has been a sticky problem in S-R analyses. The same thing holds true for the stimulus. While most verbal-learning tasks seem to have explicit stimuli, we will see in this section that these explicit stimuli may not be the actual stimuli and that very often we just do not know what the real stimuli are.

Paired-Associate Learning and Stimulus Selection. The paired-associate task seems to identify rather specifically what the stimulus is in an operational sense. However, the subjects often appear to behave as if the stimulus were quite different from that intended by the experimenter. Suppose a subject is faced with a paired-associate task in which the stimuli are low meaningfulness trigrams and the responses are single-digit numbers, e.g., *JZH-7*. If the first letter of each trigram is different, the subject could utilize this letter as his stimulus and ignore the other two letters in each trigram. Rather than struggle with *JZH-7*, the subject would learn *J-7* which is probably a much easier task. Postman and Greenbloom (1967) have shown clearly that subjects do just that, a phenomenon known as *stimulus selection* or *cue selection*. Postman and Greenbloom also demonstrated that cue selection is influenced by pronounceability of the trigrams such that if the trigram is easy to pronounce as a unit, e.g., *JOP*, subjects tend to use the entire three letters as a stimulus.

Underwood, Ham, and Ekstrand (1962) have distinguished between the *nominal stimulus* and the *functional stimulus:* the nominal stimulus is the entire stimulus presented by the experimenter and the functional stimulus is that part of the nominal stimulus which is actually used by the subject. They had subjects learn trigram-digit pairs or word-digit pairs. In addition, each trigram or word was surrounded by a different color border. Thus, a nominal stimulus might be *JZH* surrounded by a blue border or the word *TOP* surrounded by a red border. They reasoned that their conditions might lead the subjects to select a functional stimulus that was quite different from the nominal stimulus. With the trigram-color list, the subjects might choose to ignore the trigrams during learning, using only the colors to cue the responses. In this case, the functional stimulus (the color) would be different from the nominal stimulus (the trigram-color combination). In order to test these notions, Underwood and his associates employed a transfer design.

The transfer design is an extremely useful technique for determining what a subject has learned in a task. Suppose you think that subjects will select the colors as the functional stimuli in the trigram-color list and will select the words in the word-color list. How do you find out what the subject did use as his functional stimulus? If he used only colors as functional stimuli and you transfer him to a list which has had the trigrams or the words removed from the stimulus position, he should show very little decrement in performance. If he used the verbal unit, then transfer to a list with only the color stimuli present should be very poor.

The Underwood, Ham, and Ekstrand experiment used a 2 × 3 design. Subjects learned either a trigram-color or a word-color list and then they transferred to a second list which was related to the first list in one of three ways: (1) it was identical to the first list, a control condition; (2) the verbal unit (either the word or the trigram) from the first list was removed leaving only the colored borders as stimuli; or (3) the colored borders from the first list were removed leaving only the verbal units as stimuli. The transfer results are shown in Figure 8-2, where it can be seen that if the original list contained trigrams (left-hand panel) transfer to colors only (condition TC-C) was just as good as continuing on with the trigram-color combinations (TC-TC). In other words, deleting the trigrams had no effect, suggesting that the colors were the functional stimuli. In condition TC-T, where the colors were deleted leaving only the trigrams, there was very little transfer at all. In contrast with this finding, the right-hand panel shows the groups that began with word-color (WC) combinations. You can see that there was some decrement in performance when the colors were deleted leaving only the words (WC-W) but an even larger decrement when the words were deleted leaving only the colored borders (WC-C). The results of this and many other experiments (e.g., Postman and Greenbloom, 1967) make a strong case for stimulus selection. In other words, subjects select a functional stimulus when they attempt to learn, and this functional stimulus is not necessarily the nominal stimulus.

There is some evidence that subjects tend to select the more meaningful elements of a stimulus as their functional stimulus. Since we know that stimulus meaningfulness influences the rate of learning, we can suggest that stimulus selection should be designed to make the functional stimulus more meaningful than the nominal stimulus. Cohen and Musgrave (1964) had subjects learn paired associates where the stimuli were two-unit compounds and the responses were single letters. In some conditions, one unit of the compound was a three-letter word and the other unit was a low-meaningfulness nonsense syllable. A sample pair might be, *QAZ JOY-K*. Under these circumstances, there was clear evidence that the subjects selected the words as functional stimuli.

Do subjects ever learn anything about the nonfunctional elements of a compound stimulus? According to James and Greeno (1967), overlearning a list will result in substantial amounts of transfer to the nonfunctional elements. They have suggested that subjects restrict their attention to the functional stimulus until the task has been mastered, after which attention is "relaxed" such that information about the nonfunctional stimulus is learned.

We suggest that stimulus selection is thoughtful behavior. Thought often deter-

FIGURE 8–2. Transfer results of an experiment demonstrating cue selection in paired-associate learning.

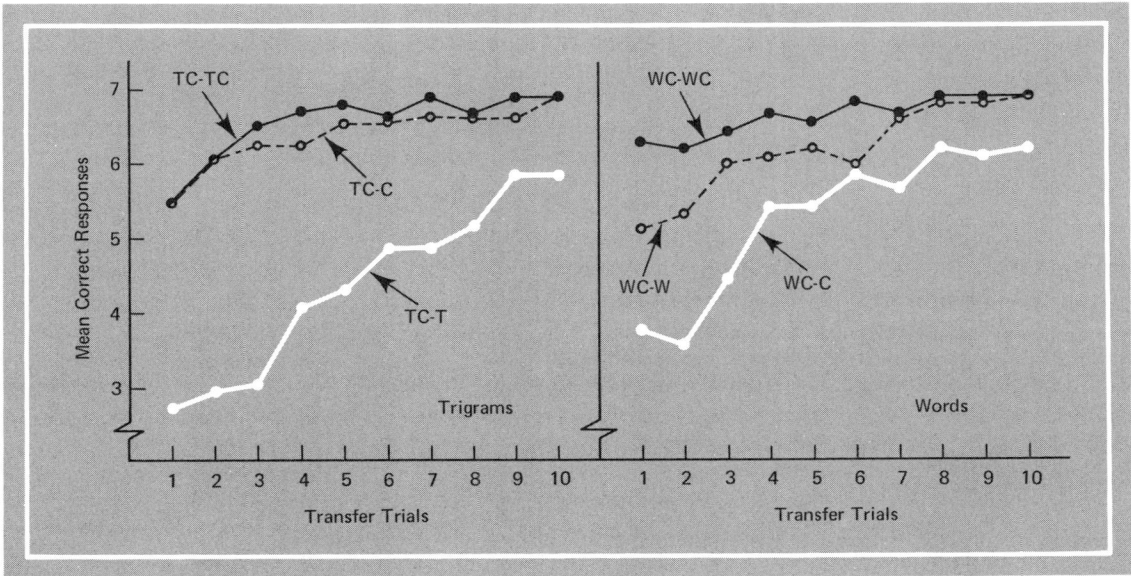

Source: From B. J. Underwood, M. Ham, and B. R. Ekstrand, Cue selection in paired-associate learning. *Journal of Experimental Psychology*, 1962, 64, 405-9. Copyright 1962 by the American Psychological Association and reprinted by permission.

mines what stimuli will be attended to and selected as functional stimuli. Stimulus selection seems to be virtually identical to the concept of attention, and as such it must be a factor in practically all behavior. It is a basic requirement of abstracting type conceptual tasks. When an individual is faced with a problem to solve, for example, he does not attend equally to all the stimuli present in the situation. He has learned that some stimuli are generally more relevant to solutions than others and he will typically attend to these stimuli first. Generally, such behavior is economical and efficient, for stimuli that have been relevant in the past are likely to be relevant in the present. However, stimulus selection will often be detrimental to problem solving, whenever the most relevant stimuli are not included in the functional stimulus.

In the candle-mounting problem, the box is necessary for solution, but subjects apparently have difficulty in recognizing this fact. Perhaps this can be described as the selection of a functional stimulus, differing from the nominal stimulus in at least one critical element, the box. Solution will occur only after the functional stimulus has been changed to include the box.

Stimulus selection in paired-associate learning certainly seems to qualify as thoughtful behavior—these subjects are not passive minds on which the experimenter is printing his associations. It is an outstanding example of the fact that subjects learning such lists are using all the knowledge and tricks that they can to make the task as easy as possible—in many respects, they appear to be treating these learning tasks as problems to be solved, which certainly means that descriptions of behavior will be very complex.

The complexity of paired-associate learning was hinted at earlier when we mentioned that Battig (1968) has suggested that at least ten different processes are involved in learning a paired-associate list. While stimulus selection itself does not seem readily amenable to explanation in terms of stimulus-response theory, it is by no means an exceptional phenomenon in this respect. Battig, in his review of paired-associate research, has said:

> The sum total of all PA [paired-associate] learning processes, however, clearly cannot be accounted for on the basis of presently available S-R principles . . . (p. 164). General S-R behavior theory has provided researchers in PA learning with an oversimplified set of concepts grossly inadequate to handle the complexities of the learning processes involved therein . . . (p. 166).

The complexity of this apparently simple task attests to the role that thinking must play in verbal learning, and evidence suggests that S-R constructs alone will be incapable of describing this behavior.

Stimulus in Serial Learning. The paired-associate task is not the only task in which there has been some problem in identifying the stimulus. In serial learning, where the subject must learn the exact order of a list of verbal items, the stimulus has yet to be determined. In the anticipation method, one item is presented to the subject and he is supposed to anticipate the next item in order. This procedure naturally suggests that the stimulus for any item is the preceding item. If the serial list consists of items A, B, C, D, and E, the associations that are learned would be A-B, B-C, C-D, D-E, each item serving once as a stimulus and once as a response, except for the first and last items in the list. This conception of the serial learning process is called the *chaining hypothesis* and for years this hypothesis was accepted as fact. Today, however, we are not at all sure about what the functional stimulus is in serial learning.

The controversy about the serial stimulus originated with the work of Young in 1959 when he demonstrated that there was very little transfer from a serial list to an appropriately derived paired-associate list. For example, if the serial list were A-B-C-D-E, the paired-associate list would have as pairs, A-B, C-D, B-C, and D-E. In paired-associate learning the pairs would be presented in a different random order on each trial. Obviously, if the chaining hypothesis were correct, we should expect tremendous positive transfer, since the learning presumably required to perform the paired-associate list would have been accomplished in the serial list. In terms of trials to a one-perfect criterion, however, no positive transfer was observed. This finding seriously questioned the validity of the chaining hypothesis. (Again note the value and utility of the transfer design.) Instead, Young (1962) suggested and found support for the *serial-position hypothesis* which says that the stimulus is the serial position that each item occupies. In an A-B-C-D-E list, this hypothesis says that the learned associations are something like 1-A, 2-B, 3-C, 4-D, 5-E; it is as if the subject were saying "the first item is A, the second is B, etc."

Young (1968) has recently provided us with an outstanding review of the status of this problem, and the picture is becoming more complex every moment. Chaining and serial position still seem the major candidates, but it now appears that neither hypothesis will account for the learning of all the items in the list. Some have suggested that early and late items are learned one way and middle items learned the other way. But there is no agreement on which items are learned which way. The best we can say is that, as yet, no one has been able to figure out just what associations, if any, a subject learns during a serial task.

Stimulus in Free-Recall Learning. The free-recall task provides us with an example of a task that exemplifies most clearly the thinking that human subjects do while learning. As we have seen earlier, free-recall learning involves learning a list of items using a study-test procedure where the subject is "free" to recall the items in any order he wishes. But, again, it is difficult to identify the stimulus. Does the subject learn a series of inter-item associations in this task that can explain his behavior? Such an analysis seems too simple to account for the facts. Two closely related phenomena of free-recall, clustering and subjective organization, are of special interest since they are indicative of the substantial amount of thinking involved in the performance of this rather simple-looking task.

The first of these phenomena was discovered by Bousfield in 1953 and is known as *clustering in recall*. Suppose the free-recall list consists of sixteen words: names of four countries, four birds, four diseases, and four elements. The sixteen words are scrambled and presented to subjects one at a time at a five-second rate; the subjects are given two and a half minutes to write down as many of the words as they can remember, in any order. What happens is that they write down the words in a highly organized fashion in comparison to the order in which they heard the words. All of the country names are written together, then perhaps the four bird names, then the diseases, and finally the elements. In other words, the subjects recall clusters of words from the same category. Certainly such subjects appear to be thinking.

There are two kinds of clustering that have been demonstrated in free-recall experiments. The example given above is known as *category clustering*, since the words are related by the fact that they are instances of some conceptual category. It is possible to collect category norms (Battig and Montague, 1969) by presenting subjects with category names and asking them to write down as many instances of the category as they can think of. These data then can be used to determine the relative strength of the association between a given instance and the category name. For example, *dog* is a high-strength instance and *aardvark* a low-strength instance of the category *four-footed animal*.

The second kind of clustering depends on the existence of strong associations between items that are not necessarily instances of the same category. Thus, *mother* and *love* are associated but are not generally considered as instances of the same category. Using available unrestricted free-association norms, it is possible to isolate pairs of words that are strongly associated to each other and present these pairs for free-recall learning. Jenkins, Mink, and Russell (1958) did just that and, in addition, they manipulated the strength of the association between the items in each pair. Of course, on study trials the pairs were not presented contiguously. The results showed that subjects clustered in recall according to the known associations present in the list, e.g., they would recall *mother* and *love* in succession. This is generally known as *associative clustering*. As you might guess, the amount of associative clustering increased as the normative strength of the association increased.

A similar result holds for category clustering, where the amount of clustering increases as the associative strength is increased between the instances of the category and the category name. Thus, more clustering occurs with the words *cat, dog, horse,* and *cow* than with *armadillo, gnu, giraffe,* and *aardvark* (Bousfield, Cohen, and Whitmarsh, 1958). Incidentally, when clustering appears in free recall, the absolute amount of recall is usually higher than is recall of an unclustered list of words. In other words, there is a positive correlation between the amount of clustering and the total number of words recalled. As Underwood (1966) has pointed out, however, it is extremely difficult to determine whether the clustering is causally related to the increased recall. Nevertheless, Mandler (1967, 1968) has found a strong positive linear relationship between the number of categories that subjects use (or are required to use) to sort a long list of words and the number of words they can recall from the list. Thus, a subject recalls more words from a list that he has learned to sort into seven stable categories than from a list he has learned to sort into only two categories. Such results strongly suggest that the number of categories used in organizing a list is causally related to the amount of recall.

It is possible to think of category clustering as a special case of associative clustering since in categorized lists there is usually a reasonable amount of associative strength among the instances of a category (e.g., dog-cat-horse-cow are associated with each other) and substantial strength between each instance and the category name. Strongly categorized lists might be stored in such a way that the category name itself is the basic memory unit. In recall, the subject first remembers the category names, each of which suggests the instances that occurred. In other words, recall of one item suggests, via previously existing associations, a related item (items) which is written down next and this constitutes an instance of clustering. The facts which show that clustering varies neatly with the degree of suspected associative strength are consistent with such a description. In addition, at the time of recall the category labels could serve to elicit a string of category instances and, as each instance is elicited, the subject would recognize it as being in the list or not. The words recognized as being in the list would then be printed on the recall sheet in a clustered fashion; furthermore, since recognition is presumably easier than recall, this description would explain the finding that recall is generally higher with categorized than with unrelated word lists.

The category names are likely to become memory units because the instances of the category presented during the study trials will probably elicit the category names as implicit associative responses. Thus, part of the problem in long lists of categorized words will be in remembering all the categories. Tulving and Pearlstone (1966) have compared *cued recall* (the subject is given the category names at the time of recall) with the normal noncued procedure. They found that cued recall was superior to noncued recall, and this advantage of cued recall increased as the number of categories increased. Tulving and Pearlstone also showed that the recall of categories was independent of the recall of words within categories. If the subject remembered at least one instance of a category, that category was said to be "accessible." Now, presentation of the category names at recall acted to increase the number of accessible categories but, surprisingly, had no effect on the number of words recalled within a category. In other words, once a subject gets into a category, he recalls some standard number of items.

A complete explanation of clustering is not presently possible. It does seem clear, however, that associative connections among the clustered items and between the clustered items and a superordinate are crucially involved. Nevertheless, it seems that a subject's knowledge of a free-recall list is more than purely associative as the following material will indicate.

The phenomenon of clustering indicates that subjects will structure a free-recall list, transforming it from the random list the experimenter presents into an organized list. The basis for the organization is provided by the experimenter who deliberately selects associated groups of words. But what about the case when the experimenter has deliberately tried to avoid building a list of related items? It appears that subjects will organize the list anyway, using their own schemes. This phenomenon has been called *subjective organization* by Tulving, the pioneer researcher in this area.

Tulving (1962, 1968) has inferred the existence of such organization from the facts of multitrial free-recall experiments using unrelated lists of words. He found that across trials the subjects organize the list such that they recall the words in the same order or similar orders on successive trials. According to his notions, subjects might organize an eighteen-word list into six units, each unit containing three words. The six units might be recalled in different orders on successive trials but the order of the words within each unit would be relatively constant. Eventually the six units themselves might be organized in recall at which time the subject would be recalling all eighteen words in the same order on each trial. All this takes place, remember, in free recall where the subjects could give the words in any order they choose.

Tulving (1968) distinguishes between E-units and S-units. E-units are the units the experimenter thinks he is asking his subjects to recall, such as the eighteen words in the list. S-units are the units that result when the subject organizes the E-units for recall, the six S-units of three words each. Again, suppose the subject is faced with a list of six low-meaningfulness trigrams, e.g., *JZQ, HZB,* etc. Actually, when he recalls a trigram he is recalling three items: *J, Z,* and *Q.* Thus the six-item list actually contains eighteen items. But gradually as the subject learns the list, the nature of the unit being remembered seems to shift from letters to trigrams (response integration) such that the subject is recalling a six-item list. *JZQ* is no longer recalled as three letters, *J-Z-Q,* but as one trigram, *JZQ.*

Miller (1956) has called this *recoding,* and it is often called *chunking,* because what was once three individual letters is now one chunk, a unified trigram. Note that words are perfect examples of this chunking phenomenon. The word *ape* is actually a trigram, but it has already been "unitized" in such a way that a letter-by-letter recall is unnecessary. For example, when rehearsing this item, one does not say "a-p-e, a-p-e," but "ape, ape, ape." In letter chunking to make words or unitized nonsense items, there is a restriction on the order of the letters—the experimenter generally expects the subject to spell the trigrams correctly. In free recall, however, he does not care about the order in which the subject recalls the trigrams; therefore each subject is free to chunk or organize the trigrams in the way he finds most efficient.

Just as three letters are chunked to make the single unit *ape,* the subject might proceed to chunk three words to make one higher-order S-unit so that instead of having to recall three words, he recalls one S-unit, and the three words in that S-unit just "fall out" automatically, in the same way that recalling the one word *ape* results in the automatic recall of three letters. There is a great deal of evidence to support the notions of organization in free recall and Tulving (1968) has provided an excellent summary of this information.

Such behavior is obviously very important. Miller (1956) has argued that humans cannot handle many more than seven items at a time. Without organizing abilities, we perhaps could only remember one seven-letter word. But, if a person recalls a seven-item list of trigrams he has actually recalled twenty-one letters. Suppose a subject can recall a list of eighteen five-letter words. By chunking the letters into words, he reduces the problem from recall of ninety letters to recall of eighteen words (by having learned English spelling he presumably has accomplished this chunking before the experiment begins). Then, by chunking or organizing the words into S-units the subject reduces the memory problem even further, perhaps reducing the eighteen-word list down to six S-units of three words each.

We suggest that organization and chunking reflect thought. Thinking is organizing. The problem then becomes one of understanding how chunking takes place, and we know very little about this process. One might chunk the three words *ape, cement,* and *rope* by composing a sentence incorporating these words—*The ape swung over the cement floor on a rope*—thus making the sentence a S-unit Or, one might chunk them by imagining a bizarre situation with the three words in conjunction (Wood, 1967): an image of a zoo keeper trying to pull an ape out of a huge vat of fresh cement with a rope. By thinking of sentences or bizarre images containing more than three of the words in a list, one could chunk more and more into each S-unit, but again probably no more than seven or so items could be incorporated into any given S-unit.

The facts of subjective organization behavior in free recall suggest that subjects are using rather complicated strategies and systems for organizing the material into larger units for recall. Such behavior does not lend itself well to a treatment in terms of direct associations between items in the list. Furthermore, it is difficult to specify the stimulus and response units in the free-recall task. The experimenter presents no stimulus for recall other than signaling the subject in some way to start recalling. And the delineation of a response in this task is not easy, for the recoding strategies employed by the subjects result in changes in the response unit across trials.

Finally, with respect to a theory of free-recall learning based on associations, consider the results of two transfer studies. In one study (Garner and Whitman, 1965) subjects learned a free-recall list of sixteen words and then transferred to another free-recall list that consisted of eight words. All eight words had been in the first list of sixteen. The result showed no positive transfer—these subjects took as long to learn the eight-word list as another group that learned the eight-word list without the prior experience with the sixteen-word list. If each item in a free-recall list was learned as a response to some stimulus (perhaps the stimulus might be the general experimental context) enormous positive transfer should have obtained, but it did not occur. Even if the stimulus were some other item in the list, some positive transfer should have occurred. The other study (Tulving, 1966) reversed the procedure. Subjects learned a list of thirty-six words. Prior to learning this list, however, one group of subjects learned an eighteen-word sublist of the thirty-six-word list. The other group of subjects learned an eighteen-word list, but none of the words occurred in the subsequent thirty-six-item list. The learning curves on the second, thirty-six-word list, for these two groups are shown in Figure 8-3. For the first three trials on this list, the group that had learned the relevant sublist (open circles) was superior to the group that had learned the irrelevant list, but after the fourth trial they were inferior.

In summary, these two studies demonstrate that learning part of a list will not necessarily benefit subsequent learning of the whole list, and learning a whole list will not necessarily benefit subsequent learning of a part of that list. These findings are indeed difficult to interpret with a theory that suggests that free-recall learning is a matter of S-R associations between items or between items and some unspecified contextual stimulus.

The work in free-recall learning is extremely fascinating, and many interesting phenomena are being discovered. Obviously, subjective organizational behaviors are instances of thinking, and as such the knowledge gained about organization in free recall should contribute importantly to our understanding of thought.

Stimulus in Verbal-Discrimination Learning. Finally, we can ask about the stimulus in verbal-discrimination learning where the subject is trying to learn the correct item in each of a set of pairs of items. The experimenter has arbitrarily selected one of the two items to be correct. As we mentioned in the last chapter, the task apparently does not require any response learning or associative learning (although we did show that associations do develop). Just how does the subject learn this task? Each time he utters a choice, he has made a response. But what was the stimulus for that response?

Instead of an associative theory of verbal discrimination, the facts of verbal-discrimination learning seem best interpreted by a theory based on the subjects' ability to behave in a manner that can be described by simple rules. Ekstrand, Wallace, and Underwood (1966) have suggested that subjects base their choice of one or the other item in a pair on simple frequency rules. Basically, they assumed that part of the knowledge of a

FIGURE 8-3. *Learning curves from an experiment on the effect of learning part of a list prior to learning the whole list. The open circles represent the group that had learned 18 of the 36 words before attempting all 36. The filled circles represent a group starting "from scratch" on the list of 36 words.*

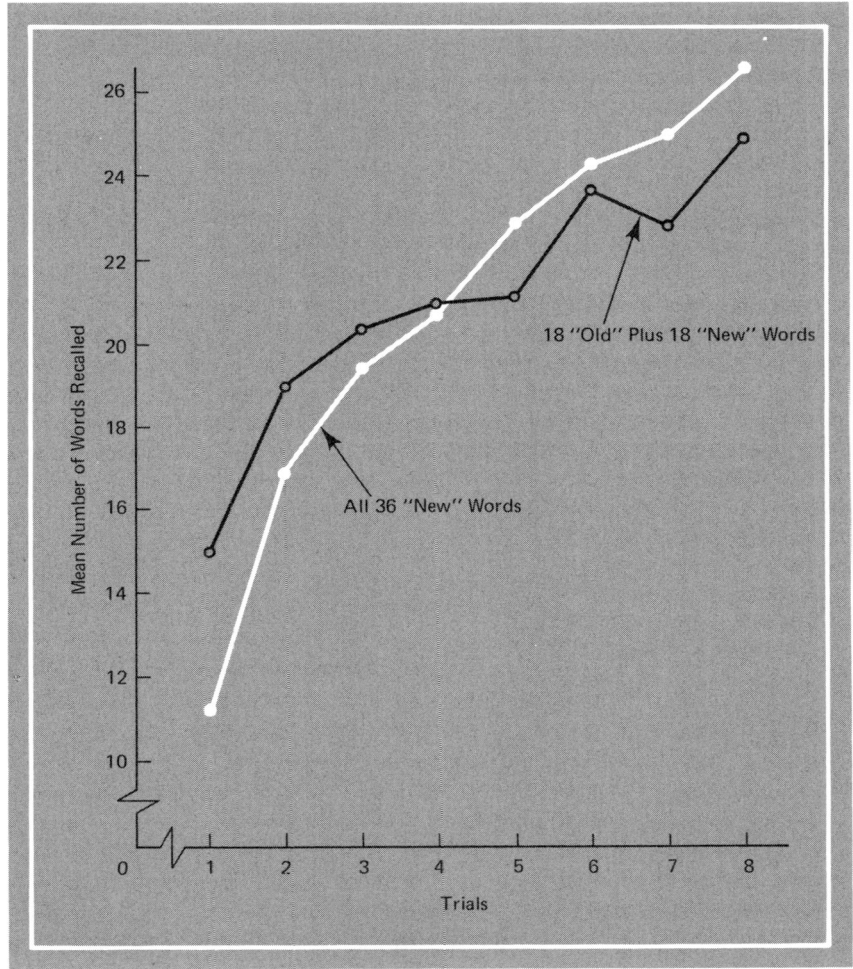

Source: From E. Tulving, Subjective organization and effects of repetition in multi-trial free-recall learning. *Journal of Verbal Learning and Verbal Behavior,* 1966, 5, 193-97. Copyright © 1966 by Academic Press.

subject consists of information about how frequently an item has been experienced. If in each pair, one item (the correct item) had been seen, heard, and pronounced more often than the other item, the subject could perform perfectly if he applied the rule, "select the more frequent item," which Ekstrand and his associates referred to as Rule 1. If the correct item was always the less frequent member of each pair, Rule 2 would apply, "select the less frequent one." Now in learning a verbal-discrimination list, the correct items tend to occur more often according to the frequency theory, since the correct item is seen, pronounced, seen again during feedback, and perhaps rehearsed. The incorrect item, however, is not pronounced as often and is not rehearsed and may not be seen during feedback. Thus, a frequency difference between the correct and incorrect items in each pair builds up across trials in favor of the correct item. The subject's behavior can then be described by Rule 1: he examines the pair for a difference in subjective frequency and selects the more frequent item in the pair.

Suppose after learning such a list, we reversed all the correct and incorrect items. We might intuitively expect some interference unless the subject is operating with rules. Thus, a rule which said, "just do the opposite of what you were doing before" would enable the subject to perform the reversal task rather proficiently. Rule 2 in the Ekstrand, Wallace, Underwood theory is just such a rule. The data on reversal learning (Paul, 1966, 1968; Paul, Callahan, Mereness, and Wilhelm, 1968; Raskin, Boice, Rubel, and Clark, 1968) show that at least early in the reversal task, subjects can perform almost perfectly, particularly when they are instructed ahead of time about the impending reversal. The reversal data as a whole seem most easily understood if we view the behavior as being governed by rules and not associations.

Comment. In summary, we have seen that identifying the stimulus and the response in verbal learning tasks is not always as straightforward as might appear from a cursory analysis of the tasks. This certainly represents a problem for any S-R theory of verbal learning. It is such a problem that we can expect a great deal of research to be devoted to understanding the nature of the stimulus. We can also expect that disenchantment with a purely S-R analysis will continue to grow and that future theories of verbal learning will involve constructs more adequately reflecting the cognitive abilities of the subjects, such as their ability to abstract and behave in accordance with simple rules.

Does Knowledge Consist of Associations?

We have stated that an adequate description of behavior must include some statement about the knowledge of the behaver. And, we have said that S-R association theories of learning have attempted to limit knowledge to associations. This has been particularly true of most theoretical attempts in verbal learning, where the knowledge that a subject has is often presumed to be nothing but associative, although everyone realizes that the associations must be fantastically complex in their interrelationships. Free-association norms are meant basically to measure the association repertoire of the average subject, and, this repertoire is used to mediate anything and perhaps everything. *Meaningfulness* of an item is sometimes measured by seeing how many associations the item will "elicit." The *meaning* of an item is sometimes defined as its associates. The whole emphasis is on associations.

In this section, we question the idea of assuming that knowledge is purely associative. We know of no better way of pointing out the difficulty with a purely associative theory of knowledge than to examine the effects of some linguistic variables on verbal learning. As we will see in Chapter 14, linguistic behavior has been extraordinarily difficult to describe with a stimulus-response theory. Many linguists feel that it is logically impossible given the present definitions of stimulus, response, and association. Here we wish merely to present some evidence suggesting that part of a subject's knowledge must be his knowledge of the language he speaks and writes; this knowledge is usually called his linguistic competence. If linguistic competence must be a part of a subject's knowledge and if this competence cannot be described in purely associative terms, then we cannot hope to explain verbal-learning behavior without some resort to nonassociative constructs such as rules, hypotheses, strategies, and the like.

Approximation to English. In 1950, Miller and Selfridge investigated the effects of a variable they called approximation to English on free-recall learning of lists of words. The basic idea was to have subjects learn strings of words that differed in degrees of similarity to a string of words that was actually an acceptable English utterance. A zero-order approximation to English, representing maximum dissimilarity, was obtained by drawing words at random from a list of the 30,000 most common words in the English language. A first-order approximation was obtained by drawing words in relation to their probability of occurrence in English, such that common words were used more often than uncommon words; however, the determination of the order of the words in a sequence was still random. At the second-order approximation and beyond, the determination of word order was contingent upon previous words. Just how many previous words enter into the determination of what word will come next defines the order of approximation. If the next word is contingent upon only one previous word, it is considered a second-order approximation. If it is contingent upon two previous words, a third-order approximation, and so on. Miller and Selfridge used eight orders: 0,1,2,3,4,5,7, and actual English text. A ten-word sample of each order is presented in Table 8-4.

The procedure for obtaining the second-order approximation was as follows: A subject was asked to use the word *was* in a sentence and might respond, "Was *he* the man who stole the car?" *He,* the word which occurred after *was,* is then given to another subject to use and he replies, "He *went* home." Then *went* is given to the next subject and so on until nine subjects have re-

TABLE 8–4. Ten-Word Lists Representing Various Approximations to English

Order of Approximation	Sample Ten-Word List
zero	byway consequence handsomely financier bent flux cavalry swiftness weather-beaten extent
first	abilities with that beside I for waltz you the sewing
second	was he went to the newspaper is in deep and
third	tall and tin boy is a biped is the beat
fourth	saw the football game will end at midnight on January
fifth	they saw the play Saturday and sat down beside him
seventh	recognize her abilities in music after he scolded him before
text	the history of California is largely that of a railroad

From G. A. Miller, and J. A. Selfridge. Verbal context and the recall of meaningful material. *American Journal of Psychology,* 1950, *63,* 176-85.

plied. The words succeeding the stimulus words then constitute the second-order list: *was he went to the newspaper is in deep and*. For a third-order list, each subject would be given two words to use, *in order*, in a sentence. The word succeeding the two stimulus words is then used as the next word in the list. The first of the two stimulus words is dropped and the remaining two words are presented to the next subject and so on. The procedure is comparable for the higher-order approximations. The first-order approximation was actually obtained by randomizing words from the higher orders. By examining the samples in Table 8-4 you can see how the word sequences approach that of text as the level of approximation increases. But remember that from the second-order on up, any two words have occurred contiguously in a sentence so that the contiguous interword association should be the same for the second-order approximation as for the seventh. For example, *he went* occurs in the second-order approximation and *he scolded* occurs in the seventh. If anything, *he* and *went* are more closely associated than *he* and *scolded*.

Next, Miller and Selfridge asked new subjects to learn the different sequences; sequences of 10, 20, 30, and 50 words were used at each approximation. The instructions asked for recall of the words in order, but a recalled word was scored as correct regardless of order. If this task consisted of just memorizing a chain of associations where each word in the sequence elicits the next word in order, then there should be no difference in recall from the second to the textual material, but orders zero and one should be significantly inferior since presumably no previous associations of any strength would be involved. The results, in terms of percentage of words correctly recalled as a function of list length are shown in Figure 8-4. It can be seen, particularly with the longest list, that there is a continued improvement in percent recalled as the order of approximation gets closer to actual English, despite the apparent equality in the association from one word to the next word for orders two through text. At the very least, the results of this experiment should have suggested in 1950 that the chaining hypothesis mentioned earlier would not adequately account for serial learning in serial recall. Instead, it appears that performance is facilitated whenever the material can be organized into larger units according to some already existing structure. Just as a knowledge of categories facilitates free recall when the words can be organized into these categories, so does knowledge of English facilitate recall when the words to be recalled are presented in an order that partially reflects the ordering rules of English syntax. The difference, however, is that no associative relationship, such as one between an instance and a superordinate, seems capable of explaining the increased recall in the case of approximations to English. One might say that the S-unit, in Tulving's analysis, becomes larger and larger, thereby reducing the memory load, as the approximation gets closer and closer to English. Certainly the subjects' knowledge of English is a necessary consideration in an explanation of these results.

Syntactic Endings. Epstein (1961) has done an experiment which shows that adding "grammatical tags" or appropriate syntactic endings to nonsense words makes it easier to learn a serial list. The materials used by Epstein are presented in Table 8-5. There are six different categories of materials, and two "sentences" in each category. Category I represents a list of nonsense words (and two function words, *A* and *the*) with appropriate syntactic endings attached in a manner designed to simulate English syntax. Category II is the same nonsense material but without the syntactic endings. Category III is a randomized order of the Category I material. Category IV has the syllables in the same order as Category I, but the endings are placed differently, in a manner designed to be incompatible with English syntax. Categories V and VI both use English words instead of nonsense words. In V, the order of

FIGURE 8–4. Results of an experiment on the effect of approximation to English on learning.

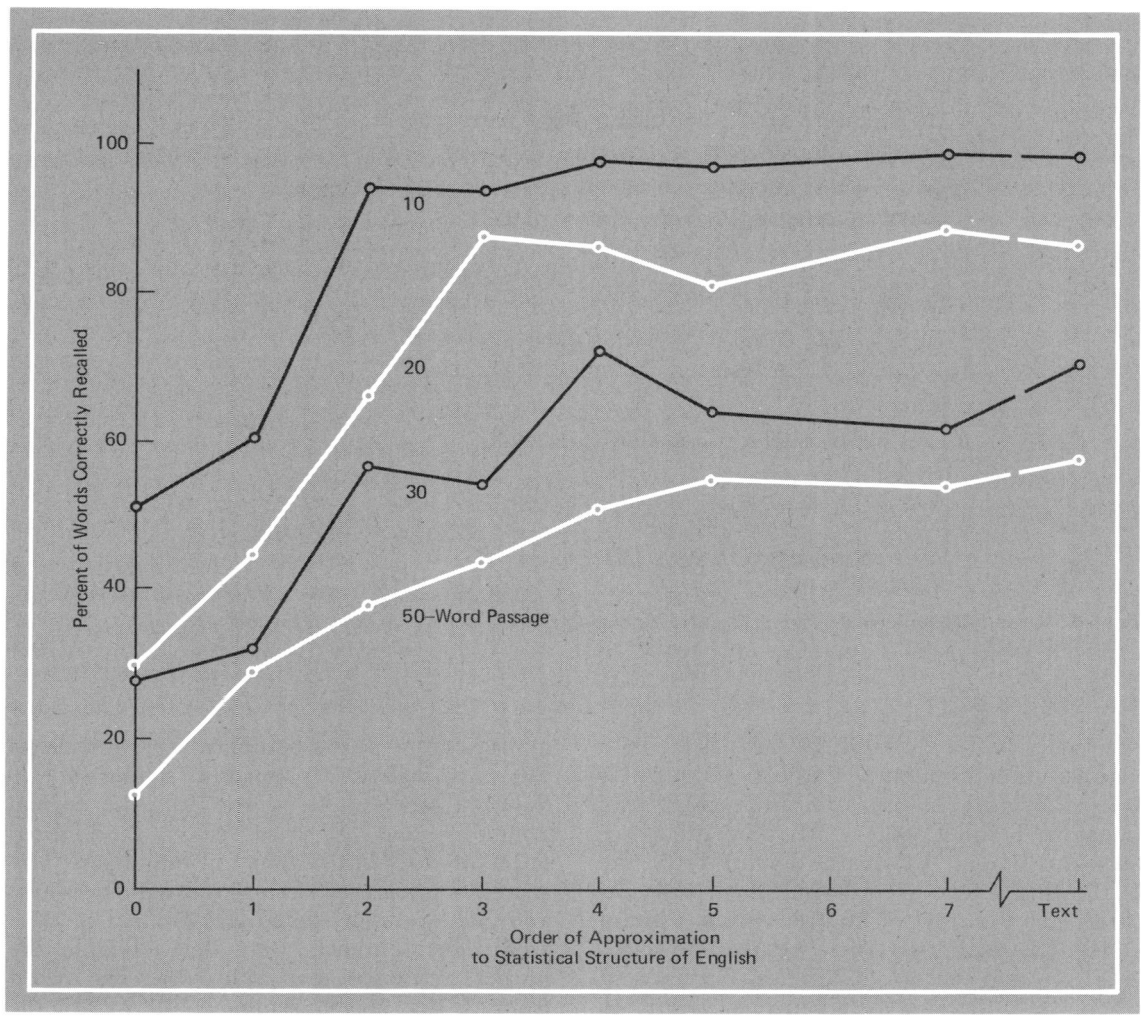

Source: From G. A. Miller and J. A. Selfridge, Verbal context and the recall of meaningful material. *American Journal of Psychology,* 1950, **63,** 176-85.

the words is designed to simulate English, while in VI the words are randomly arranged.

Each subject was required to learn both "sentences" in a category. Each sentence was presented for a seven-second study period followed by a thirty-second test, then another study period, and so on until the subject could recall the sentence perfectly. The mean number of trials to this perfect criterion is also shown in Table 8-5. Category I materials were significantly easier to learn than Category II and III materials, showing quite clearly

Verbal Learning: The Relationship to Thinking

TABLE 8–5. *Sentences Used in a Study of the Effect of Syntactic Endings on Serial Learning*

Category	Sentences	Trials to Learn
I	A vapy koobs desaked the citar molently um glox nerfs.	
	The yigs wur vumly rixing hum in jegest miv.	5.77
II	a vap koob desak the citar molent um glox nerf	
	the yig wur vum rix hum in jeg miv	7.56
III	koobs vapy the um glox citar nerfs a molently	
	yigs rixing wur miv hum vumly the in jegest	8.15
IV	A vapy koobed desaks the citar molents um glox nerfly.	
	The yigly wur vums rixest hum in jeging miv.	6.90
V	Cruel tables sang falling circles to empty bitter pencils.	
	Lazy paper stumbled to shallow trees loudly from days.	3.50
VI	sang tables bitter empty cruel to circles pencils falling	
	lousy trees paper from days lazy shallow to stumbled	5.94

From W. Epstein. The influence of syntactical structure on learning. *American Journal of Psychology*, 1961, 74, 80–85.

that when syntactic endings are placed in a manner that simulates English, learning is faster. Category V was significantly easier than Category I and Category VI. The difference between V and VI again demonstrates the facilitating effect of ordering the words according to the rules of English syntax. Epstein (1962) has replicated these results; however, he also found that the differences disappeared when the subjects were given one "word" to study at a time instead of given the entire sentence all at once.

Semantic and Grammatical Structure. Finally, let us consider an experiment by Marks and Miller (1964) which shows quite clearly that linguistic competence is a factor in the learning of structured materials. Four different types of lists of words were used: (1) normal sentences; (2) semantically anomalous sentences—the sentence is grammatical but meaningless; (3) anagram strings—a randomized order of the words from the normal sentences; and (4) word lists—a randomized order of the words from the anomalous sentences. One set of materials used by Marks and Miller is presented in Table 8-6. The anomalous sentences were derived from the normal sentences by taking the first word from the first normal sentence, followed by the second word from the second sentence, the third word from the third sentence, and so on. Note that the anomalous sentences are comparable to Category V in Epstein's study (1961) and the anagram strings are comparable to Category VI. The subjects listened to all five strings of one type and then attempted to recall the strings. Five study-test trials were given. The results, in terms of percentage of complete sentences recalled, are shown in Figure 8-5. The normal sentences which pre-

TABLE 8-6. *A Set of Materials Used to Study the Effects of Semantic and Syntactic Structure on Verbal Learning*

Type	Sentences
Normal sentences	Rapid flashes augur violent storms. Pink bouquets emit fragrant odors. Fatal accidents deter careful drivers. Melting snows cause sudden floods. Noisy parties wake sleeping neighbors.
Anomalous sentences	Rapid bouquets deter sudden neighbors. Pink accidents cause sleeping storms. Fatal snows wake violent odors. Melting parties augur fragrant drivers. Noisy flashes emit careful floods.
Anagram strings	Rapid augur violent flashes storms. Bouquets pink odors fragrant emit. Deter drivers accidents fatal careful. Sudden melting cause floods snows. Neighbors sleeping noisy wake parties.
Word lists	Rapid deter sudden bouquets neighbors. Accidents pink storms sleeping cause. Wake odors snows fatal violent. Fragrant melting augur drivers parties. Floods careful noisy emit flashes.

From L. E. Marks, and G. A. Miller. The role of semantic and syntactic constraints in the memorization of English sentences. *Journal of Verbal Learning and Verbal Behavior*, 1964, *3*, 1-5. Copyright © 1964 by Academic Press.

serve both semantic (meaning) and syntactic constraints of English are far superior to the other three types. The anomalous sentences, which preserve syntactic constraints but not semantic, are superior to the anagram strings which contain the semantic *components* of the normal sentence, but lack the syntactic components. Finally, the word lists which preserve neither semantic nor syntactic constraints are the most difficult to learn. It is interesting that Marks and Miller found the anagram strings to be superior to the anomalous sentences when recall was scored in terms of the number of words recalled, disregarding order of recall. This probably means that the subjects were reorganizing the anagram strings into normal sentences, which obviously would interfere with recall in the exact order in which the words were presented. These results show clearly that a subject's knowledge of language influences the rate at which he is capable of learning verbal materials that differ in the degree of correspondence with his linguistic knowledge or competence.

This study, together with the work on approximations to English and syntactic endings, leaves little doubt that linguistic competence is a part of the knowledge that an adult subject brings with him when he enters the verbal-learning laboratory. There can be no doubt that he uses this knowledge when he is learning. In Chapter 14, we will present additional evidence that the constructs of linguistic competence are in fact reflected in the behavior of subjects. And, furthermore, we will see that it may very well be impossible to describe linguistic competence in purely associational terms. In short, subjects use their knowledge when learning and this knowledge does not seem totally describable in S-R terms.

FIGURE 8–5. *Percent correct "sentences" recalled across trials as a function of semantic and syntactic constraints.*

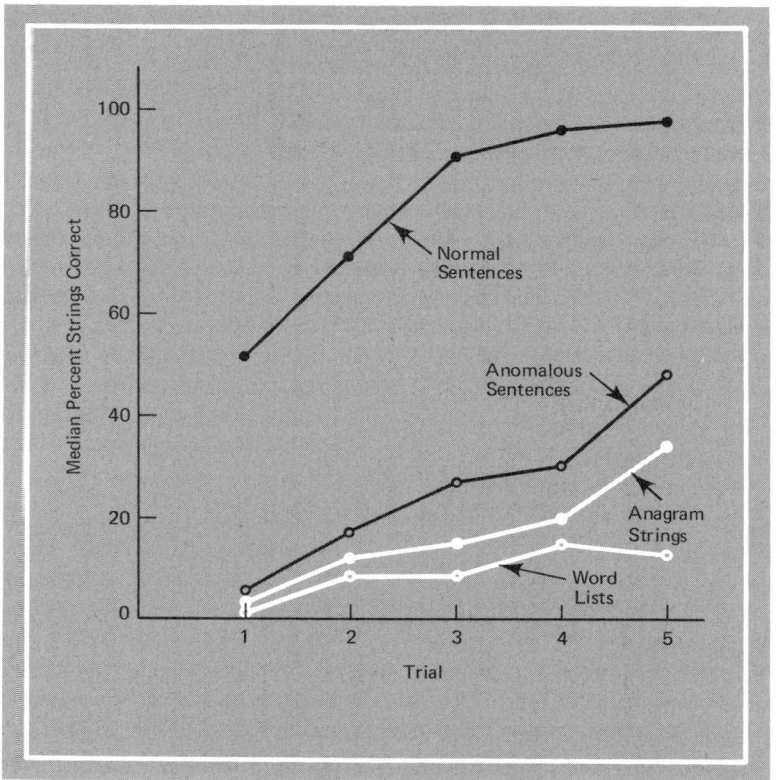

Source: From L. E. Marks and G. A. Miller, The role of semantic and syntactic constraints in the memorization of English sentences. *Journal of Verbal Learning and Verbal Behavior,* 1964, **3**, 1-5. Copyright © 1964 by Academic Press.

What Does the Subject Know How to Do?

In this final section, we will examine two of the more complex skills that subjects possess and use in many verbal-learning tasks, coding, and mnemonics. Both are indicative of the complexity of verbal learning. Both are quite clear indicators of thought. Since verbal-learning tasks seem ideally suited for studying these abilities, we have another example of an area where learning research can contribute to an experimental psychology of thinking.

Coding. Many times we are faced with a learning problem of extraordinary difficulty, one that is well beyond the capacity of our sharply limited memory system. Remember that Miller (1956) has said our capacity is about seven units. Now what if we are required to learn a sequence of many more than seven units? We know this is possible, but how is it possible if we can only remember seven units? Consider the following sequence of yes's and no's to be learned exactly in order (Miller, 1962): no, yes, yes, yes, no, yes, yes, no, no, no, yes, no, yes, yes, no. This sequence of fifteen items would be rather difficult to memorize by rote, due to its length and the large amount of formal similarity produced by the repetition of only two words. What we would like to do is transform this sequence into another sequence that is both shorter in length and lower in formal similarity. Or in the jargon, we would like to *code* (or recode as Miller has said) this sequence in a way that reduces its length and similarity. Let our code be the following:

no–no–no	=	0	yes–no–no	=	4
no–no–yes	=	1	yes–no–yes	=	5
no–yes–no	=	2	yes–yes–no	=	6
no–yes–yes	=	3	yes–yes–yes	=	7

If we have memorized this code (an octal code for binary sequences) and apply it to the sequence of yes's and no's to be learned we come up with a new sequence of numbers: 3-5-4-2-6. This sequence will be very easy to learn and recall at which time it is just a matter of decoding from the numbers to the yes's and no's. Since the typical subject can handle seven items, he should be able to handle seven numbers, which, in turn, can be decoded into a sequence of twenty-one yes's and no's. Of course, knowing the code makes the learning trivial, but we have to learn the code which might not be a trivial task. And, unless you happen to have great need for recalling sequences of yes's and no's, it would probably not be worth the effort. If you already know the code, however, it would be wise to employ it.

We all know one extremely complicated and valuable coding system, the English language. By coding experience with language responses, the memory problem can be reduced considerably, in just the same way that the number code can reduce the yes-no learning problem. Basically, the problem is that there often is much more information to be learned and retained than our memories can handle. The solution is to code the information in a way that will reduce the number of units that must be dealt with. From the verbal-learning research, it is known that meaningfulness and similarity are the two most important variables affecting the rate of learning; therefore, we would want a code that would increase the meaningfulness of the items to be learned and decrease their formal similarity. An ideal code builder would also consider the effects of semantic and conceptual similarity on the learning task. Applying this code to the stimulus materials would then result in a transformed set of items that is much easier to learn than the original set. At the time of recall, the learner recalls the transformed set and decodes these items into the original items which are then recalled.

Underwood and Erlebacher (1965) have presented interesting data on such coding strategies in verbal-learning tasks employing nonsense syllables which are anagrams and thus can be recoded into words. The syllable *TPU* can be coded as *PUT*, a transformation which reduces the memory load from three letter units to one word unit, increases the meaningfulness of the item, and probably reduces the formal similarity (orthographic) of this item to other items in the list (e.g., psychologically, *TPU* and *NTU* are probably more similar than the words *PUT* and *NUT*). However, the Underwood and Erlebacher experiments clearly demonstrated the limited abilities of humans to deal with complex situations of this sort, particularly when decoding. Our language code is so rich that we generally can encode a stimulus with ease, but unless the decoding process is rather simple and direct, we will encounter difficulties. We can easily recall *PUT* and *NUT*, but the task may require recall of the exact nonsense syllables. And since the "rule" for decoding *PUT* into *TPU* is different than the rule for decoding *NUT* into *NTU*, the subject would have to learn which rules go with which items. Underwood and Erlebacher demonstrated that subjects don't markedly benefit from the anagram coding scheme unless all the items can be handled with a single decoding rule. Certainly, the ideal code builder will want to examine carefully the decoding problems he will encounter in order to guard against decoding errors.

It is important to note that the capacity of our short term memories appears to be limited by the number of items or units and not by the amount of information conveyed by each unit. Thus, remembering seven words is about as difficult as remembering seven unrelated single letters, although in the former case one may actually be remembering well over 30 to 40 letters. In other words, by coding the letters as words we are increasing the amount of information contained in each unit of memory, but we do not substantially change the number of units that can be handled. One could then proceed to recode the words as sentences, attempting to make the memory unit a sentence, a feat that would make our memory for letters appear prodigious. Murdock (1961) has studied the short term retention of single words, trigrams (three-consonant syllables), and word triplets (e.g., *hat-dog-eat*). An item (a word, a trigram, or a word triplet) was presented briefly to the subjects for inspection. A retention interval followed which varied from 0 to 18 seconds in length during which time the subjects were prevented from rehearsing the item. At the end of the specified time, the subject attempted to recall the item. The results are shown in Figure 8-6 as the percentage of subjects correctly recalling the various types of items as a function of the length of the retention interval. Here there is clear evidence that the forgetting rate of word triplets is about the same as that of the three-consonant trigrams, both of which are forgotten more rapidly than single-word items. Such results strongly support the contention that the memory is limited by the number of items and not by the amount of information contained in each item. Recoding material to be learned into larger items (chunks) will substantially increase the amount of information we can retain in immediate memory.

Much the same analysis has been suggested for free-recall learning discussed earlier. For example, Underwood (1964), speaking about the free-recall performance of subjects who learned a sixteen-item list which consisted of four instances of each of four concepts, suggested that the memory unit was the category name, and not the individual words. Subjects may code the words *rumba, foxtrot, tango,* and *waltz* as dances. Thus, "dances" would be one item in memory but could be decoded into four words at the time of recall. The entire sixteen-word list could be coded as four items. At the time of recall the subjects presumably decode into instances, relying on recency to determine the exact dance names that had just occurred on the previous study trial. By putting category clusters in a free-recall list, one may just be providing the subject with an obvious and easy way of recoding the words into larger chunks.

Tulving's (1962) concept of subjective organization reflects the notion that when no obvious recoding scheme is available (such as category clusters) the subjects will nevertheless have to code the items into larger chunks in order to be able to recall a list that is beyond the memory span. Three words such as *hat, dog,* and *eat* might be recoded as one sentence, *the dog eats the hat.* As mentioned earlier, Tulving (1968) argues that the units of the experimenter (E-units) are single words, but these are not the same as the units of the subject (S-units), which are higher-order units or chunks, each of which contains more than one word. Free-recall learning is then largely a matter of organizing the single words into larger chunks. The evidence for such organizational behavior in the free-recall tasks is indeed impressive.

Mnemonics. Closely related to coding is the research on mnemonic devices or memory aids. In fact, one can think of most of the mnemonic "tricks" as coding schemes that

FIGURE 8–6. *The results of a short-term memory experiment.*

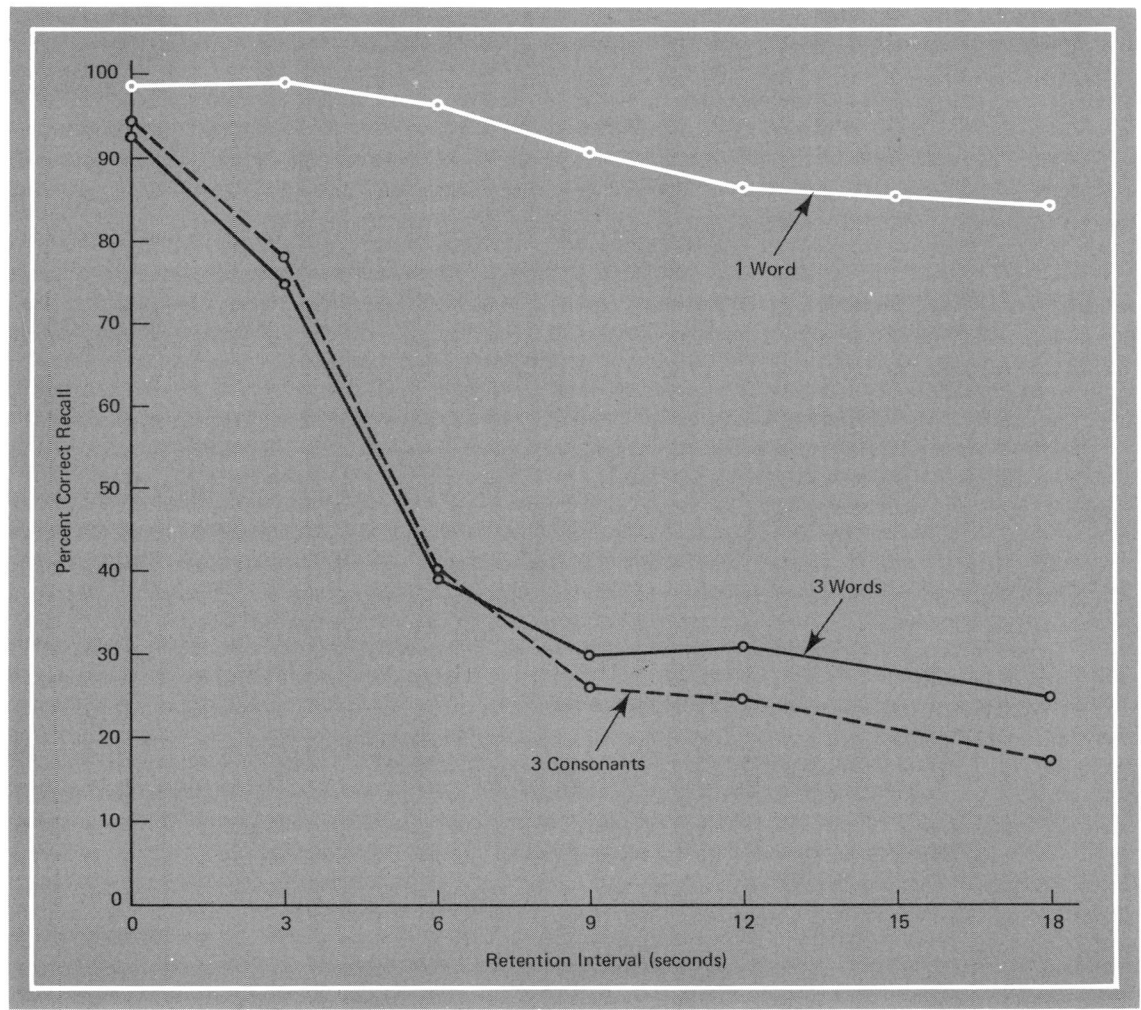

Source: From B. B. Murdock, Jr., The retentions of individual items. *Journal of Experimental Psychology*, 1961, **62**, 618-25. Copyright 1961 by the American Psychological Association and reprinted by permission.

transform the learning materials into (1) something more meaningful, (2) something that reduces the problem of decoding (retrieval), or (3) something that is a higher-order chunk. Some of the mnemonic devices accomplish more than one of these goals.

Take, for example, the recoding-cue device studied by Lindley (1963) where a trigram

Verbal Learning: The Relationship to Thinking

such as *XPO* would be coded as *expose*. This represents an example of Goal 1 (above) since the transformation raises the level of meaningfulness of the item which would make it much easier to learn. Note, however, that Goal 2 is not necessarily achieved by this strategy since the subject may have difficulty decoding from *expose* to the exact trigram. Of course, if he always codes the trigram into a word by adding one letter in front of the trigram, he will have no trouble since he could easily remember the one decoding rule necessary.

The second goal of ensured retrieval is best exemplified by an old memory scheme described by Miller, Galanter, and Pribram (1960). Briefly, the subject is taught an ordered system of "peg" words:

1—bun
2—shoe
3—tree
4—door
5—hive
etc.

As each word to be recalled is presented, the subject is instructed to construct (imagine) a bizarre image consisting of the peg word and the test word. If the first word in the list is *football,* the subject might imagine a hotdog *bun* with arms and legs that is handing off a *football* to a huge hamburger bun, or he might imagine eleven hotdog buns playing football against eleven hamburger buns before a huge throng of hot cross buns. Each successive word would be attached to its corresponding peg word in a similar manner. At recall, the subject would always be able to retrieve the peg words in order since they were well memorized beforehand and rhyme with the number designating their order. Ideally, the peg word would instantly conjure up the bizarre image which would contain the test word. Wood (1967) has studied this device and found it to work extremely well. He has also demonstrated, however, that using the same peg list over and over in order to learn several different lists of words leads to some difficulty. Since this would correspond to the A-B, A-C paradigm of negative transfer, interference would be expected. Thus, if the first word in a second list were *apple* and you imagined a live hamburger bun eating a juicy red apple, the football image from the first list might interfere at the time of retrieval. Alternatively, the football image might be completely displaced by the apple image which is fine if you don't need to remember *football* any more, but worthless if you need to remember both lists. To overcome this, one might memorize a new set of pegs for every list, but this would defeat the purpose of the system. A better strategy would be to incorporate the item from the second list into the image from the first list, perhaps by imagining eleven hotdog buns playing football against eleven apples.

The third goal involves recoding the items into larger chunks. For example, earlier we mentioned the strategy of chunking words into sentences where the words *ape, cement,* and *rope* became the sentence, *The ape swung over the cement floor on a rope.* We also mentioned the similar device of coding several of the words into a single bizarre image, the zoo keeper who was retrieving his ape from a vat of cement with a rope. Wood (1967) has studied this technique also and finds that it greatly enhances free-recall performance.

It is quite obvious from the reports of subjects and from the experimental data that subjects are terribly talented and tricky when it comes to accomplishing verbal-learning tasks. They actively employ mnemonic and coding strategies in an apparent effort to make the task as easy as possible. These abilities make it quite difficult for the experimenter who is interested in pure rote learning, uninfluenced by complex strategies, since he would have difficulty inducing adult subjects to learn without the aid of these strategies. But, because subjects employ these abilities so frequently, the verbal-learning situation offers an ideal means for the direct analysis of learning strategies.

In conclusion, there is little doubt that the typical adult subject in a verbal-learning experiment is thinking, and this is quite clearly reflected in his performance. Rules, strategies, concepts, and codes are an integral part of his repertoire, and verbal-learning tasks seem to be an excellent means for assessing this repertoire—for finding out what the subject can do with these abilities. It is time that verbal-learning theorists take greater account of these abilities. It is also time that they realize that their subjects are thinking and that thinking is not purely a matter of association, mediational or otherwise. Once this realization is accomplished in full, we can expect verbal-learning research to contribute considerably more to our understanding of thinking.

SUMMARY

In this chapter, we have examined those areas of verbal-learning research that are closely related to thinking. The first half of the chapter dealt with two crucial concepts, transfer of training and mediation, both of which have played important roles in the experimental psychology of thinking. Since thinking must involve the utilization of previously acquired knowledge, it must be dependent on the ability to transfer this knowledge to new situations. An understanding of what variables influence the amount and direction of transfer is absolutely necessary to an understanding of thinking. Verbal-learning research has been the major contributor to this understanding. Transfer of previous learning is also at the heart of mediation, a construct which has served a critical role in thinking. Covert mediational responding has been identified as thinking and has served as a process for explaining thought in associative terms. Again, verbal-learning research has been the major contributor to an understanding of mediation.

While it is obvious that mediational phenomena represent thinking, it is also obvious that all of thinking cannot be described in associative terms. In the second half of this chapter, we selected various topics which we feel most clearly demonstrate that (1) subjects are thinking while learning, and (2) this thinking is not easily described in associative terms. We have emphasized the importance of linguistic knowledge in verbal learning and have suggested that this knowledge is more than associative. We have shown that identification of the stimulus and of the response has been a difficult task, and that subjects possess abilities that reflect rather nicely the complexity of thinking. In conclusion, we have stressed the value of verbal-learning research to a psychology of thinking and we have emphasized the necessity to escape from purely associative interpretations of verbal learning. If the escape is successful, we should expect verbal-learning research to contribute as much to a psychology of thinking as to a psychology of learning.

IV Concept Formation

Nine The Nature of Concepts

The acquisition of concepts is what converts the booming, buzzing confusion of an infant's world into a relatively systematic and well-organized environment. Human beings learn to make sense of the stimuli that affect them. At least in part, that transition is based on abstracting and attending to relevant aspects of a situation, finding correct relations among stimuli, and coding distinguishable objects and events.

As a way to begin this discussion, we shall define a *concept* as any describable regularity of real or imagined events or objects. We shall say that a person understands a concept when he can identify and employ instances of the regularity in a manner appropriate to his circumstances. To learn a concept is to acquire an understanding of a formerly unrecognized regularity. All of this might sound a little too broad or vague, but it supplies some preliminary ideas which we can try now to develop and to refine in the light of certain formal and empirical considerations.

FORMAL CHARACTERISTICS OF CONCEPTS

A concept can be described by identifying the critical features or characteristics of the objects or events to which it applies and by specifying the appropriate relationship between those features. While there are many different kinds of concepts, we shall focus temporarily on a particular variety, studied extensively in experimental work—*class concepts*—to show in detail the nature of these descriptions.

Class Concepts

A class concept prescribes a partitioning of a population of stimulus objects into groups. Any describable population is partitionable. Table 9-1 portrays three distinctly different stimulus populations generated by geometric, physiognomic, and semantic dimensions, on which a large number of concepts can be

TABLE 9–1. Several Illustrative Populations of Stimulus Patterns

A: Geometrical Designs*
A population with three dimensions, each with four levels

red

yellow

green

blue

*Dimensions (and values) are: Color (red, yellow, green, and blue); Shape (circle, cross, triangle, and star); and Number of figures (one, two, three, and four).

B: Faces**
A population with three dimensions, each with three levels

**Dimensions (and values) are: Height of brow (low, medium, and high); Length of nose (long, medium, and short); and Strength of chin (strong, medium, and weak).

TABLE 9-1. Continued

C: Words***
A population with three dimensions, each with two levels

+++	++-	+-+	+--
college	bird	bridge	beauty
progress	child	metal	evening
-++	-+-	--+	---
force	burn	black	poor
tax	worry	rock	sorrow

***Dimensions (and values) are: Evaluation (good, +; bad, -), Activity (fast, +; slow, -), and Potency (strong, +; weak, -). Plus-minus designations in the examples above refer to the values on the dimensions in the order listed. Two examples for each combination of values are given. Examples are taken from a normative study of semantic dimensions reported by Heise (1965). Note that the attributes of this population are defined more abstractly, by use or by function, than those of populations A and B which are concrete, physical stimulus features.
From D. D. Heise, Semantic differential profiles for 1000 most frequent English words. *Psychological Monographs*, 1965, 79, No. 8. Copyright 1965 by the American Psychological Association and reprinted by permission.

defined. We refer occasionally to these populations in later examples. It might be also noted that these or similar populations have been used frequently for research purposes.

The partition of a population can vary in its elaborateness. The simplest concepts generate two-group partitions in which every stimulus object belonging to some general domain is assigned unambiguously to one of two categories—usually called *examples* and *nonexamples*, or *positive* and *negative instances*—of the concept. A simple, concrete illustration would be the concept *triangle*. This concept partitions the world of perceptible things into two classes—those which are and those which are not describable as closed figures with three straight-line sides. The attributes of a concept might not always be as clearly specifiable in physical stimulus terms. Think of the concept *money*, for example. Here it seems more comfortable and familiar to speak of function or use as the critical attribute, the physical characteristics of which are set by local rules (coins, shells, paper, letters of credit, etc.). Not all class concepts are binary, of course. Another possibility is some sort of color system generating a variety of discriminable categories such as *red, yellow, green,* and *blue* objects. A different dimension of concept complexity is defined in terms of the number of characteristics which are relevant to the stimulus partition. An example would be the concept of *red triangles* or of *large red triangles* for which two and three stimulus characteristics, respectively, are critical.

The description of any class concept, C, will have the function form

$$C = R(x, y, \ldots),$$

where $x, y, \ldots$ are distinguishable characteristics of instances of the stimulus population and R is the relationship between those characteristics which elaborates and completes the partition.

Reconsider the class concept, *red triangle*, from above. In its definition, the critical characteristics are redness and triangularity. For all people whose understanding of the concept is roughly the same, these characteristics must be discriminable from all other possibilities.

Knowing these characteristics, however, does not uniquely determine the concept. One must also specify the function of or relation between stimulus characteristics. In the example, one clear way to write that relation is as a conjunction—in order for a stimulus object to qualify as an example of red triangles, both aspects, redness *and* triangularity, must characterize the object. Otherwise the object is not an example.

Thus, one ordinarily understands by the concept "red triangle" the following descriptive expression

$$C_{red\ triangle} = \text{Conjunction (redness, triangularity)}$$

Attributes and Principles

Any class concept, indeed any concept, is a regularity of objects or events specified by a relation or set of relations among certain characteristics of those objects and events. To understand, recognize, and employ the concept, one must know a particular relationship among a particular set of stimulus characteristics.

Characteristics which enter into the definition of a concept are, by convention, called the defining or *relevant attributes* of the concept (e.g., redness and triangularity, from above) to distinguish them from other variable characteristics (*irrelevant attributes*) of the stimuli (e.g., largeness, tiltedness, etc.). Likewise the conceptual relationship is called the *relevant* relationship or *principle* to distinguish it from other possibilities. These two components of any concept are independent in the sense that, within limits, a given set of attributes can be related in a number of different ways to form different concepts and, conversely, a given principle can relate a number of different sets of attributes to form different concepts. For example, the conjunctive relationship between redness and triangularity forms one concept—*red triangle*—and the disjunctive relationship forms another—the class of all objects which are *red, triangular,* or *both red and triangular*. Moreover, it is obvious that almost any pair of attributes can be conjoined to form a potential concept or class (e.g., red triangle, large solid objects, male students, and so on) although many will be nonsensical (e.g., triangular students, male solids, and the like). Clearly understanding any concept depends on knowing both its attributes and its defining principles.

There is a large number of principles for defining class concepts of which disjunctive and conjunctive relationships are only two. Many of them can be expressed as compound conjunctions and disjunctions (Neisser and Weene, 1962); these principles obviously are more complex and more difficult to learn than one-attribute concepts or single conjunctions. Table 9-2 provides verbal and symbolic descriptions of several relatively (though not necessarily equally) familiar principles. To demonstrate the uniqueness of these conceptual principles, Table 9-3 shows the partitions produced when each of them is used to join a particular pair of attributes of population A in Table 9-1. It is easy to provide conjunctive and disjunctive concepts from everyday life. With greater difficulty, we can think of conditional and biconditional cases. Some examples are mentioned in Table 9-2.

These principles and our discussion thus far have been limited to fully determined class concepts—concepts which prescribe unambiguously whether each object is a positive or negative instance. In addition to these, there are concepts of a probabilistic sort which, in the current state of knowledge, do not permit perfect classification of instances. Some medical diagnoses—the patient has some or all of the critical symptoms (attributes) but doesn't get sick—or weather forecasts are familiar examples of that. Finally, it should be emphasized that there are other types of concepts beside those which assign objects to classes. Particularly common are concepts which prescribe temporal and spatial orderings of instances. Numerical sequences (e.g., the geometric series 1, 4, 9, 16 . . .) and grammatical structures in the language (articles and adjectives precede the noun they qualify in English) are examples of these ordinal concepts.

TABLE 9–2. Conceptual Rules Describing Binary Partitions of a Stimulus Population

Rule Name	Symbolic Description*	Alternative Symbolic Description	Verbal Description	Real-Life Examples
Affirmative	R	None	Every red pattern is an example of the concept	Any attribute will do
Conjunction	R ∩ S	None	Every pattern which is red and a star is an example	A *volume: large and book-ish*
Inclusive disjunction	R ∪ S	None	Every pattern which is red or a star or both is an example	An eligible *voter: a resident and/or a property owner*
Conditional	R → S	R̄ ∪ S	If a pattern is red then it must be a star to be an example; if it is nonred then it is an example regardless of shape	A *well-mannered male: If a lady enters, then he will stand*
Biconditional	R ↔ S	(R ∩ S) ∪ (R̄ ∩ S̄)	A red pattern is an example if and only if it is also a star; any red nonstar or nonred star is not an example	An *appropriate behavior: wearing an overcoat if and only if it is cold*

*R and S stand for red and star (relevant attributes), respectively.

TABLE 9–3. Assignments of Stimulus Patterns to Response Categories (+ and —) Under the Five Rules Described in Table 9–2

Stimulus Class	General Notation	Stimulus* Set	Affirmation (R)	Conjunctive (R ∩ S)	Disjunctive (R ∪ S)	Conditional (R → S)	Biconditional (R ↔ S)
RS	TT	RS	+	+	+	+	+
RS̄	TF	RTr, RC	+	−	+	−	−
R̄S	FT	GS, BS	−	−	+	+	−
R̄S̄	FF	GTr, GC BTr, BC	−	−	−	+	+

*The following abbreviations are used: T, true (or present); F, false (or absent); R, red; G, green; B, blue; S, star; Tr, triangle; C, circle. The stimulus population is a reduced form of population A in Table 9-1, having two dimensions each with three levels. Extension to larger populations is straightforward.

Indeed, as we have claimed earlier, any describable regularity is a concept; learning new concepts and applying those that are already known constitute a considerable segment of human activity.

Comment

In concluding this section, two comments are appropriate. First, it must be clear that any attribute, e.g., redness, is descriptive of a class or range of stimulation and is itself a concept. Some concepts, defined in terms of the physically measurable characteristics of things, such as color or size, are essentially unanalyzable and incapable of being reduced to a combination of other attributes. These might well be called the most primitive of concepts. More complex concepts are readily derived from simple attributes, by combinative principles and by other relational operators. The greater the number of simple attributes and the larger the number of combinations or relations, the greater the complexity of the concept. Experimental evidence on these variables as determiners of concept complexity will be given in a later section. We shall also show later how the principles themselves are interpretable as still another, higher order kind of concept.

Second, not all regularities are physical or structural regularities of inanimate stimulus objects. Much of the behavior of animals and people is also regular, predictable, and describable in conceptual terms. Some concepts, then, are concepts about behavior, including the behavior of the concept user. We learn to behave in accord with certain principles and we learn to detect particular classes of behavior on the part of others. We learn, for example, what is and what is not an "act of aggression" or a case of "bad manners" and we behave accordingly in any circumstances. Behavioral concepts such as these are not just frequent; they serve as the basis of both ordinary social interaction and the science of psychology. They are some of the most important concepts we might study.

CONCEPTUAL BEHAVIOR

Conceptual behavior is the collection of activities of organisms, especially human beings, that involves learning and using concepts. We learn the regularities of objects, events, people, etc., through a variety of means. Sometimes the concept is "discovered" or "inferred" from a series of instances, some of which are examples and some nonexamples of the concept. A child might form the concept, *dog*, largely by observation of several four-legged animals identified for him as "dogs" or "not dogs" by a companion. Similarly, a newcomer to the big city might learn the customs of the subway via a series of encounters with experienced travelers. On other occasions, the concept is explained or learned by formal instruction rather than by example. Our concepts of unicorns, genes, and other derivative ideas are certainly learned without the benefit of point-at-able instances. In any case, once the concept is understood it can generally be used to solve new problems or to serve as a basis for learning even more complex or abstract concepts of which it is only a part or an example.

Learning About Attributes and Rules

Concepts of any kind are said to be defined by a relationship among attributes of the things to which the concept applies. Learning about a concept means learning about the defining attributes and the relevant principles. While formally it is possible to distinguish between these aspects of a concept, it seems unlikely in normal circumstances that a person learns the components as separate and distinct entities. We wouldn't normally dissect the concept of white church buildings in New England into its several attributes and their conjunctive relationship. That would take an unusually analytic orientation by the learner. Rather, the learner probably understands the concept as a single coherent regularity, a single kind of structure.

Still, when a person learns a concept, it is possible that he acquires information that is useful in other problems involving the same attributes but a different conceptual principle or the same principle but different attributes. It is on that basis that, in experimental work, a distinction is made between attribute learning and principle (or relational) learning.

Attribute learning problems generally consist of a series of events or trials on which the subject acquires new information about a stimulus property (or a set of properties) of objects. *Principle learning problems* represent a series of occasions for learning a new relationship among known stimulus properties.

Examples. A couple of illustrations will help clarify the general nature of the distinction between attribute and principle learning. From infancy on, human beings with normal sensory abilities can make exceedingly fine discriminations between values on stimulus dimensions, such as size or color (Bell, 1965). But this ability guarantees nothing about the organism's understanding of or ability to use a particular dimension, the relationship (ordering) of multiple values of the dimension, or the verbal label (description) of the dimension or its values. Indeed, a familiar, primitive dimension such as size or brightness might not even be recognized as a dimension by a young child (Johnson and White, 1967). Rather, its values might be treated as unique and unrelated entities. Children probably learn, for example, to differentiate "bigness" of objects into the subdimensions, height, width, and length, only after considerable experience and training (Bruner, Olver, and Greenfield, 1966). While discriminations between red and green objects can probably be accepted as innate, and while approximately the same wave lengths of light produce the "best instances" of color categories for nearly all cultures, still the ordering and the naming of color categories is almost certainly learned. There are then some things to be found out through experience about all stimulus dimensions. The process involved in finding out is called attribute (sometimes, stimulus) learning.

Other examples illustrate the learning of relationships which are indifferent to particular stimulus properties. Suppose, for example, a series of trials is arranged on which the subject is always rewarded for choosing the unique (different or odd) member of an array of objects. Depending on a number of conditions, notably the intelligence of the subject and his motives, we might expect him in time to select invariably the unique item regardless of the stimulus properties of the array. He would pick the red object among a collection of blues, the large one from a set of small, the symmetrical one in a group of irregular figures, and so on. What the subject has learned is a general relationship among stimulus attributes, in this case the oddity principle, which does not depend on what the attributes are as long as the relevant discriminations among them are possible. For another example, see the discussion of problem-solving set in Chapter 6. This is the process called relational learning or the learning of principles.

Learning vs. Utilization

Knowledge, in general, is useful. A fact or a skill, once acquired, can be expected to manifest itself with some frequency in the subsequent activities of the learner. Once something has been learned, it is ready to be used. In fact, learning is just a brief, early, and transitory (though obviously vital) aspect of the history of a known fact or skill.

The point at which some human performance is fully mastered is, of course, debatable. But clearly under some circumstances it is more appropriate to describe the subject's behavior in terms of the utilization rather than the learning of a fact or a skill. Many, perhaps most, everyday situations for an adult admit to the utilization of known behaviors rather than require the attainment of entirely new ones.

Illustrations will help here. When we discover that the wiring in a complex electronic device is "color-coded" to distinguish subcircuits or different functional units we are utilizing known and readily discriminated attributes (values on the color dimension) to solve a conceptual problem. Likewise, circuit designers used the same concept(s) to solve problems involved in the fabrication of the device in the first place. Our discovery of color-coding depends on "seeing" the relation between this one set of obvious stimulus properties and the abstract components of the electrical scheme. Note that the device iself presents a host of stimuli and that we detected the appropriate set. Many laboratory tasks have been modeled after this general type of situation in which the subject must abstract or identify and use one or more relevant attributes from among many variable dimensions. A large body of research deals with behavior in these problems. More of this later.

Similarly, many everyday problems require for solution the utilization of known relationships or principles rather than the acquisition of new ones. Consider, for example, a simple form of arithmetic problems involving the computation of distance (D) covered by a moving object. If the rate of movement (attribute R) and lapse of time (attribute T) are known, the solution is determined by the relationship (formula), $D = R \cdot T$. Knowing the principle, as most adults do, turns this potentially difficult intellectual exercise into a triviality. In contrast to attribute utilization problems, only a meager amount of research and empirical information is available on the use of known principles.

Theoretical Remarks

It might be useful at this point to make contact with some conventional terminology and theory in psychology. Attribute learning, as that term is used here, can be redescribed in terms of the formation of stimulus-response (S-R) associations. Both descriptions have direct reference to the linking of a particular way of responding to what appears to be a physically specifiable stimulus or stimulus complex. Much of classical learning theory is predicated on the notion of association formation as *the* basic form of learning. Once an association has been formed, it is often referred to as a habit—an S-R habit—and the strength of the association is called *habit strength*. Thus, learning appropriate behaviors with respect to the attributes of objects has a seemingly straightforward and natural interpretation within classical learning theories which were developed originally to handle much simpler forms of behavior, e.g., conditioning. Moreover, the phenomena referred to as attribute utilization are interpretable in terms of the laws of associative transfer, especially those concerning the variables of stimulus and response similarity. There is more to be said on these theoretical issues in a later section.

Like attribute learning, the learning of new principles is a familiar phenomenon in experimental psychology. What is involved basically is an increasing facility with successive tasks of the same type; the more crossword puzzles or maze problems, say, that one solves, the better he becomes (up to some limit) at solving new ones. Similarly, the more conceptual problems one solves based on one or another principle, the more quickly he solves a new one. Figure 9-1 shows how performance, measured in terms of the number of instances the subject must be shown before he finds a solution, improves with practice, over a series of conceptual problems. The principles used are two of those described in Tables 9-2 and 9-3.

Unlike attribute learning, the learning of principles has no easy interpretation in classical learning theory. Heroic attempts (e.g., Restle, 1958) have been made to reduce this process to more familiar S-R terms, but these attempts have been uniformly unconvincing. One of the major problems has been the failure to identify anything in the situation which constitutes the constant and repeatable physical stimulus to which the subject's new behavior becomes associated. Is the stimulus a relationship? If so, what are its common and distinguishable physical features from problem to problem? It is not necessarily true that there are any. Consider, for example, the oddity principle. A similar dilemma could be developed on the response side of any imputed associational process. So as Hunt (1962) notes, the learning of principles ". . . has remained

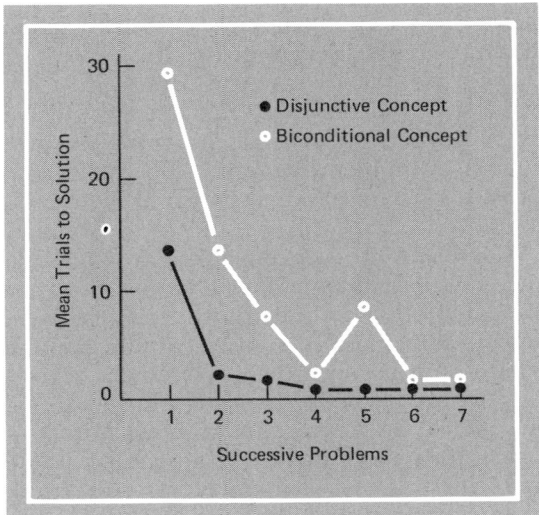

FIGURE 9-1. Mean number of trials to solution for each of seven successive concept problems. Half the subjects solved for disjunctive concepts and half for biconditionals.

Source: Redrawn from L. E. Bourne, Jr., Learning and utilization of conceptual rules. In B. Kleinmuntz, ed., *Memory and the Structure of Concepts.* New York: John Wiley & Sons, Inc., copyright 1967. Reprinted by permission of the publisher.

something of an unexplained scandal to learning theory" (p. 94).

Comment. When there are demonstrable inconsistencies between a theory and a properly coordinated and executed observation, then the theory is wrong. Either we try to elaborate or otherwise modify the theory or we seek a different approach. Although currently accepted theory appears to be compatible with many of our observations, it is clearly inadequate to explain others. A new approach will inevitably come forth.

This, however, is not the place to present a new theory, even in outline form. The primary function of this volume is to review available literature and to summarize the present state of knowledge. Thus we describe in a later section the conventional theoretical account(s) of conceptual behavior, even though they have some difficulty accounting for the learning of principles. We note in passing, however, here and on later occasions that a reasonable alternative is a pragmatic account which describes man's behavior as a rule-following system (Ossorio, 1966; Bourne, 1969). There are many fundamental differences between the rule-following model and the classical theory, not the least of which are a rejection of the notion that behavior is a determined product of underlying causal processes (e.g., associations) and an emphasis on relations rather than physical invariants (stimulus and response) as primitive terms.

For present purposes, the only point that needs to be made is that the alternative model does not limit behavior and behavioral concepts merely to observable movement caused by physical absolutes. Rather, it describes behavior in terms of rules (regularities or concepts), of which any particular movement pattern is an attribute and of which any particular behavioral episode is an instance. This form of description is appropriate whether the task in question requires attribute or principle learning, for, as we have noted, the attributes themselves are conceptual in nature. No new or different theoretical postulates are required by these apparently different processes. Thus, while there is an important functional distinction to be made between attribute and principle learning, largely based on procedural considerations, the subject's behavior is to be understood and explained in the same way in both cases. Clarifying remarks will be made where appropriate later in the text.

METHODOLOGICAL CONSIDERATIONS

In experimental work on conceptual behavior, the experimenter usually puts before the subject a contrived problem which can be solved only by learning or utilizing one or more concepts. The paradigm provides a variety of options for the experimenter, and a simple, introductory summary of these possibilities will be given in this section.

Type of Problem

Roughly speaking, there are three basic types of conceptual problems which differ in terms of what the subject knows at the outset about the solution. Recall that concepts are specified in terms of attributes and principles. In a particular problem either or both the attributes and the principle of the concept might be unknown to the subject.

Attribute Learning and Identification. In some studies, interest lies in the characteristics of the subject's performance when new stimulus distinctions are to be learned or old ones are to be utilized in some new way. Under these conditions, the experimenter might tell the subject about the general form of solution, that is, about the principle to be used. The primary task requirement is then to determine the relevant attributes of the concept from all the variable stimulus characteristics. The principle is a "given" and the attributes the unknowns for which the subject must solve. For example, the subject might be told that the concept is a conjunction of some number, say two, of attributes—C = Conjunction (x, y)—with the attributes left unspecified.

Principle Learning and Application. In the complementary problem format, the attributes are the "givens" and the relationship between them is an unknown. Here the subject must determine, on the basis of trial-by-trial information supplied by the experimenter, the manner in which one or more named attributes are related to the response system. For example, the subject might be told only that redness and triangularity are the relevant attributes—C = R (redness, triangularity).

To the extent that the principle is new and unfamiliar, some learning is required, as might be the case with a principle such as "if and only if"—red figures are exemplars of the concept *if and only if* they are triangular. Otherwise the problem requires the utilization of a previously learned principle.

Principles obviously can differ in their familiarity and difficulty. But if the subject is given practice on a particular principle over a series of problems he tends to become proficient in its application, as shown in Figure 9-1.

Comment. It is, of course, logically possible and not uncommon for a problem to be presented in such a way that the naive subject knows neither the relevant attributes nor the relationship between them. Here both aspects of the concept must be determined and, as one might anticipate, this problem format is significantly more difficult than a comparable problem with one component of the concept given (Haygood and Bourne, 1965).

Most experimental work to date has focused on problems in which the attributes are unknowns and the principle is given. In many additional cases the principle might not be stated explicitly, but it can be reasonably assumed that the subject knows and will use it. For example, when adult subjects are told that the concept involves two relevant attributes, say, *red* and *star,* most think initially in terms of a conjunctive relationship, *red star.* Because conjunctions are commonly used concepts in experiments, it is probably fair to say that most of the available empirical information concerns the processes of attribute learning and utilization. There are, however, signs of increasing interest in the potentially more complex behavior involved in learning conceptual principles.

Type of Concept

We have had occasion to note earlier that the majority of experimental problems have been based on class concepts. Even within this limitation, however, there is a large variety of possible conceptual forms and conceptual systems.

Unidimensional Concepts. The simplest concepts generate two categories and are defined on a single relevant attribute. Only objects characterized by that attribute are positive instances; any which lack the attribute are negative instances. The basic form of unidimensional concept is defined by some primitive sensory quality. Examples might be the class of all red objects, of all fragrant odors, or all tonal sounds. But increasingly more complex combinations of sensory qualities and relationships come, through learning and experience, to have all the essential features of single attributes and therefore can serve as a basis for categorizing objects. Examples of this might be the class of all bananas, all animals, all nouns, all declarative sentences, etc.

Multidimensional Concepts. Obviously, what have just been described as unidimensional concepts based on complex attributes could just as easily be described as multidimensional concepts. Objects can be classified depending on whether or not they have the attribute "banana-ness." But one could also redefine "banana-ness" in terms of a conjunction of more elementary attributes such as "yellowness and softness and sweetness . . . ." Thus, strictly speaking, except for the most primitive of sensory qualities, every concept is multidimensional. However, in this discussion, we use the term "multidimensional" arbitrarily to refer to concepts defined by a combination of two or more well-integrated (primitive or well-known) attributes in a population which includes stimulus objects of all possible attribute combinations. For example, "red triangle" is considered to be a definable bidimensional concept if the stimulus population contains red triangles, red objects which are not triangular, triangular objects which are not red, and objects which are neither red nor triangular. In a world in which all triangles were red and all nontriangles were some other color, there would be no point in (perhaps no opportunity for) holding to a distinction between redness and triangularity. Here, as in the case of yellow, soft, sweet-tasting, etc. (banana-ness), redness and triangularity would be sensibly integrated into a single attribute.

So, when the situation calls for combining two or more distinct attributes, the concept is multidimensional. There are, as we noted earlier, many ways of (principles for) combining attributes, and some of these relationships have been described and illustrated in Tables 9-2 and 9-3.

Multicategory Concepts. We have been concerned so far with binary partitions of a stimulus population, concepts prescribing two classes of stimulus patterns—positive and negative instances. This, again, is a limiting case. One can form, even on the basis of a single dimension, a number of categories or a conceptual system, constrained only by the ability to make discriminations and identifications. And even though human beings do not by any means make full use of the theoretical resolving power of their sensory systems, fairly detailed category systems are common. A familiar example is the categories of the color spectrum, hue.

Multiple-category systems can be defined on one or more dimensions. In the case of several dimensions, the separate categories might be specified by the conjunctive combinations of attributes from these dimensions—red triangles, red squares, red circles, green triangles, blue circles—or by some more complex principles.

Another example of conceptual tasks with multiple categories is used frequently in the study of concepts based on the dimension of verbal meaning. In the task, the subject must determine how a large number of common words, e.g., nouns, are to be classified. The system is sometimes related to the sensory qualities or impressions suggested by or associated with the words, so that all words eliciting the impression "white" are to be responded to in the same way, all words eliciting "round" take another response, and so on (Underwood and Richardson, 1956). An illustrative, and simplified, stimulus population for such a task is shown in Table 9-4. Note the difference in population structure between Table 9-4 and Table 9-1C. In Table 9-1C each item could be located on each of three dimensions and could be categorized with respect to any one or some combination of those dimensions, as for example, all "good" words or all "good and fast" words might be positive instances. In contrast, the category differences represented in Table 9-4 are not easily dimensionalized. One cannot easily describe either the relevant or irrelevant dimensions, though it is obviously possible to name the relevant attributes of each category.

The subject's job is to figure out which words are grouped together or assigned to the same response category on the basis of trial-by-trial hints given by the experimenter. Similar conceptual groupings of verbal items could be arranged on other bases, such as parts of speech. Some important recent work, as we have seen in Chapter 8, is concerned with the classification schemes subjects derive for themselves when their task is to commit

TABLE 9-4. *Illustrative Materials Used for the Study of Multiple-Category Verbal Concepts*

As Presented		*Proper Groupings*	
Stimulus	Required Response	*Stimulus*	Response
Chalk	White	Barrel (72)	
Mansion	Big	Derby (33)	
Onion	Smelly	Eye (32)	Round
Eye	Round	Moon (30)	
Barrel	Round	Bandage (73)	
Boulder	Big	Chalk (80)	
Derby	Round	Teeth (72)	White
Bandage	White	Milk (83)	
Cigar	Smelly	Cigar (40)	
Moon	Round	Sardine (30)	
Milk	White	Onion (49)	Smelly
Sardine	Smelly	Pine (44)	
Pine	Smelly	Boulder (46)	
Ocean	Big	Mansion (72)	
Teeth	White	Ocean (83)	Big
City	Big	City (33)	

*Materials taken from B. J. Underwood and J. Richardson, Some verbal materials for the study of concept formation. *Psychological Bulletin*, 1956, 53, 84-95. Copyright 1956 by the American Psychological Association and reproduced by permission.

Each stimulus (concept instance) is of Rank 1, meaning that its concept name is the most frequently given sensory associate to it. Number in parentheses after each stimulus is the frequency with which each concept was associated with it, relative to all other conceptual associates. See Underwood and Richardson (1956) for further details.

The first two columns show an order of stimulus items that might be used in an experiment. The second two columns show how the subject must eventually group the items.

a fairly long list of verbal items to memory (Tulving, 1968). A very complicated example of linguistic concepts is the classification of sentences according to function, e.g., declarative, interrogative, imperative, etc.

The categories prescribed by a particular concept often fall out in a "natural" order, e.g., red, orange, yellow, small, medium, large. In these cases, the system can usually be redefined in terms of some quantitative underlying variable. The extreme case of an ordered system is a continuum in which categories, as such, no longer exist. The concept admits to an infinity of values. Many concepts or functions in mathematics are, clearly, of this sort. The particular designation (value) of any stimulus, S_{ijk}, characterized by quantitative attributes x_i, y_j and z_k, is given by some function,

$$C_{ijk} = f(x_i, y_j, z_k).$$

A relatively familiar case might be a unidimensional log function. Thus,

$$C_i = \log x_i, \text{ where } x_i \text{ is a numerical attribute of } S_i.$$

The conceptual response, C_i, on each trial is some quantity on a continuous scale. The way subjects learn and use these quantitative concepts has been the focus of a number of experiments (e.g., Uhl, 1966).

Experimental Procedures

There are two major experimental paradigms currently used to study conceptual behavior. The difference between the two is basically a matter of whether the subject or the experimenter determines the sequence of concept instances encountered in the course of a problem. Each paradigm is merely a set of loose rules for the arrangement of events in an experiment. These rules are subject to change and adjustment to fit the purposes of any particular study. Further, special arrangements for independent variables and allowances for the recording of response measures must be made on an experiment-by-experiment basis.

Instructions and Other Preliminary Considerations. Before describing the paradigms, we might note that almost every experiment begins with a set of instructions to the subject. The purpose of these instructions is to direct the subject's attention to the critical aspects of the problem so that he doesn't bog down in irrelevant details. Thus, the instructions typically will include (1) a general definition of concepts, (2) a description of the stimulus population, complete with dimensions and values, (3) a statement about the manner in which stimulus instances will be presented, (4) information about response requirements and how and when responses are to be made, and (5) a statement outlining the meaning of corrective feedback which might follow a response. Any additional instructions of pretraining will depend on the special purpose of the study. For example, in a principle learning experiment, the subject might be given the names of the relevant attributes. In an attribute identification experiment, he will be told about the principle or general solution form; if the principle is new or unusual, he might also be given some preliminary examples of it and practice in its use. Instructions to the subject provide the "givens" of the problem. Everything about the task except the particular aspect which the subject must learn or use (and in which the experimenter has primary interest) should be known. Experimenters have learned by experience to pay special attention to instructions in their research. Instructions must be considered a powerful variable (or set of variables) in work on conceptual behavior.

Reception Paradigm. The most frequently used procedure in concept studies is the reception paradigm. After instructions, the experimenter presents a single stimulus object. The subject responds by classifying that object (or by somehow indicating its place within a set or system of possible responses). The subject's response is followed by *informative feedback*—a signal to indicate whether or not the response was correct and, in case of error, which response was actually correct. Then, another stimulus is shown and is followed by response and feedback. This routine continues until the subject demonstrates an ability to categorize or respond to stimuli without error.

The three events—stimulus, response, and feedback—are usually said to constitute a *trial*. One common measure of performance in these experiments is the number of trials taken by the subject before he stops making errors. In addition, the relationships among these three critical intratrial events—e.g., time between response and feedback or the availability of the stimulus object during and after feedback —have been shown to be significant variables.

Variations on the Reception Paradigm. The foregoing description of the reception procedure is a distillation of many experiments. There are some common and important variations of the theme that ought to be mentioned.

First, ordinarily stimulus objects are presented to the subject one at a time. Before a new stimulus is shown the last one is removed. Because no single stimulus (plus its associated feedback) is sufficient to solve a problem, the subject must remember the information provided on a series of trials. This mode of stimulus presentation is called *successive*.

A significant variation is to lay out the entire stimulus population before the subject, permitting him access to all previously identified and yet to be identified stimuli. On each trial, the experimenter merely designates the stimulus he wants the subject to respond to. This is the method of *simultaneous presentation*. It simplifies the problem for the subject because he can "look back" at earlier stimuli (Cahill and Hovland, 1960). A further simplification is introduced if the stimuli from early trials are marked as positive or negative instances of the concept. A related variation is to display for the subject some number of stimuli, greater than zero but less than the total number in the population. An example would be to show the stimuli of n preceding trials, where $n = 1, 2, 3, \ldots$. As you might expect, number of available stimuli is a powerful determiner of problem-solving performance (Bourne, Goldstein, and Link, 1964).

Second, it is typical to require a category response on each trial. The subject could, however, be asked to state his hypothesis as well, either before or after the presentation of informative feedback. An hypothesis in advance of feedback is essentially a rationale for the category named. After feedback, the hypothesis should reflect, and be consistent with, the new information made available on that trial. In some studies the category response requirement is dropped altogether, with the subject merely giving his best guess about the concept after each successive stimulus object is identified by the experimenter as a positive or negative instance.

One final variant of the reception procedure calls for the display of two or more stimuli on each trial, with the requirement that the subject indicate the positive instances. Like simultaneous presentation, this method should facilitate problem solving for it provides a contrast on each trial between different types of instances.

Selection Paradigm. The main alternative procedure permits the subject to choose the test stimulus for himself on each trial. The problem begins, after pertinent instructions, with the experimenter's laying out the entire stimulus population. Typically the experimenter designates one of the stimuli as a positive instance, and asks the subject for an hypothesis. Next, the subject selects a stimulus which the experimenter, in turn, identifies as positive or negative. Again, the subject gives his best guess. This routine continues until the subject can state the solution.

Variations on the Selection Paradigm. As with the reception paradigm, this procedure can be modified to fit the aims of any particular experiment. For example, the subject might be asked to categorize each of his stimulus selections, or, similarly, to try to select only positive instances. Another possibility, designed to increase the memory demands of the problem, is to require that the task be "done in one's head" without the benefit of a physically present stimulus array or, alternatively, to show the subject, at his request, only one stimulus at a time.

A final variation relates to the systematic nature of the stimulus array. It is probably most convenient for the subject if the stimulus patterns are laid out in a regular fashion so that all of a certain type, say, all the red ones, are together. Examples of that sort are shown in Table 9-1. This arrangement helps the subject keep track of which patterns and stimulus dimensions have been tested. An alternative is to introduce different amounts of irregularity (randomness) into the placement of stimuli, a variable which might easily change the subject's strategy as well as the quality of his performance.

Comment. Several comparisons have been made of performance in the reception and selection paradigms, but the outcome is still somewhat in doubt. Adult subjects seem to achieve solutions faster under the selection procedure (Hunt, 1965), while children are better under reception (Huttenlocher, 1962a). Methodological differences between studies and artifacts involved in these comparisons (Lowenkron and Johnson, 1968) make any general conclusion tenuous at this time.

Measures of Performance

Table 9-5 sets forth an illustrative subject protocol in an attribute identification problem, showing the sequence of events—stimulus, response, feedback, and hypothesis, in that

TABLE 9–5. A Sample Subject Protocol Showing the Trial-by-Trial Sequence of Events Leading to Problem Solution

Trial	Stimulus*	Subject's Category Response	Feedback	Subject's Hypothesis
1	1LR △ T	+	Correct	LR △
2	2LG ○ M	−	Correct	LRT
3	2SR □ T	+	Incorrect	R △
4	1LR □ Bo	−	Incorrect	LR □
5	3LB △ Bo	−	Correct	LR □
6	2LR □ M	+	Incorrect	SR
7	1LR △ M	−	Incorrect	1LR △ M
8	3LR △ M	−	Correct	1LR △ M
9	1SR △ M	−	Correct	1LR △ M
10	1LG △ M	+	Correct	1L △ M
11	1LR □ M	−	Incorrect	1LM
12	1LR △ Bo	−	Incorrect	1L

Solution: 1L

Total trials: 12
Total category response errors: 6

*The dimensions in the order listed are: Number of figures (1, 2, 3), Size (large, medium, small), Color (red, green, blue), Shape (square, triangle, circle), and Position (top, middle, bottom).

order—trial by trial from the first stimulus through solution. One can imagine that the stimulus sequence is determined either by the experimenter (reception procedure) or by the subject (selection procedure). The subject is required both to categorize each stimulus and to state an hypothesis. Note that if the subject knows the rule (conjunction), sufficient information to solve the problem is available after Trial 10.

Both experimental paradigms give rise to a number of performance measures, some of which are demonstrated in Table 9-5. The easiest measures to take are number of trials (number of instances or number of wrong hypotheses) and number of categorization errors before problem solution is achieved. These are counting measures which reflect the efficiency of performance, over all, but provide little detailed information about how the subject solved the problem. A derived measure would be the determination of the average number of errors made by a group of subjects on each successive trial or block of trials.

Conceptual behavior is systematic and organized. It is difficult to see its systematic nature, however, if one looks only at a single overall measure such as trials to solution, or at the individual category responses. Much more informative are analyses of the relatedness of the subject's category responses and hypotheses trial by trial with each other and with themselves. For example, how often, if at all, does the subject name a category for a particular stimulus which is inconsistent with his hypothesis statement? (See Trial 3.) Does the subject revise his hypothesis in the appropriate way and at appropriate times, e.g., after it has been disconfirmed on the preceding trial? (See Trial 4.) Does the subject make card selections on successive trials to ensure new information? (Compare the transition from Trial 1 to 2 and from Trial 7 to 8.)

There are many useful measures of this general form designed to reveal the pattern or plan, if any, in the subject's behavior. As with paradigms, however, the details of analysis will vary from study to study, depending on purpose and need, making it impossible to list them all here. The general idea always is to elucidate the complex patterns of response or *strategies* which characterize conceptual problem solving. Note that the performance exemplified in Table 9-5 is rather haphazard through the first six trials. On Trial 7, the subject gives all attributes of the stimulus, a positive instance, as his working hypothesis. From that point on, he systematically eliminates irrelevant attributes as each is infirmed. The stimulus sequence on Trials 6 through 12 allows the subject to test the attributes, one at a time, for their relevance. Such a sequence would be unlikely to appear randomly in the reception paradigm. If the subject is allowed to select successive stimuli, however, this sequence would not be unexpected and would reflect the utilization by the subject of a sophisticated, yet simple, strategy of problem solving. This approach has been observed by Bruner, Goodnow, and Austin (1956), among others, and has been labeled *conservative focusing* to emphasize the manner in which irrelevant attributes of a single (positive) focal instance are successively and systematically eliminated. Analyses such as these, and the strategies they reveal, will be reviewed in detail in later chapters.

SUMMARY

The primary purpose of this chapter has been to introduce to the reader the vocabulary and the methods of concept formation research. We have given a semi-formal analysis of concepts as a rule-form relationship among several relevant attributes of stimulus objects, commonly producing a division of those objects into two or more categories. Using this analysis, it has been possible to show how concepts tend to be hierarchically arranged, with concepts at one level—dogs—being embedded within and subsumed by concepts at a higher level—animals.

Conceptual behavior is a phrase we apply

to learning and using concepts or parts of concepts, viz., attributes and rules. Several preliminary theoretical and methodological problems that arise in an attempt to study conceptual behavior in the laboratory were discussed. Distinctions were drawn between attribute learning and rule (or principle) learning problems. Several kinds of concepts, differing primarily in their rule form or principle, were described and illustrated. The two primary experimental procedures, called the selection and the reception paradigms, were outlined in detail. Finally, the most commonly used measures of performance, dealing both with overall quality and with the subject's problem strategy, were described.

With this technical information at his disposal, the reader is now prepared to study the more sophisticated theoretical and empirical work in this area.

Ten Contemporary Theories of Concept Formation

SECTION I: The Theories

Four theoretical approaches to the interpretation of conceptual behavior are to be reviewed and summarized here. With the possible exception of the last of these—information processing models—all have developed rather directly from classical learning theory. This follows naturally from the fact that all concepts are probably learned, i.e., acquired through experience. To account for conceptual behavior one must account for its acquisition, and this requires some sort of learning theory. In addition, learning theories are generally formulated broadly enough to encompass at least some transfer phenomena, i.e., some cases of concept application or utilization in situations different from the one in which the concept was learned. Thus available theory has the *potential* to give an adequate characterization of all aspects of human conceptual behavior.

The theories will be summarized first without much logical or empirical evaluation. Tests and comparisons pertinent to an evaluation are presented in Section II of this chapter and, where appropriate, in Chapters 11 and 12.

THEORY OF ASSOCIATIONS

The oldest and easily the most influential construct in psychology is *association*. As has been discussed (especially in Chapters 4 and 7), the general notion is that for a given individual, an association between two events forms as these events are repeatedly presented together; whenever the one event occurs it tends to suggest, to that individual, the other event. If the two events in question are a stimulus (some energy change that affects one or more sensory systems) and a response (some movement on the part of the organism), we have the basic parameters of stimulus-response (S-R) associational learning theory. All learning, no matter how complex, is by assumption analyzable into its separate S-R components. More generally, the attempt is to explain behavior in terms of the acquisition of skills (responses or response sequences), supplemented by ancillary (secondary) principles of motivation and performance.

Associative Theories of Concept Formation

In a simple sense, class concepts always involve making the same response (a classificatory response) to discriminably different stimuli. The concept partitions a population into positive and negative instances, though this does not preclude the subject's ability to tell one positive instance from another.

The associationistic account is to describe concept formation as a process which forms associations between every positive or negative instance presented to or encountered by the subject and its response category. There are only two categories, so we find several stimuli all associated with the same response.

The associations are considered independent, so that one positive instance can be highly associated with that category while another is only weakly associated. However, positive instances usually tend to be more alike among themselves, and negative instances are more alike among themselves. Thus stimulus generalization—the parasitic effect of one stimulus on the associative strength of another, similar stimulus—is likely to produce more rapid acquisition of later S-R connections. In fact, one of the trade marks of concept learning is that once the concept has been mastered for a large set of stimulus instances (not exhausting the population), novel stimuli elicit the correct response, positive or negative, without hesitation or error by the subject. An interpretation within the associative framework would be that generalization from all the previously learned instances was great enough to establish associations for the "novel" stimulus without any prior reinforcement for it.

If the foregoing analysis based on stimulus generalization effects is correct, one would expect to be able to control the rate of concept learning by manipulating the degree of similarity among positive and among negative instances. The more similar positives are to each other and the more dissimilar they are to negatives, the faster the concept should be learned. The same holds true for similarity among negatives and their dissimilarity to positives. Baum (1954) provided a partial test of this hypothesis showing that frequency of between-category stimulus confusions is directly related to the difficulty of the learning task. The results are confirmatory of a stimulus generalization hypothesis, but the issue merits further empirical examination.

An alternative associationistic interpretation takes cognizance of the fact that typically it is not necessary for the subject to consider all aspects of stimulus objects in identifying or using a concept. When we talk about red triangles, we can ignore their size; when we talk about "good" words, we can ignore their *potency* and *activity* characteristics in the semantic differential sense (see Table 9-1). Thus, it seems reasonable to describe the learning process as the formation of associations only between certain aspects of the stimuli—arising from the relevant dimensions—and responses. To train a subject to respond positively to red triangles, we confirm or reinforce (through informative feedback) a positive response whenever a red triangle is presented, regardless of context, and we confirm a negative response whenever the stimulus is something other than a red triangle. Because both positive and negative instances can be large or small, tilted or upright, and so on, these dimensions—the irrelevant dimensions—are inconsistently (randomly or probabilistically) reinforced. The subject should learn to attend and respond only to the relevant aspects.

Restle (1955; Bourne and Restle, 1959) has advanced this type of theory. It asserts that on all reinforced trials associations develop between the attributes of the relevant dimensions and response categories. More precisely, each stimulus attribute is supposed, in theory, to give rise to many elements or cues. Some of these hypothetical elements, from both relevant and irrelevant dimensions, are sampled on each trial and become associated with the reinforced response at the time of reinforcement. Over the course of several trials, all or nearly all of the elements from relevant dimensions are sampled and properly associated. Elements from irrelevant dimensions, because they appear in both positive and negative instances, never stay associated with one response. Rather, because of the inconsistency of reinforcement, they are said to become adapted or neutralized, i.e., the subject learns to ignore them. When the concept has been attained, all relevant elements are in a state of association with a response, and all irrelevant elements are ineffective. The main structural parameter of the theory is the rate of association formation and adaptation, taken to be a function of the proportion of relevant elements in the entire population of elements. A mathematical statement of the theory has been used in the interpretation of several experiments (Bourne and Restle, 1959; Bourne, 1963a).

Comment

The theoretical ideas summarized above do not exhaust the variety of interpretations of conceptual behavior offered by associational theorists. Other possibilities were introduced in Chapters 4 and 7, and it is relatively easy to see how they might be translated for applicability here. This presentation is intended to give some basic and commonly accepted associational principles and an indication of their relationship to concept learning and concept utilization. The reader interested in the more detailed and complete expansion of the associative point of view of learning is encouraged to look elsewhere (e.g., Hilgard and Bower, 1966).

THEORY OF HYPOTHESES

An idea nearly as popular in learning theory as association is *hypothesis*. This notion has been incorporated in several psychological theories of conceptual behavior. The general idea is that learning how to perform properly in any given situation is a matter of testing various possibilities until the correct way is discovered. In theory, the subject's behavior is always guided by some hypothesis, some internal representation of behavior. Learning is conceived as a discrete process—an all-at-once change in behavior from an inadequate to an adequate way of responding.

Restle's Strategy-Selection Theory

Differences among the various hypothesis theories of learning are largely a matter of how hypotheses are selected for test. Restle (1962) has suggested a variety of alternatives ranging all the way from (1) a theory which permits the subject to test all allowable (determined by the conditions of the task) hypotheses at once, arriving at a solution by eliminating subsets of wrong hypotheses with each successive trial, through all intermediate cases to (2) a theory which permits the subject to test only one hypothesis at a time. Restle has given formal, mathematical development to this variety of theoretical models. In the process, he proves the counter intuitive theorem that predictions about the subject's overall performance in problems are unaffected by the size of the hypothesis sample he selects and works with. Because there is no logical connection between the terms of the theory and behavior in the real world, it is impossible to test this theorem decisively. Still it would seem that a careful study, apparently yet to be undertaken, would show that subjects who are able to keep more than one hypothesis in mind *will* perform better in conceptual problems than those who cannot.

Some Special Considerations. One critical assumption of all of Restle's models is that subjects resample from the hypothesis pool only on error trials, i.e., trials on which the hypothesis or hypotheses which guide his response lead him to miscategorize a stimulus.

When the subject entertains only a single hypothesis on each trial, the implication is that he stays with the selected hypothesis until it leads him to make a category error. (Note that the correct hypothesis never leads to error so the subject will never encounter an occasion to change.) The further implication is that the subject can learn, i.e., can solve the problem, only on or just after an error trial; correct category response based on an erroneous hypothesis does not lead him to change his approach.

When the subject entertains more than one hypothesis, significant changes are presumed to occur on correct response trials. In this case, some hypotheses will suggest a positive response and others a negative response for any stimulus. The subject responds in accord with the greater proportion of hypotheses in his sample. If the subject is correct, he is assumed to set aside all hypotheses which would have led to an alternative response, working in terms of a smaller sample in the next trial. If he is wrong, then, as in the first case, he resamples from the entire hypothesis population.

A second noteworthy assumption, implicit in the preceding discussion, is that a subject can remember only the hypothesis, or hypotheses, he is currently using. If he makes an error, he rejects his current hypothesis but cannot remember which hypotheses have been disconfirmed in earlier trials. Therefore, he randomly samples from the hypothesis population and, in effect, starts the problem over again. Mathematically this description is based on the theory of uncertain, recurrent events (Feller, 1957). An error resets the subject back to zero, and he works as if the problem had just started.

As do other aspects of Restle's model, this assumption seems patently wrong. Yet empirical data on memory in concept learning, which will be summarized in a later section, do suggest that subjects typically remember only a limited amount of information from preceding trials. (In a special situation to be discussed later, however, Levine [1966] has shown that subjects remember all or nearly all of the information from preceding trials.) While the existence of some memory effects might be sufficient to reject Restle's model, his approach is still clearly useful as an approximation to the quantitative features of performance in some conceptual problems.

The Bower-Trabasso Model

Bower and Trabasso (1964) have proposed a related approach which adopts many of the assumptions of Restle's one-hypothesis-at-a-time model. The model has advanced through a series of revisions (Trabasso and Bower, 1964a, 1964b, 1966, 1968) designed to take account of new data as they have appeared. At present the theory supposes two fundamental processes: (1) a stimulus selection process by which the subject is said to attend only to the attributes of a single stimulus dimension and (2) a conditioning process by which attributes of a dimension, once selected, are associated with the available response categories. As with Restle's hypotheses, dimensions are selected randomly and rejected on the basis of error signals. The more important behavioral component of concept learning is dimension selection; conditioning, mainly because there are few responses involved in these tasks, is said to happen rapidly (in a single trial). The major difference between this and Restle's hypothesis models is that it assumes that the subject has a memory, although a limited one, for preceding events. More precisely, on each error trial the subject is said to make a "consistency check," comparing information given in that trial with the one preceding it. Dimensions which fail to pass the consistency check are set aside and not considered in the selection process. Thus, if the same attribute were assigned to different categories or different attributes from the same dimension were assigned to the same category on these two trials, the dimension in question would not be a member of the pool from which the subject makes his next selection. Both the number of trials involved in the consistency check and the length of the trial run during which inconsistent hypotheses are excluded from the hypothesis pool can be made parameters of the formal model. Attesting to the limited use by subjects of memory for previously disconfirmed hypotheses, Trabasso and Bower (1966) find it possible to account for a large block of data by postulating that the subject remembers only one previous stimulus-category outcome for a span of only three to four trials.

Learning on Correct Response Trials

Contrary to the preceding models, Levine (1966; see also Suppes and Schlag-Rey, 1965) reported that subjects make active use of information provided by, and therefore they learn on, correct response trials. He found that a subject's category response on any particular trial tends to be consistent with *all* previous trials. This led Levine to conclude that subjects compare the information (stimulus and feedback) given on each trial with what they remember was available on earlier trials and that they can, and often do, learn more, in the sense of eliminating incorrect hypotheses, on correct as opposed to incorrect response trials.

Levine devised an alternative to the Restle-type models based on the idea that subjects formulate a new hypothesis on each trial at the time of stimulus selection or presentation and in advance of feedback. Imagine that the subject is presented with two stimuli on each trial and has to choose the positive one. On the first trial, the subject's selection is clearly a guess. But once the experimenter indicates which of the two is positive, the subject is assumed to take its attributes (e.g., one large red triangle) as his first composite hypothesis. The subject then narrows that hypothesis on successive trials—each consisting of a pair of stimuli, one positive and one negative—as some of the attributes are proved irrelevant. The process of attribute elimination is said to involve formulating an hypothesis on each trial which includes only those instances in common to the hypothesis of the preceding trial and the instance selected as positive. If the subject correctly selects the positive instance, he simply accepts the new hypothesis and proceeds to the next trial. He has been able, in this correct response trial, to eliminate straightforwardly some of the stimulus attributes. But if he selects the negative instance, and is therefore wrong, he must formulate another hypothesis, consistent (if he can remember) with the hypothesis of the last trial and with the attributes of the stimulus he did not select. This, Levine claims, is a more difficult inferential task and is likely to be mishandled frequently by the subject. For this reason, subjects probably learn more (make better hypothesis revisions) after correct as contrasted with incorrect trials.

Levine's theory calls for complex hypothetical operations which are assumed to be universal among all subjects. This alone might generate some skepticism. But there are other discomforting aspects of this work. First, the problems Levine uses are quite simple in structure with stimuli varying on only four two-level dimensions. Thus there are only sixteen different stimulus patterns in the entire population. Second, the subject is presented with two stimuli on each trial providing him with an opportunity to make a useful and informative comparison (Wells, 1967) of a positive and a negative instance. Finally, Levine's subjects are given detailed instructions and pretraining and a large number of experimental problems to solve. They are highly familiar with the stimulus population and the type of solutions to be achieved before experimental data are collected, thus producing a degree of sophistication in performance not likely to be characteristic of subjects used in the majority of experiments.

Levine's theory is probably restricted to situations governed by highly limiting conditions. Experiments whose results are consistent with an error-trial-only learning principle have, in contrast, tended to employ more complicated problems with a more difficult mode of stimulus presentation and less well-trained subjects. The main point of this comparison is that we need a more flexible theoretical or analytical approach to conceptual behavior than is provided by any of the currently popular models. Clearly, the subject's behavior will depend on what he knows already, the conditions under which he must work, and the complexity of the problem to be solved. It is necessary to have a theory—hypothesis model, associational model, or some other—flexible enough to interpret these variables and to suggest their possible effects.

Note also that Levine's theory is very close to, if not actually, a behavior description. It is less abstract than the Restle models and seems better to summarize the relevant behavioral facts, albeit in a somewhat circumscribed way. Similar descriptions suitable to other problem formats and experimental conditions will be discussed later when we review the work of Bruner, Goodnow, and Austin (1956) and others on strategies in conceptual problems.

Learning and Utilization of Concepts

Most psychological theories subscribe to some sort of distinction between the acquisition of a fact or skill and its subsequent utilization. Hypothesis theories, at least those currently used to interpret conceptual behavior, are unique in the sense that they fail to make that distinction. Hypotheses (ways of behaving) are said to exist, but there are no principles which describe their coming to exist. The subject is presumed at the outset of any conceptual problem to know the requisite way or ways of responding. Solving the problem, or learning the solution, is a matter of selecting that known way from among other known possibilities.

From this one might conclude either (1) that hypothesis theories simply do not consider the acquisition of new facts to be a real phenomenon or (2) that conceptual behavior is entirely a matter of utilizing known skills and facts, possibly in unique combinations. Is isn't clear whether either possibility is favored by the majority of hypothesis theorists. Proponents have not yet addressed themselves seriously to the origin of hypotheses; a plausible suggestion as to how hypotheses do come to exist appears in a theoretical development of a different sort, which is reviewed next.

THEORY OF MEDIATION

An explanation based entirely on discriminations among properties of physical stimuli is, even for most S-R theorists, far too simple to handle the phenomena of concept learning and utilization. There are many familiar concepts (e.g., food) for which no stimulus element or combination of elements is common to all positive instances, and the learning of these would seem resistant to interpretation within such an impoverished system. One suggestion is that the basis of such concepts lies less in the characteristics of external stimulus objects than in the internal activities they initiate. This possibility attributes important functional significance to intervening or *mediational processes* in an integrated chain of events beginning with an external stimulus and terminating in an overt movement or response. Note that the idiom here is entirely consistent with S-R associational theory, while at the same time it makes allowances for what, in an alternative approach, is called an hypothesis. We will note also that the theory of mediation suggests a way in which "hypotheses" might originate.

Many psychologists have contributed to the formulation of mediational theory, but the most detailed and explicit developments come from the work of Osgood (e.g., 1953). Let us review briefly the general idea, which was laid out in earlier chapters. Overt responses are associated with stimulus objects, either reflexively or by learning. Of the total set of responses associated with a particular object, some are dependent on the actual presence of the object while others are "detachable" and can occur independently of the presence of the object. Stimuli which occur regularly or semi-regularly in conjunction with the stimulus object tend to become associated with all overt responses elicited by the object. But when they occur alone (without the stimulus object) they elicit only the detachable responses. Thus a wide range of stimuli can become associated with fragments of a behavior (response set or response sequence) associated with an object and thereby serve as a sign of the object.

These fragments represent the total behavior ordinarily elicited if the object itself had occurred and are called, by Osgood and others, mediational responses. Hull (1930), perhaps the first experimental psychologist to use this theoretical construct (or, more precisely, a related construct), referred to them as pure stimulus acts, for their main, or only, function is to produce self-stimulation—a pattern of physiological activity internal to the subject. This internal stimulation is often triggered off in anticipation of the real stimulus object and can initiate overt behaviors aimed at achieving the object. For example, an animal may stumble across a sign of its natural prey—a smell possibly—and this is sufficient to set off complex "hunting responses."

Concepts and Concept Learning

Stimulus patterns, acting as signs, are often associated with systems of mediating responses. For example the approaching mailman may be the sign of an uncollected bill, a friendly letter, an anxiously awaited periodical, etc. In each case there might be a different anticipatory reaction, mediating appropriate approach or avoidance responses to the sign. These systems were called *habit-family hierarchies* by Hull and are critical in the interpretation of concept learning by mediational theorists.

The foregoing example of the approaching mailman is what would be called a "divergent hierarchy"—one stimulus (the mailman) is associated with and elicits a number of alternative mediational responses. The importance of divergent hierarchies of behavior is best illustrated in the context of research on problem solving as we have seen in earlier chapters. The more relevant case for concepts is the convergent hierarchy in which a number of different stimuli are associated with the same mediating response. Thus, beefsteak, watermelon, cornflakes, and artichoke are all stimulus instances of the concept "food," not because they share any physical stimulus attributes, but because they (or their signs) elicit common mediational responses of a motor, glandular (e.g., anticipatory salivating), or verbal type (e.g., "good," "wholesome," "nourishing," "tasty").

Part of what is meant by concept learning is the formation of these convergent hierarchies between stimuli and a common mediational response. Their acquisition follows the usual principles of S-R learning, including the formation of associations largely as a function of the repeated contiguous occurrence of stimulus, response, and reinforcement. The critical difference is the allowance that unobserved, and perhaps unobservable, responses can occur as a part of any behavioral episode. For Osgood (1953), the existence of common (symbolic) mediational responses is the hallmark of a true concept.

Concept Utilization

The existence of these mediators and S-R hierarchies provides the basis for transfer of training and concept utilization. To illustrate, suppose the subject has the concept of shape (number, color, and other simple stimulus dimensions) and is asked to solve an attribute identification problem, i.e., to find the dimension or dimensions which are the basis for dividing the population of geometrical designs shown in Table 9-1a into two groups.

After the usual instructions, the subject is presented with a series of designs according to the reception procedure. The first design will elicit mediational "looking" or attending responses to each of the dimensions, or better to the attribute on each dimension represented in the stimulus. Diagrammatically:

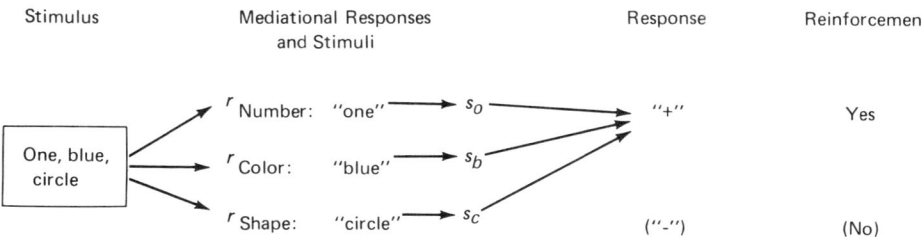

The subject responds because the conditions of the task require a response to each stimulus. The response is probably an outright guess, though the subject may have some inkling based on prior experience (e.g., "My favorite color is blue, so I think this blue circle should be 'plus.' ").

Note that the needed mediational processes for this task already exist. The subject understands all the stimulus dimensions, and we shall assume that a mediational response to each of them is automatically elicited by the stimulus with equal strength. The task for the subject is to associate a new response, say "Plus" or "Minus," to this and every other stimulus in the population.

Problem solution is achieved through the effects of reinforcement. Suppose the solution is a unidimensional concept: circles ⟶ "Plus," triangles (crosses and squares) ⟶ "Minus." Over a series of trials, attentional responses to the shape dimension will be strengthened, relative to color and number through their consistent connection with reinforcement. Every time the subject attends to shape, notices the pattern is circular (or triangular, crossed, or square), and responds "Plus" (or "Minus"), he is reinforced. In contrast, attending to color or number (or any other variation) and responding in accord with that dimension results in no better than chance reinforcement (i.e., no better than guessing based on no mediational process at all). Thus, the shape mediator becomes dominant, under the imposed task conditions, and comes to control the subject's outward category responses. The subject learns to ignore, so to speak, or not to bother attending to any characteristic other than shape. Therefore, after problem solution is attained, his behavior may be represented as diagrammed below.

Using existing mediational responses as a way of codifying stimulus objects, and putting them into categories perhaps in novel ways, would constitute an interpretation of attribute identification within this form of theory. In general within this theory, conceptual behavior is a special, mediated, associative chain of events, involving multiple converging linkages between external stimuli and overt responses, passing through a discriminatory mediational process. Concept learning is the *acquisition* of this mediational ability.

Comment

Mediational responses are a product of overt performance. They are internalized representations of that performance. They are, then, a form of internal, covert, or implicit behavior. We have seen that many mediators are likely to be elicited in any particular situ-

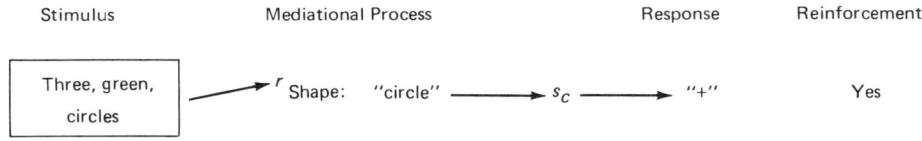

ation and that the subject's overt responses are guided by one or another of these mediational processes at any given time. The strongest mediator elicited is dominant at the outset, but if it leads the subject to make incorrect responses, it loses its control for lack of positive reinforcement or confirmation and gives way to the next strongest mediational response. So it goes until eventually the appropriate mediator becomes dominant and strengthened or sustained by consistent reinforcement (or until the subject exhausts his mediational repertoire).

Under these circumstances the subject will appear to be shifting his response basis until he "hits upon" the correct way to respond. The shifting might give the appearance of discontinuity, an all-or-none testing of one thing, then another. This is the type of performance which others have called hypothesis testing and which led to the development of hypothesis theories to account for conceptual behavior. Mediational theories attempt to explain the same performance characteristics by reference to a different internal process—a stimulus elicitation process as contrasted with a random selection process for hypotheses—but both theories do lead to somewhat similar expectations and predictions. One point on the side of mediational theory which is of heuristic significance is that it does, in contrast to hypothesis theories, make explicit statements about the origin of the assumed internal, controlling process. It seems reasonable that the subject must learn to differentiate some stimulus attributes before he can use them as a basis for hypotheses. The prior learning requisite to hypothesis testing might derive from the acquisition of associations between stimulus attributes and responses and their internalization as mediational processes.

THEORY OF INFORMATION PROCESSING

This discussion might be titled more familiarly "computer theories of behavior," for most of the work to be summarized shows clearly the influence of computing science and technology. In the first place information processing theories are predicated largely on analogies between man and high speed, electronic computing machines. The general idea is that both consist of a system which accepts external information (stimuli or input), operates on it in a variety of ways (internal responding or information processing), and delivers up an answer (behavior or output). Since we typically have direct sensory access to input and output, the theory largely concerns the information processing functions which convert one into the other.

A secondary effect has come from the use of computers to expand and test theoretical structures. One difficulty of theoretical work involves keeping the system internally consistent as it is developed to accommodate additional, new empirical results. Another is the problem of generating predictions. Both become increasingly more severe as the theory is elaborated. But these are human limitations; people have an ability to process just so much information and still keep things straight. So do computers, of course, but there is a vast difference in the upper limits for human beings and for contemporary computing systems. Clearly, computing hardware has enlarged the range and complexity of theoretical problems with which psychology can deal successfully and, as a consequence, it has had a direct influence on the recent development of psychological science.

The use of computer programs as a theoretical format has already been discussed (see Chapter 4). The idea is to write a program which has the computer behave (test hypotheses, form associations, etc.) as a human being might behave and at the same time come to solutions similar to those people are likely to produce. It is worth repeating that, in principle, simulating human behavior with computer programs is indifferent to the theoretical assumptions made by the programmer-theorist. It turns out, however, that most of the computer models which have been popular in the area of conceptual behavior are best characterized as extensions of the hypothesis-testing idea. They are theories that make performance dependent on antecedent, internal cognitive activities. But, rather than being limited to the simple one-hypothesis-at-a-time, independence-of-selection assumptions which have been typical of many other theoretical structures written in the same idiom, this approach affords the organism considerable flexibility. This, incidentally, is a good example of the constraints placed on theoretical work by the limited capacity of the unassisted human being—a theorist—to deal adequately with a large amount of data. The subject is assumed to have a variety of information processing skills and is expected to generate a complex, highly integrated series of hypothesis operations in the course of achieving problem solution.

Hunt's Concept Learning System

There have been several attempts to simulate conceptual behavior with computing programs. To illustrate the approach we summarize a program developed by Hunt (1962; see also Hunt, Marin, and Stone, 1966), which solves problems based on some unknown class concept. As with other models of this type, the program consists of a set of routines and subroutines which carry out elementary operations on input and stored information. These information processing operations are flexibly organized so that any of a number might be tried as a way of achieving problem solution on each of the steps toward that goal.

The theory assumes that the learner stores away in memory the attributes of each stimulus as it is presented. Positive and negative instances are stored separately. He, the subject or the program, "learns" by constructing a decision rule for placing each new stimulus into the positive or negative category, depending on whether it exhibits one or more of the attributes presumed at the time to be relevant.

Construction of the decision rule is the critical process. At the outset the program is assumed to know neither the relevant attributes nor the principle of the concept. It has at its disposal a conditional focusing routine. This routine periodically scans the several instances stored as positive and negative to determine whether there are one or more attributes common to the members of one of these sets but not the other. If such a set of characteristics can be found—as would be the case for a unidimensional or conjunctive concept—it is used as the basis of the decision rule and the problem is promptly solved. (The procedure thus far is recognizable as a wholist or focusing strategy, first reported by Bruner, Goodnow, and Austin, 1956, and described in detail in the next section. It appears to be a commonly used problem-solving technique among reasonably sophisticated subjects.)

If no common feature is found—as is the case with nonconjunctive concepts—the program settles for the attribute (if there is one), say attribute x, which occurs most frequently among positive instances. It then divides both the positive and the negative instances into those which do and those which do not have attribute x. Having completed this operation, the program scans to determine whether among those instances with x there is any attribute, y, common to the positives (or negatives) which is missing in the negatives (or positives). If the answer is yes—as it will always be if there are only two relevant attributes and the principle is one of those given in Table 9-2—a decision rule is formed on the basis of x and y and the problem is solved. If the answer is no, the program once again takes the most frequent attribute, z, of positive instances, performs a sort into those stimuli with and without z, and looks for some attribute common only to the "withs" (or the "withouts").

This sorting and searching process continues until a critical attribute—always the last relevant attribute—is identified. It can be shown that the number of decision points produced by this process is equal to the number of relevant dimensions, which is as it should be because each relevant attribute must be taken into account in a determination of the category for any stimulus pattern. We should note, however, that the number of sorts and searches is typically not equal to the number of relevant attributes; the program, just as human subjects, can be misled into using an irrelevant attribute if that feature shows up fortuitously in a large number of positive instances.

An Example. Suppose the concept is "red and/or square." After a sufficiently long series of stimuli the program searches and finds no attribute common to positive or to negative instances. Suppose that *redness* is the most frequently occurring attribute among the positives; the program sorts patterns on the basis of the presence or absence of red. There are at that point three kinds of patterns: red-positive, nonred-positive, and nonred-negative. The program searches again and finds, let's say, two attributes, squareness and largeness, common to the second group. Given that the problem has only two relevant dimensions, additional stimulus patterns would be necessary to determine which of those two attributes combined with redness to form the concept. Eventually one of these two will be eliminated and the program will be left with a solution in the form: red-square-positive, red-nonsquare-positive, nonred-square-positive, and nonred-nonsquare-negative. All subsequently encountered patterns are so categorized. Any concept problem of the type illustrated in Table 9-2 can be solved with the routines outlined above. Note that the form of the solution is the truth table (see Table 9-3); stimuli are categorized on the presence or absence of each of two (or more) attributes (e.g., red vs. nonred) and no consideration is given to distinctions among stimuli lacking the critical attribute (e.g., yellow, green, blue).

Additional Comments. One important positive feature of Hunt's model is its ability to contend with concepts defined by a variety of multidimensional principles, such as those listed in Table 9-2. This is not to say that all conceptual forms are soluble or learnable by the system. But the fact that Hunt has been sensitive to more than the simple unidimensional and conjunctive forms is, in itself, a significant advance over other theories heretofore outlined.

Still it is easy enough to find faults with Hunt's model as a simulation of human behavior. Some of these are common to all current theories and will be discussed later. We mention here a few points which are peculiar to his approach. First, to carry out its search routine, the program must have perfect memory for a large number of stimulus patterns. Such an impeccable memory is simply inconsistent with a vast amount of empirical information (e.g., Dominowski, 1965a). Second, the program depends essentially on one overall strategy, conditional focusing, despite the well-known fact (e.g., Bruner, Goodnow, and Austin, 1956) that there is a fair amount of variability in the problem-solving methods employed by human beings. Third, the program is infallible, carrying out its information processing routines errorlessly which stands in marked contrast to the often irregular performance of real subjects. Fourth, the theory gives no hint of the origin of its assumed processes. Again, we encounter the crucial question as to whether they are learned and, if so, how.

These problems are technically soluble, even given the current state of knowledge in computing science. Better simulations can be achieved with elaborations in the parameters of the program. The solutions lead, however, to significant complications, reducing both the elegance and the comprehensibility of the theory. Still, if the aim of this enterprise is to build theories which are tested by their capacity to simulate human behavior, then these or other complications are patently unavoidable.

Simon-Kotovsky Sequential "Concept Learner"

One type of problem outside the scope of Hunt's program is based on sequential concepts. The idea here is that the subject must induce a conclusion consistent with a series of prior events. The conclusion is in the form of a principle which generates the series. A simple example is a-z-b-y-c-x . . . . If one knew the principle, which is discoverable from a sufficiently large number of entries, he could supply the next or any succeeding letter. Here, the principle is "every other letter must be the next in the alphabet reading either (for odd numbered items) forward or (for even numbered items) backward." The next letter above would then be d. While we use ordered letters for the sake of this example, numbers, colors, sizes, or almost any other property of objects could be operated on by some principle to produce a structured series.

Simon and Kotovsky (1963) assumed that subjects solve problems of this sort (i.e., learn or discover the principle) by developing a description of the sequential pattern in some of the items, by using that description to generate the next item, and by then comparing the generated item for consistency with the real next item. They wrote a computer program to carry out just these operations and, as always, built into the program certain facts (knowledge) and routines (skills) such as the order of letters in the alphabet, the ability to compare items, simple cycling operations, which serve as the primitive (given) information processing repertoire. There are some free, or empirical, parameters in the program, such as the amount of memory and the limits on ability to keep track of several series and subseries at once, as might be necessary for the example given above. Using these as a way of adjusting the program's output, Simon and Kotovsky were able to match rather closely the performance of real subjects solving sequential problems.

Comment

In this discussion we have merely illustrated the current work in computer simulation or information processing theories as it pertains to concept learning. The positive contributions of computing science to psychology are fairly obvious. Using the computer as a tool, the theorist is able to expand the range of variables, processes, and forms of behavior far beyond what he might otherwise be able to handle. Computer-based theories are still in rather primitive form and are far from reaching their full potential for systematizing psychological knowledge. Here, despite the cautions expressed in Chapter 4, is the promise of a more detailed and exacting account of human behavior than has yet been developed.

SECTION II: Preliminary Evaluation of Theories

The theoretical positions just outlined provide plausible accounts of at least some aspects of conceptual behavior. The way in which these theories are coordinated with experimental work will be demonstrated more fully in the review of experimental literature presented in the next chapter. But before leaving the theoretical discussion it is appropriate to discuss several conceptual and empirical problems which currently lack resolution.

CONCEPTUAL ISSUES

Learning vs. Utilization

Of the theories outlined, only the associational and mediational positions make a clear conceptual distinction between the learning or acquisition of new behaviors and the performance or utilization of already learned behaviors. Both systems assume that behaviors are strengthened in accord with some orderly growth process, usually predicated on response repetition and reinforcement. Both assume that behaviors are connected with environmental events (stimuli) via some internal (hypothetical) trace, and both assume that when that trace achieves any significant, not necessarily maximal, strength, the behavior in question may transfer or "be used" in other contexts. It should be noted that the similarity between associational and mediational interpretations is more than incidental. Both theories are representative of the stimulus-response (S-R) tradition in psychology and have historical roots both in philosophical associationism, or empiricism, and in Behaviorism.

In contrast to these positions, hypothesis and information processing theories begin with the assumption that the subject has a sufficient repertoire of behaviors, the origin of which is unspecified, for the problem at hand and that solving is largely a selection and utilization affair. Neither of these theories necessarily excludes the acquisition of new behaviors. As we have noted earlier, one could imagine the development of hypotheses following much the same rules as those governing mediational processes. Or it might be reasonable to allow for the "building" of complex behaviors via an integration or sequencing of simpler ones in an information processing theory. But, so far, hypothesis and processing theories simply have not dealt adequately with the phenomena of learning.

Attributes vs. Principles

In none of the theories does there seem to be a clear distinction between the learnable components of a concept: attributes and principles. Responses associated with attributes, attribute discriminations, attribute labeling, and other aspects of attribute learning and utilization have relatively clear and natural interpretations with all the systems covered. But anything that involves learning or knowledge of a relationship among attributes, as is the the case in learning even the simplest conceptual principles, presents awkward theoretical problems.

Strange as it might seem, there have been no serious attempts to represent principles generalizable over wide classes of stimuli within any model of conceptual behavior. This is true even of Hunt's approach which attempts explicitly to account for performance in problems based on a variety of conceptual principles. Hunt's assumption (made tacitly in other theories) seems to be that all cases of the learning and use of principles are reducible to cases of attribute learning. Thus all problems, regardless of principle, are said to be learned in roughly the same way, with differences in principle represented only by the way in which stimuli (or stimulus subsets) are assigned to response categories.

More on the Learning of Principles. The difficulty involved for any theory which fails to represent principle and attribute separately is easy to demonstrate. Present the subject with a series of problems, each based on the same conceptual principle. Suppose the principle is "x if and only if y" which is known to be an initially difficult relationship even for sophisticated, adult subjects (Neisser and Weene, 1962). Suppose further that x and y, the relevant attributes in each problem, are given, i.e., are named for the subject at the beginning of each problem. Over the course of the problem series the subject will improve, become proficient at solving "if and only if" problems, and indeed eventually will achieve errorless performance on each new "problem." Here we can say the subject has learned the principle. And what he has learned has nothing to do with stimulus attributes per se.

The learning of principles is a well-known phenomenon. Theories which fail to give representation to principles are logically incapable of accounting for their acquisition and use. None of the theories summarized in the preceding discussion has made even a passing attempt at showing how the subject can transfer knowledge of the principle from one problem to the next or can achieve with practice its full mastery.

EMPIRICAL ISSUES

Solution Shifts

Consider the following. The subject is given a simple unidimensional conceptual problem to solve. Red figures are assigned to Category A and green ones to Category B. Once the subject has attained the concept (demonstrated by, say, 10 errorless category responses in a row), the solution, without any forewarning or interruption, is changed. The new solution might have one of two forms, either a reversal of stimulus-category assignments (green figures in Category A and red ones in B)—called a *reversal shift*—or a change to another relevant dimension (e.g., triangular figures in Category A and squares in B)—called a *nonreversal shift*.

The empirical question is, which shift, reversal or nonreversal, is more difficult? Diametrically opposed answers to this question can be derived from some associational and mediational theories. Consider the diagram below, representing the learning that occurs in both the training and shift phases of the experiment according to simple associational principles. At first the subject establishes connections between each of the red objects and Category A and between each of the green objects and Category B. In a reversal shift, all the initial associations must be extinguished and new ones formed in their places. After a nonreversal shift, some (here, 50 percent) of the original associations are still valid; red triangles are still assigned to Category A and green squares to Category B. Thus, if

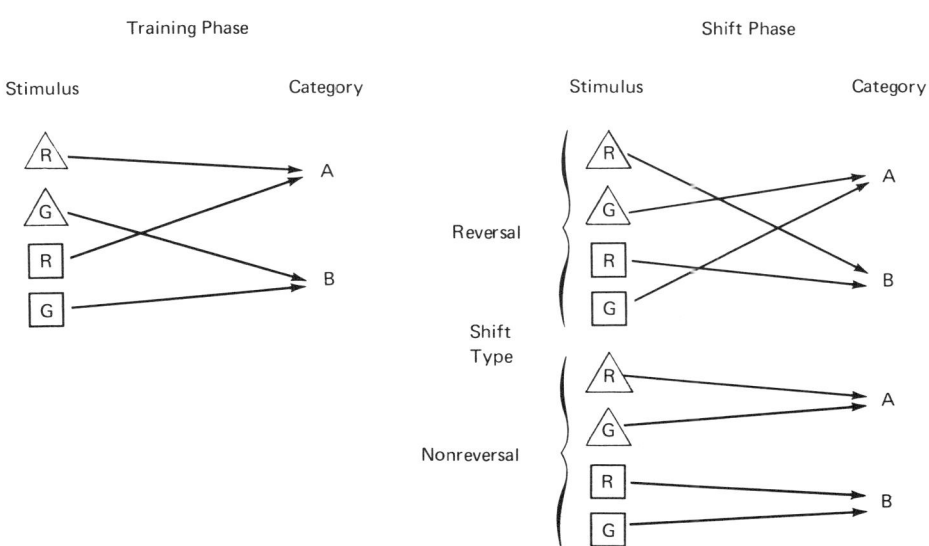

number of old connections to be extinguished and of new connections to be formed is a measure of task difficulty, as is commonly taken to be the case in associative theories, one would expect the reversal shift to be more difficult than the nonreversal shift.

But suppose the subject's behavior is somehow mediated:

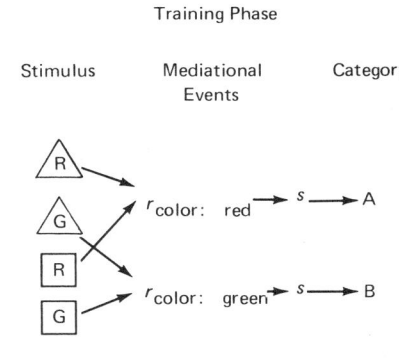

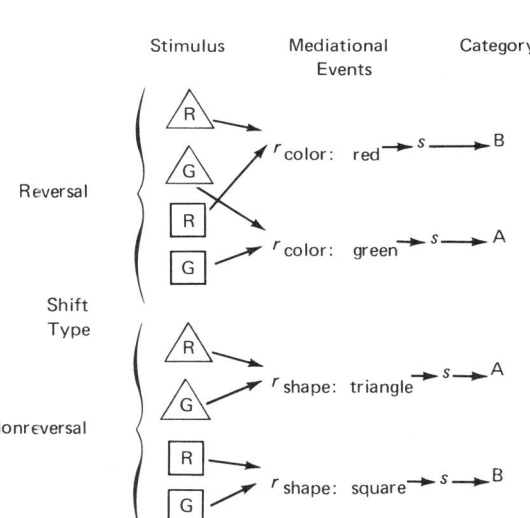

At first the subject learns to attend to color and, if the figure is red, to respond with Category A; if green, with Category B. The same dimension is relevant before and after a reversal shift. Thus the mediational response established during training is the correct one after the shift. The subject needs only to reverse his overt category responses. But after a nonreversal shift, the initial mediational process must be suppressed and replaced by a new one, corresponding to the new relevant dimension. This, according to mediational theory, should make the nonreversal shift considerably more difficult than the reversal shift.

Which of these two predictions—associative (nonreversal easier than reversal) or mediational (reversal easier than nonreversal)—is consistent with the facts? As it turns out, the answer to that question depends among other things on the subject's age and verbal ability. If the subject is younger than four years and verbally unskilled, he tends to find the nonreversal shift easier. If he is over seven years and has some appreciable command of the language, he tends to find the reversal shift easier (Kendler and Kendler, 1962).

These results have been taken to mean that the behavior of young, inexperienced, and inarticulate organisms is adequately described by simple associational principles. Their behavior is based largely on direct, unmediated associations between objects in the environment and overt responses. However, with age, experience, and the acquisition of language skill, some behaviors are internalized, that is, become capable of vicarious performance without necessarily any outward signs. These are referred to as mediational behaviors; attentional responses to a particular stimulus dimension (as described above) are an example. The capacity to mediate comes through a developmental process. Once subjects have achieved that capacity, then behavior under all stimulus conditions is based on mediated (sometimes complex, multistage mediation) associations (Kendler and Kendler, 1962). But the upshot of research on solution shifts, at least for some significant number of psychologists, is that adult conceptual behavior is more adequately represented by mediational principles than by simple associational principles.

Comment. In the foregoing interpretation we see once again a distinction between two types of behavior: (1) external and overt, usually identified with relatively gross bodily movements, e.g., categorizing a stimulus object; and (2) internal and covert, identified by various theorists with physiological processes (Osgood, 1953), as purely representational or hypothetical (Kendler and Kendler, 1962), or identified with faint or miniaturized bodily movements not ordinarily detectable by the unaided eye (McGuigan, 1966). The antecedent, covert behavior is seen as the controlling agent for overt behavior.

Whether the antecedent, mediational process exists is impossible to determine for, as things now stand, there is no direct access to it, i.e., no way to collect direct evidence. It might or might not enter into some "ultimate" explanation of the performance phenomena in solution shifts. But in the meantime a simpler account of these phenomena seems to be emerging.

Johnson and White (1967) gave children of roughly the same age as those used by the Kendlers, i.e., six and seven years, a test designed to determine their knowledge of simple stimulus dimensions such as size and brightness. The test basically required the subject to place sample objects in their proper order according to a particular dimension, e.g., from smallest to largest. The subjects also solved two unidimensional conceptual problems in the conventional solution shift paradigm. The relevant dimensions were those represented in the preceding dimensions test.

Subjects who performed better on the dimensions test also performed better on a reversal than on a nonreversal shift. The poorer subjects on the dimensions test performed better on the nonreversal shift. These results were taken by the authors to signify that a reversal shift is truly a reversal only for subjects who recognize and understand the dimension in question as an independent descriptive property of things, viz., subjects who pass the dimensions test. Those subjects who have not achieved this degree of understanding learn more or less by the independent assignment of objects to categories. This account of the change in relative difficulty of solution shifts is simple and direct, making no reference to imaginary aspects of behavior. Other things being equal, such an explanation is surely to be preferred to other, open-ended efforts.

Incremental versus All-or-None Learning

Associational and mediational theories are generally construed to imply that concept learning is a gradual process, with the subject coming to respond errorlessly only after a series of trials during which the probability of correctly classifying stimulus patterns increases from chance to 1.0. Taken at face value, this means that subjects should show some incremental improvement in performance over the successive trials of a problem. The change in performance is said to reflect the growth (with reinforcement) of direct or mediated associations between stimulus objects or their attributes and the appropriate response categories.

Hypothesis theories postulate discrete, discontinuous changes in a subject's performance, reflecting underlying changes in the cues, dimensions, or hypotheses used as a basis for categorizing patterns. In a simple unidimensional problem, for example, probability of making a correct response should lie close to chance (i.e., .5 with two response categories) until the subject selects or hypothesizes the relevant dimension, at which time this probability should change instantly to 1.0.

The issue is seemingly straightforward and should be decided by inspection of those trials immediately preceding the last error made by a subject on any problem. The test appears to be definitive and might permit the rejection of one or the other theory.

One type of potentially useful data portrayal is the backward learning curve. All subjects solving a particular problem are synchronized at the trial of last error, Trial n. Using the pooled data, one can then compute the probability, over all subjects, of an error on the trial preceding the last error, Trial n-1. Similarly we can compute the probability of an error on all preceding trials, n-2, n-3, etc. Note that in this analysis the data of some subjects, i.e., those who solve in few trials, are exhausted earlier than others. For example, if a subject made his last error on Trial 3, he would contribute to the probability computations on Trials n, n-1, and n-2, but not thereafter.

Usually these learning curves are carried back only over a few trials preceding last error, for these are the critical ones. If subjects are responding at a chance level on Trials n-1 through n-5, say, it would seem to be clear evidence of their not profiting from the experience of any preceding trials. Bower and Trabasso (1964) report data from one experiment in which error probabilities were computed over 60 trials preceding solution. The problem was a two-category, unidimensional task in which positive and negative instances were equally likely. These data are reproduced in Figure 10-1.

Clearly, response probabilities as computed did not change significantly over the trials preceding solution. Subjects seemed to be responding at a chance level until that error trial (Trial n), on which the relevant dimension assumedly was selected. Similar results have been obtained by other investigators (e.g. Erickson, Zajkowski, and Ehmann, 1966). This might be taken as disproof of incremental learning notions. But the issue is not so easily settled.

Suppes and Ginsberg (1963) found stationary learning curves in a variety of studies, but noted the possibility that in some cases these functions might arise as an artifact of pooling the data of fast and slow learners. Fast learners, whose probability of a correct response might be *relatively* low just prior to the solution, could depress the probability computed over all subjects. To avoid the possible bias introduced by individual differences in the trial numbers of last errors, Suppes and Ginsberg constructed Vincent-type learning curves. In a Vincent curve the trial sequence (prior to last error) for each subject individually is divided into percentiles (quartiles in the Suppes and Ginsberg study). Then average probabilities for each percentile are computed. This procedure tends to align all subjects at separate stages of problem solving.

An example of the trends produced by this procedure, on data that appeared in backward curves to be stationary, is shown in Figure 10-2. The functions clearly show a substantial, gradual rise prior to solution, which demonstrates that backward curves can introduce significant distortion and a misleading impression of presolution performance. From this, Suppes and Ginsberg concluded that response probabilities are clearly not always constant prior to solution and that some compromise between incremental and all-or-none learning models is necessary.

A variety of compromises are possible and have been suggested. For example, Suppes and Ginsberg (1963) propose that probabilities change discretely, but in two steps, rather than in one. Thus the probability of a correct response can exceed chance for each individual subject and still be less than 1.0. When this is the case, pooled curves will give the impression of gradualness. Another possibility lies in the Bower and Trabasso (1964) assumption of both an initial hypothesis selection and a subsequent paired-associates process in concept identification. The establishment of associations between levels of the relevant dimensions and response categories could in principle take several trials beyond the point at which the relevant dimension has been found. During these trials, the probability of a correct response is likely to increase systematically. Still a third alternative is Restle's (1962) more general theory which allows for the possibility that subjects respond in accord with several hypotheses at once, working to solution through a process of elimination. This

FIGURE 10–1. Backward learning curve: Percentage of successes plotted over trials from last error.

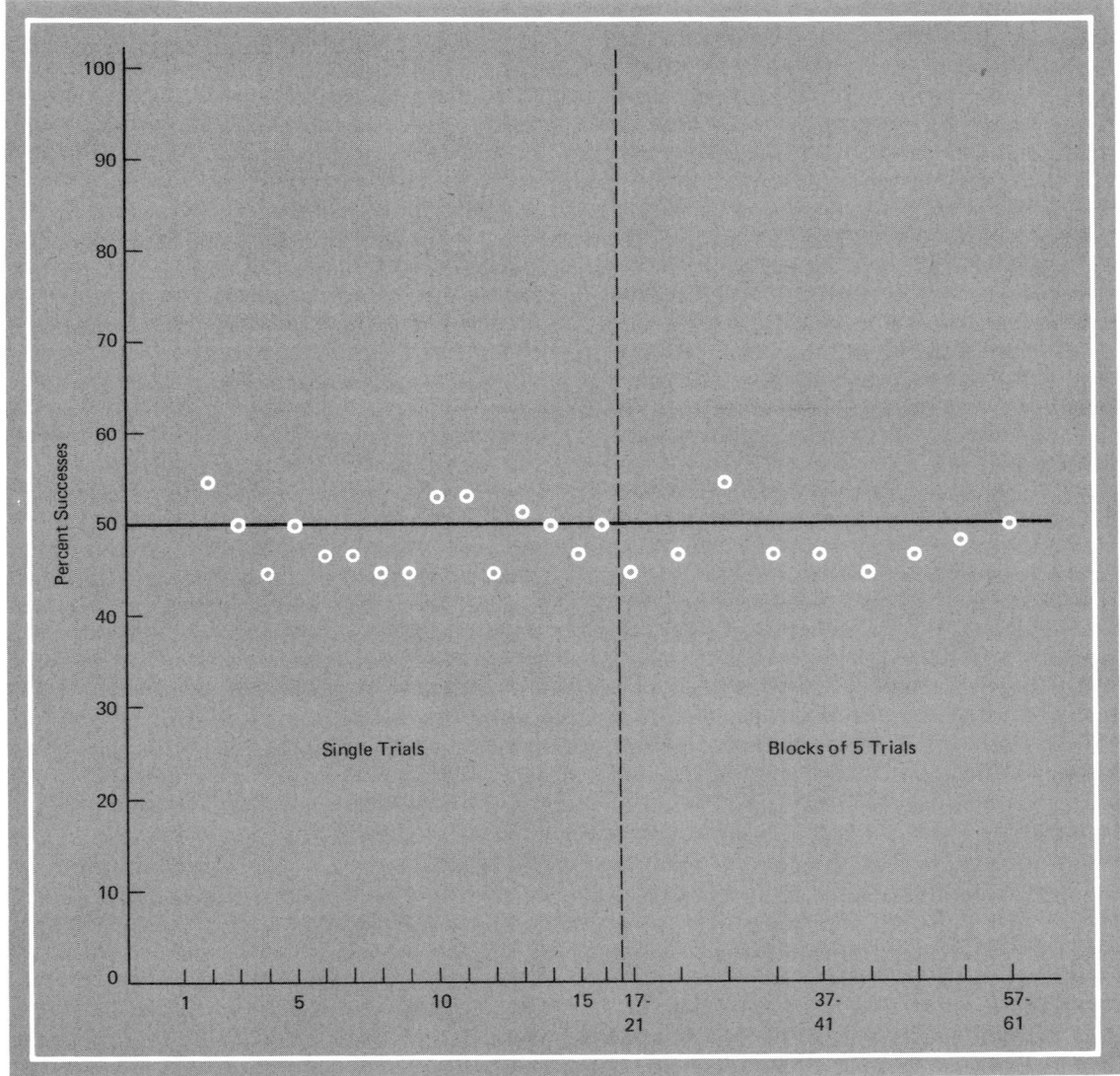

Source: Adapted from G. H. Bower and T. Trabasso, Concept identification. In R. C. Atkinson, ed., *Studies in Mathematical Psychology*. Stanford: Stanford University Press, 1964.

FIGURE 10–2. *Vincent learning curves in quartiles for proportion of correct responses prior to last error. There are three different concepts involving A, identity of sets; B, binary numbers; and C, probability.*

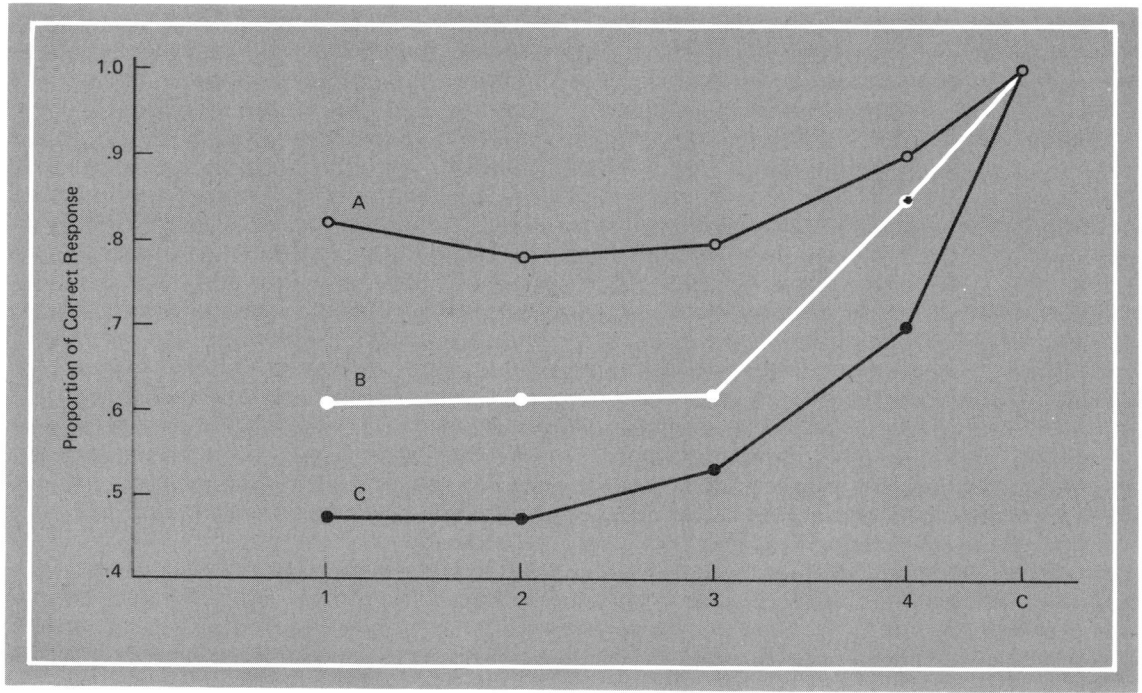

Source: Redrawn from P. Suppes and Rose Ginsberg, A fundamental property of all or none models, binomial distribution of responses prior to conditioning, with application to concept formation in children. *Psychological Review,* 1963, **70,** 139-61. Copyright 1963 by the American Psychological Association and reprinted by permission.

position captures the notion of incremental learning—a gradual homing in on the correct way of responding—even though the probability of responding correctly on any particular trial changes discretely with changes in the subject's hypothesis set.

Thus, the seemingly straightforward question—Does a subject learn in an all-or-none or in an incremental fashion?—has no easy answer. Special theoretical developments from either associative or hypothesis testing assumptions can be made to be consistent with most or all of the data. This outcome should neither surprise nor dishearten the reader. It is probably a mistake to assume that there is one true state of affairs to be found out. In every conceivable case, several theories, starting from different premises, are likely to be useful in accounting for available data and as bases for predictions about and control of future events.

Let us note one final point on this issue. Bower and Trabasso explicitly describe their work as a theory of *concept* (attribute) *identification* in contrast to *concept learning* or *concept formation.* They are concerned with a person's skill in discovering which of several well-known concepts is correct in a particular problem. Presumably, if the correct concept was unfamiliar, the characteristics of the subject's performance would be different. Now, when one reviews the relevant literature it becomes clear that experiments producing stationary learning curves have certain characteristics in common: (1) the concept to be identified is invariably one which the subject already knows; (2) the stimulus dimensions are primitive and well known; (3) the attributes within dimensions are highly discriminable and have, typically, unambiguous labels; (4) the responses are simple and highly integrated; and (5) the subject is given detailed instructions or practice problems designed to acquaint him with the form of problem solution (i.e., the principle). In these experiments the subject knows all there is to know except the relevant dimension. He can hardly show anything but a discontinuous change from chance to perfect performance.

Each of the aforementioned conditions can be varied to make the task more difficult. While a systematic research program has yet to be reported, the expectation might be that with increasing difficulty performance functions would tend to become more gradual. Thus, a seemingly more reasonable question for concern at the moment might be, "Under what conditions should we expect gradual and discontinuous learning or behavioral changes?"

Presolution Shifts

A literal interpretation of some theories yields the implication that until the subject selects the correct hypothesis, he learns absolutely nothing of relevance to problem solution. That is, for all intents and purposes, the subject remains in the same state (of ignorance) from the first through the last presolution trial (i.e., the trial of last error). If this is the case, then random reinforcements (informative feedback signals) or reinforcement of some other dimension during presolution trials should have no effect on the subject's attainment of the solution. In contrast, of course, almost all other theories would lead one to expect some influence on performance from presolution events.

Bower and Trabasso (1963, 1964; Trabasso and Bower, 1964b, 1966) have conducted a series of experiments designed to reveal the possible effects of presolution events. In the first of these studies, they used three groups of subjects, whose problems are described in Table 10-1. Reversal subjects were given feedback over the first 10 trials which was consistent with just the opposite of the final solution. Nonreversal subjects were given feedback during the first 10 trials which was consistent with the values of a different dimension from that eventually relevant to solution. Control subjects solved a normal problem with no solution shift. The idea was to determine whether early incorrect training retards learning on the final problem. Since this early training was intended to be limited to the presolution trials, any subject who stopped making errors prior to the tenth trial was eliminated.

According to Bower and Trabasso's theory, an error on any trial indicates that the subject has not yet learned anything useful. All usable subjects made at least one error after

TABLE 10–1. Schematic Outline for Reversal Experiments

Stimulus	Dimensions	Control	Reversal	Nonreversal	Final Assignment
Red	Square	A	B	A	A
Red	Triangle	A	B	B	A
Green	Square	B	A	A	B
Green	Triangle	B	A	B	B

This is an illustration of the three conditions used in a study of presolution shifts by Trabasso and Bower (1964b). A and B are the two response categories.

Trial 10, and, for all subjects, the solution was the same after Trial 10. Therefore, on the average, subjects in all three conditions should perform equivalently. On the basis of other theories, especially those which describe learning as a process of gradual conditioning or association formation, one would expect that early training leads to the partial establishment of response habits which have to change when the solution is changed. Performance on the final problem should suffer from the interference of presolution training, and control subjects should solve more rapidly than reversal or nonreversal subjects. Consistent with the Bower-Trabasso theory, however, there was no detectable difference in performance among the three groups on the final problem.

A second experiment seems even more critical for the different theories. Here, in contrast to the preceding study, shifts in problem solution were made repeatedly. Control subjects learned a normal two-category, unidimensional concept problem. For experimental subjects, the stimulus-category assignments defining solution were reversed on every other error trial. The procedure used with experimental subjects is illustrated in Table 10-2. The correct category assignments over the first three trials are red-positive, green-negative. On Trial 4, this hypothetical subject makes his second error so the assignments are reversed, red-negative, green-positive. In other words, the subject is told that his response on Trial 4 was correct. The solution remains unchanged through the next three trials but on Trial 8, when the subject makes his second error relative to the current S-R assignments, the solution is again reversed. And so on through the problem until the subject stops making errors.

The assumption of Bower and Trabasso, that learning occurs all at once on some error trial, leads to the expectation that there will be no difference between experimental and control groups in number of *informed errors*. From the assumption of gradual learning made by many other theorists, these authors conclude either that subjects should not learn at all or, at best, should learn very slowly because of the interference due to the inconsistency of feedback or reinforcement. In the experiment, performance differences between the groups appeared to be trivial and the authors concluded in favor of their own theory.

While these early studies were completely consistent with a "one-trial-learning, no-memory-for-previous-events" principle, other evidence is not so easily reconciled. For example, Levine (1962) showed that random feedback (or random reinforcement) during the early trials of a concept problem significantly delayed solution. This random reinforcement stage, varying in Levine's experiment from 4 to 60 trials, is in all important respects comparable to the various presolution shift conditions explored in the preceding

TABLE 10–2. Schematic Outline for Repeated Reversal Experiment

Stimulus	Category	1	2	3	4	5	6	7	8	9	10	11	12	13	14	...
Red	A	C	E	C	(E)			C	E	(E)			C	E		...
Blue	B															
Blue	A					C	C	E	C	(E)	C	E	C	(E)		
Red	B															

This is an illustrative subject-protocol in a repeated reversal experiment. The solution, always involving color, is reversed on every other error trial. Circled errors represent trials on which the solution is shifted, the subject being told "correct" on these occasions.

experiments and should not, in the Bower-Trabasso scheme of things, affect performance. Trabasso and Bower (1966) provided a difficult example of their own in a study of dimensional shifts, i.e., presolution shifts between two different dimensions on every other error trial. This problem also was reliably harder to solve than was predicted by the model.

To account for these apparent exceptions, Trabasso and Bower (1966) amended their model by introducing the assumption that a subject can remember one stimulus-category assignment from previous trials. On an error trial, the subject selects a new hypothesis which is consistent with the S-R assignments shown on both the error-trial and the immediately preceding trial. Thus, in the revised model, a subject is ascribed a modest ability to remember.

With this new set of assumptions, Trabasso and Bower show that it is possible to account for the random reinforcement and dimensional shift data without sacrificing the capacity to handle other presolution shift experiments. But one must become accustomed to continual change in all scientific enterprise, and studies are currently being reported which present problems even for the revised model. For example, Dodd and Bourne (1969) have shown that hypotheses selected by subjects are often inconsistent with information given on the trial preceding an error. Further they have presented evidence that subjects change hypotheses on correct response trials (see also Suppes and Schlag-Rey, 1965; Levine, 1966). Thus, it is clear that hypothesis (and other) models must be continually open to change if they are to keep pace with available data.

The "Error-Trial-Only" Learning Principle

An assumption which characterizes several of the previously discussed hypothesis theories (Restle, 1962; Bower and Trabasso, 1964) is that subjects learn, i.e., can solve the problem, only on error trials. In these theories, the subject's category responses are assumed to be controlled by his current hypothesis. Further, an error trial is the only event which occasions a change of hypothesis. Thus, the only opportunity the subject has to achieve the correct classification scheme for stimuli is an error trial. Of course, this assumption is not logically connected to hypothesis theory for, as we have seen, Levine's (1966) model allows for hypothesis changes on every trial, and conceivably one could assemble a theory of associations which form only on error (or correct response) trials. The question of "when concepts are attained" is strictly empirical and has been subjected to a number of tests, some of which will be reviewed here.

The most direct tests were performed by Suppes and Schlag-Rey (1965) and by Levine (1966). In the Suppes and Schlag-Rey experiments, subjects were asked on each trial to make a two-group classification of the entire stimulus population (equivalent to a verbalized hypothesis) contingent on the information provided by the stimulus-response-feedback sequence given on that trial. They found the proportion of changes in classifications on correct response trials to be quite high (up to .65 in some cases) and to be nearly as large as the proportion on error trials. Tendencies to change on correct response trials were pervasive and were limited neither to particular subjects nor to particular problems.

Levine (1966) adopted a similar approach. Between each learning trial (Levine calls them outcome trials) consisting of stimulus, response, and feedback, the subject had to classify four stimuli selected to reveal his current unidimensional hypothesis. The data demonstrated that when the subject received a "wrong" signal on some outcome trial, he almost always changed his way of classifying stimuli. After "right" signals, he almost never changed his classification scheme. So far, so good for conventional hypothesis theory. However, although his classifications remained stable after positive outcomes, the subject was able to use this information to reject other, previously untested hypotheses which were inconsistent with it. Indeed, Levine's data show that subjects were able to execute the hypothesis elimination process *more efficiently* on the basis of positive information (i.e., "right") than negative information (i.e., "wrong"). As we noted earlier, Levine has outlined an hypothesis theory which assumes important, though not identical, learning or information processing events to occur on *both* correct and incorrect trials.

Bower and Trabasso have explicitly limited their theory to a standard unidimensional concept problem, following the reception paradigm. Thus, one may argue on strictly methodological grounds that the Suppes and Schlag-Rey and the Levine experiments are not fair tests of their position. Both these studies used complicated, time-consuming intertrial probe procedures, designed to externalize the subject's hypothesis. Both used a variation of simultaneous stimulus presentation. Suppes and Schlag-Rey used, in some cases, complex bidimensional concepts. Granting these differences, however, the conclusion of Suppes and Schlag-Rey—that the error trial learning principle ". . . is unsound for a significant class of concept learning experiments [and] should be made a special case rather than a postulate in a comprehensive theory of concept learning" (p. 662)—seems justified.

Indirect Evidence on the Error-Trial Learning Principle: Novel Stimulus Dimensions. There is more research indirectly related to the conditions under which one can expect learning in conceptual tasks to occur primarily on error trials. Some of this work will be discussed in a later section. For now we present only one additional finding which questions the pervasiveness of this principle.

Once a subject achieves a solution and ceases to make errors, he has no opportunity, in theory, to learn or to change his hypothesis. Just as during the presolution trials, nothing of any significance happens during the post-solution trials. Thus, no matter what changes the experimenter might make in the task—just so long as they don't affect the solution or cause errors—the subject should remain insensitive to them.

Guy, Van Fleet, and Bourne (1966) executed two experiments in which the effects of events during post-solution trials on the subject's subsequent behavior were assayed. Their interest lay more precisely in the effects of introducing a new dimension of variation into the stimulus patterns after the subject had learned a correct way of classifying those patterns. The experimental paradigm of the study included three phases. In Phase I, the subject learned a simple, two-category unidimensional concept. In Phase II, which was continuous with Phase I and began immediately upon the attainment of the Phase I performance criterion (10 consecutively correct responses), stimuli varied in one additional dimension—a dimension which was constant during Phase I. For example, all stimulus patterns might have been red in Phase I and then red or green in Phase II. The solution remained unchanged, and no subject made any category errors during Phase II. The beginning of Phase III, which was continuous with Phase II, was marked by a nonreversal (NR) shift in problem solution to the new dimension, i.e., the dimension first introduced in Phase II.

In the first experiment two variables were investigated. First, the novel dimension was introduced in two different ways. For some subjects (those in Condition R) its values were perfectly correlated with the values of the relevant dimension. In other words, if the subject had learned to place all large figures in Category A and all small figures in Category B (i.e., size was the Phase I relevant dimension) and if background was the novel dimension, then in Phase II all large figures (Category A) would appear on a crosshatched background and all small figures (Category B) on a stippled background. During Phase II the subject could respond either on the basis of size or background or both and be 100 percent correct. For other subjects (Condition I), the novel dimension was irrelevant in Phase II; its values were uncorrelated with the Phase I solution. Thus the subject could not base his Phase II responses on the novel dimension and still be correct. The second main variable was length (in trials) of Phase II, taking the values 10 and 20. Two conditions were introduced as controls: (1) in Condition 0, subjects were shifted immediately from Phase I to Phase III, with no Phase II trials, and (2) there were two groups of subjects in Condition N (10 and 20 trials in Phase II), for both of which the novel dimension was introduced on the first trial of Phase III, coincidentally with the nonreversal shift.

Expectations about the outcome of this experiment seem relatively clear. If the subject learns on all trials, a principle common to but not limited to incremental learning theories, he can and should learn about the novel dimension in Phase II. When it is relevant, he should learn that it is possible to base category responses on it; when it is irrelevant he might learn to ignore it (Bourne and Restle, 1959). Considering Phase III performance, subjects should perform best in Condition R (because they have already learned partially to respond to the new relevant dimension), worst in Condition I (because they have learned to ignore the now relevant dimension, and at some intermediate level in Condition N for lack of any predisposition regarding the relevant dimension. Further, the magnitude of these differences should increase with the length of Phase II, as the subject's knowledge of the relevance or irrelevance of the novel dimension increases. If the subject learns only on error trials then, given that no errors are made in Phase II, there should be no differences in Phase II performance. The subject should execute the shift just as if Phase II did not exist.

The results of the study, shown in Figure 10-3, indicate clearly that the events of Phase II significantly affect post-shift performance. Performance in Condition I is inhibited in increasing amounts as the length of Phase II

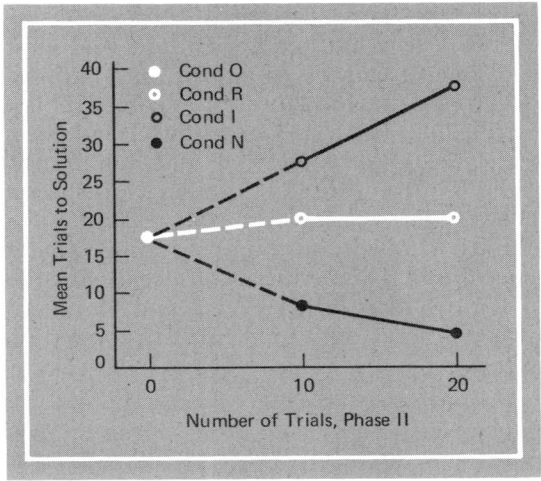

FIGURE 10–3. Mean number of trials to solution in Phase III as a function of the trial length of Phase II and the manner in which the novel (to-be-relevant) dimension was introduced in Phase II.

Source: Redrawn from D. E. Guy, F. Van Fleet, and L. E. Bourne, Jr., Effects of adding a stimulus dimension prior to a nonreversal shift. *Journal of Experimental Psychology,* 1966, **72**, 161-78. Copyright 1966 by the American Psychological Association and reprinted by permission.

increases. Performance in Condition N improves with length of Phase II, possibly a consequence of both the attention-getting value of a new dimension when it is introduced simultaneously with a solution shift and of an overlearning effect which has been shown by others (e.g., Grant and Berg, 1948) to facilitate post-shift performance. Data from Condition R are surprisingly constant. Solutions here are achieved significantly more rapidly than in Condition I, but there appears to be no effect of length of Phase II. This result bears further experimental evaluation. But whatever the outcome of further work, the overall pattern of evidence here is inconsistent with the notion that subjects acquire solution-relevant information only on error trials.

In a second experiment, Guy, Van Fleet, and Bourne (1966) replicated these findings and showed in addition that if the novel dimension is partially correlated with the relevant dimension during Phase II—i.e., if most (75 percent) large patterns (Category A) appear on a cross-hatched background and most small ones (Category B) appear on a stippled background—performance in Phase III lies intermediate between Conditions I and R in which the correlation is 0 and 1.0, respectively. Thus a partially correlated dimension achieves some distinction (for at least some subjects) through intermittent reinforcement or feedback. This result is consistent with the possibility that subjects can and do learn during a series of uninterrupted correct responses.

Bidimensional Concepts and the Independence of Subproblems

So far, the empirical evaluation of theories has been limited to investigations of performance in two-category problems with unidimensional solutions. Of course, if these theories have any generality they must account for a broader domain of behavior than is involved in these simple tasks. One more complicated and frequently used problem is based on a concept or conceptual system in which the conjunctive combinations of two levels on each of two stimulus dimensions represent four distinct categories of patterns. Suppose color (red vs. green) and form (square vs. triangle) are the relevant dimensions. Then the subject would have to learn to sort red squares, green squares, red triangles, and green triangles into four separate categories, ignoring other irrelevant properties of the stimuli such as their size, orientation, and the like. This two-dimensional concept problem is much more difficult to solve than the unidimensionals discussed in preceding sections and provides at least a step in the direction of the multidimensional problems people encounter in everyday life.

There are several possibilities for theoretical analysis of these tasks. One might suppose that they are solved through a decision-tree approach in which patterns are first subclassified on the basis of common or frequent attributes of one or another category (Hunt, 1962). Alternatively, one might think in terms of paired combinations of attributes (e.g., red and square) being conditioned to response categories. An interesting alternative has been suggested by representatives of both the hypothesis-testing (Bower and Trabasso, 1964) and the associative (Bourne and Restle, 1959) points of view. The idea is that the subject learns about the two relevant dimensions separately and independently. He solves these problems as if performing on two distinct unidimensional subproblems. Thus in the foregoing example, the subject learns that red objects belong to Categories 1 and 3, green to 2 and 4, and that square objects belong to Categories 1 and 2 and triangular to 3 and 4. The probability of a correct response to any particular pattern, say a red square, is then a multiplicative function of the probabilities of responding correctly to red and to square, individually. This assumption of the independence of dimension or subproblem learning allows all the theoretical apparatus developed initially in the context of simpler problems to be carried over to the more complicated case.

But, is the independence assumption tenable? This question has been approached indirectly in a number of ways. For example, Bourne and Restle (1959) showed that performance (e.g., mean trials to solution) by a group of subjects on a four-category problem was quantitatively predictable from knowledge of the performance of separate groups solving the two separate subproblems. That is, knowing how well subjects do on a unidimensional color concept and unidimensional form concept, one can accurately predict how well they will do on a bidimensional color-form concept. Trabasso and Bower (1964a) showed further that one could predict the probability of a correct response on each trial of the four-category problem from comparable knowledge of subproblem probabilities. Crawford, Hunt, and Peak (1967) showed that a similar analysis can be made of performance in disjunctive concepts.

Despite the success of predictions based on the subproblem assumption, it should not be thought of as a universal, for it too has its significant exceptions. Studies reported by Bourne, Dodd, Guy, and Justesen (1968) and White (1967), which are primarily addressed to other issues and will be discussed elsewhere (Chapters 11 and 12), have shown that under some important conditions subproblem independence is an inappropriate assumption. Thus this principle is at best an approximate description, useful only in limited circumstances and subject to modification as more empirical information about behavior in complex conceptual tasks is accumulated.

The Relative Difficulty of Different Conceptual Principles

As has been noted earlier, concepts are describable in terms of many different principles, i.e., relationships among relevant stimulus properties, examples of which were presented in Table 9-2. While there has been recent empirical study of the way in which people learn and use concepts based on different principles, to date there has been little progress in the theoretical analysis of this problem.

Two relatively obvious theoretical questions arise immediately: Are some principles harder to work with than others? If so, why? The earliest systematic approach to this question was a study by Hunt and Hovland (1960). These authors showed their subjects a series of positive and negative instances which were logically consistent with three different concepts, a conjunctive ("and"), an inclusive disjunctive ("and/or"), and a relational concept. There are several types of relational concepts that might be used; the one chosen for this experiment was the concept of equality, as in "all triangles with two *equal* sides are positive instances of the concept" (isosceles triangles).

The question asked in the study was, Which of the three types of concept will a subject discover or notice first? It was found that conjunctive and relational solutions were discovered significantly more often than disjunctive solutions, suggesting the possibility that principles do differ in familiarity and in ease of learning and application. In a subsequent, related experiment, Wells (1963) replicated the Hunt-Hovland result and, in addition, demonstrated that exclusive disjunctive ("or") concepts (see Table 9-2) are even more difficult to learn than inclusive disjunctive concepts.

The most extensive comparison of different conceptual principles was reported by Neisser and Weene (1962). These experimenters constructed problems based on all the principles outlined in Table 9-2 and on all the complements of those principles. (A complementary principle is one which merely reverses the categories of positive and negative instances. Thus, while only the instances with both relevant attributes are positive in a conjunctive concept, either attribute or both must be *missing* for an instance to be *positive* in the complementary concept—which Neisser and Weene called disjunctive absence. Only those instances in which both attributes are present are considered as *negative* in the complement of conjunction.) All subjects were required to solve problems based on all the different principles.

Considerable variability in problem difficulty was observed. To account for this variability, the authors suggested that human beings work with only three primitive logical operators, viz., conjunction, disjunction, and negation. All principles used in the Neisser-Weene study can be redefined in those terms. According to the authors, differences in difficulty among the principles reflect three levels of logical complexity described as follows. Level I: The unidimensional concept in which the presence or absence of a single attribute determines the difference between instances. Level II: Those bidimensional concepts in which a single conjunction or disjunction (and, possibly, negation) is involved (i.e., conjunction, disjunction, conditional, and their complements). Level III: Those bidimensional concepts which involve both conjunctions and disjunctions (i.e., the biconditional and its complement). Neisser and Weene suggested that adult human beings are able to form conjunctions, disjunctions, and negations without special training. The main determiner of the difficulty of a conceptual problem then is a matter of how many operations—simple affirmation or negation (Level I), affirmation and/or negation plus conjunction or disjunction (Level II), or affirmation and/or negation plus conjunction and disjunction (Level III)—the subject must apply to solve a problem.

This conclusion is pleasingly simple and neat. However, there is in these data a good deal of within-level variation in difficulty and at least one case of a Level II concept which is just about as difficult as those at Level III. Extensive as it was, the Neisser-Weene study left a number of questions in need of further exploration.

The Neisser-Weene results are ambiguous for one important procedural reason. The problem situations in which they collected data presented the subject with two unknowns: (1) Which, among several possibilities, are the *relevant attributes* of the concept, and (2) what is the *relationship* between those attributes, i.e., the conceptual principle? The subject was given neither the relevant attributes nor the principle at the outset and, thus, had to determine both to solve the problem. Differences among the various concepts, then, could be a function of differences among the principles in the difficulty they present for identifying relevant attributes or differences inherent in the principles themselves or both. To separate out these potential effects, one needs to construct problems wherein either attributes or principle, but not both, are unknown.

The first attack on this issue was a study by Conant and Trabasso (1964). These experimenters studied the identification of the two relevant attributes of conjunctive and inclusive disjunctive concepts when the principle or form of solution was known to the subject at the outset. Using the selection paradigm, Conant and Trabasso found that disjunctives were more difficult to solve than conjunctive problems. In addition, subjects selected more redundant cards—i.e., cards which eliminate an hypothesis or hypotheses which had been ruled out by earlier selections—when solving disjunctive as contrasted with conjunctive problems. Overall the results suggested that the difference in difficulty was probably a function of the greater informational content of the positive instances of conjunctive concepts, which must contain both relevant attributes, than that of the positive instances of disjunctions, which may contain only one of the relevant attributes. More important for the immediate issue, however, is the apparent fact that the disjunctive principle presents greater difficulty than the conjunctive principle for the attribute identification process.

A second question of theoretical importance concerns the stability of the differences among principles. Is it the case that some principles are inherently more difficult, or is it a matter of familiarity and differential prior training and experience? Suggestions that it might be the latter are contained in the studies of Neisser and Weene (1962) and of Wells (1963). In the former, performance was considerably better on the second of two problems based on the same principle, and differences among concepts appeared to be reduced on the second problem. Wells made an explicit effort to train subjects to solve disjunctive problems, and then tested them, using a technique similar to that of Hunt and Hovland (1960), in a problem that could be solved either conjunctively or disjunctively. He found that four training problems significantly increased the frequency of disjunctive solutions.

These results suggest that with sufficient training the subject can be brought to a level of equivalent mastery on all, or a wide variety of, principles and that initial differences are primarily a matter of differential experience.

In both of the foregoing cases, however, there was still significant variation in difficulty among the concepts even after training. Thus, to demonstrate that differences among principles can be eliminated, a considerably more intensive training routine is necessary. It is also to be noted that the Neisser-Weene and Wells experiments presented subjects with problems with two unknowns—principle and attributes. We have discussed earlier the ad-

FIGURE 10–4. Mean trials to solution of rule-learning and attribute-identification problems based on the four primary bidimensional rules described in Table 8–2.

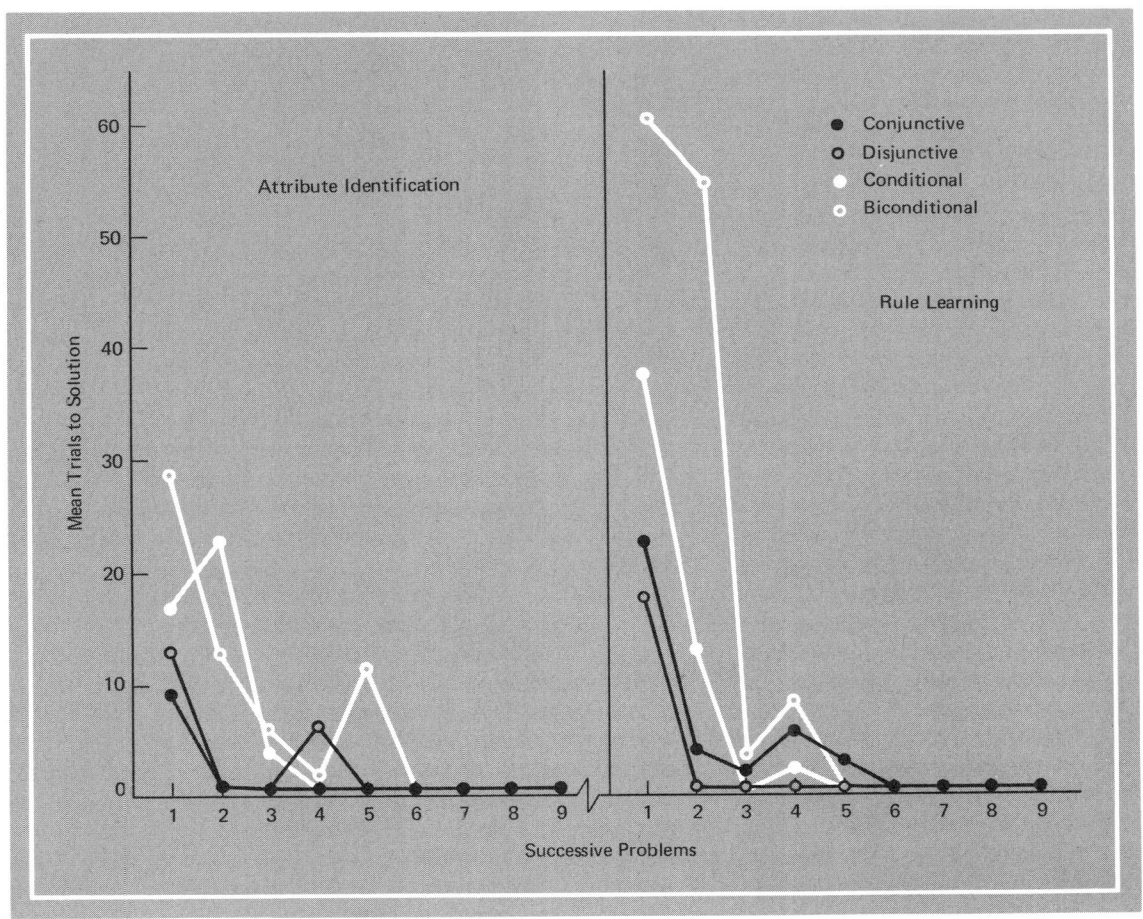

Source: Redrawn from L. E. Bourne, Jr., Learning and utilization of conceptual rules. In B. Kleinmuntz, ed., *Memory and the Structure of Concepts*. New York: John Wiley & Sons., Inc., copyright 1967. Reprinted by permission of the publisher.

vantages of making one of these aspects of the concept a "given."

A study designed to take both of these considerations into account was reported by Bourne (1967). Subjects were required to solve a series of conceptual problems each of which was based on the same bidimensional principle but on a different pair of relevant attributes. All four bidimensional principles described in Table 9-2 were used, each for a different group of subjects. These four groups were subdivided, moreover, so that for half the subjects the principle was an unknown and the relevant attributes were given and for the remaining half the attributes were unknown and the principle was given.

The results are shown in Figure 10-4. Clearly, the principles differ in initial difficulty, whether the task requires attribute identification (principle given) or principle learning (attributes given). The order of difficulty is essentially the same in both cases as that observed by Neisser and Weene (1962) and others. Thus, the principles themselves seem to differ inherently and to create unique difficulties for the task of attribute identification. But equally clear is the fact that these differences are transient and can be overcome by practice. At the end of six successive problems, all subjects reached the point of maximal performance. Initial differences apparently were a matter of familiarity and experience. Given the appropriate training, these differences vanish.

SUMMARY

We have reviewed specific examples of several theoretical positions regarding conceptual behavior. While other theoretical ideas and theory-relevant data will be taken up later, we have come now to the end of our immediate concern with these issues. It is obvious that the whole matter of theory of conceptual functioning is unsettled. There are many knotty problems still to be worked out. Perhaps the most serious, in retrospect, is the one we have just been dealing with, viz., the learning of principles. It seems clear that all the theories detailed earlier fail to give an adequate account of this phenomenon. S-R associational and mediational orientations seem inappropriate, for principles cannot be defined in conventional S-R terms. The stimuli and the responses of successive problems can be completely different, and still subjects will learn the principle common to them all. Some elaboration of theoretical concepts, designed to give representation to this kind of learnable knowledge, is an obvious necessity. Hypothesis and information processing theories have suitable representations for conceptual principles, e.g., the form of hypothesis might be conjunctive or disjunctive or some other, but fail to specify how these forms are learned as guidelines for a subject's hypothesis testing. It is not enough merely to say they exist, for marked changes in the precision, accuracy and frequency of their use have been repeatedly demonstrated by experiment. Thus some greater specificity of the learning process, as it concerns conceptual principles, must be given.

These remarks are not meant as an indictment of contemporary theory. Many phenomena are adequately and usefully interpreted as things now stand. The idea here is merely to suggest one issue of importance which, when it is addressed, will represent a step forward in our understanding of human conceptual behavior.

Eleven: Empirical Studies of Conceptual Behavior: The Problem Solver

Human behavior follows a notoriously complex set of rules. So much so that it isn't difficult to reach the conclusion that either there is no system to what people do or that the system is far beyond our present capability to decipher and to understand. In psychology we normally take it for granted that behavior is rule-governed or lawful and that its rules are discoverable. We think that there has been fair progress toward this end though a vast amount of detail is still unknown. What is apparent from research to date is that many variables or conditions of both the subject and his environment are intimately bound up in and influence behavior. This is no less true of conceptual behavior than behavior of any other sort. The aim of the next two chapters is to outline some of the directions of research and to summarize what is known empirically about the properties of conceptual behavior.

PERFORMANCE

It is appropriate to begin this review with research aimed at defining and developing useful measures and descriptions of conceptual behavior—studies with the primary purpose of detailing the various components of conceptual behavior.

Strategies for Solving Conceptual Problems

Despite its complexity, the behavior of subjects solving conceptual problems does present a detectable amount of organization and structure. People ordinarily do not attack situations in a totally random and haphazard fashion. Their approach tends to be structured in terms of and guided by hypotheses, expectations, and rules based on prior experiences. Most conceptual problems are logical and straightforward. Their solutions can be achieved in a statable sequence of steps or operations. Subjects' behavior can often be seen as a reflection of this sequence. The degree to which subjects' performance actually does approximate the logic of the problem is, as expected, a function in part of their training and experience with other problems of the same or a similar type.

An organized sequence of responses by a subject, made in an effort to achieve the solution of a problem, has come to be called a *strategy*, and a good deal of attention has been given in recent years to the strategies subjects might have or might learn in the context of conceptual tasks. The pioneer work was undertaken by Bruner, Goodnow, and Austin (1956). Their research has many facets and is, therefore, difficult to summarize concisely. The essential outcome of it is that they were able to show, contrary to prevailing (primarily associationistic) opinions at the time, that conceptual problem solving is intentional, consciously planned, and highly organized behavior.

Focusing. Most of the research of Bruner and associates was conducted with a task which required the subject to identify the relevant attributes of a conjunctive concept. Strategic approaches to these problems were not determinable in the performance of all subjects on all problems. However, by sifting through the data, these experimenters did discover two general strategies which were characteristic of many of the problem solvers. One of these was termed "focusing." *Focusing* yields the relevant attributes of a concept by a process of elimination based on the comparison of each successively encountered instance with a positive instance which is chosen as a focus.

Consider Example A, portrayed in Table 11-1. The problem is arranged according to the selection paradigm. From a large array of patterns, the experimenter designates one (1), large (L), red (R), square (□) as a positive instance. Conformance with the focusing strategy requires the subject to accept all attributes of this (or possibly some later) focal stimulus as (potentially) relevant, so that his first hypothesis is 1LR□. The subject then selects Pattern 2, 1LR triangle (△) and the experimenter indicates that it, too, is a positive instance. Comparing Pattern 2 to the focal instances reveals that form (□ vs △) is an irrelevant dimension and that the next hypothesis should be 1LR. Pattern 3, selected by the subject, is 1L green (G) □, which is called negative. Comparison with the focal instance indicates that red must be a relevant attribute, for red patterns but not green are positive; the hypothesis remains 1LR. The selection and test procedure continues, in this case, through two more patterns, after which the subject has achieved all the necessary information to specify the concept.

The system in the subject's behavior is revealed by the sequence of stimulus choices and hypotheses. He used the initial positive instance as a focus and began with a composite hypothesis based on all its characteristics. He selected successive stimuli to differ in one and only one respect from the focus, allowing him to check the relevance of one attribute on every trial. When the concept is a conjunction of attributes, this strategy is guaranteed to yield the solution in a specifiable number of selections.

Bruner named the approach outlined above *conservative focusing*, to make note of the fact that it carried a built-in guarantee of some information on each trial. But this is not the only form of focusing observed in experiments. Sometimes subjects adopt a more reckless method and select cards that differ from the focus in not one but in two or more attributes. Consider Example B in Table 11-1. Here the subject has chosen 1SR △ as Pattern 2, changing two attributes from the initial positive instance. Because both size and form are irrelevant dimensions, Pattern 2 is positive, and this subject has achieved in two trials what the conservative subject required three trials to learn. There is, therefore, some potentially greater payoff to be had from larger changes in successive stimuli. But suppose Pattern 2 had been a negative instance. The subject would know that size, form, or both size and form were relevant dimensions, but would need to make additional selections (changing one attribute at a time) to determine the status of each separately. Under these circumstances the subject would need

TABLE 11-1. *Examples of Focusing Strategies*

A: *Conservative focusing*

	Stimulus Patterns	Category	Hypothesis
Focal stimulus	1 LR □	+	"1 LR □"
Subject's selections			
1.	1 LR △	+	"1 LR"
2.	1 LG □	−	"1 LR"
3.	1 SR □	+	"1 R"
4.	2 LR □	−	"1 R"
	Concept: 1 R		

B: *Focus gambling*

	Stimulus Patterns	Category	Hypothesis
Focal stimulus	1 LR □	+	"1 LR □"
Subject's selections			
1.	1 SR △	+	"1 R"
2.	2 LR □	−	"1 R"
3.	1 LG □	−	"1 R"
	Concept: 1 R		

more trials to gather the same evidence as the conservative focuser. There are then both greater payoffs and greater risks involved in this strategy, thus the name, given by Bruner, *focus gambling*.

A form of focusing can be and, according to Levine (1966), probably is used in reception problems. Bruner and his associates reported that some of their subjects took the first positive instance presented by the experimenter as a focus, forming a working hypothesis based on all its attributes, and then attempted to close in on the true concept by comparing successively presented stimuli to it. Ideally the subjects' hypothesis is always a composite of the still potentially relevant attributes. For this reason the strategy has been called the *wholist* or *wholist focusing* approach. The rules for eliminating irrelevant attributes and for holding relevant attributes in the hypothesis are the same here as in the focusing strategies of the selection paradigm. They are, however, harder to follow because the stimulus sequence typically follows no simple pattern.

One particularly common, although indirect kind of evidence of focusing in the reception procedure is a "primacy effect" in memory for preceding instances. Subjects typically remember best the first (or first few) stimulus patterns presented in the problem (Cahill and Hovland, 1960; Trabasso and Bower, 1964c). Apparently they attend more carefully to the initial stimulus, suggesting its use as a focal instance for subsequent hypothesis testing.

As noted, the reception method does not permit the subject to select the instances he wants to test and leaves him rather at the mercy of the experimenter for evidence on the relevance of attributes. For this reason, the reception paradigm probably makes any consistent strategy difficult to follow. Moreover, because it eliminates one critical aspect of performance—stimulus selection—the experimenter has less data on which to make conjectures about the subject's strategy. It is clear then that most research designed to elucidate methods of problem solving would more profitably employ some variation of the selection paradigm rather than reception techniques.

Scanning. The second general strategy observed by Bruner and his associates bears resemblance to the operations assumed to be used in some hypothesis theories. Rather than adopt a focal instance as a basis for eliminating irrelevant attributes of the stimuli, some subjects appear to form simple hypotheses about the solution, e.g., "all large squares are positive instances," and to categorize stimuli accordingly until proved wrong. Stimuli are selected to provide tests of hypotheses. Bruner termed the general approach *scanning* and distinguished between those subjects who seemed to test hypotheses one at a time, *successive* scanning, and those who could work in terms of several possibilities concurrently, *simultaneous* scanning.

Subjects generally have only limited success with the scanning strategy. It is clearly a more difficult, though logically no less appropriate, strategy than focusing. To scan optimally the subject must make considerable use of memory. In the successive case, he must remember, among other things, all previously tested and rejected hypotheses in order to avoid redundant stimulus selections and tests. The same is true in the simultaneous case, with the addition that the subject must keep a large number of tenable possibilities in mind at once. Given the limitations on the ability of human beings to remember and to keep track of several variables simultaneously (Yntema and Mueser, 1960), it is not surprising to find scanning a generally less efficient problem-solving strategy than focusing (Laughlin and Jordan, 1967).

Scanning, like focusing, is usable in either the selection or reception paradigms. When reception procedures are used, scanning subjects often adopt some attributes of the first positive instance as a working hypothesis (or hypothesis set) ignoring others. To distinguish this approach from the superior wholist strategy of focusers, Bruner coined the term *partist* strategy.

A "Truth-Table" Strategy. Scanning, focusing, and their variations are strategies which are revealed in the context of attribute identification problems. They describe a series of steps leading to the discovery of the attributes that are relevant to the categorization of objects. They are not applicable, at least not directly, to a problem in which the subject is *given* the relevant attributes and is required to discover the general principle of the concept. On the other hand, performance on principle learning problems is also systematic and regular.

A series of experiments reported by Bourne (1967) provides a description of some of the systematic features of principle learning. In the main the results showed that with practice most subjects acquire essentially the same general strategy. The paradigm of this research is to have the subject solve a series of problems based on an unknown principle and two given relevant attributes. The principle is changed from problem to problem, varying among the four primary bidimensional principles portrayed in Table 9-2. The subject's performance is complex, irregular, and inefficient in the early problems, but improves with practice. Eventually, most subjects come to be able to solve each new problem within four trials.

Detailed study of the performance of sophisticated subjects in these experiments revealed a rather general pattern. Subjects seemed to reduce the stimulus population to four types of patterns and then merely to learn the associations between these four stimulus types and the two response categories (positive and negative instances). Usually, this 4:2 paired-associates task could be mastered after inspection of one example of each of the four types, thus effecting a solution within four trials.

The four types of patterns have a familiar, though apparently not an immediately obvious, characterization. They correspond to the rows of a two-dimensional truth table. The four types could be described, that is, as patterns containing the two given relevant attributes (TT), patterns containing the first but not the second (TF), patterns containing the second but not the first (FT), and patterns containing neither (FF). Any of the rules assigns these types uniquely to response categories. Knowing the category for each type, which is signified by one example, is tantamount to knowing and successfully using the required principle. Apparently the terminal strategy achieved by nearly all subjects in this kind of problem is an informal or intuitive version of the logical truth table.

A Note on Response Requirements. In general, the selection procedure supplies more information than the reception paradigm, permitting the experimenter to make a more complete and confident description of the subject's strategy. The difference in informational output is a consequence of the differing response requirements of the two procedures. The selection paradigm necessitates both a stimulus selection and, usually, an hypothesis on each trial, while the reception procedure often requires only a category response from the subject. These differential requirements are not only connected with the subject's strategy but also affect the overall quality of his performance. For example, Hunt (1965) had two groups of subjects solve the same conceptual problem, one under selection and the second under reception procedures. The results show clearly that subjects come more quickly and efficiently to problem solution if they are allowed to make stimulus selections for themselves. Among the possible facilitating effects of the selection procedure are that (1) it makes a greater demand for attention to the task, and (2) it permits the subject to select, if he is able, a highly efficient sequence of stimuli. Consistent with the first possibility is a result reported by Byers and Davidson (1967). These experimenters discovered that requiring the subject to give an hypothesis periodically, rather than just a category response, improved overall problem solving significantly in the reception paradigm. Making stricter demands on the subject apparently will contribute favorably to his performance, at least up to a point.

The generality of the selection-reception difference, it should be noted, is still in question, not only because of the procedural limitations of Hunt's study, which are discussed in some detail by Lowenkron and Johnson (1968), but also because other comparisons, e.g., Huttenlocher's (1962a) investigation of children's performance, have led to the opposite conclusion. Possibly the greater demands on attention and performance interfere with problem solving by young subjects, who are more easily overloaded or distracted than adults. In any case, there appears to be some need of further exploration of both procedural and developmental variables in determining behavior in selection and reception problems.

Conditions Affecting the Subject's Strategy

Cognitive Strain. A major factor contributing to the difficulty of scanning as a strategy is what Bruner calls "cognitive strain," i.e., the heavy demand scanning makes on a subject's memory and ability to process information. Focusing affords the subject an excellent bookkeeping system for all attributes which are, at any given time, still potentially relevant. On every trial, his hypothesis is a composite which includes all untested solution possibilities. In contrast, an efficient scanner has to keep in mind all the hypotheses he has tested (or all the hypotheses which remain as possibilities) in order to avoid redundant tests. Even with a stimulus population of limited dimensionality, there may be hundreds of possible solutions, making the memory task in scanning formidable for most people. As a consequence, scanners typically remember only a few of the rejected (or untested) hypotheses at any given time; they do indeed often test the same possibility two or more times; and generally, they are poorer problem solvers than the focusers.

This argument would imply that any increase in the memory requirements or cognitive strain of a conceptual problem will affect the performance of scanners more than focusers, because the former are already working near the limits of capacity. To test this notion, Bruner and his associates had subjects solve the third of three successive selection problems "in their heads" with the stimulus array no longer in view. Focusers had a relatively easy time, taking no more trials to solve the memory task than they had on the first two conventional problems. Scanners, in contrast, showed a significant increase in trials to solve the memory task. As had been expected, subjects who use an approach which does not make particularly heavy demands on memory, i.e., focusers, can contend with the additional task requirements which have adverse effects on the performance of those who follow a more difficult strategy.

Strategies in the Reception Paradigm. Bourne (1963a) reported an evaluation of several variables affecting the use of reception strategies. Certain of these observations are of interest here. First, using size of initial hypothesis as a basis of distinction, Bourne found, in contrast to the results of Bruner, Goodnow, and Austin, that most subjects adopt an apparent scanning or partist approach, only 9 percent qualifying as focusers or wholists. Given the facts that the number of wholist subjects increased over three successive problems in this experiment, that the wholist approach is generally more successful than the partist, and that Bruner's subjects participated in a series of 14 problems, the contrast suggests the importance of amount of previous relevant experience in the development of an efficient strategy. Subjects become more whole-oriented with practice.

The two main variables explored in the study were problem complexity (concepts with one, two, or three relevant attributes) and method of stimulus presentation (simultaneous or successive). Both variables affected the difficulty of the problem. The effects were different, however, depending on the subject's strategy. As complexity increased, fewer partist subjects were able to solve the problem within a theoretically minimal number of trials. The percentages of solvers were 76, 52, and 31 for the three levels of complexity, respectively. Wholists, in contrast, solved 100 percent of the one and two relevant attribute problems and 75 percent of the three attribute problems with minimal information. In the successive condition, 39 percent of partists and 75 percent of wholists solved with minimal information; in the simultaneous condition, 68 percent of partists and 100 percent of wholists solved. Thus, the wholist strategy was clearly a superior mode of performance, and incidentally was also associated with less inter-subject performance variance than the partist strategy. While it was difficult to establish a trend because of the relatively few clear wholist solutions, it appeared in general that this strategy tended to be adopted primarily in the simpler (i.e., one relevant attribute, simultaneous presentation) problems.

One of the critical differences between partists and wholists revealed by this study is the difference in accuracy of handling certain stimulus contingencies. There are four types of instances that might be encountered in a problem: positive instances which confirm the subject's hypothesis, negative instances which confirm his hypothesis, positive instances which disconfirm his hypothesis, and negative instances which disconfirm his hypothesis. There were only minor differences among subjects in their handling of positive and negative confirming and negative disconfirming instances. A marked discrepancy for positive disconfirming instances was noted however. Wholists responded properly to 85 percent of these cases by making proper modifications in their hypothesis; partists handled only 45 percent of them correctly. Subjects who did make proper hypothesis revisions, whether partists or wholists, discovered quick solutions. The failures were, generally, the poor problem solvers overall.

Bourne argued that the partist-wholist dichotomy does not clarify some of the important differences in strategy. There is a continuum, quantifiable in terms of the number of attributes the subject includes in his initial hypothesis, underlying the dichotomy. Subjects in this experiment represented every possible size of initial hypothesis. The question of differences between partists and wholists then is basically a question of the relationship between performance and initial hypothesis size. This relationship is essentially linear, with overall performance improving directly with the breadth of initial hypothesis.

Quantification of Strategies. Laughlin (1965, 1966; Laughlin and Jordan, 1967) working more closely with the methods of Bruner, Goodnow, and Austin, developed a set of rules for scoring the degree of focusing and scanning each subject exemplifies in the course of a problem. In one experiment, Laughlin (1965) explored the behavior of subjects working alone and in two-person groups. His hypothesis was that groups would perform better both because of their greater capacity for retaining relevant information and because of the greater likelihood that one member of the group would use the more workable focusing strategy. The prediction was confirmed: groups required fewer examples to reach solution, they were less repetitive (or redundant) in their stimulus selections, and they showed significantly more focusing behavior than did individuals. Laughlin noted that the opportunity for discussion aided groups in the realization that focusing reduces the memory requirement of the task and ensures a constant amount of new information on each trial.

In a second experiment Laughlin (1966) argued that a subject might be induced to use a focusing strategy under certain conditions. In particular, a problem which in its own right is difficult and carries heavy memory requirements might influence a subject to adopt a strategy (focusing) which minimizes the necessity to remember previously encountered instances. To test this notion, subjects were given a series of problems. For half of them solutions were relatively simple two-attribute concepts; for the remaining subjects, four attributes were relevant. Greater use of focusing was hypothesized for those subjects solving four-attribute problems and this prediction was confirmed. Moreover, the four-attribute problems, which seem intrinsically more difficult than two-attribute problems, required no more trials (stimulus selections) to solve. Laughlin argued that this secondary finding was a consequence of the greater use of the more efficient focusing approach in complex tasks.

More recently, Laughlin and Jordan (1967) have demonstrated that strategic behaviors of the type outlined are not limited to problems with conjunctive solutions. Variations of both the focusing and scanning approaches were observed in problems based on disjunctive and biconditional principles. It is noteworthy that focusing was least common on disjunctive concepts. Disjunctives require some sort of negative approach. Either (1) the subject must focus on a positive instance, select a stimulus in which all but one attribute are different, and then infer the relevance of the unchanged attribute from knowledge of its category; or (2) he must focus on a negative instance and change attributes one at a time as in normal focusing. In either case, the inferential task is intuitively and empirically difficult, which might account for the limited use of focusing in disjunctive problems. Bruner and his associates (1956) and Conant and Trabasso (1964) reported results similar to these.

Acquisition of the Truth-Table Strategy. According to Bourne (1967), a systematic truth-table strategy emerges in a subject's behavior as he solves a series of principle learning problems. That is, most people come to attack each new task first by reducing the stimulus population to four types of patterns and then learning the associations between these types and the categories of positive and negative instances. The four types correspond to the four rows of a bidimensional truth table, constructed on the basis of the presence or absence of each of the two relevant attributes.

While not all subjects acquire the strategy, it was shown in one experiment that 83 percent of those who have solved three problems based on each of the four primary logical bidimensional connectives outlined in Table 9-2 do give evidence of its development and use. One set of variables that appears to be critical has to do with the breadth and type experience that the subject gains in a problem series. Bourne and Guy (1968) and Dodd (1967) reported that subjects are more likely to acquire the truth-table strategy as the number of principles they learn increases. They compared groups of subjects who solved a series of problems based on one, two, three, or all four principles (they also used a no practice control group) and found that as more different principles were experienced in the series, there was more evidence of "truth-table" behavior. They further showed that some principles—particularly the conditional, "if x, then y"—are more conducive to learning the strategy than are others, presumably because they draw the subject's attention more forcefully to the various types of patterns.

A related experiment by Haygood and Kiehlbauch (1965) showed that teaching the truth-table strategy directly, by having the subject learn to sort patterns into the four types in a pretraining exercise, facilitates later learning of the principles. In a sense this finding is the converse of those above, in which the strategy was allowed to evolve from problem experience. It supports the general idea that systematic, well-organized behaviors, designed to simplify the information to be dealt with, are at the root of efficient thinking and problem solving in conceptual tasks.

Comment. The pioneering work of Bruner, Goodnow, and Austin has stimulated important progress toward an understanding of the organizational properties of conceptual behavior. The general approach exemplified by the research reviewed in the preceding pages and elsewhere (see the discussion of Levine's model, 1966, in Chapter 10) has been to write out a logical analysis of the necessary and sufficient steps or operations for achieving problem solution. (In at least some cases it is obvious that the subject can solve in more than one way, as for example with scanning or focusing strategies.) Levine (1966) and Huttenlocher (1967) provide perhaps the clearest statements of this form of analysis. The logical sequence then serves as a normative model of the subject's behavior and the experimenter looks for evidence of this logic in the subject's actual behavior. Erroneous responses are defined in terms of deviations from the model (e.g., the dimension-selection and value-specification errors of Glanzer, Huttenlocher, and Clark, 1963, or the perceptual-inference and memory errors described by Cahill and Hovland, 1960).

While it is quite plain that behavior does follow some set of rules, often approximating the logical models and strategies outlined here, the deviations from these idealized models are just as important to understand and account for. In the next section we explore some of these individual differences among subjects and the conditions that create them.

Analyses of Individual Differences

People differ in the overall efficiency of their work in any problem. This is revealed plainly in the spread of performance scores in almost any experiment. Not so obvious are the factors that are involved in producing these differences, the finer characteristics of a subject's trial-by-trial performance which might be correlated with overall success, and the consistent styles of approach which different subjects exemplify. It is these considerations that the complete study of individual differences must address.

To begin, we know that it is possible to determine logically the one or more paths to the solution of a conceptual problem. The strategies described by Bruner and by others are representative of this possibility. We know further that subjects, even when giving evidence of a particular strategy, typically fail to follow it rigidly. That is, people may approximate a certain systematic approach while at the same time making errors of one or another type. These deviations vary from subject to subject, though a particular subject might quite characteristically commit a distinguishable pattern of deviant responses.

Internal Relationships. Deviations from a strictly logical approach to a problem are probably to be expected on the part of all but the most highly trained and sophisticated subjects. Some deviations might be more frequent than others or more important sources of interference in the general problem-solving process. To find out, one might study the relationship between response patterns on the successive trials of a problem and overall performance measures.

A study which illustrates this approach was reported by Bourne (1965). Attribute identification problems were presented to subjects in the context of the reception paradigm. On each trial of a problem, the subject was required to announce both a category response and an hypothesis about the solution. He was instructed to try to make his responses consistent with all the information about solution he had accumulated up to that particular trial.

The general purpose of the study was to search for whatever relationships might exist between hypothesis and trial-to-trial hypothesis revisions and overall level of performance on the problem. To this end, subjects were divided into two groups at the median number of errors required for solution, those who made more than the median being considered "poorer" problem solvers than those who made fewer. Next, ten unique hypothesis characteristics were determined, separately for subjects below and above median performance. These characteristics were based on considerations such as the frequency, the occasion, and the type of hypothesis revisions expressed. Marked and reliable differences on any characteristic between the two subgroups of subjects could then be taken as evidence suggestive of a particularly important aspect of hypothesis behavior insofar as general problem-solving performance is concerned.

The results gave a reasonably clear picture of the patterns of trial-by-trial responses, the relationships between hypotheses and category responses, and the correlation between these detailed features and overall performance in one simple type of conceptual task. First, the better subject is one who starts with a comprehensive initial hypothesis, considering most or all of the stimulus attributes of the first positive instance as potentially relevant. This finding is consistent with an earlier report (Bourne, 1963a) of a direct relationship between size of initial hypothesis and problem-solving performance and, in general, with the various studies (e.g., Laughlin and Jordan, 1967) suggesting the superiority of focusing strategy over any other in these tasks.

Second, the better problem solver made hypothesis revisions when they were indicated by the available evidence and made no revisions when there was no indication, both with greater probability than the poorer subject. In other words, better subjects are more properly responsive to trial-by-trial information. The occasion of their changes is quite predictable, while the poorer performers are more capricious. Third, the better subject made simpler and more systematic hypothesis revisions. His changes tended to be limited to a single attribute at a time and to be consistent with the information given on that trial. His revisions were reminiscent of those of a focuser in the experiments of Bruner and his associates (1956). In contrast, the poorer performer's revisions were characteristically large and variable, resembling more the random sampling scanner or focus gambler than the conservative focuser. These large changes on occasion produced an early solution. More often, however, they were associated with a long period of categorizing at chance level. The end result was much more variability in number of errors to solution among subjects who made complex hypothesis changes.

Finally, the majority of hypotheses by all subjects were inconsistent in one or another way with information given on preceding trials. The task requires effective use of memory and the ability of human beings to remember is limited. In this connection, it is important to note that the hypothesis revisions of better subjects were consistent with previous information a greater percentage of the time than were those of poorer subjects.

In summary, then, these results suggest that efficient problem solving in simple attribute identification tasks involves working initially with a global hypothesis, changing it when the evidence so indicates, changing it in a simple and systematic way, and changing it to be consistent with the information provided on earlier trials. The outcome is certainly not unexpected, but yet it is useful for it helps to complete the empirical picture of conceptual problem solving. The outcome is consistent with and serves to elaborate the evidence provided in the earlier work of Bruner, Goodnow, and Austin (1956).

In a more recent and somewhat more elaborate study, using similar techniques, Schwartz (1957) produced some supplementary findings. Among other variables, Schwartz studied both unidimensional and disjunctive concept problems, whereas only conjunctive concepts were used in Bourne's experiment. Moreover, Schwartz presented problems via both the reception and selection paradigms. Despite the technical differences, experimental results, where comparable, seemed to be roughly the same in both investigations. For example, Schwartz reported a significant correlation between number of trials required for solution and consistency of stated hypotheses with available information.

Among the unique performance measures developed by Schwartz was an index of hypothesis validity, defined for any hypothesis as the proportion of stimuli in the population which would be correctly classified as positive or negative instances by its use. To illustrate, suppose that "large square" is the solution (a conjunctive concept) in a particular problem defined on a population of stimuli having all two-valued dimensions. If the subject's hypothesis were "red square," its validity would be .75 because its application to the entire population would result in 75 percent correct stimulus classifications. The index actually used was the average validity of all hypotheses stated by the subject prior to problem solution. The data indicate a strong negative correlation between mean hypothesis validity and the number of trials to solution, at least in the more complex disjunctive tasks. The better subjects not only adopt generally more valid or useful hypotheses, but also produce a series of hypotheses, the validity of which increases more sharply over trials than those produced by the less apt subjects. Clearly the systematic formulation and trial-by-trial revision of hypotheses are basic skills in solving conceptual problems despite assumptions to the contrary in many contemporary theories.

The better subjects in Schwartz's experiment made large rather than small and simple changes in their hypotheses. This result conflicts with that obtained by Bourne (1965) and is inconsistent with the general observations that focusing is the most workable strategy in this type of conceptual problem. The explanation for the apparent discrepancy is clear, however, after careful inspection of procedures and data. First, a significant correlation between trials to solution and mean number of attributes changed between successive trials occurs only for problems with a unidimensional solution. In the manner in which these problems were presented a subject always had one marked positive (and one negative) instance available for inspection.

Logically, the most efficient way to pinpoint the one relevant dimension among several is to use a split-half strategy. That is, after the first positive instance has been identified, the subject should select a new card which differs from the positive one in half the number of variable dimensions. If that card is positive also, the relevant dimension is among those not changed. If it is negative, the relevant dimension is among those changed. He should then select another card differing in half the dimensions not yet eliminated. This operation is repeated until all irrelevant dimensions are eliminated. Naive subjects fail, no doubt, to use the split-half strategy unerringly (Goldbeck, Bernstein, Hillix, and Marx, 1957). But any approximation will yield large differences from one card selection to the next and will probably be related to better than average performance. This possibility is not only compatible with the present data but is consistent with the general notion that the higher the quality of overall human performance in a task, the more closely its details take the form of a reasonable logical model.

External Relationships. An alternative and complementary approach to the analysis of individual differences is to search for correlations between performance in conceptual tasks and scores on other tests administered separately. Because of the nature of the behavior of interest, tests of basic human intellectual abilities are particularly useful and informative. Reliable correlations between test scores and problem solving are indicative of particular abilities that are necessarily involved in conceptual behavior and, at the same time, help to specify in detail the basis of differences among performers. Several studies of this type have been conducted.

One of the more comprehensive and revealing investigations was reported by Bunderson (1965). Bunderson administered 30 abilities tests measuring general reasoning, flexibility in thinking, memory, and visual search speed, and a large number of concept problems to a sample of university students. Strongest relationships were observed between conceptual performance and tests of visual speed and of logical reasoning. From the pattern of results, Bunderson suggested the possibility of three stages in solving of concept problems: *problem analysis,* i.e., finding out what the elements of the problem are; *search* for the relevant elements; and *organization* of the relevant elements into an acceptable solution. Visual search is more closely related to activities in the first two stages, while reasoning abilities are required in the first and third stages. Subjects who scored highest on these tests did best in general in a variety of conceptual problems, with particularly high correlations in evidence on the earlier trials between concept and visual speed measures and on the later trials between concept and reasoning scores. Supplementary and confirmatory results were reported by Dunham, Guilford, and Hoepfner (1968), who, using a different set of conceptual tasks, were able to demonstrate the relevance of good general memory and ideational fluency (an ability to generate a large number of new ideas) to efficient problem solving.

Cognitive Style. The preceding studies attempt to isolate the significant dimensions of individual differences in intellectual ability and to show the degree to which each of these is bound up in concept learning. They describe, as it were, a cross-section of conceptual performance. While many measures of many different types of behavior are taken, each measure is relatively unique and there is no direct assessment of the stability of performance as might be revealed by repeated testing with the same task (or closely related tasks). Given that there are individual differences and that people perform in detectably different ways on conceptual and other problems, it is of some interest to know whether those differences will persist over repeated measurements spanning significant periods of time and variations in task structures.

A term that has been used in connection with persistent individual differences in modes of behavior is *cognitive style.* One study which illustrates the way a person's cognitive style pervades his behavior in a variety of settings and over a period of years was reported by Kagan, Moss, and Sigel (1963). Their general technique was to ask subjects to sort freely several different sets of drawings, e.g., of human figures, into "groups that go together." The groups so produced could be classified, according to the experimenters, into six basic types, based on the apparent orientation of the subject (egocentric or stimulus centered) and the formal features of the group itself (analytic, relational, or inferential).

Prior to the free-sorting experience, subjects were given a lengthy battery of assessment tests, designed to yield ratings on 36 personality variables. The relationships that obtained between performances on the conceptual tasks and personality variables suggested several remarkably stable individual differences, especially in degree of structural analysis demonstrated by subjects. Analytic conceptual groupings were based on careful and purposeful distinctions among stimulus attributes. The concepts so derived were well conceived and unambiguous. People who produced this type of concept did so regularly and consistently in contrast to the more variable performance of nonanalytic subjects.

If the so-called analytic style were limited only to the free-sorting conceptual task, it would have little general interest. On the contrary, Kagan and his associates were also able to show evidence of analysis and stimulus differentiation on the part of the same subjects in perceptual, specifically visual, vigilance and other tasks. More impressive, however, is the tendency for analytic concept formers to be analytic in their extra-laboratory behaviors and their personalities. In particular, analytic subjects, in contrast to the nonanalyzers, have better articulated life goals, are more systematic in intellectual performance, make clearer distinctions between themselves and other people, and so on. Analysis is a pervasive human characteristic and clearly one on which people systematically differ.

Other styles which are pertinent to conceptual problem solving are, of course, identifiable. Whitman (1966), for example, isolated two types of people, exemplifying the analytic and an inferential style. These subjects were asked to solve conceptual problems which were either compatible or incompatible with their styles, and it was observed that compatibility was an even more important determiner of performance than intelligence.

Cognitive styles are ways of achieving intellectual goals which are general enough to be characteristic of a large segment of one individual's activity and to distinguish him from other individuals in search of the same goals. Their stability suggests that considerable use can be made of these concepts in the description and explanation of human behavior.

GENERAL CHARACTERISTICS AND PROCESSES OF THE LEARNER

Memory

Conceptual problems can be solved only by the accumulation of information, in some way, from a number of examples. This follows from the fact that concepts, by their very nature, are descriptions which cover a multitude of possibilities. No single exemplifying event can reflect these possibilities fully. The basic behavioral process involved in solving conceptual problems is called *inference*. The subject must take evidence available in several instances and infer a description that fits those instances and excludes noninstances. But, as Underwood (1952) has argued, the inferential task is often complicated by the necessity to remember information in previously given but no longer available instances. On these occasions memory, too, plays an important role in conceptual problem solving.

Experimentally, the importance of memory is emphasized when stimuli are presented successively, i.e., one at a time with the last being removed before the next is given. Elements of both stimulus and feedback must be retained by the subject across trials. Even with a simultaneous presentation procedure, the subject might have to remember the category of previously encountered items if no feedback marking system is provided.

"No Memory" Theories. Certain theories hold that a subject makes no use of memory at all in conceptual tasks (Bower and Trabasso, 1964; Restle, 1962). This assumption seems a little extreme, although it is logically possible to solve a problem by chance, simply by testing one hypothesis after another. Blind luck is essentially the process of problem solving implied by these notions.

There is a fair amount of evidence to suggest that subjects do remember stimuli and their response assignments from trial to trial. But it is also clear that human memory is fallible in conceptual tasks. The fallibility phenomenon appears to be attributable in large measure to interference factors. Even in the simplest, two-category problem, the subject must deal with the response assignments of several multidimensional and highly similar stimuli in order to infer the concept. As the dimensionality of the stimuli or the number of response categories increases, the memory requirements are compounded. These conditions are precisely the kind that produce competition and interference among the associations to be learned. The role of these factors in concept learning has been outlined by Underwood (1952) who predicted that in a multiple concept problem, the greater the number of examples of other concepts interpolated between successive examples of the same concept, the harder that concept would be to learn. This expectation has been confirmed repeatedly (e.g., Kurtz and Hovland, 1956; Bourne and Jennings, 1963), although more than simple interference is involved (Anderson and Guthrie, 1966). A related, more powerful result was obtained by Hunt (1961) who showed that the probability of identifying a concept consistent with a particular "key" instance was inversely related to the number of different intervening instances between the "key" and the concept test. Thus, again, it would appear that each interpolated instance offered some possibility of competition so that the more there were the greater the amount of interference (and in this case the less the likelihood of arriving at a consistent concept).

Trabasso and Bower (1964c) provided a direct empirical evaluation of what a subject remembers in a conceptual problem. The subject was given successively a sufficient number of positive and negative instances (six) to delimit a particular concept. After stating a solution, he tried to recall each stimulus and category in its proper serial position. The probability of correct recall was quite low, exceeding chance only at the initial and terminal positions in the series.

Despite these apparently negative data, it is clear that a subject does make some use of his memory in solving conceptual problems. The more interpolated instances of other concepts, the poorer concept learning is. But that result, in and of itself, and the fact that a person can learn at all in the interpolated case, can be turned around to document the importance of memory. If a subject were not remembering, there would be nothing to be interfered with, and any number of interpolated instances of another concept should have the same effect. Moreover, while instance recall was poor in the Trabasso-Bower data, there were reliable primacy and recency effects. Subjects do remember rather well the very first and last instances presented to them, as one might expect if he were using some sort of focusing strategy. These and other data have forced changes in the simplistic "no memory" theories, allowing for information processing in the absence of stimulus or feedback (Restle and Emmerich, 1966) and for short term memory of one or more stimulus-category associations persisting over several trials (Trabasso and Bower, 1966). Thus liberalized, these models afford a much closer and more natural fit to available data.

Artificial Memory. We noted earlier, without proof, that it would be helpful to relieve a subject of the necessity to remember previous instances, reducing his task to its fundamental inferential component. This assertion is based on the assumption, of course, that subjects do use their memory in solving problems employing a successive stimulus presentation procedure. It is testable, as an empirical hypothesis, by comparing performance levels in the same conceptual problem by subjects serving in simultaneous and successive presentation conditions.

Cahill and Hovland (1960) made that comparison. One group of subjects saw the instances of a concept one at a time. Another group received the stimuli in cumulative fashion, each new instance being added to those already available. The result is obvious; subjects with a cumulative record of instances did reliably better. The poorer performance of "successive" subjects was traced directly to their inability to remember and therefore their repeated test of hypotheses infirmed by preceding instances in the series. An interesting sidelight of the study was the appearance of primacy (early) and recency (late) memory effects similar to those reported in a different context by Trabasso and Bower (1964c). Better memory for more recent instances is consistent with well-known interference phenomena, while the primacy effect suggests that at least some subjects used a focusing-type strategy in problem solving.

These results indicate that a complete artificial memory is better than none at all. But what about intermediate cases, where some but not all previously encountered stimuli are still available for inspection? Is it possible in the complete memory case that the subject does not use all the information provided for him? Bourne, Goldstein, and Link (1964) investigated this question and, in the first of their studies, arrived at a partially affirmative answer. They made zero through ten previously seen stimuli, identified as positive and negative instances, available to the subject and observed a progressive improvement in performance as the number increased to four —but a mild deterioration thereafter. A subsequent study, however, implicated the length of the permissible response interval in the secondary effect. If the interval is limited (in this case, to 15 seconds) the subject apparently has insufficient time to make use of more than four previous instances. If the interval is unconstrained, an increase in this artificial form of memory, at least to eight stimuli, reliably benefits the identification of relevant attributes. Thus, with a memory (real or artificial) and an opportunity to use it, human performance in concept tasks takes a more efficient form, limited, in essence, only by the subject's inferential skills.

Some Related Findings. There are several other observations which bear on the usability of an artificial memory. Pishkin and Wolfgang (1965; see also Pishkin, 1967), for example, have extended the general result to a more complicated four-category conceptual problem. They demonstrated that the major effects of availability are identified with the first instance of each category, a total of four exposed instances. Providing additional exemplars has no significant beneficial effect. The available instances, in this case, must be positive instances of the category they represent. Somewhat surprisingly, making available one or more nonexemplars of each category does not change performance. While it is impossible to give any unambiguous interpretation of this result, it might be that the confusion developed by putting noninstances into a positive category counteracts the logical information, indirect though it might be, embedded in negative instances. This result requires further examination, designed to separate the two sources of potential influence.

Kates and Yudin (1964) added a third condition to the standard simultaneous and successive presentation comparison. Called the *focus condition,* it provided the subject with continuous access to the initial focus card in the stimulus sequence. As might be expected, from the results of Bourne, Goldstein, and Link (1964), performance in the focus condition was intermediate to that of the two extreme stimulus arrangements. A final variation was Wells' (1967) comparison of a contrast condition (i.e., presenting one positive and one negative instance on each trial) with a noncontrast condition (i.e., presenting two positives or two negatives on each trial). From his results, which we have reviewed earlier, it is clear that contrasting positive and negative instances are much more informative to the subject than is a pair of positives or negatives.

Comment. Obviously, the use of real and artificial memory in concept learning requires further examination. Several straightforward questions, as yet unanswered, are raised by the research reviewed here. For example, in all the preceding experiments when an instance was available to the subject, both the stimulus and its category were designated. Either stimulus or feedback alone, because it provides incomplete information, might be of no use to the subject. Alternatively, judging by the facilitative effects of exposing one of these components throughout the intertrial interval (Bourne, et al., 1965), some benefit might be anticipated, particularly from cumulative stimulus exposure. Another example pertains to the type of stimulus exposed. Would it be more helpful to have a running record of preceding positive or negative instances? Earlier work has made no comparison, usually adopting a procedure which reveals all previous stimuli consisting of a mixture of positive and negative instances. Knowing what we do about conceptual principles (Bourne and Guy, 1968), it is reasonable to expect type of instances retained in artificial memory to depend on the type of concept (e.g., conjunctive or conditional) and type of problem (i.e., attribute identification or principle learning) that must be solved.

These and other important studies apparently have not yet been conducted. Significant as it is, our knowledge of human memory in conceptual tasks remains fragmentary. Despite this uncomfortable state of affairs, there is enough information to conclude that memory for preceding events, while limited, is an important skill in the typical problem-solving task. We suspect that, in the future, investigators of concept learning will begin to turn their attention to the strategies and techniques that subjects possess or acquire for retaining solution-relevant information over time.

Motivation

Behavior is purposeful, intentional, and goal-directed; in a word, behavior is characteristically motivated. The primary property of the psychological concept of motivation is intention, e.g., the intention to act in such a way to achieve a quick and efficient solution to a conceptual problem. In most experimental work, instructions are phrased to establish an intention to perform well. Indeed, the proper and necessary intention on a subject's part is typically assumed. It is feasible to manipulate degree of intention. In concept experiments, however, this seems to have been attempted in very few cases—for example, by Romanow (1958) who used instructions to create different levels of ego involvement in the task—and without much success.

There are severe methodological problems, which are more clearly evident in other research areas (Postman, 1964) with the control, measurement, and manipulation of the intentional aspect of motivation. These problems have, no doubt, dissuaded many experimenters from tackling the substantive issues that are involved. A promising new approach to solving the measurement problems is evidenced in the work of Dulany (1968), which relies heavily on the trial-by-trial verbal reports of subjects. These techniques have been developed and used primarily in verbal conditioning tasks, however, and are as yet relatively untried in conceptual problems. Still, it is possible that some modification of these procedures will provide an opening wedge into the general study of intentional action.

Activation, Arousal, or Generalized Drive. In addition to goal-directedness, motivation is seen also to have an energizing property, at least in some theoretical systems. In other words, to say one is motivated is to say, among other things, that he is active, aroused, or driven. This aspect of motivation, too, provides methodological problems. But there is at least some agreement on techniques, and some headway toward empirical study has been made.

Physiological recordings of heart rate, skin resistance, breathing rates, etc., have been successfully used in some psychological research areas, including other types of human learning research (Andreassi, 1966), as measures of arousal. To date, no significant psychophysiological studies of concept learning have been reported, although it seems reasonable to anticipate a good deal of work in the near future. Rather, research thus far has employed a somewhat more indirect attack using as its primary tool paper and pencil tests of manifest anxiety.

Anxiety and Generalized Drive. It is conventionally agreed that one form of generalized drive is anxiety. The argument is that many specific needs of the organism, e.g., hunger, thirst, need for social approval or achievement, can all give rise to general feelings of anxiety. The anxiety that typifies a given individual might not be tied to any single or immediate goal, but it does reflect his general level of arousal or drive. A measure of general anxiety would be expected then to correlate reliably with the arousal or energizing component of motivation.

In almost all psychological theories, motivation is assumed to be importantly related to performance. For example, according to Hull (1952), motivation converts habits (knowledge and skill) into action; the higher the motivation the more vigorous the action. Thus, at least up to the point at which motivation begins to arouse irrelevant habits to compete with the appropriate responses in a task, increasing activation (or anxiety) should facilitate performance. In some tasks, presumably where there are few competing habits, people who are most anxious should perform best. In all tasks there should be some important relationship between anxiety and performance.

This prediction has been examined in a number of studies using concept formation problems and Taylor's (1953) test of manifest anxiety. The results of these evaluations appear somewhat inconsistent. Wesley (1953) observed that "high-anxious" people—those who scored in the upper 25 percent on the test—solved a series of attribute identification problems faster and made fewer perseverative errors (erroneous responses that would have been correct on the just-preceding problem in the series) than "low-anxious" people, in the bottom 25 percent of Taylor's scale. Many other researchers (e.g., Romanow, 1958; Denny, 1966; Zaffy and Bruning, 1966) have found no overall difference in the performance of anxious and nonanxious subjects, although anxiety might be facilitative under certain experimental conditions. There is an occasional report of nonanxious subjects' performing better than anxious subjects (Dunn, 1968). Clearly no single overall statement about the effects of anxiety in conceptual problems is adequate. This conflict-filled pattern of results is partly clarified, however, by an examination of the variables with which anxiety interacts.

Task Complexity. A well-known result in psychological research is the Yerkes-Dodson effect—that for every task there is an optimal level of activation (Woodworth and Schlosberg, 1954). One interpretation of the effect has it that activation below the optimum fails to elicit the correct habits at full strength, while activation above the optimum calls out weaker incorrect habits which compete and interfere with required performance (Spence, 1956). In both cases, performance suffers relative to the optimal activation level.

Another variable, task complexity, has a related interpretation within the theory. The more complex the task, the greater the number of irrelevant responses to compete with the correct response and the greater the strength of competing habits relative to correct habits. Putting the arousal and the task complexity interpretations together, this theory predicts that a low level of anxiety will be optimal for more complex tasks. Or, alternatively stated, anxious subjects are likely to perform best on simple problems, where the correct habits are relatively strong and free of competition, while nonanxious subjects are likely to be superior on complex problems.

These expectations have been partially confirmed in two studies, both using a verbal concept task. Romanow (1958) adopted the procedure of Underwood and Richardson, defining task complexity in terms of the dominance of the concept-instance relationships to be learned. She found high-anxious subjects clearly inferior to subjects of low and moderate anxiety on the most complex and difficult, low-dominance concepts. They learned in fewer trials and with fewer errors. In two easier problems, however, there were no differences among anxiety levels.

Dunn (1968) used a variation of this task, in which the subject was asked to identify the adjectival concept exemplified by five key nouns, embedded within five, ten, or fifteen distractor nouns. These nouns were presented to subjects in five rows of two, three, or four columns, each row containing one of the key words. The three levels of distraction were used to define three levels of task complexity. The results, some of which are portrayed in Figure 11-1, are similar to those of Romanow. While there are performance differences favoring subjects in the low-anxiety category at all levels of task complexity, the difference is greatest on the most difficult problem. The overall effect of anxiety was not statistically reliable in this study, but the result, coupled with those of Romanow and other considerations to be discussed next, offers reasonably good evidence supporting the habit by drive interaction theory.

Stress. Dunn's study was complicated by the inclusion of a second motivational variable —stress associated with some of the concepts

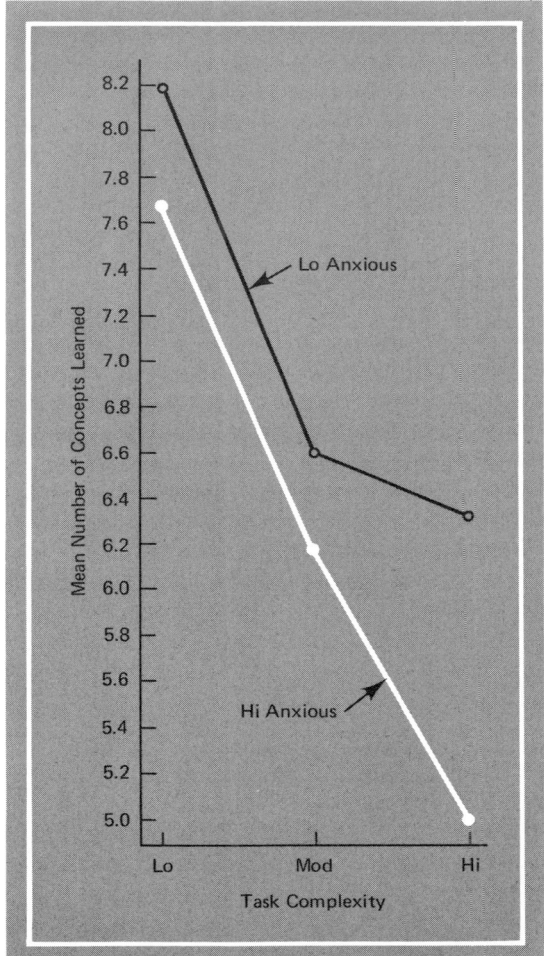

FIGURE 11-1. *Performance by anxious and nonanxious subjects averaged over a series of verbal concept problems. For different groups of subjects the problems were relatively easy, moderately difficult, or very hard.*

Source: Data from R. F. Dunn, Anxiety and verbal concept learning. *Journal of Experimental Psychology,* 1968, **76,** 286-90. Copyright 1968 by the American Psychological Association and reprinted by permission.

to be learned. The rationale was that stress should not only enhance the subject's general level of activation but also depress the positive habit strength with which it is associated. To establish the necessary relationships, Dunn put all subjects, prior to concept learning, through an aversive conditioning task in which instances of half of the concepts were associated with an irritating electrical shock. The consequences of this operation confirmed the activation theory in a new way. In the simplest concept problem, stressed concepts were identified more easily than nonstressed, while just the opposite was the outcome in the most complex problems. The result is once again reasonably consistent with expectations if it is assumed that the *existing* level of activation for a subject is suboptimal for easy problems but supraoptimal for hard problems. Stress should enhance activation, leading to better performance in the first case, worse in the second. The results are not altogether consistent, however, for even in the simplest problem used in this study, high-anxiety subjects were poorer than low; if the average level of anxiety was suboptimal, high-anxious subjects probably would be expected to exceed low anxious. There are various interpretations of this anomaly. High-anxious subjects might have been supraoptimally aroused for all problems; alternatively, the aversive aspect of the conditioning procedure might have specific effects, not fully accounted for in this analysis and that might in some way sensitize subjects to stress concepts. Obviously, to work out the details of this effect, additional and more incisive experiments are required. A suggestive lead is provided by Kinsman (1968) in an experiment considered in the next section.

Cue Utilization. We have explored an interpretation of motivational arousal that emphasizes its effects on existing habits or associations, and we find it compatible with many available empirical facts. As with most issues, however, there are other viable theoretical descriptions of the same phenomena. One of these alternatives stresses the effects of generalized drive in perceptual processes. In brief, the proposal is that strength of drive is inversely related to breadth of attention or of cue utilization. Imagine a situation in which a large number of either necessary or sufficient cues to solution is available; high drive or anxiety should be detrimental because, theoretically, the subject would be sensitive only to a limited subset of those cues at any time. Alternatively, imagine a task that requires a narrowing of attention to one or at most a few of the available cues; here, high drive might work to the subject's benefit.

Zaffy and Bruning (1966) conducted a test of this hypothesis in a learning task which basically required a series of positional responses. For one group of subjects, a redundant cue was added to the task giving two bases, positional and numerical, on which the correct response sequence could be learned. For a second group, an irrelevant (numerical) cue was added which could not easily be used as a basis for learning the series. A third, control group learned to perform with no additional cues involved.

As they expected, Zaffy and Bruning found a significantly greater difference among these conditions when the subjects measured low rather than high on Taylor's anxiety scale. Low-anxious subjects should, in theory, be sensitive to a broader range of cues than high-anxious subjects. The addition of redundant cues should help them; but if irrelevant cues are added, that should interfere—relative to the effects of these experimental manipulations on the performance of the insensitive, high-anxious group. Zaffy and Bruning predicted correctly that high-anxious subjects would perform better in the irrelevant cue condition but worse in the relevant cue condition, thus adding some credence to the hypothesis that heightened drive is associated with a reduction in the range of cues utilized.

A similar test of the same hypothesis, performed within the context of a more conventional conceptual problem, was reported by Kinsman (1968). Kinsman used the three-phase procedure introduced by Guy, Van Fleet, and Bourne (1966) which begins with a simple, unidimensional attribute identification task (Phase I), involves the introduction of a novel dimension after the first problem has been solved (Phase II), and shifts the solution to the novel dimension after a fixed number of trials (Phase III). In effect, two successive problems are solved, with one dimension relevant in Phases I and II and a second dimension relevant in Phase III. The three phases are continuous, with no interruption or forewarning to the subject of changes at any point.

Kinsman's experiment contained four independent groups of subjects. For half of them the novel dimension was irrelevant to solution and could not be used as a basis for correct responding in Phase II. For the remaining subjects, the novel dimension was relevant in Phase II and therefore redundant with the Phase I solution; the subject could use either dimension as a basis for correct responding. Half of the subjects within each of these conditions were given a mildly painful electrical shock on the finger three times during Phases I and II. This technique was used to raise anxiety, arousal, or generalized drive. No shock was administered to the remaining subjects.

On the basis of Dunn's results, some difference in the performance between the shocked and nonshocked subjects in Phase I might be expected. None was observed, however, an outcome which might be attributable to the intermediate level of difficulty of the task, the fact that only one shock was actually given in Phase I, or to some other unknown consideration. The more impressive and interesting data, shown in Figure 11-2, were obtained in Phase III. While there was no overall difference in the performance of shocked and nonshocked subjects, shocked subjects were quicker than nonshocked to solve in Phase III when the novel dimension has been relevant in Phase II and slower to solve when the novel dimension has been irrelevant. If it is assumed that shock arouses the subject, then it follows that arousal makes him more sensitive to novel sources of stimulation—arousal sensitizes the subject to a wider range of stimuli.

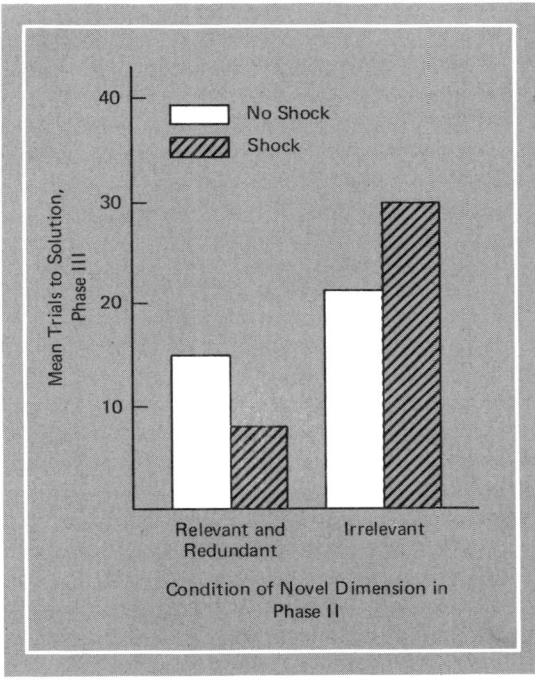

FIGURE 11-2. Performance in Phase III of a concept problem which involved a nonreversal shift. Some subjects were aroused by electrical shock and some were not. For some subjects the novel dimension, which was relevant to solution in Phase III, was relevant in Phase II and for others it was irrelevant. See text for details.

Source: Data from R. A. Kinsman, The effects of induced anxiety on the identification of a novel stimulus dimension. Cognitive Processes Report No. 109, Boulder, Colo., 1968.

This outcome plainly conflicts both with the results of Zaffy and Bruning and with the arousal-cue utilization hypothesis. Instead of the induction of cue focusing, shock-generated arousal produced a sensitization process. Assuming the available results are valid, one must invoke some sort of curvilinear relationship between level of arousal and range of cue utilization. It is possible that moderate (or induced, as in Kinsman's study) anxiety is associated with supranormal sensitization, a trend which is reversed at higher (manifest) anxiety levels. This interpretation is based, of course, on a number of untested assumptions about the comparability of experimental tasks, reproducibility of results, and relative levels of arousal. Obviously, the implied approach is a more detailed experiment in which arousal, induced or chronic, is varied over several values within the same experimental context. An adequate study remains to be conducted.

Comment. As we have noted, there are other aspects to motivation besides generalized drive, arousal, or anxiety, but these seem to have been given little attention by researchers. For example, in many learning situations, reinforcers, i.e., rewards and punishments, are given on a trial-by-trial basis as added inducements to performance. The characteristics of reinforcement, such as magnitude, frequency, and the like, are traditionally categorized as motivational variables. But only on rare occasion have any added inducements—above and beyond informative feedback which is considered by some to have reinforcing properties in its own right (Buss and Buss, 1956)—been included in a study of concept learning.

What studies are available in this issue seem neither to be systematic nor unambiguous in outcome. Wallace (1964) used tones and verbal remarks derogating performance as signals to the subject that his hypothesis was incorrect. As the degree of tone intensity and the degree of derogation increased, fewer premature hypotheses were offered, and overall performance in some problems was facilitated, despite the fact that logically the same information was contained in each signal. The result suggests that feedback, especially verbal feedback, can have motivating effects as well as effects strictly assignable to its informational content. In contrast to this outcome, Bourne, Guy, and Wadsworth (1967) reported that coupling "right" signals with a monetary payoff and "wrong" signals with monetary loss in an attribute identification problem had no effect on performance. Subjects performed just as well, whether or not money was at stake. Here it would appear that all the information and all the motivation necessary to solve was provided by instructions and verbal feedback, the effects of added reinforcers being nil. These two sets of results lead to different conclusions. But there are many substantive and procedural differences between these studies, and neither can be said to be definitive.

Another apparently important motivational variable is related to the affective nature of the stimulus materials. Rhine (1965) demonstrated that a positive evaluative concept is learned more rapidly and is more resistant to change than a negative evaluative concept, indicating that the emotional tone of the materials to be categorized enters importantly into the learning process.

These and other observations are at best suggestive of possible relationships between motivation and performance. The questions are important but have been given little attention by researchers of concept formation. What is needed is a systematic analysis of motivational properties and a programmatic approach to the problems involved. There are no signs of this development at present.

Intelligence

Through contact and interaction with the environment, people acquire knowledge and skills which then manifest themselves in subsequent behavior. What a person knows and knows how to do at any point in time is a major dimension or property of behavior which enters importantly into descriptions and explanations of human activities. While there are many ways to elaborate and to categorize the different manifestations of this property it is known collectively as intelligence, i.e., intelligent behavior.

Several facts are fairly well established about intelligence. First, as a concept it has reference both to nativistic and experiential considerations. Knowledge and skill are dependent on learning, but natural aptitude seems to govern the rate at which acquisition occurs. Second, general and specific features of intelligence can be measured reliably in various ways—most familiarly by IQ tests—and a person can be characterized by a number indicative of his intelligence level. Third, intelligence is related to performance in nearly every task or problem; we can reasonably expect that learning new concepts and solving conceptual problems will be directly correlated with the intelligence a person brings to the situation.

Denny (1966) had subjects who scored above and below the median on a general intelligence test solve an attribute identification problem. He found overall that subjects with higher intelligence made few errors, drew a large number of correct conclusions from the information provided by the experimenter, and reached a satisfactory solution in a larger number of cases than did the less intelligent group. This is an impressive result in view of the fact that the subjects were college students—an intellectually homogeneous group which does not represent the full range of variation found in the normal population. This result has been confirmed, moreover, over a wider range of intelligence and ages by other investigators (e.g., Hoffman, 1955; Osler and Fivel, 1961).

Intelligence and Anxiety. While on the subject of Denny's experiment, it would be appropriate to mention its connection with work discussed in the preceding section to point up one type of interaction between intelligence and motivation. The primary purpose of the study was to test an hypothesis that on particular tasks, anxiety will facilitate the performance of bright individuals and interfere with the performance of dull ones. The hypothesis rests on the assumption that a task which is easy for intelligent individuals can be rather complex and difficult for the less intelligent. Some of the results of Denny's

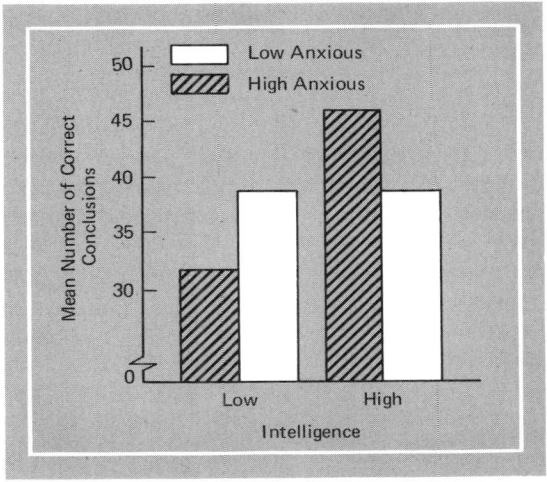

FIGURE 11–3. *Performance on a logical, conceptual problem by anxious and nonanxious subjects of differing intelligence levels.*

Source: Data from J. P. Denny, Effects of anxiety and intelligence on concept formation. *Journal of Experimental Psychology,* 1966, **72**, 596-602. Copyright 1966 by the American Psychological Association and reprinted by permission.

study are given in Figure 11-3 where it can be seen that, for this particular problem which was empirically constructed to achieve a moderate degree of difficulty for the average person, intelligence level is practically unimportant for subjects who test at the low end of the Taylor scale but exerts enormous control over the performance of high-anxious subjects. These data are (1) in agreement with predictions from the drive-habit interaction theory, (2) serve further to clarify the inconsistent effects of manifest anxiety in learning processes, and (3) demonstrate one of the ways in which intelligence, as a general construct, is embedded in the overall picture of human problem solving.

Components of Intelligence. Intelligence is often thought of as a unitary attribute of behavior, quantified on some fundamental unidimensional scale. The use of a single test score, as in Denny's experiment and many others, helps to convey that impression, which is a vast oversimplification of the facts. Intelligent behavior is predicated on knowledge, skills, and aptitudes in various areas and of various types. Knowledge of political history and mathematics, musical and athletic skills, memory and inferential abilities, and other specific considerations are all of some potential relevance to a person's performance in any task at any time. To date researchers have looked almost exclusively at the relationship between some overall composite measure of intelligence and performance in conceptual tasks. Although progress toward a detailed understanding of the intellectual components of some types of learning has been made, e.g., Games's (1962) investigation of serial and paired-associates verbal learning, little is known about these specific relationships in concept learning.

The most extensive available studies were reported by Bunderson (1965) and by Dunham, Guilford, and Hoepfner (1968). As discussed earlier in this chapter, the general purpose of this work was to identify which of several intellectual abilities—knowledge of classes, fluency of ideas, memory, and the like—are correlated with performance in a conceptual problem and then to show how this relationship changes as the subject proceeds through several stages of progress toward the solution of the problem. It is difficult to summarize all the data reported by these investigators. Moreover, the details of their results are limited by the particular tests and measures used and it is difficult, without additional work, to specify their generality. These studies are important because they provide a preliminary analysis of intelligence into component properties and a demonstration that components are unequally related to performance on conceptual tasks. Perhaps the greatest contribution of this work will be as a source of hypotheses about independent variables which other researchers can pursue in detail in more refined experimentation.

DEVELOPMENT OF CONCEPTUAL BEHAVIOR

For many years, the study of human psychological development consisted primarily of statistical and psychometric reports of correlations between changes in one or another behavioral characteristic and chronological age. This research provided a great amount of useful standardization data, descriptive of the human organism at various points in his life span, but it was wholly empirical and based on no particular general theoretical or interpretative system. The dominant learning theorists in the early part of this century (and even many popular contemporary theorists) had little to add about specific developmental processes, and, by their neglect, might have discouraged programmatic, experimental research in the area. In any case, the work that was done was rather cut and dried, stimulating little interest and lacking systematization and integration with the general body of psychological knowledge.

There have been recent changes in this picture, triggered largely by extensions of theoretical research into the domain of developmental processes. The pertinent theories represent several different traditions and points of view in psychology, some of which were discussed earlier. They provide interesting contrasts in interpretation, and this, as much as anything, is responsible for an upsurge in experimentation. There is considerable activity at the present time, and the results are beginning to provide a coherent description of the growing human being which can sensibly be integrated with knowledge of mature behavior. A fair proportion of this current experimental work is related to concept learning and its changing characteristics at early ages.

Developmental Processes

The two fundamental developmental processes are experience and biological growth.

They are so obvious and so familiar that neither should require any elaborate clarification. Normally, as the organism gets older, maturational changes in various biological systems take place. Sensory, motor, and nervous systems all develop according to a certain pattern and rate. Commonly, we think of these changes as achieving a particular level, usually described as full maturation. Both the time course of these developments and the level eventually achieved will vary from person to person, and even from system to system within the same person, but the general trends are characteristic of all normal individuals. It is also clear, however, that biological changes continue to take place throughout life. One can clearly develop new and enlarged muscle tissue through proper exercise at almost any age. In addition, there are aging processes which, later in life, more or less reverse some of the positive maturational changes. It is fair to say that "biological growth," in the general sense, is a continuing process that has ramifications for all aspects and all phases of human activity.

Experience, the cumulative totality of an organism's behavioral interaction with his environment, is also correlated with age. One can conceive of the process as a kind of "psychological growth." While the patterns are not nearly as well known, nor apparently as regular as the corresponding biological patterns, it is still reasonable to think analogously of the development of experiential systems, such as one's knowledge of music or skill as a pianist, at characteristic rates. Like biological changes, specific experiential systems achieve certain levels which are subject to inter- and intra-individual and to temporal variations. Psychological growth is clearly a primary process in human behavior.

It is useful, though simplistic, to think of the products of maturation as "tools" for use in behavioral processes and of the products of experience as knowledge and skills in the use of these tools. But processes, and their products, place limitations on behavior. One can achieve some level of mastery in, say, piano playing, only when and if the biological development of necessary sensory-motor and neural equipment and the appropriate training experiences have taken place.

The description is oversimplified, however, in many ways, two of which are particularly notable. First, psychological and biological processes are interrelated. Training often leads to biological change (as in exercise) which otherwise would not occur. Conversely, biological changes often result in behavioral effects (for example, brain tumors) of a reliable sort. Second, these systems, like all processes, are time-dependent. Both are correlated with age, especially in the earlier years of life. These conditions make it extremely difficult to separate experience effects from maturation, so that in many cases the kind of change observed is impossible to categorize.

Theoretical Problems

The confounding of processes is often reflected in the interpretations given for developmental data. Extant theories of behavioral development—all of which tend to emphasize early as contrasted with gerontological changes —run the entire range, from heavy emphasis on innate, nativistic, or biological concepts to systems that are completely experience oriented. The fact that such fundamentally different accounts can sensibly be given for the same data is attributable largely to the empirical confusion of maturational and experiential phenomena.

Many of the theories in question were outlined in their basic forms in an earlier section. Associational and mediational theory present an extreme emphasis on learning in human development. No theory denies that human beings are biological organisms and subject to biological change. But the importance of those considerations for behavior is de-emphasized in this approach. The general idea is that behavioral development is accounted for by a stockpiling of associative connections between stimuli and responses.

The more we experience and the more we learn, the more associations and, in that sense, the more knowledge and skills we have. Each new behavioral episode is a function in part of the generalization and transfer of older associations.

In contrast, classical Gestalt theory (Koffka, 1928, 1935) and the modern nativistic theories of language and linguistic behavior put a heavy burden on biological considerations. For example, organisms are said to be biologically equipped with a "language acquisition device" which automatically takes perceived speech in its physical form and distills from it a set of grammatical rules, i.e., a theory of language (Chomsky, 1965). From that theory the device then generates its own speech and, thereby, the organism becomes verbal. Note, experience is not ignored—the corpus of spoken utterances produced by others is vital to the acquisition-developmental process. But the primary determiners of behavior at every stage are biophysical, not psychological.

Piaget's Theory. Lying somewhere between these extremes is an elaborate theoretical system created by Piaget (1957). Unlike the others, this system is specially conceived as an interpretation of developmental processes, though it does of course terminate in a description of the mature behavioral characteristics of an adult. It is predicated on two assumed invariant properties of behavior, *organization* and *adaptation*. These are the general governing functions of the organism at every stage of his development. Thus, at any point, a person's behavior reflects some integrated form of knowledge and skill, achieved through prior, diverse experiences, and a tendency to achieve an adaptive equilibrium with his environmental circumstances. It is pertinent to note that organization and adaptation are as applicable to biological as to psychological growth. They are often cited as major functional properties of all living matter. A formally trained biologist, Piaget is given to reasoning about behavior through biological analogy.

Behavior, in Piaget's system, is governed by internalized representations known as schemas or knowledge units. Schemas are learned. Each is predicated on and influenced by existing schemas. One can acquire only what his present knowledge prepares him to acquire. New schemas rest on a base of old ones. Thus schemas, and as a consequence behavior itself, are organized pyramidally or hierarchically.

As for adaptation, there are two primary forms. *Accommodation* is an adjustment on the part of the person (his schemas and his behavior) to the realities of his circumstances. *Assimilation* is a subjective adjustment (distortion) of the environment by the person so that things are perceived to conform with existing schemas. Both processes provide the means for adjusting behavior to the momentary circumstances.

The organism is in continual interaction with the environment. His behavior and its internalized representations are continually adapting and reorganizing. The most dramatic changes take place in early life during which the basic behavioral forms are acquired. On the basis of long and detailed observations of children and adolescents, Piaget has described several periods or stages of development which mark off the most significant behavioral changes. As they relate to thinking and conceptual processes, these include periods of (1) sensory-motor intelligence (0-2 years); (2) concrete quasi-logical behaviors (2-11 years); and (3) formalized abstract behaviors (11-15 years). There are, of course, inter-individual variations in the timing of these epochs, but the sequence is said to be constant. Each period rests on developments at the preceding stage, leading to increasingly more complicated behaviors up to a certain age at which the physiological and psychological maxima are reached.

Piaget's theory is particularly pertinent in a discussion of the developmental psychology of conceptual behavior. As noted above, his is primarily a theory of human development. In addition, it focuses on the issues of complex, logical activity. Since its introduction into the American literature (see particularly Flavell, 1963), it has generated many interesting empirical studies of conceptual processes, examples of which are considered below.

Chronological Age

Common sense would lead one to expect performance on conceptual and most other types of tasks to improve up to a point with age. Age is identified with growth in both a maturational and an experiential sense and the products of both processes are intimately involved in quality considerations of human behavior. But chronological age is just a temporal marker. It, in itself, could hardly be the critical determiner of behavior. What are more important and more interesting are the events and processes that cumulate over time and terminate in a particular behavioral ability or episode.

The general age trend in conceptual performance has been established over a wide range of tasks. These include learning sequential concepts (Friedman, 1965) and oddity concepts (Strong, 1966), identifying the attributes of class concepts (Pishkin, Wolfgang, and Rasmussen, 1967), acquiring discrimination learning set (Harter, 1967), learning the rule—conjunctive or disjunctive—of class concepts (King, 1966), and solving verbal logic problems involving class concepts (Saltz and Sigel, 1967). In the main, these studies have concentrated on early life, covering among them approximately the ages 3 to 20. They typically report improvement in performance on any of the tasks with increasing age.

Several studies (e.g., Strong, 1966) included samples of older individuals, in this case seniles over 65 years of age, showing a not unexpected deterioration in performance, reminiscent of the decline in general intelligence with old age (e.g., Jones and Conrad, 1933) and usually attributed to a combination of biological changes (e.g., arteriosclerosis) and psychological changes (e.g., waning concentration). At the other extreme, a very few experiments have assessed the behavior of animals and human beings on substantially the same problems. This introduces, of course, a new dimension into the picture but provides interesting comparative data which can further be used to evaluate age effects. Some of the results of Strong, who studied the formation of a simple oddity learning set in cats, raccoons, monkeys, chimpanzees, and human beings of varying ages, are reproduced in Figure 11-4. This representation provides a simple, yet broad picture of the overall changes associated with developmental processes.

The arrangement of data in Figure 11-4 is not meant to suggest that animals and human beings, or even all human beings, solve conceptual problems in the same way. There are profound differences in the details of performance, illustrated by the developmental changes in behavior that have already been discussed. Strong reported a few observations suggesting that young children (three years) give performance curves much like the best infrahuman subjects, showing a gradual acquisition of the oddity concept. Older subjects (including some seniles), on the other hand, learned in an apparently insightful fashion, as if at some point in the training sequence they "discovered" the correct concept in their repertoire and began to apply it. A different kind of evidence on species differences was provided by Wells and Deffenbacher (1967) who compared the performance of squirrel monkeys and college sophomores on two types of problem, one conjunctive and one disjunctive. As one would anticipate, human subjects were better in both cases. But whereas the disjunctive problem was significantly more difficult than the conjunctive for humans, there was a small difference in favor of disjunctions for monkeys. Detailed analyses

FIGURE 11-4. *Number of trials to achieve mastery of the oddity principle for several species and by age among human beings.*

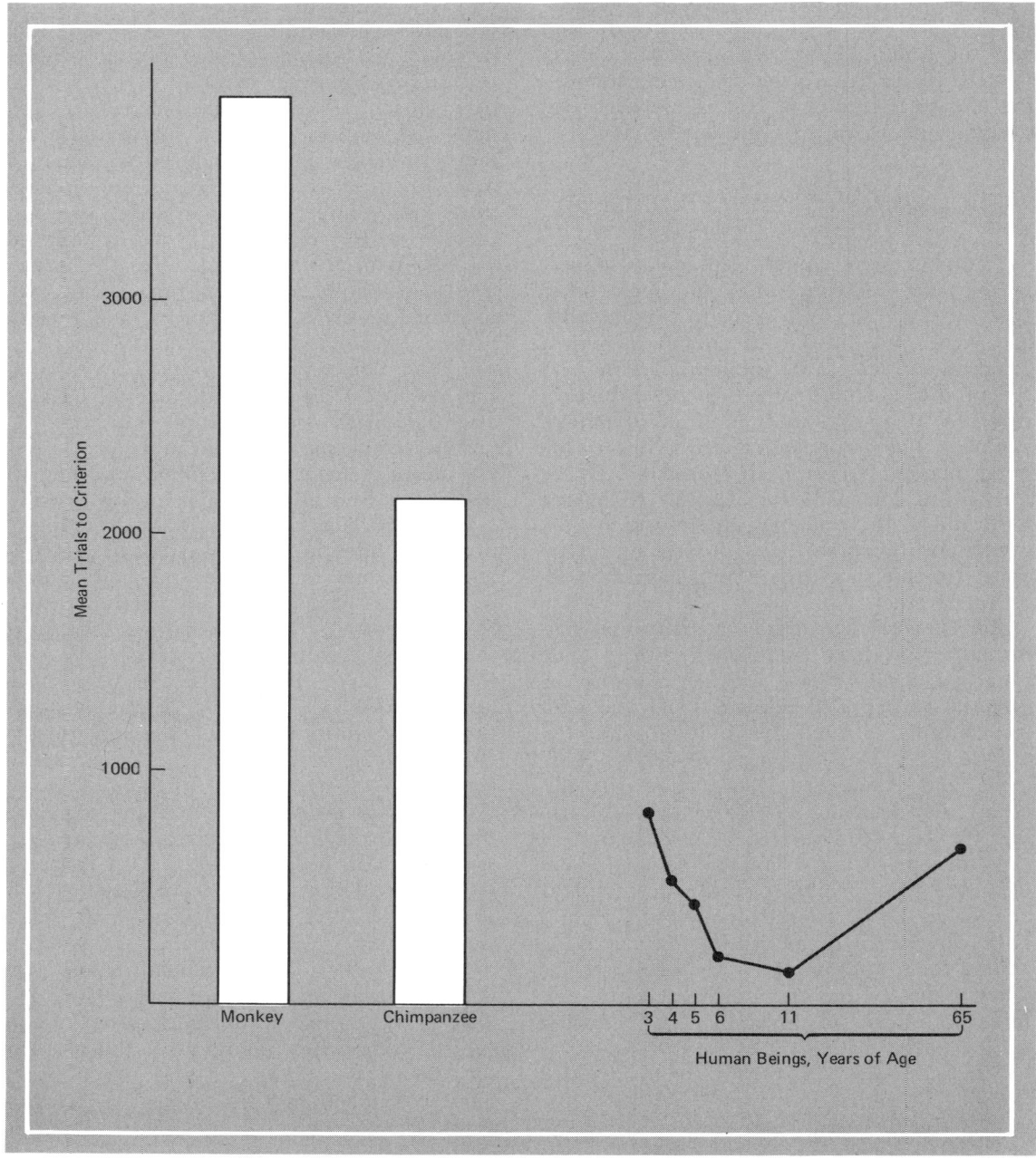

Source: Data from P. N. Strong, Jr., Comparative studies in simple oddity learning: II. *Psychonomic Science,* 1966, **6**, 459-60.

of these results indicated that monkeys learned the cue value of each relevant attribute independently, while adults searched and tested combinations of attributes. Logically the first strategy favors disjunction for, in an "x and/or y" problem, anything that contains attribute x is positive regardless of its other features, and anything that contains y is positive regardless of its other features. The subject can learn the problem as two simple unidimensional discriminations. In contrast, a contingent combination of attributes must be learned to solve a conjunctive problem. Adults, with less of an inclination toward unidimensional responding, adopt a strategy which is more appropriate to conjunctive solutions. It is interesting, though probably coincidental, that the approach exemplified by monkeys seems consistent with the "independence of subproblems" assumption of some theoretical models (see Chapter 10), originally proposed as an account of human concept learning.

The Possibility of an Inverse Relationship. It is normal to expect performance to improve with age during the early years of life. Skills grow in complexity and sharpness as the subject accumulates experience and practice. But it is conceivable that this very complexity in behavior can be a source of interference in certain situations. It has been shown, for example, that training on a series of three-step arithmetic problems often leads to failure on a subsequent, simpler, two-step problem (Luchins, 1942). The more complex set established by preliminary training was simply inappropriate for the test.

There is the suggestion of a similar kind of phenomenon in some developmental studies of conceptual behavior. For example, Klugh, Colgan, and Ryba (1964) observed and Friedman (1965) confirmed an apparent reversal in the typical age-performance relationship. In tasks involving sequential concepts, Klugh and his associates found a deterioration of performance with increasing grade level, first through fourth, while Friedman reported a dip at the fourth grade level only. Using a unidimensional attribute identification problem King (1966) compared first, fourth, and seventh graders with adults and found steady improvement with age except for a significant drop at the seventh grade level. Finally, in a problem which required the subject to learn a certain conceptual principle (either conjunction or disjunction), King reported that performance shows a reversal at the adult level, i.e., seventh graders solved more rapidly than adults.

All of these results are consistent with the notion that developmental changes do not necessarily work to the benefit of problem solving. New knowledge and skills take time and practice to perfect. The subject might be handicapped during the acquisition of some new skill, for his old approach has been rejected but the new one has not been completely mastered. This idea was suggested by Friedman to account for the fourth grade dip in sequential problems. According to him, fourth graders have rejected a strategy based on rote memorization of individual responses, e.g., "1," then "3," then "5," in favor of a coding-rule approach, e.g., "every odd-numbered response." But the replacement, coding strategy has not been fully mastered at the fourth grade level, putting the subject at a disadvantage relative even to younger people. In some cases, as King suggests, the new approach may simply be "too powerful" for the problem. He observed that seventh graders, far more often than first or fourth graders, tested multidimensional hypotheses. This approach is simply inappropriate and, as King observed, will lead to difficulties in a unidimensional attribute identification problem.

In both King's and Friedman's experiments, performance dips were transient. Older children and adults recovered from whatever the source of deficit might have been at any earlier age. This result is indicative of the continuing process of development, suggesting that subsequent changes are of the sort that provide the subject with a means of selecting appropriate action patterns from various hierarchical levels for utilization in accord with the demands of the task.

IQ and Mental Age

The normal individual has been the primary point of discussion in the preceding section and in most theoretical work. This idealized person matures at an "average" rate and has a "normal" set of familial, educational, etc., experiences. His pattern of behavioral development is a standard by which variations and deviations are evaluated. But obviously not all human beings develop in the same way and at the same rate. Chronological age is not a magical regulator of behavior, but rather just a convenient yardstick by which to measure the opportunity for changes. There are many types and a wide range of maturational and experiential differences, and since these are intimately connected with behavior, extreme variations in performance on any task at any age are to be expected.

One sensitive measure of individual differences in knowledge and skill at a particular chronological age (CA), which is of considerable use with young children, is mental age (MA). This index is based on the subject's performance on a standardized battery of paper and pencil tests. For the average child, MA is equal to CA. Roughly speaking, the MA of any particular child is said to be equal to the CA at which the average child passes the same test items. Thus, a bright child tends to pass items in advance of his chronological years and achieves an MA which is greater than his CA. Conversely, the CA of a dull child will be greater than this MA. A derived measure of differences among individuals is the IQ, operationally defined

$$IQ = 100 \times \frac{MA}{CA},$$

which gives a direct means of comparing the intellectual ability of individuals of different ages.

Chronological age, in a crude sense, is a measure of a person's opportunity to learn; MA is an index of how much has been learned and thereby of ability to learn. It is likely then that MA is more strongly related to and therefore a better predictor of the adequacy of a subject's behavior in conceptual problems. While there are few pertinent studies, available data tend to support this conjecture. Harter (1965, 1967), for example, trained subjects on a series of discrimination problems which involved learning to choose the correct one of two objects. Training continued until the subject could solve any new problem in one trial, at which point he had learned the general principle for problems of this type. This principle boils down simply to a "win-stay, lose-shift" strategy, i.e., select the same object if it was rewarded last trial, select the alternate object if it was not.

Between the CAs of roughly 4 and 14 years, Harter found a significant correlation between MA (and IQ) and number of problems required to learn the principle. There was, however, only a trivial relation between CA and performance when MA was held constant.

Harter's research is, of course, limited to a particular task and procedure. There are, moreover, only a few other well-controlled studies of CA-MA (IQ) effects. Thus it is difficult to defend any strong general conclusions. But, while there no doubt are certain cases in which CA plays a significant role, it is clear from the evidence at hand that general knowledge and ability (as measured by MA) are more important determiners of problem solving than age (CA) or opportunity to learn. Furthermore, as has been noted in another section, individual differences in performance at any particular chronological age on specific conceptual tasks are at least partly accounted for in terms of general intellectual factors.

Verbal-Mediational Processes

While there are occasional inversions in the trend, it is clear that performance on conceptual tasks generally improves with age up to adulthood. In any particular task, it is possible to study and to describe the detailed aspects of this change. For example, one can explore the possibility that certain strategic approaches to a problem are characteristic of one age and not another. A good deal of contemporary research is invested in working out these details for different specific problem formats (Harter, 1967; Weir, 1964). The results tend to be too specialized to consider here. However, various theorists have attempted to summarize the array of empirical changes, using one or another hypothetical construct.

As discussed in Chapter 10, Kendler and Kendler (1962) have extended the theory of mediation into the area of developmental processes. One of their primary experimental techniques is a comparison of reversal and nonreversal shifts in the solution of unidimensional attribute identification problems. Noting that nonmediated performance—quicker solutions to nonreversals than to reversals—is characteristic of infrahuman animals and young children, while mediated performance—quicker solutions to reversals than to nonreversals—is characteristic of older children and adults, and that language is one system that distinguishes these two groups, the Kendlers proposed that mediators are likely to be linguistic in nature. As humans mature and become more fluent with language, there is an increased tendency to code abstract or general features of the physical world, e.g., stimulus dimensions of objects, in words and to use these verbal responses to mediate overt performances, such as categorizing objects. Coding and responding verbally on a mediational level to dimensions of objects, rather than to objects (with many attributes) as units, facilitates those conceptual problems which involve a dimensional abstracting process and favors reversal (one-dimensional) over nonreversal (two-dimensional) shifts.

Another pertinent result obtains in a study by Sanders, Ross, and Heal (1965) comparing normal and retarded children, both with average MAs of about 10 years. On the assumption that retardates suffer from a mediational deficit—an inability to control one's own behavior by implicit verbalization—these experimenters predicted no difference in difficulty between forced reversal or nonreversal shifts for retarded subjects. The usual difference was expected for normals. The data were entirely consistent with these expectations. House and Zeaman (1962) in a similar study did find that both normal and retarded subjects with 6-8 year MA performed better on reversals than nonreversals, but, later, Ohlrich and Ross (1966) determined that this result was attributable to a procedure which involved extensive overtraining on the preshift concept. Overtraining is known from other studies (e.g., Grant and Cost, 1954) to simplify subsequent shifts in performance and might have been especially effective for reversal shifts by providing both substantial reinforcement for the relevant dimension and an opportunity for the subject to learn the appropriate dimensional mediational response after the correct category responses for the different stimulus objects had been mastered. Tighe and Tighe (1965 and Youniss and Furth (1965) have shown similar overtraining effects for normal children of a younger age who otherwise perform better on a nonreversal shift. The main point, however, is that once again the evidence is in line with the Kendlers' notions of verbal mediation and its fundamental role in the development of conceptual behavior.

Schemas

Piaget's interpretation of developmental changes is, as has been noted, predicated on the assumption of internal cognitive structures called schemas. Schemas are representations of the real world having both concrete sensory and motor properties and abstract relational properties. In many ways, schemas are like the representational constructs used by other theorists. Their sensory-motor aspects seem indistinguishable from the mediational stimuli and responses of Osgood (1953) and the Kendlers (1962). The manner in which they are acquired through training and their assumed capacity to represent in detail a real behavioral episode are entirely consistent with Mandler's (1962) description of a symbolic analogue of overt behavior. As internal knowledge units describing abstract as well as concrete characteristics of the world, they can play much the same role as the internalized multidimensional hypotheses assumed to be at the root of performance by Restle (1962), among others.

There is no question that the schema concept as developed by Piaget is broader and more general than any of these related notions. Furthermore, when it comes to human development, it is clear that Piaget's theory covers more of the ground than any other. Despite all this, definitive evidence in support of the theory—especially experimental evidence—is practically nonexistent. Piaget's data, while voluminous, are mostly naturalistic and anecdotal or, in his own words, "clinical-experimental." His theory has been popularized among experimental child researchers only for roughly a decade or so, which is relatively little time to accumulate a body of tested facts. Thus the utility and adequacy of concepts like the schema are largely unknown.

The research work that has been undertaken within the framework of Piaget's theory has been largely devoted to the evaluation of his proposed stages of growth and to the possibility of accelerating stage-wise development through specialized training routines. For example, Youniss and Furth (1964) demonstrated that the ability to transfer bidimensional logical principles such as conjunction and disjunction from one set of stimuli to another increases systematically with age (9-14 years) and grade in school (fourth through seventh) even though there is no reliable age trend in the initial acquisition of these principles. They suggested that the older the child the greater the likelihood of his being in what Piaget calls the formal (or abstract) stage of development as contrasted with the concrete stage. Thus older children are more likely to learn the logical principles as abstract or content-free responses, allowing them to use these principles in an appropriate way, independent of the context in which they were attained.

But many of these studies, including that of Youniss and Furth (1964; see also Sigel, Saltz, and Roskind, 1967), find no signs of a gap or an all-or-none change between stages as Piaget's notions might be taken to imply. Rather, the evidence points to a smooth transition with age in the direction of increased ability to perform logical operations in the context of varying irrelevant stimulus circumstances. Thus, the appropriateness of any form of stage analysis remains at issue at the present time.

SUMMARY

We have reviewed available empirical information about the characteristics of a problem solver as they relate to performance in conceptual tasks. The initial issue had to do with ways of characterizing performance, and several possibilities for evaluating overall quality of performance (e.g., number of erroneous responses before solution) and details of the process leading to solution (e.g., type of strategy) were discussed. There is considerable variability among subjects on any of these measures, even within the same experimental conditions. Some of this variability can be traced to individual differences in problem solving or even more general life style.

As a result of recent detailed experimental investigation, a clearer picture of the effects of some ability variables (e.g., memory) and state variables (e.g., motivation) has emerged. These data were summarized, and the importance of interaction between subject variables and task conditions was noted and illustrated. Difficulties posed by these interactions for theoretical accounts of cognition, competence, and motivation in conceptual behavior were explored.

Finally, this chapter considered the origin and development of individual differences and subject variables. Both theoretical evidence and empirical evidence, primarily from studies with chronological or mental age as one variable, were reviewed. It can be concluded that only in the past 10-15 years, partly through the growing influence of Piaget and partly through an interest in testing learning theory and certain experimental procedures at early ages, have important, developmental problems been approached. Progress has been good, but the work is still primitive, and definite answers to these questions are still few in number.

Twelve Empirical Studies of Conceptual Behavior: The Task

As with all learning tasks, conceptual problems can be described in terms of three major recurrent events: stimulus, response, and informative feedback. On every trial, a stimulus is presented or selected, the subject responds to it, and his response is followed by some indication of its correctness. These trials continue until the subject achieves a predetermined experimenter-defined criterion. Note that the description as presented is not intended to be exhaustive of all the events of every conceptual problem, nor does it necessarily prejudice theoretical interpretations of concept learning. It is, however, a convenient, familiar, and useful way to talk both theoretically and empirically about the events of learning tasks.

The characteristics of these events and of the relationships among them are generally important determiners of performance. The form in which stimulus information is presented, the nature of the response requirements, and the completeness of the feedback provided for the subject have been shown to affect the difficulty of a problem and the strategic features of the subject's efforts to solve. A review of recent empirical assessments of selected variables is presented in this section.

COMPLEXITY OF THE RESPONSE SYSTEM

On other occasions we have noted cases in which response variables changed the complexion of a subject's achievement in a conceptual problem. For example, Hunt (1965) has demonstrated that the more demanding requirements of the selection, in contrast to the reception paradigm, seem to facilitate problem solving, at least for adult subjects. The added necessity to state an hypothesis along with each category response, moreover, has been shown by Byers and Davidson (1967) and by Bower and King (1967) to contribute positively to a subject's overall success in reception problems. The manner in which a subject is called on to display what he knows at any point is clearly an important constituent of the task.

A basically different response factor, which

has been given systematic examination in recent research is the complexity of the response system which the subject must use to solve a problem. The importance of this variable comes to light in a comparison of two experiments which were intended as studies of *stimulus* complexity. In both experiments, subjects were required to solve for concepts with one, two, or three binary dimensions. In the multidimensional cases all concepts were conjunctive. In the earlier of the two reports, Walker and Bourne (1961) constructed problems in which the number of response categories (or individual concepts) increased with the number of relevant dimensions. Unidimensional problems had two categories: Category A for red objects and B for green. Two-dimensional problems had four categories: A, red squares; B, red triangles; C, green squares; D, green triangles. Three-dimensional problems had eight categories: A, large red squares; B, small red squares; ... H, small green triangles. The performance on these problems systematically deteriorated with increases in problem complexity, number of trials to solution increasing exponentially with number of relevant dimensions.

In a comparable study reported shortly thereafter, Bulgarella and Archer (1962) used problems in which the number of response categories was held constant at two across changes in the number of relevant dimensions. Thus, their unidimensional problem was identical, in terms of response to that of Walker and Bourne. The two-dimensional problem was formed by collapsing over three categories: Category A, red square; B, green square, red triangle, and green triangle. The three-dimensional problem collapsed over seven categories: A, large red square; B, large green square, small red square ... small green triangle. (For ease of comparison with Walker and Bourne, geometrical stimuli are used to illustrate the problems of Bulgarella and Archer. Actually, multidimensional auditory stimuli were presented in the latter study.) Once again, increasing the relevant dimensionality interfered with performance, but this time the trend was linear rather than exponential. In other words, each new relevant dimension produced the same increment in problem difficulty.

Because both the response complexity variable and the mode of stimulus presentation were different—visual versus auditory—in the two studies, it is treacherous to draw any strong conclusions. Number of relevant dimensions might affect performance in two different ways depending on whether the relevant information is heard or seen. It is more likely, however, that the greater, exponential effect observed in the Walker-Bourne experiment was the outcome of variable response complexity. Number of relevant dimensions in and of itself probably increases problem difficulty linearly regardless of the sense modality involved. But response complexity should affect performance adversely also, if for no other reason than the changing number of S-R connections it generates. The exponential trend observed by Walker and Bourne would then be a reflection of the combination of two sources of affect in performance—a stimulus source and a response source.

An investigation by Kepros (1965) puts this interpretation on reasonably sound empirical grounds. Response complexity and number of relevant dimensions were varied independently in this study. Problems with two, three, or four relevant dimensions were constructed. These problems were arranged in such a way that the subject would have to use two, three, four, six, or eight response categories. For example, one group of subjects solved a three-dimensional problem with two categories: Category A, large red square versus B, all other patterns. Another group solved the same problem with four categories: Category A, large red square; B, small green square; C, large green triangle; versus D, everything else. A third group solved with eight categories, corresponding to all eight conjunctive combinations of the two levels on the three relevant dimensions. (Note that only the 2, 3, and 4 category conditions could be used with two-dimensional problems.)

In the evaluation of data, number of relevant dimensions as an independent factor was shown to affect performance, and the trend was linear as in the results of Bulgarella and Archer. This is consistent with a review of experiments on search problems reported in Chapter 5. Response complexity had an even more powerful influence on performance. Number of errors to solution increased with number of responses, and again the effect was linear. These two sources of problem difficulty summate. If the data are rearranged to show the mean number of errors subjects make in a set of conditions analogous to those used by Walker and Bourne, in which response complexity and number of relevant dimensions change concomitantly, the trend is curvilinear. Such a portrayal of Kepros's data is given in Figure 12-1.

Drawing on analytical work in verbal paired-associate learning (Underwood and Schulz, 1960), Kepros argued that concept identification in its simplest form is a two-component process involving (1) the search for relevant dimensions and (2) the associative hookup of levels on the relevant dimensions and responses. A similar analysis of conceptual performance was proposed earlier by

FIGURE 12–1. Performance in an attribute identification problem as a function of the confounded variables, number of response categories, and number of relevant dimensions.

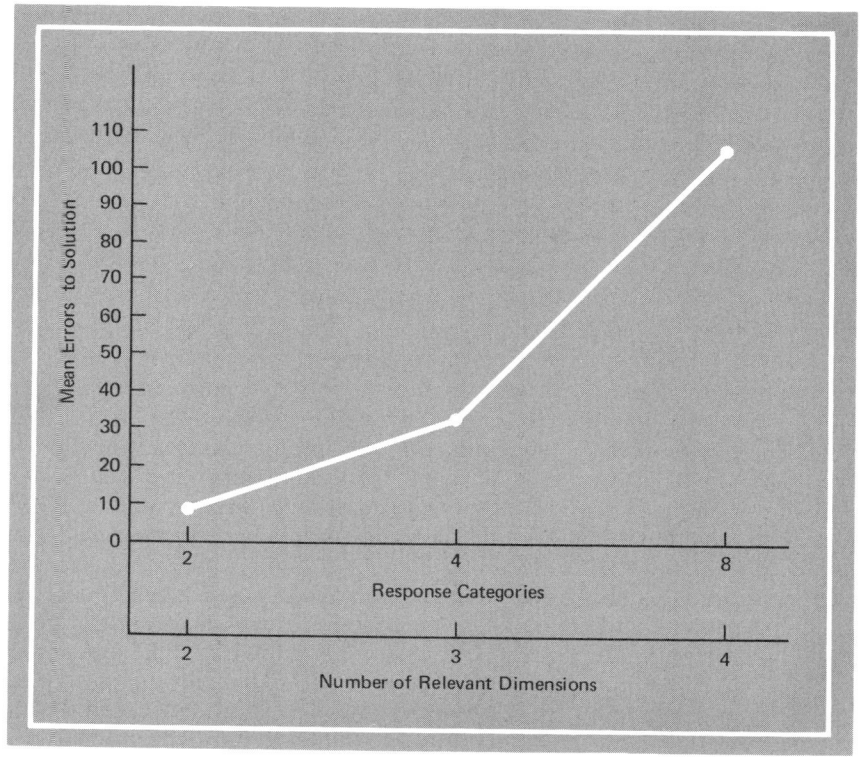

Source: Data from P. G. Kepros, Identification of conjunctive concepts as a function of stimulus and response complexity. Unpublished doctoral thesis, University of Utah, 1965.

Richardson and Bergum (1954). Kepros theorized that the significant effect of response complexity was primarily associated with the second component, associative hookup, for it seems reasonable that the length of this stage should depend on the number of associations to be formed.

Kepros offered only indirect evidence in support of his two-component analysis. One datum of interest in this respect would come from a comparison of learning curves across groups. Logically, associative hookup cannot begin until at least one of the relevant dimensions has been identified. Identification might take a constant number of trials regardless of the response complexity factor. Therefore, we would expect all groups of subjects working on problems with a given number of relevant dimensions to show nearly identical learning curves up to a point in the trial sequence, after which the curves should diverge with those representing fewest response categories achieving problem solution earliest.

PROPERTIES OF THE CONCEPT

Conceptual problems differ both in overall difficulty and in the kind of strategies they elicit from subjects. These differences are traceable to the concept itself and to the conditions under which it must be learned and used. We consider first some of the properties of concepts which make a difference in performance. Two structural properties—the number of relevant stimulus attributes and the type of principle—are the main variables to be considered in this section.

Concept Complexity

The complexity of a concept is conventionally defined by the number of stimulus attributes it implicates, i.e., the number of relevant dimensions. It has been fairly well established now that general performance measures, such as number of trials to solution, bear a linear relationship to concept complexity (e.g., Bulgarella and Archer, 1962; Schvaneveldt, 1966). A similar trend is typically observed in other tasks requiring a search for relevant elements (see Chapter 5). We reported earlier that the conflicting results of Walker and Bourne (1961), indicating an exponential change in performance, have been more or less resolved by Kepros (1965), who separated the variables of concept and response complexity which were confounded in the Walker-Bourne experiment. To date there have been no detailed studies of the relationship between number of relevant attributes and the subject's strategy, with the exception of Laughlin (1966), who found that subjects have a greater tendency to adopt a focusing-type approach in more complex problems.

Incidentally, Laughlin's results (see also Glanzer, Huttenlocher, and Clark, 1963) seem to conflict with the typically observed effects of concept complexity. Laughlin reported no difference between problems with two and four relevant attributes, and Glanzer and his associates found a U-shaped performance-complexity relationship. One reason for these exceptions to the general rule of a linear change in performance is not difficult to find. In conventional studies of the number of relevant dimensions, the number of irrelevant dimensions is either held constant or is systematically varied. Neither was the case in the Laughlin and the Glanzer, Huttenlocher, and Clark experiments, which held the *total* number of stimulus dimensions constant and thus confounded the numbers of relevant and irrelevant dimensions. That is, in both these experiments, as concept complexity increased, the number of nonrelevant dimensions—a variable of considerable influence in its own right—decreased. This confounding of variables could easily account for the nontypical results in these experiments.

Other Considerations in Concept Complexity. In the context of this discussion, it is convenient to make note of the effects of two variables related to the number of relevant dimensions. The first, mentioned above, is the number of irrelevant dimensions—a parameter of the stimulus population on which the concept is defined. Time, trials, or errors to solution of a concept identification problem all increase linearly with this variable, as they do with number of relevant dimensions (e.g., Bourne, 1957; Bulgarella and Archer, 1962). This is an extremely stable and general observation. It has been reported over a wide range of concept complexity (unidimensional and multidimensional concepts) and for a number of different conceptual principles including conjunctive (Bulgarella and Archer, 1962), biconditional (Kepros and Bourne, 1966), disjunctive (Haygood and Stevenson, 1967), and oddity (Lordahl, Berger, and Manning, 1967), and with both visual and auditory (Keele and Archer, 1967) stimuli.

It is quite likely that the same process characterizes the effects of both relevant and irrelevant dimensions. To solve for a concept of any complexity, a subject must test the relevance of all variable dimensions and generally can be counted on to do so (Bruner, Goodnow, and Austin, 1956; Glanzer, Huttenlocher, and Clark, 1963). The dimensions that are connected with response categories are used for sorting patterns, while those that are unconnected are disregarded. The test of each dimension can, on the average, be considered to take a certain fixed number of trials, and that number might depend on a multitude of other variables. Thus, the more dimensions to contend with, whether relevant or irrelevant, the more trials to complete the testing routine, the increase being a constant number per dimension. Of course, it would be an error to rule out axiomatically the possibility that with continual increase in the number of dimensions, the limit of man's ability to cope with the problem will be passed. At the limit there is either a discontinuity in the performance function or it must become curvilinear. Problems used in experiments to date, however, seem to be well within the region in which performance and number of dimensions are related in a strictly linear way (Wolfgang, 1967).

Parenthetically, we should note that these effects of number of irrelevant dimensions in a stimulus population hold only for attribute identification problems, i.e., problems in which it is unclear to the subject at the outset which of the variable dimensions is implicated in the concept. In principle-learning problems, theoretically, it should not make any difference how many irrelevant dimensions vary, for the subject is told which dimensions to attend to and which to ignore. Haygood and Stevenson (1967) and Bower and King (1967) have shown this expectation to be essentially valid. Haygood and Stevenson found no discernible effect of irrelevant dimensions; Bower and King observed a minor effect, and then only on the first of three successive problems.

Another variable related to concept complexity is stimulus redundancy. Normally, when we talk about the number of relevant attributes of a concept, we have in mind independent attributes, each of which plays a separate and necessary role in defining the concept. But two or more defining attributes might be partly or completely redundant. While each enters into the definition of the concept, only one needs to be used as a basis of response. Consider, for example, automatic traffic signals. The stop signal appears at the top of a row of three lights and is always red; the "go" signal is always at the bottom and green. Color and position of light are completely redundant in informational content. Their values—red, green, yellow and top, bottom, middle—occur together in perfect correlation, and either alone provides a fully sufficient source of information.

These built-in redundancies are, of course, not merely a matter of poor planning on the part of an inventor or an engineer. Rather they are consistent with a general principle that the more cues to the same response, the more likely is that response, at least up to a point. Obviously, the consequences of missing a traffic signal or failing to make the correct response could be disastrous, making redundancy a desirable feature of the concept.

This general principle has been documented in laboratory research on concept learning. Bourne and Haygood (1959, 1961) have shown that increasing the number of perfectly redundant relevant dimensions in an essentially unidimensional concept identification problem reduces trials to criterion and that this effect is more marked in normally difficult problems, i.e., problems with a large number of irrelevant dimensions. Keele and Archer (1967) have confirmed this general result using meaningful verbal concepts presented orally in contrast to the abstract geometrical stimuli presented visually in the studies of Bourne and Haygood. From these results it is clear that the more possible bases for correct response, the more rapidly the problem is solved. The outcome is directly related to the necessity for the subject to test possible solutions on a dimensional or focusing basis. The probability of selecting a relevant dimension is logically related to the proportion of variable dimensions that are relevant. That this involves more than simply finding one relevant dimension, however, is suggested by the observation that subjects often can name several usable dimensions once solution has been achieved (Bourne and Haygood, 1959). While the subject might discover relevant dimensions one at a time, learning doesn't cease once a workable solution has been reached. Subjects remain sensitive to alternative possibilities throughout their participation in the task.

There has been relatively little work on partially redundant relevant dimensions. These are cases in which one dimension (or set of dimensions) provides the solution, but others are better than chance cues to correct response. Some data suggest beneficial effects of partial redundancy (Haygood and Bourne, 1960)—possibly by calling the problem solver's attention to the fully relevant dimension—but, as Trabasso and Bower (1968) suggest, the function is in need of more thorough examination.

The Conceptual Principle

Attributes are integrated into a concept description by some principle. This property of concepts, as a variable affecting behavior, has been considered in an earlier section, and there is no need to repeat that discussion here. Comparative studies (e.g., Hunt and Hovland, 1960; Neisser and Weene, 1962; Bourne, 1967) have clearly demonstrated that principles differ in their difficulty. The concept "red if-and-only-if square" is considerably more difficult to learn than the concept "red and square," despite the fact that the same two relevant attributes are implicated in the solution. Several interpretations have been advanced to account for these observations. Among them the arguments that (1) some principles are more "primitive" than others (Neisser and Weene, 1962); (2) some principles are more directly generated from "natural" strategies (Hunt, 1962); and (3) some principles are informationally "richer" than others (Haygood and Bourne, 1965).

Whatever the most useful interpretation of the differences, it is clear that principles themselves are learnable and that with sufficient practice differences among them tend to vanish (Bourne, 1967). In many known cases, subjects come to use difficult conceptual principles errorlessly, suggesting the acquisition of strategies appropriate for each principle or, as seems more likely, the acquisition of a general strategy such as the truth table for solving problems based on any of a number of related principles.

Quantitative Principles. We consider briefly at this juncture some recent research on a special type of principle. Most studies in the area use problems based on deterministic class concepts. Clearly these are neither the only, nor even necessarily the most interesting concepts that people learn and use in their everyday lives. Another type of concept of obvious importance is quantitative, i.e., the type of concept that prescribes a numerical value for each stimulus, using some combination of the numerical values of selected stimulus attributes as the principle. To attain the concept, the subject must learn to rate each stimulus in a population on some unitary scale. To accomplish the goal, he needs to determine (1) which of the several stimulus dimensions are involved in the concept, (2) what weight to assign to each relevant dimension as a determiner of response, and (3) how the relevant dimensions are combined within the principle.

To illustrate quantitative concepts, consider the general relationship

$$R_{ijk} = xA_i + yB_j + zC_k, \text{ where}$$

R_{ijk} is the correct numerical response for stimulus (ijk); A_i, B_j and C_k are stimulus values on dimension A, B, and C, and x, y, and z are the weightings of these dimensions. A specific example

$$R_{ijk} = 1.0A_i + .5B_j + 0C_k$$

A, B and C might correspond to three rows of numbered lights (i to n, from left to right), their values in any stimulus pattern corresponding to the particular element which is lighted. In the course of solving this problem, the subject must learn to base his responses on dimensions A and B, ignoring C which bears no relationship to the correct response. In working with these dimensions, the subject must give more weight to the value of A which has twice as much control of the correct response as B. Finally, he must note that R depends on an additive, as opposed to some other, say, multiplicative, relation between A and B. All these considerations must be taken into account for a complete solution.

In principle a person's behavior should be no less systematic in quantitative than in qualitative problems. To the extent that the general problem and its solution form are unfamiliar, his performance will be variable. But, with practice, well-organized methods of attack should appear. Unfortunately, to date, there have been relatively few attempts to describe empirically the properties of performance in quantitative concept tasks.

One of the earliest studies was reported by Azuma and Cronbach (1966). These experimenters had their subjects respond with values between one and four to each of a large number of stimulus patterns, portraying positional variations of two objects on a matrix. Using as a measure the degree of correlation across trials between the subject's responses and the four different stimulus dimensions, they were able to show that subjects do progressively come to depend only on variations in relevant dimensions (in this case, two) and with proper weighting. When reporting their own solutions, however, subjects typically did not even approximate the compact quantitative formula which governed the solution. Many revealed a rather unexpected strategy. Instead of giving a universal rule, they often reported dealing with subsets of stimuli each associated with a unique numerical response, one, two, three, or four. That is, they appeared to solve the problem in parts, and the conceptual response for each part was commonly given in nonquantitative rather than quantitative terms. The analysis given by Azuma and Cronbach is suggestive of a general theoretical approach outlined by Hunt (1962), in which subjects are said to solve all but the simplest unidimensional and conjunctive problems by a method of parts.

The effects of several significant variables on performance in quantitative problems have been explored in related work. Hammond and Summers (1965), for example, have shown that subjects are able to approximate the solution to problems involving nonlinear (e.g., $R = \sin A$) as well as linear relations between dimension and response and, in fact, can successfully combine these two types of relationship in a complex concept (e.g., $R = \sin A + xB$). Uhl (1963) has shown that as the degree of relevance of two dimensions changes from equality to extreme disparity, with one dimension relevant and the other irrelevant, overall performance improves. As in nominal concept problems, then, it is easier to learn to respond to one than to a combination of two dimensions. In a later study, Uhl (1966) reported on the interfering effects of irrelevant stimulus variability. In each of these cases, the experimenters were able to describe the subjects' growing reliance on the relevant dimensions with multiple correlational techniques, but were unable to specify in detail any of the strategies they used in achieving this solution.

PROPERTIES OF THE STIMULUS

Every concept prescribes an arrangement of stimulus objects. What characteristics those stimulus objects have and how they are presented can make a difference in the ease with which a person learns the concept and then subsequently uses it. For example, Bruner, Goodnow, and Austin (1956) have shown that formally identical concepts are more difficult to identify when defined on a population of thematic stimulus materials (two persons shown in some type of social interaction) than on a population of abstract materials (geometric designs). Bruner suggested that the difference might very well result from interference in the thematic problem arising from pre-experimental experience with the various forms of social interaction portrayed.

Other stimulus variables which are known to affect ease of concept learning include: (1) *systemization in the stimulus display*—subjects solve selection paradigm problems more rapidly when the stimulus population is placed in an orderly arrangement as contrasted with a random arrangement (Bruner, Goodnow, and Austin, 1956); (2) *compactness of stimulus information*—in a variety of problem types, subjects seem to learn more slowly when the stimulus dimensions are assigned singly to spatially separate objects than when they are compactly represented in a single object (Shepard, Hovland, and Jenkins, 1961; Bourne and Parker, 1964); and (3) *sequential contiguity*—in a multiconcept problem, quality of performance is a direct function of the probability with which instances of the same concept occur in adjacent positions in the stimulus sequence (Kurtz and Hovland, 1956; Newman, 1956; Bourne and Jennings, 1963).

We have preliminary information identifying these and other variables as important determiners of problem difficulty. Detailed information, beyond that given above, however, is lacking, and what we know is not very well integrated. Rather than listing the various isolated conditions that have been explored, we devote the remainder of this section to a consideration of the few stimulus variables on which a substantial body of knowledge has begun to develop.

Positive and Negative Instances

The General Rule. In the course of learning about a single concept, a person encounters and responds to both positive and negative instances. There was a time when the behavioral processes involved in utilizing positive and negative instances were thought to be fairly straightforward and well understood. That is, positive instances were assumed to be more useful than negatives to the problem solver. In recent years, however, new experimental techniques have reopened the question, suggesting that the situation may be more complex than was initially imagined.

The earliest significant studies of the problem were reported by Smoke (1933) who observed that subjects were able to use positive instances much more readily than negative as clues to the concept. While negative instances were not worthless, Smoke felt that they did little more than provide a background or context against which subjects were able to evaluate the information provided by positive instances. Negative instances were used essentially to establish the limits of the stimulus population on which the concept was defined.

Smoke's work was crude by modern standards. Later, Hovland (1952) showed that his results might be attributable to a number of unique methodological conditions, among them the fact that negative instances of the concepts and problems used by Smoke contained less information, logically, than their positive counterparts. Subjects might have learned less from negative examples simply because there was less to be learned.

Subsequently, Hovland and Weiss (1953) undertook a study in which the logical content of positive and negative instances was equated. While they did show that people can identify concepts from negative instances only, they found that positive instances are used more efficiently than negatives. Later still, Schvaneveldt (1966) found a direct relationship at several different levels of stimulus complexity between the percentage of positive instances in the sample shown and overall efficiency of performance.

There are of course several interpretations of this general outcome. One obvious one, that has been suggested by Bruner, Goodnow, and Austin (1956) among others, is that most natural and formal educational processes are structured around examples of what the concept "is," not around what the concept "is not." To teach the child about horses, one ordinarily doesn't point out dogs or houses or automobiles or clouds. Thus, people might have trouble inferring concepts from nonexamples simply for lack of experience and skill in making such inferences. If making inferences is a learnable skill, however, the imbalance between positive and negative instances should be correctible. People should be able to learn to use negative examples just as well as positive.

This is a testable proposition and has been evaluated by Freibergs and Tulving (1961). In their experiment, subjects were given 20 consecutive concept problems to solve. For half the subjects, only positive instances of each concept were shown—in sufficient number, of course, to define the solution. The remaining subjects saw only a set of negative instances of each concept. Subjects were allowed a fixed interval to discover the solution (3.5 minutes) and time to solution was the main dependent variable. On the first few problems of the series, subjects with positive instances were vastly superior to those with negative. In fact, none of the subjects working with negative instances attained a solution to any of the first four problems.

With practice all subjects improved, average time to solution decreasing reliably from problem to problem. Subjects working with negative instances improved more rapidly, however, attaining a performance level nearly equivalent to the other group by the eleventh problem of the series. For all practical purposes, there was no difference between the groups from that point on through the end of the series.

Incidentally, the minor difference in average time to solution that remained between the two groups after 20 problems, can probably be accounted for by an additional step in problem solving required by subjects working with negative instances. Negative instances prescribe what the concept *is not*. To state an acceptable solution to the problem, the subject must convert his conclusion to positive form. Evidence for the importance of this conversion operation can be found in the work of Huttenlocher (1962). It could easily account for the small additional time interval required in the negative case.

Special Cases. As a general rule, then, people are more efficient concept problem solvers if they have positive instances of the concept to work with, but they can be trained to use negative instances with nearly equal facility. There are some significant qualifications of this rule, however, that have been uncovered in recent research and that need to be taken into account as special cases.

First, consider the experiment by Huttenlocher (1962). Her subjects solved for unidimensional concepts defined on a population generated by binary (two-level) dimensions.

Under these circumstances, exactly the same logical amount of information about solution can be supplied either by a positive or a negative instance. Problems were arranged such that only two instances—both positive, both negative, or a combination—were sufficient to solve. Consistent with the general rule, even in these simple problems, subjects generally gained more from positive than from negative instances. But the data showed further that the sequence in which instances are given can be an even more powerful variable than the type. Specifically, a sequence consisting of a negative followed by a positive instance resulted in more solutions than even a sequence of two positive instances. A combination of two positives was slightly better than a positive-negative combination and grossly better than two negatives. Huttenlocher attributed this outcome to the logical operations required to solve a problem. In a negative-positive sequence only two simple steps are required: (1) to notice the dimension that changes between the first and second stimulus and (2) to name the value of that dimension in the second stimulus. Other sequences require more steps, including the conversion of a negative conclusion into a positive statement in the sequences ending in a negative instance.

Wells (1967) has a related finding. His experiment was designed to compare three different stimulus presentation methods. Subjects solved a bidimensional conjunctive concept problem under (1) a *contrast* condition in which one positive and one negative stimulus were shown on each trial, (2) a *pairs* condition in which either two positive or two negative instances were given on each trial, or (3) a *successive* condition in which only one instance, positive or negative, was presented on each trial. In terms of both trials and number of instances to problem solution, the contrast condition was superior to the other two. That this effect is probably not attributable to the availability of more stimuli for the contrast as opposed to the successive condition is indicated by better performance with successive than with pairs-type presentation. The overall inferiority of the pairs condition is difficult to explain in view of the general facilitation usually associated with simultaneous stimulus arrangements (e.g., Cahill and Hovland, 1960). The superiority of contrast, however, seems to result from its provision of the relatively obvious strategy of taking the intersect of the positive and negative instance on each trial as a working hypothesis (Levine, 1966). In any case the data help to clarify the significance of negative instances in the process of learning and identifying concepts.

In the conceptual problems used in nearly all the available research, including that reported above, positive instances are those which embody all the relevant attributes (one or more). In other words, almost always the conceptual principle has been simple affirmation or conjunction. It is clear, however, that many concepts have the structure of a disjunctive or conditional or some other relationship between relevant attributes. In these cases, a positive instance does not necessarily embody all (or even any) of the relevant attributes (see Table 9-2). When this is the state of affairs, it is not quite so clear that positive instances will be any better than negative instances as sources of information to the subject.

Haygood and Devine (1967) were the first to study this question. They surmised, from a logical analysis, that instances which contain all the relevant attributes are the most useful to subjects. When there are two relevant attributes, these can be designated the TT instances (see Table 9-3), using the truth-table analogy. These are, of course, the only positive instances of a conjunctive concept. In a nonconjunctive concept, Haygood and Devine argued that increasing the percentage of TT instances in a series of trials following the standard reception paradigm would facilitate problem solving, while increasing the percentage of other, non-TT positive instances (holding TTs roughly constant) would have little effect.

This is precisely their finding in an experiment which employed both disjunctive and biconditional concepts, learned in the context of both attribute identification and principle learning paradigms. Their results are summarized in Figure 12-2. They argued that the

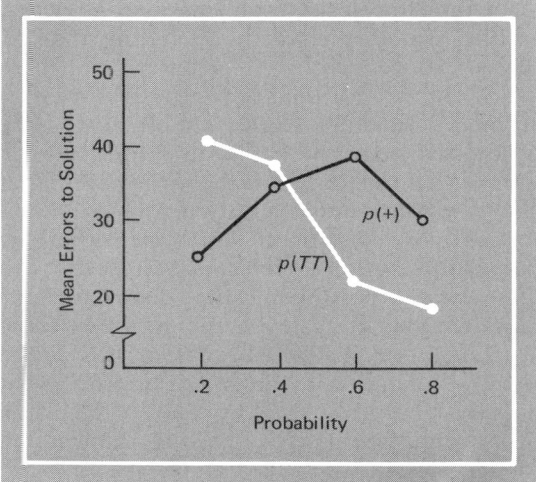

FIGURE 12–2. Performance averaged over attribute identification and rule learning problems based on disjunctive and biconditional rules as a function of the probability with which positive instances, p (+), and TT instances, p (TT), occur in the stimulus series.

Source: From R. C. Haygood and J. V. Devine, Effects of composition of the positive category on concept learning. *Journal of Experimental Psychology,* 1967, **74**, 230-35. Copyright 1967 by the American Psychological Association and reprinted by permission.

superiority of the positive instance in conjunctive problems is an artifact of its identity as a TT stimulus. The beneficial effects are said to be primarily a consequence of making the relevant attributes perceptually more obvious to a subject which in turn might effect a more rapid utilization of a problem-simplifying strategy such as the truth table described by Haygood and Bourne (1965; see also Bourne, 1967).

The Haygood-Devine results help to define what it is that makes positive instances informative to the typical problem solver. They do not, however, provide any direct evidence on the *relative* usefulness of positive and negative instance within different conceptual principles and different conceptual tasks. That question was the subject of an investigation by Bourne and Guy (1968).

These experimenters presented subjects with alternating informational and test stimulus series. For different groups of subjects each informational series of eight stimuli was all positive, all negative, or 50 percent of each type. The subject passively observed these instances, learning from the experimenter whether each was positive or negative. Then he tried to categorize correctly, without feedback, four test stimuli, one each from the four truth-table categories, TT, TF, FT, and FF. Problem solution was achieved when the subject could categorize test instances errorlessly. In addition to the type of instance condition, subjects were divided according to the principle involved in the concept and according to whether the principle or the attributes were to be learned.

The pattern of results was complex. Considering first attribute identification problems, results for conjunctive concepts replicate those of other investigators. All positive instances led to fastest learning, all negative to slowest. There was, however, little difference between the instance conditions for disjunctive problems; for conditional concepts, all negatives produced fastest solutions and all positives slowest. When the problem was to learn the principle, a mixture of positive and negative instances was best in the case of all principles, with positive instances *worst* for conjunctions and negatives worst for disjunctions and conditionals.

These data imply important qualifications, in terms of the givens and unknowns of a problem, of the general rule of thumb that positive instances are more useful than negative instances in learning a concept. To wit, when the task is to identify the relevant attributes (principle given), subjects perform best if information is presented in the form of instances from the *smaller* and more homogeneous of the two conceptual categories. Which of the two is smaller depends on the principle—positive instances (TT) in conjunctions and negative instances (TF) in conditionals. (For the population used in this experiment, positives and negatives were roughly equal in disjunctive problems.) The fact that the smaller category gives a person fewer attribute combinations and fewer distinctly different stimuli to keep track of is, in all probability, critical in this outcome.

In the case of principle learning problems, performances improve as a direct function of the *variety* of informational instances the subject is exposed to. Whether positives only or negatives only are better depends on which category represents the greater variety, a result which is in sharp contrast to the outcome for attribute identification.

Comment. In this summary, we have seen a relatively complicated, though regular and comprehensible picture emerge. The available results indicate that in the most common cases of unidimensional and conjunctive concepts, learning the concept (a matter primarily of attribute identification) proceeds most efficiently on the basis of positive instances. This situation is a product primarily of the presence of *all relevant attributes* in every positive instance of concepts of this type. While negative instances are less effective sources of information to the naive subject, even when equated logically with positives, they are not without some value, particularly in establishing the boundaries of the concept. In the rarer cases of nonconjunctive concepts, particularly in principle learning problems, the relative usefulness of the two types of instances changes markedly, showing that the most important consideration for understanding how people use stimulus information is, in all probability, the number of different instances contained in the positive and negative categories.

Stimulus Saliency

General. For a variety of reasons, some properties of physical stimuli are more salient, impressive, or obvious than others. The hue of a traffic signal, for example, probably would be a more compelling characteristic to a motorist than its brightness. The reason would clearly be traceable, in part, to the learning history of the individual, for there seems to be no intrinsic reason for a man to notice hue before brightness. In another case, the backfire of a nearby automobile would be more noticeable than the background hum of an engine, here for reasons of an intensity differential. The saliency of a stimulus and of the information it carries about solution would certainly be expected to affect its rapidity of use and, therefore indirectly, the efficiency of problem solving. As suggested, saliency has several separable properties. The effects of these variable properties in concept learning situations are reviewed in the following section.

Intradimensional Considerations. Incidental to their main observations, several investigators have noted differences in the usability of seemingly quite neutral dimensions of stimulus objects. For example, in a visual display, Brown and Archer (1956) found that positional dimensions (i.e., the location—top vs. bottom, right vs. left—of an object, geometrical design, on a viewing screen) were relatively more difficult to use as a basis for solving attribute identification problems than were properties of the object itself, e.g., form or size. Moreover, quantitative analyses of a series of attribute identification experiments (Bourne and Restle, 1959) indicated that color is an extremely compelling property, having roughly twice the weight of other dimensions of the objects to be categorized.

These effects are not limited to visually presented geometric stimuli. Pishkin and Blanchard (1964) conducted an extensive study of the relative saliency of variations in auditory signals, such as the duration, frequency, amplitude, and laterality (a positional dimension) of a pure tone. Not only did they find differences among these dimensions—with the positional dimension being a difficult one to use for categorizing purposes—they also observed certain peculiar interactions with sex, which were reproducible in three separate experiments. Although Pishkin and Blanchard offered no detailed explanation of their results, it is plain that the usability of a dimension is not purely and simply a function of its physical features.

Observations made in the foregoing studies were incidental to their purposes. None of them was especially designed to evaluate what differences among dimensions might contribute to their saliency. The first systematic step in this direction was taken by Archer (1962). His technique was to vary the physical difference between the levels of a given dimension, on the assumption that this characteristic would make the dimension more or less obvious to the subject as a possible basis of solution. Care was taken to ensure that the levels of a dimension even at their smallest degree of physical difference were 100 percent discriminable so that any resulting performance effects could be assigned unambiguously to the obviousness of the dimension (rather than an inability to tell the difference between its levels). The stimuli were geometrical designs which the subject had to learn to sort into four categories defined by the four conjunctive combinations of two dimensions. The relevant dimensions were unknown to the subject at the outset.

When a particular dimension, say, size, was represented at very distinct levels it was quickly noticed by the subject and tested as a possible component of problem solution. Thus, when size was relevant, the problem was solved more rapidly than usual; when size was irrelevant, problem solving was delayed. Just the opposite outcome was observed when the same dimension, size, was represented by closely spaced values. Solution was achieved more quickly when such a dimension was irrelevant than when relevant. Archer's results show clearly that inter-level difference is one of the properties contributing to dimensional saliency.

Attesting to the generality of this effect is a similar result obtained by Lordahl (1967), in the context of an oddity problem. Here the subject had to learn to respond to the odd (unique) value of one among several variable stimulus dimensions. Problem solving was significantly more rapid when the odd versus nonodd difference within the relevant dimension was perceptually more dominant (by subjective judgment) and physically larger than the corresponding differences within irrelevant dimensions. In the same type of problem, moreover, Gollin, Saravo, and Salten (1967) showed that the distinctiveness of the odd value of a relevant dimension, and therefore overall performance by children, can be enhanced by increasing the number of stimuli taking the nonodd (i.e., identical) value.

The most detailed study of this issue was conducted by Trabasso (1963). The single relevant dimension of an attribute identification problem was emphasized, i.e., made more salient, in a number of different ways, which were compared both in original learning (problem solving) and in transfer. Briefly, three techniques of emphasis—(1) removing all irrelevant dimensions of variation during original learning, (2) increasing the difference between levels on the relevant dimension (the same operation used by Archer, 1962, and Lordahl, 1967), and (3) adding a marker (a semi-redundant cue) to the relevant dimension—all produced faster original learning and significant positive transfer as contrasted with a control condition involving none of these emphasizers. As did Archer, Trabasso concluded that the primary function of emphasis or saliency is not a matter of discriminating among the values within a dimension but of attending to dimensions as a whole. Any technique which attracts subjects' attention to a particular dimension, generally by making it unique and different from other dimensions, will, thereby, speed or slow problem solving, depending on the relevance of that dimension. The effects, according to Trabasso, carry over to a second problem involving the same dimensions but in which the emphasizing operation has been deleted.

Modality

The exemplars of most everyday concepts are not only multidimensional but also multimodal. Think, for example, of a piece of furniture. Clearly it has visual and tactual components, and in fact might also have a characteristic sound—as with the creaking noise of an old rocker. A concept itself is often defined by properties which are specifiable in the terms of two or more stimulus modalities.

In recent years, there has been some interest in research into the relative usability of information from different senses in solving conceptual problems, particularly the modalities of vision and hearing. In one of the earliest comparative evaluations Lordahl (1961) defined four-category conjunctive problems in terms of one auditory and one visual stimulus dimension. Subjects knew the general form of solution, but had to identify the two relevant dimensions from an equal number of variable dimensions of each type. The total number of dimensions, and therefore the number of irrelevant dimensions, was a major variable in the study. Lordahl reported that subjects have considerably more difficulty using auditory than visual information, though they were warned in advance that either type might enter into the solution. The visual dimensions were, moreover, more potent distractors, when irrelevant. Changing the number of visual dimensions had, as it normally does, an immense effect on trials to problem solution; changing the number of auditory dimensions had practically no effect at all. The visual stimulus apparently overpowers auditory signals in this type of problem. The performance differences reported by Lordahl are similar to those obtained from more and less obvious dimensions (of the same modality) in Archer's experiment (1962).

Auditory dimensions were almost totally ignored by subjects in Lordahl's study. This fact seems to conflict with the important role that auditory information plays in everyday learning and problem solving. Later research by Haygood (1965) and Keele and Archer (1967) helps to elucidate some aspects of the situation.

With a primary interest in some applied questions about the utilization of audio-visual materials, Haygood compared performance on structurally identical unidimensional and bidimensional attribute identification problems in which the solutions depended on visual only, auditory only, visual plus auditory, or either visual or auditory (i.e., redundant) information. For simple, unidimensional concepts, the availability of two redundant solutions, one visual and one auditory, was of no benefit to a subject. Visual only and the redundant problem were solved with roughly equal rapidity and both were easier than the comparable, auditory only concept. Having alternative possible solutions (visual, auditory, or some combination) was of some advantage in the more difficult bidimensional task. Fewer errors were made prior to solution in the redundant case than in either the visual or auditory problem. Again, auditory only information was more difficult to use than visual only. The most difficult problem by far, however, was the one in which the subject had to integrate one visual and one auditory dimension into a single solution. Subjects made over twice as many errors in this case as in any other.

Haygood concluded that, in general, nonverbal auditory information is only slightly more difficult (perhaps for reasons of familiarity, obviousness, or discriminability) to use than visual. When the task is complex, some redundant combination of visual and auditory data—so that essentially the same message is presented via different channels—can be quite helpful. It is relatively inefficient, however, to *require* a person to use both channels simultaneously, e.g., to require a crossmodal combination of data. Attending simultaneously to two types of signals is apparently a task that most people perform inefficiently. The information processes which constitute human thinking are, with the possible exception of highly trained individuals, primarily single channel (modality) affairs (Broadbent, 1958).

The results of Keele and Archer add further clarification to the importance of sense modality. First of all, they showed that irrelevant auditory information can be just as deleterious to performance as visual information, depending on its form. Lordahl, who found very limited effects of auditory signals, used the relatively neutral dimensions of pure tone, e.g., loudness, pitch, etc. With linguistic stimuli, i.e., spoken words, varying in gender, tense, and the like, Keele and Archer observed highly reliable effects of number of irrelevant auditory dimensions (equivalent to those of visual dimensions). Second, these experimenters demonstrated that auditory information of the same type, made redundant, can be facilitative even in simple two-category, unidimensional problems.

One important conclusion to be drawn from a comparison among these studies is that the saliency and usability of information is a function not only of its modality but also of its meaningfulness. It would be worthwhile to undertake an experiment involving independent variations in the meaningfulness of visual and auditory signals, perhaps both of which are verbal in nature. There are probably circumstances under which auditory signals will be even more potent sources of problem-solving data than visual. This, and other possibilities involving the investigation of other modalities such as touch remain, however, for further research to investigate.

Concept Dominance

Still another source of saliency differential, in addition to the individual stimulus dimensions and the sense modality through which information is registered, is the stimulus instances themselves and the concept they exemplify. This property is defined by the compellingness with which particular stimuli illustrate a concept and the obviousness of that concept among other possibilities. As with other aspects of saliency, this variable exerts a significant influence on performance in conceptual problems.

Curiously, most of the empirical work on concept *dominance,* as this saliency property has come to be called, has been undertaken with verbal stimulus materials and "verbal" concepts. The theory, procedures, and results of this research have been outlined elsewhere (Bourne, 1966); the connection provided by this work between the often independently treated domains of concept formation and language learning has been described in a preceding chapter. For these reasons, only a brief summary of methods and findings is given here.

Human beings learn language as a way of codifying their perceptions of the real world. A single term, e.g., "kitten," is used to represent a multitude of possibilities, i.e., many different kittens. The objects covered by any term have specifiable features which are also codified linguistically, e.g., "soft," "small," and "hairy." These features are not only common to all (or most) objects of a particular class, but they are also shared by objects of other classes, e.g., linen, moss, cotton, and bread, as well as kittens, are all soft. Thus the characteristics of objects, or other linguistic counterparts, can serve as a basis for classifying those objects.

But, it should also be noted that any characteristic such as softness is more prominently associated with some objects than others. Soft seems more closely connected with cotton or kitten than, say, with linen. If we were to play a word-association game, soft would more often and more quickly be elicited by kitten than by linen.

Underwood and Richardson (1956a) were the first to make systematic use of these facts and arguments. Their first step was to calibrate a set of verbal materials—213 common nouns—in terms of the frequency with which each item elicited, as an associate, certain descriptive property characteristics. The characteristics were considered to be concepts, and the nouns their exemplars. The strength of a concept-exemplar relationship, called its dominance value, was defined by the percentage of subjects in the standardization population who responded with the concept, given the exemplar. Thus, to the exemplar *kitten* 40 percent of the subjects responded with *soft,* 25 percent with *small,* 13 percent with *hairy,* etc. Examples of these materials are given in Table 9-4.

Different exemplars will, of course, elicit the same (as well as different) concepts with nearly the same or quite different dominance values. Thus it is possible with these materials to construct several sets of words, each set representing the same concept at some controlled level of dominance, which amounts to controlling the saliency of the concept or its instances.

This aspect of concept saliency has been explored experimentally in several ways. In the initial study, Underwood and Richardson (1956b) had subjects learn a paired-associate list containing exemplars of six different concepts. In the list, two concepts were represented by high-dominance (approximately 75 percent) instances, two others by medium-dominance instances (41 percent), and the remaining two by low-dominance instances (16 percent). As expected, the order in which subjects learned the correct conceptual response for each set of instances corresponded with their level of dominance. The lower the dominance value of an instance, the greater the probability of its eliciting incorrect responses from a subject in the form of other highly salient features of that instance. These prepotent responses interfered, of course, with the attainment of the required concept.

In the foregoing experiment, conditions were defined by the absolute dominance value of an item. Mednick and Halpern (1962) repeated this work, using dominance rank—the ordering of conceptual associates of a noun—as a variable. Holding absolute dominance value constant, they constructed lists of Rank 1 associates of certain concepts and Rank 2 associates of others (where Rank 1 items all elicit the same most frequent concept word and Rank 2 elicit the same second most frequent concept). Rank 1 concepts were learned more rapidly than Rank 2 despite the fact that the two sets were equal in absolute dominance.

In a related study, Freedman and Mednick (1958) demonstrated that dominance variability is also a factor of importance in concept learning. Of two sets of instances with equal average dominance values, the concept for the set with greater variability will generally be learned first. The reason seems to be that a high-variance set will by definition contain one or more instances of high dominance. All other things being equal, this instance calls forth the correct conceptual response from the subject earlier than any other (including those in the low variance set). Once the correct response has been elicited, the subject is apparently able to make the connection between it and its other instances in the list. The high dominance of a single item might then be sufficient to account for the effects reported by Underwood and Richardson (1956b) and others. Moreover, if the influence of a single item is mainly to call out the correct response, a procedure in which correct responses are given, leaving the subject only the task of properly connecting them up with instances, should eliminate dominance effects altogether. Plainly, we need more data to clarify the essential effects of dominance.

Before concluding this discussion, we might make note of two secondary points. First of all, studies of the type just outlined make use of normative or group data in the construction of materials to be learned. The average dominance values so determined are not the exact values for any single subject in the original standardization group, not to mention an individual who serves in a subsequent experiment. Moreover, the experimenter himself has no means of control over the value of any particular "instance-concept" association, for these are determined by the extra-laboratory experience of his subject. Thysell and Schulz (1964) suggested a refinement of the Underwood-Richardson procedure which seems appropriate in many cases. It amounts to using nonsense items, e.g., cojak, as instances, for which the subject learns a certain set or pattern of meaningful associates, i.e., adjectives, in the laboratory. In other words, the subject is given some amount of training (this being the main determiner of dominance) with some number, 1 through n, of adjectival associates of each of several instances (nonsense words). After the instance-concept relationships have been established, under controlled laboratory conditions, the experimenter can proceed to arrange lists for the experiment proper, with greater certainty about the number of associates and dominance value of each pair in the list. Despite the fact that Thysell and Schulz have used this procedure with good results, it has not been adopted widely, undoubtedly because of the additional experimental time and effort involved in developing the necessary associations *de novo* for each subject.

Second, although it was stated at the outset that work on dominance had been constructed mainly with verbal materials, there is at least one study in which the Underwood-Richardson normative technique was applied to nonverbal stimuli, in this case geometric designs. Wallace (1964) asked subjects to state as many bidimensional conjunctive concepts as they could, using a four-dimensional (color, form, number of figures, and number of borders) stimulus population as a reference. The dominance of concepts was computed using order and frequency of naming by subjects in a normative group. High- and low-valued concepts were then incorporated into a larger experiment with results completely consistent with studies of dominance in verbal material.

Novelty

Not unexpectedly, the novelty of a stimulus dimension with respect to the context in which it appears is still another significant aspect of saliency. A number of investigators (e.g., Berlyne, 1958) have discussed the attention-getting value of novel stimulation, but Braley (1962) appears to be the first to experiment with novelty in a conceptual task.

In Braley's initial study, subjects worked through a three-phase paradigm. First, they solved a unidimensional attribute-identification problem. Immediately thereafter, and without any interruption, there followed 10 trials of overtraining, with exposure to an additional, irrelevant dimension of variation for half the subjects, and without that exposure for the rest. Finally, and again without interruption, they switched to a new problem based on the dimension added in Phase II. For subjects without Phase II exposure, the Phase III relevant dimension appeared for the first time at the beginning of Phase III and was therefore relatively novel. Unlike the others, these subjects had not had a chance to adapt to the added dimension during Phase II. Apparently as a consequence of its novelty, nonexposed subjects noticed and used the new dimension, achieving the Phase III solution in significantly fewer trials than subjects with prior exposure.

These results were replicated later by Braley and Johnson (1963) and by Guy, Van Fleet, and Bourne (1966). The latter group of investigators showed that this effect holds whether the added dimension is irrelevant (as in Braley's studies) or relevant (redundant with the Phase I solution) in Phase II. However, novelty has less of an advantage over a Phase II relevant than a Phase II irrelevant dimension. Presumably then, a subject attends to and learns about a novel dimension when it is first introduced, either in Phase II or III. It might further be noted that the facilitating effects of novelty on Phase III performance increased with the length of Phase II. Thus, the more familiar a subject becomes with a particular stimulus population, the greater the impact of a new dimension when first introduced.

INFORMATIVE FEEDBACK

Stimulus, response, and feedback are the three primary events defining a trial in any learning process. Both stimulus and feedback are objective events, providing information to the learner about how to respond or to solve the problem. In research, they are typically controlled by an experimenter. The primary function of feedback is response correction. Feedback is any signal that indicates to the learner whether his last response was right or wrong or, alternatively, which of several possible responses should have been made. In any case, the learner gets some information about what to do the next time the same stimulus or one like it is presented. Incidentally, telling the learner on each trial which response he should have made is a more effective form of feedback for learning than is merely telling him whether or not his response was correct (Bourne and Pendleton, 1958).

Variations in the characteristics of feedback signals can have significant effects on the usability of the information they carry. A detailed review of these variables is available elsewhere (Bourne, 1966) so that this discussion will be limited primarily to what appears to be the major property of feedback, its frequency of occurrence.

Omission of Feedback

Simple Omission. Learning, of course, cannot occur in the absence of feedback. The subject must have periodic information about the adequacy of his responses. But suppose feedback is omitted on some percentage of trials. How does this affect learning? If it is true that the subject does not use the feedback on some trials—perhaps because he knows his response is correct from an earlier trial—solution might not be delayed very much at all. Alternatively, there would be a disproportionately adverse effect if the blank trials created a source of distraction or interference. This becomes a reasonable hypothesis if one notes that stimulus information is meaningless without feedback and, if omission is random, that the subject has no way of knowing on any trial whether or not feedback will be given.

Actually the effects of omitting some feedback signals at random in attribute identification tasks is relatively minor, except when the problem is very difficult, in which case there is some slight delay in solution. In general, the subject acts as if he merely ignores no-feedback trials; solution is achieved in approximately the same number of regular feedback trials, no matter what the frequency of non-feedback up to 40 percent (Bourne and Pendleton, 1958) and perhaps beyond (Namikas, 1967).

Selective Omission. These results hold for the case in which the occurrence of feedback is not contingent on the correctness of the subject's response. Suppose it is contingent. This question is addressed in a series of experiments by Buss (e.g., Buss and Buss, 1956) and others (e.g., Spence, Lair, and Goodstein, 1963). These experimenters gave feedback on selected trials depending on whether the subject's response was correct or not. Specifically, they compared the performances on an attribute identification problem of three groups: one given feedback ("Right") only after correct responses—the Right-Nothing group; one given feedback ("Wrong") only after incorrect responses—the Nothing-Wrong group; and one given feedback on every trial regardless of the response—the Right-Wrong group. It is reasonable to expect Right-Wrong subjects to perform best, simply because of the greater completeness of feedback in this condition. The results, however, are not entirely in accord with expectations. A typical experimental outcome is shown in Table 12-1. When one counts trials or errors to problem solu-

TABLE 12–1. *Number of Trials (and Estimated Trials with Feedback) to Learn a Concept as a Function of Feedback Conditions*

Condition	Trials	Estimated Feedback Trials
Right-Wrong	29.7	29.7
Nothing-Wrong	42.5	31.8
Right-Nothing*	97.7	24.4

Data from A. H. Buss and E. H. Buss. The effect of verbal reinforcement combinations on conceptual learning. *Journal of Experimental Psychology*, 1956, 52, 283-87. Copyright 1956 by the American Psychological Association and reprinted by permission.

*Only one of 15 subjects achieved solution within 100 trials. Nonsolvers were assigned the arbitrary score 100.

tion, both Right-Wrong and Nothing-Wrong groups perform better than Right-Nothing, but do not appear to differ very much from each other.

This result has led Buss and Buss (1956) to ascribe a greater reinforcing effect to "Wrong" signals than to "Right." Subjects come to solution faster in any Right-Wrong and Nothing-Wrong conditions because of the greater effectiveness of negative reinforcement as contrasted with positive (Right) reinforcement in this experimental situation. It is possible, for example, that being wrong appeals more to an individual's ego-involvement in the task than being right does, according to the authors.

But these results and their explanation leave certain issues in doubt. For one thing, Buss used a four-category sorting problem, which means that the probability of making an error (at least on the initial trials) is .75. Thus, it is probably true that the subject received more Wrong signals than Right signals, which (keeping in mind the effects of frequencies of feedback discussed earlier) could account for the superiority of the Nothing-Wrong group over the Right-Nothing group. Another consideration is that Wrong signals might be less ambiguous than Right signals. That is, any Wrong signal tells the subject that whatever sorting basis he used is incorrect and does so in no uncertain terms.

Right signals on the other hand occur at a chance rate even before the subject solves the problem. A Right signal does not necessarily mean that the subject is on the right track. Thus, there might be no motivational involvement in Right and Wrong signals at all, but rather a difference between the two in informational content.

These possibilities were explored in a subsequent study by Bourne, Guy, and Wadsworth (1967). They argued that the most appropriate measure of performance in experiments of this type is the number of trials *accompanied by feedback*, not the total number of trials. Nonfeedback trials do not provide the necessary information for learning and should be ignored in scoring the subject's performance. They noted that, if one corrects the mean trials scores observed by Buss and Buss and presented in Table 12-1 by deducting an estimate of the percentage of nonfeedback trials, differences among the group disappear. That is, assume that Wrong signals occur on 75 percent of trials and Right on only 25 percent. Then, the values in Table 12-1 all approach 30. As noted in Table 12-1, 14 of 15 subjects in the Right-Nothing group failed to solve and were assigned arbitrarily a score of 100. This could easily account for the slightly superior estimated performance of the Right-Nothing group. The results suggest that subjects actually ignored nonfeedback trials, taking a constant number of informative trials to master the problem.

Of course, it is not clear that these percentages are accurate, for the probability of Right and Wrong signals might change over trials as the subject begins to zero in on the solution. Thus, Bourne and his associates conducted an extended replication of the earlier studies, using not only the basic Right-Wrong, Right-Nothing, and Nothing-Wrong arrangements, but also intermediate conditions involving Right and Wrong signals on some, but not all trials. While there were the usual adverse effects of omitting feedback when total errors and trials were used as measures, no reliable differences among conditions in number of feedback trials were observed. The authors concluded that some fixed number of trials with feedback is needed for solving conceptual problems; under the conditions used, nonfeedback has a relatively minor effect on performance at best. While Right and Wrong signals obviously convey different *types* of information, the data cast serious doubt on Buss's interpretation which emphasizes a strong difference in the *degree* of their effects on learning. Both are valuable as guides to the required behavior.

Theoretical Note. In an earlier chapter we noted that some hypothesis models of concept learning draw important distinctions between positive (right) and negative (wrong) feedback. In an early development (e.g., Bower and Trabasso, 1964), positive feedback was equated with nonfeedback, as it was by Buss and Buss (1956); neither was supposed to have an effect on the subject's hypothesis or his category responses.

The bulk of the empirical evidence, cited above and in a preceding chapter, weighs heavily against this assumption. While subjects probably ignore blank (nonfeedback) trials, they do learn and do modify their hypothesis on the basis of information in positive feedback This is not to say that learning is indifferent to the kind of feedback given. Subjects logically must take different steps after an error as contrasted with a correct response signal. Levine (1966) has been clearest in spelling out the likely distinctions. But learning, as a general phenomenon, is connected in roughly equal degree with both positive and negative feedback.

Misinformative Feedback

In the foregoing studies, feedback frequency has been manipulated by the omission of information on some trials. This manipulation has little serious effect on performance. But instead of omitting feedback, suppose one presents misinformation—telling the subject that he is "Right" when in fact his response was inconsistent with the concept to be learned or telling him "Wrong" when his response was really correct—on some trials. The situation is not unlike many real-life conceptual problems which are probabilistic rather than fully determined. Conceptual techniques involved in weather forecasting or medical diagnosis, where attributes of the cases in question are not perfect signs or predictors of outcome (feedback), are familiar examples of probabilistic concepts.

A few experimenters (e.g., Goodnow and Postman, 1955; Pishkin, 1960; Bourne, 1963b) have investigated misinformative feedback, and it should come as no surprise to learn that its effects are far more serious than the effects of merely omitting feedback on some trials. The effects are able to prevent the subject from achieving a maximally correct level of responding for a substantial period of time. Rather, subjects typically try to "outguess" the environment, learning to respond most of the time to the relevant attributes of the concept but switching periodically in hopes of guessing correctly on a misinformative trial. Despite his inefficiency in using the available information, however, the subject can identify the relevant attributes under conditions which involve up to 40 percent misinformed trials (Pishkin, 1960). Moreover, given sufficient opportunity most subjects eventually do find the most rational way of using the relevant attributes which is to respond to them consistently despite the occasional error signals This approach will maximize number of "correct response" signals. Not only do most subjects eventually attain the rational solution or use of cues, they also readily transfer that strategy to other probabilistic concepts involving new relevant attributes and a different schedule of misinformation (Bourne, 1965b). Thus, while the effects of misleading feedback are severe, normal adults are able to sort out the reliable information and to use it properly and efficiently as a basis of response.

TIMING OF CRITICAL EVENTS

It takes time to process information. Each trial of a conceptual problem contains some information which is necessarily related to the solution, and it takes time to make use of it. If the stimulus or the feedback signals are too brief, the subject predictably will miss some relevant information. If the overall time within a trial is short, the subject might not be able to make the necessary and possible inferences from the information given. Clearly, information can come at a supraoptimal rate, and its use, consequently, will be inefficient. It is also possible, however, for long intra- and intertrial time intervals to have deleterious effects, as when feedback is extensively delayed or when trials are widely spaced allowing forgetting to occur.

Timing variables have been widely explored in more traditional areas of human performance such as verbal learning (Underwood, 1961). However, while there is some experimental evidence to support the general statements made above, much remains to be done to understand these variables in concept learning. For example, to date there are no systematic comparisons of stimulus durations or rates of stimulus presentation comparable to those in paired-associate learning (e.g., Nodine, 1963), most experiments using a subject-paced presentation procedure in concept problems. Timing conditions have significant effects on conceptual performance, as the following review of experiments will show, and also enter importantly into certain theoretical distinctions. Thus, this general area should attract increasing research interest in the near future.

Intertrial Interval

Discussion of the effects of intertrial interval begins in an unlikely place, with a study of delayed feedback. Following up a considerable amount of earlier work on delayed reinforcement, Bourne (1957) varied the time interval between response and feedback in attribute identification problems. As anticipated at the time, the longer the interval—during which the stimulus was not available to the subject for his inspection—the poorer the performance, and this effect was magnified by increases in problem complexity.

The result seemed reasonable and consistent with most contemporary data and theorizing in related areas. Delayed feedback, analogous to delayed reward, was presumed to be weaker than immediate feedback in its effect on the establishment and growth of stimulus-response associations. The results of the experiment became suspect, however, when other investigators reported an inability to produce reliable delayed feedback effects in other complex human learning situations such as stimulus selection and perceptual-motor skills (Noble and Alcock, 1958; Bilodeau and Bilodeau, 1958).

An examination of experimental procedures used by Bourne (1957) revealed a confounding of delay interval and intertrial interval (defined as the blank time between feedback on one trial and the onset of the stimulus for the next). As delay increased, intertrial interval decreased. Because of this, the apparent deleterious effects of delay might be ascribed with equal cogency to an abbreviation of the intertrial interval. This is reasonable not only on logical grounds but also on the basis of empirically shown facilitative effects of lengthening the intertrial interval in some verbal-learning situations (Underwood, 1961). Thus the necessity arose to explore delay and intertrial interval independently within the same experiment to determine whether one or the other or both exerted reliable effects on attribute identification.

Bourne and Bunderson (1963) conducted an experiment to assess these variables separately. Some of the results are portrayed in Figure 12-3. They indicate that under the con-

FIGURE 12–3. *Performance in attribute identification problems as a function of the length of delay of informative feedback and the length of the intertrial interval.*

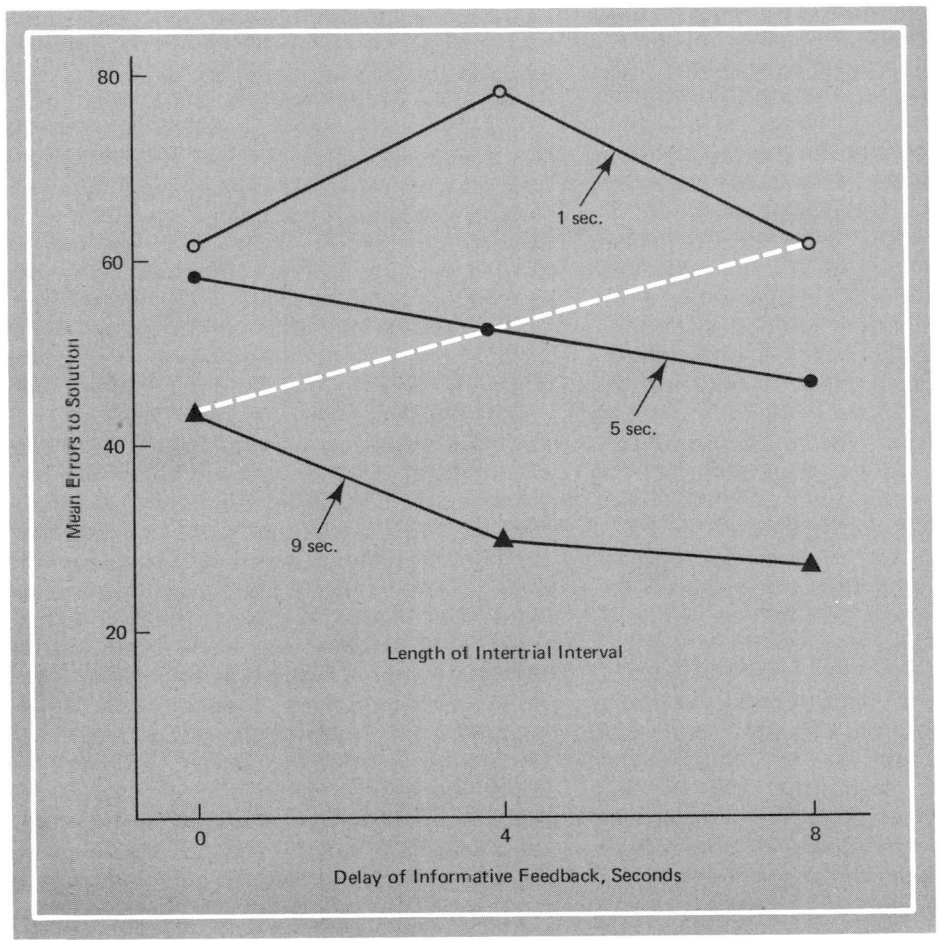

Source: Redrawn from L. E. Bourne, Jr. and C. V. Bunderson, Effects of delay of informative feedback and length of the postfeedback interval on concept identification. *Journal of Experimental Psychology,* 1963, **65,** 1-5. Copyright 1963 by the American Psychological Association and reprinted by permission.

ditions used in these studies only length of intertrial interval has any major effect on performance. As the intertrial interval is increased up to 9 seconds, attribute identification is facilitated. Some relevant problem-solving activities obviously take place during the interval; the more time the subject has, the greater the opportunity for these activities to run their course.

Delay of feedback has essentially no effect in this experiment. How can this be rationalized with the earlier results and conclusion of Bourne (1957)? An answer is provided by an inspection of those timing conditions which were identical in the two studies. The data points for these conditions are specially marked and interconnected in Figure 12-3. Performance does seem to deteriorate with increased delay, but only because the intertrial interval is correspondingly decreased.

These results are not to be taken, of course, as a general indication of the ineffectiveness of feedback delay. Longer delays or delay intervals filled with some sort of distracting activity clearly could impede performance. Further research is needed to establish the general influence of these parameters. Within the limited conditions used in these studies, however, delay is unimportant—subjects have no trouble bridging the time gap (maximum, 8 seconds) between response and feedback. The significant factor is intertrial interval which the subject somehow uses to process the retained information from stimulus and feedback.

Additional Work on Intertrial Intervals. Average performance improved over the range of intertrial intervals used by Bourne and Bunderson (1963). Their maximal interval was only 9 seconds, however, and it is reasonable to expect to reach a point of diminishing returns with further increases. Bourne, Guy, Dodd, and Justesen (1965) investigated this possibility using attribute identification problems of two levels of complexity and intervals as long as 25 seconds. The results of the study are presented in Panel A of Figure 12-4; performance improved as the interval was lengthened up to an optimum. The optimal interval was shorter for the less complex problem. Apparently it takes a certain amount of time for a subject to use the information he retains from the preceding stimulus and feedback display. The processing time is less for simpler problems which embody a smaller amount of information. Increases beyond the optimum actually seem to have a deleterious effect.

There are several plausible interpretations of these results. All of them ascribe important learning, information processing, and problem-solving activities to the intertrial interval, and all provide adequate accounts of the facilitation observed. Empirical attempts to distinguish among these possibilities will be mentioned in a later section. The deterioration that occurs with supraoptimal intervals suggests either a forgetting phenomenon or a loss of attention or vigilance to the task resulting from a prolonged period of relative inactivity.

Bourne, et al. (1965) conducted a second experiment to explore one aspect of the later deterioration of performance. On the assumption that the major source of performance deficit is forgetting, they arranged experimental conditions in which (1) both stimulus and feedback, (2) either one but not the other, and (3) neither persisted and were available to the subject for inspection throughout the intertrial interval. These results appear in Panel B of Figure 12-4. Having either of these sources of information is of some utility, though it is more important to have access to the stimulus. Having both available seems completely to wash out the performance deficit observed when the intertrial interval is blank. It would appear then that forgetting the solution-relevant information presented on a trial is a major factor in the intertrial interval effect, and can be counteracted by making the informational components of the trial physically available to the subject. Access to the clues provided by a trial and sufficient time to make use of these clues are both significant determiners of problem-solving effi-

FIGURE 12–4. Performance in attribute identification as a function of intertrial interval and (Panel A) number of irrelevant dimensions and (Panel B) the availability of stimulus or feedback during the intertrial interval.

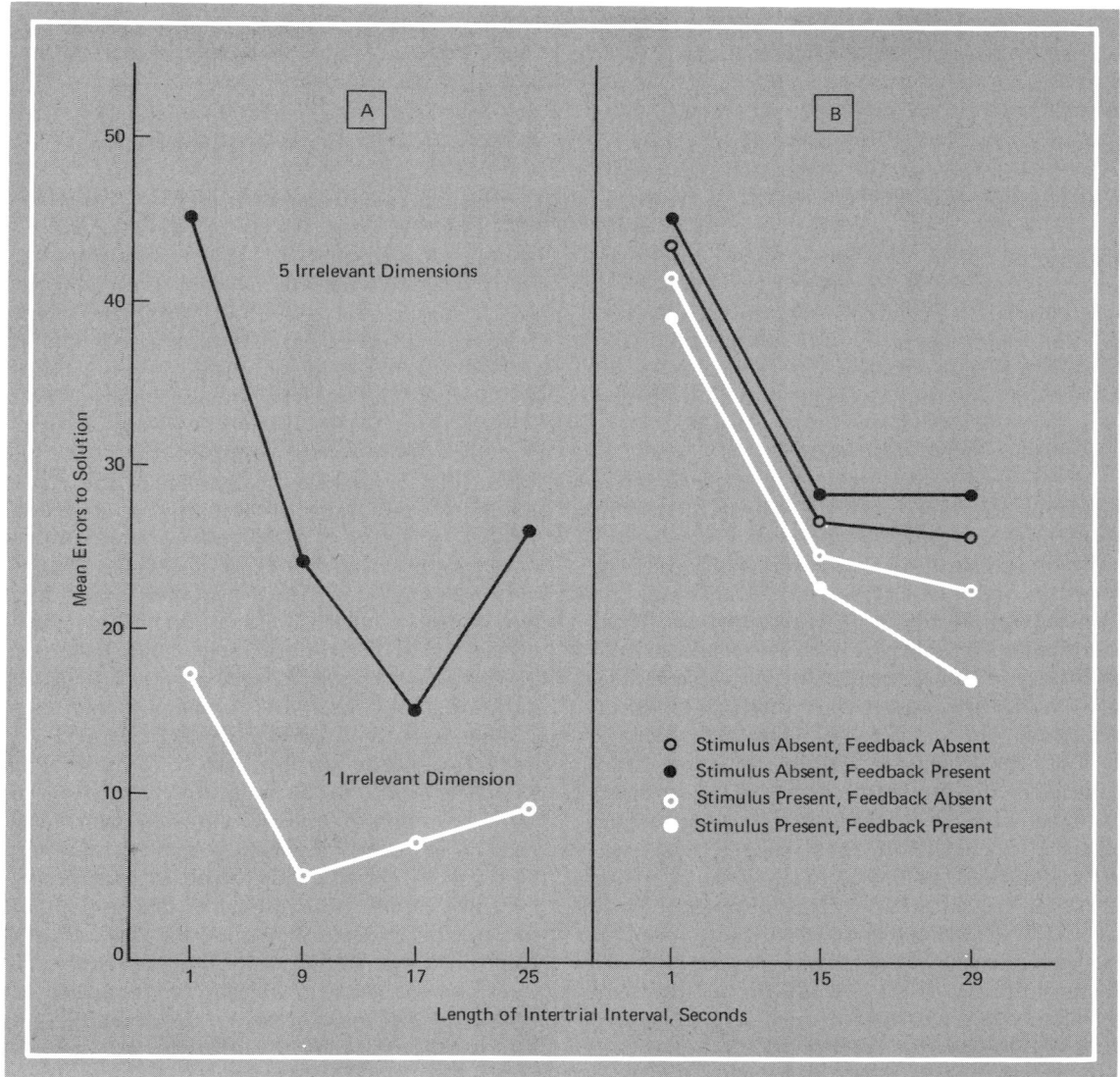

Source: Redrawn from L. E. Bourne, Jr., D. E. Guy, D. H. Dodd, and D. R. Justesen, Concept identification: The effects of varying length and informational components of the intertrial interval. *Journal of Experimental Psychology*, 1965, **69**, 624-29. Copyright 1965 by the American Psychological Association and reprinted by permission.

ciency. The greater importance of stimulus over feedback follows naturally from the fact that there is a greater degree of variation and therefore more potentially usable information within the stimulus as contrasted with the feedback system.

A Qualification

The results of the foregoing studies are rather consistent; providing a certain interval of time between trials for the subject to "mull over" what has thus far been given has a marked positive effect on performance. Two other experiments suggest some limits on this conclusion. Oseas and Underwood (1952) and Brown and Archer (1956) investigated the length of rest intervals interpolated between blocks of trials in attribute identification problems. In the Oseas-Underwood study, intervals of 6, 15, 30, or 60 seconds were inserted after every 9 stimuli. Brown and Archer gave rests of 0, 30, or 60 seconds after every 16 trials. Both experiments revealed only a minor, and in one case insignificant, improvement in performance resulting from increasing the rest interval.

There are at least three plausible explanations for the discrepancy between these data and those reviewed in the preceding section. First it is possible that intervals beyond the shortest used by Oseas and Underwood and Brown and Archer were supraoptimal. Their subjects might have found the rest intervals too short in some cases and too long in others, giving the impression that interval length is generally an ineffective variable. Alternatively, the difference might be procedural. Studies with interblock intervals, in contrast to those with intertrial intervals, required the subject to engage in an unrelated task (e.g., color-naming) during rest.

There is a third, more interesting possibility. If we assume that the subject uses rest intervals in some way to process available information toward the formulation of problem solution, then the blocking of trials between rests might be the critical factor. A subject can work only with the information he can remember, for the rests used in these studies were blank. Human memory for prior events is notoriously poor, especially in concept problems of this type (Trabasso and Bower, 1964c), meaning that a person, at best, probably remembers only the last or the last couple of stimulus-feedback pairings. A rest every 9 or 16 or n trials is therefore minimally useful to a subject in contrast to a rest on every or every other trial. This possibility suggests an experiment in which size of trial block between rests is manipulated. If the argument is sound, the facilitating effect of intertrial should decrease with increasing block sizes, even with total rest time held constant.

Response-Contingent Intertrial Intervals. The facilitating effects of lengthening the interval indicate that a subject continues actively to work with whatever he can remember for at least some period of time after feedback has been given. There are, of course, several alternative descriptions of the kind of problem-solving activity subjects engage in— for example, we might suppose that associative or conditioning processes carry on mechanically for as long as "traces" of the given stimulus and response remain or that the subject uses the available time to formulate an hypothesis in the light of retained information—but the evidence discussed so far does not permit a clear choice among these possibilities. The one thing that is clear, however, is that learning on a particular trial is not an immediate, automatic function of the reinforcing properties of feedback.

Manipulation of the intertrial interval is a rather crude probe technique, unlikely to provide much definitive data on what the subject is actually doing. There is, however, one variation that needs to be considered. We have made note in an earlier section of the emphasis that some theories (e.g., Bower and Trabasso, 1964) put on error trials. In fact, it has been argued that an incorrect response is the only occasion for learning, on the assumption that the subject bases his responses on hypotheses and that an hypothesis is infirmed only when it leads him to make an error. If learning occurs only on error trials, then variables which affect learning are significant only on error trials. In contrast, of course, some theories imply that learning does or can occur on any trial, so the influence of any imposed condition should be indifferent to the type of trial on which it happens. It is possible to get some leverage, then, on the theoretical issue of when learning takes place by arranging a comparison of response-contingent conditions. Specifically, if the error-trial learning principle is accurate, there should be no performance difference between subjects who are given an optimal interval after every trial and subjects who are given an optimal interval only after error trials; if the every-trial learning principle is accurate, there should be a difference in favor of the first group.

A comparison of these conditions was reported by Bourne, Dodd, Guy, and Justesen (1968). These experimenters arranged four conditions: (I) the intertrial interval was suboptimal (1 second in length) on all trials, (II) the interval was optimal (15 seconds) on error trials and suboptimal on correct response trials, (III) the interval was suboptimal on error trials and optimal on correct response trials, and (IV) the interval was optimal on all trials. From the *error-trial* principle they predicted a performance ordering from best to worst of IV = II > III = I. From the *all-trials* principle, they predicted IV > III = II > I. Results obtained in a complex four-category attribute identification problem favored the *all-trials* model, mean trials to solve being 91.6, 52.8, 48.5, and 43.8, for Conditions I, II, III, and IV, respectively. In a simpler two-category unidimensional problem, Condition I was clearly inferior to the other three, which did not differ from each other.

In both cases, the results are more closely aligned with the notion that subjects learn or process available information on all trials. The small difference among Conditions II, III, and IV in the first experiment and the complete lack of difference in the second suggests that some percentage of intervals less than 100 percent of optimal might be sufficient. Conditions II and III, in which the contingency is based on errors and correct responses, respectively, provided around 50 percent optimal intervals in both experiments. This suggests another experiment yet to be conducted, in which percentage of trials, associated with optimal intervals, is varied irrespective of the subject's response. Presumably one would observe a monotonic improvement in performance with increasing percentage up to around 50-60, after which the effect would be minimal.

Pretraining and Response-Contingent Intervals. While it is clear that learning can occur on all trials, some of the details of the foregoing results are not strictly congruent with classical, incremental, associational theory. White (1967) pointed out that in the data of Bourne, et al. (1968), error trials do seem to be slightly more important than nonerror trials and that analyses of presolution responses show discrepancies from both the *all-trials* and *error-trials* notions. It seems possible, according to White, that these data were produced not by a homogeneous group of subjects, all of whom learned according to the same incremental process, but rather by a mixture of at least two types of subjects, some of whom learned incrementally on all trials and others of whom learned insightfully on some error trial. He showed that several of the unaccounted-for discrepancies in the data could be explained if this mixture were the case.

It is difficult to determine the general nature of a subject's learning process from an examination of his trial-by-trial response protocol. Category responses in a conceptual problem are affected by many factors in addition to the subject's knowledge at any point in time; thus there is normally a good deal of variability in performance. A re-analysis of the available data offered little hope of accurately classifying subjects as to type. White, therefore, took a different approach to the problem. He argued that one ought to be able to train subjects to behave as "hypothesis testers" or "scanners," fitting the description of performance implied by hypothesis theories, or as "incremental associators," performing in accord with associational principles. One would expect that performance in the response-contingent intertrial interval conditions described above would follow either the error-trial order, I = III > II = IV, or the every-trial order, I > II = III > IV, depending on how the subject had been pretrained.

White gave all subjects two problems to solve, one for pretraining and the second as a test. To train hypothesis testers, an initial conceptual problem was used which had a general solution principle identical with the test, i.e., identifying the attributes of a conjunctive concept. The subject was encouraged to formulate and test hypotheses as a problem-solving procedure. To train associators, an initial paired-associates problem (using the same stimuli and responses as in the hypothesis-training case) with no conceptual solution was given; the subject could learn only by connecting individual stimuli with individual responses. Subjects were divided evenly between these pretraining methods. Half within each group were given brief pretraining (25 trials) and half were given prolonged pretraining (75 trials) with the expectation of magnifying differences in test performance. Subjects from each pretraining condition were assigned randomly to one of the four response-contingent intertrial arrangements for the test problem.

With extensive pretraining (75 trials) results followed theoretical expectations. The data are presented in Figure 12-5. Preliminary experience with the hypothesis selection and test approach produced data which suggests that the subject makes use primarily of error-trial information (disconfirming his current hypothesis) in problem solving. Experience which reinforces an associational approach leads to the apparent utilization of information from all trials. Trends obtained with abbreviated pretraining of either type follow neither model in all details but are more like the associational outcome reported above and in Bourne, et al. (1968), who also gave only a few pretraining trials. White concluded that a relatively untrained group of subjects will consist of a mixture of types. Only those subjects with the appropriate preliminary training, given in sufficient amount, will conform to the specifications of a uniprocess theory.

Comment. In a random sample of subjects, there will be considerable variability, not only in the quantitative aspects of overall performance but also in the strategies used. Some subjects clearly try to form connections between stimuli and responses, some test successive hypotheses, some attempt to identify the relevance of independent attributes, and so on, and some subjects might do several or all of these things, even within a single problem. Any theory which assumes strict homogeneity among untrained subjects is bound to be wrong. Performance is going to reflect the subject-mixture and, except for chance, is unlikely to conform neatly to the predictions of a single model. White's results illustrate this fact, but beyond that they verify the perhaps not-so-surprising conclusion that one can create homogeneity (to an approximation) through training. Data from artificially homogenized groups fit nicely with expectations from a theory which assumes homogeneity, and that is always gratifying (at least to the theorist). To have a comprehensive account of conceptual behavior, however, some more elaborate model which admits to heterogeneity in the "learning process" is plainly a "must."

SUMMARY

In this chapter, we have reviewed and evaluated the evidence on major task variables—stimulus, response, informative feedback—and their temporal relationships. Relative to subject variables discussed in Chapter 11, the evidence is fairly clear and straightforward. Any manipulation which (1) reduces or obscures relevant information about solution, derived primarily from stimulus and feedback on each trial, or (2) complicates the performance requirements for a subject will slow the

FIGURE 12–5. *Performance on attribute identification problems as a function of the type of pretraining and the contingency between length of intertrial interval and the correctness of the subject's response.*

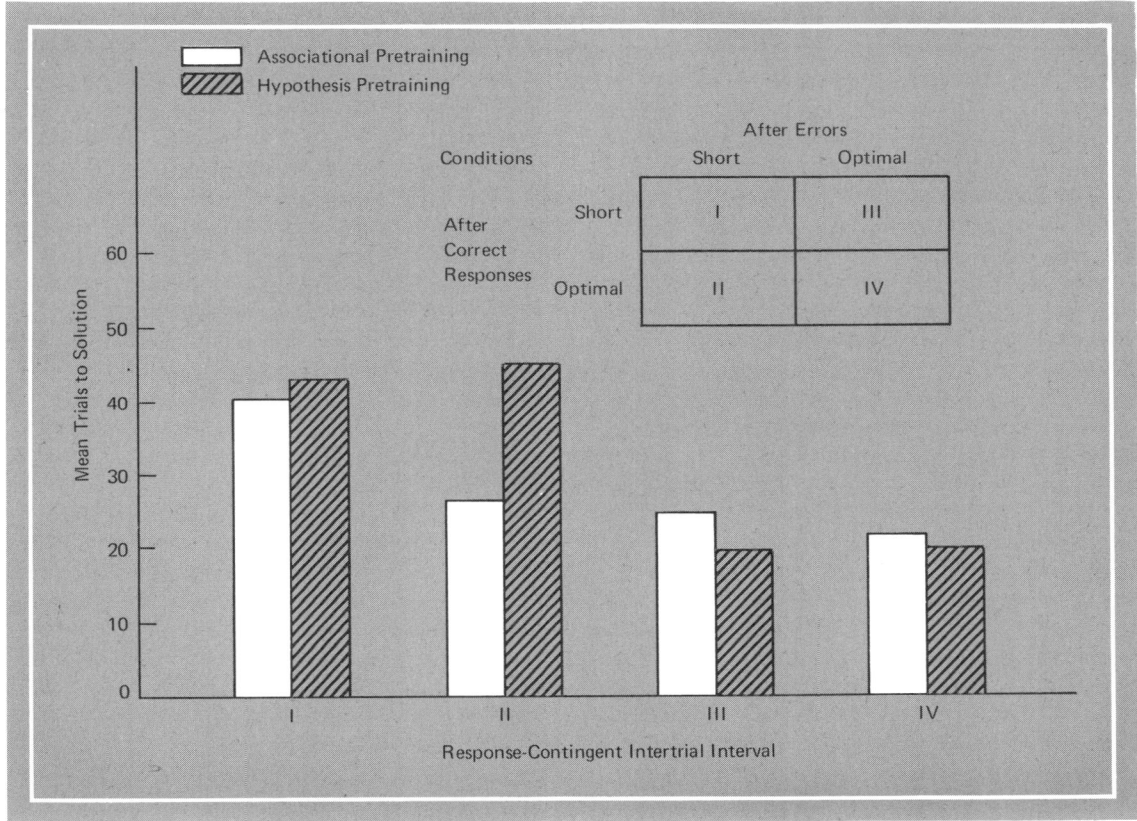

Source: Redrawn from R. W. White, Jr., The effects of some pretraining variables on concept identification. Unpublished doctoral dissertation, University of Colorado, 1967.

problem-solving process. These variables exercise considerable control over both the quantitative and qualitative aspects of a subject's performance. They are not powerful enough to obliterate individual differences within a given condition, however, and we end both this chapter and the section on conceptual behavior by noting the necessity to consider both task and subject variables in a complete theoretical account.

V Language

Thirteen Language and Thought

The Arabs have about 6000 different ways of naming camels (Thomas, 1937). The Hanunoo people in the Philippine Islands have a name for each of 92 varieties of rice (Brown, 1965). And, the color spectrum is differentiated in strikingly different ways in different languages, as can be seen in Figure 13-1 (Gleason, 1961). In what way does the language we speak influence our behavior, particularly our ability to think about experience? Can the Hanunoo see differences in varieties of rice that we cannot? Would the people of Liberia who speak the Bassa language make terrible interior decorators? Just what is the role of language in thought?

SOME BASIC RESEARCH FINDINGS

In writing about the problem of language and thought, it is extremely difficult to avoid a great philosophical discourse devoid of any experimental data. This is so because much of the writing on the problem has been done by philosophers, while relatively little successful empirical research has been reported.

In this section we will present four examples of research findings that are directly related to the problem in various ways. Later, we will refer to these experiments in an effort to give a concrete example of what is being said. Each of the experiments is interesting in its own right and each can probably be interpreted in more than one way. It almost goes without saying that establishing the relationship between language and thought as a result of empirical research is indeed a monumental task since both the language (the so-called "inner speech") and the thought are behavioral events with minimal movement (actional) correlates.

Howard B. Ranken

First consider the ingenious experiment by Ranken (1963) which seems to suggest that language can either facilitate or inhibit performance on tasks that require symbolic manipulation. Ranken made up eight novel stimulus shapes which are shown in Figure 13-2. The tops and bottoms of the shapes had

FIGURE 13-1. *Verbal labels for the spectrum of visible wavelengths in three different languages.*

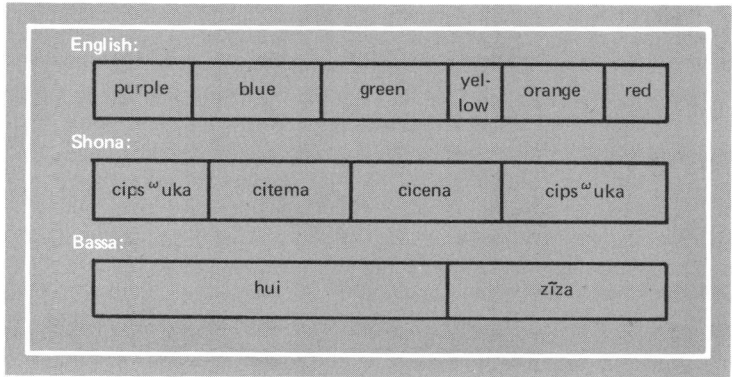

Source: Redrawn from H. A. Gleason, Jr., *An Introduction to Descriptive Linguistics*, Rev. Ed., Chapter 1. New York: Copyright © 1955, 1961 by Holt, Rinehart & Winston, Inc. Reprinted by permission of the publisher.

FIGURE 13-2. *The eight shapes with corresponding animal labels used by Ranken to study the effects of labeling on thinking. The numbers correspond to the position that each shape occupied in a ring designed to facilitate communication with the subjects. See text for full explanation.*

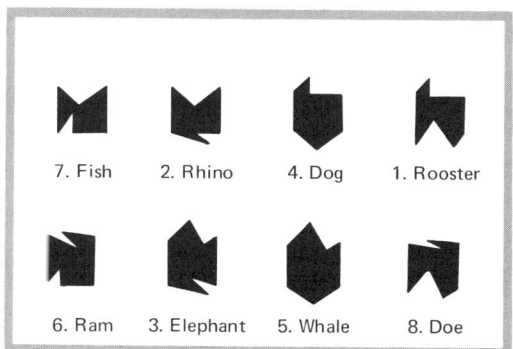

Source: Redrawn from H. B. Ranken, Language and thinking: Positive and negative effects of naming. *Science*, 1963, **141**, 48-50. Copyright 1963 by the American Association for the Advancement of Science.

jagged contours that interlocked with each other so that the eight shapes could be joined in jigsaw fashion to form a vertical column. Two groups of subjects were used. One group (Named Condition) was taught a different animal name for each shape and then was given training at recognizing the shapes. The second group (Unnamed Condition) was not provided with names for the shapes, but was simply asked to study the shapes and try to memorize the appearance of each shape without using names. This group also then received recognition training with the shapes. We can suggest at this point that the subjects in the Unnamed Condition have memorized images of the shapes, images that contain information about the various jagged edges. We might also suggest that subjects in the Named Condition have memorized animal names for the shapes, with relatively little storage of images of the shape. Here we are suggesting the essence of language—*language encodes experience*. The name of a shape presumably encodes some information about the edges (the edges which contribute to the similarity of the shape to the animal) but little information about the remaining edges would be encoded by the animal name. An image, however, might contain information about all the edges. If we ask the subjects to solve a problem that requires information about the edges that are not encoded by the name, we might expect the Named subjects to do more poorly than the Unnamed subjects. However, if the problem did not require specific information about these edges, we can expect the Named subjects to be superior.

To test these notions, Ranken had the subjects in the two groups perform two different tasks. One task involved solving the vertical jigsaw puzzle which required having specific information available about the jagged edges. They never saw any of the shapes during the problem, but instead had to solve it "in their heads." It is interesting to note at this point that Ranken had to be able to communicate with his subjects—they had to have some way of telling him the order of the shapes in the puzzle. The Named people could just use the animal names, but the Unnamed subjects had no way to communicate with the experimenter. What Ranken did was to have all the subjects learn the locations of the eight shapes in a clock-like ring with positions numbered from one to eight. Thus, the Named subjects really learned two "names" for each shape, one an animal name and the other a number corresponding to the location of the shape in this ring. The Unnamed subjects just learned the locations and numbers in the ring. All communication with the subjects was by number—the subject called out the number of the shape that went next in the jigsaw problem.

The second task which Ranken used presumably did not require specific information about the jagged edges. This was a serial learning task in which the subjects were shown the shapes one at a time in a random order, and were then asked to recall the exact order of the shapes by calling out the numbers of the shapes in the order presented. Since the shapes were randomly arranged for the serial learning task, specific information about the edges was irrelevant to recalling the serial order. Presumably, the Named subjects could learn a serial list of names, while the Unnamed subjects would have to memorize the order by the shape. It should be noted, however, that one can argue that the numbers which had to be used for communication purposes could certainly serve as verbal labels for the shapes in the Unnamed condition—these subjects may very well have learned the serial order by memorizing numbers rather than by memorizing images of the shapes. We can see instantly the difficulty in designing an experiment where some subjects are supposed to be thinking about something without verbal assistance. But suppose for the moment that the Unnamed subjects were at least less likely to have language assistance in memorizing the serial order.

The results, in terms of mean number of errors on the two different problems, are presented in Figure 13-3. On the jigsaw problem, subjects provided with the animal names were inferior to the subjects without the names. The difference was reversed on the memory task, however, where the Named condition was superior to the Unnamed condition. It is also interesting to note that in terms of time to solve, there were no differences between the groups on either problem. Finally, Ranken asked the subjects in each group to draw the shapes from memory. The Unnamed subjects made 14.8 errors in drawing (omitting a line segment) while the Named subjects made 20.2 errors, the difference being significant at the .01 level. The results of the drawing are consistent with the notion that the Named subjects had encoded the shapes by the animal name which resulted in a loss of information about the exact nature of the edges, while the Unnamed subjects had coded the shapes as images which would result in more coding of information about the edges.

The jigsaw-puzzle and the serial-learning results can be construed as supporting the notion that language can either facilitate or inhibit thinking (problems solving) depending mainly on whether or not the language responses of the subject encode relevant or irrelevant aspects of an experience. In the serial-learning tasks, the animal names code all the information the subject would need to learn a serial order of the shapes. The fact that the names facilitated learning suggests that language can facilitate thinking. And, the time

FIGURE 13–3. *Mean errors in serial learning and in jigsaw problem solving.*

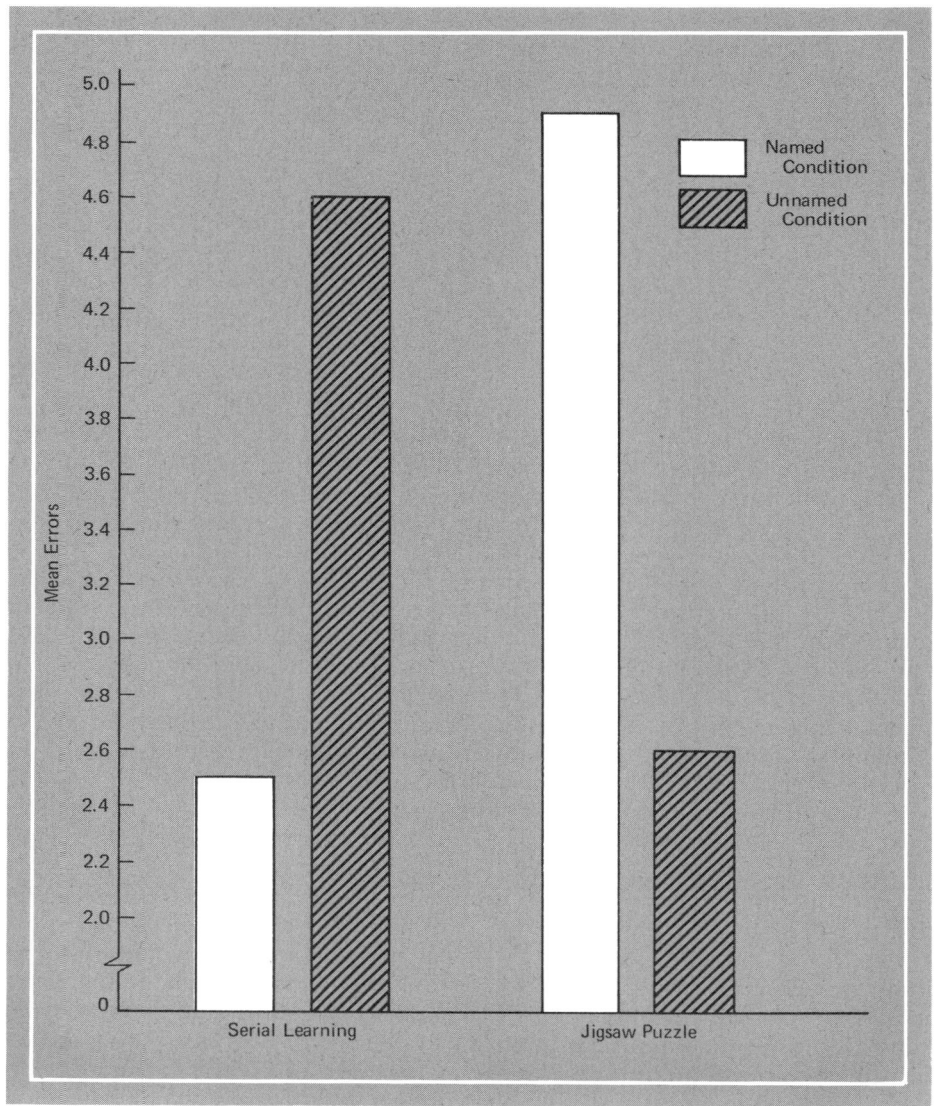

Source: Data from H. B. Ranken, Language and thinking: Positive and negative effects of naming. *Science,* 1963, **141,** 48-50. Copyright 1963 by the American Association for the Advancement of Science.

data suggest that this facilitation cannot easily be attributed to a difference in the speed of linguistic, as opposed to image-based thinking. The puzzle results suggest that if the linguistic encoding does not contain information that will definitely be necessary to solve the problem, then it will be better to encode the experience by images.

Ranken's experiment suggests two basic points about language and thought. First, it suggests that not all thinking is verbal in nature. If we assume that the Unnamed subjects did not make up their own verbal labels for the shapes and did not perform the task using the numbers in the location ring as labels, then their excellent performance on the jigsaw problem and the shape-drawing test can be taken to imply that we can think in basically nonverbal ways. Of course, it is difficult to determine whether these subjects did in fact think only in images. Post-experimental interviews revealed that some of them did attempt to verbalize descriptions of the shapes. Interestingly, these verbalizers did worse on the jigsaw puzzle than nonverbalizers. This problem, ensuring that one group thinks in nonverbal terms, is one important reason why experimentation on language and thought is so difficult to devise and interpret unequivocally. We are probably so accustomed to verbalizing experience that we find it difficult not to make up names (or verbal descriptions) for the shapes, even though we are requested not to.

Nevertheless, it seems reasonable to assume that at least part of the thinking of subjects in the Unnamed condition was nonverbal in nature. In other words, there are nonlinguistic aspects of thinking. Deaf people can perform quite well on all types of tasks that involve thinking (Furth, 1964); indeed, they are surprisingly efficient on such tasks, typically being only slightly behind people with normal hearing. Of course, one could argue that these deaf individuals have developed a language of some kind, such as sign language, and thus they really are not thinking without language. The assumption that thinking is possible without language, however, is more consistent with introspective evidence, and it seems unduly restrictive to assume that such behavior is not possible.

Second, Ranken's experiment suggests that a major function of language in thought is to encode experience into memory. The next experiment to be described will make this function even more apparent. Whether or not language facilitates the subsequent use of this memorized information will depend on the nature of the attributes that the language code ignores. English has only one or two words for encoding snow while Eskimo has many. If one is faced with a problem about snow, such as why the skiing is poor, and the answer has something to do with the texture of the snow, we can imagine that an Eskimo would solve the problem more rapidly than an American. If the differences in texture that are encoded in Eskimo but not English are irrelevant to the solution, the Eskimo should have no advantage.

L. A. Carmichael, H. P. Hogan, and A. A. Walter

This is a classic study investigating the effects of verbal labels on memory for shapes (1932). The subjects were exposed to the shapes shown in Figure 13-4. Before each figure was presented, the experimenter said, "The next figure resembles a _____," filling in a name that resembled the figure. Two sets of names were made up for the 12 shapes and these are presented in Figure 13-4 as Word Lists I and II. One group was exposed to the figures labeled according to List I, one group heard List II labels, and a third group heard no labels at all. When the subjects attempted to recall the figures by drawing them, there was clear evidence that the labels influenced their reproductions. Subjects who heard the label, *eye glasses*, for the fifth figure might put a bend in the shaft between the two circles and those who heard the label, *dumbbells*, might put a double shaft between the two circles.

FIGURE 13-4. *Stimulus figures and verbal labels.*

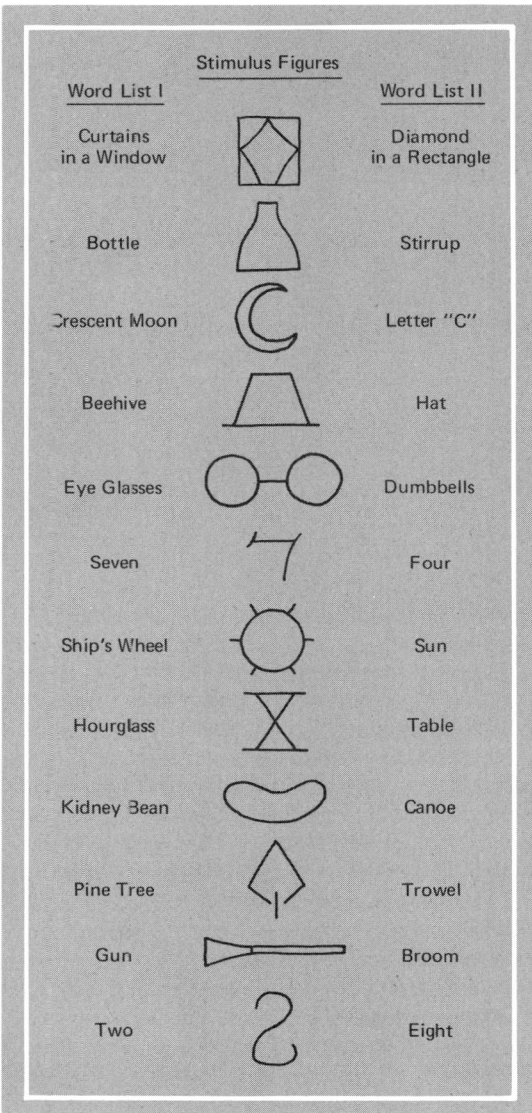

Source: L. Carmichael, H. P. Hogan, and A. Walter, An experimental study of the effect of language on the reproduction of visually perceived form. *Journal of Experimental Psychology,* 1932, 15, 73-86.

For all reproductions that were in error, those of subjects who heard the label, *eye glasses,* were judged to be more similar to eye glasses than dumbbells, and just the reverse was true for the subjects who heard the label, *dumbbells.*

These results suggest the encoding function of language. At least part of the time the shapes were encoded by the label rather than by images of the shapes, or lengthy verbal descriptions of the figures (e.g., "two identical circles alongside each other with a single horizontal line joining them at 3 and 9 o'clock"). The storage of the experience in memory was influenced by the verbal labels supplied by the experimenter. One supposes that at the time of recall, the subjects recalled the labels and from this attempted to reproduce the figure. When they failed in correct reproduction they made errors suggested by the verbal label itself. Language provides us with an encoding system by which we "dissect nature" and categorize experience. These subjects probably memorized a free-recall list of the names rather than a list of figures, although it is quite certain that some figure information (image) was also stored along with the name. Thus, their thinking at the time of recall was not totally verbal in nature, but the verbal aspects of the memories did influence their reproductions.

*Sam Glucksberg
and Robert W. Weisberg*

In this experiment (1966), the subjects were confronted with the candle-mounting problem that is used in research on functional fixedness. You may remember from earlier chapters (see Chapters 3 and 5 and Figure 3-5) that one group of subjects is presented the equipment with the tacks inside the box (fixated version) while another group is presented with the box and the tacks separated. The box, of course, is highly relevant to the solution. The basic phenomenon to be explained is that the fixated version is more difficult to solve. If a subject is confronted with a box full of tacks, his linguistic coding of this experience might be, "There is a box present and there are some tacks present, and the tacks are in the box." This encoding contains all the relevant information, but it certainly is cumbersome and highly unlikely that subjects would respond this way. A more likely encoding of the experience would be, "There is a box of tacks present" or "There are some tacks present." Notice that these encodings of the experience seem to treat the box itself as irrelevant. But since the box is highly relevant to solution of the candle problem, these encodings, if they are made by the subject, should interfere with solution. If the subject is presented the nonfixated version of the problem (box and tacks separate) he will probably encode the experience in a way that makes it clear that two things, a box and some tacks, are available for solution. Thus, the fixated version may be more difficult solely because of the nature of the linguistic encoding of the experience. The basic problem seems to be that the subject does not realize that the box can be used to solve the problem. Is this lack of realization due to the nature of the linguistic encoding of the situation, or does the subject misperceive the situation but label his perception correctly (he does not perceive the box and, hence, does not encode it)?

Glucksberg and Weisberg had two groups of subjects solve the candle problem in fixated form. One group saw the regular fixated version as was shown in Fig. 3-5. The other group saw the version shown in Fig. 13-5. Here separate labels pointing out the presence of the tacks and the presence of the box were included. In three different experiments, subjects in the condition which labeled the box as a separate entity solved the problem more rapidly than subjects in the no-label condition. Just what did the labels do that facilitated solution?

There is a temptation to say that they resulted in a change in the linguistic encoding of the situation such that in thinking about

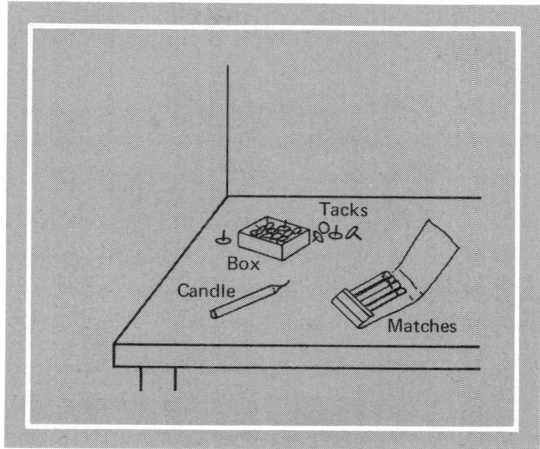

FIGURE 13–5. The labeled versions of the candle problem used by Glucksberg and Weisberg.

Source: From S. Glucksberg and R. W. Weisberg, Verbal behavior and problem solving: Some effects of labeling in a functional fixedness problem. *Journal of Experimental Psychology,* 1966, **71**, 659-64. Copyright 1966 by the American Psychological Association and reprinted by permission.

the problem, the subjects would have included the box in their thoughts. The emphasis here is on the encoding function of language which determines which attributes of an experience will be treated as relevant and thus encoded into memory and which will be treated as irrelevant and ignored in the encoding experience. On the other hand, the verbal labels may have facilitated performance only by calling attention to the box, by ensuring that the subject realized or perceived that a box was available. We suggest that the problem is not totally one of perception—the subjects probably perceive the box but do not encode the experience in such a way that when thinking linguistically about the solution the box will be included in thought. The labels may call attention to the box and thus result in a different linguistic encoding of the situation, but this is different from say-

Language and Thought 291

ing that the box was never perceived in the first place.

Roger Brown and Eric Lenneberg

In a classic experiment in the field of language and thought, Brown and Lenneberg (1954) attempted to measure the ease with which colors can be linguistically coded in English. Subjects looked at numerous color patches and attempted to give each color a name. Colors which were named rapidly and easily (generally given short names) and for which there was high agreement among the subjects on the appropriate name, were said to be high in *codability;* those colors not easily named and for which agreement among subjects was low were said to be low in codability. Thus, in the first stage of the experiment, Brown and Lenneberg measured the codability of a series of colors.

In the second phase, subjects were asked to "solve" recognition problems with the colors that had been scaled in codability in phase one. For example, patches of four different colors were shown to the subjects for three seconds and after a delay the subjects had to pick these four colors out from a set of 120 different colored patches. The results showed a significant correlation ($r = .415$) between a color's codability and the ease with which it was recognized (see also Lantz and Stefflre, 1964). In addition, they showed that the effect of color codability on recognition increased as the delay between exposure and recognition test increased. When the delay between color exposure and test was very short, the subjects appeared to rely on perceptual memory (an image of the color), but as the delay increased, the subject relied on his memory of the linguistic encoding response. We can speculate that during the exposure interval, the subject names the colors (encodes them linguistically) and that these names are stored in memory. At the time of testing, when the 120 patches are exposed and the subject must find the four he saw earlier, he uses the names to find a match in the array. In other words, he searches the array for colors that he would name exactly as he named the four original colors. Thus, if a subject had labeled one of the original colors *misty green,* he would search the array of 120 colors until he found one that would also fit the label *misty green.* During the original exposure of four colors, the subjects' problem was to think up distinctive names for the colors, and in the test portion, the problem was to find colors that would fit the distinctive names that were stored in memory. It is then reasonable to expect and not unusual to find that colors for which there is little agreement as to an appropriate name, and which individual subjects have difficulty naming, tend to be the same colors that are difficult to remember over the delay between exposure and test.

THE LINGUISTIC RELATIVITY HYPOTHESIS

In the remainder of this chapter, the discussion will focus on the most widely known hypothesis about the relationship between language and thought, the *linguistic relativity hypothesis,* which was the joint product of Benjamin L. Whorf and his linguistics professor, Edward Sapir. Whorf is generally credited with the most extreme and popular version and so it is often referred to as the *Whorfian hypothesis.* The hypothesis states that the structure and semantics of the language one speaks control the manner in which he will perceive and understand the world, and this in turn will influence his actions in that world. The most important emphasis seems to be placed on the effect that language has in determining the contents and processes of thought. In other words, language is said to determine to a large extent how one thinks about the world.

The hypothesis was elaborated in several papers (see Carroll, 1956, for a collection of

Whorf's writings) and has received a great deal of at least rhetorical attention from linguists, anthropologists, and psychologists. One of the most often quoted passages from Whorf's writings gives a clear indication of the importance he placed on the role of language in thought:

> ... the background linguistic system (in other words, the grammar) of each language is not merely a reproducing instrument for voicing ideas but rather is itself the shaper of ideas, the program and guide for the individual's mental activity, for his analysis of impressions, for his synthesis of his mental stock in trade. Formulation of ideas is not an independent process, strictly rational in the old sense, but is part of a particular grammar and differs, from slightly to greatly, as between different grammars. We dissect nature along lines laid down by our native languages [Carroll, 1956, pp. 212-213].

Whorf relied heavily on evidence gathered while completing his linguistic analyses of various American Indian languages, particularly Hopi, evidence which is largely anecdotal in character. He was impressed by the fact the various languages "dissect nature" using differing numbers of words for describing what English describes with only one word (e.g., Eskimo words for snow). But it was not only the lexical differences which he thought were important, as the above quotation clearly indicates. For example, he claimed that English, by dividing sentences into two basic components, the noun phrase and the verb phrase, seems to emphasize a distinction between objects or things and actions or events. Some Indian languages, however, appeared not to make such a distinction. Whorf has argued that this distinction in English guides our thinking about the real world such that we are highly prone to analyze experience into things and actions. He suggests that the Hopi Indians do not make such an analysis because their language does not make such a distinction, although this argument has been criticized as being tautological.

The Whorfian Hypothesis—Four Levels

Fishman (1960) has divided the linguistic-relativity hypothesis into four separate levels, each one dealing with a different aspect of the effect of language on behavior. The four levels come from separating language into vocabulary and grammar and asking about the effects on either world view (essentially as expressed verbally) or nonverbal behavior. The four levels thus correspond roughly to (1) the effects of vocabulary on world view, (2) vocabulary effects on nonlinguistic behavior, (3) the effects of grammar on world view, and (4) the effects of grammar on nonlinguistic behavior.

Level 1: Vocabulary Differences and World View. The first level of the hypothesis deals with the facts of differences in vocabulary among languages which are said to influence the world outlook of the people speaking them. Here the basic pieces of evidence are facts such as those stated in the first paragraph of this chapter. The Hanunoo have many more words for rice and the Arabs have more names for camels than English speakers do. This is also the level we hear much about when considering translations from one language to another. Because there is no direct word-for-word correspondence among languages, the argument is that a great deal of meaning is lost in translation. As Fishman points out in his analysis, this kind of difference has long been known and is by no means an original contribution of Whorf. The real question, however, is what is the significance of this difference?

We suggest that most if not all experiences of men can be coded in any language, but the complexity of the encoding responses may vary greatly from one language to the next. We might say, "I saw a camel on your front lawn this morning" while an Arab might say something like, "I saw a zerba on your front lawn this morning." Now a *zerba* might just be a small, young, female camel with a long, shaggy, tawny-beige coat. The Arab can communicate this information in a single word, whereas we would require a linguistic construction of several words, but we could in fact convey what the Arab conveys if we wanted to. Presumably, for us, a camel is a camel so that 5000 camel names are not very useful additions to our vocabulary. It is unlikely that we care whether it is a camel or a zerba in our yard. As Brown (1965) wrote, "The world close up is more differentiated than the world farther off" (p. 336) and presumably camels are more important (closer) to Arabs and snow is more important to Eskimos than to most Americans. If a distinction is an important one for a group of speakers we can expect that it will be represented in the lexicon. The fact that another language has lexical items that convey many distinctions certainly gives us information about what the speakers of the more finely coded language consider important in their culture—camels, snow, and rice. But does it really suggest anything at all about how they perceive the world?

If the American culture suddenly depended as heavily on camels as that of the Arabs, we can be sure that new words would enter the American vocabulary, words that would code all of the important distinctions among camels. If camels were so important, we would be communicating about camels all the time, and we would want a highly differentiated vocabulary to facilitate this communication (just think for a moment of the vocabulary we have for talking about automobiles). At this level, then, the hypothesis merely tells us that what is close up in one culture may be far off in another and that this difference in closeness is reflected in the verbal behavior of the speakers of the two languages in question. The Hanunoo people obviously know more about rice than we do, talk about rice more than we do, and think about rice more than we do. In looking at different kinds of rice, they will obviously be more aware of the differences than we would be, not necessarily because of the language they speak, but because of the knowledge they possess.

Level 2: Codability and Nonverbal Behavior. The question at this level is whether the differences that exist in codability in various languages can influence nonverbal behavior. The verbal behavior of the Arabs with respect to camels and the Hanunoo with respect to rice is clearly different from ours, but what about nonverbal behavior? If the Whorfian hypothesis is to be confirmed at all, we must be able to demonstrate that linguistic differences among languages correspond to differences in nonlinguistic behavior.

The Brown-Lenneberg study of color codability is the classic study in support of Level 2 of the Whorfian hypothesis. Phase I of their study reflects Level 1 of the hypothesis by showing that some color experiences are easier to encode in English than others. Phase II of their study, however, went on to show that this linguistic difference did correspond to a nonlinguistic difference—the ability to recognize colors from memory. If you have a single word that encodes all the relevant information of an experience, you will be able to remember that experience more easily than if you had a multiple-word encoding that perhaps did not encode all of the attributes necessary to recognize that experience. The important point is whether or not the information necessary to solve the problem at hand is encoded in the linguistic response. Coding a color as *green* is useful if you only have to recognize one green from among a series of reds, yellows, and blues. But if the matching array contains twelve different shades of green, then recognition memory will undoubtedly be poor.

Suppose that Brown and Lenneberg had decided to study codability of rice instead of colors and that they used Hanunoo and American subjects, and 92 varieties of rice. The subject is shown four types for study and then is asked to recognize the four from among the 92. It is quite obvious that the Hanunoo will surpass the Americans at the task, not so much because the American has to use multiple-word encodings (e.g., *small, brown grains with darker brown spots*) but because the Hanunoo encodings will contain all the relevant information. At the time of recognition, the American may find two varieties that are small and brown with darker brown spots. These two grains may differ in shape, something the American did not include in his encoding. The single words of the Hanunoo would encode all of the relevant attributes that would be necessary to pick one variety from the 92. The words then serve as concept labels—they encode the relevant attributes and the rule for combining these attributes. The American does not know the concepts and so can only guess about the relevant attributes, and if he fails to include shape as a relevant attribute, he will surely not perform very well on the task. In other words, when we compare these two groups on rice recognition, we do not know for sure whether performance differences are due to differences in language or to differences in knowledge that are reflected in language.

But, consider the cross-cultural study of Stefflre, Vales, and Morley (1966) on color coding and recognition. Presumably the color dimension is one about which all people have roughly comparable knowledge so that differences in performance can be more unequivocally attributed to the differences in the ease of linguistic encoding. Speakers of Spanish and of Yucatec (a language of the Mayan people in Yucatan) were the subjects. Each group was used to scale color patches on ease of communication. For example, Spanish speakers named the colors and these names were then given to other Spanish speakers who tried to pick out the named color from a large array of colors. The ease with which this could be done for each color was the communication accuracy score for that color. Still other Spanish speakers were tested on the color recognition task. The same procedure was carried out with the Yucatec speakers. The results showed a significant correlation between the communication accuracy scores and the recognition accuracy scores for the colors within a language. The correlation was .448 in Yucatec and .588 in Spanish. However, there were no correlations *between* the two languages in either communication ease or recognition ease. The correlation between communication scores for the colors in the two languages was .113 and the correlation between recognition scores was −.064. Thus, the colors that were easy to communicate in one language were not necessarily easy to communicate in the other—and the same was true for ease of recognition. These data along with Brown and Lenneberg's findings (see also Lenneberg and Roberts, 1956) suggest that the language one speaks can influence his nonlinguistic behavior independent of the knowledge he has about the materials employed in testing. However, these differences in linguistic ease of encoding seem much less important than the differences in knowledge possessed by speakers of various languages. Camels, snow, and rice are more highly codable by the Arabs, Eskimos, and Hanunoo mainly because they know more about these things than most Americans do and not typically because their languages encode them differently. The language differences merely reflect the knowledge differences.

Of course, the language differences *per se* will be more important whenever one language user is forced to employ an extremely complex verbal encoding for the relevant information. A long construction such as *small, young, female camel with a long, shaggy, tawny-beige coat* is going to be more difficult to remember than the single word, *zerba*. And if there are several camels to be described that differ slightly in these attributes, then there will be very high similarity among the constructional encodings and perhaps very little similarity among the single-word encodings. A *barez* may be just like a *zerba* except for coat color. Most assuredly, the English equivalents of *barez* and *zerba* would be easily confused, and so an English-speaking subject could have great difficulty in a camel-recognition experiment just trying to remember his linguistic encodings. He may know all of the relevant attributes of the camel kingdom, but the description of one camel would be so similar to that of another that we could predict with certainty that his learning and memory ability would be impaired.

In this regard, consider the *verbal-loop hypothesis* of Glanzer and Clark (1962). They suggest that subjects encode experience into language and store the linguistic encoding for subsequent use. The stored encoding then allows the subject to "get back to" the world of experience, forming a "verbal loop." The length of the covert verbalization or encoding of an experience will depend on the complexity of the stimulus being encoded and on the nature of the coder's language, as the Brown and Lenneberg data suggest. In general, within any one language, the more complex the stimulus is, the longer and more complex the verbalization will be. From this it follows that it will take longer to encode a complex stimulus than a simple one, and, therefore, encoding will be less adequate as the duration of the stimulus exposure is decreased. Also, it will be more difficult to store and retrieve the information if it is necessary to encode the stimulus in a complex manner. In other words, forgetting of the encoded information will occur, and we can expect more information loss over time with complex codes than with simple ones.

Preliminary support for the verbal-loop hypothesis was presented by Glanzer and Clark. They reasoned that the length of the covert verbalization (the verbal encoding) could be determined by measuring the length of overt verbalization. Their subjects were asked to describe in words several stimulus arrays of black and white shapes (see Fig. 13-6) presumed to vary in complexity. Other subjects were shown the arrays for very brief intervals and were then asked to reproduce them. These latter subjects showed reliable differences in reproduction accuracy among the different arrays, and these differences were highly correlated ($r = -.826$) with the length of the overt verbal description of the arrays. For example, arrays that took eight words to describe were reproduced with only about 15 percent accuracy, while arrays that could be adequately encoded with only two words were recalled with essentially 100 percent accuracy.

Furthermore, Glanzer, Taub, and Murphy (1968) have found support for the notion discussed above that long verbal encodings of several similar things will result in poor performance because there will be a great deal of formal similarity in the words used to encode different but highly similar objects. Since we know that formal similarity is terribly detrimental to learning, this poor performance is understandable. The Arabs have different words for encoding similar camels; in English, these camels would have to be encoded with long linguistic descriptions which are bound to be highly similar to one another. And this similarity is bound to affect performance.

Notice that the verbal-loop hypothesis gives a very good account of the data from the Carmichael, Hogan, and Walter (1932) study on memory for various shapes. Presumably, the verbal encoding of each shape was influenced by what the experimenter had called it. This linguistic response was stored and retrieved at the time of testing. The subjects then structured their drawings to correspond to the stored verbal encoding, and this resulted in distortions of the original figures that more closely resembled the names. Clearly the name applied to each figure influenced the nonverbal behavior (drawing) of the subjects and therefore the study by Carmichael and his associates is consistent with the relativity hypothesis at Level 2.

Finally, consider the results of an experiment by Thomas and DeCapito (1966). Subjects were shown a colored test patch of light and asked to name it. Following this naming, a test of generalization was given. A series of colors was shown that bracketed the original color. The subject was pressing down on a key and was to release the key whenever he thought he saw the original color. For example, a "blue-green" (490 millimicrons in wavelength) was shown to 49 subjects; 27 labeled it blue and 22 labeled it green. During the test, colors surrounding 490 were

FIGURE 13–6. *Sample stimulus arrays used by Glanzer and Clark to study the verbal-loop hypothesis. The subjects had to encode verbally the pattern of black-white across a row of constant shapes. The accuracy score represents the proportion of subjects who recalled the colors correctly for each array.*

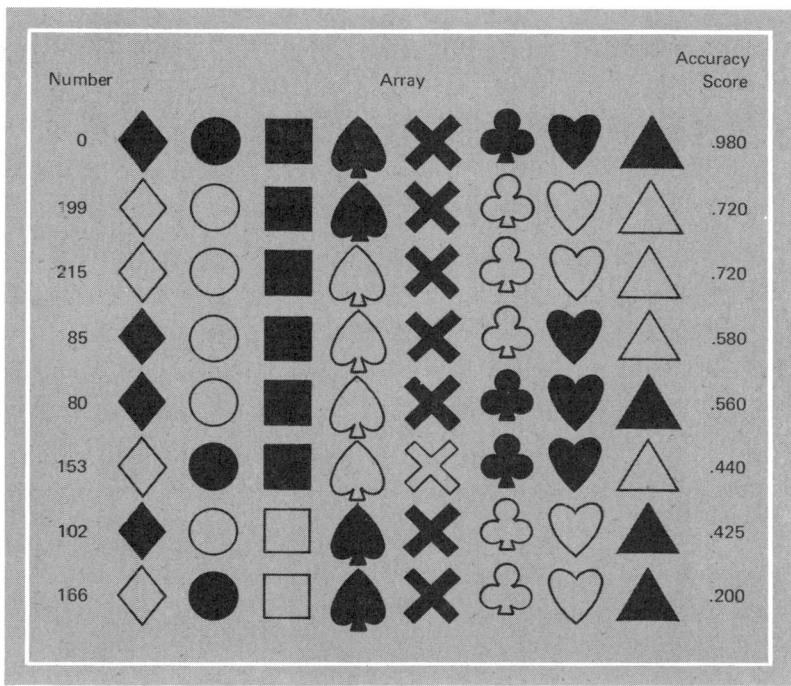

Source: From M. Glanzer and W. H. Clark, Accuracy of perceptual recall: An analysis of organization. *Journal of Verbal Learning and Verbal Behavior,* 1962, **1**, 289-99. Copyright © 1962 by the Academic Press.

shown (475, 480, 485, 490, 500, 505). Colors above 490 approach a pure green (they are "greener" than 490) and colors below 490 approach a pure blue (they are "bluer" than 490). The results showed that subjects who had labeled the original 490 stimulus as blue responded more to the lower wavelengths (the blues) during the test phase, and subjects who labeled it green responded more to higher wavelengths (the greens). The label certainly seemed to affect their nonverbal behavior. Thomas, Caronite, LaMonica, and Hoving (1968) have replicated this effect with the experimenter providing the label for the subject rather than the subject providing his own label.

The research dealing with Level 2 of the relativity hypothesis has provided substantial support. Quite clearly the names applied to experiences can influence the nonverbal behavior of the namer with respect to these experiences. The work on color coding indicates that within a language different colors are differentially codable and that this can influence the accurate recognition of colors. Languages differ in the ease with which various colors

Language and Thought 297

can be coded, and these language differences correspond to differences in the behavior of the speakers. It is also clear, however, that language differences are often merely reflections of differences in knowledge possessed by the speakers. In other words, we can conceive of differences in nonlinguistic experience giving rise to differences in the knowledge parameter of behavior. Speakers of different languages will also generally have experienced different cultures, which results in differences in knowledge. Thus we see that knowledge differences are confounded with cultural experience differences. A clear separation of these two kinds of differences may be impossible, and it will be equally impossible to attribute behavioral differences solely to language differences or solely to knowledge differences that are correlated with the language differences. When Whorf suggests that language differences are responsible for the behavioral differences between the speaker of different languages, we must remember this confounding of knowledge and language.

Level 3: Linguistic Structure and World View. The third level of the Whorfian hypothesis is much like the first level except that it suggests that linguistic structure, particularly grammar, determines the way the world is viewed in a gross sense. The German word, *Weltanschauung*, is often employed to describe just what it is that language structure determines at this level. The third level of the hypothesis, as with Level 1, has been criticized for its circular nature. Grammatical differences between languages are noted, and then there is a tendency to suggest that these differences are so unusual that they must reflect a different world view, or *Weltanschauung*. The same grammatical differences are then cited as evidence for the different world outlook. The Chinese language, for example, does not require a distinction between singular and plural, and there are no relative clauses in Chinese. Whorf believed the Hopi language had no tenses for verbs (it does, as later work demonstrated) and a set of grammatical features for designating the certainty of the speaker about a particular utterance. And Navaho does not perfectly separate subject, verb, and object.

Evidence at Level 3 is confined to this kind of catalogue of grammatical differences followed by an intuitive analysis about how these differences might reflect different world views. Thus, Whorf felt that the absence of verb tenses in Hopi and other Hopi grammatical features indicated that the Hopi people had a "timeless" outlook on the world. But the evidence for these outlook differences was always verbal behavior. The language determined the outlook which determined the verbal behavior—thus the circularity of the evidence.

The third level not only suffers from the circularity of the reasoning behind it and in support of it, but it fails to make clear just what is being influenced by the linguistic structure. Just what is the *Weltanschauung*, the world outlook, or one's orientation to the world? At Level 3, the hypothesis only suggests that speakers of different languages speak about experience in different ways and from these differences in verbal behavior, a rather giant leap is made to different world outlooks. Most serious students of the Whorfian hypothesis have disregarded this third level and have concentrated on Level 2, or on attempting to determine whether linguistic structure determines nonverbal behavior, and this brings us to the fourth level of the hypothesis.

Level 4: Grammatical Structure and Nonverbal Behavior. At Levels 3 and 4 we find Whorf's most provocative statements. Here he suggests that the language one speaks plays an extremely important role in all of his behavior because it determines the world outlook (Level 3) which in turn will greatly influence the verbal behavior (again Level 3) and the nonverbal behavior as well (Level 4). Level 4 seems to be the most appropriate level of analysis for this position since it breaks the circularity implied in Level 3. Here we can seek nonverbal behavioral differences that correspond to differences in linguistic structure.

There is apparently only one study that supports this fourth level of the hypothesis, done by Carroll and Casagrande (1958, Experiment II). The Navaho language requires different verb forms depending on the nature of the thing being acted upon, particularly depending on shape, rigidity, and material. A different form of some verbs is required if the thing being acted upon is spherical or round and thin, long and flexible or rigid, and so on. Carroll and Casagrande reasoned that Navaho children might learn to attend to the attributes marked by Navaho verbs before English-speaking children. They compared Navaho-speaking children with other Navaho children who spoke only English on a "matching" task. Each child was shown two objects which differed in two attributes (e.g., color and shape). Next a third object was presented which was similar to each of the original two in only one dimension. The subject then was asked to indicate which of the original two objects "went with" the third object. For example, the first two objects might have been a yellow stick and a piece of blue rope, the rope being as long as the stick. The third object would be a yellow rope. Since Navaho verbs require different forms for sticks (rigid) than for ropes (flexible), the Navaho-speaking children should say that the blue rope goes best with the yellow rope. The results did in fact support the hypothesis: the Navaho-speaking children tended to match on the basis of similar verb forms in Navaho, while the English-speaking children matched more on color. Interestingly enough, Carroll and Casagrande also tested English-speaking children from Boston and found that these children did not match on color as much as the English-speaking Navaho children. The Boston children were more like the Navaho-speaking children, tending to match on form or shape rather than color. Carroll and Casagrande suggest that the Boston children learned about form and shape earlier than the English-speaking Navahos because of all the experience with different toys of the form-board variety that are so popular with middle-class mothers and fathers.

The data of Carroll and Casagrande's experiment indicate that differences in linguistic structure do correspond to differences in nonverbal matching behavior, but they do not unequivocally show that the language differences caused the matching differences, since the Navaho speakers could have differed in many respects other than the language they spoke. Nevertheless, the data are cited in support of Level 4 of the Whorfian hypothesis and are indeed quite suggestive. At the same time, however, the data from Boston children indicate that experience can easily overcome any differences that might result from linguistic differences. As Fishman (1960) has pointed out, the overall picture one gets from the data is that linguistic relativity, where it might exist, probably does not influence thinking in a very potent manner. Furthermore, it seems that any such influence can easily be counteracted by relevant experience.

The Whorfian Hypothesis—Discussion and Comment

Consider the candle-mounting problem once again (Glucksberg and Weisberg) and the fact that labeling the separate items available for solution facilitated problem solving. This task is used to demonstrate functional fixedness; the problem is no problem if the box is empty and the tacks are alongside. But when the subjects experience the function of the box as a container for the tacks, they have difficulty in realizing that the box is something that can also be used to solve the problem. In many functional fixedness situations the critical object has to be used in a very unusual manner, so unusual that subjects do not always think of it even though they are trying (e.g., Glucksberg and Danks, 1968). But this does not appear to be the case in the candle problem. Here the problem is not that subjects cannot think of using the box as a platform, but that they do not seem to perceive the box itself as part of the problem; they don't even try to think of using the box. The fact that labeling the box separately facilitated solution can be explained by saying that the label merely called attention to the box as a separate entity and probably implied that the box was to be used in some fashion. The fact that the labels were linguistic (words) does not necessarily mean that language itself facilitated solution. Any means of calling attention to the box might have done the same thing.

Suppose instead that the subject was given a totally verbal description of the problem—including a statement that, "a box of tacks" is available. Or we could argue that a subject looking at the real problem encodes the perceived information as, "a box of tacks." If all further thinking is done linguistically and "in the head" without re-examining the picture, the subject must discover the relevant piece of information from the encoding. Now "a box of tacks" does in fact encode the fact that a box is available for solution, but perhaps the nature of English grammar makes it more difficult to perceive the box as a separate entity. Some other language might encode this as "a box and some tacks" or "a box with tacks in it," and these constructions might suggest more clearly that a box is present. The English form, "a box of tacks," seems to suggest that tacks are present and a part of the problem more than it suggests the presence of the box. Thus, it is conceivable that the nature of the English construction could contribute to the difficulty of the problem and this would constitute support for Level 4 of the Whorfian hypothesis.

The more important question we suggest is whether the linguistic encoding contains the relevant information. For example, in Rankin's experiment with the jigsaw shapes, we saw that the animal names did not encode the information that was necessary to solve the puzzle and in this case the names appeared to inhibit solution. The question boils down to one of knowledge—just how much knowledge is represented in the linguistic encoding of an experience, and is that knowledge relevant to the problem at hand. Names often act as labels for concepts; so, if the person using the name knows the concept, then the name encodes information about relevant attributes and the rule for combining these attributes. The vast majority of vocabulary differences among languages probably just reflect differences in knowledge commonly possessed by the average speaker of that language. Of course these differences are translated into performance differences, but to say that such differences are due to language alone is misleading. The Arabs can encode information about camels better than we can; the Arabs will be more aware of differences among camels than we are; and they will probably solve any camel problems that arise sooner than we do. But to suggest that they see the world differently than we do in any substantive sense is drastically overstating the facts.

At the same time, it must be remembered that there is a reasonable body of evidence to support the weaker Level 2 of the hypothesis —that semantic differences do correspond to nonverbal behavioral differences. This level reflects the fact that much of thinking is linguistically based and that different languages differ in the *ease* with which certain kinds of information can be encoded. If certain attributes of experience can be more easily encoded in one language than in another, speakers of those two languages should differ in the ease with which they can solve problems depending on those attributes. For example, suppose the Hanunoo language codes the pattern of spots on rice grains more easily than English and suppose we then ask Hanunoos and Americans to solve an attribute identification problem with rice grains, the relevant attribute being the pattern of the spots. Certainly, finding that the Hanunoos do better than the Americans would not be surprising. We do think about things in words and these words encode information—but it is the information, or knowledge, that is primarily responsible for the success of our problem-solving efforts and not the language which conveys this knowledge. The fact that the Hanunoos are superior on the rice problem may suggest but does not necessitate the conclusion that their way of solving the problem is different from that of an English-speaking person.

Finally, in those cases where the relativity hypothesis may apply, there is no reason to believe that the differences produced by language are of very substantial magnitude or are insurmountable. It may be easier to encode some things in one language than in another, but there is no reason to believe that things codable in one language simply cannot be encoded in some other language. As Brown has indicated, somewhere in the U.S. there must exist an English-speaking rice expert who can tell you (in English) how the 92 varieties differ.

LANGUAGE AND THOUGHT— ADDITIONAL CONSIDERATIONS

Stimulus Predifferentiation and Verbal Labeling

Closely related to the second level of the linguistic-relativity hypothesis is the work on the effects of verbal predifferentiation. Most of this work has not been directed toward an analysis of language and thought, but it is quite closely related. The predifferentiation experiment is basically a study of transfer of training. First there is some kind of criterion task on which different groups are to be compared, say, learning to move a control lever up in response to a red light and down in response to a green light. Suppose we gave different groups of subjects different kinds of pretraining with the colored lights to see if this would facilitate learning the up-down response sequence.

Arnoult (1957) has distinguished five different types of pretraining as is shown in Table 13-1. The type of most interest to us here is called *Relevant-S pretraining* because stimuli (S) relevant to the transfer task are used during the pretraining phase. In this case, Relevant-S pretraining consisted of having the subjects learn verbal labels (*cow* and *horse*) for the two lights. The *Irrelevant-S pretraining* is used to control for the nonspecific transfer effects due to warm-up and learning to learn. It is irrelevant because the subjects learn verbal labels for stimuli which are not used in the transfer task. If the Relevant-S group surpasses the Irrelevant-S group on the transfer task, we have a demonstration of positive transfer which is sometimes said to be due to the fact that the verbal labels during pretraining resulted in greater differentiation between the stimuli and hence the name stimulus predifferentiation. The other groups represent additional types of control groups (Attention and No Pretraining) and a group that learns relevant verbal responses to relevant stimuli (Relevant-S-R).

Very often the stimuli are objects for which no labels are typically available to the subject (e.g., random shapes); therefore, we can see that the Relevant-S pretraining is studying the effects of having a verbal label for a stimulus on learning some response to that stimulus. Thus, in Rankin's experiment, where he taught some subjects animal names for the shapes, we have a case of Relevant-S pretraining. Of course, the nature of the transfer task can be manipulated to determine the effects of verbal labels on learning (as in Rankin's serial-learning task), or on thinking (as in Rankin's jigsaw-puzzle task). One other transfer task is of interest. After pretraining we can test the subject on the ease with which the stimuli can be detected in a perceptual-recognition task. In short, these experiments are getting at the question, How does having a name for something influence one's ability to perceive, learn, or think about that thing?

A rather substantial number of experiments has been done on the effects of Relevant-S pretraining when the transfer is either to a motor task or a perceptual-recognition task. The results of all the experiments are not always in agreement, but it probably would be fair to say that Relevant-S pretraining usually results in positive transfer to a

TABLE 13-1. *The Basic Types of Pretraining Used in the Study of Stimulus Predifferentiation*

Type	Pretraining Task		Transfer Task	
	Stimuli	Verbal Response	Stimulus	Motor Response
Relevant S-R	red light green light	"up" "down"	red light green light	up down
Relevant S	red light green light	"cow" "horse"	same as above	
Irrelevant S	bright light dim light	"cow" "horse"	same as above	
Attention	red light	none — just told to examine the stimuli	same as above	
No Pretraining	none		same as above	

Adapted from M. D. Arnoult, Stimulus predifferentiation: Some generalizations and hypotheses. *Psychological Bulletin*, 1957, *54*, 339-50. Copyright 1957 by the American Psychological Association and reproduced by permission.

motor task but only occasionally in positive transfer to a perceptual recognition task. For example, consider an experiment by Ellis and Muller (1964). Subjects were pretrained to give verbal labels to a set of six-point random shapes. A six-point shape is one that is made by connecting six points with straight lines. Another group of subjects was given no labels during pretraining but merely told "to inspect the shapes and differentiate among them." This group is comparable to the Attention pretraining condition in Table 13-1. In their first experiment, Ellis and Muller transferred the subjects to a perceptual-recognition task. A deck of 16 cards was constructed, with five six-point shapes on each card in a row. Eight of the cards displayed one of the original eight shapes (the prototypes) together with four variations of the prototype. The other eight cards displayed five variations of the prototype but did not contain any prototype shapes. The subjects had to point to a prototype whenever they saw one, and if they thought the card contained no prototype, they were to say "none." The results showed that the Relevant-S pretraining group was somewhat *inferior* to the Attention pretraining group. However, Ellis and Muller also found that with more complex shapes (24 points) the Relevant-S group was superior to the Attention group.

In a second experiment, Ellis and Muller transferred subjects to a "motor" task which required them to learn to press one of eight switches for each of the eight shapes that had been pretrained. Only six-point shapes were used. The results showed that the Relevant-S pretraining group was significantly superior to the Attention group. Thus, with six-point shapes Ellis and Muller found that the distinctive labels facilitated transfer to a motor task but inhibited transfer to a perceptual task in comparison to an Attention condition. Quite similar results have also been reported by others (Vanderplas, Sanderson, and Vanderplas, 1964).

Katz (1963) has also shown that distinctive verbal labels applied to similar shapes can facilitate subsequent discrimination learning with those shapes. Her subjects were children averaging about 8 years in age. Four random shapes were used. The subjects in the Common-Label condition learned two nonsense-syllable names for the four shapes, each name referring to two different shapes. The Distinctive-Label condition involved learning a different name for each shape. Finally, there was a No-Label condition which corresponds somewhat to Attention pretraining—these subjects were just shown the shapes and asked to count them. Two transfer tasks were used, one perceptual and one discrimination task. In the perceptual task, pairs of figures were shown and the subject had to indicate whether or not they were "twins" by pressing a key marked "same" or "different." In the discrimination task, three figures were used. One figure was chosen by the experimenter as the correct figure. When the three figures were displayed, there was a paper goldfish always under the correct figure and the child had to learn to pick up the correct figure and find the goldfish. The results of the perceptual task showed that when the two figures in a pair were actually different (but had been labeled identically in the Common-Label condition) the subjects in the Distinctive-Label condition called them different more often than the No-Label group, which in turn was superior to the Common-Label condition. In the discrimination task, the mean number of correct responses was 16.31, 21.25, and 25.92 for the Common-Label, No-Label, and Distinctive-Label groups, respectively, indicating that distinctive labels facilitated and common labels inhibited learning.

The Katz study is one of few that has found labeling effects in a perceptual task, as did the Ellis and Muller study with the 24-point shapes. In the Katz study, however, we cannot entirely dismiss the possibility that the children were making their judgments of "twins" on the basis of the label rather than on the basis of the physical attributes of the shapes. They may have perceived the physical differences but responded "same" because they knew the two shapes had the same name. In other words, we cannot be sure that the subjects understood the task as a perceptual one. If asked whether there was any physical difference between the two shapes that had common labels they might have performed differently. The same criticism can be applied to a more recent experiment by Katz and Zigler (1969), where these labeling effects were replicated with second-grade children, but no labeling effects were found for fourth-grade children. The fourth-grade children may have understood the task better than the second graders, and this could explain the Katz and Zigler findings. This would also make these results more consistent with others that have failed to find labeling effects when the transfer task was perceptual in nature (Arnoult, 1953; Ellis, Bessemer, Devine, and Trafton, 1962; Ellis and Muller, 1964; Robinson, 1955; Vanderplas, Sanderson, and Vanderplas, 1964). However, we cannot make a final judgment that labeling will not influence perceptual transfer since some positive effects of labeling have been found (Ellis and Muller, 1964, with the complex shapes; Ellis, Feuge, Long, and Pegram, 1964; and the studies by Katz, 1963, and Katz and Zigler, 1969, if one is willing to assume that the children understood the instructions appropriately). We must agree with Katz and Zigler, that the developmental level of the subjects is probably a relevant variable determining the amount of positive transfer. In summary, the experiments clearly show that Relevant-S pretraining will influence transfer to a discrimination task. In those cases where Relevant-S pretraining has failed to have effects, the transfer task was most likely perceptual in nature.

The data then clearly indicate that having different names for different objects can facilitate learning different responses to these objects. Furthermore, learning to call two physically different objects by the same name can in some cases retard acquisition of different responses to these objects. In terms of thinking tasks, we have the demonstration by Rankin (1963) that distinctive labels for shapes can in fact interfere with performance on the "mental jigsaw" problem while facilitating a serial-learning task.

Consider also a study by Kendler and Kendler (1961). The subjects, four- and seven-year-old children, were taught a discrimination problem in Stage I of the experiment. A large, black square was the correct stimulus, and a small, white square was incorrect. One group at each age level was forced to respond in terms of the color dimension—they labeled the two figures as "black" or "white." A second group labeled them by size, "large" or "small," and a third group was not required to label the figures at all. After learning the Stage I discrimination problem, the subjects were transferred to a second task involving four figures (large+black, large+white, small+black, small+white). On this problem, size was the relevant dimension—the large figures were incorrect regardless of color, and the small figures were correct regardless of color. Given the nature of the second task, we can see that if the subjects were labeling according to size in Stage I, then Stage II ought to be a reversal shift for these subjects (large was correct in Stage I but incorrect in Stage II, and size was the relevant dimension in both Stages). If, however, the subjects labeled according to color in Stage I, then the Stage II task ought to be like a nonreversal shift (color relevant in Stage I and size relevant in Stage II with color irrelevant). The results showed quite clearly that the verbal labels in Stage I influenced Stage II performance. The groups that labeled the dimension that would lead to a reversal shift learned the Stage II task faster than the no-label group which was superior to the group which labeled the dimension leading to a nonreversal shift. The difference between the reversal and nonreversal label groups was also more pronounced in the seven-year-old children than in the four-year olds. The seven-year olds should find a nonreversal shift more difficult than a reversal shift based on earlier work of the Kendlers and so the labels should have affected them more than the four-year olds. Within the four-year olds, the reversal labels in Stage I did facilitate Stage II performance in comparison to the no-label group. The findings provide support for the Kendlers' mediational analysis of reversal shifting. The experiment as a whole is a fine example of how verbal labels can affect performance.

Theoretical Interpretations of Labeling. Given that having a name for something can influence the way it is used, the next question is, How do the names produce these effects? There are at least three interpretations of the naming effects. We will examine each one briefly.

Probably the most well-known theory of labeling is the *acquired distinctiveness* and *acquired equivalence of cues* theory of Miller and Dollard (1941). The theory is basically associative in nature, suggesting that labeling practice results in an associative link between the object (the stimulus) and the label (the response). Whenever the object is presented, it will tend to elicit the label (a kind of implicit associative response). The label response is postulated to have stimulus properties; so, the label acts as a mediator. After label training is completed, presentation of the object as a stimulus elicits the label which also has stimulus properties. The total stimulus is then considered to be the object *and* the stimulus properties of the label it elicits. In terms of this total stimulus (object plus label), the label will affect the similarity of any two stimuli. If two different objects ($0_1 + 0_2$) have a common label (L_1), the total stimulation produced by 0_1 will be more similar to that produced by 0_2 than if no labels were attached ($0_1 + L$ is more similar to $0_2 + L$ than 0_1 is to 0_2). The objects are said to have acquired greater similarity due to the common label, or they have become more equivalent and thus the name *acquired equivalence of cues*. Conversely, if two similar objects have different labels attached to them, the similarity of the two total stimulus patterns (object plus distinctive label) elicited by the objects will be reduced. The objects are said to have acquired distinctiveness as a result of the different labels and hence the name *acquired distinctiveness of cues*. The theory is thus basically associative and mediational suggesting that the labels serve as common or distinctive mediators in subsequent performance. The changes in similarity would be expected to produce changes in stimulus generalization (increased generalization for equivalence and decreased for distinctiveness) which would show up as inferior or superior performance on a transfer task that required learning a different response to each object.

In contrast to this position is the *differentiation theory* of Gibson and Gibson (1955). According to the Gibsons, labeling pretraining does not affect performance by attaching associations to the objects which then mediate later performance. Rather, in order for the subject to learn to give different names to relatively similar objects, he will have to learn to differentiate the objects. Perceptual learning will be required during pretraining—the objects must be perceived as different if the subject is to learn different names for them. Thus, the labels in a sense force the subject to differentiate between the objects on the basis of physical attributes that were there all along but were not perceived. This learned differentiation, in turn, will reduce the amount of stimulus generalization among the stimuli, making it easier to attach different overt responses to the objects, although the reasoning is rather circular at this point. This theory minimizes the role of the labels during the transfer task. The labeling task produced increased differentiation during the pretraining, and there is then no need to postulate that the labels are used during the transfer task. The transfer task is facilitated because the stimuli which had labels attached are more highly differentiated before the transfer task begins due to perceptual learning, not associative learning.

Finally, the third theory of interest, *attention theory,* is based on the work of Hake and Eriksen (1955). Basically, these authors suggest that the labels merely call attention to various distinctive attributes of the objects. Labeling a particular random shape *cow* calls the subjects' attention to any aspects of the shape that might resemble a cow. The label may continue to direct the subjects' attention to these aspects during the transfer task. The subjects' attention is thus directed toward those aspects which will tend to differentiate the stimuli from each other. We have suggested an attention mechanism earlier with regard to the labeling of the box in the candle-mounting problem.

All three theories are designed to account for the same sets of data and it is difficult to choose among them. They are also similar enough that designing experiments to distinguish among them has proved to be a difficult task. Unfortunately, at present, we cannot render a judgment about their respective validities. More likely is the possibility that labels function in all three ways, sometimes acting as additions to the total stimulus complex, sometimes producing differentiation, and sometimes merely calling the subjects' attention to certain features of the labeled objects.

Comment

It seems rather clear that at least a substantial portion of thought is linguistic in nature. This is most commonly reflected in the term "inner speech." In solving a problem "in our heads" we seem to be talking to ourselves, and in this sense having a distinctive label for the objects of our thoughts can certainly be beneficial. Again, however, we feel that the most relevant point about linguistically based thought is not whether it is possible (it is) and not whether all thinking is linguistically based (it is not). It is, rather, the encoding function of language that is most important. We encode much but not all of experience linguistically. Whether or not this will facilitate thinking will depend on whether the attributes relevant to the solution of the problem at hand are encoded by the linguistic responses.

One of the most distinguishing features of thought is that the behavior of the thinker becomes relatively independent of the immediate external stimulus situation. It is in this regard that linguistically based thinking assumes a major role. Language encodings of information result in particular abstractions of the attributes of an experience. Thinking about the experience linguistically will then maximize the independence of thought from the immediate stimulus situation. By classifying experiences into concepts, linguistic encodings collapse experience over uncoded dimensions and thus focus thinking on the coded features, thereby facilitating problem solution if these features are relevant or inhibiting solution if they are not. In contrast, if thinking were totally dominated by images of experience, then behavior would more often appear to be dominated by the exact nature of the stimulus situation to the extent that an image is less likely than a verbal label to collapse experiences across minute, and generally irrelevant, attributes.

In this regard, consider the conservation of volume experiment conducted by Bruner, Olver, and Greenfield (1966). In this experiment, children of four to seven years were shown two equal-sized beakers filled with water to the same level; the children judged the amount of water in the two beakers to be equal. Then the water from one beaker was poured into a third beaker which was taller and thinner than the first two beakers so that the water level in the third beaker was much higher. The child of five years or younger typically said that there was more water in the tall, thin beaker because the water level was higher. Bruner and his associates reasoned that the perceptual information provided by the different water levels was responsible for the children's inability to conserve volume. If the children could be made to solve the problem "in their heads," without seeing the different water levels, they should do better. So a screen was placed between the child and the beakers such that he could only see the tops of the beakers but not the water levels. The water was poured from one beaker into the taller beaker behind the screen and the child was then asked to say which beaker would have more water. Under this condition, some of the four-year olds and all of the older children said there still was the same amount of water, i.e., they conserved volume. Without the screen, all four- and five-year olds and many six- and seven-year-old children do not conserve volume. If a four-year old conserves with the screen in place and the screen is subsequently removed, he often changes his mind upon seeing the different water levels. None of the older children changed when the screen was removed. It is as if the youngest children are not confident of their reasoning abilities, and so they change their minds when faced with conflicting perceptual data. Language, by providing a means of encoding experience, allows behavior to become relatively independent of the immediate stimulus situation, and generally this will facilitate problem solving.

Of course, we have also argued that linguistically based thought will not invariably be superior to image based thought. Whenever the linguistic encoding ignores relevant features of an experience, thinking will be inhibited. The Rankin experiment in which animal names retard solution of the jigsaw puzzle demonstrates this quite clearly. The animal names did not encode enough information about the exact nature of the edges, and this information just happened to be relevant to the puzzle.

In short, as we have argued in Chapter 1, there is a strong relationship between thinking and that parameter of behavior we call knowledge—what the subject thinks of, what he knows, and whether this knowledge is relevant or irrelevant to solution of the problem. In some cases, he will have more relevant information available if he encodes experience linguistically and thinks linguistically. In other cases, linguistically based thinking will contain less relevant information. In this sense, thinking most certainly depends on language and on the subject's ability to use his linguistic repertoire to encode and store information.

Thinking is probably never totally linguistic in nature in the sense that it follows perfectly the rules of overt speech. Likewise, it is very unlikely that adult thinking is ever totally without an influence of language or totally nonlinguistic in nature. In this sense, language is always a part of thought.

SUMMARY

In this chapter we have tried to examine the difficult problem of the relationship between language and thought. The guiding hypothesis in this endeavor was the linguistic-relativity hypothesis of Benjamin L. Whorf, which was considered at four levels. Substantial support exists for the proposition that language can and does influence nonverbal behavior. Different languages encode experiences differently—some things are more easily encoded in one language than in another. But there is no evidence that some languages can encode experiences that cannot be encoded in some way in another language. Lexical and grammatical differences among languages can influence nonverbal behavior, but no evidence suggests very convincingly that such differences result in or are responsible for different ways of perceiving reality. Most of the language differences probably reflect differences in the knowledge commonly possessed by speakers of these languages rather than any differences in the way these speakers think about the world.

Evidence was also presented which indicates that having names for objects can facilitate or inhibit performance with those objects. The most important feature of language is that it represents a system for coding experience into existing concepts represented by words. The words of a language encode the attributes and rules of experience and whether this encoded information will facilitate or inhibit thinking will depend mainly on the relevance of the information. In this regard, knowledge is the most important parameter of behavior, and the nature of the linguistic encoding of the world can undoubtedly influence the nature or the amount of knowledge available to the thinker.

Fourteen Language: A System for Thinking

Language and its acquisition distinguish mankind from other animals. Yet, what we learn and how we do it remain much of a mystery.

In this chapter, we will examine some of the basic features of language. The initial emphasis will be on the structural aspects of languages. We will attempt to show that our understanding of language will be enhanced by a study of the conceptual nature of language systems. Language behavior is extraordinarily complicated; in this chapter we touch only on the basic components. Several excellent books, which present a much fuller account, are available for the interested student. We have found the writings of Brown (1956, 1958, 1965, especially Chapters 7 and 8) to be particularly useful introductions. Introductory treatments of the science of linguistics will also be necessary reading for the serious student (e.g., Gleason, 1961; Hall, 1964).

COMPETENCE AND PERFORMANCE

We begin by assuming that there is a distinction between the language user's knowledge about his language and his observed linguistic activities. What he knows, and knows how to do, is called *competence* and what he actually does is *performance*. Certainly we all utter language constructions that would horrify us if they were written down and shown to us because we would realize instantly that these utterances violate many of the rules we know about our language. The science of linguistics is mainly concerned with a description of competence, while the branch of psychology known as psycholinguistics deals with both competence and performance but emphasizes the latter. We argued in the first chapter that a truly adequate description of behavior must include some description of the knowledge and skills that a person possesses as well as a description of what he does in fact do. The competence-performance distinction that is emphasized in current linguistic research represents a clear recognition of this necessity. In fact, modern linguistics has been one of the most effective influences in bringing experimental psychologists to realize that descriptions of overt performance without due regard to competence do not provide much in the way of understanding or explanation of behavior.

The complexity of language is simply illustrated by the fact that the competent speaker could, if he lived long enough, speak an infinite number of grammatically correct (acceptable) sentences and never repeat himself. Furthermore, he could understand the infinite number of sentences spoken by another person. In other words, each of us is capable of speaking and understanding sentences we have never heard before, which means we could not have learned to say and understand each sentence independently. Miller (1965) has illustrated this point compellingly by suggesting that 10^{20} sentences each 20 words long are easily possible in our language. We might suppose learning to speak and understand each of these sentences required learning each one as an individual response. Such learning would make available an enormous library of sentences to draw upon, some to be used at cocktail parties, others for fraternity bull sessions, and so on. The stimulus conditions would call forth the appropriate sentences at the appropriate times, presumably because of our past experience at hearing and saying the sentences and receiving appropriate reinforcements. We must, however, realize that any such interpretation, based on either classical or instrumental learning of specific stimulus-response units is preposterous. As Miller points out, just listening once to 10^{20} 20-word sentences read at a reasonable rate would require "1000 times the estimated age of the earth." What we learn *must* be something different from a catalogue of independent sentences. One possibility is that we, as language users, learn a system of rules by which we can generate and understand an infinite number of sentences. Our knowledge of this system is our linguistic competence.

We can illustrate the notion of competence with a familiar example. A successful subject in a simple concept-identification experiment possesses a certain competence when he has identified the correct solution to the problem, *What is a dax?* Suppose that patterns which are both red and square are positive instances (they are daxes) of the concept; all other patterns are negative instances (nondaxes). If the subject had an infinite amount of construction paper and enough time, theoretically, he could generate an infinite number of patterns that are both red and square. In other words, he is a competent producer of daxes because he knows what it takes to make a dax. Similarly, this hypothetical subject could look at an infinite number of patterns which we had constructed and classify them as positive and negative instances. When we say, then, that the subject has learned the concept of *dax* or knows the concept, we are making a statement about competence. And we assume that such competence allows him to perform an infinite number of specific but not necessarily identical responses.

By *linguistic competence* we mean much the same thing. When we say that someone knows a language or has learned a language, we are talking about the competence that he possesses which permits him to engage in certain performances. A theory of linguistic competence can be viewed as an attempt to describe what it is that a person knows that allows him to perform in a certain variety of ways. Such a theory consists of a system that would generate all the sentences of a language and none of the nonsentences. Such a theory, then, is like an elaborate concept that divides all possible utterances into positive and negative instances corresponding to sentences and nonsentences. The competent speaker knows what it takes to produce a positive instance, and he knows how to separate positive instances from negative instances. In other words, we are saying that this subject knows the concept, *sentence in Language* X (say, English), in much the same way that someone knows the concept, *dax*. Now, knowing that someone knows *dax* does not really explain why when told to make daxes he often comes up with nondaxes (say, parallelograms that are not quite square). Or, in other words, competence does not fully explain performance. Actually these are interdependent but separate parameters of behavior and require separate consideration.

The child who is learning a language is participating in the most complicated concept-learning task he will ever face (cf. Brown, 1958, "The Original Word Game"). The concept he acquires is so complex that no one has as yet been able to describe it adequately. He is presented with ostensibly positive instances of the concept when he hears others speak (a reception paradigm) and he produces both positive and negative instances of the concept when he attempts to speak (a selection paradigm) and receives feedback about his attempts. By the time he is four or five years old, he seems to have developed a reasonable level of competence. From the set of utterances he has experienced, he has abstracted a system that enables him to generate and understand an infinity of utterances. Note again that the system is a set of rules that generatively describes the utterances, but not a description of how this generation takes place. "Red and square" describes all positive instances of *dax*, but says nothing about the physical attributes of a device that recognizes or produces daxes.

LEVELS OF LINGUISTIC ANALYSIS

In our brief treatment of language we will consider three levels of linguistic analysis: (1) *phonetics* and *phonemics*, or the study of *phonology;* (2) *morphology;* and (3) *syntax*. A sentence consists of a series of speech sounds called *phones*. When these sounds are ordered in certain ways they constitute words. (Linguists prefer the concept of *morpheme* to the concept of *word*. However, for the time being, we can consider a morpheme to be a word). The study of the ordering of sounds to produce morphemes is called morphology. Finally, the words or morphemes are ordered to produce sentences; the study of this ordering is known as syntax. Both morphology and syntax are concerned with the problem of sequencing of units, the former with the sequencing of sounds to make words and the latter with the sequencing of words to make sentences. Morphology and syntax together constitute *grammar,* the study of the sequencing of units to produce acceptable utterances.

Phonology

The basic units of sound of every known language are called *phonemes*. There are 46 phonemes in the "standard" dialect of English language; other known languages have as few as 15 sounds or as many as 85. But even 85 does not seem like very many different sounds when we think of the fantastic variety of utterances a speaker can produce. Obviously, the variety comes from the phoneme combination rules of a language, not from the speaker's ability to produce a very large variety of basic sounds.

The phoneme is an abstraction, because a phoneme never actually occurs. The sounds that do actually occur when we speak are called *phones*. Conventionally, phones are symbolized by enclosing them in brackets (e.g., [b]) and phonemes by enclosing them with slash marks (e.g., /b/). Phones and phonemes correspond very roughly to the letters of the alphabet, but they are not pronounced as the letter name. The phoneme /b/ is pronounced, not as "bee" but as the initial sound in the word *bill* or *bullet* is pronounced.

If a speaker pronounces the word *bill* over and over, he will produce many instances of the concept, the phoneme /b/. Each instance is a phone, [b], but all the phones could be slightly different. The speaker would not produce an acoustic signal that was exactly the same each time he uttered the initial sound in the word *bill*. The differences may be very slight (it would take sophisticated acoustic equipment, a sound spectrograph, to detect most of them) and they obviously are not important differences to the listener, for he hears the same word each time. In describing this speech we would want to classify all of these phones together since the speaker did not intend for them to be different sounds, the listener did not detect the differences, and since it would be horribly cumbersome otherwise. Enter the phoneme.

All phones that are mutually substitutable, i.e., make no difference to the listener, are instances of a single phoneme. The differences among them that make no difference are the irrelevant attributes of the phoneme concept. Such phones are said to be in *free variation*, for the speaker can feel free to vary his exact pronunciation without worrying about the listener's varying his interpretation of what was said. Some phones are not in free variation, not typically substituted for each other, but are nevertheless classified as instances of the same phoneme. Such phones are said to be in *complementary distribution*. For example, the k sounds in the words *key* and *ski* are consistently different from each other, the former being an aspirated sound (produced with a puff of air which you can feel on the back of your hand) while the latter is generally unaspirated. However, these phones are classified together as instances of /k/, because following /s/, /k/ is always unaspirated, while not following /s/, /k/ is always somewhat aspirated. One can predict perfectly which sound will occur from the preceding context. These two varieties of /k/ are called *allophones* of /k/. In a sense they are in free variation because one could pronounce *key* with an unaspirated sound and it would still be interpreted as the word *key*. However, since speakers do not freely vary the aspiration in these words, the two phones are not technically in free variation, and the term *complementary distribution* is used instead.

What about the relevant attributes of the concept of a particular phoneme? What are the attributes that distinguish one phoneme from another? In 1952, Jakobson, Fant, and Halle presented the elements of a *distinctive-feature theory* of phoneme identification. Briefly, they suggest that a phoneme can be conceived of as a conjunctive combination of several binary features. Each phoneme consists of a different combination of the basic features. For example, one feature might be whether the sound is voiced (produced with a vibration of the vocal cords) or voiceless (no vibration). The English phonemes /b/ and /p/ differ only in this one feature of voicing, /b/ being the voiced phoneme. By having enough features (which are comparable to binary dimensions), the phonemes in any language can be differentiated.

Presumably, phoneme identification by listeners is based heavily on their analysis of the features that are present in the sound, and since each phoneme differs from every other one by at least one feature or attribute, the listener can determine which phoneme is meant by the speaker. In this theory, then, similarity between any two phonemes is determined by the number of distinctive features they have in common. Phonemes that differ by only one feature (e.g., /b/ and /p/) are maximally similar. Thus, distinctive-feature theory predicts that when listeners misperceive a phoneme, they will most likely confuse it with a phoneme that differs by only one distinctive feature. The more features that differentiate two phonemes, the less likely it is that listeners will confuse the two. Research on phoneme confusions (e.g., Miller and Nicely, 1955; and particularly Shepard, 1966) has provided considerable support for this prediction. Similarly, if subjects are asked to judge the similarity of pairs of sounds, we should find that judged similarity is positively correlated with the number of features the two sounds share. Greenberg and Jenkins (1964) have indeed found that two sounds differing by only one feature are regularly judged more similar to each other than two sounds that differ by two features. In addition, there is evidence that distinctive features may underlie the effects of acoustic similarity on learning. For example, both Hintzman (1967) and Wickelgren (1966) have shown that confusion errors in short term memory are predictable from a knowledge of distinctive features.

It has also been shown that a distinctive-feature dimension (voiced or voiceless) can serve as a cue for learning (Jenkins, Foss, and Greenberg, 1968). These authors asked subjects to learn the paired-associate list presented in Table 14-1. Each stimulus-response

TABLE 14–1. *Stimulus-Response Pairings Used by Jenkins, Foss & Greenberg (1968)*

Stimuli	Responses
pa	ba
ta	da
ka	ga
fa	va
sa	za
cha	ja

Each stimulus is paired with a response that, in terms of distinctive features, is identical with the exception of voicing. Thus, each response term is the "voiced version" of its stimulus. The learning of this paired-associate list was facilitated when the subjects were requested to pay attention to their mouths.

From J. J. Jenkins, D. J. Foss, and J. H. Greenberg. Phonological distinctive features as cues in learning. *Journal of Experimental Psychology*, 1968, 77, 200-205. Copyright 1968 by the American Psychological Association and reproduced by permission.

pair differed only in one feature; the stimulus term was a *voiceless* consonant and a vowel; the corresponding response was the matching *voiced* consonant paired with the same vowel. The only feature difference between the stimulus consonant and the corresponding response consonant was the difference in voicing. Thus, the response term in each pair could be perfectly determined by taking the stimulus term and pronouncing it in exactly the same manner but with the addition of voicing. In a gross sense, however, the list looks as if it would be difficult to learn because of extremely high acoustic similarity and fairly high orthographic similarity. The learning of this list was markedly facilitated, however, when the subjects were told to "pay attention to what your mouth is doing as you say the syllables." These results then give psychological validity to distinctive features and they demonstrate again that we must consider linguistic competence in our psychological theories of verbal learning.

The data, then, indicate that distinctive features are psychologically important, and they support the idea that a phoneme is basically a conjunctive concept—a conjunction of a set of distinctive features. The dimensions of the concept are the distinctive features, each dimension consisting of two attributes (the presence or absence of that particular feature), and the rule is one of conjunction. Since the phoneme is a basic unit of any language, we can see that conjunctive-concept learning will be an early necessity in learning any language.

Morphology

The next level of linguistic analysis is concerned with the ordering of phonemes to construct morphemes. You may think of a morpheme as the *smallest* unit of language that conveys meaning. Rather than deal with the word as the unit of meaning, linguists employ the concept of a morpheme because the word is not the smallest unit. Take, for example, the word *hats*. To the linguist, this word consists of two morphemes, {hat} + {Z_1} where {Z_1} is a symbol standing for the plural morpheme. Morphemes are typically enclosed in braces.

There are two types of morphemes. *Free morphemes* are words—they are free to stand alone in sentences, the word {hat} being a free morpheme. The other type is known as the *bound morpheme*. Bound morphemes are not words and as such cannot stand alone in sentences—they are bound to other morphemes. The plural morpheme {Z_1}, is an example. Prefixes and suffixes are the most common bound morphemes. You can see that *hats*, although a single word, actually is composed of two units, each of which conveys some meaning, and thus, words are certainly not the minimal meaning units.

Just as an allophone is a variety of a phoneme that occurs in predictable linguistic contexts, so is the *allomorph* a variety of a morpheme that occurs in definable contexts. Consider the plural morpheme, $\{Z_1\}$, which has three common allomorphs exemplified by the words, *hats, losses,* and *rugs*. Respectively, the allomorphs of the plural morpheme in these three examples are phonemically described as /s/, /iz/, and /z/. But since the occurrence of these can be perfectly predicted by the preceding phonemic context, they are classified as allomorphs of a single morpheme, the plural morpheme, $\{Z_1\}$. Since the morphology specifies the phonemes, we have what are known as *morphophonemic rules*.

It seems clear that speakers of English have learned morphological rules. For example, they have not memorized the plural of each and every noun, but instead have learned a rule for pluralizing nouns, as can be judged from the way they pluralize nonsense words. Berko (1958) has developed materials for the study of children's knowledge of these morphological rules. The subject is asked to pluralize such "words" as *wug, bik,* and *niss*. The child is shown a picture of one wug (see Figure 14-1), then a picture of two of these creatures, while the experimenter recites, "This is a wug. Now there are two of them. There are two _____."

Adult speakers will show knowledge of the rules by pluralizing *wug* with the allomorph /z/, *bik* with /s/, and *niss* with /iz/. The rules are of the conditional variety. First, the noun in question must be an instance of the class of morphemes called *count nouns* as opposed to *mass nouns* (e.g., *dirt, air,* and *water*) which are not subject to the rule for pluralizing nouns. So the rule specifies that if X is a count noun, then pluralize with $\{Z_1\}$. Next comes the morphophonemic rule which specifies the allomorph of $\{Z_1\}$ according to the phonemic ending of the singular form (e.g., if X ends in /k/ then pluralize with /s/). This rule is also of the conditional variety, the particular allomorph being conditional upon the phonemic ending of the

FIGURE 14–1. *An example of the materials used to study morphological rules.*

Source: Redrawn from Jean Berko, The child's learning of English morphology. *Word,* 1958, 14, 150-77.

count noun. The ease with which speakers pluralize nonsense count nouns according to the rules is strong evidence that such behavior is rule governed. It is especially interesting because the average speaker knows nothing at the verbal descriptive level about phonemics and morphology and cannot accurately tell you what the rules are that describe his behavior even though his behavior is lawful and he "knows what to do."

Note that morphology also involves classifying groups of morphemes into large categories that correspond somewhat to the parts of speech. Some rules apply only to count nouns, others only to verbs, and so on. Thus, language learning must involve the development of the concepts of *morpheme classes* or *form classes* as they are usually termed. The learning of these classes constitutes a fundamental necessity for learning the language. Jenkins and Palermo (1964; see also Palermo, 1966) have attempted to apply the principles of mediation theory to this learning. They have argued that the stimulus-equivalence and response-equivalence paradigms of mediation represent the basic process involved in the development of these form classes. For example, count nouns are always associated with the indefinite articles *a* or *an,* whereas mass nouns are not (we do not say, "a dirt"). The count nouns become a differentiated class because they have the same or similar privileges of occurrence in sentences, which is to say that they have occurred as responses to the same or similar antecedent stimuli. In the utterance, "Get me a _____," all single words that are acceptable fillers are count nouns, and count nouns could become a response class because of their common association with such utterances. This would be an instance of response-equivalence training.

Linguists have long known the ambiguity of the concepts of the various parts of speech and generally prefer the term, form class, where form class is defined by privilege of occurrence. For some linguists (e.g., Fries, 1940), a noun is not defined as a person, place, or thing, but as a word with certain privileges of occurrence in various sentence positions (e.g , words that fit the blank in, "The _____ is [or was] good."). Such definitions of form classes seem to suggest that equivalence paradigms might very well represent the nature of the learning involved in the development of form classes. However, the mediational interpretation implies that a sentence can be divided up, with the early words serving as stimuli for the later words, indeed, with each word serving first as a response in its own right and secondly as a stimulus for subsequent words. To the linguist, such an analysis means that the grammar of language is a *finite-state grammar* (each word being dependent in a probabilistic manner on preceding words). And, it has been suggested that finite-state grammars are inadequate descriptions of the grammatical structure of language (Bever, Fodor, and Garrett, 1968).

There are also morphological rules for changing the form class of a word and these are known as *derivational* rules. Thus, adjectives are transformed into nouns and adverbs (*quick* becomes *quickness* or *quickly*) and nouns into adjectives (*dirt* becomes *dirty*). The words we sometimes "invent" (e.g., orangey, complexness, systematicity, criterial) when applying morphological rules are further testimony to the rule-governed nature of linguistic behavior. A detergent commercial tells us that our white things will be whiter and our plaid things will be "plaider." The morphological rules make the language extremely flexible, tremendously increasing the generative power of the competent speaker.

English morphology is complex, and we have examined only the simplest features and rules. The competent speaker, however, by learning morphology has accomplished an enormously intricate rule-learning task.

Syntax

Syntax deals with the arrangement of words or morphemes to form larger constructions, phrases and sentences. Syntactic theory attempts to set forth rules that will generate an infinity of grammatically correct sentences and no incorrect sentences. The theory should reveal the structure of each sentence so that we may see the relationships among sentences. Adequate structural descriptions will also be necessary if we are to understand the relationships between the various parts (words and phrases) of a single sentence. Finally, structural information will be necessary for the correct semantic interpretation of a sentence, i.e., we will have to know something about sentence structure in order to decide what the sentence means.

Finite-State Grammars. The simplest models or theories of grammar are called *finite-state grammars,* often called *regular grammars.* Regular grammars view the sentence-generating process in a left-to-right manner, i.e., begin with word A which is followed by word Q, and Q is followed by word X, finally arriving at the sentence AQX, where AQX might represent *I hate spinach.*

The rules in such grammars are all of the same variety, namely, they specify what can come after what. A schematic illustration of a regular grammar is shown in Figure 14-2. The generation of a sentence can be viewed

FIGURE 14–2. A "road map" of a possible finite state or regular grammar.

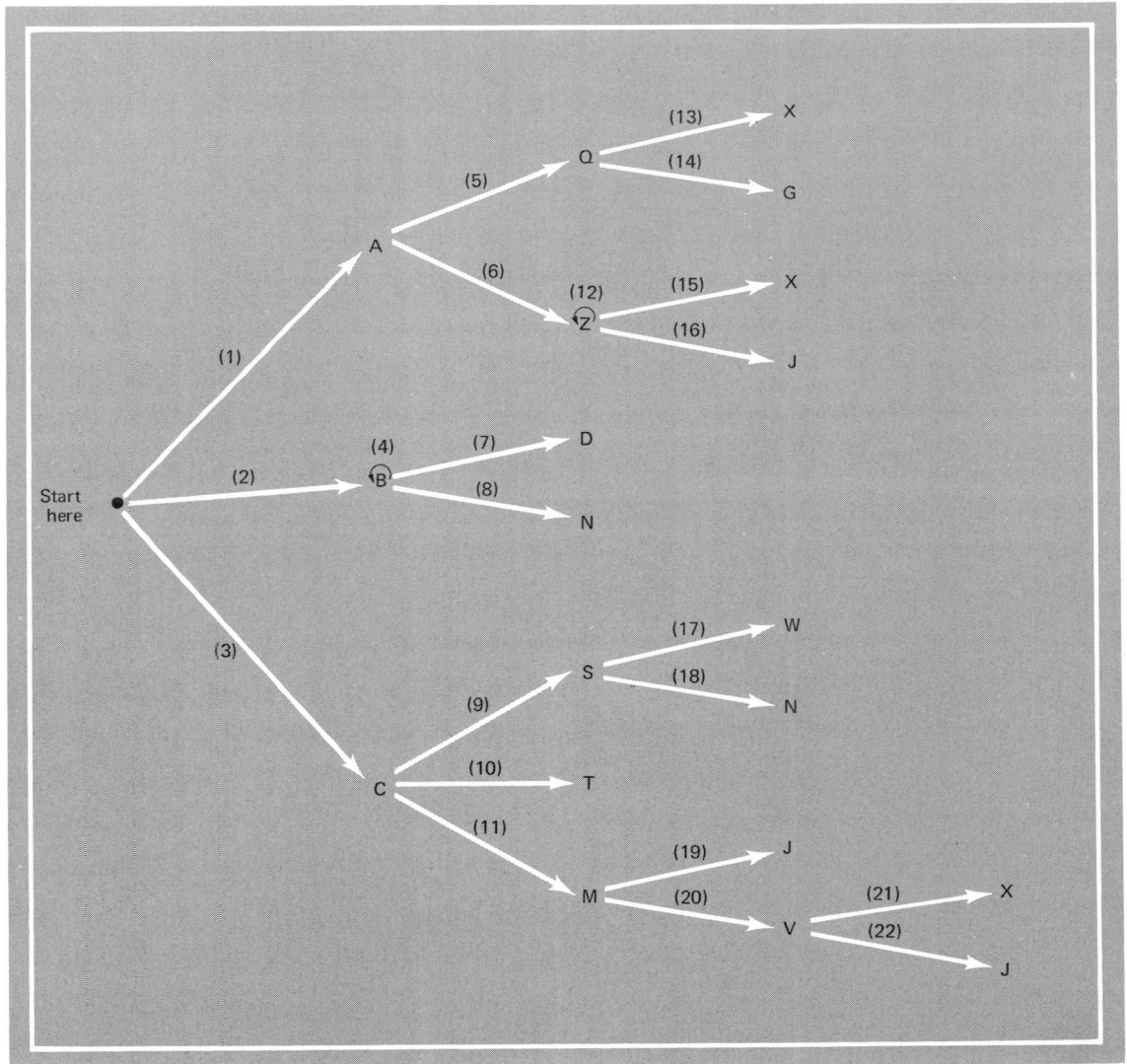

as traveling down a series of paths, beginning at point zero and proceeding from left-to-right until reaching a stopping point. Each time a person selects a path, a word or morpheme is generated, and by the time he hits a dead end he will have generated a string of words that is supposed to be grammatically acceptable. It will, of course, be grammatically correct only if that person's map correctly portrays the language he is trying to describe. The whole idea is to try to construct such a map.

There are 22 numbered paths in Figure 14-2. Beginning at zero and following paths 1, 5, and 13, we would generate the sentence AQX. Path 3-11-20-22 would likewise generate CMVJ. Since we have two paths that are recursive (numbers 4 and 12), there is no longest sentence in this grammar and there is no limit to the number of different sentences that could be generated by this system. Thus, we could generate BBBBBB . . . . . . D by following 2-4-4-4-4-4 . . . . . . 7. The finite-state rules specify what can come after what, e.g., after C comes either S, T, or M. Finite-state grammars are usually formulated as *Markov chains,* where a probability is assigned to the various paths leading from a single point. For example, from State C we can proceed in one of three ways (9, 10, or 11) and we could assign probabilities to these paths. Thus, the probability of S given C (which is the probability that we will traverse path 9) might be .60; the probability of T given C might be .20, leaving the probability of M given C as .20.

The most important thing to realize about finite-state grammars is that the application of most any currently available theory of learning, such as those summarized in previous sections, to the problem of language learning will result in some variety of finite-state grammar. These applications can usually be stated as Markov processes where what is learned are the various probabilities at the transition or choice points. And, typically, this is because the choice points in a Markov model can be viewed as representing stimuli in a stimulus-response learning theory. Assume we are at point C or state C in Figure 14-2, which means we are about to generate either CS, CT, or CM. We can easily think of these possibilities as being analogous to the strength of the associations between C and S, C and T, and C and M, respectively. In other words, association models are almost certain to reduce to some variety of finite-state grammar. If one could prove that a finite-state grammar could not possibly describe the grammar of some natural language, he could then essentially dismiss S-R association learning theories as being logically incapable of explaining language learning. And this is just what many linguists are telling their psychologist "friends." A suggested "proof" of the inadequacy of left-to-right Markov processes is available (see Bever, Fodor, and Garrett, 1968), and so it is argued a learning theory that is reducible to such processes cannot explain language learning and performance.

Phrase-Structure Grammars. A promising alternative to the finite-state grammars is provided by the phrase-structure grammars, the name deriving from the fact that such grammars give detailed descriptions of the structure of sentences so that one can see the relations between the various phrases that constitute a sentence. Phrase-structure grammars consist of a series of rewrite rules of the general form X→Y which is read as "X can be rewritten as Y," meaning that we can substitute Y wherever X occurs. Phrase-structure rules rewrite single symbols as other symbols, and they require this rewriting of X as Y whenever X occurs. These rules, then, do not rewrite a series of symbols, but rather they rewrite symbols one at a time. Using a series of rewrite rules, we can derive sentences, the process being shown in **Figure 14-3** for three very simple sentences.

The top portion of Figure 14-3 presents the rewrite rules, and the bottom portion displays the steps in the derivation of the sentence. The process is of the "top-down" variety, as opposed to the left-right nature of

FIGURE 14–3. *A simple phrase-structure grammar and three sample derivations.*

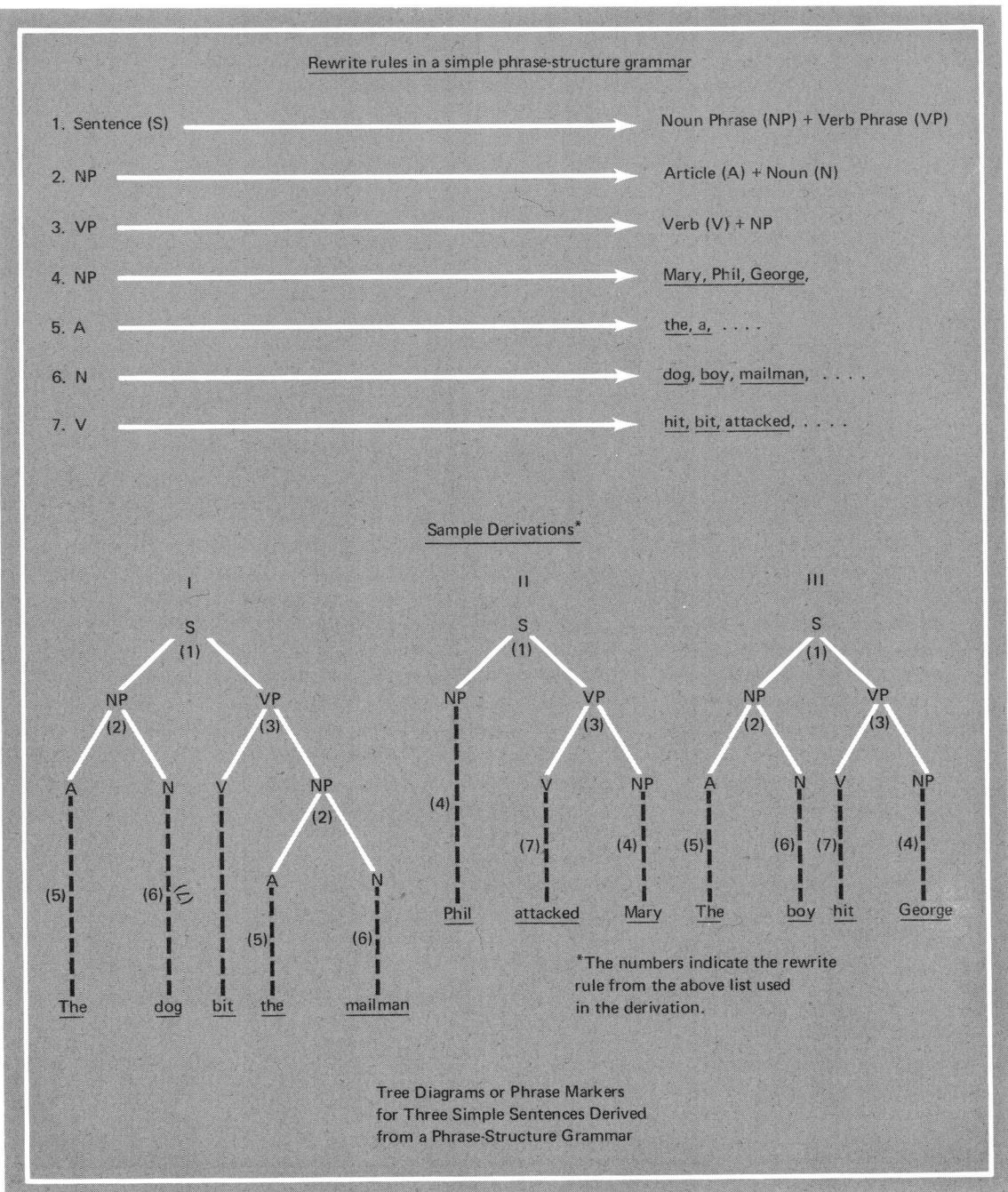

finite-state grammars. The three diagrams in the lower portion are called phrase markers (P-markers) for they mark the relations between the various parts of the sentence.

Let's examine Sentence I, *The dog bit the mailman*. Beginning at the top of the tree with the largest construction, the sentence, we rewrite this as noun phrase plus verb phrase employing Rule 1. What we are saying, in other words, is that the *construction* (the sentence) is composed of two parts or *constituents*, a noun phrase (NP) and a verb phrase (VP). The noun phrase, in turn, is a construction which, according to Rule 2, has as one possible set of constituents an article (A) and a noun (N). As we descend the tree diagram we descend levels of construction, and the units below any given construction are called the *immediate constituents* of that construction. Thus, the immediate constituents of the noun phrase when rewritten by Rule 2 are an article and a noun; the noun phrase is one of the two immediate constituents of the entire sentence.

Modern linguistic analysis of syntax places heavy emphasis on the description of utterances in terms of constitutents at various levels. The process is somewhat like the old exercises of sentence parsing. The task is to figure out the immediate constituents at each level and to determine the relationships among them. When this is accomplished, the *phrase structure* or *constituent structure* of the utterance has been described. Ideally, such descriptions would reveal the similarities and differences among various sentence types. Also, such descriptions would explain why some utterances are ambiguous. Ambiguity would be explained by demonstrating that more than one structural description is possible for the same terminal utterance. Consider the sentence, *They are eating apples,* and examine the P-markers in Figure 14-4. The sentence is ambiguous: we do not know whether it is the answer to the question, *What kind of apples are those?* or to the question, *What are they doing?* The reason for the ambiguity is seen in Figure 14-4, where it is shown that two different P-markers are possible for this sentence, with the left-hand marker describing the answer about the kind of apples and the right-hand marker describing the answer about what they are doing. A finite-state grammar would not represent the ambiguity that is most assuredly present, whereas the analysis in terms of constituent structure reveals the exact source of the ambiguity.

There is a fair amount of evidence that constituent structure is psychologically important. Consider an experiment by Fodor and Bever (1965). Subjects listened to sentences played into one ear while click sounds were played into the other ear at the same time. The subjects had to write down each sentence after it was played and had to indicate the point in the sentence where the click had occurred. The results showed a marked tendency for the subjects to displace the click from its actual point of occurrence toward a constituent break. A constituent break is the boundary between two words that do not belong to the same constituent, e.g., in Figure 14-4, Derivation I assigns *are* and *eating* to different constituents, whereas Derivation II assigns *are* and *eating* to the same constituent. Thus, the break between *are* and *eating* is a constitutent break in Derivation I but not in Derivation II. In the results, it appeared as if the constituents were the perceptual units and that displacing the perceived location of the click allowed the subjects to perceive the sentences without disruption of their basic processing units. Alternatively, the subjects' knowledge of phrase structure led them to process the sentence in chunks larger than a single word, these chunks being determined by the constituent structure. The structure provides a natural basis for chunking which would be destroyed if the clicks determined the chunks instead of the more powerful system imposed by the linguistic structure. Garrett, Bever, and Fodor (1966) have subsequently demonstrated that the physical features of the auditory stimulus (such as stress, intonation, and pause), which are some-

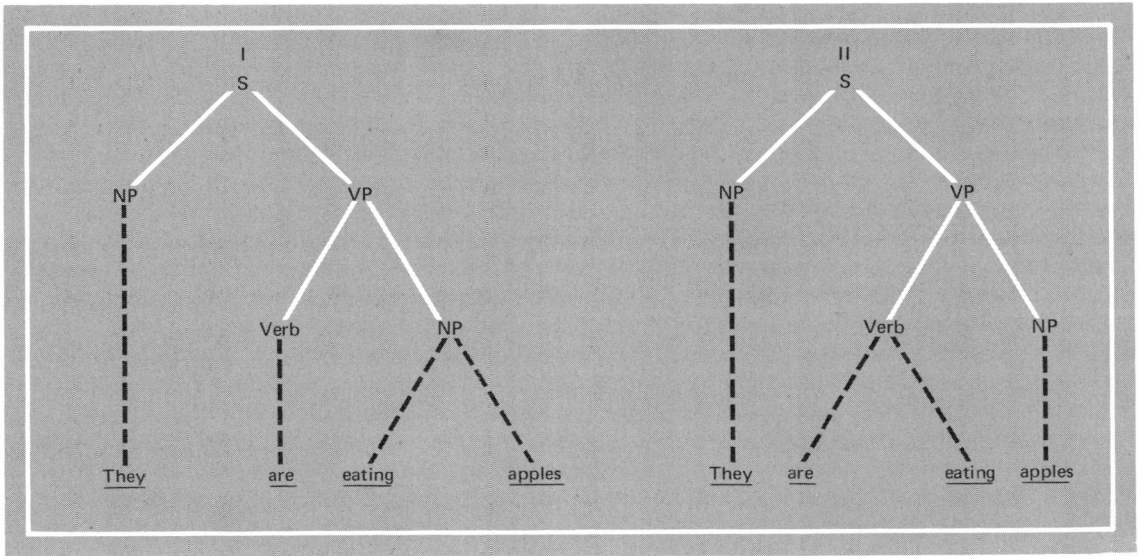

FIGURE 14-4. *Two alternative phrase markers for an ambiguous sentence. The sentence, "They are eating apples," has two possible derivations or phrase markers when a phrase-structure grammar is used to derive it. This corresponds nicely with the fact that the sentence has two semantic interpretations, i.e., it is semantically ambiguous.*

what correlated with constitutent boundaries, cannot account for the click displacement. These results and others (see Garrett and Fodor, 1968) suggest that subjects are in a sense analyzing the constituent structure while they are listening to sentences.

Riegle (1969) has recently presented some convincing evidence for the psychological validity of the phrase-structure rule system. His materials consisted of eight-letter consonant strings, e.g., FDZHMKWR. It is possible to set up a tree diagram corresponding to a set of phrase-structure rules that would generate such eight-letter sequences. Figure 14-5 shows such a diagram with the various nodes labeled from 1 to 7, the final output being FDZHMKWR. Note, however, that the phrase-structure diagram seems to provide for a grouping of the elements into three major constituents: FD ZHM KWR. Next, Riegle devised a set of "permutation rules"

which reverse the order of the elements within a particular constituent. Rule 1 is applied at node one reversing the order of the two constituents below that node. Thus, applying Rule 1 to the original sequence FDZHMKWR results in DFZHMKWR. Similarly, Rule 6 would result in FDKWRZHM. With seven nodes in the diagram, there are seven rules for permutation which are illustrated in Figure 14-5. It may be noted here that the permutation rules may be viewed as transformational rules which we will discuss later.

The subjects were required to learn the permutation rules based on phrase-structure rules that segment the sequence on a 2-3-3 basis, i.e., the first two letters (FD) form one segment, the next three form another (ZHM), and the last three form a third (KWR). However, 2-3-3 is not the only basis for segmenting the sequence, although it is the only basis that would correspond to the above tree dia-

Language: A System for Thinking 319

FIGURE 14–5. Tree diagram, permutation rules, and resulting materials used in a study on the validity of phrase-structure grammar.

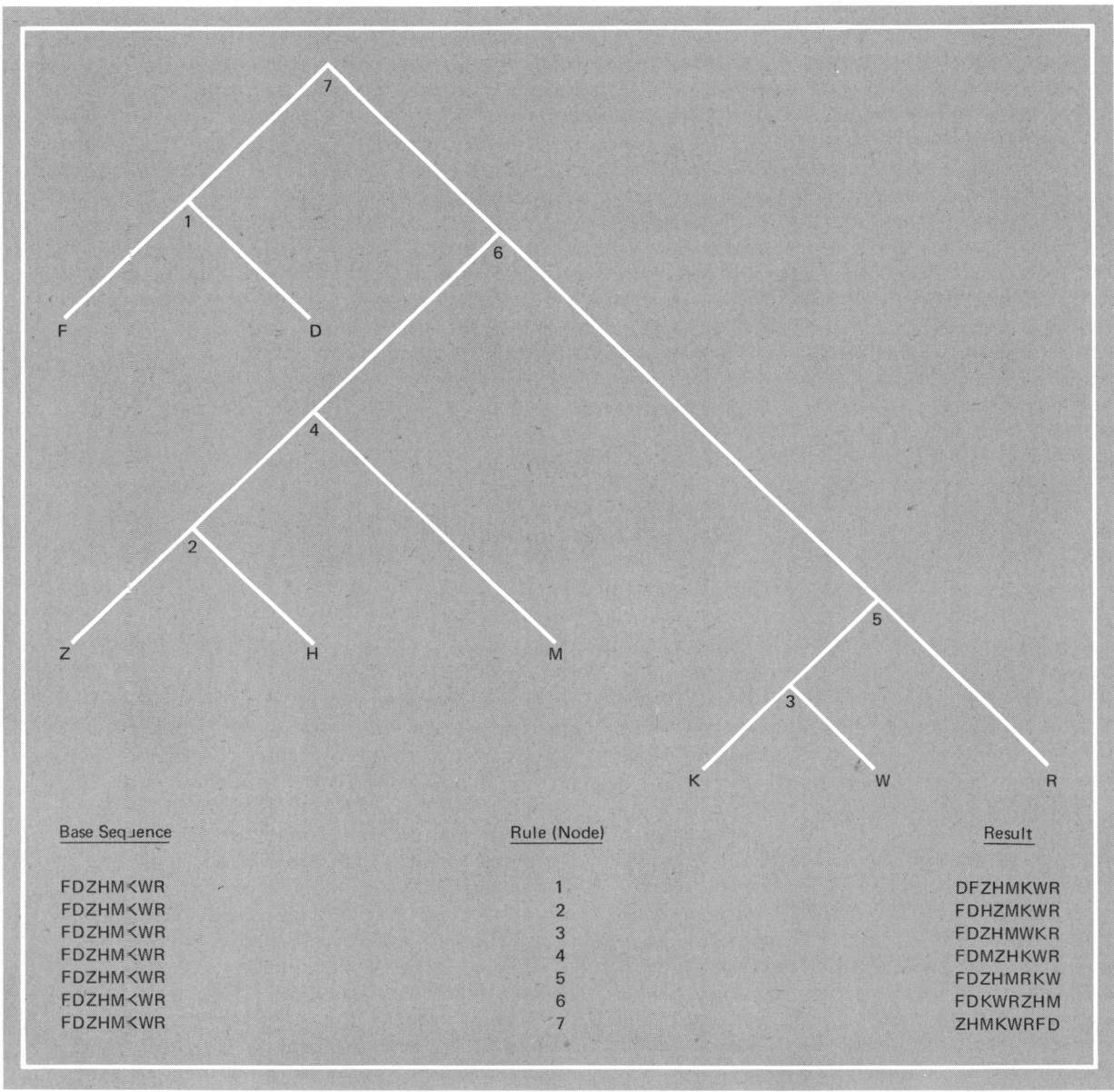

Source: Redrawn from E. M. Riegle, Some perceptual characteristics of phrase structure rule learning. Unpublished doctoral dissertation, University of Minnesota, 1969.

gram. Other possible bases for segmentation are 3-3-2 corresponding to FDZ HMK WR or 2-2-2-2 corresponding to FD ZH MK WR. Of course, numerous other bases are possible, but note that only the 2-3-3 segmentation corresponds to the tree diagram in Figure 14-5. In presenting the material visually, we can let spaces between segments represent breaks between constituents. Thus, Riegle can define a "facilitation" condition in which the sequences are presented to the subject parsed or spaced according to the tree diagram which is used to define the permutation rules the subjects will have to apply to the sequence. A facilitation subject would see FD ZHM KWR. Alternatively, Riegle devised an "interference" condition where the spacing did not correspond to the constituents of the intended tree diagram. He used a 3-3-2 grouping as opposed to the 2-3-3 grouping resulting from the phrase-structure rules. An interference subject would be shown the following: FDZ HMK WR. Finally, a third condition, "unparsed," was shown the sequences with no spacing between letters, FDZHMKWR.

The subject was shown a sequence (either with facilitation spacing, interference spacing, or no spacing) followed by a number indicating the permutation rule, and then he was required to respond with the sequence that would result from application of that rule. This was followed by presenting him with the correctly permuted sequence, always in unparsed form. Of course, at the beginning of learning, the subjects did not have any idea of what the rule numbers meant. The prediction was that learning the rules would be easier if the subjects saw the spacing that corresponded to the segments from the tree diagram that was used to determine the rules. The results strongly supported the hypothesis. After nine trials the subjects in the facilitation condition were able to employ an average of 6.4 of the 7 rules correctly, whereas subjects in the interference condition could only use 2.5 of the rules correctly. The unparsed condition fell in between with a mean of 3.9 rules correctly performed.

Two additional experiments supported the idea that it is not the visual spacing that is important but the auditory input. For example, the results were the same when all subjects saw unparsed sequences but were trained to read them aloud with pauses which grouped letters on a 2-3-3 basis (facilitation) as opposed to a 3-3-2 basis (interference). The same results also obtained when the sequences were read to the subject by an experimenter using either the 2-3-3 or 3-3-2 grouping. It also seems quite clear that the subjects were learning rules rather than memorizing a particular response to the combined stimulus of a sequence and rule number. Subjects could readily apply the acquired rules to a new sequence of letters they had never seen before. The results are thus a clear example of "rule-governed behavior" as well as a demonstration of the psychological validity of phrase structure.

Finally, as evidence for the psychological validity of phrase-structure rules, consider some data collected by Johnson (1965). He asked subjects to learn paired-associate lists with single digits as stimulus terms and complete sentences as response terms. Some of the sentences were "two-phrase" sentences and others were "three-phrase" sentences, but the number of words was the same in both types. An example of each type is presented in Figure 14-6.

Johnson was interested in the kinds of errors subjects would make while learning the response sentences, specifically transition errors. A *transition error* is defined as a response with a correct word followed by an incorrect word. For the first sentence in Figure 14-6, a response of *The tall man saved the dying dog* would mean that a transition error was made in going from *tall* to *boy* and from *dying* to *woman*. With seven-word sentences, there are six places where a transition error could take place. The question Johnson asked was whether or not the probability of a transition error varied across the six positions and between the two types of sentences. The results showed clearly that errors were

FIGURE 14–6. *Tree diagrams for the "two-phrase" and "three-phrase" sentences used by Johnson.*

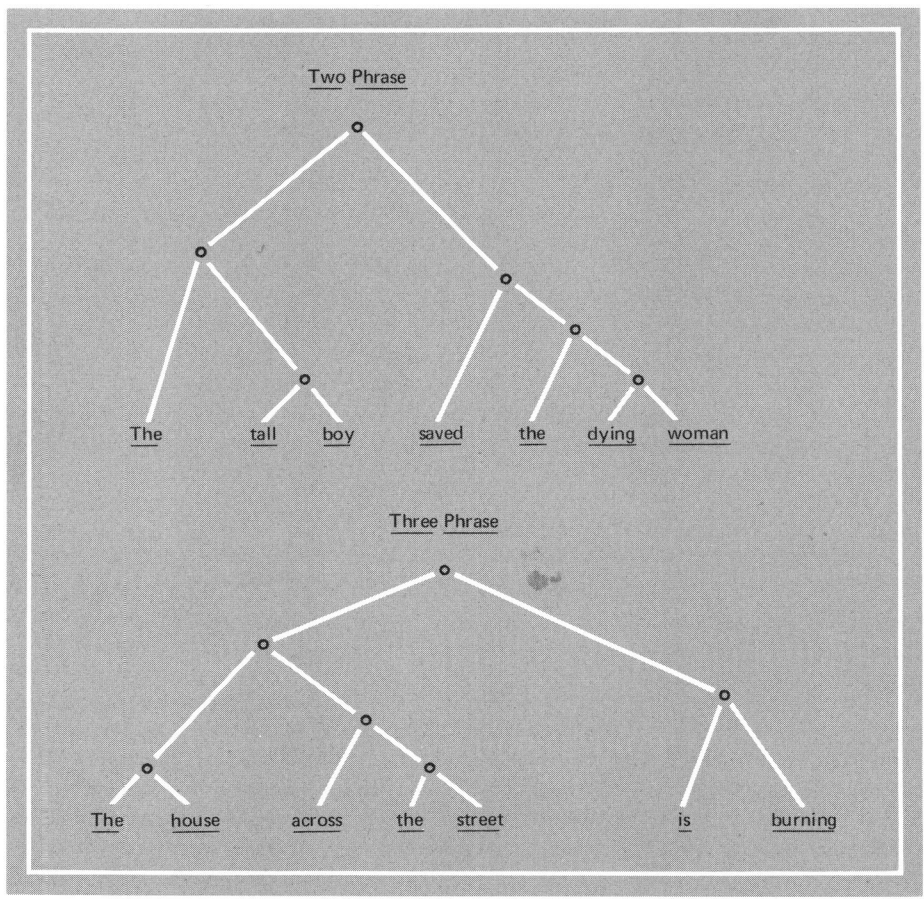

Source: Redrawn from N. F. Johnson, Linguistic models and functional units of language behavior. In S. Rosenberg, ed., *Directions in Psycholinguistics.* New York: Macmillan, 1965.

not equally likely at the six positions and that the pattern of errors was different for the two types of sentences. Thus, in the first sentence, the highest error rate occurred between *boy* and *saved* (the third position), whereas in the second sentence the highest error rates occurred between *house* and *across* and between *street* and *is*. You can see that these positions represent transitions between major constituents of these sentences (e.g., the *boy-saved* break is a break between NP and VP). The overall error patterns were remarkably in accord with the constituent structures of the sentences, suggesting that the subjects were learning the sentences by learning the major constituents and then organizing these into the entire sentence. In other words, the error data indicate that the subjects were learning units larger than a single word and these units correspond rather strikingly with the constituents deduced from a phrase-structure analysis of the sentences. Again, a finite-state grammar would seem incapable of predicting such behavior since such grammars would suggest a word-by-word learning process without any particular grouping of sets of words into larger units.

In summary, the data leave little doubt about the psychological validity of phrase-structure rules in contrast to finite-state systems. Phrase-structure grammars assign a structural description to every sentence, making possible: (1) detailed comparisons of the similarities between sentences, (2) analyses of the relationships among various constitutents within a single sentence, and (3) explanations of sentence ambiguity. Besides all of these linguistic advantages, phrase-structure grammars seem to correspond to psychological data on sentence perception and learning more accurately than finite-state grammars.

Transformational Grammar. However reasonable the phrase-structure grammars appear to be, they fail to capture all of the distinctions we need to describe the entire syntactic system. In 1957, Chomsky argued persuasively that phrase-structure rules must be supplemented by transformational rules. Both transformational and phrase-structure rules are rewrite rules, but the former rewrite entire strings of symbols, while the latter rewrite only single symbols. Some transformational rules are optional, but phrase-structure rules must be applied whenever they can be. Finally, the appropriateness of a transformational rule depends on the structure of the string of symbols to which it might be applied, whereas phrase-structure rules are automatically applied to a symbol regardless of the structure of the string that contains the symbol.

To illustrate transformational rules, consider the set of sentences presented in Table 14-2. It seems clear that these sentences are related to each other in a very definite way, but a way which is not revealed by phrase-structure descriptions. Transformational grammar suggests that the sentences are related because they represent the results of applying various transformational rules to a single underlying string, known as the kernel string. For example, the passive transformation (P) is a rule that rewrites the kernel string: *The mechanic fixed my car* as *My car was fixed by the mechanic*. The appropriateness of the rule depends on the structure of the string to which it is applied; if a sentence is already written in passive voice, then the passive transformation cannot be applied. The passive transformation is optional—when a string is of the kernel variety where a passive transformation could be applied, the grammar does not *require* the transformation. Two other transformations, the negative (N) and the question (Q), are also illustrated in Table 14-2. The entire set of eight sentences has

TABLE 14–2. *P,N,Q Sentence Family*

Sentence	Transformations Applied
The mechanic fixed my car.	Kernel
My car was fixed by the mechanic.	Passive (P)
The mechanic did not fix my car.	Negative (N)
Did the mechanic fix my car?	Question (Q)
My car was not fixed by the mechanic.	P + N
Was my car fixed by the mechanic?	P + Q
Didn't the mechanic fix my car?	N + Q
Wasn't my car fixed by the mechanic?	P + N + Q

been called a P,N,Q sentence family (Clifton and Odom, 1966), for it consists of all possible combinations of the three transformations. Each of these three transformations rewrites a single string as another single string and for this reason they are known as *singulary transformations*. In contrast, *generalized transformations* rewrite two or more strings as a single string: *The mechanic fixed my car, My car is blue*, and *The mechanic is old* can be rewritten as *The old mechanic fixed my blue car*.

In order to understand the necessity for transformational rules, consider the important distinction made by Chomsky between surface and deep structure in grammar. Examine the following sentences:

(1) The theorem was proved by induction.
(2) The theorem was proved by John.

The *surface structures* of these two sentences are identical, which is to say that they can be analyzed into the same set of constituents. Note, however, that the relationship among the constituents is different for these sentences. For example, we can change (2) into *John proved the theorem*, but an analogous change in (1) results in the incorrect utterance, *Induction proved the theorem*. On the surface, these sentences are identical, but the surface is deceiving, because syntactically they are clearly not identical. Since the phrase-structure descriptions are the same for these two sentences, such descriptions do not adequately characterize the difference in syntax that we know is there. To describe the difference, we must imagine an underlying structure, the *deep structure*. We might imagine the following deep structure for (1) and (2), respectively:

(3) Someone proved the theorem by induction.
(4) John proved the theorem.

If we look at the phrase structure of (3) and (4) we see that indeed they are slightly different. In Chomsky's theory, the phrase-structure rules are moved to the level of deep structure, to produce the underlying sentences (more accurately speaking, they produce the strings that underlie the surface sentence). Phrase-structure rules generate the tree diagrams or P-markers of the underlying strings (the underlying P-marker). Now, in order to get from (3) to the surface sentence (1) and from (4) to (2), a new set of rules will be required, the transformational rules.

The transformational rules operate on the output of the phrase-structure rules (the underlying P-marker) to transform the underlying structure into the surface structure (the derived P-marker). Thus, a passive transformation would be applied to (4) to produce (2), and a passive followed by a deletion transformation would be applied to (3) to produce (1). That is, (3) would be changed first to *The theorem was proved by induction by someone* and then by deletion of the underlying subject to (1). Actually, the entire process takes place below the surface, the utterance not being complete until after application of morphophonemic rules that change the string of morphemes into a string of phonemes which constitute the actual utterance.

Transformational grammars have caused a revolution in linguistics and have had great impact on psycholinguistics. Furthermore, the transformational theorists, led by Chomsky, have pointed out the immense difficulties that modern theories of learning based on S-R associationism will have in accounting for language phenomena. You can get a good idea of these difficulties by reading Chomsky's review (Chomsky, 1959) of Skinner's book, *Verbal Behavior* (Skinner, 1957). The argument has been presented so persuasively by the linguists that many psychologists now feel that association models must be discounted. It now seems quite possible that transformational grammar theory may precipitate a revolution in experimental psychology as well.

An immense amount of work is still being done to refine the details of transformational grammar. The field is moving so rapidly that early versions of the theory are now out of date, and it is difficult to keep pace. For example, originally the passive transformation was a so-called optional transformation that was applied to the output of the phrase-structure rules. In more recent versions of the theory (Chomsky, 1965), the phrase-structure output specifies (requires) the passive form in the underlying, deep structure—the idea of some transformational rules being optional is being questioned. Thus, the deep structures of (1) and (2) would be more like:

(1′) Someone proved the theorem by induction —passive

(2′) John proved the theorem—passive

Remember that the deep structure forms, the underlying strings, are not in fact sentences. The underlying, terminal strings are more closely characterized as a set of explicit instructions for producing particular sentences.

It seems clear that sentences such as (1) and (2) are not identical in grammatical form and the phrase-structure rules alone cannot capture the difference, without the aid of transformational rules and the surface-deep structure distinction. The question remains, however, as to whether there is any psychological significance to the concept of deep structure. It might appear that, behaviorally, sentences such as (1) and (2) could be treated identically in every respect. The deep-structure distinction could be a difference that is important to linguists but has no manifestation in performance. If deep structure is a necessary component of a description of competence, however, we would certainly bet that it is important to the speaker and listener.

Consider some additional examples on resolving the ambiguity of sentences. Phrase-structure grammars are capable of explaining or resolving ambiguity in some sentences, and this is not possible with finite-state grammars. Now, it can also be shown that certain types of ambiguity are impossible to resolve through phrase-structure descriptions alone. For a now classic example, take the phrase, *The shooting of the hunters,* as in the sentence, *The shooting of the hunters was terrible.* We are not sure whether the hunters possessed poor shooting ability or somebody shot some hunters. And phrase-structure is of no help here because the P-marker is the same regardless of which meaning was intended.

However, transformational grammar will elucidate the difference as in Figure 14-7. A transformation (T_1) is available that converts *Lions growl* into *The growling of lions.* A second transformation (T_2) operates on sentences such as *They raise flowers* and results in the phrase *The raising of flowers.* When we consider *The shooting of the hunters,* we see that this could be the result of either one of two operations: (1) the application of T_1 to *The hunters shoot* or (2) the application of T_2 to *They shoot the hunters.* *The growling of lions* and *The raising of flowers* are not ambiguous because we do not have deep-structure forms such as *They growl lions* and *Flowers raise.* Thus, the ambiguity is not resolved at the surface but only when we examine the deep structure underlying an utterance. Deep-structure analysis surely plays a role in the interpretation of ambiguous utterances.

Experimental evidence that deep structure plays a role in performance is beginning to accumulate. Mehler and Carey (1967) asked subjects to recognize sentences that were played in noise. Using a procedure like that of Luchins in his water-jar experiments (see Chapter 6), Mehler and Carey attempted to produce a "syntactic set" in their subjects for a particular underlying structure. The subject heard ten set-inducing sentences with the same deep structure followed by a test sentence with a different underlying structure. The surface structures of the set-inducing and test sentences were identical. The notion was that the first ten sentences would induce a deep-structure set in the subjects which would make it difficult for them to hear the test sentence correctly. The results showed some support for the hypothesis. When the test sentence, *They are troublesome to employ,* followed ten sentences all with the structure of *They are hesitant to travel,* subjects made significantly more errors on the word *trouble-*

FIGURE 14–7. *An illustration of ambiguity that is not explained by phrase-structure rules alone. It is only after a consideration of deep structure and transformational history of a sentence that the ambiguity is resolved.*

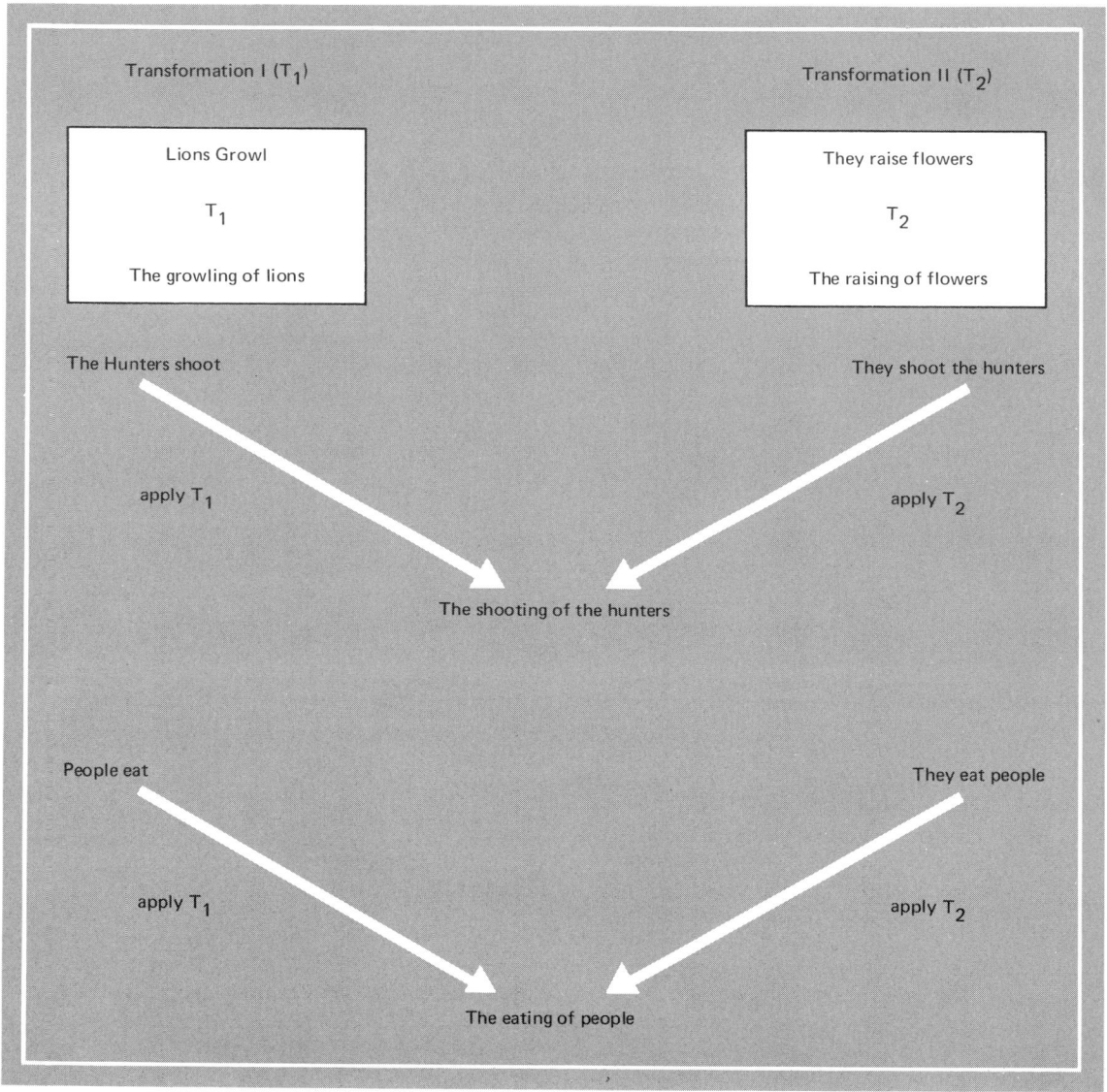

some than did control subjects. A second set of sentences, however, failed to produce a significant effect, mainly because the control scores were so low that it would have been difficult for the set effect to decrease recognition significantly further. Overall, the results were not terribly impressive. Mehler and Carey did find a rather substantial effect when both the surface and deep structure changed between the set-inducing and test sentences, suggesting a strong effect of surface structure on sentence recognition.

Blumenthal (1967) has done an experiment on cued recall of sentences that provides support for the psychological validity of deep structure. He used two types of sentences differing in deep structure as in sentences (1) and (2) above. The sentence, *Gloves were made by tailors,* is a standard passive sentence where the "by-phrase" designates the agent (*tailors*) of the action, and the underlying string is something like *Tailors made gloves—passive*. In the second type of sentence, the agent by-phrase was replaced with an adverbial by-phrase to yield what Blumenthal called the *replaced-agent passive*. An example of a replaced-agent passive would be *Gloves were made by hand,* where the underlying form is something like *Someone made gloves by hand—passive*. A list of ten standard or ten replaced-agent passive sentences (mixed with 15 filler sentences) was read three times to a subject. On the test for recall, a word from the sentence was given as a prompt or cue and the subject had to reproduce the entire sentence. Two types of prompt words were used, either the final noun (*tailors* or *hand*) in the sentence or the initial noun (*gloves*). The critical comparison is between recall of the two kinds of sentences with the final noun prompt. On the level of surface structure it should make no difference whether the cue for recall is the word *tailors* in the standard passive or the word *hand* in the replaced-agent passive, so that the two types of passive sentences should be recalled equally well. However, at the level of deep structure, *tailors* seems to be a much better cue for *Tailors made gloves* than *hand* seems for *Someone made gloves by hand*. The results supported this intuitive hypothesis; when the final noun was the prompt word, recall of the standard sentences was superior to recall of the replaced-agent sentences. Standard and replaced-agent recall did not differ when the initial noun was the prompt word. Blumenthal and Boakes (1967) have replicated these results with somewhat more carefully controlled materials, the results again supporting the notion that the most effective prompt word will depend on the deep structure rather than the surface structure.

Comment. It should be clear from the above discussion that grammar, both morphology and syntax, is obviously a generative system based on rules. That is to say that the acquisition of language depends crucially on the learner's discovering the systematic, structured nature of the utterances he hears. And he makes these discoveries despite the fact that a very substantial proportion of the utterances he hears does not conform to the rules. In other words, rule learning is a basic part of language acquisition, and until psychological theories can give an adequate account of rule learning we can expect them to provide inadequate accounts of language learning.

In earlier chapters, we have emphasized the basic nature of concept formation in thinking. Language acquisition must be at least partly a matter of concept formation, involving the discovery of relevant attributes and the abstraction of rules for combining attributes in prescribed ways. The child learning a language is much like a subject in a concept-formation experiment employing the reception paradigm. He hears many instances of the concept and on the basis of this information he identifies the relevant attributes and learns the rules. Certainly, the basic research on concept formation should provide a firm theoretical basis for the understanding of language learning.

The persistent criticism of the linguists who have forced the recognition of the generative nature of language has highlighted the role that thinking plays in linguistic performance. The inadequacies of finite-state grammars make it painfully clear that presently available stimulus-response learning theory contributes little to our understanding of language learning. The emphasis on phrase-structure grammars supplemented with transformational constructs makes linguistic performance appear to be a monumental achievement that is only possible because humans can think and behave in ways that are perhaps impossible for other animals. We can expect, then, that psychological theories of language performance will rely more and more on the cognitive skills possessed by humans and less and less on classical and operant conditioning, reinforcement, and the basic notion of an S-R association. We have seen earlier that even relatively simple verbal-learning tasks require, for understanding, that we consider the cognitive skills of the subjects. In comparison, the thinking that must be involved in linguistic performance seems enormously complex. Uttering a novel grammatical sentence just cannot be explained as the result of a series of S-R connections. It is the product of the cognitive structure and abilities of human beings—it is a most impressive display of thinking. "Speech is the best show man puts on. It is his own 'act' on the stage of evolution, in which he comes before the cosmic backdrop and really 'does his stuff'" (Whorf, 1956, p. 249).

SEMANTICS

In this section we turn to the most important yet least understood component of language: meaning, the study of which is known as semantics. Meaning is at the heart of the basic linguistic functions, coding and communicating. Meaning is what languages are all about. Knowing how to pronounce all the words of a foreign language and knowing the rules for generating grammatical sentences is totally inconsequential if one does not know what the words and sentences mean. Our discussion of semantics will unfortunately, yet necessarily, be brief, for progress in this area seems to be minimal. We hope only to present some of the current psychological analyses and some of the difficulties with each.

It seems clear at the outset, though there have been arguments to the contrary, that the meaning of a word is not specifiable in physical terms, i.e., in terms of sounds or visual patterns. Meaning is learned, a product of human experience. As such, it is a behavioral concept, involving primarily a person's knowledge of the functions and uses of his circumstances, including words. The details of how meaning is best conceived, psychologically, are a subject of some dispute. We shall consider first several possibilities which emphasize the performance or response aspects of meaning.

Meaning as a Response to a Referent Stimulus

Some psychologists have reduced the problem of meaning to one of reference. Words are said to have meaning when they refer to experience, either experience in the real world or in the content of thought. Meaning is thus a sign process—words are signs of their referents. The semantic system is a sign system.

Carroll (1964) lists three basic features of all sign systems. First, they consist of a finite number of discrete signs, sounds, and sound combinations (morphemes). Second, and most important, the signs serve a referential function; i.e., each sign refers to something other than itself. For example, the word *table* is said to refer to a class of objects, a concept. Thus, words are often labels for concepts that have been acquired by the speaker. Some problems arise in this connection. What about the word *table* in utterances such as, *He wants to table the motion.* This use of the term refers neither to a specific object nor to the general class. Consider words such as *loyalty, happiness, democracy,* and *love*. It is difficult to think of objective referents for such abstract words. One is then forced to define a referent in a rather loose manner to include not only physical objects, but also subjective states, events, and relationships between referents. The third feature of sign systems is that signs are arbitrarily paired with the referents, although all speakers of the same language must agree on the same arbitrary assignments. Thus, the class of objects which we call *tables* could logically have been labeled *chairs* and the chairs could have been called *windows*.

Accepting the sign process, where one stimulus refers to or stands for another stimulus, as basic, some theorists have argued that meaning derives from the fact that a word comes to elicit responses which are closely related to the responses elicited by its object referent. If a word elicited exactly the same responses as its referent, the word obviously would be a very good substitute for the object. At first glance this seems to be exactly what is needed since we want to talk, read, write, and hear about things that are not physically present. So, many psychologists have concentrated on understanding how the responses toward an object are related to the responses toward the sign of that object, the word.

First, consider *meaning as a simple conditioned response*. Here the object serves as an unconditioned stimulus (UCS) eliciting some kind of unconditioned response (UCR) in the observer of that object. For example, a snake (UCS) might elicit UCRs of turning, running, yelling, and a "fear response" in the autonomic nervous system. Assuming the presence of a "teacher" who is not screaming and is not so scared that he cannot name the observed object, the word *snake* would be contiguously paired with the object snake. We thus have a standard classical conditioning paradigm. The principles of classical conditioning then tell us that eventually we can expect the word *snake* to elicit the UCR responses at which point they are called conditioned responses (CRs). The word *snake* has become a substitute for the real thing, and the meaning of the word *snake* consists of these CRs. In other words, meaning is viewed as a CR—the learner reacts to the word as he would toward the real object. Note that this view assumes what is called a *stimulus-substitution description* of classical conditioning in that the CR is assumed to be an exact replica of the UCR. It is this assumption that makes this view of meaning so unbelievable. If it were true, a great many readers would have been screaming and filled with fear when they encountered (read) the word *snake* several times in this paragraph. It is patently obvious that people do not behave toward the word *snake* in the same manner that they might behave had they really seen a snake.

This view is based on the idea that a CR is identical to the UCR. However, it is now generally believed, even in simple classical conditioning, that the CR is not a replica of the UCR (Kimble, 1961). Two alternative views of the CR have been suggested: (1) the CR is a fractional part of the UCR, or (2) the CR is a response designed to prepare the subject for the occurrence of the UCS. Both of these conceptions of the relationship between CR and UCR have their counterparts in psychological interpretations of the semantic process.

Osgood (1952, 1953) has suggested that meaning is a *fractional implicit conditioned response* (r_m), a mediational response. Two modifications of the simple conditioning notion described above are involved. First, it is clear that responses to the word are not identical to responses to the object. Some of the responses typically elicited by the object just cannot occur if the object is not present. Food may elicit salivation, chewing, and swallowing, but the word *food* cannot be chewed or swallowed. Those responses that can occur without the object's being present (e.g., salivation) are called detachable responses, and it is these responses that get conditioned to the CS word. The second modification is that in Osgood's theory, the responses which carry meaning are implicit, which seems to be a logical necessity for any performance-oriented theory of meaning.

Presumably, the fractional responses become smaller and less observable with repeated exposures so that eventually they have been reduced to the minimal response that is discriminable from the responses to other words. Thus, the r_m's become unobservable, implicit responses that can serve as stimuli for additional, perhaps overt, responses.

There is a reasonable amount of evidence consistent with the mediational conditioning model of the Osgood variety, but the evidence is largely confined to laboratory situations with individual words employed in an often nonlinguistic manner (see Staats, 1968). For example, pairing the CS *large* with the UCS of shock which elicits a galvanic skin response (GSR) as a UCR, results in the word *large* eliciting a GSR. Furthermore, ratings of the pleasantness of the word *large* are affected by this aversive conditioning and generalization will occur to other words not physically, but semantically similar to *large* (e.g., *big*). As we have seen earlier, this is known as semantic generalization, and semantic generalization does seem to be adequately covered by the postulation of the implicit mediating response suggested by Osgood. *Large* and *big* are synonyms because they elicit essentially the same implicit response pattern. Conditioning the GSR to the implicit responses of *large* is practically the same as conditioning the GSR to the implicit responses of *big*. Subsequent presentation of *big* will elicit the mediating response pattern which in turn will elicit the GSR.

It is not surprising that the evidence suggests that words can serve as conditioned stimuli. Flashing a word on a screen ought to be just as good as flashing a light or ringing a bell. The real question, however, is not whether words *can* serve as conditioned stimuli, but whether they *do* serve as conditioned stimuli in linguistic situations. No one has satisfactorily demonstrated that they do.

Finally, consider *meaning as a preparatory response*. This position is closely related to the conception of the CR as a response that prepares the subject for the presentation of the UCS (Zener, 1937). Thus, the conditioned salivation to a bell prepares the dog's mouth for the forthcoming food. Moreover, the dog approaches the food pan and appears to be expecting the food, not eating an imaginary food. One might say the dog gets *set* to eat or is now disposed to eat. In semantics, this notion is translated into a view of meaning as a *disposition to behave* (Morris, 1946; Brown, 1958). The bell has "meaning" for the dog because it prepares or disposes or sets him to behave in particular ways, namely, to eat. Words have meanings to the extent that they *dispose* someone to behave in a manner that is relevant to the objects being symbolized by the words. The problem then becomes one of specifying the nature of dispositions and this is not without a great deal of vagueness. Did the word *snake* which you read several times earlier dispose you to behave as if a real snake were present or forthcoming? Were you prepared to run or set to scream? Probably not. Again, no one has yet shown that words serve as conditioned stimuli when they are heard in a conversation or read in a book.

We have examined three positions on meaning, each with a different view of the classical conditioning process: (a) stimulus substitution where the CR is presumed to be identical to the UCR; (b) fractional responding, where the CR is viewed as a fraction of the UCR; and (c) preparatory responding, where the CR is viewed as a response designed to prepare the organism for the forthcoming UCS. While it is reasonable to treat meaning as a behavioral phenomenon, all three of these views seem inadequate, mainly because they are predicated on the orthodox, but impoverished, concept of behavior as performance or response. This compels convoluted and unconvincing assertions about the locus of meaning in bodily movements, or their hidden analogues. We have argued for a descriptive system which admits intention, competence, and skill as parameters of behavior. The meaning of anything, including words, seems to lie more naturally in what a person knows about it and knows how to do with it.

Meaning, Understanding, and Knowledge

An alternative to the response-oriented position, that introduces a formal competence feature, has been given by Katz and Fodor (1963). The fluent speaker can understand an infinite number of sentences he has never heard. He can, moreover, generate an infinite number of sentences that will be understood by others. According to Katz and Fodor, the basic fact to be explained by a semantic theory is that the competent speaker can comprehend a sentence in terms of its parts (the individual words) and the manner in which the principles of grammar combine those parts. This sounds very much like attributes and rules again.

What constitutes the knowledge component of this behavior? According to Katz and Fodor, two ingredients are necessary. First, the speaker must have the analogue of a dictionary of the words in the language and, second, he must know some rules (called *projection rules* by Katz and Fodor) for deriving the meaning of a sentence from the meanings of the constituent items and the nature of the grammatical structure of the sentence (the order of combination of the constituents). Knowing only the meanings of the individual words and the exact grammatical structure of the sentence is not sufficient information for understanding many sentences. The grammar may tag a word as a noun and the dictionary may have only one meaning of that word—in such cases the projection rule is simple. But very often this is not the case; the dictionary will have more than one meaning for a word with the same form class. The semantic projection rules take account of the relationships between different words in a sentence, and they analyze the relationship between the grammar and the individual word meanings to result finally in a semantic interpretation of the entire sentence.

When we speak of the dictionary component of semantic knowledge we are suggesting that the speaker has acquired a large number of concepts and their linguistic codes. The concept-learning process, as we have seen, consists basically of learning the relevant attributes and the rules for combining them. The label that is learned for a concept then serves as a sign for those attributes and rules. In communication, the label succinctly conveys information about the attributes and rules that would be extremely cumbersome to convey in any other way. The encoding function of language also stems from the fact that words are concept labels. Experiences are categorized as instances of particular known concepts and are encoded by the concept label. But the most powerful aspect of language is not in words as concept labels, but in words in combinations that can express meanings for which individual labels are not available. If one wants to write an article or give a lecture on *the joy of living,* he is not really hampered by the fact that English does not have a single word to express this. Language X may have such a word, *xuthia,* which means something that has to be expressed in a four-word construction in English, but the speaker of Language X has little advantage over the speaker of English, thanks to the constructive power of language. A knowledge of the projection rules of a language is, of course, basic to this ability to construct and understand new meanings by combinations of lexical items. The projection rules determine the meaning by specifying the relationships between words and the relationships between grammatical structure and the individual word meanings. Without these rules, the meaning of a sentence would just be the sum of the meanings of the individual words and this is very seldom the case.

Comment. Words, singly and in combination, code the objects, events, processes, and states of affairs that constitute a person's circumstances. We use the code for describing, communicating, or otherwise dealing with these circumstances. It seems to us that the various uses, both actual and possible, by a person of a particular utterance constitute the quantitative and qualitative aspects of the meaning of that utterance for that person. This argument gives rise naturally to many other, seemingly disparate, definitions and measures of meaning (or meaningfulness) that have been suggested by psychologists over the years. What a person thinks about or associates in response to a particular linguistic item, its associative value (e.g., Archer, 1960), is a commonly adopted measure of its degree of meaning. We would conceive of these associates as representing different behavioral functions or uses of the item. The relation of an item to other scalar terms representing certain fundamental dimensions has been used to locate that item in semantic space (Osgood, 1957). We think of the place of an item on semantic dimensions as primarily a matter of how the item, or what it codes, can be or is primarily used.

Rather than identify these uses of linguistic items strictly with performance aspects of behavior, we think of them as largely a matter of knowledge and skill. To the extent that a person knows facts about an item and how to make use of those facts, the item has meaning. A meaning is most directly exhibited when in fact an item is used in a recognizably sensible way. But the meaning exists even when the item is used in a different sense or not used at all. And this is the cash value of saying the meaning belongs as much in the competence parameters as it does in the performance parameters of behavior.

THE DEVELOPMENT OF LANGUAGE

The acquisition of language by a child represents one of the most remarkable achievements of man. The complexity of the language system is so great that it still lacks an adequate description. And yet, there is evidence that a child learns the basic system in as little as 30 months' time. It is not until the age of approximately 18 months that the child begins to utter more than one word at a time; nevertheless, by the age of four years, the child can utter sentences of every known grammatical type (e.g., Menyuk, 1963).

The Prelinguistic Phase

The overt vocalization of the infant, of course, begins at birth with the birth cry. During the first year of development, three stages can be identified (Ervin-Tripp, 1966): (1) a period of organically based sounds, (2) vocal play and babbling, and (3) imitative behavior and "intentional" speech. These three stages appear prior to the occurrence of the first words and are collectively called the prelinguistic phase.

The earliest sounds of the infant are cries and coos which seem to be organic in origin, connected with the physical needs of the infant and satisfaction of these needs. Somewhere around three to four months, the babbling stage begins to appear with the vocalizations sounding more like adult speech. It has been maintained that all phonemes, including phonemes that do not occur in English, are produced by the child in this stage. At least, sounds which can be classified by trained phoneticians as instances of the various phonemes have been recorded (Osgood, 1953). A real question can be raised, however, about whether these early sounds are in any psychological sense actually instances of phoneme concepts. In any case, such observations lead naturally to the position that the infant is capable of making and does make all the sounds of any language. His experience with the language of his own community then shapes his phonemic repertoire, extinguishing the sounds that do not occur in the language and strengthening the sounds that do occur. However, some of the sounds of the adult languages are extremely rare occurrences in the babbling stage. A more accurate and conservative model based on general learning principles would suggest that the infant is capable of making any adult speech sound and that his language experience results in both acquisition of new sounds and extinction of others. Note, however, that this view treats the phoneme as a simple response subject to the laws of conditioning, which we have rejected on other grounds.

Babbling certainly seems to be organically based. Infants babble sounds that they have never heard in the speech of the parents, and furthermore, congenitally deaf children initially babble as much as hearing children, the deaf and hearing infants being indistinguishable in babbling for several months (Ervin-Tripp, 1966). There is not, however, universal agreement on the importance of the prelinguistic phase to the development of adult speech. As indicated above, one is tempted to say that the infant is learning and practicing the basic sounds that he will need for speech production. However, Fry (1966) suggests that babbling serves two general functions not specific to the learning of particular sounds: (1) the child is developing, in a very general way, control and knowledge of the effects of the motor systems involved in speech, and (2) the child is establishing feedback circuits linking the kinesthetic feedback from the muscular systems with the auditory sensations produced and heard by the child. It is the failure in this second aspect that distinguishes the deaf from the hearing child during this period. Carroll (1964) suggests that the sounds of babbling have "little bearing" on the phonemes the child will employ in his adult language. And Ervin-Tripp says that there is no known relationship between the vocalizations in the prelinguistic phase and the patterns of later linguistic behavior.

There is no doubt about there being a gradual shift in the nature and frequencies of the various phonemes as the child develops. Irwin (1948a) has presented frequency distributions of various phoneme classes for children ranging in age from newborn infants to 30 months. The distributions show clearly a shift in phoneme frequencies from one quite unlike adult frequencies to one rather similar to adult behavior by the age of 30 months. One might be tempted to apply the operant conditioning term of *shaping* to this shift behavior.

In the learning-theory tradition, the most often cited hypothesis about the basis for this early language learning was suggested by Mowrer in 1954. His theory asserts that infant vocalizations become increasingly similar to adult speech because adult speech is a secondary reinforcer. The adults speak to the child while they are satisfying the child's primary needs. This pairing of adult speech and primary need reduction is a paradigm of secondary reinforcement with the adult speech taking on reinforcing properties. The child in his babbling then is seen to shape his own speech, for production of an adult-like sound gets immediate secondary reinforcement. Babblings which do not sound like adult speech are presumably extinguished because of the lack of any such reinforcement. Note here that the emphasis is on the acquisition and extinction of individual responses. While Mowrer's hypothesis is an important one, no one has adequately demonstrated that language learning is based on reinforcement. There is very little evidence that these principles apply because appropriate tests are extremely difficult to implement.

Is the child learning individual responses as he acquires the phonemic system of the adult speaker? Earlier, we presented the notion that the system is best characterized as a set of binary distinctive features (Jakobson, Fant, and Halle, 1952). Working from distinctive-feature theory, one can suggest that the child is not learning individual phonemes as responses but rather is learning the distinctive features. The child may begin with a totally undifferentiated set of sounds and proceed by learning the features, one at a time. Each binary feature, when acquired, would result in a further differentiation of the sound system and a greater similarity of the speech to the adult model. When all the features had been learned, the child would presumably have acquired the adult phonemic system. Ervin-Tripp (1966) presents the findings of Shvachkin, a Russian investigator, who found substantial support for this analysis of phoneme development. Note that here the emphasis is on acquiring attributes and rules that constitute the knowledge and skills necessary for producing new responses rather than on learning the responses individually and directly.

First Words

Somewhere around 12 months of age, the child will utter his first word. There is reason to believe that he can understand simple words and commands by 10 to 11 months of age, but his first word utterance does not generally occur until he is one year old. There seems to be very little progress in word acquisition for the next six months, after which the child's vocabulary seems to grow at a very rapid rate. The results of one developmental study of vocabulary growth (Smith, 1926) are presented in Table 14-3. Carroll (1964) suggests that this rapid growth in vocabulary is due to the discovery by the child of the coding concept, that things have names. Carroll suggests that thinking begins to exert an influence on language development at this point, the development of the concept of *name* being related to the development of vocabulary.

The process of single-word acquisition seems most like those of simple learning based on classical and instrumental conditioning principles. In classical conditioning terms, the parent might say the word *dog* in the presence of a real dog. If the child imitates the parent, this will result in another contiguous pairing of the child's imitation with the stimulus object. On subsequent occasions, the real dog may then elicit the child's imitative response, thus constituting an instance of a naming response.

Even more important perhaps is the role of operant or instrumental conditioning in early word acquisition. Skinner (1957) has de-

TABLE 14-3. Vocabulary Growth

Age		Vocabulary Size
Years	Months	
0	8	0
0	10	1
1	0	3
1	3	19
1	6	22
1	9	118
2	0	272
2	6	446
3	0	896
3	6	1222
4	0	1540
4	6	1870
5	0	2072
5	6	2289
6	0	2562

Data from M. E. Smith, An investigation of the development of the sentence and the extent of vocabulary in young children, University of Iowa *Studies in Child Welfare*, 1926, *3*, No. 5.

scribed several ways in which speech acquisition might be viewed as a product of operant conditioning. For example, the tendency of children to imitate a parent, necessary to the classical conditioning of names, may be a result of the parents' providing social reinforcement (smiling, laughing, etc.) whenever the child reasonably imitates the parent. Skinner called these imitations *echoic responses*.

If a dog is present and the child emits an utterance that sounds anything like the word *dog,* the parent is likely to show approval (reinforcement) which increases the probability that the child will say something of a similar nature when the next dog appears. Skinner calls this approximation *shaping,* and the strength of naming as a response is considered important in the development of reporting the world or *tacting*.

The earliest words learned by a child are probably acquired as a result of the operations of classical and instrumental conditioning. Once the child has acquired the concept of name, however, there is a real question about the role of conditioning factors. The child now seems more accurately described as playing the *original word game* (Brown, 1958). In this "game" the child is actively trying to determine the attributes and rules of the concepts to which the names apply. He is receiving information from adult speakers about the correctness of his labels and is continually modifying the concepts in the light of this feedback. The child may learn the motor skills necessary to produce the label long before he has acquired the concept, as when the child calls the milkman "daddy." Being able to pronounce the adult labels soon becomes a trivial task for the child, while learning the concepts signified by the labels assumes the major portion of his efforts. In this context, the principles of conditioning seem less applicable.

Two-Word Utterances

Somewhere around the age of 18 months, two-word utterances begin to appear in the child's speech. It is this point, most psycholinguists feel, that marks the real beginning of language acquisition, most importantly the beginning of abstraction by the child of the structural properties of his language. It is at this point that we begin to see evidence of grammatical rules. There seems to be substantial agreement that the two-word utterances of children are like sentences, i.e., they have a describable grammar. Brown and Fraser (1963) provide an extensive discussion of these early utterances. They refer to the child's speech at this point as *telegraphic speech* because the child appears systematically to omit all but the most important words as if he were sending a telegram to the listener and didn't want to pay for a single unnecessary word. The child may say *more milk* and mean, *I would like some more milk*.

Three investigations (Braine, 1963a; Brown and Fraser, 1963; Miller and Ervin, 1964) have supported the idea that these utterances are constructed from two word classes that the child has developed. Consider the following utterances obtained by Braine from a boy not quite two years old:

allgone shoe	my mommy	byebye plane
allgone egg	my daddy	byebye man
allgone watch	my milk	byebye hot

Utterances such as these suggest to the psycholinguists that the child has developed two classes of words. Class I words are called *pivot words*. The pivot class is made up of a small number of words each of which occurs rather frequently in the child's speech but is almost always paired with a second word from the other class. This second class of words is called the *open class,* and it consists of a large number of words (mostly nouns) each of which occurs rather infrequently (compared to the pivot words) in the child's speech.

In the above examples, *allgone, my,* and *byebye* are the pivot words. The grammar of the child can be described by a rule which rewrites an utterance as pivot word plus an open-class word:

U ⟶ Pivot + Open
Pivot ⟶ allgone, my, byebye
Open ⟶ shoe, egg, watch, mommy, daddy, etc.

The child may also have a complementary grammar that has the open-class words in the initial position and the pivot words second. Thus, the earliest two-word utterances suggest that the child has developed response classes and is behaving according to a rule. As mentioned earlier, Jenkins and Palermo (1964) have argued that the development of response classes may be based on stimulus- and response-equivalence mediation. For example, if the child hears and produces the utterances *my mommy, my daddy,* and *my milk* and then subsequently hears *my dog*, response-equivalence principles suggest that *dog* will become associated with *mommy, daddy,* and *milk*; in essence, this might mean that dog would become a member of the open class. Once *dog* has been assimilated into the open class we might then expect, based on the rewrite rules above, such utterances as *allgone dog* and *byebye dog*. The simplicity of the mediational notion is appealing, but the complexity of even the earliest utterances suggests that we must be cautious before accepting this interpretation (see McNeill, 1968).

The stimulus- and response-equivalence paradigms can also be applied to the problem of word sequencing. Suppose the child had encountered the following utterances:

Mary is happy	Mary is happy
John is happy	Mary is sad
The coach is happy	Mary is quiet
Daddy is happy	Mary is sick

The sentences in the left-hand column may constitute a stimulus-equivalence situation which might result in the association (into a class) of *Mary, John, coach,* and *daddy*. Presumably, the words *John, coach,* and *daddy* would then be likely to occur in utterances that had contained the word *Mary* (those in the right-hand column). Thus, we might expect the child to be able to say such things as:

| John is sick | John is sad |
| Daddy is sick | The coach is quiet |

Similarly, the right-hand column is like a response-equivalence paradigm, establishing a class of associated words (*happy, sad, quiet, sick*). Thus *sad, quiet,* and *sick* might occur in places that *happy* had occurred (the left-hand column), again resulting in new sentences. Thus, the combined influence of stimulus and response equivalence could result in the production of novel utterances.

A somewhat similar notion about the acquisition of grammar has been presented by Braine (1963b). The basic proposition is that the child learns *locations of linguistic units* within larger linguistic constructions based on a principle called *contextual generalization*. If the child hears the sentence, *The angry coach was yelling at his players,* he notices that the noun phrase *The angry coach* occurs in the first part of the sentence (i.e., he learns the location of the phrase within a sentence). Contextual generalization (presumably quite similar to ordinary stimulus and response generalization) would result in this phrase's showing up in the initial position of some other utterance, e.g., *The angry coach was penalized by the referee*. According to Braine, there is a hierarchy of locations, so that that child learns the locations of morphemes within words, words within phrases, and phrases within sentences. This multiple-location learning would then result in the child's understanding (developing competence in) the hierarchical nature of the language.

This ability of Braine's theory to give an account of what might constitute competence is a crucial advantage his theory has over the mediational model of Jenkins and Palermo (see McNeill, 1968). Braine's model, however, suffers from some severe limitations. The order of the constituents of a sentence is extremely flexible, and it is thus difficult to see how a child could learn much about grammatical structure if he learned constituent positions and simple ordering rules. It seems that the underlying abstract, transformational nature of language is not adequately characterized by a theory based on generalization of constituent location at the surface level (see

Bever, Fodor, and Weksel, 1965). While Braine's proposal does describe competence, in contrast to Jenkins and Palermo's model, it does not appear to be sufficient to the task of accounting for the acquisition of abstract linguistic structure. But it is also not clear that the processes suggested by Braine are irrelevant to linguistic behavior; generalization may, in fact, play a crucial role in performance even though the speaker's knowledge cannot be completely described as resulting from a generalization process.

Process and Experience in the Development of Language

Brown (1965) has identified three processes in the acquisition of grammar. The first process is *imitation with reduction*. This refers to the behavior of beginning speakers who imitate a heard utterance but reduce it to its bare essentials, omitting everything but the basic content words. For example, one of Brown's subjects heard someone say, "It's not the same dog as Pepper," to which the child replied, "Dog Pepper." The reductions made by the child are quite systematic, tending to preserve the word order of the model being imitated, and omitting the function words and morphemes instead of the content words. The content words may be retained in the imitation because they are the most informative (convey the most information), but they may also be retained simply because they are the words that receive the most stress in speaking and are thus the words the child most likely heard. The reduction to telegraphic speech is not due to an immediate memory problem according to Brown, but rather to an inability to "program" or "plan" longer utterances. However, this does not explain the reduction phenomenon; it appears to be just a restatement of the fact that the child's imitation is not as long as the model sentence he is imitating. Furthermore, reduced memory capacity of children could be responsible for this inability to program long utterances.

The second process described by Brown is *imitation with expansion* by a listener. Brown's records of parent-child "conversations" show that very often the parent expands the child's telegraphic constructions, filling in the function words and morphemes. For example, one child said, "There go one" and his mother replied, "Yes, there goes one," her expansion adding the third person verb inflection. It would seem quite reasonable to suggest that this kind of feedback from the parents about the adequacy of an utterance is crucial for the development of grammatical competence. Many learning situations seem to be of this type where the learner attempts to perform appropriately after which the teacher provides feedback in the correct form.

Cazden, in an unpublished dissertation (see Ervin-Tripp, 1966), tried to demonstrate the effectiveness of expansion with children whose home environment was apparently deficient in parent-child conversations. For a three-month period, Cazden spent 40 minutes a day expanding every utterance of her subjects who were two and one-half years old. These subjects showed somewhat greater language development than a control group of children who did not receive the expansion experience, although the differences were not very impressive. Surprisingly, a third group of children that received a "modeling" treatment showed the most rapid progress. The modeling treatment consisted of responding to the child's utterance with a comment that might follow in an ordinary conversation (a grammatical reply to the child) rather than repeating what the child had presumably meant. Cazden's results may cast some doubt on the importance of expansion, but they do show the effectiveness of increased linguistic experience, even as little as 40 minutes a day, on language acquisition.

Experience is undoubtedly crucial. Brodbeck and Irwin (1946) have shown that children raised in orphanages, where their language experience is presumably limited, seem to be retarded in language acquisition when compared to children raised in normal homes.

The mean length of the orphans' utterances is less than normals, as is their frequency of speaking. Irwin (1948b,c) has also presented data that indicate both length and frequency of vocalization are greater in middle-class children than in children from lower-class homes. More importantly, Irwin (1960) has demonstrated the effects of manipulating experience. He persuaded working-class mothers to read to their children for at least 10 minutes a day for several months. Reading began when the children were about one year old. A control group of children whose parents were not specifically encouraged to read to their children was also observed. The assumption was that these working-class parents would normally be unlikely to read to their children, especially at this early age. The results showed clear differences in fluency favoring the experimental children, the differences being apparent after four to six months. As Ervin-Tripp (1966) suggests, this study implies that just hearing speech is crucial to development, although it is possible that the reading resulted in a changed relationship between mother and child such that more "conversations" occurred in the experimental group.

It certainly is no surprise that the data bear out the obvious fact that experience with language is crucial to learning. The interesting question is, What kinds of experience are most responsible for the development of language? One is tempted, on the basis of available research, to conclude that it is not the *exact* nature of the experience that is crucial, but it is, rather, the amount and variety of language experience that govern development. This leads some to speculate that human infants are born with a capacity for abstracting the structure of language and that when they are given enough opportunities to hear utterances representative of this structure, competence will develop automatically. Lenneberg (1964, 1967) has been the strongest proponent of this biological view. For Lenneberg (1964), five major points strongly suggest that man is uniquely capable of speech due to his genetic history: (1) speech is apparently closely related to a number of morphological features of the human body; (2) the onset of speech in young children tends to occur in a very regular age pattern in all cultures; (3) speech behavior appears in humans despite tremendous handicaps such as congenital blindness; (4) no nonhumans have ever acquired language, despite a number of extended efforts to teach them; and (5) all languages of the world seem to be based on the same basic principles of semantics, syntax, and phonology. Obviously, genetic endowment and experience are both crucial, but Lenneberg's analysis begins to suggest that genetic factors are much more important than most psychologists had ever suspected.

Finally, we come to Brown's third process, *induction of the latent structure*. In some fashion, which presently defies detection, the child begins to abstract the structural properties of his language. Note that Lenneberg's position suggests that the basic nature of this abstraction might be genetically determined. In any case, the child begins to "figure out" the rules for generating acceptable sentences. The process seems much like a rule-learning problem in concept formation in that the child is presented with instances (mostly positive instances from his parents and a mixture of positive and negative instances from his own lips) of the concept, and out of this experience he is able to learn the rules which will describe his present and future language behavior. The task set for the child seems so complex and the conditions of learning seem so difficult that it is tempting to place an extremely heavy emphasis on genetics.

The inference that the child is abstracting rules which govern his own language production comes most convincingly from an examination of the errors the child makes. In this regard, a great deal of attention has been directed to the child's learning of morphological rules, particularly rules for inflecting verbs into the past tense and rules for pluralizing nouns. Thanks to the careful work of Berko

(1958) and Ervin (1964), the development of these morphological characteristics has been well-described. Consider the inflection of verbs for past tense. Verbs are of two types: (1) regular or weak verbs which are inflected by adding *-ed* (e.g., *walk-walked*), and (2) irregular or strong verbs which are not inflected in any standard way (e.g., *go-went, run-ran, eat-ate*). Children learn irregular forms earlier than the regular inflection; however, acquisition of the regular inflection is followed by an overgeneralization of this inflection to the irregular verbs. This results in the child's saying such things as *eated, runned,* and *goed*. The child may use the two past-tense forms interchangeably, saying *I ran away* on one occasion and *I runned away* on another. Such errors suggest that the child has acquired a regular rule for inflecting past tense, especially when the past-tense form is applied correctly by the child to a verb he has just learned.

Palermo and Eberhart (1968) have recently examined this rule-learning behavior in *adult* subjects who are learning miniature languages. These experiments showed that the adults exhibited exactly the same kinds of regularities and irregularities in their performance as the child learning the past-tense inflection. The Palermo and Eberhart experiment was done using a learning paradigm first employed by Esper in 1925. This paradigm and Esper's results are worthy of further consideration.

Esper had subjects learn two-syllable names for colored shapes. In one condition, however, the assignment of names to shapes followed a system; an example of such a system taken from Foss (1968*b*) is shown in Figure 14-8. Each color has a name and each shape has a name, so that the name of the entire figure is generated by combining the color and shape names. Thus, referring to Figure 14-8, a red circle would be called a *Zintep,* a yellow triangle would be a *Jorfub,* etc., the first syllable of the name being determined by the color and the second syllable by the shape. Esper showed that learning was facilitated by this systematic assignment of names to figures. Furthermore, during learning, the subjects never saw two of the sixteen possible figures, i.e., learning was carried out with only fourteen stimuli. After the subjects had learned the fourteen name-figure pairs, Esper presented the two figures that the subjects had not seen before. Interestingly enough, the subjects named these new figures correctly according to the matrix and, surprisingly, they did not realize that these were new figures. Such results argue strongly that the subjects had abstracted the rule-like properties of the matrix and were responding on the basis of these rules and not on the basis of simple associations between figures and names. The similarity between a matrix such as that shown in Figure 14-8 and certain linguistic situations is apparent, as is the kind of learning (rule learning) that takes place when subjects tackle such material. This similarity makes these systematic learning situations worthy of further study (see Foss, 1968*a,b*).

Palermo and Eberhart (1968) used the "Esper squares" to simulate the situation confronting a child learning verb inflections. Thus, an Esper square can be set up with a few items that don't follow the system; these items correspond to the irregular verbs which are fewer in number than the regular verbs. Some of the items are not presented during the learning phase but are reserved for use in the test phase only. Two-digit numbers were used as stimuli and two-letter combinations (bigrams) were used as responses (see Figure 14-9 for an example from Palermo and Eberhart). The irregular pairs were presented more frequently to correspond with the fact that irregular verbs are more frequently used in English (although there are fewer of them) than the regular verbs. The results, based on college students learning number-bigram pairs, corresponded remarkably with the data of children learning verb inflections. The more frequently presented irregular pairs were learned sooner than the regular pairs. Once the regular pairs had been learned, how-

FIGURE 14–8. *An Esper square. The matrix contains the names of the 16 possible stimulus figures, e.g., a red circle is a Zintep and a green heart is a **Nidgom**.*

Stimuli	○	△	□	♡
Red	Zintep	Zinfub	Zinpir	Zingom
Yellow	Jortep	Jorfub	Jorpir	Jorgom
Blue	Kestep	Kesfub	Kespiv	Kesgom
Green	Nidtep	Nidfub	Nidpiv	Nidgom

Source: Redrawn from D. J. Foss, Learning and discovery in the acquisition of structured material: Effects of number of items and their sequence. *Journal of Experimental Psychology*, 1968, **77**, 341-44. Copyright 1968 by the American Psychological Association and reprinted by permission.

ever, errors which consisted of overgeneralization of the rules became fairly frequent on the irregular pairs. Performance on the omitted, test pairs was as good as that on the pairs that had actually been experienced, corresponding to the fact that children apply inflection rules to newly acquired verbs.

The results suggest that at least some language-acquisition phenomena can be reproduced in the laboratory where experimental manipulations can be accomplished, a finding that bodes well for the future development of an understanding of such phenomena. Since it is extremely difficult to control a child's experience with language, we cannot expect many definitive experiments on language acquisition until we can develop laboratory tasks that parallel this acquisition. The Esper paradigm shows a great deal of promise in this regard. The materials to be learned in an Esper paradigm are structured according to rules so that an understanding of how subjects abstract these rules will contribute to our knowledge of how children accomplish

FIGURE 14–9. *A modified Esper square for the study of morphological rules. Each pair consisted of a two-digit stimulus and a bigram response, e.g., 61-DL, 84-RK, etc.*

	Second Digit			
Stimuli	1	2	3	4
6	DL*	VF	VG	VK
7	HM	PC*	HG	HK
8	RM	RF	TJ*	RK
9	XM	XF	XG	WS*

(First Digit on vertical axis)

*Irregular pairs

Source: Redrawn from D. S. Palermo and V. L. Eberhart, On the learning of morphological rules: An experimental analogy. *Journal of Verbal Learning and Verbal Behavior,* 1968, **7**, 337-44. Copyright © 1968 by the Academic Press.

Brown's third process, induction of the latent structure. Since the basic task can be described as rule learning, it is obvious that studies of rule learning in concept formation also will provide information about this process.

The elaboration of language skills is a continuing process, one that is certainly not complete by the time the child is four years old. For example, Brown and Berko (1960), in a fascinating study of syntactic rules, found clear improvement in the ability of children to use new words in grammatically correct ways as the children got older. Performance was not by any means perfect by the third grade (the highest grade tested). The point is not that continued improvement in language does not occur after four years of age, but rather that the four-year old exhibits all the complexities of adult language behavior even though he may not be very consistent about it. It is not possible to say at what age essentially full acquisition has been accomplished, but much of the acquisition is complete at a very young age. The fact that thinking may not appear to develop as rapidly as language tempts one to suggest that thinking is not highly dependent on language. However, any lack of a developmental correlation may only mean that the more complex varieties of thinking are impossible until the child has a sufficient command of language skills and competence, which in some cases may not be until age ten or eleven.

SUMMARY

In this chapter we have examined language as a system within which thought and behavior are expressed. We have emphasized the conceptual nature of linguistic knowledge and skill. The basic components of the language system were examined: (1) phonetics and phonemics, (2) morphology, (3) syntax, and (4) semantics. All of these aspects of language show the conceptual nature of the system, composed of attributes and rules. The most thorough analysis has been made at the level of grammar, while semantics remains the area most poorly understood. Modern grammatical theory, as exemplified by the work of Noam Chomsky, has provided a severe challenge to classical psychological theories, especially those predicated on S-R notions, as applied to linguistic behavior. Those theories have not adequately described the rule-governed aspects of behavior. Research in grammar suggests that the finite-state models that result from present association theories are probably incapable of adequate descriptions of linguistic performance. At present, some type of phrase-structure principles in combination with transformational rules seem most capable of such a description. Finally, we examined briefly the development of linguistic behavior. Just what aspects of experience are crucial to this development remains unclear. It is clear, however, that in its complexity and rapidity, the acquisition of language is the most astounding achievement of mankind.

VI Conclusion

Fifteen Concepts, Thoughts, and Behavior

It should be clear from the preceding review and discussion of the literature that psychology is caught up currently in a determined attempt to elucidate the concept of thought. Unlike the situation some 15 years ago or so, when experimental psychology was still in the grips of theoretical Behaviorism and thinking was considered an ephemeral mentalism unfit for laboratory study (Osgood, 1953), cognitive psychology is now a focal area for many investigators. Real progress has been made. If laboratory successes act as rewards to the experimenter, then we should see no slackening, but rather a continued increase in scientific work on the problem for some time to come.

We have not tried in these pages to give an exhaustive review of cognitive psychology. Such an effort might require covering all of psychology, for thinking is a pervasive aspect of behavior. Try to find some human activity which is completely devoid of thinking! Rather, the approach has been to use examples. We have attempted a summary of contemporary empirical and theoretical research in four fundamental topical areas which we hope capture sufficiently psychology's current understanding of human thinking.

THINKING AND BEHAVIOR

A general position was announced in Chapter 1. Thinking was said to be a behavioral concept, a noncommittal descriptive term properly applied to some of the activities of man (and animals). The particular application with which we have been concerned primarily is to a person's behavior in problematical situations.

We claim that the concept of thought is logically descriptive rather than causal. It is a matter of coding and communicating a state of affairs rather than "explaining" via hypothetical underlying processes. It says what thinking is—overtly and recognizably—rather than relegating it to some theoretical or nonpsychological status in a special domain.

In this sense, the position taken here conflicts with traditional psychological theory, which is written in a cause-effect idiom, distinguishes between thinking (usually semantically disguised as symbolic processes) and behavior, and views thinking as an explanation (the cause) rather than something to be explained. The traditional approach is predicated on what seems to us to be an impoverished concept of behavior, originally imposed on psychology by the Behaviorists and from which most psychologists—their profound protestations to the contrary (Newell, 1969; Deese, 1969)—have not recovered. The tradition maintains that behavior is performance (movement). It is to be distinguished substantively and empirically from motivation (intention), knowledge (stimuli, circumstances), and skill (habit, competence). Once that distinction is made, the theorist becomes consumed in the unnatural task of reconnecting the parts he has dissected, usually by way of physiology or some causal, underlying process model. Stimulus, motivation, habit, competence, cognitive structure, symbolic process, and their variants are then the explanations of behavior (performance), rather than the natural properties of behavior.

We have no inclination to controvert the established arguments. The value of a position is best judged by what it allows its holder to accomplish, and we have already said that orthodox psychology has come a long way in its understanding of thinking. The point to be made here is that there are alternatives. The view of thought as a change in behavior potential, of thinking as characteristic of behaving organisms, and of behavior as a concept with cognitive, competence and intentional as well as performance attributes is, we believe, logically more general and includes the established, causal arguments as a special case.

It is important to note that radical changes have taken place in psychologists' conceptions of thinking and that these changes have been dictated largely by experimental data. The traditional point of view is most closely tied to associative theory, which has been described and referenced in several earlier chapters. The attempt to extend the principles of conditioning to thinking, primarily through the postulation of mediating processes, may be judged to have come up short of accounting for a considerable portion of the findings previously described.

Perhaps the clearest indication of the limitations of associative theory is provided by the study of language; recall that arguments exist claiming to demonstrate the logical impossibility of fully describing linguistic competence in associative terms (Chapter 14). The data on sentence production and comprehension are difficult to account for in S-R language, however modified. The associative approach to conceptual behavior has led to consideration of only the simplest concepts and has neither generated nor accounted for the findings regarding strategies, differences in conceptual rules, or interproblem transfer. Although the study of verbal learning was initially viewed as a means of determining how associations are formed, the data have led modern investigators to characterize verbal-learning tasks in a problem-solving mode, with an emphasis on the subject's knowledge and skills (strategies) relevant to successful completion of the task. Associative theory has had its greatest success in the study of simple problem solving, but the approach has been fragmented and has not yielded any unified theoretical account. In other words, psychologists have looked at the data and have been essentially forced to create more complex descriptions of thinking than are afforded by associative theory.

Behavior as Rule Following. Throughout this book, we have been emphasizing the utility of describing behavior as rule governed, and it seems appropriate at this point to illustrate the variety of behaviors to which this description applies. Some instances are obvious—the description of linguistic competence as well as of the production and comprehension of sentences. A strategy for solving concept-identification problems, for example, *focusing,* can be described as follows: *Form a* *working hypothesis consisting of all of the attributes of the first positive instance encountered. Select a stimulus differing in one attribute from this hypothesis. Determine its category membership. If positive, eliminate the changed dimension from the working hypothesis; if negative, mark the changed attribute as relevant. Select another stimulus differing from the hypothesis in one attribute. Determine.... If positive...; if negative.... (Repetitively) Continue until X relevant attributes have been marked (if the number of relevant attributes is known) or until all attributes in the working hypothesis have been marked as relevant or eliminated.*

In paired-associate learning, the phenomenon of *stimulus selection* seems to be rule governed: *Select the minimal part of the stimulus complex that can be easily used as a cue for response recall.* As indicated, in Chapter 8, *verbal-discrimination* learning can be described in terms of rules based on differences in (subjective) frequency between correct and incorrect items: *Select the item that has occurred most frequently.* Certain transfer phenomena with verbal-discrimination tasks can be attributed to the continued use of now inappropriate rules. Rules based on differential frequencies of another sort describe the changes which occur in the effect of varying the language frequency of the correct item when a subject solves a series of selection tasks whose solutions have similar (language) frequencies. In general, phenomena related to problem-solving *set* involve the acquisition of rules: e.g., *Try to produce only words which are animal names,* or *Fill the largest jar, fill the medium jar from it, etc.* It should be clear that rule following is a pervasive aspect of the variety of behaviors characterized as thinking. As a final point, keep in mind the tremendous importance of *instructions* in determining the behavior of human organisms; instructions can be usefully viewed as either providing rules for the subject or requesting him to follow certain rules.

Knowledge and Skills. The importance of knowledge and skill in behavior has been repeatedly stressed throughout the book. We believe that improving our understanding of these components of behavior constitutes a major goal for future research. It is obvious that an adequate description of behavior requires identification of the skills a person brings to a task—what he knows how to do, how he will approach the task. Identifying these skills is not easy, but it seems clear that one worthwhile technique for obtaining relevant information has been used too infrequently in studying thinking—asking the subject. Of course, describing a person's behavior in terms of a skill does not require that he be able to tell us about it, but subjects are able to tell us about some skills, and this source of information should not be overlooked.

The critical problem with respect to the cognitive component of behavior description is to characterize adequately its organization or structure. Noticeable advances have been made in psycholinguistics, but our understanding of the organization of knowledge relevant to a wide variety of instances of thinking is poor indeed. Consider, for example, a person's knowledge of a single word. There is an indefinite number of things a person can tell us about a word such as *horse*—"it's an animal name," "the name of a wooden structure used to block streets," "a verb in slang," " it has five letters," "my uncle had a horse once," "horses are stupid," and so on, ad infinitum. Similarly, the number of relations a person can construct among items is infinite. How should the knowledge which enables a person to do these things be characterized? Some have suggested that the concept of *list* is useful, e.g., horse: English word; noun; brown, gray; etc. (Reitman, 1965). The history of describing linguistic competence strongly suggests that an adequate description will be based on generative and recursive rules. Some ideas on the organization of knowledge stemming from studies of conceptual behavior will be presented shortly, but first, some comments on how changes in behavior should be characterized.

LEARNING TO THINK

Changes in behavior are primarily a matter of experience—observation and practice; it seems clear that human beings learn to think. The changes are most cogently described as the acquisition of cognitions and competences, as coming to know and to know how. A person's behavior at any time is contingent not only on his "external" circumstances but also on what he knows and what he knows how to do. It makes sense to describe episodes of behavior as processes with empirically discoverable parameters. But note, these are parameters of behavior, not of some hypothetical, invisible, currently indeterminant, nonbehavioral, underlying processes.

Behavior is contingent on specifiable parameters, e.g., the person's skills. But obviously behavior is not static; the parameters change in time. The manner and extent of change depend on the person's momentary behavioral repertoire. Thus, in agreement with Piaget (1957) and others, we would say that psychological growth is an evolving process, with developmental changes being essential elaborations of the present stage. Each new developmental epoch is dependent on the events of the preceding stage. This holds not only in childhood, where the changes are most dramatic, but throughout life.

To describe this process of psychological growth completely is too large a task to handle in this discussion. There are, moreover, too many unknowns to contend with. In its place, we shall give an illustration, using concept formation, which has been worked out in some empirical detail and which might be prototypical of the general case of learning to think.

LEARNING AND USING CONCEPTS

Concepts are defined by relationships among constituents, which commonly are certain attributes of objects, events, processes, or states of affairs. The class concepts, *red triangle* or *Republican senator,* to take two widely disparate examples, can be described as conjunctive relations between two simple physical attributes (redness, triangularity) in the first case and two more complicated and abstract attributes (Republican-ness, senatorness) in the second. When a person learns a new class concept, he learns a new, and presumably utilitarian, way of combining attributes. The process, as has been noted, is predicated on existing discriminations (knowledge), as, for example, between triangles and nontriangles and between reds and nonreds. With the new concept he can engage in a myriad of new behaviors, such as recognizing and treating novel cases as examples or nonexamples of the concept or generating a subset of examples or nonexamples.

Concepts: Attributes and Principles. The distinction between attributes and relations (principles) proposed in this analysis implies that attributes are specific and unique characteristics of physical stimuli while relations are conceptual and abstract. A qualification needs to be introduced, for the distinction is arbitrary and partly semantic. Attributes, as well as relations, are conceptual and cover in all cases a multitude of discriminable possibilities. Consider that redness, triangularity, Jesuit-ness and priest-ness are all applicable as descriptions to innumerable objects. In this sense we treat everything as a concept rather than as a matter of ultimate, physical reality. That is why theories and philosophies of sciences predicated on a reduction of behavior to physics, or some other more elementary system, are likely to be inadequate. Logically, behavior requires a theory of relations, not a theory of physical absolutes.

A Specific Concept. A concept is composed of a series of interrelated concepts. The system of concepts which characterizes a person's behavior at a given time comprises his knowledge. It is a continually changing system, of course, with new concepts being added, dependent on what is presently known, giving the definite impression of an hierarchical organization and growth pattern.

What does a person learn when he forms some class concept, say the disjunction, Dj_1, or "x and/or y"? For one thing, he learns to treat some things, the $d_1,_i$'s, as examples of the concept, and others, the $\bar{d}_{1,i}$'s, as nonexamples. He has learned a new discrimination and some of the consequences of making that discrimination. The new discrimination is, of course, based on prior discriminations between x's and non-x's, and between y's and non-y's, the relevant attributes of the new concept. The particular x's and y's involved might represent any kind of discrimination, such as the primitive properties, redness and one-ness or the complex constructions, Jesuit-ness and priest-ness.

We can describe the new concept hierarchically, as follows:

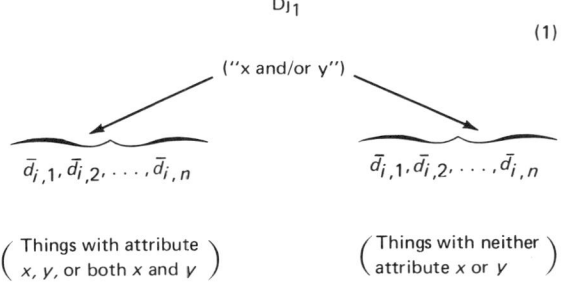

(1)

A Somewhat More General Concept. It is not inconceivable that the subject learned more than a particular new discrimination from the foregoing experience. He might learn something about the place of the specific class concept, Dj_1, in a larger system. Imagine an experimental procedure, patterned after the learning set paradigm (Harlow, 1959), in which the subject solves a series of problems (learns several class concepts successively), all of which are based on a disjunctive principle. It has been shown that, as a consequence of this training routine, subjects learn to solve disjunctive problems with the minimal amount of information (Bourne, 1967, 1968b). If in each problem the attributes are given, leaving the subject to combine those attributes disjunctively, he comes to employ the disjunctive principle errorlessly within a reasonably short series of problems.

In any particular problem based on a class concept, the subject encounters and must derive a solution from a series of stimulus objects. The objects might be all positive, all negative, or a mixture of positive and negative instances (Bourne and Guy, 1968b). In any case, he learns to categorize objects appropriately. The paradigm for learning a principle is analogous. The instances are not objects, but problems, or rather the conceptual solutions to problems, presented successively. We can think of the paradigm as providing the subject with a series of positive instances of the disjunctive principle, from which the concept of *disjunctivity* is learned. We can describe the form of this higher-order concept as follows:

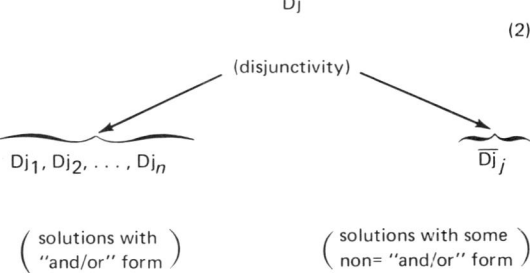

(2)

where each Dj_i and Dj_j is described as in (1). Just as each instance of a particular disjunctive class concept provides the subject with useful information about the discrimination it codifies, so, too, each disjunctive problem supplies information on a more general relation. At some level of performance or achievement, we would say not only that the subject understands each of the disjunctive concepts, Dj_i, but that he knows the principle or concept of disjunctivity. He can use the principle in solving novel disjunctive problems, he can construct disjunctive classes, and he can recognize instances of "disjunctivity" when they occur.

The outcome of such a training routine, in which independent groups of subjects solved problems based on conjunctive, disjunctive, conditional, and biconditional principles, is shown in Figure 10-4. These were typical principle-learning problems in which the subject knew the relevant attributes to begin with. Early problems provide a basis for learning the principle, allowing the subject to perform errorlessly later in the series, regardless of the initial difficulty of the principle.

A Set of Coordinate Concepts. Without a chance to observe and to work with contrasting counter examples, i.e., negative instances, the subject probably cannot be said to have a thorough or well-formed concept. The negative instances of a specific class concept help to establish its limits or boundaries (Smoke, 1933). Likewise, familiarity with concepts of a nondisjunctive sort can be expected to contribute to the precision of the subjects' knowledge of disjunctivity. It is possible to arrange a problem series in which the principle changes from one concept to the next, to provide the subject with examples and counter examples of several principles. An experiment approximating this routine, in which each subject solved three principle-learning problems based on each of four bidimensional concept types—conjunctive, disjunctive, conditional, and biconditional—was reported by Bourne (1970). Principles were counterbalanced across subjects, for order of presentation, but the three problems illustrating a given principle were successive. As can be seen in Figure 15-1, three problems per principle were not sufficient to ensure full mastery, but, owing to general positive transfer effects between principles, performance near the end of the series approached maximal efficiency.

With a sufficiently long training series, it would be reasonable to expect the subject to acquire a thorough understanding of all four principles. In any subsequent test, he should distinguish among them with minimal information. For the system of principles used in this example, minimal information is provided by a bidimensional truth table (see Table 9-3). That is, if the trained subject is shown a single object with both, neither, one, and the other relevant attribute present (xy, $x\bar{y}$, $\bar{x}y$, and $\overline{xy}$), he should be able to classify all subsequent examples correctly and, in that sense, apply the proper principle. (Note that no xy example would be necessary, since these are positive under all four principles. The experiment might have been conducted with different principles, however, in which this was not the case. In general, an example of all four classes of stimuli would be required.)

Actually, a test of this sort was administered in the preceding experiment. Having solved three problems on each of the four principles, the subject was given one more task in which he had to decide, with as few stimulus examples as possible, which one of the four principles governed solution. Forty of 48 subjects in the experiment found the unknown principle with minimal information—one example of each truth-table class. In other words, 83 percent of the subjects did demonstrate complete understanding of the four principles. It seems reasonable to assume that all subjects would have attained this level of performance, if a longer series of practice problems had been arranged.

One way to describe the competent subject's knowledge at this point would be as follows:

Cj.	Dj.	Cd.	Bd.
(Conjunctivity)	(Disjunctivity)	(Conditionality)	(Biconditionality)
$Cj_1, Cj_2, \ldots, Cj_n$	$Dj_1, Dj_2, \ldots, Dj_n$	$Cd_1, Cd_2, \ldots, Cd_n$	$Bd_1, Bd_2, \ldots, Bd_n$

He understands a principle of conjunctivity, transcending any particular conjunctive concept, and covering a multitude of different

FIGURE 15–1. *Performance on a series of rule learning problems. Each set of three successive problems is based on the same principle. All four primary concept types are represented with the order counterbalanced across subjects.*

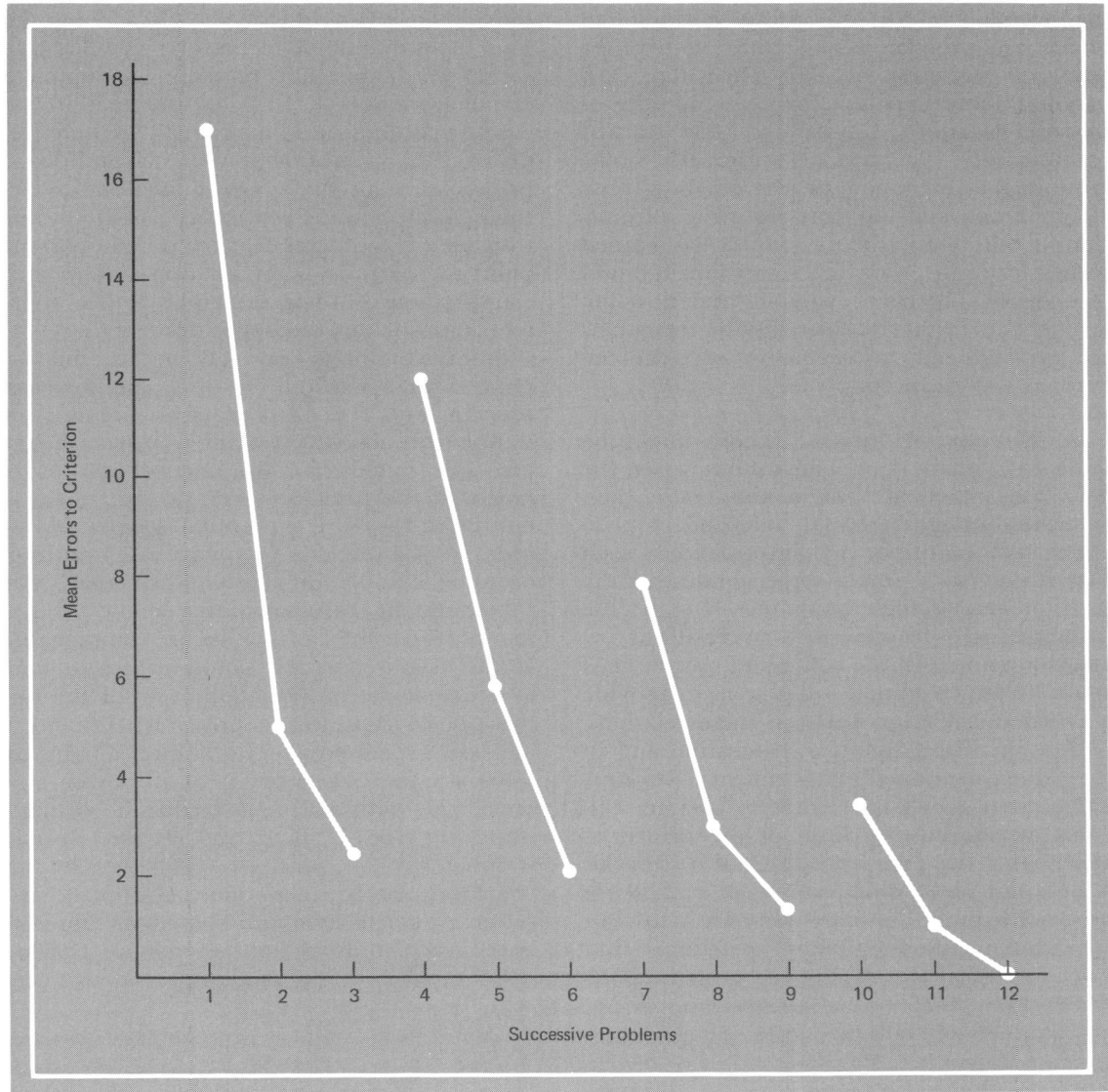

Source: Redrawn from L. E. Bourne, Jr., Development of conceptual rules, Fig. 3. *Psychological Review,* 1970, **77,** No. 6, 546-56. Copyright 1970 by the American Psychological Association and reprinted by permission.

class concepts with varying stimulus features. The several conjunctive concepts which the subject has learned and used represent the positive instances of conjunctivity, much as the several stimulus objects he encountered within any problem served as the positive (or negative) instances of that particular class concept. From experience with a number of problem-examples, the subject has learned conjunctivity, i.e., to treat properly some groupings as conjunctions and others as nonconjunctions and to generate new conjunctions at will. Similarly, the subject has learned principles of disjunctivity, conditionality, and biconditionality from examples and now understands them in the sense that he treats new concepts correctly as members, or nonmembers, of those concept types.

A Conceptual System. There might be more to it than that. The subject, after the preceding experience, might know more than just the four separate and independent principles. The nature of his performance is such that it suggests a deeper understanding of the relation among these principles. Just as the principles can be described as relations between attributes in the context of specific class concepts, superordinate rules seem to provide a systematic relation between these relations.

The principles used for illustration and in the aforementioned experiment (Bourne, 1970) are a subset selected from a larger calculus of possibilities. Each of the principles generates a two-group partition of a stimulus population based on the presence or absence of two attributes. Actually there are a total of 16 different types of binary partitions that can be formed using two attributes, the system being based on the logical calculus of propositions. Reference to the bidimensional truth table once again clarifies the 16 possibilities. Each is a distinct way of assigning the four types of stimuli to positive and negative categories. Table 15-1 presents the complete layout. Partitions F, L, B, D, and H illustrate the now familiar unidimensional, conjunctive, disjunctive, conditional, and biconditional principles, respectively. Other labels are sometimes applied to the remaining partitions, but they need not concern us here. The important point to recognize is the relation among, and coordination of, these principles within a system, the calculus of propositions.

Stimulus objects, say, 1LR△, are the instances (or noninstances) of a specific class concept, say, R△. Class concepts are the instances (or noninstances) of a more general principle, in this case, conjunction. It appears now that the principles serve as instances (or noninstances) of a conceptual system. Moreover, from a series of problems based on four or some number of different principles, the subject might learn something about the system of which these principles are components. If this is the case, we would expect to find evidence of the proper application of the system (the concept) to new principles (instances) not yet experienced. The subject ought to solve a type C, E, I, or N partition or any other type with the same facility he demonstrates on types L, B, D, and H, used during training.

Unfortunately, there are no directly applicable data to refer to. The closest approximation is a study by Bourne and Guy (1968a)

TABLE 15–1. *Sixteen Bidimensional Partitions of a Stimulus Population*

Truth-table Class	Partition															
	A	B	C	D	E	F	G	H	I	J	K	L	M	N	O	P
xy (TT)	+	+	+	+	−	+	+	+	−	−	−	+	−	−	−	−
x̄y (TF)	+	+	+	−	+	+	−	−	+	+	−	+	−	−	−
x̄y (FT)	+	+	−	+	+	−	+	−	+	−	+	−	−	+	−	−
x̄ȳ (FF)	+	−	+	+	+	−	−	+	+	−	+	−	−	−	+	−

showing that the greater the number of principles experienced during preliminary training, the greater the transfer to a problem based on a new principle within the same system. The data are only suggestive, however, for too few problems (12), training principles (0 to 3), and test principles (1) were used to make a definitive conclusion. In general, the training was insufficient in all cases to bring subjects to a high level of mastery of the system.

But these data, and other results discussed here, strongly imply that subjects will learn (abstract) the full system with sufficient partial training (examples). The basic superordinate approach to each of these principles is the bidimensional truth table—inspect one instance of each stimulus class, xy, $x\bar{y}$, $\bar{x}y$, $\overline{xy}$, and then categorize all subsequent instances of that class in the same way. Once this approach is mastered or discovered, any problem can and probably would be solved in, at most, four instances, one from each truth-table class. An understanding of the system, and problem-solving facility throughout, is no doubt acquirable with relatively few examples.

Knowledge and Its Skillful Use. What the subject knows after a sufficient number of training examples is not just a subset of four (or some number of) principles, but rather a well-developed system of possibilities, or, in other words, a still higher-order concept. The system can be represented as follows:

number of problems to which the system is applicable. He can *generate* from any level downward: Given that he is working within the system, he can give the various principles and examples of their application, using any two attributes, x and y, of a stimulus population. Further, he can, with sufficient preliminary information, *abstract* upward in the hierarchy, from a particular concept or its denotation to the system as a whole.

FINAL REMARK

The system of concepts used in this example is closed and fully determined. We know the parameters and the conditions for its application. It is a relatively simple system to learn—taking perhaps an hour or two for a reasonably bright person—which makes it desirable for many research purposes. Despite its simplicity, the manner of its acquisition might be a useful model for the acquisition of knowledge generally, in everyday circumstances. Furthermore, to generalize from the model is relatively straightforward. With appropriate training, a person can learn to use other systems, coordinate with the two-valued calculus of propositions, such as a three-valued or an n-valued logical system or a system based on continuous functions. He might learn the interrelations of these systems, which are fundamental to more general domains of

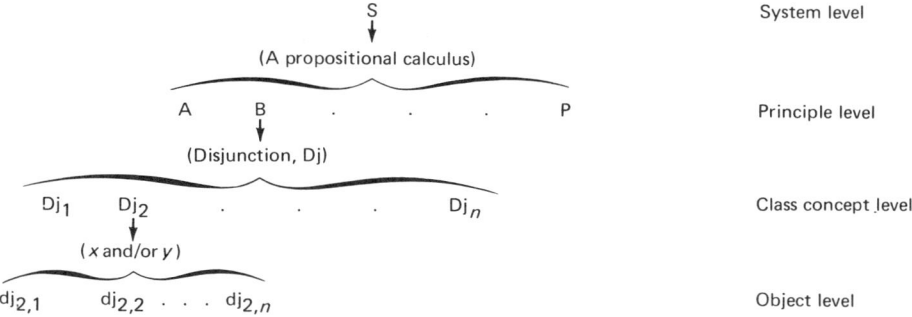

The sophisticated subject understands the system at every level as a network of interrelated concepts. He can solve the infinite

mathematics—in themselves, still higher-order conceptual systems. It is also pertinent to note that modern linguists of the generative persuasion (Chomsky, 1965) have used methodologically similar hierarchical rule-form models to portray the linguistic competence of human beings, which is both an indeterminate system and clearly more complex than the research example used here. But the available experimental data on conceptual rule learning have run out. We might speculate on more complicated conceptual systems, but it is unnecessary to belabor the point.

Concepts and Language. Some of the ways in which people behave are fundamentally nonlinguistic. Use of language seems to be involved neither in the acquisition nor in the execution of these activities. For examples, we need only think of the things that a preverbal child comes, with experience, to be able to do. It might be that an elementary, associative, or conditioning analysis will provide an acceptable account of these activities. Given this measure of success, some theorists have extrapolated simple conditioning ideas in an attempt to account for all behavior, including linguistic behavior. That this is a naive and inadequate interpretative framework is attested to by much of the research reviewed in Chapters 13 and 14. Pavlov himself recognized the limited implications of simple conditioning and proposed the necessity of higher-order signalling systems, especially language, to account for the full complexity of mature human behavior.

The kind of knowledge and skill implied by the conceptual example given in this chapter does not make sense in a nonlinguistic context. What the subject learns is not only coded linguistically but primarily expressed that way as it is used in subsequent problematic situations. A person who knows propositional calculus is capable of certain achievements which he would otherwise fail. He can discriminate conjunctive and disjunctive possibilities, pick either of them out of a variety of others, produce real or hypothetical examples. In general, his position, vis-à-vis a certain domain of tasks, is not unlike that of the Eskimo who can discriminate and categorize varieties of snow. In both cases, we have reference to linguistically coded, abstract attributes which are then used in solving problems. It is impossible to imagine a nonlinguistic, physical-stimulus—physical-response conditioning mechanism which could accomplish the same tasks.

Knowledge and Its Skillfull Use. Human knowledge is the knowledge of concepts. It is most conveniently described hierarchically. It is achieved primarily by abstraction from example. It is used primarily to generate more specific outcomes which, it seems, is at least one of the basic processes of problem solving as presented in Chapter 3. On any occasion, a person is likely both to be abstracting and generating, learning and using, and his knowledge and skills are likely to be in a continual state of change.

Knowledge and skill are basic descriptive parameters of behavior. Combined with intention and performance, they define the concept of a person. The four parameters are clearly relevant to the particular type of behavioral processes emphasized in this book, thinking. When used in the noncommittal, and perhaps most familiar form, this description says only that the person (1) is trying to achieve a solution to a problem (intention), (2) has the necessary knowledge and skills (or is believed to have them), and (3) is making relatively slow progress, exhibiting little successful overt action (performance). The goal of psychological research has been to go beyond this usage, to add substance and detail, to identify cognitions and competences, to develop the most informative performance measures, and to show how they all fit together in a well-formed description of behavioral processes.

We have reviewed a considerable amount of work aimed at characterizing thoughtful behavior in a variety of problematic situations. Despite the magnitude of the task, visible progress has been made toward the elucidation of thinking as a concept within the system of behavior. With continued research at the present level, there is every hope that the current, still cloudy view of the solution will gradually become clear.

Bibliography

ABBOTT, D. W., and L. E. PRICE. Stimulus generalization of the conditioned eyelid response to structurally similar nonsense syllables. *Journal of Experimental Psychology,* 1964, **68,** 368-71.

ADAMS, J. A. *Human Memory.* New York: McGraw-Hill, 1967.

―――, and W. E. MONTAGUE. Retroactive inhibition and natural language mediation. *Journal of Verbal Learning and Verbal Behavior,* 1967, **6,** 528-35.

ADAMSON, R. E. Functional fixedness as related to problem solving: A repetition of three experiments. *Journal of Experimental Psychology,* 1952, **44,** 288-91.

―――. Inhibitory set in problem solving as related to reinforcement learning. *Journal of Experimental Psychology,* 1959, **58,** 280-82.

ANDERSON, B., and W. JOHNSON. Two kinds of set in problem solving. *Psychological Reports,* 1966, **19,** 851-58.

ANDERSON, R. C., and J. T. GUTHRIE. Effects of some sequential manipulations of relevant and irrelevant stimulus dimensions on concept learning. *Journal of Experimental Psychology,* 1966, **72,** 501-4.

ANDREASSI, J. L. Some physiological correlates of verbal learning task difficulty. *Psychonomic Science,* 1966, **6,** 69-70.

ANISFELD, M., and M. KNAPP. Association, synonymity, and directionality in false recognition. *Journal of Experimental Psychology,* 1968, **77,** 171-79.

ARCHER, E. J. A re-evaluation of the meaningfulness of all possible CVC trigrams. *Psychological Monographs,* 1960, **74,** 10, Whole No. 497.

―――. Concept identification as a function of obviousness of relevant and irrelevant information. *Journal of Experimental Psychology,* 1962, **63,** 616-20.

ARNOULT, M. D. Transfer of predifferentiation training in simple and multiple shape discrimination. *Journal of Experimental Psychology,* 1953, **45,** 401-9.

―――. Stimulus predifferentiation: Some generalizations and hypotheses. *Psychological Bulletin,* 1957, **54,** 330-50.

ARONSON, E., and D. LANDY. Further steps beyond Parkinson's Law: A replication and extension of the excess time effect. *Journal of Experimental Social Psychology,* 1967, **3,** 274-85.

ATKINSON, R. C., and R. M. SCHIFFRIN. Human memory: A proposed system and its control processes. In K. W. Spence and Janet T. Spence, eds., *The Psychology of Learning and Motivation: Advances in Research and Theory,* Vol. 2, New York: Academic Press, 1968.

AZUMA, H., and L. J. CRONBACH. Cue response correlations in the attainment of a scalar concept. *American Journal of Psychology*, 1966, **79**, 38-49.

BARNES, J. M., and B. J. UNDERWOOD. "Fate" of first-associations in transfer theory. *Journal of Experimental Psychology*, 1959, **58**, 97-105.

BATTIG, W. F. Some factors affecting performance of a word-formation problem. *Journal of Experimental Psychology*, 1957, **54**, 96-104.

―――. Procedural problems in paired-associate learning research. *Psychonomic Monograph Supplements*, 1965, **1**, No. 1.

―――. Paired-associate learning. In T. R. Dixon and D. L. Horton, eds., *Verbal Behavior and General Behavior Theory*. Englewood Cliffs, N.J.: Prentice-Hall, 1968.

―――, and W. E. MONTAGUE. Category norms for verbal items in 56 categories: A replication and extension of the Connecticut category norms. *Journal of Experimental Psychology Monograph*, 1969, **80**, No. 3.

BAUM, MARIAN. Simple concept learning as a function of intra-list generalization. *Journal of Experimental Psychology*, 1954, **47**, 89-94.

BEACH, L. E., and C. R. PETERSON. Man as an intuitive statistician. *Psychological Bulletin*, 1967, **68**, 29-46.

BEILIN, H. Developmental determinants of word and nonsense anagram solution. *Journal of Verbal Learning and Verbal Behavior*, 1967, **6**, 523-27.

―――, and R. HORN. Transition probability effects in anagram problem solving. *Journal of Experimental Psychology*, 1962, **63**, 514-18.

BELL, R. Q. Developmental psychology. In P. R. Farnsworth, O. McNemar, and Q. McNemar, eds., *Annual Review of Psychology*, 1965, **16**, 1-38.

BENDIG, A. W. Practice effects in "Twenty Questions." *Journal of General Psychology*, 1957, **56**, 261-68.

BERKO, JEAN. The child's learning of English morphology. *Word*, 1958, **14**, 150-77.

BERLYNE, D. E. The influence of complexity and change in visual figures on orienting responses. *Journal of Experimental Psychology*, 1958, **55**, 289-96.

BERNBACH, H. A. Stimulus learning and recognition in paired-associate learning. *Journal of Experimental Psychology*, 1967, **75**, 513-19.

BEVER, T. G., J. A. FODOR, and M. GARRETT. A formal limitation of associationism. In T. R. Dixon and D. L. Horton, eds., *Verbal Behavior and General Behavior Theory*. Englewood Cliffs, N.J.: Prentice-Hall, 1968.

BEVER, T. G., J. A. FODOR, and W. WEKSEL. On the acquisition of syntax: A critique of "contextual generalization." *Psychological Review*, 1965, **72**, 467-82.

BILODEAU, E. A., and INA McD. BILODEAU. Variation of temporal intervals among critical events in five studies on knowledge of results. *Journal of Experimental Psychology*, 1958, **55**, 603-12.

BIRCH, H. G., and H. S. RABINOWITZ. The negative effect of previous experience on productive thinking. *Journal of Experimental Psychology*, 1951, **41**, 121-25.

BIRREN, J. E., E. A. JEROME, and S. M. CHOWN. Aging and psychological adjustment: Problem-solving and motivation. *Review of Educational Research*, 1961, **31**, 487-99.

BLUMENTHAL, A. L. Promoted recall of sentences. *Journal of Verbal Learning and Verbal Behavior*, 1967, **6**, 203-6.

―――, and R. BOAKES. Prompted recall of sentences. *Journal of Verbal Learning and Verbal Behavior*, 1967, **6**, 674-76.

BORING, E. G. *A History of Experimental Psychology*. New York: Appleton-Century-Crofts, 1950.

BOURNE, L. E., JR. Effects of delay of information feedback and task complexity on the identification of concepts. *Journal of Experimental Psychology*, 1957, **54**, 201-7.

―――. Some factors affecting strategies used in problems of concept formation. *American Journal of Psychology*, 1963, **75**, 229-38 (a).

―――. Long-term effects of misinformation feedback on concept identification. *Journal of Experimental Psychology*, 1963, **65**, 139-47 (b).

―――. Hypotheses and hypothesis shifts in classification learning. *Journal of General Psychology*, 1965, **72**, 251-61.

―――. *Human Conceptual Behavior*. Boston: Allyn & Bacon, 1966.

―――. Learning and utilization of conceptual rules. In B. Kleinmuntz, ed., *Memory and the Structure of Concepts*. New York: John Wiley, 1967.

―――. Concept attainment. In T. R. Dixon and D. L. Horton, eds., *Verbal Behavior and General Behavior Theory*. Englewood Cliffs, N.J.: Prentice-Hall, 1968 (a).

―――. Development of conceptual rules. Invited

address. *American Psychological Association Convention*, San Francisco, September, 1968 (b).

———. Concept learning and thought. In J. Voss, ed., *Approaches to Thought*. Columbus, O.: Charles E. Merrill, 1969.

———, and C. V. BUNDERSON. Effects of delay of informative feedback and length of postfeedback interval on concept identification. *Journal of Experimental Psychology*, 1963, **65**, 1-5.

BOURNE, L. E., JR., D. DODD, D. E. GUY, and D. R. JUSTESEN. Response-contingent intertrial intervals in concept identification. *Journal of Experimental Psychology*, 1968, **76**, 601-8.

BOURNE, L. E., JR., S. GOLDSTEIN, and W. E. LINK. Concept learning as a function of availability of previously presented information. *Journal of Experimental Psychology*, 1964, **67**, 439-48.

BOURNE, L. E., JR., and D. E. GUY. Learning conceptual rules: I. Some inter-rule transfer effects. *Journal of Experimental Psychology*, 1968, **76**, 423-29 (a).

———. Learning conceptual rules: II. The role of positive and negative instances. *Journal of Experimental Psychology*, 1968, **77**, 488-94 (b)

———, D. DODD, and D. R. JUSTESEN. Concept identification: The effects of varying length and informational components of the intertrial interval. *Journal of Experimental Psychology*, 1965, **69**, 624-29.

BOURNE, L. E., JR., D. E. GUY, and N. WADSWORTH. Verbal-reinforcement combinations and the relative frequency of informative feedback in a card-sorting task. *Journal of Experimental Psychology*, 1967, **73**, 220-26.

BOURNE, L. E., JR., and R. C. HAYGOOD. The role of stimulus redundancy in the identification of concepts. *Journal of Experimental Psychology*, 1959, **58**, 232-38.

———. Supplementary report: Effects of redundant relevant information upon the identification of concepts. *Journal of Experimental Psychology*, 1961, **61**, 259-60.

BOURNE, L. E., JR., and P. C. JENNINGS. The relationship between contiguity and classification learning. *Journal of General Psychology*, 1963, **69**, 335-38.

BOURNE, L. E., JR., and B. K. PARKER. Differences among modes for portraying stimulus information in concept identification. *Psychonomic Science*, 1964, **1**, 209-10.

BOURNE, L. E., JR., and R. B. PENDLETON. Concept identification as a function of completeness and probability of information feedback. *Journal of Experimental Psychology*, 1958, **56**, 413-20.

BOURNE, L. E., JR., and F. RESTLE. Mathematical theory of concept identification. *Psychological Review*, 1959, **66**, 278-96.

BOUSFIELD, W. A. The occurrence of clustering in the recall of randomly arranged associates. *Journal of General Psychology*, 1953, **49**, 229-40.

———, B. H. COHEN, and G. A. WHITMARSH. Associative clustering in the recall of words of different taxonomic frequencies of occurrence. *Psychological Reports*, 1958, **4**, 39-44.

BOUSFIELD, W. A., G. A. WHITMARSH, and J. J. DANICK. Partial response identities in verbal generalization. *Psychological Reports*, 1958, **4**, 703-13.

BOWER, A. C., and W. L. KING. The effect of number of irrelevant stimulus dimensions, verbalizations, and sex on learning. *Psychonomic Science*, 1967, **8**, 453-54.

BOWER, G. An associational model for response and training variables in paired associates learning. *Psychological Review*, 1962, **69**, 34-53.

———, and T. TRABASSO. Reversals prior to solution in concept identification. *Journal of Experimental Psychology*, 1963, **66**, 409-18.

———. Concept identification. In R. C. Atkinson, ed., *Studies in Mathematical Psychology*. Stanford: Stanford University Press, 1964.

BRAINE, M. D. S. The ontogeny of English phrase structure: The first phase. *Language*, 1963, **39**, 1-13 (a).

———. On learning the grammatical order of words. *Psychological Review*, 1963, **70**, 323-48 (b).

BRALEY, L. S. Some conditions influencing the acquisition and utilization of cues. *Journal of Experimental Psychology*, 1962, **64**, 62-66.

———, and D. M. JOHNSON. Novelty effects in cue acquisition and utilization. *Journal of Experimental Psychology*, 1963, **66**, 421-22.

BROADBENT, D. E. *Perception and Communication*. New York: Pergamon Press, 1958.

BRODBECK, A. J., and O. C. IRWIN. The speech behavior of children without families. *Child Development*, 1946, **17**, 145-56.

BROWN, F. G., and E. J. ARCHER. Concept identification as a function of task complexity and distribution of practice. *Journal of Experimental Psychology,* 1956, **52,** 316-21.

BROWN, R. W. Language and categories. Appendix in J. S. Bruner, Jacqueline J. Goodnow, and G. A. Austin, *A Study of Thinking.* New York: John Wiley, 1956.

———. *Words and Things.* Glencoe, Ill.: The Free Press, 1958.

———. *Social Psychology.* Glencoe, Ill.: The Free Press, 1965.

———, and J. BERKO. Word association and the acquisition of grammar. *Child Development,* 1960, **31,** 1-14.

BROWN, R. W., and C. FRASER. The acquisition of syntax. In C. N. Cofer and Barbara S. Musgrave, eds., *Verbal Behavior and Learning.* New York: McGraw-Hill, 1963.

BROWN, R. W., and E. H. LENNEBERG. A study in language and cognition. *Journal of Abnormal and Social Psychology,* 1954, **49,** 454-62.

BROWN, R. W., and D. MCNEILL. The "tip of the tongue" phenomenon. *Journal of Verbal Learning and Verbal Behavior,* 1966, **5,** 325-37.

BRUNER, J. S. The course of cognitive growth. *American Psychologist,* 1964, **19,** 1-15.

———, JACQUELINE J. GOODNOW, and G. A. AUSTIN. *A Study of Thinking.* New York: John Wiley, 1956.

BRUNER, J. S., R. R. OLVER, and P. M. GREENFIELD. *Studies in Cognitive Growth.* New York: John Wiley, 1966.

BUGELSKI, B. R. Presentation time, total time, and mediation in paired associate learning. *Journal of Experimental Psychology,* 1962, **63,** 409-12.

———, and E. M. HUFF. A note on increasing the efficiency of Luchin's mental sets. *American Journal of Psychology,* 1962, **75,** 665-67.

BULGARELLA, ROSARIA, and E. J. ARCHER. Concept identification of auditory stimuli as a function of amount of relevant and irrelevant information. *Journal of Experimental Psychology,* 1962, **663,** 254-57.

BUNDERSON, C. V. Transfer of mental abilities at different stages of practice in the solution of concept problems. Unpublished doctoral dissertation, Princeton University, 1965.

BURACK, B., and D. MOOS. Effect of knowing the principle basic to the solution of a problem. *Journal of Educational Research,* 1956, **50,** 203-8.

BURKE, R. J., and N. R. F. MAIER. Attempts to predict success on an insight problem. *Psychological Reports,* 1965, **17,** 303-10.

———, and L. R. HOFFMAN. Functions of hints in individual problem-solving. *American Journal of Psychology,* 1966, **79,** 389-99.

BUSS, A. H., and EDITH H. BUSS. The effect of verbal reinforcement combinations on conceptual learning. *Journal of Experimental Psychology,* 1956, **52,** 283-87.

BYERS, J. I., and R. E. DAVIDSON. The role of hypothesizing in the facilitation of concept attainment. *Journal of Verbal Learning and Verbal Behavior,* 1967, **6,** 595-600.

CAHILL, H. E., and C. I. HOVLAND. The role of memory in the acquisition of concepts. *Journal of Experimental Psychology,* 1960, **59,** 137-44.

CAMPBELL, D. T. Blind variation and selective retention in creative thought and in other knowledge processes. *Psychological Review,* 1960, **67,** 380-400.

CAREY, G. L. Sex differences in problem-solving as a function of attitude differences. *Journal of Abnormal and Social Psychology,* 1958, **56,** 256-60.

CARMICHAEL, L. A., H. P. HOGAN, and A. A. WALTER. An experimental study of the effect of language on the reproduction of visually perceived form. *Journal of Experimental Psychology,* 1932, **15,** 73-86.

CARON, A. J., S. M. UNGER, and M. B. PARLOFF. A test of Maltzman's originality training. *Journal of Verbal Learning and Verbal Behavior,* 1963, **1,** 436-42.

CARROLL, J. B., ed. *Language, Thought, and Reality, Selected Writings of Benjamin Lee Whorf.* Cambridge, Mass.: M.I.T. Press, 1956.

———. *Language and Thought.* Englewood Cliffs, N.J.: Prentice-Hall, 1964.

———, and J. B. CASAGRANDE. The function of language classifications in behavior. In Eleanor E. Maccoby, T. M. Newcomb, and E. L. Hartley, eds., *Readings in Social Psychology* (3rd ed.). New York: Holt, Rinehart, and Winston, 1958.

CAZDEN, C. B. Environmental assistance to the child's acquisition of grammar. Unpublished doctoral dissertation, Harvard University, 1965.

CHOMSKY, N. *Syntactic Structures.* The Hague: Mouton, 1957.

———. A review of B. F. Skinner's *Verbal Behavior. Language,* 1959, **35,** 26-58.

———. *Aspects of the Theory of Syntax*. Cambridge, Mass.: M.I.T. Press, 1965.

———. *Language and Mind*. New York: Harcourt, Brace, Jovanovich, 1968.

CHRISTENSEN, P. R., J. P. GUILFORD, and R. C. WILSON. Relations of creative responses to working time and instructions. *Journal of Experimental Psychology*, 1957, **53**, 82-88.

CLIFTON, C., JR., and P. ODOM. Similarity relations among certain English sentence constructions. *Psychological Monographs*, 1966, **80**, No. 613.

COFER, C. N., F. DIAMOND, R. A. OLSEN, J. S. STEIN, and H. WALKER. Comparison of anticipation and recall methods in paired-associate learning. *Journal of Experimental Psychology*, 1967, **75**, 545-58.

COHEN, B. H., W. A. BOUSFIELD, and G. A. WHITMARSH. Cultural norms for verbal items in 43 categories. Tech. Report No. 22, ONR Contract Nonr-631, University of Connecticut, 1957.

COHEN, J. C., and BARBARA S. MUSGRAVE. Effect of meaningfulness on cue selection in verbal paired-associate learning. *Journal of Experimental Psychology*, 1964, **68**, 284-91.

COHEN, J. L. The effect of letter frequency on anagram solution times. *Psychonomic Science*, 1968, **11**, 79-80.

CONANT, M. B., and T. TRABASSO. Conjunctive and disjunctive concept formation under equal-information conditions. *Journal of Experimental Psychology*, 1964, **57**, 250-55.

CONRAD, R. Acoustic confusions in immediate memory. *British Journal of Psychology*, 1964, **55**, 75-84.

CORMAN, B. R. The effect of varying amounts and kinds of information as guidance in problem solving. *Psychological Monograph*, 1957, **71** (Whole No. 431).

CRAWFORD, JUNE, E. B. HUNT, and G. PEAK. One-trial learning of disjunctive concepts. *Journal of Verbal Learning and Verbal Behavior*, 1967, **6**, 207-12.

DANKS, J. H., and S. GLUCKSBERG. Asymmetric transfer between the Remote Associates Test and functional fixedness. *Psychological Reports*, 1966, **19**, 682.

DARWIN, C. *Origin of Species* (2nd ed.). London: Collier, 1909.

DAVIS, G. A. Detrimental effects of distraction, additional response alternatives, and longer response chains in solving switch-light problems. *Journal of Experimental Psychology*, 1967, **73**, 45-55.

———, and M. E. MANSKE. An instructional method for increasing originality. *Psychonomic Science*, 1966, **6**, 73-74.

DAVIS, G. A., A. J. TRAIN, and M. E. MANSKE. Trial and error versus "insightful" problem solving: Effects of distraction, additional response alternatives, and longer response chains. *Journal of Experimental Psychology*, 1968, **76**, 337-40.

DAVIS, K. G., and H. E. HESS. The effectiveness of concepts at various levels of awareness. *Journal of Experimental Psychology*, 1962, **63**, 63-67.

DEESE, J. On the prediction of occurrence of particular verbal intrusions in immediate recall. *Journal of Experimental Psychology*, 1959, **58**, 17-22.

———. On the structure of associative meaning. *Psychological Review*, 1962, **60**, 161-75.

———. *The Structure of Associations in Language and Thought*. Baltimore: Johns Hopkins, 1965.

———. Behavior and fact. *American Psychologist*, 1969, **24**, 515-22.

deGROOT, A. D. Perception and memory versus thought: Some old ideas and recent findings. In B. Kleinmuntz, ed., *Problem Solving: Research, Method, and Theory*. New York: John Wiley, 1966.

DENNY, J. P. Effects of anxiety and intelligence on concept formation. *Journal of Experimental Psychology*, 1966, **72**, 596-602.

DEWEY, J. *How We Think*. Boston: Heath, 1910.

DiVESTA, F. J., and R. T. WALLS. Transfer of object-function in problem solving. *American Educational Research Journal*, 1967, 4, **62**, 596-602 (a).

———. Transfer of solution rules in problem solving. *Journal of Educational Psychology*, 1967, **58**, 319-26 (b).

DODD, D. H. Transfer effects from rule learning to logical problems. *Cognitive Processes Report* No. 105, University of Colorado: Mimeo, 1967.

———, and L. E. BOURNE, JR. A test of some assumptions of a hypothesis-testing model of concept identification. *Journal of Experimental Psychology*, 1969, **80**, 69-72.

DOMINOWSKI, R. L. Role of memory in concept learning. *Psychological Bulletin*, 1965, **63**, 271-80 (a).

———. Problem difficulty as a function of relative frequency of correct responses. *Psychonomic Science*, 1965, **3**, 417-18 (b).

———. Anagram solving as a function of letter moves. *Journal of Verbal Learning and Verbal Behavior*, 1966, **5**, 107-11.

———. Anagram solving as a function of bigram rank and word frequency. *Journal of Experimental Psychology*, 1967, **75**, 299-306.

———. Anagram solving as a function of letter-sequence information. *Journal of Experimental Psychology*, 1968, **76**, 78-83.

———. The effect of pronunciation practice on anagram difficulty. *Psychonomic Science*, 1969, **15**, 99-100.

———, and C. P. DUNCAN. Anagram solving as a function of bigram frequency. *Journal of Verbal Learning and Verbal Behavior*, 1964, **3**, 321-25.

DOMINOWSKI, R. L., and B. R. EKSTRAND. Direct and associative priming in anagram solving. *Journal of Experimental Psychology*, 1967, **74**, 85-86.

DULANY, D. E., JR. Awareness, rules, and propositional control: A confrontation with S-R behavior theory. In T. R. Dixon and D. L. Horton, eds., *Verbal Behavior and General Behavior Theory*. Englewood Cliffs, N.J.: Prentice-Hall, 1968.

DUNCAN, C. P. Transfer after training with single versus multiple tasks. *Journal of Experimental Psychology*, 1958, **55**, 63-72.

———. Recent research on human problem solving. *Psychological Bulletin*, 1959, **56**, 397-429.

———. Attempts to influence performance on an insight problem. *Psychological Reports*, 1961, **9**, 35-42.

———. Effect of instructions and information on problem solving. *Journal of Experimental Psychology*, 1963, **65**, 321-27.

———. Problem-solving within a verbal response hierarchy. *Psychonomic Science*, 1966, **4**, 147-48 (a).

———. Effect of word frequency on thinking of a word. *Journal of Verbal Learning and Verbal Behavior*, 1966, **5**, 434-40 (b).

———. Response hierarchies in problem solving. In C. P. Duncan, ed., *Thinking: Current Experimental Studies*. Philadelphia: Lippincott, 1967.

———, and G. WOOD. Norms for successive word associations. *Psychonomic Science Monograph Supplement*, 1966, **1**, 203-6.

DUNCKER, K. On problem-solving. *Psychological Monographs*, 1945, **58**, 5 (Whole No. 270).

DUNHAM, J. L., J. P. GUILFORD, and R. HOEPFNER. Multivariate approaches to discovering the intellectual components of concept learning. *Psychological Review*, 1968, **75**, 206-21.

DUNN, R. F. Anxiety and verbal concept learning. *Journal of Experimental Psychology*, 1968, **76**, 286-90.

DUVALL, A. N. Functional fixedness: a replication study. *Psychological Record*, 1965, **15**, 497-599.

EBBINGHAUS, H. *Uber das Gedachtnis*. 1885. Reprinted *On Memory*. H. A. Ruger and C. E. Bussenius (trans.). New York: Teachers College, 1913.

EKSTRAND, B. R. A note on measuring response learning during paired-associate learning. *Journal of Verbal Learning and Verbal Behavior*, 1966, **5**, 344-47.

———, and R. L. DOMINOWSKI. Solving words as anagrams. *Psychonomic Science*, 1965, **2**, 239-40.

———. Solving words as anagrams: II. A clarification. *Journal of Experimental Psychology*, 1968, **77**, 552-58.

EKSTRAND, B. R., W. P. WALLACE, and B. J. UNDERWOOD. A frequency theory of verbal-discrimination learning. *Psychological Review*, 1966, **73**, 566-78.

ELLIS, H. C., D. W. BESSEMER, J. V. DEVINE, and C. L. TRAFTON. Recognition of random tactual shapes following predifferentiation training. *Perceptual and Motor Skills*, 1962, **10**, 99-102.

ELLIS, H. C., R. L. FEUGE, K. K. LONG, and V. G. PEGRAM. Evidence for acquired equivalence of cues in a perceptual task. *Perceptual and Motor Skills*, 1964, **19**, 159-62.

ELLIS, H. C., and D. G. MULLER. Transfer in perceptual learning following stimulus predifferentiation. *Journal of Experimental Psychology*, 1964, **68**, 388-95.

EPSTEIN, W. The influence of syntactical structure on learning. *American Journal of Psychology*, 1961, **74**, 80-85.

———. A further study of the influence of syntactic structure on learning. *American Journal of Psychology*, 1962, **75**, 121-26.

ERICKSON, J. R., M. M. ZAJKOWSKI, and E. D. EHMANN. All-or-none assumptions in concept identification: analysis of latency data. *Journal of Experimental Psychology*, 1966, **72**, 690-97.

ERVIN, SUSAN M. Imitation and structural change in children's language. In E. H. Lenneberg, ed., *New Directions in the Study of Language.* Cambridge, Mass.: M.I.T. Press, 1964.

ERVIN-TRIPP, SUSAN. Language development. In L. W. Hoffman and M. L. Hoffman, eds., *Review of Child Development Research,* Vol. 2. New York: Russell Sage Foundation, 1966.

ESPER, E. A. A technique for the experimental investigation of associative interference in artificial linguistic material. *Language Monographs,* 1925, No. 1.

FEATHER, N. T. Effects of prior success and failure on expectations of success and subsequent performance. *Journal of Personality and Social Psychology,* 1966, **3**, 287-98.

FEIGENBAUM, E. A., and J. FELDMAN, eds. *Computers and Thought.* New York: McGraw-Hill, 1963.

FELLER, W. *An Introduction to Probability Theory and Its Applications,* Vol. I (2nd ed.). New York: John Wiley, 1957.

FISHMAN, J. A systematization of the Whorfian hypothesis. *Behavioral Science,* 1960, **5**, 323-39.

FLAVELL, J. H. *The Developmental Psychology of Jean Piaget.* New York: Van Nostrand Reinhold, 1963.

———, A. COOPER, and R. H. LOISELLE. Effect of the number of pre-utilization functions on functional fixedness in problem-solving. *Psychological Reports,* 1958, **5**, 343-50.

FODOR, J., and T. BEVER. The psychological reality of linguistic segments. *Journal of Verbal Learning and Verbal Behavior,* 1965, **4**, 414-20.

FORGUS, R. H., and R. J. SCHWARTZ. Efficient retention and transfer as affected by learning method. *Journal of Psychology,* 1957, **43**, 135-39.

FOSS, D. J. An analysis of learning in a miniature linguistic system. *Journal of Experimental Psychology,* 1968, **76**, 450-59 (a).

———. Learning and discovery in the acquisition of structured material: effects of number of items and their sequence. *Journal of Experimental Psychology,* 1968, **77**, 341-44 (b).

FREEDMAN, J. L. Increasing creativity by free-association training. *Journal of Experimental Psychology,* 1965, **69**, 89-91.

———, and S. A. MEDNICK. Ease of attainment of concepts as a function of response dominance variance. *Journal of Experimental Psychology,* 1958, **55**, 463-66.

FREEMAN, G. L. Mental activity and the muscular process. *Psychological Review,* 1931, **38**, 428-47.

FREIBERGS, VAIRA, and E. TULVING. The effect of practice of utilization of information from positive and negative instances in concept identification. *Canadian Journal of Psychology,* 1961, **15**, 101-6.

FRENCH, E. G. The interaction of achievement motivation and ability in problem-solving success. *Journal of Abnormal and Social Psychology,* 1958, **67**, 306-9.

FRIEDMAN, S. R. Developmental level and concept learning: Confirmation of an inverse relationship. *Psychonomic Science,* 1965, **2**, 3-4.

FRIES, C. C. *American English Grammar.* New York: Appleton-Century-Crofts, 1940.

FRY, D. B. The development of the phonological system in the normal and the deaf child. In F. Smith and G. A. Miller, eds., *The Genesis of Language.* Cambridge, Mass.: M.I.T. Press, 1966.

FURTH, H. G. Research with the deaf: Implications for language and cognition. *Psychological Bulletin,* 1964, **62**, 145-64.

GAGNÉ, R. M. Problem-solving and thinking. *Annual Review of Psychology,* 1959, **10**, 147-72.

———, and E. C. SMITH, JR. A study of the effects of verbalization on problem-solving. *Journal of Experimental Psychology,* 1962, **63**, 12-18.

GAMES, P. A. A factorial analysis of verbal learning tasks. *Journal of Experimental Psychology,* 1962, **63**, 1-11.

GARDNER, R. A., and W. N. RUNQUIST. Acquisition and extinction of problem-solving set. *Journal of Experimental Psychology,* 1958, **55**, 274-77.

GARNER, W. R., and J. R. WHITMAN. Form and amount of internal structure as factors in free-recall learning of nonsense words. *Journal of Verbal Learning and Verbal Behavior,* 1965, **4**, 257-66.

GARRETT, M., T. BEVER, and J. FODOR. The active use of grammar in speech perception. *Perception and Psychophysics,* 1966, **1**, 30-32.

GARRETT, M., and J. FODOR. Psychological theories and linguistic constructs. In T. R. Dixon and D. L. Horton, eds., *Verbal Behavior and General Behavior Theory.* Englewood Cliffs, N.J.: Prentice-Hall, 1968.

GAVURIN, E. I. Anagram solving under conditions of letter order randomization. *Journal of Psychology,* 1967, **65,** 179-82.

GIBSON, J. J., and E. J. GIBSON. Perceptual learning: Differentiation or enrichment? *Psychological Review,* 1955, **62,** 32-41.

GLANZER, M., and W. H. CLARK. Accuracy of perceptual recall: An analysis of organization. *Journal of Verbal Learning and Verbal Behavior,* 1962, **1,** 289-99.

GLANZER, M., JANELLEN HUTTENLOCHER, and W. H. CLARK. Systematic operations in solving concept problems: A parametric study of a class of problems. *Psychological Monographs,* 1963, **77,** No. 1 (Whole No. 564).

GLANZER, M., T. TAUB, and R. MURPHY. An evaluation of three theories of figural organization. *American Journal of Psychology,* 1968, **81,** 53-66.

GLEASON, H. A., JR. *An Introduction to Descriptive Linguistics.* New York: Holt, Rinehart, & Winston, 1961.

GLUCKSBERG, S. The influence of strength of drive on functional fixedness and perceptual recognition. *Journal of Experimental Psychology,* 1962, **63,** 36-51.

———. Functional fixedness: Problem solution as a function of observing responses. *Psychonomic Science,* 1964, **1,** 117-18.

———, and J. H. DANKS. Functional fixedness: stimulus equivalence mediated by semantic-acoustic similarity. *Journal of Experimental Psychology,* 1967, **74,** 400-5.

———. Effects of discriminative labels and of nonsense labels upon availability of novel function. *Journal on Verbal Learning and Verbal Behavior,* 1968, **7,** 72-76.

GLUCKSBERG, S., and R. W. WEISBERG. Verbal behavior and problem solving: some effects of labeling in a functional fixedness problem. *Journal of Experimental Psychology,* 1966, **71,** 659-64.

GOLDBECK, R. A., B. B. BERNSTEIN, W. A. HILLIX, and M. H. MARX. Application of the half-split technique to problem-solving tasks. *Journal of Experimental Psychology,* 1957, **53,** 330-38.

GOLLIN, E. S., ANNE SARAVO, and CYNTHIA SALTEN. Perceptual distinctiveness and oddity-problem solving in children. *Journal of Experimental Child Psychology,* 1967, **5,** 586-96.

GOODNOW, JACQUELINE J., and L. POSTMAN. Probability learning in a problem solving situation. *Journal of Experimental Psychology,* 1955, **49,** 16-22.

GRANT, D. A., and E. A. BERG. A behavioral analysis of degree of reinforcement and ease of shifting to new responses in a Weigl-type card sorting problem. *Journal of Experimental Psychology,* 1948, **38,** 404-11.

GRANT, D. A., and J. R. COST. Continuities and discontinuities in conceptual behavior in a card sorting problem. *Journal of Experimental Psychology,* 1954, **50,** 237-44.

GREENBERG, J. H., and J. J. JENKINS. Studies in the psychological correlates of the sound system of American English. *Word,* 1964, 157-77.

GUILFORD, J. P. Creativity: Yesterday, today, and tomorrow. *Journal of Creative Behavior,* 1968, **1,** 3-14.

GUY, D. E., F. VAN FLEET, and L. E. BOURNE, JR. Effects of adding a stimulus dimension prior to a nonreversal shift. *Journal of Experimental Psychology,* 1966, **72,** 161-68.

HABER, R. N. Perception and thought: an information-processing analysis. In J. F. Voss, ed., *Approaches to Thought.* Columbus, O.: Charles E. Merrill, 1969.

HAKE, H. W., and C. W. ERIKSEN. Effect of number of permissible response categories on learning of a constant number of visual stimuli. *Journal of Experimental Psychology,* 1955, **50,** 161-67.

HALL, R. A., JR. *Introductory Linguistics.* Philadelphia: Chilton, 1964.

HAMMOND, K. R., and D. A. SUMMERS. Cognitive dependence on linear and nonlinear cues. *Psychological Review,* 1965, **72,** 215-24.

HARLESTON, B. W. Test anxiety and performance in problem-solving situations. *Journal of Personality,* 1962, **30,** 557-73.

HARLOW, H. Learning set and error factor theory. In S. Koch, ed., *Psychology: A study of a science.* New York: McGraw-Hill, 1959.

———. Analysis of discrimination learning by monkeys. *Journal of Experimental Psychology,* 1960, **40,** 26-39.

HARTER, SUSAN. Discrimination learning set in children as function of IQ and MA. *Journal of Experimental Child Psychology,* 1965, **2,** 31-43.

———. Mental age, IQ, and motivational factors in the discrimination learning set performance of normal and retarded children. *Journal of Experimental Child Psychology,* 1967, **5,** 123-41.

HASELRUD, G., and S. MEYERS. The transfer value of given and individually derived principles. *Journal of Educational Psychology,* 1958, **49,** 239-44.

HAYES, J. R. Problem topology and the solution process. *Journal of Verbal Learning and Verbal Behavior,* 1965, **4,** 126-32.

HAYGOOD, DANIELLE. Audio-visual concept formation. *Journal of Educational Psychology,* 1965, **56,** 126-32.

HAYGOOD, R. C., and L. E. BOURNE, JR. Effects of intermittent reinforcement of an irrelevant dimension and task complexity upon concept identification. *Journal of Experimental Psychology,* 1960, **60,** 371-75.

———. Attribute- and rule-learning aspects of conceptual behavior. *Psychological Review,* 1965, **72,** 175-95.

HAYGOOD, R. C., and J. V. DEVINE. Effects of composition of the positive category on concept learning. *Journal of Experimental Psychology,* 1967, **74,** 230-35.

HAYGOOD, R. C., and J. B. KIEHLBAUCH. Effects of logical pretraining on concept rule-learning performance. Unpublished report, Kansas State University, 1965.

HAYGOOD, R. C., and M. STEVENSON. Effects of number of irrelevant dimensions in nonconjunctive concept learning. *Journal of Experimental Psychology,* 1967, **74,** 302-4.

HEBERT, J. A., and C. A. ROGERS, JR. Anagram solution as a function of pronounceability and difficulty. *Psychonomic Science,* 1966, **4,** 359-60.

HEISE, D. D. Semantic differential profiles for 1000 most frequent English words. *Psychological Monographs,* 1965, **79,** No. 8.

HILGARD, E. R., and G. BOWER. *Theories of Learning.* New York: Appleton-Century-Crofts, 1966.

HILGARD, E. R., R. P. IRVINE, and J. E. WHIPPLE. Rote memorization, understanding, and transfer: An extension of Katona's card trick experiments. *Journal of Experimental Psychology,* 1953, **46,** 288-92.

HINTZMAN, D. L. Articulatory coding in short-term memory. *Journal of Verbal Learning and Verbal Behavior,* 1967, **6,** 312-16.

HOFFMAN, H. N. A study in an aspect of concept formation, with subnormal, average and superior adolescents. *Genetic Psychological Monographs,* 1955, **52,** 191-239.

———, and N. R. F. MAIER. Sex differences, sex composition, and group problem solving. *Journal of Abnormal and Social Psychology,* 1961, **63,** 453-56.

HOROWITZ, L. M., M. A. WHITE, and D. W. ATWOOD. Word fragments as aids to recall: the organization of a word. *Journal of Experimental Psychology,* 1968, **76,** 225-32.

HORTON, D. L., and P. M. KJELDERGAARD. An experimental analysis of associative factors in mediated generalization. *Psychological Monographs,* 1961, **75,** No. 11.

HOUSE, BETTY J., and D. ZEAMAN. Reversal and nonreversal shifts in discrimination learning in retardates. *Journal of Experimental Psychology,* 1962, **63,** 441-51.

HOVLAND, C. I. A "communication analysis" of concept learning. *Psychological Review,* 1952, **59,** 461-72.

———, and W. WEISS. Transmission of information concerning concepts through positive and negative instances. *Journal of Experimental Psychology,* 1953, **45,** 165-82.

HULL, C. L. Knowledge and purpose as habit mechanisms. *Psychological Review,* 1930, **57,** 511-25.

———. *A Behavior System.* New Haven: Yale University Press, 1952.

HUNT, E. B. Memory effects in concept learning. *Journal of Experimental Psychology,* 1961, **62,** 598-604.

———. *Concept learning: An Information Processing Problem.* New York: John Wiley, 1962.

———. Selection and reception conditions in grammar and concept learning. *Journal of Verbal Learning and Verbal Behavior,* 1965, **4,** 211-15.

———, and C. I. HOVLAND. Order of consideration of different types of concepts. *Journal of Experimental Psychology,* 1960, **59,** 220-25.

HUNT, E. B., JANET MARIN, and P. J. STONE. *Experiments in Induction.* New York: Academic Press, 1966.

HUNTER, I. M. L. Further studies on anagram solving. *British Journal of Psychology,* 1961, **52,** 161-65.

HUTTENLOCHER, JANELLEN. Effects of manipulation of attributes on efficiency of concept formation. *Psychological Reports,* 1962, **10,** 503-9 (a).

———. Some effects of negative instances on the formation of simple concepts. *Psychological Reports,* 1962, **11,** 35-42 (b).

———. How certain formal reasoning problems

are solved. *Journal of Verbal Learning and Verbal Behavior,* 1967, **6,** 802-8.

IRWIN, O. C. Infant speech: Development of vowel sounds. *Journal of Speech and Hearing Disorders,* 1948, **13,** 31-34 (*a*).

———. Infant speech: The effect of family occupational status and of age on use of sound types. *Journal of Speech and Hearing Disorders,* 1948, **13,** 224-26 (*b*).

———. Infant speech: The effect of family occupational status and of age on sound frequency. *Journal of Speech and Hearing Disorders,* 1948, **13,** 320-23 (*c*).

———. Infant speech: Effect of systematic reading of stories. *Journal of Speech and Hearing Research,* 1960, **3,** 187-90.

JACOBSON, E. Electrical measurements of neuromuscular states during mental activities: IV. Evidence of contraction of specific muscles during imagination. *American Journal of Physiology,* 1930, **95,** 703-12.

JACOBUS, D. A., and N. F. JOHNSON. An experimental set to adopt a set. *Psychological Reports,* 1964, **15,** 737.

JAKOBSON, R., C. G. M. FANT, and M. HALLE. *Preliminaries to Speech Analysis, the Distinctive Features and Their Correlates.* Cambridge, Mass.: M.I.T. Press, 1952.

JAMES, C. T., and J. G. GREENO. Stimulus selection at different stages of paired-associate learning. *Journal of Experimental Psychology,* 1967, **74,** 75-83.

JAMES, W. *The Principles of Psychology.* New York: Holt, 1890.

JENKINS, J. J. Mediated associations: Paradigms and situations. In C. N. Cofer and Barbara S. Musgrave, eds., *Verbal Behavior and Learning: Problems and Processes.* New York: McGraw-Hill, 1963.

———. Meaningfulness and concepts: Concepts and meaningfulness. In H. Klausmeier and C. W. Harris, eds., *Analyses of Concept Learning.* New York: Academic Press, 1966.

———, D. J. Foss, and J. H. GREENBERG. Phonological distinctive features as cues in learning. *Journal of Experimental Psychology,* 1968, **77,** 200-5.

JENKINS, J. J., W. D. MINK, and W. A. RUSSELL. Associative clustering as a function of verbal association strength. *Psychological Reports,* 1958, **4,** 127-36.

JOHNSON, D. M. *The Psychology of Thought and Judgment.* New York: Harper, 1955.

———. Solution of anagrams. *Psychological Bulletin,* 1966, **66,** 371-84.

———, and J. W. JENNINGS. Serial analysis of three problem-solving processes. *Journal of Psychology,* 1963, **56,** 43-52.

JOHNSON, D. M., D. O. LYNCH, and J. G. RAMSEY. Word frequency and verbal comparisons. *Journal of Verbal Learning and Verbal Behavior,* 1967, **6,** 403-7.

JOHNSON, D. M., G. R. PARROTT, and R. P. STRATTON. Productive thinking: Produce one solution or many. *Proceedings of the 75th Annual Convention of the American Psychological Association,* 1967, **2,** 299-300.

JOHNSON, D. M., and D. J. ZERBOLIO. Relations between production and judgment of plot titles. *American Journal of Psychology,* 1964, **77,** 99-105.

JOHNSON, N. F. Linguistic models and functional units of language behavior. In S. Rosenberg, ed., *Directions in Psycholinguistics.* New York: Macmillan, 1965.

JOHNSON, P. J., and R. M. WHITE, JR. Concept of dimensionality and reversal shift performance in children. *Journal of Experimental Child Psychology,* 1967, **5,** 223-27.

JOHNSON, T. J., and A. P. VAN MONDFRANS. Order of solutions in ambiguous anagrams as a function of word frequency of the solution words. *Psychonomic Science,* 1965, **3,** 565-66.

JONES, H. E., and H. S. CONRAD. The growth and decline of intelligence. *Genetic Psychological Monographs,* 1933, **13,** 223-98.

JUDSON, A. J., C. N. COFER, and S. GELFAND. Reasoning as an associative process: II. "Direction" in problem solving as a function of prior reinforcement of relevant responses. *Psychological Reports,* 1956, **2,** 501-7.

JURCA, N. H., and C. P. DUNCAN. Problem solving within a word-frequency hierarchy. *Journal of Verbal Learning and Verbal Behavior,* 1969, **8,** 229-33.

KAGAN, J., H. A. MOSS, and J. E. SIGEL. Psychological significance of styles of conceptualization. In J. C. Wright and J. Kagan, eds., *Basic Cognitive Processes in Children. Monographs of Social Research, Child Development,* 1963, **28,** 73-112.

KAPLAN, I. T., and T. CARVELLAS. Effect of word length on anagram solution time. *Journal of Verbal Learning and Verbal Behavior,* 1968, **7,** 201-6.

KAPLAN, I. T., and W. N. SCHOENFELD. Oculomotor

patterns during the solution of visually displayed anagrams. *Journal of Experimental Psychology,* 1966, **72,** 447-51.

KATES, S. L., and L. YUDIN. Concept attainment and memory. *Journal of Educational Psychology,* 1964, **55,** 103-11.

KATZ, J. J., and J. A. FODOR. The structure of a semantic theory. *Language,* 1963, **39,** 170-210.

KATZ, P. A. Effects of labels on children's perception and discrimination learning. *Journal of Experimental Psychology,* 1963, **66,** 423-28.

———, and E. ZIGLER. Effects of labels on perceptual transfer: stimulus and developmental factors. *Journal of Experimental Psychology,* 1969, **80,** 73-77.

KEELE, S. W., and E. J. ARCHER. A comparison of two types of information in concept identification. *Journal of Verbal Learning and Verbal Behavior,* 1967, **6,** 185-92.

KENDLER, H. H., A. GREENBERG, and H. RICHMAN. The influence of massed and distributed practice on the development of mental set. *Journal of Experimental Psychology,* 1952, **43,** 21-25.

KENDLER, H. H., and TRACY S. KENDLER. Effect of verbalization on reversal shifts in children. *Science,* 1961, **134,** 1619-20.

———. Vertical and horizontal processes in problem-solving. *Psychological Review,* 1962, **69,** 1-16.

KENDLER, TRACY S. Verbalization and optional reversal shifts among kindergarten children. *Journal of Verbal Learning and Verbal Behavior,* 1964, **3,** 428-33.

KEPROS, P. G. Identification of conjunctive concepts as a function of stimulus and response complexity. Unpublished doctor's thesis, University of Utah, 1965.

———, and L. E. BOURNE, JR. Identification of biconditional concepts: effects of number of relevant and irrelevant dimensions. *Canadian Journal of Psychology,* 1966, **20,** 198-207.

KIMBLE, G. A. *Hilgard and Marquis' Conditioning and Learning.* New York: Appleton-Century-Crofts, 1961.

———. Mediating association. *Journal of Experimental Psychology,* 1968, **76,** 263-66.

KING, W. L. Learning and utilization of conjunctive and disjunctive rules: a developmental study. *Journal of Experimental Child Psychology,* 1966, **4,** 217-31.

KINSMAN, R. A. The effects of induced anxiety on the identification of a novel stimulus dimension. Cognitive Processes Report No. 109, Boulder, Colorado, 1968.

KJELDERGAARD, P. M. Transfer and mediation in verbal learning. In T. R. Dixon and D. L. Horton, eds., *Verbal Behavior and General Behavior Theory.* Englewood Cliffs, N.J.: Prentice-Hall, 1968.

KLUGH, H. E., DAY COLGAN, and JUDITH A. RYBA. Developmental level and speed of relational concept formation: a possible inverse relationship. *Psychonomic Science,* 1964, **1,** 89-90.

KOFFKA, K. *The Growth of the Mind.* New York: Harcourt, Brace, 1928.

———. *Principles of Gestalt Psychology.* New York: Harcourt, Brace, 1935.

KOHLER, W. *The Mentality of Apes.* New York: Harcourt, Brace, 1925.

KUCERA, H., and W. N. FRANCIS. *Computational Analysis of Present-day American English.* Providence: Brown University Press, 1967.

KURTZ, K. H., and C. I. HOVLAND. Concept learning with different sequences of instances. *Journal of Experimental Psychology,* 1956, **51,** 239-43.

LANTZ, D., and V. STEFFLRE. Language and cognition revisited. *Journal of Abnormal and Social Psychology,* 1964, **69,** 471-81.

LAUGHLIN, P. R. Speed versus minimum choice instructions in concept attainment. *Journal of Experimental Psychology,* 1964, **67,** 596.

———. Selection strategies in concept attainment as a function of number of persons and stimulus display. *Journal of Experimental Psychology,* 1965, **70,** 323-27.

———. Selection strategies in concept attainment as a function of number of relevant problem attributes. *Journal of Experimental Psychology,* 1966, **71,** 773-77.

———, and R. M. JORDAN. Selection strategies in conjunctive, disjunctive and biconditional concept attainment. *Journal of Experimental Psychology,* 1967, **75,** 188-93.

LENNEBERG, E. H. A biological perspective of language. In E. H. Lenneberg, ed., *New Directions in the Study of Language.* Cambridge, Mass.: M.I.T. Press, 1964.

———. *Biological Foundations of Language.* New York: John Wiley, 1967.

———, and J. M. ROBERTS. *The Language of Experience: A Study in Methodology.* Memoir 18, Indiana University publications in Anthropology and Linguistics, 1956.

LEVINE, M. Cue neutralization: The effects of

random reinforcement in discrimination learning. *Psychological Review,* 1962, **63,** 438-43.

———. Hypothesis behavior by humans during discrimination learning. *Journal of Experimental Psychology,* 1966, **71,** 331-36.

LEVITT, E. E. The water-jar Einstellung test as a measure of rigidity. *Psychological Bulletin,* 1956, **53,** 347-70.

LEVY, L. H. Originality as a role-defined behavior. *Journal of Personality and Social Psychology,* 1968, **9,** 72-78.

LINDLEY, R. H. Effects of controlled coding cues in short-term memory. *Journal of Experimental Psychology,* 1963, **66,** 580-87.

LORDAHL, D. S. Concept identification using simultaneous auditory and visual signals. *Journal of Experimental Psychology,* 1961, **62,** 282-90.

———, S. E. BERGER, and A. A. MANNING. The effects of irrelevant information and stimulus dominance in an oddity problem. *Psychonomic Science,* 1967, **8,** 325-26.

LOWENKRON, B., and P. J. JOHNSON. Yoked group comparison of selection and reception paradigms of concept attainment. *Psychological Reports,* 1968, **23,** 1143-49.

LUCHINS, A. S. Mechanization in problem solving: the effect of Einstellung. *Psychological Monographs,* 1942, **54,** 6, Whole No. 248.

———, and EDITH H. LUCHINS. *Rigidity of Behavior: A Variational Approach to the Effect of Einstellung.* Eugene, Oregon: University of Oregon Press, 1959.

LURIA, A. R. *The Role of Speech in the Regulation of Normal and Abnormal Behavior.* New York: Liveright, 1961.

McGUIGAN, F. J. *Thinking: Studies of Covert Language Processes.* New York: Appleton-Century-Crofts, 1966.

McNEILL, D. On theories of language acquisition. In T. R. Dixon and D. L. Horton, eds. *Verbal Behavior and General Behavior Theory.* Englewood Cliffs, N.J.: Prentice-Hall, 1968.

MAIER, N. R. F. Reasoning in humans: I. On direction. *Journal of Comparative Psychology,* 1930, **10,** 115-43.

———. The behavior mechanisms concerned with problem solving. *Psychological Review,* 1940, **47,** 43-58.

———, and R. J. BURKE. Test of the concept of "availability of functions" in problem solving. *Psychological Reports,* 1966, **19,** 119-25.

MAIER, N. R. F., and J. C. JANZEN. Are good problem-solvers also creative? *Psychological Reports,* 1969, **24,** 139-46.

MALMO, R. B. Activation: A neuropsychological dimension. *Psychological Review,* 1959, **66,** 367-86.

MALTZMAN, I. Thinking: From a Behavioristic point of view. *Psychological Review,* 1955, **66,** 367-86.

———. On the training of originality. *Psychological Review,* 1960, **67,** 229-42.

———, M. BELLONI, and M. FISHBEIN. Experimental studies of associative variables in originality. *Psychological Monographs,* 1964, **78,** 3, Whole No. 580.

MALTZMAN, I., W. BOGARTZ, and L. BREGER. A procedure for increasing word association originality and its transfer effects. *Journal of Experimental Psychology,* 1958, **56,** 392-98.

MALTZMAN, I., L. BROOKS, W. BOGARTZ, and S. S. SUMMERS. The facilitation of problem solving by prior exposure to uncommon responses. *Journal of Experimental Psychology,* 1958, **56,** 399-406.

MALTZMAN, I., E. EISMAN, and L. O. BROOKS. Some relationships between methods of instruction, personality variables, and problem-solving behavior. *Journal of Educational Psychology,* 1956, **47,** 71-78.

———, and W. M. SMITH. Task instructions for anagrams following different task instructions and training. *Journal of Experimental Psychology,* 1956, **51,** 418-20.

MALTZMAN, I., S. SIMON, D. RASKIN, and L. LICHT. Experimental studies in the training of originality. *Psychological Monographs,* 1960, **74,** 5, Whole No. 493.

MANDLER, G. From association to structure. *Psychological Review,* 1962, **69,** 415-27.

———. Organization and memory. In K. W. Spence and Janet T. Spence, eds., *The Psychology of Learning and Motivation,* Vol. 1. New York: Academic Press, 1967.

———. Organized recall: individual functions. *Psychonomic Science,* 1968, **13,** 235-36.

MANSKE, MARY E., and G. A. DAVIS. Effects of simple instructional biases upon performance in the Unusual Uses Test. *Journal of General Psychology,* 1968, **78,** 25-33.

MARKS, L. E., and G. A. MILLER. The role of semantic and syntactic constraints in the memorization of English sentences. *Journal of*

Verbal Learning and Verbal Behavior, 1964, **3,** 1-5.
MARTIN, E. Transfer of verbal paired-associates. *Psychological Review,* 1965, **72,** 327-43.
———. Stimulus recognition in aural paired-associate learning. *Journal of Verbal Learning and Verbal Behavior,* 1967, **6,** 272-76.
———. Stimulus meaningfulness and paired-associate transfer: An encoding variability hypothesis. *Psychological Review,* 1968, **75,** 421-41.
MAYZNER, M. S. The effects of the competition of various strengths of sets in problem solution. *Psychological Newsletter,* 1955, **6,** 134-55.
———, and M. E. TRESSELT. Anagram solution times: a function of letter order and word frequency. *Journal of Experimental Psychology,* 1958, **56,** 376-79.
———. Anagram solution times: a function of letter order and word frequency. *Journal of Experimental Psychology,* 1959, **47,** 117-25.
———. Anagram solution times: A function of multiple-solution anagrams. *Journal of Experimental Psychology,* 1966, **71,** 66-73.
———. Anagram solution times: a function of word transition probabilities. *Journal of Experimental Psychology,* 1962, **63,** 510-13.
———. The effect of the competition and generalization of sets with respect to manifest anxiety. *Journal of General Psychology,* 1956, **55,** 241-47.
———. Tables of single letter and digraph frequency counts for various word-length and letter-position combinations. *Psychonomic Science Monograph Supplement,* 1965, **1,** 2.
———, and G. HELBOCK. An exploratory study of mediational responses in anagram problem solving. *Journal of Psychology,* 1964, **57,** 263-74.
MAX, L. W. An experimental study of the motor theory of consciousness: IV. Action-current responses in the deaf during awakening, kinesthetic imagery and abstract thinking. *Journal of Comparative Psychology,* 1937, **24,** 301-44.
MEDNICK, S. A. The associative basis of the creative process. *Psychological Review,* 1962, **69,** 220-32.
———, and S. HALPERN. Ease of concept attainment as a function of associative rank. *Journal of Experimental Psychology,* 1962, **64,** 628-30.
MEDNICK, S. A., and M. T. MEDNICK. *Examiner's Manual: Remote Associates Test.* Boston: Houghton-Mifflin, 1967.
MEHLER, J., and R. CAREY. Role of surface and base structure in the perception of sentences. *Journal of Verbal Learning and Verbal Behavior,* 1967, **6,** 335-38.
MENDELSOHN, G. A., and B. B. GRISWOLD. Differential use of incidental stimuli in problem solving as a function of creativity. *Journal of Abnormal and Social Psychology,* 1964, **68,** 431-36.
———, and M. L. ANDERSON. Individual differences in anagram-solving ability. *Psychological Reports,* 1966, **2,** 429-39.
MENYUK, P. A preliminary evaluation of grammatical capacity in children. *Journal of Verbal Learning and Verbal Behavior,* 1963, **2,** 429-39.
MILLER, G. A. The magical number seven, plus or minus two: some limits on our capacity for processing information. *Psychological Review,* 1956, **63,** 81-96.
———. *Psychology, the Science of Mental Life.* New York: Harper & Row, 1962.
———. Some preliminaries to psycholinguistics. *American Psychologist,* 1965, **20,** 15-20.
———, E. GALANTER, and K. L. PRIBRAM. *Plans and the Structure of Behavior.* New York: Holt, Rinehart & Winston, 1960.
MILLER, G. A., and P. E. NICELY. An analysis of perceptual confusions among some English consonants. *Journal of the Acoustical Society of America,* 1955, **27,** 338-52.
MILLER, G. A., and J. A. SELFRIDGE. Verbal context and the recall of meaningful material. *American Journal of Psychology,* 1950, **63,** 176-85.
MILLER, N. E., and J. DOLLARD. *Social Learning and Imitation.* New Haven: Yale University Press, 1941.
MILLER, W., and SUSAN ERVIN. The development of grammar in child language. In Ursula Bellugi and R. W. Brown, eds., *The Acquisition of Language. Monographs of the Society for Research in Child Development,* 1964, **29,** Serial No. 92.
MILTON, G. A. The effects of sex-role identification upon problem solving. *Journal of Abnormal and Social Psychology,* 1957, **55,** 208-12.
MORRIS, C. *Signs, Language and Behavior.* Englewood Cliffs, N.J.: Prentice-Hall, 1946.
MORRISETT, L., JR., and C. I. HOVLAND. A comparison of three varieties of training in

human problem solving. *Journal of Experimental Psychology,* 1959, **58**, 52-55.

MOWRER, O. H. The psychologist looks at language. *American Psychologist,* 1954, **9**, 660-94.

MURDOCK, B. B., JR. The retention of individual items. *Journal of Experimental Psychology,* 1961, **62**, 618-25.

NAMIKAS, G. Concept identification as a function of relevance of pretraining and percentage of informative feedback. *Psychonomic Science,* 1967, **8**, 261-62.

NEIMARK, EDITH D. Information-gathering in diagnostic problem solving. *Psychological Record,* 1961, **11**, 243-48.

———, and H. WAGNER. Information-gathering in diagnostic problem solving as a function on number of alternative solutions. *Psychonomic Science,* 1964, **1**, 329-30.

NEISSER, V., and P. WEENE. Hierarchies in concept attainment. *Journal of Experimental Psychology,* 1962, **64**, 644-45.

NEWELL, A. Thoughts on the concept of process. In J. Voss, ed., *Approaches to Thought.* Columbus, O.: Charles E. Merrill, 1969.

———, J. C. SHAW, and H. A. SIMON. Elements of a theory of human problem solving. *Psychological Review,* 1958, **65**, 151-66.

———. Chess-playing programs and the problem of complexity. In E. A. Feigenbaum and J. Feldman, edc., *Computers and Thought.* New York: McGraw-Hill, 1963.

NEWMAN, S. E. Effects of contiguity and similarity on the learning of concepts. *Journal of Experimental Psychology,* 1956, **52**, 349-53.

———, and C. W. Gray. S-R vs. R-S recall and R-term vs. S-term recall following paired-associate learning. *American Journal of Psychology,* 1964, **77**, 444-50.

NOBLE, C. C., and N. T. ALCOCK. Human delayed-reward learning with different lengths of task. *Journal of Experimental Psychology,* 1958, **56**, 407-12.

NODINE, C. F. Stimulus durations and stimulus characteristics in paired-associates learning. *Journal of Experimental Psychology,* 1963, **66**, 100-6.

OHLRICH, ELIZABETH S., and D. E. ROSS. Reversal and nonreversal shift learning in retardates as a function of overtraining. *Journal of Experimental Psychology,* 1966, **72**, 622-24.

OSBORNE, A. F. *Applied Imagination.* New York: Scribner's, 1957.

OSEAS, L., and B. J. UNDERWOOD. Studies of distributed practice: V. Learning and retention of concepts. *Journal of Experimental Psychology,* 1952, **43**, 143-48.

OSGOOD, C. E. The nature and measurement of meaning. *Psychological Bulletin,* 1952, **49**, 197-237.

———. *Method and Theory in Experimental Psychology.* New York: Oxford University Press, 1953.

———. A behavioristic analysis of perception and language as cognitive phenomena. In *Contemporary Approaches to Cognition.* Cambridge, Mass.: Harvard University Press, 1957.

OSLER, SONIA F., and M. W. FIVEL. Concept attainment: I. The role of age and intelligence in concept attainment by induction. *Journal of Experimental Psychology,* 1961, **62**, 1-8.

OSSORIO, P. G. *Persons.* Boulder, Colorado: Linguistic Research Institute Report, No. 3, mimeo, 1966.

PAIVIO, A. Abstractness, imagery, and meaningfulness in paired-associate learning. *Journal of Verbal Learning and Verbal Behavior,* 1965, **4**, 32-38.

———, and S. A. MADIGAN. Imagery and association value in paired-associate learning. *Journal of Experimental Psychology,* 1968, **76**, 35-39.

PAIVIO, A., P. C. SMYTHE, and J. C. YUILLE. Imagery versus meaningfulness of nouns in paired-associate learning. *Canadian Journal of Psychology,* 1968, **22**, 427-41.

PALERMO, D. S. On learning to talk: Are principles derived from the learning laboratory applicable? Research Bulletin No. 61, 1966, National Science Foundation, Research Grant GB-2568, The Pennsylvania State University.

———, and V. L. EBERHART. On the learning of morphological rules: An experimental analogy. *Journal of Verbal Learning and Verbal Behavior,* 1968, **7**, 337-44.

PALERMO, D. S., and J. J. JENKINS. Mediation processes and the acquisition of linguistic structure. In Ursula Bellugi and R. W. Brown, eds., *The Acquisition of Language. Monographs of the Society for Research in Child Development,* 1964, **29**, No. 1.

PARNES, S. J. Research on developing creative behavior. In C. W. Taylor, ed., *Widening Horizons in Creativity.* New York: John Wiley, 1962.

PAUL, C. Verbal discrimination reversal as a function of overlearning and percentage of items reversed. *Journal of Experimental Psychology,* 1966, **72,** 271-75.

———. Verbal discrimination reversal as a function of overlearning and percentage of items reversed: An extension. *Journal of Verbal Learning and Verbal Behavior,* 1968, **7,** 270-72.

———, C. CALLAHAN, M. MERENESS, and K. WILHELM. Transfer-activated response sets: Effect of overtraining and percentage of items shifted on a verbal discrimination shift. *Journal of Experimental Psychology,* 1968, **78,** 488-93.

PIAGET, J. *Logic and Psychology.* New York: Basic Books, 1957.

PISHKIN, V. Effects of probability of misinformation and number of irrelevant dimensions upon concept identification. *Journal of Experimental Psychology,* 1960, **59,** 371-78.

———. Experimenter variable in concept identification feedback of schizophrenics. *Perceptual and Motor Skills,* 1963, **16,** 921-22.

———. Availability of feedback-corrected error instances in concept learning. *Journal of Experimental Psychology,* 1967, **73,** 318-19.

———, and R. J. BLANCHARD. Auditory concept identification as a function of subject sex and stimulus dimensions. *Psychonomic Science,* 1964, **1,** 177-78.

PISHKIN, V., and A. WOLFGANG. Number and type of available instances in concept learning. *Journal of Experimental Psychology,* 1965, **69,** 5-8.

———, and ELIZABETH RASMUSSEN. Age, sex, amount and type of memory information in concept learning. *Journal of Experimental Psychology,* 1967, **73,** 121-24.

POSTMAN, L. Short-term memory and incidental learning. In A. W. Melton, ed., *Categories of Human Learning.* New York: Academic Press, 1964.

———, and R. GREENBLOOM. Conditions of cue selection in the acquisition of paired-associate lists. *Journal of Experimental Psychology,* 1967, **73,** 91-100.

RANKEN, H. B. Language and thinking: Positive and negative effects of naming. *Science,* 1963, **141,** 48-50.

RASKIN, D. C., C. BOICE, E. W. RUBEL, and D. CLARK. Transfer tests of the frequency theory of verbal discrimination learning. *Journal of Experimental Psychology,* 1968, **76,** 521-29.

RAY, W. S. Three experiments on functional fixedness. *Psychological Record,* 1965, **15,** 489-95.

REITMAN, W. R. *Cognition and Thought: An Information-processing Approach.* New York: John Wiley, 1965.

RESTLE, F. A theory of discrimination learning. *Psychological Review,* 1955, **62,** 11-19.

———. Toward a quantitative description of learning set data. *Psychological Review,* 1958, **65,** 77-91.

———. The selection of strategies in cue learning. *Psychological Review,* 1962, **69,** 320-43.

———, and J. H. DAVIS. Success and speed of problem solving by individuals and groups. *Psychological Review,* 1962, **69,** 520-36.

RESTLE, F. A., and D. EMMERICH. Memory in concept attainments: effects of giving several problems concurrently. *Journal of Experimental Psychology,* 1966, **71,** 794-99.

RHINE, R. J. The relation of achievement in problem solving to rate and kind of hypotheses produced. *Journal of Experimental Psychology,* 1959, **57,** 253-56.

———. Preference for positive evaluative response in concept learning. *Journal of Experimental Psychology,* 1965, **70,** 632-36.

RICHARDSON, J., and B. O. BERGUM. Distributed practice and rote learning in concept formation. *Journal of Experimental Psychology,* 1954, **47,** 442-46.

RIEGLE, E. M. Some perceptual characteristics of phrase structure rule learning. Unpublished doctoral dissertation, University of Minnesota, 1969.

ROBINSON, J. S. The effect of learning verbal labels for stimuli on their later discrimination. *Journal of Experimental Psychology,* 1955, **49,** 112-15.

ROMANOW, CONCETTA V. Anxiety level and ego-involvement as factors in concept formation. *Journal of Experimental Psychology,* 1958, **56,** 166-73.

RONNING, R. R. Anagram solution times: A function of the "Rule-out" factor. *Journal of Experimental Psychology,* 1965, **69,** 35-39.

RUNQUIST, W. N., and B. SEXTON. Supplementary report: spontaneous recovery of problem solving set. *Journal of Experimental Psychology,* 1961, **61,** 351-52.

RUSSELL, D. G., and I. G. SARASON. Test anxiety, sex, and experimental conditions in relation to anagram solution. *Journal of Personality and Social Psychology,* 1965, **1,** 493-96.

Russell, W. A., and J. J. Jenkins. The complete Minnesota norms for responses to 100 words from the Kent-Rosanoff word association test. Tech. Rep. No. 11, 1954, University of Minnesota, Contract N8-onr066216, Office of Naval Research.

Saflen, M. A. Associations, sets, and the solution of word problems. *Journal of Experimental Psychology*, 1962, **64**, 40-45.

Saltz, E., and I. E. Sigel. Concept overdiscrimination in children. *Journal of Experimental Psychology*, 1967, **73**, 1-8.

Samuels, A. L. Some studies in machine learning using the game of checkers. In E. A. Feigenbaum and J. Feldman, eds., *Computers and Thought*. New York: McGraw-Hill, 1963.

Sanders, B., L. E. Ross, and L. W. Heal. Reversal and nonreversal shift learning in normal children and retardates of comparable mental age. *Journal of Experimental Psychology*, 1965, **69**, 84-88.

Saporta, S., A. L. Blumenthal, and D. G. Rieff. Grammatical models and language learning. *Monograph Series on Language and Linguistics*, 1963, **16**, 133-42.

Sarason, I. G. The effects of anxiety and threat on the solution of a difficult task. *Journal of Abnormal and Social Psychology*, 1961, **62**, 165-68.

Saugstad, P. Problem-solving as dependent on availability of functions. *British Journal of Psychology*, 1955, **46**, 191-98.

———. An analysis of Maier's pendulum problem. *Journal of Experimental Psychology*, 1957, **54**, 168-79.

———, and K. Raaheim. Problem solving and the availability of functions. *Acta Psychologia*, 1957, **13**, 263-78.

Scandura, J. M. Algorithm learning and problem solving. *Journal of Experimental Education*, 1966, **34**, 1-6.

Scheerer, M. Problem-solving. *Scientific American*, 1963, **208**, 118-28.

Schulz, R. W. Problem solving behavior and transfer. *Harvard Educational Review*, 1960, **30**, 61-77.

Schvaneveldt, R. W. Concept identification as a function of probability of positive instances and number of relevant dimensions. *Journal of Experimental Psychology*, 1966, **72**, 649-60.

Schwartz, S. H. Trial-by-trial analysis of processes in simple and disjunctive concept-attainment tasks. *Journal of Experimental Psychology*, 1967, **72**, 456-65.

Shepard, R. N., C. I. Hovland, and H. N. Jenkins. Learning and memorization of classifications. *Psychological Monographs*, 1961, **75**, No. 13 (Whole No. 517).

Shepard, R. N. Invited address, Division 3, American Psychological Association Annual Meeting, 1966.

Sigel, I. E., E. Saltz, and W. Roskind. Variables determining concept conservation in children. *Journal of Experimental Psychology*, 1967, **74**, 471-75.

Simon, H. A., and K. Kotovsky. Human acquisition of concepts for sequential patterns. *Psychological Review*, 1963, **70**, 534-46.

Simon, H. A., and A. Newell. Information processing in computers and man. *American Scientist*, 1964, **52**, 281-300.

Skinner, B. F. *Verbal Behavior*. New York: Appleton-Century-Crofts, 1957.

Smith, M. E. An investigation of the development of the sentence and the extent of vocabulary in young children. University of Iowa, *Stud. Child. Welfare*, 1926, **3**, No. 5.

Smoke, K. L. Negative instances in concept learning. *Journal of Experimental Psychology*, 1933, **16**, 583-88.

Solley, C. M., and F. W. Snyder. Information processing and problem solving. *Journal of Experimental Psychology*, 1958, **55**, 384-87.

Solley, C. M., and R. Stagner. Effects of magnitude of temporal barriers, type of goal, and perception of self. *Journal of Experimental Psychology*, 1956, **51**, 62-70.

Spear, N. E., B. R. Ekstrand, and B. J. Underwood. Association by contiguity. *Journal of Experimental Psychology*, 1964, **67**, 151-61.

Spence, J. T., U. L. Lair, and L. D. Goodstein. Effects of different feedback conditions on verbal discrimination learning in schizophrenic and nonpsychiatric subjects. *Journal of Verbal Learning and Verbal Behavior*, 1963, **2**, 339-45.

Spence, K. W. Theoretical interpretations of learning. In S. S. Stevens, ed., *Handbook of Experimental Psychology*. New York: John Wiley, 1951.

———. *Behavior Theory and Conditioning*. New Haven: Yale University Press, 1956.

Staats, A. W. Verbal and instrumental response hierarchies and their relationship to problem solving. *American Journal of Psychology,* 1957, **70,** 442-46.

———. *Learning, Language, and Cognition.* New York: Holt, Rinehart & Winston, 1968.

STACHNICK, T. Transitional probability in anagram solution in a group setting. *Journal of Psychology,* 1963, **55,** 259-61.

STEFFLRE, V., V. C. VALES, and L. MORLEY. Language and cognition in Yucatan: A cross-cultural replication. *Journal of Personality and Social Psychology,* 1966, **4,** 112-15.

STERNBERG, S. High speed scanning in human memory. *Science,* 1966, **153,** 652-54.

STRONG, P. N., JR. Comparative studies in simple oddity learning: II. Children, adults and seniles. *Psychonomic Science,* 1966, **6,** 459-60.

SUEDFELD, P., S. GLUCKSBERG, and J. VERNON. Sensory deprivation as a drive operation: effects upon problem solving. *Journal of Experimental Psychology,* 1967, **75,** 166-69.

SUPPES, P. and ROSE GINSBERG. A fundamental property of all-or-none models, binomial distribution of responses prior to conditioning, with application of concept formation in children. *Psychological Review,* 1963, **70,** 139-61.

SUPPES, P., and M. SCHLAG-REY. Observable changes in hypotheses under positive reinforcement. *Science,* 1965, **148,** 661-62.

TAFT, R., and J. T. ROSSITER. The Remote Associates Test: Divergent or convergent thinking? *Psychological Reports,* 1966, **19,** 1313-14.

TAYLOR, C. W., ed., *Widening Horizons in Creativity.* New York: John Wiley, 1962.

TAYLOR, D. W., P. C. BERRY, and C. H. BLOCK. Does group participation when using brainstorming facilitate or inhibit creative thinking? *Administration Science Quarterly,* 1958, **3,** 23-47.

TAYLOR, D. W., and W. L. FAUST. Twenty questions: Efficiency in problem solving as a function of size of group. *Journal of Experimental Psychology,* 1952, **44,** 360-68.

TAYLOR, J. A. A personality scale of manifest anxiety. *Psychological Bulletin,* 1953, **48,** 285-90.

TECCE, J. J. Relationship of anxiety (drive) and response competition in problem solving. *Journal of Abnormal Psychology,* 1965, **70,** 465-67.

THOMAS, D. R., A. D. CARONITE, G. L. LAMONICA, and K. L. HOVING. Mediated generalization via stimulus labeling: a replication and extension. *Journal of Experimental Psychology,* 1968, **78,** 531-33.

THOMAS, D. R., and A. DECAPITO. Role of stimulus labeling in stimulus generalization. *Journal of Experimental Psychology,* 1966, **71,** 913-15.

THOMAS, W. I. *Primitive Behavior.* New York: McGraw-Hill, 1937.

THORNDIKE, E. L. Animal intelligence. *Psychological Monographs,* 1898, No. 8.

———. *Animal Intelligence.* New York: Macmillan, 1911.

———, and I. LORGE. *A Teacher's Word Book of 30,000 Words.* New York: Teachers College, Columbia University, 1944.

THYSELL, R. V., and R. W. SCHULZ. Concept-utilization as a function of the strength of relevant and irrelevant associations. *Journal of Verbal Learning and Verbal Behavior,* 1964, **3,** 203-8.

TIGHE, LOUISE S. Effects of perceptual pretraining on reversal and nonreversal shifts. *Journal of Experimental Psychology,* 1965, **70,** 379-85.

———, and T. J. TIGHE. Overtraining and discrimination shift behavior in children. *Psychonomic Science,* 1965, **2,** 365-66.

TIGHE, T. J. Effect of overtraining on reversal and extradimensional shift. *Journal of Experimental Psychology,* 1965, **70,** 13-17.

TOMBAUGH, T. N., and J. TOMBAUGH. The effects of apparent task solubility and reward upon the duration of problem solving behavior. *Psychological Record,* 1963, **13,** 83-87.

TRABASSO, T. Stimulus emphasis and all-or-none learning of concept identification. *Journal of Experimental Psychology,* 1963, **65,** 395-406.

———, and G. BOWER. Component learning in the four-category concept problem. *Journal of Mathematical Psychology,* 1964, **1,** 143-69 (a).

———. Presolution reversal and dimensional shifts in concept identification. *Journal of Experimental Psychology,* 1964, **67,** 398-99 (b).

———. Memory in concept identification. *Psychonomic Science,* 1964, **1,** 133-34 (c).

———. Presolution dimensional shifts in concept identification: a test of the sampling with replacement axiom in all-or-none models. *Journal of Mathematical Psychology,* 1966, **3,** 163-73.

———. *Attention in Learning.* New York: John Wiley, 1968.

TRESSELT, M. E., and M. S. MAYZNER. Anagram solution times: a function of single- and double-letter solution words. *Journal of Ver-*

bal Learning and Verbal Behavior, 1968, **7**, 128-32.

TULVING, E. Subjective organization in free recall of "unrelated" words. *Psychological Review*, 1962, **69**, 344-54.

———. Subjective organization and effects of repetition in multi-trial free-recall learning. *Journal of Verbal Learning and Verbal Behavior*, 1966, **5**, 193-97.

———. Theoretical issues in free recall. In T. R. Dixon and D. L. Horton, eds., *Verbal Behavior and General Behavior Theory*. Englewood Cliffs, N.J.: Prentice-Hall, 1968.

———, and Z. PEARLSTONE. Availability versus accessibility of information in memory for words. *Journal of Verbal Learning and Verbal Behavior*, 1966, **5**, 381-91.

UHL, C. N. Learning of interval concepts: I. Effects of differences in stimulus weights. *Journal of Experimental Psychology*, 1963, **66**, 264-73.

———. Effects of multiple stimulus validity and criterion dispersion on learning of interval concepts. *Journal of Experimental Psychology*, 1966, **72**, 519-25.

UNDERWOOD, B. J. An orientation for research on thinking. *Psychological Review*, 1952, **59**, 209-20.

———. Ten years of massed practice on distributed practice. *Psychological Review*, 1961, **68**, 229-47.

———. The representativeness of rote verbal learning. In A. W. Melton, ed., *Categories of Human Learning*. New York: Academic Press, 1964.

———. False recognition produced by implicit verbal responses. *Journal of Experimental Psychology*, 1965, **70**, 122-29.

———. *Experimental Psychology*, 2nd ed. New York: Appleton-Century-Crofts, 1966.

———, B. R. EKSTRAND, and G. KEPPEL. An analysis of learning with experiments on conceptual similarity. *Journal of Verbal Learning and Verbal Behavior*, 1965, **4**, 447-62.

UNDERWOOD, B. J., and A. H. ERLEBACHER. Studies of coding in verbal learning. *Psychological Monographs*, 1965, **79**, No. 13.

UNDERWOOD, B. J., M. HAM, and B. EKSTRAND. Cue selection in paired-associate learning. *Journal of Experimental Psychology*, 1962, **64**, 405-9.

UNDERWOOD, B. J., and J. RICHARDSON. Verbal concept learning as a function of instructions and dominance level. *Journal of Experimental Psychology*, 1953, **51**, 229-38.

———. Some verbal materials for the study of concept formation. *Psychological Bulletin*, 1956, **53**, 84-85 (*a*).

———. Verbal concept learning as a function of instructions and dominance level. *Journal of Experimental Psychology*, 1956, **51**, 229-38 (*b*).

UNDERWOOD, B. J., W. N. RUNQUIST, and R. W. SCHULZ. Response learning in paired-associate lists as a function of intralist similarity. *Journal of Experimental Psychology*, 1959, **58**, 70-78.

UNDERWOOD, B. J., and R. W. SCHULZ. *Meaningfulness and Verbal Learning*. Philadelphia: Lippincott, 1960.

VAN DE GEER, J. P. *A Psychological Study of Problem Solving*. Haarlem: Uitgeverig De Toorts, 1957.

VANDERPLAS, J. M., W. A. SANDERSON, and J. N. VANDERPLAS. Some task-related determinants of transfer in perceptual learning. *Perceptual and Motor Skills*, 1964, **18**, 71-80.

VIGOTSKY, L. S. *Thought and Language*. Cambridge, Mass.: M.I.T. Press, 1962.

VOSS, J. F., ed., *Approaches to Thought*. Columbus, O.: Charles E. Merrill, 1969.

WAKIN, A. H., and J. R. BRAUN. Semantic satiation and problem solving. *Psychonomic Science*, 1966, **5**, 469-70.

WALKER, C. M., and L. E. BOURNE, JR. Concept identification as a function of amounts of relevant and irrelevant information. *American Journal of Psychology*, 1961, **74**, 410-17.

WALLACE, J. Concept dominance, type of feedback, and intensity of feedback as related to concept attainment. *Journal of Educational Psychology*, 1964, **55**, 159-66.

WALLACH, M. A., and N. KOGAN. *Modes of Thinking in Young Children*. New York: Holt, Rinehart & Winston, 1965.

WALLAS, G. *The Art of Thought*. New York: Harcourt, Brace, 1926.

WEAVER, H. E., and E. H. MADDEN. "Direction" in problem solving. *Journal of Psychology*, 1949, **27**, 331-45.

WECHSLER, D. *The Measurement and Appraisal of Adult Intelligence*, 4th ed. Baltimore: Williams & Wilkins, 1958.

WEINGARTNER, H. The free recall of sets of associatively related words. *Journal of Verbal Learning and Verbal Behavior*, 1964, **3**, 6-10.

WEIR, M. W. Developmental changes in problem solving strategies. *Psychological Review*, 1964, **71**, 473-90.

———. Age and memory as factors in problem solving. *Journal of Experimental Psychology,* 1967, **73,** 78-84.

WELLS, H. Effects of transfer and problem structure in disjunctive concept formation. *Journal of Experimental Psychology,* 1963, **65,** 63-69.

———. Facilitation of concept learning by a "simultaneous contrast" procedure. *Psychonomic Science,* 1967, **9,** 609-10.

———, and K. DEFFENBACHER. Conjunctive and disjunctive concept learning in humans and squirrel monkeys. *Canadian Journal of Psychology,* 1967, **21,** 301-8.

WERTHEIMER, M. *Productive Thinking.* New York: Harper, 1945.

WESLEY, ELIZABETH L. Perseverative behavior in a concept formation task as a function of manifest anxiety and rigidity. *Journal of Abnormal and Social Psychology,* 1953, **48,** 129-34.

WHITE, R. M., JR. Effects of some pretraining variables on concept identification. Boulder, Colo.: Cognitive Process Report, No. 105, Mimeo, 1967.

———, and P. J. JOHNSON. Concept of dimensionality and optional shift performance in nursery school children. *Journal of Experimental Child Psychology,* 1968, **6,** 113-19.

WHITMAN, R. N. Concept attainment as a function of intelligence and conceptual styles. *Center for Study of Cognitive Processes report,* Wayne State University, 1966.

WHORF, B. L. *Language, thought, and reality.* New York: M.I.T. Press–Wiley, 1956, p. 249.

WICKELGREN, W. A. Acoustic similarity and retroactive interference in short-term memory. *Journal of Verbal Learning and Verbal Behavior,* 1965, **4,** 53-61.

———. Distinctive features and errors in short-term memory for English consonants. *Journal of the Acoustical Society of America,* 1966, **39,** 388-98.

WILSON, R. G., J. P. GUILFORD, and P. R. CHRISTENSEN. The measurement of individual differences in originality. *Psychological Bulletin,* 1953, **50,** 363-70.

WOLFGANG, A. Exploration of upper limits of task complexity in concept identification of males and females in individual and social conditions. *Psychonomic Science,* 1967, **9,** 621-22.

WOOD, G., Mnemonic systems in recall. *Journal of Educational Psychology Monograph,* 1967, **58,** No. 6.

———, and B. J. UNDERWOOD. Implicit responses and conceptual similarity. *Journal of Verbal Learning and Verbal Behavior,* 1967, **6,** 1-10.

WOODWORTH, R., and H. SCHLOSBERG. *Experimental Psychology,* rev. ed., New York: Holt, Rinehart & Winston, 1954.

YNTEMA, D. B., and G. E. MUESER. Remembering the present states of a number of variables. *Journal of Experimental Psychology,* 1960, **60,** 18-22.

YOUNG, R. K. A comparison of two methods of learning serial associations. *American Journal of Psychology,* 1959, **72,** 554-59.

———. Tests of three hypotheses about the effective stimulus in serial learning. *Journal of Experimental Psychology,* 1962, **63,** 307-13.

———. Serial learning. In T. R. Dixon and D. L. Horton, eds., *Verbal Behavior and General Behavior Theory.* Englewood Cliffs, N.J.: Prentice-Hall, 1968.

YOUNISS, J., and H. G. FURTH. Attainment and transfer of logical connectives in children. *Journal of Educational Psychology,* 1964, **55,** 357-61.

———. Discrimination shifts as a function of degree of training in children. *Journal of Experimental Psychology,* 1965, **70,** 424-29.

ZAFFY, D. J., and J. L. BRUNING. Drive and the range of cue utilization. *Journal of Experimental Psychology,* 1966, **71,** 382-86.

ZENER, K. The significance of behavior accompanying conditioned salivary secretion for theories of the conditioned response. *American Journal of Psychology,* 1937, **50,** 384-403.

Author Index

Abbott, D. W., 137, 149
Adams, J. A., 131
Adamson, R. E., 88, 98, 107
Alcock, N. T., 274
Anderson, B., 109
Anderson, M. L., 99-103
Anderson, R. C., 235
Andreassi, J. L., 238
Anisfeld, M., 129
Archer, E. J., 255-59, 265-67, 278
Arnoult, M. D., 301, 303
Aronson, E., 85
Atkinson, R. C., 12
Atwood, D. W., 83
Austin, G. A., 192, 203-4, 224, 232, 258, 261-62
Azuma, H., 260

Battig, W. F., 106, 123, 156-57
Baum, M., 195
Beach, L. E., 12
Beilin, H., 85, 99
Belloni, M., 110, 113-15
Bendig, A. W., 106
Berg, E. A., 217
Berger, S. E., 258
Bergum, B. O., 257
Berko, J., 313, 338, 341
Berlyne, D. E., 270
Bernbach, H. A., 126
Bernstein, B. B., 111, 233
Berry, P. C., 116
Bessemer, D. W., 303

Bever, T. G., 314, 316, 318, 337
Bilodeau, E. A., 274
Bilodeau, I. McD., 274
Birch, H. G., 109
Birren, J. E., 99
Blanchard, R. J., 265
Block, C. H., 116
Blumenthal, A. L., 327
Boakes, R., 327
Bogartz, W., 110, 114
Boice, C., 162
Boring, E. G., 18, 28, 35-36
Bourne, L. E., Jr., 185-86, 190, 195-96, 215-19, 222, 226-32, 235-37, 240, 242, 255-61, 264-65, 268-75, 278-80, 349-52
Bousfield, W. A., 127, 138, 157
Bower, A. C., 254, 258
Bower, G., 196-97, 210, 213, 215, 218, 225, 235-36, 259, 273, 278
Braine, M. D. S., 335-36
Braley, L. S., 270
Braun, J. R., 110
Breger, L., 114
Broadbent, D. E., 268
Brodbeck, A. J., 337
Brooks, L. O., 84, 99, 101, 110
Brown, F. G., 265, 278
Brown, R. W., 83, 285, 292, 294, 308, 310, 330, 335, 337, 341
Bruner, J. S., 4, 183, 192, 203-4, 224, 229, 231-32, 258, 261-62, 306
Bruning, J. L., 238
Bugelski, B. R., 107-8, 131

Bulgarella, R., 255, 257-58
Bunderson, C. V., 233, 244, 275-76
Burack, B., 111
Burke, R. J., 68, 97, 99, 104
Buss, A. H., 242, 271-73
Buss, E. H., 242, 271-73
Byers, J. I., 227, 254

Cahill, H. E., 190, 225, 230, 236, 263
Callahan, C., 162
Carey, G. L., 100
Carey, R., 325
Carmichael, L. A., 289, 296
Caron, A. J., 114
Caronite, A. D., 297
Carroll, J. B., 292, 299, 328, 333-34
Carvellas, T., 55, 82
Casagrande, J. B., 299
Chomsky, N., 118, 246, 322, 324-25, 353
Chown, S. M., 99
Christensen, P. R., 59, 113
Clark, W. H., 162, 230, 257-58, 296
Clifton, C., Jr., 324
Cofer, C. N., 110, 123
Cohen, B. H., 157
Cohen, J. C., 154
Cohen, J. L., 88
Colgan, D., 249
Conant, M. B., 220, 229
Conrad, H. S., 247
Conrad, R., 137

375

Cooper, A., 109
Corman, B. R., 84, 111
Cost, J. R., 251
Crawford, J., 219
Cronbach, L. J., 260

Danick, J. J., 127
Danks, J. H., 89, 104, 113, 299
Davidson, R. E., 227, 254
Davis, G. A., 90, 100, 106, 113, 115-16
Davis, J. H., 62, 81, 84, 90
Davis, K. G., 109
DeCapito, A., 296
Deese, J., 127, 139, 146, 346
Deffenbacher, K., 247
deGroot, A. D., 73
Denny, J. P., 238, 243
Devine, J. V., 263, 303
Diamond, F., 123
DiVesta, F. J., 109-11
Dodd, D. H., 215, 219, 230, 276, 279
Dollard, J., 304
Dominowski, R. L., 83, 85-87, 94, 106, 110, 145, 204
Dulany, D. E., Jr., 237
Duncan, C. P., 51, 84, 92-95, 97-98, 100, 106
Duncker, K., 37, 66, 109
Dunham, J. L., 233, 244
Dunn, R. F., 238-39
Duvall, A. N., 109

Eberhart, V. L., 339
Ehrmann, E. D., 210
Eisman, E., 84, 99, 101
Ekstrand, B. R., 85-86, 110, 125, 131, 145, 153, 160
Ellis, H. C., 302
Emmerich, D., 235
Epstein, W., 164, 166
Eriksen, C. W., 305
Erickson, J. R., 210
Erlebacher, A. H., 169
Ervin, S. M., 335, 339
Ervin-Tripp, S., 333-34, 337-38
Esper, E. A., 339

Fant, G. M., 311, 333
Faust, W. L., 106
Feather, N. T., 102
Feigenbaum, E. A., 47, 75
Feldman, J., 47, 75
Feller, W., 197
Feuge, R. L., 303

Fishbein, M., 110, 113-15
Fishman, J., 293, 299
Fivel, M. W., 243
Flavell, J. H., 109
Fodor, J., 314, 316, 318-19, 331, 337
Forgus, R. H., 111
Foss, D. J., 312, 339
Fraser, C., 335
Freedman, J. L., 115, 269
Freeman, G. L., 35
Freibergs, V., 262
French, E. G., 99
Friedman, S. R., 247, 249
Fries, C. C., 314
Fry, D. B., 333
Furth, H. G., 251-52

Gagné, R. M., 4, 54, 90, 111
Galanter, E., 73, 75-76, 172
Games, P. A., 244
Gardner, R. A., 107
Garner, W. R., 160
Garrett, M., 314, 316, 318-19
Gavurin, E. I., 104
Gelfand, S., 110
Gibson, E. J., 305
Gibson, J. J., 305
Ginsburg, R., 210
Glanzer, M., 230, 257-58, 296
Gleason, H. A., 285, 308
Glucksberg, S., 88-89, 102, 104, 113, 290, 299
Goldbeck, R. A., 111, 233
Goldstein, S., 190, 236
Gollin E. S., 266
Goodnow, J. J., 192, 203-4, 224, 232, 258, 261-62, 273
Goodstein, L. B., 271
Grant, D. A., 217, 251
Gray, C. W., 126
Greenberg, H. A., 107
Greenberg, J. H., 134, 311-12
Greenbloom, R., 153
Greenfield, P. M., 183, 306
Greeno, J. G., 154
Griswold, B. B., 99-101, 103, 110
Guilford, J. P., 59, 111, 113, 233, 244
Guthrie, J. T., 235
Guy, D. E., 216, 218-19, 230, 237, 240, 242, 264, 270, 272, 276, 279, 349, 352

Hake, H. W., 305
Hall, R. A., 308
Halle, M., 311, 333

Halpern, S., 269
Ham, M., 153
Hammond, K. R., 260
Harleston, B. W., 101
Harlow, H., 14, 349
Harter, S., 247, 250-51
Haselrud, G., 111
Hayes, J. R., 90-91
Haygood, D., 267
Haygood, R. C., 186, 230, 258-59, 263-64
Heal, L. W., 251
Hebert, J. A., 86
Helbock, G., 55
Hess, H. E., 109
Hilgard, E. R., 111, 196
Hillix, W. A., 111, 233
Hintzman, D. L., 311
Hoepfner, R., 233, 244
Hoffman, H. N., 68, 100, 243
Hogan, H. P., 289, 296
Horn, R., 85
Horowitz, L. M., 83
Horton, D. L., 152
House, B. J., 251
Hoving, K. L., 297
Hovland, C. I., 106, 190, 219-20, 225, 230, 235-36, 259, 261-63
Huff, E. M., 107-8
Hull, C. L., 200, 238
Hunt, E. B., 184, 191, 203, 218-20, 227, 235, 254, 259-60
Hunter, I. M., 87
Huttenlocher, J., 191, 227, 230, 257-58, 262

Irvine, R. P., 111
Irwin, O. C., 333, 337-38

Jacobus, D. A., 108
Jakobson, R., 311, 333
James, C. T., 154
James, W., 30
Janzen, J. C., 113
Jenkins, J. J., 93, 130, 134, 151, 153, 157, 261, 311-12, 314, 336
Jennings, J. W., 57
Jennings, P. C., 235, 261
Jerome, E. A., 99
Johnson, D. M., 56-57, 76, 96, 98, 115-16, 270
Johnson, N. F., 108, 321
Johnson, P. J., 183, 191, 209, 227
Johnson, T. J., 93
Johnson, W., 109
Jones, H. E., 247

Jordan, R. M., 226, 229, 231
Judson, A. J., 110
Jurca, N. H., 94
Justesen, D. R., 219, 276, 279

Kagan, J., 233
Kaplan, I. T., 55, 82, 106
Kates, S. L., 236
Katz, J. J., 331
Katz, P. A., 303
Keele, S. W., 258-59, 267
Kendler, H. H., 73, 107, 153, 208-9, 251-52, 304
Kendler, T. S., 73, 153, 208-9, 251-52, 304
Keppel, G., 125
Kepros, P. G., 255, 257-58
Kiehlbach, J. B., 230
Kimble, G. A., 129, 329
King, W. L., 247, 249, 254, 258
Kinsman, R. A., 240
Kjeldergaard, P. M., 147, 151-52
Klugh, H. E., 249
Knapp, M., 129
Koffka, K., 246
Kogan, N., 111, 113
Kotovsky, K., 205
Kurtz, K. H., 235, 261

Lair, U. L., 271
LaMonica, G. L., 297
Landy, D., 85
Laughlin, P. R., 226, 229, 231, 257
Lenneberg, E. H., 292, 295, 338
Levine, M., 197-98, 214-15, 225, 230, 263
Levitt, E. E., 107
Levy, L. H., 114
Licht, L., 114
Lindley, R. H., 171
Link, W. E., 190, 236
Loiselle, R. H., 109
Long, K. K., 303
Lordahl, D. S., 258, 266-67
Lowenkron, B., 191, 227
Luchins, A. S., 107, 249
Luchins, E. H., 107
Luria, A. R., 153
Lynch, D. O., 96

McGuigan, F. J., 4, 209
McNeill, D., 83, 336
Madden, E. H., 68
Madigan, S. A., 143

Maier, N. R. F., 49, 68, 97, 99-100, 104, 113
Malmo, R. B., 35
Maltzman, I., 45, 69, 71, 84, 99, 101, 110, 113-15
Mandler, G., 4, 13, 22, 157, 252
Manning, A. A., 258
Manske, M. E., 84, 90, 113, 115-16
Marin, J., 203
Marks, L. E., 166
Martin, E., 126, 136, 148
Marx, M. H., 111, 233
Max, L. W., 35
Mayzner, M. S., 55, 86-87, 93, 96, 106-7
Mednick, M. T., 113
Mednick, S. A., 72, 104, 111, 113, 116, 269
Mehler, J., 325
Mendelsohn, G. A., 99-101, 103, 110
Menyuk, P. A., 332
Mereness, M., 162
Meyers, S., 111
Miller, G. A., 73, 75-76, 159, 163, 166, 168-69, 172, 309, 311
Miller, N. E., 304
Miller, W., 335
Milton, G. A., 100
Mink, W. D., 157
Montague, W. E., 131, 157
Moos, D., 111
Morley, L., 295
Morris, C., 330
Morrisett, L., Jr., 106
Moss, H. A., 233
Mowrer, O. H., 333
Mueser, G. E., 226
Muller, D. G., 302-3
Murdock, B. B., Jr., 170
Murphy, R., 296
Musgrave, B. S., 154

Namikas, G., 271
Neimark, E. D., 81, 106
Neisser, U., 180, 206, 219-20, 222, 259
Newell, A., 4, 74-75, 77-78, 346
Newman, S. E., 126, 261
Nicely, P. E., 311
Noble, C. C., 274
Nodine, C. F., 274

Odom, P., 324
Ohlrich, E. S., 251
Olsen, R. A., 123
Olver, R. R., 183, 306

Osborn, A. F., 115
Oseas, L., 278
Osgood, C. E., 4, 199-200, 209, 252, 329, 332, 345
Osler, S. F., 243
Ossorio, P. G., 6, 185

Paivio, A., 141, 143
Palermo, D. S., 314, 336, 339
Parker, B. K., 261
Parloff, M. B., 114
Parnes, S. J., 115-16
Parrott, G. R., 115
Paul, C., 162
Peak, G., 219
Pearlstone, Z., 158
Pegram, V. G., 303
Pendleton, R. B., 271
Peterson, C. R., 12
Piaget, J., 246, 348
Pishkin, V., 236, 247, 265, 273
Postman, L., 153, 237, 273
Pribram, K. L., 73, 75-76, 172
Price, L. E., 137, 149

Raaheim, K., 97
Rabinowitz, H. S., 109
Ramsay, J. G., 96
Ranken, H. B., 285, 304
Raskin, D., 114, 162
Rasmussen, E., 247
Ray, W. S., 109
Reitman, W. R., 48, 77, 347
Restle, F. A., 62, 90, 184, 195-96, 210, 215, 217-18, 235, 252, 265
Rhine, R. J., 55
Richardson, J., 188, 257, 268-69
Richman, H., 107
Riegle, E. M., 319
Roberts, J. M., 295
Robinson, J. S., 303
Rogers, C. A., Jr., 86
Romanow, C. V., 237-39
Ronning, R. R., 83, 88
Roskind, W., 252
Ross, D. E., 251
Ross, L. E., 251
Rossiter, J. T., 113
Rubel, E. W., 162
Runquist, W. N., 107, 138
Russell, D. G., 101
Russell, W. A., 93, 157
Ryba, J. A., 249

Safren, M. A., 84

Salten, C., 266
Saltz, E., 247, 252
Samuels, A. L., 74, 76
Sanders, B., 251
Sanderson, W. A., 303
Sarason, I. G., 101
Saravo, A., 266
Saugstad, P., 68, 96-97
Scandura, J. M., 111
Scheerer, M., 42-44
Schlag-Rey, P., 198, 215
Schlosberg, H., 238
Schoenfeld, W. N., 106
Schulz, R. W., 44, 131, 134, 138, 145, 149, 256, 270
Schvaneveldt, R. W., 257, 262
Schwartz, R. J., 111
Schwartz, S. H., 232
Selfridge, J. A., 163
Sexton, V., 107
Shaw, J. C., 74, 77
Shepard, R. N., 261, 311
Shiffrin, R. M., 12
Sigel, I. E., 247, 252
Sigel, J. E., 233
Simon, H. A., 74-75, 77, 205
Simon, S., 114
Skinner, B. F., 324, 334
Smith, E. C., Jr., 54, 91, 111
Smith, M. E., 334
Smoke, K. L., 261, 350
Smythe, P. C., 143
Snyder, C. M., 81
Solley, C. M., 81, 102
Spear, N. E., 131
Spence, J. T., 271
Spence, K. W., 101, 238
Staats, A. W., 17, 97, 100-101, 330
Stachnik, T., 86
Stagner, R., 102
Stefflre, V., 295
Stein, J. S., 123
Sternberg, S., 7
Stevenson, M., 258
Stone, P. J., 203
Stratton, R. P., 115
Strong, P. N., 247
Suedfeld, P., 102

Summers, D. A., 260
Summers, S. S., 110
Suppes, P., 198, 210, 215

Taft, R., 113
Taub, T., 296
Taylor, C. W., 111
Taylor, D. W., 106, 116
Taylor, J., 238
Tecce, J. J., 103
Thomas, D. R., 296-97
Thomas, W. I., 284
Thorndike, E. L., 32
Thysell, R. V., 270
Tighe, L. S., 251
Tighe, T. J., 251
Tombaugh, J., 85
Tombaugh, T. N., 85
Trabasso, T., 197, 210, 213, 215, 218, 220, 225, 229, 235-36, 259, 266, 273, 278
Trafton, C. L., 303
Train, A. J., 84, 90
Tresselt, M. E., 55, 86-87, 93, 96, 106-7
Tulving, E., 158-60, 170, 189, 262

Uhl, C. N., 189, 260-61
Underwood, B. J., 108, 125, 127, 131, 134-35, 138, 141, 147, 153, 157, 160, 169-70, 188, 234-35, 256, 268-69, 274, 278
Unger, S. M., 114

Vales, V. C., 295
VandeGeer, J. P., 109
Vanderplas, J. M., 303
Vanderplas, J. N., 303
VanFleet, F., 216, 218, 240, 270
VanMondfrans, A. P., 93
Vernon, J., 102
Voss, J. F., 8
Vygotsky, L. S., 137

Wadsworth, N., 242, 272
Wagner, H., 81
Wakin, A. H., 110
Walker, C. M., 255, 257
Walker, H., 123
Wallace, J., 242, 270
Wallace, W. P., 160
Wallach, M. A., 111, 113
Walls, R. T., 109-11
Walter, A. A., 289, 296
Weaver, H. E., 68
Wechsler, D., 99-100
Weene, P., 180, 206, 219-20, 222, 259
Weingartner, H., 139
Weir, M. W., 99, 251
Weisberg, R. W., 88, 290
Weiss, W., 262
Weksel, W., 337
Wells, H., 198, 219-20, 237, 247, 263
Wesley, E. L., 238
Whipple, J. E., 111
White, M. A., 83
White, R. M., Jr., 183, 209, 219, 279
Whitman, R. N., 160, 234
Whitmarsh, G. A., 127, 157
Wickelgren, W. A., 137, 311
Wilhelm, K., 162
Wilson, R. G., 59, 113
Wolfgang, A., 236, 247, 258
Wood, G., 92, 141, 159, 172
Woodworth, R., 238

Yntema, D. B., 226
Young, R. K., 156
Youniss, J., 251-52
Yudin, L., 236
Yuille, J. C., 143

Zaffy, D. J., 238
Zajkowski, M. M., 210
Zeaman, D., 251
Zener, K., 330
Zerbolio, D. J., 116
Zigler, E., 303

Subject Index

Acoustic similarity, 137, 311
Acquired distinctiveness of cues, 304-5
Acquired equivalence of cues, 304-5
Act Psychology, 25
Age differences:
  concept formation, 247-50
  problem solving, 99
  solution shifts, 208-9
Algorithm, 74-75
Allomorph, 313
Allophone, 311
Ambiguous sentence, 318, 325-26
Anagram, 51, 82-83
  bigram frequency, 96
  letter order, 87-88
  organization, 85-88
  word frequency, 92-94
Anagram solving, individual differences, 103-4
Anticipation method, 123
Anxiety:
  concept formation, 238-42
  intelligence, 243-44
  problem solving, 101-3
Arousal (*see* Anxiety)
Association, laws of, 22-23
Associative learning:
  concept formation, 256-57
  conceptual similarity, 125-26
  linguistic rules, 339-41
  meaningfulness, 135-36
  mediation, 131-33
  paired-associate learning, 124

Associative learning (*cont.*)
  transfer, 147-50
Associative matching, 124
Associative strength, clustering, 157
Associative theory:
  concept formation, 194-96
  finite-state grammar, 316
  language development, 333
  meaning, 329-30
  philosophical tradition, 21-23
  principle learning, 184-85
  problem solving, 69-73
  transformational grammar, 324
Attention theory, 305
Attribute learning (identification), 182-83, 186
  strategies, 223-30
Attributes of concepts, 180
Aufgabe, 27-28

Backward association, 148-50
Behaviorism, 33-34
Berkeley, George, 21-22
Brainstorming, 115-16
Brown, Thomas, 23

Candle problem, 51, 88-89, 290-92
Chaining, 151, 156
Chunking, 168-69
  free recall, 159
  phrase structure, 318-22
  syntactic constraint, 163-64

Class concept, 177-80
Clustering, free recall, 157-58
Coding processes, 168-70
  concept formation, 251
  language development, 334-35
  memory, 287, 289-90, 292, 296-98
  nonverbal behavior, 294-98, 301-6
  perception, 296, 303
  problem solving, 285-89, 290-92
  solution shifts, 304
  stimulus differentiation, 301-6
  vocabulary and world view, 293-94
Cognitive strain, 227-28
Cognitive style, 233-34
Competence, acquisition, 14
Complementary distribution, phones, 311
Computer model, 73, 77-78, 202-5
Concept (*see also* Concept formation):
  attributes, 348
  definition, 177
  learning vs. utilization, 183-84, 186, 199-200, 206
  multicategory, 187-89
  multidimensional, 187, 218-19
  quantitative, 189
  unidimensional, 187
Concept formation:
  associative theory, 194-96
  Bower-Trabasso model, 197-98
  concept dominance, 268-70
  development, 244-52

Concept formation (*cont.*)
   feedback, 271-74
   hypothesis theory, 196-99, 235, 279-80
      correct response trials, 198-99, 215-18, 278-80
      error trials, 197, 215-18, 278-80
      stationarity principle, 209-13
   individual differences, 230-34
   information-processing theory, 202-5
   intertrial interval, 274-80
   irrelevant information, 258-59
   linguistic competence, 309
   mediation theory, 197-201, 250-51
   memory, 203-5, 234-37, 276-78
   motivation, 237-42
   novel stimulus dimensions, 216-18, 240-42, 270-71
   positive vs. negative instances, 261-65
   presolution shifts, 213-15
   relevant information, 255-57
   response complexity, 255-57
   solution shifts, 216-18
   stimulus display, 261
   stimulus modality, 267-68
   stimulus redundancy, 258-59
   stimulus saliency, 265-67
   stimulus sequence, 263
   strategies, 223-30, 249-50
Conceptual principles, 348
   definition, 180-82
   difficulty, 219-21, 259
   hierarchy of, 350-53
   positive vs. negative instances, 261-65
Conceptual similarity:
   clustering, 157-58
   false recognition, 129
   paired-associate learning, 125-26
   verbal learning, 138
Conceptual systems, 350-53
Consciousness, 31
Constituent structure, 318-22
Contiguity, 22
   associative learning, 130-32
   concept formation, 261
   creative thought, 116
Creativity, 72-73
   originality, 111-13
Cross cultural studies, 293, 295, 299-300

Darwin, Charles, 29
Deep structure, 324-27
Determining tendency, 27-28

Dewey, John, 31
Distinctive features, phonemes, 311-12, 333-34
Donders, F. C., 28
Dualism, 24

Ebbinghaus, Hermann, 25-26
Echoic response, 335
Esper paradigm, 339-41
Evolution, 29
Extinction, 69-70
   mediated transfer, 152
   problem-solving set, 107

Faculty Psychology, 23
False recognition, 127-30
Familiarity:
   conceptual principles, 220-22
   meaningfulness, 134
   positive instances, 262
   problem solving, 91-97
Feedback, 191 (*see also* Reinforcement)
   concept formation, 242, 271-74
   delay, 273-76
Finite-state grammars, 314-16
Focusing strategy, 224-25
Form class, 313-14
Forward association, 148-50
Free association, 127
Free recall, 123
   conceptual similarity, 138
   formal similarity, 137
   organization, 158-60
   semantic similarity, 138
   stimulus for, 156-60
Free variation, phones, 312
Functional fixedness, 37, 88-89, 102, 109-10
Functionalism, 31-33
Functional stimulus, 153
Functional value, 66-68

Generalization, 69-72
   concept formation, 195
   formal similarity, 137
   mediation, 138-40, 151
Gestalt Psychology, 36-38
Gestalt theory, problem solving, 65-69
Grammatical rules, 314-28
Grammatical structure:
   nonverbal behavior, 298-99
   recall, 166-67

Hartley, David, 22
Heuristic, 74-75
Hints, problem solving, 67-68
Hume, David, 21-22
Hypothesis, definition, 196
Hypothesis-testing experiment, 53-56

Imageless thought, 27
Imagery:
   free recall, 159-60
   mnemonics, 170-73
   thought, 306
   verbal learning, 142-43
Imitation, language development, 334-35, 337-38
Implicit associative response, 127
   false recognition, 129-30
Incremental vs. all-or-none learning, 209-13
Individual differences:
   concept formation, 230-34
   problem solving, 99-104
Induction, language development, 338
Information, amount:
   concept formation, 257-59
   problem solving, 81-85
   short-term memory, 170
Information-processing theory:
   concept formation, 202-5
   problem solving, 73-78
Insight problem, 50-51, 96-97, 104
Insight vs. trial-and-error, 65-66
Instructions, 84-85, 189
Intelligence:
   concept formation, 233, 242-44
   IQ, 250
   problem solving, 99
Introspection, 24-25
Intrusions in recall, 139
Irrelevant attributes:
   concepts, 180
   phonemes, 311

James, William, 30-31

Kernel string, 323
Knowledge:
   associations, 162-68
   skills, 347
Köhler, Wolfgang, 36-37
Külpe, Oswald, 26-29

Language development, 332-42
  experience, 337-42
  prelinguistic phase, 332-34
Learning to learn, 15-16
  conceptual principles, 229-30
  negative instances, 262
  problem solving, 105-6
  verbal learning, 146-47
Linguistic competence, 308-10
Linguistic relativity hypothesis, 292-301
Linguistic rules, 308-10
  recall, 163-68
  world view, 298
Locke, John, 21

Meaning, 85
  conditioned response, 329-30
  preparatory response, 330
  sentences, 331-32
  understanding, 331-32
Meaningfulness, 134
  familiarity, 134
  imagery, 141
  linguistic rules, 134
  number of associations, 134, 136
  paired-associate learning, 135-36
  pronounceability, 134
  response learning, 135-36
Means-end analysis, 75-76
Mediated generalization, 138-40, 151
Mediating response, 44-47
Mediation:
  associative learning, 131, 133
  concept formation, 199-201, 250-51
  imagery, 142
  language development, 336
  paradigms, 151-53
  similarity, 138-40
  solution shifts, 207-9
  transfer, 148-53
Memory:
  coding processes, 296-98
  concept formation, 197, 234-37, 276-78
  language development, 337
Mental chronometry, 28
Mental elements, 24
Mill, James, 22
Mill, John Stuart, 22-23
Mnemonics, 170-73
Morpheme, 310, 312-14
Morphological rules, 339-41
Morphology, 310, 312-14
Morphophonemic rules, 313

Motivation:
  concept formation, 237-42
  problem solving, 100-103

Nativistic theories, 246, 338
Natural language mediators, 133
Negative instance, definition, 179
Nominal stimulus, 153
Nonreversal shift, 207-9

Oddity problem, 266
Originality, 71-72
  creativity, 111-13
  training, 113-14
Original word game, 310
Orthographic similarity, 137

Paired-associate learning, 122-23
  conceptual similarity, 138
  formal similarity, 137
  semantic similarity, 138
  stages, 124-26
  stimulus selection, 153-56
  transfer, 146-53
Partist strategy, 226, 228-29
Perception, two meanings, 42-43
Permutation rules, grammar, 319-21
Phone, 310-12
Phoneme, 310-12, 332-34
Phonology, 310-12
Phrase marker, 317-20
Phrase structure, 318-22
Phrase-structure grammar, 316-23
Piaget, Jean, 246-47, 251-52
Pivot words, 335-37
Planning process, 76
Positive instance, definition, 179
Principle, 180
Principle learning, 182-83, 186, 205-7, 219-22, 263-65, 348-53
  language development, 338-42
Problem:
  anagram, 51
  ill-defined, 47-48
  insight, 50-51
  multiple solutions, 48-49
  search task, 49-50
  well-defined, 47-48
Problem solving:
  age differences, 99
  associative arousal, 44-46
  creativity, 48, 58-60
  definition, 9
  direction, 66-69
  failure, 102
  hints, 67-68

Problem solving (cont.)
  individual differences, 99-104
  judgment, 57-58
  learning, 76-77
  motivation, 100-103
  perceptual reorganization, 42-44
  preparation, 57
  production, 48, 57
  productive vs. reproductive, 49
  search process, 46-47
  selection process, 48, 94-96
  set, 70-71, 106-9
  sex differences, 100
  similarity, 87-89
  solution complexity, 90-91
  solution familiarity, 91-97
  stages, 31-32, 56-58, 62-63
  transfer, 104-17, 145
  verbalization, 54-56
Process-tracing experiment, 53-56
Pronounceability:
  anagrams, 86-87
  meaningfulness, 134
Pyramid problem, 54

Quantitative principles, 259-61

Reaction time, measure of thinking, 28
Recall of sentences, 321-22, 327
Reception paradigm, 189-90
  strategies, 225-26, 228-29
Recognition, associative learning, 126
Redundancy, concepts, 258-59
Reid, Thomas, 23
Reinforcement, 69-72
  concept formation, 195-96, 213-15
  language development, 333-35
  parasitic, 139-40
  problem-solving set, 107
Relevant attributes, concepts, 180, 255-57
Remote Associates Test, 73, 114-15
Repetition of ideas, 22
Representational response, 127
Response complexity, concepts, 254-57
Response equivalence, 151-52
  language development, 336-37
Response hierarchy, 44-47
Response integration, 150
Response learning:
  conceptual similarity, 125
  paired-associate learning, 124-26
  transfer, 147-50

Reversal shift, 207-9
Rigidity in thinking, 107
Rule following, as behavior description, 346-54
Rule learning (*see* Principle learning)

Scanning strategy, 226
Schema, 251-52
Search-scan scheme, 75
Selection paradigm, 190-91
   strategies, 223-26
Semantics, 137, 328-32
   recall, 166-67
Semantic similarity, 330
   verbal learning, 137-38
Serial learning, 123
   chaining hypothesis, 156
   position hypothesis, 156
   syntactic constraint, 163-66
Set, problem solving, 37, 106-9
Shaping, language development, 335
Similarity:
   ideas, 22
   mediation, 138-40
   problem solving, 87-89
   transfer, 146-47
   verbal learning, 137-41
Skill, description, 13
Solution probability and working time, 58-60
Solution shifts, 207-9, 250-51
Spontaneous recovery, 69-70
Stimulus discrimination, 126
Stimulus equivalence, 151-52
   language development, 336-37
Stimulus learning, 126
Stimulus predifferentiation, 301-6
Stimulus selection, 153-56

Strategies, concept formation, 192, 223-30, 249-50
   individual differences, 231-33
Stress:
   concept formation, 239-42
   problem solving, 101-2
Structuralism, 24
Study-test method, 123
Subjective organization, 158-60, 170
Surface structure, sentences, 324-26
Syntax, 310, 314-28

Tacting, 335
Telegraphic speech, 335
Thinking:
   behavior description, 7-8, 345-46
   definitions, 4-5, 8
   development, 12-17
   individual differences, 29-30
   learning, 16
   motor components, 34-35
   organization, 159-60
   perception, 36-38
Thorndike, E. L., 32-33
Titchener, E. B., 27
TOTE, 75-76
Transfer:
   concept formation, 279-80
   conceptual principles, 229-30
   creativity, 114-16
   free recall, 160
   mediation, 148-53
   operational definition, 144-45
   originality, 113-14
   paradigms, 146-47
   principles, 110-11
   problem solving, 105-10, 145
   similarity, 146-47
   solution shifts, 207-9, 250-51

Transfer (*cont.*)
   stage analysis, 147-50
   stimulus predifferentiation, 301-6
Transformational grammar, 323-28
Transition error, 321-23
Tree diagram, sentence, 320
Trial-and-error vs. insight, 32-33, 65-66
Truth-table strategy:
   acquisition, 229-30
   definition, 226-27
Two-string problem, 51

Verbal discrimination, 124
   associative learning, 131
   frequency rules, 160-62
Verbalization, problem solving, 54-56
Verbal-loop hypothesis, 296-98

Warm-up effect, 146-47
Watson, John B., 31, 33-34
Weltanschauung, 298
Wertheimer, Max, 36-37
Wholist strategy, 225
Whorfian hypothesis, 292-301
Words:
   abstract vs. concrete, 141-43
   acquisition, 334-35
   as anagrams, 85-86, 99
   development of classes, 335-36
   meaning, 328-30
   morphemes, 310
   representational response, 127
Working backwards, 76
Wundt, Wilhelm, 24
Würzburg School, 26-29

Yerkes-Dodson law, 100, 238